THE
LOST
GOSPEL

Decoding the Ancient Text that Reveals
Jesus' Marriage to Mary the Magdalene

SIMCHA JACOBOVICI
AND BARRIE WILSON

TRANSLATION OF THE SYRIAC MANUSCRIPT
BY TONY BURKE

PEGASUS BOOKS
NEW YORK LONDON

THE LOST GOSPEL

Pegasus Books LLC
80 Broad Street, 5th Floor
New York, NY 10004

Copyright © 2014 Simcha Jacobovici and Barrie Wilson

First Pegasus Books cloth edition November 2014

Interior design by Maria Fernandez

ISBN: 978-1-60598610-4

10 9 8 7 6 5 4 3 2 1

Printed in the United States of America

Distributed by W. W. Norton & Company, Inc.

Dedicated to Amnon Rosenfeld (z"l)—scholar, friend
and truth seeker.
(1944–2014)

—Simcha

For my grandchildren—
Jacob, Noah, Eden, Thalia, Jackson, Ryder
and for those yet to be born

—Barrie

CONTENTS

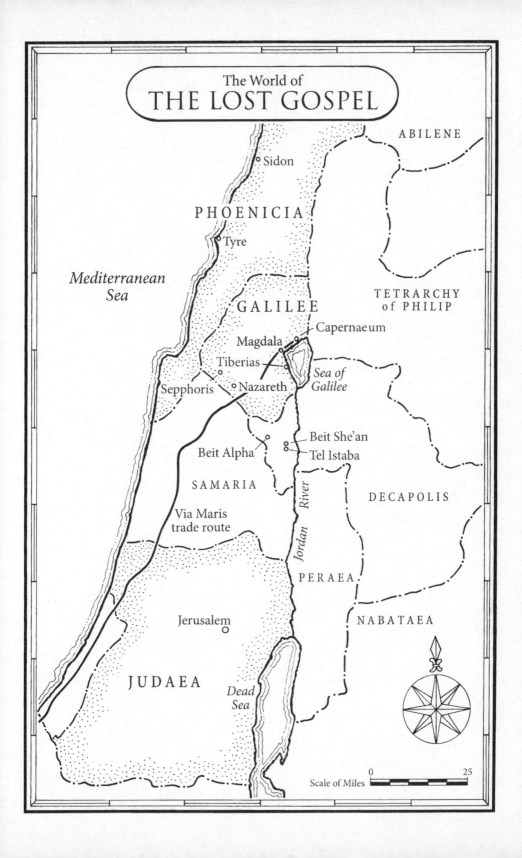

The World of
THE LOST GOSPEL

ABILENE

Sidon

PHOENICIA

Tyre

Mediterranean
Sea

GALILEE

TETRARCHY
of PHILIP

Capernaeum

Magdala

Tiberias

Sea of
Galilee

Sepphoris   Nazareth

Beit She'an

Beit Alpha   Tel Istaba

SAMARIA

DECAPOLIS

Via Maris
trade route

Jordan River

PERAEA

Jerusalem

NABATAEA

JUDAEA

Dead
Sea

0   25
Scale of Miles

MARRIAGE, SEX, CHILDREN

What you are about to read is a detective story. We have uncovered an ancient writing that is encrypted with a hidden meaning. In the process of decoding it, we'll take you on a journey into the world of this mysterious text. What the Vatican feared—and Dan Brown only suspected—has come true. There is now written evidence that Jesus was married to Mary the Magdalene[1] and that they had children together. More than this, based on the new evidence, we now know what the original Jesus movement looked like and the unexpected role sexuality played in it. We have even unraveled the politics behind the crucifixion, as well as the events and the people that took part in it.

Gathering dust in the British Library is a document that takes us into the missing years of Jesus' life. Scholars believe that Jesus was born around 5 B.C.E. (B.C.) and that he was crucified around 30 C.E. (A.D.).[2] But there is a huge gap in his biography. We know absolutely nothing about Jesus from the time he was eight days old (his circumcision, according to Jewish law), until he was in his early thirties. There is one exception. According to the Gospel of Luke (2:41–2:51), when he was twelve years old, Jesus traveled with his parents to Jerusalem to celebrate Passover. That's it. That's all we have. Otherwise, thirty years of absolute silence.

Isn't this incredible? Here is arguably the most influential individual in human history and we know nothing about him until after he starts his "ministry" (i.e., his public activism) at most three years before his crucifixion. But the fact is that we simply have no information about Jesus' early years—his upbringing, friends, schooling, or his interaction with family members. We have no knowledge of Jesus as a young adult. How did he gain access to the writings of the Hebrew Bible? Did the synagogue in Nazareth, a very small hamlet at the time, have scrolls of the Law and the Prophets? Who were his religious teachers? How well versed was he in Hebrew, in addition to the Aramaic that we know he spoke? Did he speak Greek, the lingua franca of the Roman world?

Jesus appears on the stage of history suddenly in the late 20s c.e. At this point, the mature Jesus announces the "Kingdom of God"—that is, the advent of a qualitative transformation in human history, prophesied by the Hebrew Bible, in which justice will reign upon the earth and the worship of the one true God will be universal.

But what happened to Jesus before this sudden appearance? According to the document that we uncovered, sometime during this period he became engaged, got married, had sexual relations, and produced children. Before anyone gets his/her theological back up, keep in mind that we are not attacking anyone's theology. We are reporting on a text. Theology must follow historical fact and not the other way around. Having said this, for the moment, we are not asserting that our text is historical fact. So far, we are merely stating that the Christian Bible tells us nothing about Jesus' early years, and that we have discovered a text that claims that he was married and fathered children.

On a purely historical level, this really shouldn't surprise us. Marriage and children were expected of a Jewish man, then and now. If he hadn't been married, that would have caused consternation to his family, possible scandal in the community, and the New Testament certainly would have commented on it—if for no other reason than to explain and defend Jesus' unusual behavior. But now we have a document that claims that he was indeed married and fathered children. Not only this, our document indicates that for some of his original followers, Jesus' marriage was the most important aspect of their theology.

A Sudden Insight

Before we proceed, we need to clarify one more thing: we don't claim to have excavated a long-lost text. What we do claim is to have found a centuries-old manuscript in a long-forgotten corner of a library. Such a discovery is not without precedent. For example, in 1873, in a library in Constantinople, a Greek priest found a text known as the *Didache*. It dates back to at least the beginning of the 2nd century, maybe even earlier, "making it as old as some of the books included in the New Testament canon."[3] The *Didache* gives us a glimpse into a pre-Pauline Christianity: that is, Christianity before the Apostle Paul reworked it. In the *Didache*, the Eucharist is a simple thanksgiving meal. There is no mention of Paul's idea that the bread represents Jesus' flesh and the wine his blood.[4] In similar fashion, we have also found a text that gives us a glimpse into the earliest writings concerning Jesus and his followers. Later versions of this text have been known to a small coterie of scholars for over a hundred years. They have been baffled, however, by its message and its purpose. As a result, it has occupied esoteric corners of academic research largely unnoticed and certainly unheralded.

What we also claim is to have gone back to the text's earliest existing version, translated it, and decoded its meaning. As we will demonstrate, the document in question is a very loosely disguised Gospel. It was probably encoded by a persecuted community of Christians so as to spare their group's literature from the bonfires of their oppressors.

How did we come across the manuscript, and how did we discover its meaning?

Oddly enough, the discovery of the manuscript's meaning came through an epiphany, a sudden blast of insight. We were both in Turkey en route to Ephesus in July 2008, filming an episode on Paul for the Associated Producers' History Channel documentary series, *Secrets of Christianity*. For our research, we had been mulling over puzzling texts from early Christianity—what they might mean and what new insights they could give us about the various groups that followed Jesus in the earliest days of his movement. Our discussion included a little-known text that highlights two figures from the Hebrew Bible.[5] The figures in question are Joseph, the Israelite of multi-color-coat fame who in the Book of Genesis is sold by his brothers into slavery and ends up as a ruler in Egypt, and his obscure Egyptian wife, Aseneth.

As Biblical historical researchers, we knew that the few scholars who had examined this text—dubbed *Joseph and Aseneth*—had expressed bewilderment over its meaning. We initially surmised that it might have something to do with Jesus—after all, the text was preserved in Christian monasteries. Also, the

Joseph in the story is depicted—in scholarly language—as a savior-figure. He is an ancient Israelite who saved his people from extinction and the Egyptians from starvation. Following up on this idea, we began to explore the possibility that the Joseph in question might be a stand-in for Jesus. Right away, the parallel was easy to see. After all, Joseph, like Jesus, was assumed dead and turned up alive; he too had humble beginnings and ended up a king of sorts. Despite the parallels, however, we realized that we had no smoking gun to justify equating the Joseph of *Joseph and Aseneth* with the Jesus of the Gospels.

We now turned our attention to the woman of the story. Could Joseph's partner, Aseneth, turn out to be a stand-in for Jesus' partner, likely Mary the Magdalene? We weren't at all sure about this identification. After all, even if she was a stand-in for his wife, there are other possibilities for Jesus' partner. For example, another Mary—Mary of Bethany—and her sister Martha were also close to Jesus. According to the Gospels, he often used their home in Bethany—which was within easy walking distance of Jerusalem—as his base of operations.

But the symbolism associated with Aseneth in the text—which we will be decoding throughout this book—couldn't be ignored: she lives in a tower, she has a heavenly and an earthly wedding, she partakes of a magical honeycomb, and she is especially associated with bees. In the story, they swarm her, try to sting her, die, and are resurrected. What is this all about? If the Joseph in our manuscript is Jesus, what do bees have to do with his wife, whoever she might be?

All this perplexed us as we traveled from Antioch and Tarsus in eastern Turkey toward Ephesus in the west. How could we make sense of the obscure *Joseph and Aseneth* text? We were sure that on some level it must be comprehensible. But what could we make of those strange symbols it alludes to? Into what surreal space had we landed? Since we couldn't answer these questions, we decided to shelve the idea of doing further detective work on the manuscript.

But that all changed in Ephesus.

In Ephesus, Turkish authorities allowed us to get within an inch of the imposing statue of the goddess Artemis. This statue, now in a local museum, had originally graced Ephesus' spectacular Temple of Artemis, one of the seven wonders of the ancient world. We now found ourselves standing before the great goddess. Millions—literally millions—in the ancient world had adored her and prayed to her for health, healing, and prosperity. Standing in her presence, we were able to notice details that visitors could not see from fifteen or twenty feet away. For example, we observed that her garment was covered with—bees.

More than this, multiple protrusions cling to her chest. These have perplexed scholars for centuries. Some identified them as breasts. They argued that since Artemis was a nourishing goddess, she must have had dozens of breasts. This theory was accepted by academics for many years until someone noted that the protrusions on her body were too low, didn't look anything like breasts, and don't have the requisite nipples. Others then conjectured that the protrusions must be bulls' testicles. After all, bulls were sacrificed to Artemis, and the testicles must have been something like notches in her belt. There's no need to comment on this theory, although it still has several academic adherents.

Standing before Artemis, it all came together for us. Suddenly, the meaning of the protrusions became apparent—they were bee cocoons or, more accurately, queen bee cells. Just as there were bees clinging to Aseneth, here were bees clinging to Artemis.

Our eyes now tracked to the top of the statue. There, crowning her head, was a tall tower. As in our manuscript, just as Aseneth lived in a tower, here was a tower crowning the goddess Artemis.

We looked at each other at the same time and immediately blurted out with the excitement of children: "Could these be the bees and tower we have been puzzling over in our *Joseph and Aseneth* text?" Suddenly, our text came into sharp focus. It began to make sense, and the light began to dawn. As we went back and forth between statue and text, text and statue, we gradually came to see how the image of Joseph's partner, Aseneth, was modeled on the goddess Artemis. So whomever she might represent historically, she was likened to this figure. In time, we came to see what these symbols really meant.

Put simply, in order to convey the stature of Aseneth—perhaps Mary the Magdalene—to his audience, the unknown author of our manuscript selected a dominant image of his culture, one that he could be sure his readers would readily understand. He took the well-known figure of the goddess Artemis and used her symbols to clothe the depiction of Aseneth. While headquartered in Ephesus, the worship of Artemis flourished all over the Greek and Roman world. Unlike most other local deities, the worship of Artemis boasted religious sanctuaries around the entire Mediterranean basin—from modern-day Spain, Greece, and Turkey to Africa, Jordan, and even Israel.

Now our work began in earnest. As we went through the text systematically, we figured out what the symbols meant by doing something that the few scholars who were familiar with this text had not done—we looked back in time to learn how early Christians understood these symbols. We examined ancient writings and sermons to see how the first followers of Jesus understood Biblical figures like Joseph. This was critical: we wanted to see how early Christians understood their own writings.

This detective work took us into the realm of Syriac-speaking Christianity—little understood in today's world but highly influential in antiquity—as well as into the world of so-called Gnostic Christianity: that is, early Christian mysticism. A door opened to a lost world of early Christian understanding.

We worked jointly over several years, puzzling over the clues given within the document. Without getting ahead of our story, we eventually realized that our overlooked manuscript—ostensibly about *Joseph and Aseneth*—was really about Jesus and Mary the Magdalene. Not only that, it was also about their marriage and the previously unknown politics that surrounded their activism, including the events that led up to the crucifixion. All the imagery and symbolism dovetailed.

At one point, we realized that our obscure manuscript is really a lost Gospel and that it is less about Jesus and more about Mary. What the manuscript is really about is Mary as "the Bride of God." On one level, it is a gripping love story: first meeting, first impressions, wedding preparations, the ceremony, and then the offspring. On another level, it is also a tale of politics, intrigue, betrayal, and mysticism.

As we pored through the manuscript, we realized that while knowledge of the marriage had been relegated to historical rumor, it never really went away. In fact, it is actually very impressive how this tradition refused to disappear. Over the centuries, it has been resurrected in different ways and in different places. Nonetheless, the stories are, for the most part, surprisingly consistent. In his chronicle of the Albigensian Crusade, Pierre Vaux de Cernay wrote in 1213 that the townspeople of Béziers were burned alive on the feast day of Mary Magdalene (22 July 1209) in retribution for "their scandalous assertion that Mary Magdalene and Christ were lovers."[6] During the Renaissance, Michelangelo sculpted a Pietà that was meant for his own tomb. Today, it is in the Museo dell'Opera del Duomo in Florence. The composition shows a group of people crowded around

Jesus just after the crucifixion. Surprisingly, Jesus' leg is slung over one of the women. The slung leg is a Renaissance code indicating a sexual relationship.

There is a 16th-century Renaissance painting by Luca Cambiasi that can act as a cipher for Michelangelo's sculpture. Today, Cambiasi's painting is in the Hermitage in St. Petersburg. It depicts Venus and Adonis in the same way Michelangelo depicts Jesus and Mary—slung leg and all. In other words, Michelangelo depicted Jesus and Mary the Magdalene in the way Cambiasi depicted a Greek god and his divine consort.

Another example of the enduring nature of the heavenly marriage is associated with Rennes-le-Château in France. In 1885, a parish priest named Bérenger Saunière is said to have found secret coded documents hidden in a hollow pillar in an 11th-century church in the town. This has given rise to endless *Da Vinci Code*-type speculations. According to the various theories, the secret texts reveal Mary the Magdalene's marriage to Jesus.

And it's not just in writings and art that the marriage theme finds expression. More recently, for example, a popular song by U2 ("Until the End of the World," from their album *Achtung Baby*, 1991) refers to Jesus and Mary the Magdalene as a bride and groom. In a song called "Jesus Had a Son" (from their *Long John Silver* album, 1972), Jefferson Airplane belt out "Jesus had a son by Mary Magdalene. . . ." In other words, Jesus' marriage to Mary the Magdalene is not an unknown idea. It is part of the substrata of our culture—and here we were looking at a document that took us back to the source of this idea.

But why did the marriage have to go underground? If this was historical fact, why did it have to become historical rumor? Why was it relegated to our culture's fringes? Why was Mary the Magdalene written out, as it were, from the authorized accounts of Jesus' life? In other words, why has this chapter in Jesus' life been covered up? When it came to our manuscript, why did the author have to encode the text to preserve it? Now, at last, we had a decoded document that could answer all these questions.

Surprises

Reading the document from our new perspective, readers will be startled to learn about the human side of Jesus . . . and what this aspect of Jesus meant to his early followers. The new information gleaned from our lost Gospel will flesh out an aspect of Jesus only hinted at in the canonical texts. Clearly, in their attempt to assert his divinity, the latter tend to gloss over the details of Jesus' personal life.

Unexpectedly, through this text, we came across a whole new early Christian movement—one that was vastly different from the Jewish messianic movement led by James, the brother of Jesus, and from the Gentile "Christ Movement" led by Paul which, eventually, became Christianity as we know it today. In fact, the group of Jesus followers that we've rediscovered predates Paul and takes us into a now-lost world that has been inaccessible for centuries.

The early centuries of Christianity were exciting, gut-wrenching, noisy times, as factions jostled with one another—even battled vigorously with each other—over how best to understand Jesus—the man, his mission, and his message. According to Marvin Meyer, several of these factions "showed remarkable similarities to the mystery religions" of the Roman Empire.[7] The "mystery" religions involved secret teachings and secret rituals of initiation. Often these included the use of drugs, sex, and altered states of mind. Until the interventions of the Roman emperors Constantine and Theodosius in the 4th century, there wasn't one right, orthodox, or catholic (i.e., universal) expression of the faith. But eventually, one version of Christianity—Paul's version focusing on the resurrected "Christ" as opposed to the historical Jesus—was endorsed by the power of the Roman Empire. After that, multiple Christianities disappeared. Suddenly, there was only one correct version sanctioned by the Roman state. Those versions that did not make it into the official canon were dubbed heresies and consigned to the flames.

Today, conditioned by thousands of years of Pauline Christianity, it seems outlandish to talk, for example, of a married Jesus. The simple fact is that we live inside the post-Constantine box. In the post-Constantine era, talking about a married Jesus is akin to reporting on alien abductions.[8] According to the mainstream—even the secular mainstream—the orthodox narrative is right or, at least, it is the only narrative with a shot at being right. By definition, every other narrative is wrong or at least far-fetched.

However, when we look at the first centuries of Christian development, we shouldn't make the anachronistic mistake of thinking that everyone agreed with Paul and the version of Christianity that we've inherited from him. More than this, his version did not represent the normative expression of the new faith. The original movements in Jerusalem—the Gnostics, the Ebionites, and the Nazarenes—all disagreed with Paul's version of Jesus' message.

In many ways, the Christianity of the first few centuries was much more varied than the religion is today. Some might object, saying that that we live in a multi-denominational Christian world. But in some ways, this is an illusion. The fact is that Catholics, Orthodox, Anglicans, Reformation and post-Reformation Protestants (e.g., Presbyterians, Lutherans, etc.), and Evangelicals all trace their spiritual lineage to the theology of Paul. However different they are from each other, and however important they think these theological differences are, all five contemporary Christian groupings represent variations on the same theme: Pauline Christianity.

But our text gives a voice to those who lost out. In the manuscript, for example, we encounter a non-Pauline theology of redemption. Our lost Gospel is essentially a story of salvation—but it represents a perspective that's not familiar to us today, even though it was believed by many in the early church. It advances a theology of human liberation markedly different from the one we have inherited from Paul and his followers. It is a theology based on Jesus' marriage, not his death; on his moments of joy, not the "passion" of his suffering.

An Unknown Plot

Besides giving us previously unknown details of Jesus' private life, our text reveals details of his political life. Specifically, in our manuscript, we uncover the story of a plot against Jesus' life prior to his arrest and crucifixion in Jerusalem. Jesus was clearly a marked man—and he knew it. Especially after the execution of his cousin, John the Baptizer,[9] by none other than Herod Antipas, the ruler of two Roman territories: the Galilee in northern Israel, and Peraea in modern Jordan.

Jesus had many opponents and enemies. The entire Herodian party—i.e., Herod's extended family and its supporters—was literally out to get him. Jesus' enemies also included other powerful people such as the High Priest Caiaphas in Jerusalem, as well as the Roman procurator/prefect Pontius Pilate and members of the occupying power, perhaps as far afield as Rome itself. Then, too, there were Jesus' Jewish debating partners and critics—the Pharisees and the Scribes.

The fact is that Jesus and his followers were well aware that the Roman authorities and their Jewish underlings were carefully watching them. No would-be "King of the Jews" could, of course, escape detection—at least, not for long.

Jesus' message was radical and seditious: "Coming soon—the 'Kingdom of God.'" Simply put, declaring that the Kingdom of God was on the cusp of history represented a forceful challenge to the viability and continuity of Roman rule over Jewish Judaea. Jesus went further: he claimed that many in his audience would live to see the redemption—that is, the end of Roman rule and its replacement by God's Kingdom. That's a fantastic assertion. It raised huge expectations. Jesus' powerful message tapped deeply into the messianic dream of ancient Israel. God, it was thought, would intervene in human affairs by sending a Moses-like messenger, or messiah. All evil empires—and peoples—would be swept away, Romans included, into the garbage heap of history. And all this was going to happen not in some distant future but now. Right now.

Given all this, the Romans had an excellent reason to monitor Jesus and his potentially seditious group. Equally, ordinary Jewish folk—Jesus' countrymen—had especially good reasons to become enthused. This was an explosive situation. That Jesus' period of activism—his so-called ministry—may have lasted three years is remarkable given the incendiary nature of his preaching. His message wasn't just religious: it was profoundly political and potentially threatening to established authority. Incredibly, the political side of Jesus has been vastly underrated. By highlighting an unknown plot against his life, prior to the one recounted in the Gospels, our rediscovered text places the Jesus story back in the historical/political context from which it has been extracted.

A Hidden Message

We now embark on our detective work. As we scrutinize each section, the document in question occupies center stage in our investigation. We make no assumptions. We start at the beginning and let the text speak for itself.

Along the way, as the investigation unfolds, we'll also consider why a group of early Christians would think they had to disguise this history, composing for us a narrative that requires decoding. Indeed, why did they preserve this writing for posterity?

What we will soon discover is that encoded documents were not unusual in the world of early Christianity. It may seem strange to us today, but the early Christians thought the Old Testament—which preceded Jesus—was also a coded text. They believed that its real message became apparent only after Jesus' ministry. Jesus, too, veiled his central teaching concerning the Kingdom of God in parables. This reinforced the early Christian belief in the need to decipher hidden meanings in sacred scriptures. In other words, encoding and decoding was part and parcel of early Christian theology.[10]

For our part, we'll do something that scholars so far have failed to do with respect to early Christianity. When analyzing this particular text, we're the first to use the actual decoding techniques employed by early Christians themselves. From their writings and sermons that have remarkably survived the centuries, they will tell us—in their own words—what this ancient manuscript really means. What we're presenting is not some alien, modern-day take on the material. Rather, it is one that arises organically, out of the way in which communities within early Christianity understood Biblical writings.

In this document, against those who would seek to quell its message, we hear a voice that struggles to be heard. The censors include not only Romans but also Christians who did not share the perspective of the author of our Gospel. Certainly Paul and his followers would have rejected these views, as they objected to anything pertaining to Jesus' family. Paul and his followers were, after all, hostile not only to Mary the Magdalene, but also to James, Jesus' brother, who took over the leadership of Jesus' movement after the crucifixion.

Here's the Clincher

Hidden messages, a secret history, a lost Gospel, encoding and decoding—pretty heady stuff. But, to our absolute amazement, we discovered that we weren't the first to think that our text contains a hidden meaning. In the course of our investigation, we came across an ancient Syriac letter, never before translated into any modern language, that indicated that the person in antiquity who first discovered our document also suspected that it contained a secret message, an embedded truth.

We don't know the name of that person. He was likely a monk. But we have the nearly fifteen-hundred-year-old letter he sent to the translator he commissioned. He obviously intuited that it contained something very, very important. Around 550 C.E. he found our manuscript in a Greek version. Not very familiar with that language, he sent it to a scholar named Moses of Ingila[11] for translation into Syriac. The translation he requested represents the oldest extant manuscript of our work, a copy of a now-lost, much-older Greek writing. The anonymous man who commissioned the translation also asked Moses of Ingila to tell him its inner meaning. We don't know if Moses of Ingila ever did oblige, but now, some 1,460 years after his written request, we are pleased that this book provides this ancient truth-seeker with the answer he was looking for: a disclosure of its hidden meaning.

Here's our approach: first, we will present a synopsis of our manuscript by way of an overview. Without going into all the rich details of the story, we'll give the reader a précis of what it says. Then, we'll take the reader through the surface narrative. Here we identify the questions that prompted us to look beyond its superficial story line and issues that point to a deeper underlying meaning. We invite the reader to partner with us in our detective work.

Next, we summarize what we know of this writing—its date and origin and what scholars say about the work.

After all this, we start making sense of our text by stepping into the world of early Christianity, so as to learn the original Christian approach to under-standing scripture. Bit by bit, we decode the various elements of the story. In this book, we unravel the complex symbols and retrieve the original narrative.

Finally, we provide another first: an English translation of the oldest sur-viving manuscript of this ancient writing, the one written in Syriac.[12] This translation, along with commentary, is presented as Appendix I of this book so that you—the reader—can judge for yourself what the original narrative says. Two 6th-century covering letters to the manuscript are also translated for the first time from Syriac into English as Appendix II. Most exciting, we realized that a 13th-century censor literally took a knife to the manuscript and also covered certain words with ink. Using multi-spectral imaging, we were able to see these words for the first time in almost a thousand years.

PART I
A MYSTERIOUS MANUSCRIPT

1

MANUSCRIPT 17,202

Located in the British Library is a manuscript dating to around 570 c.e. It was acquired on November 11, 1847. The man who sold it was an Egyptian by the name of Auguste Pacho, a native of Alexandria. Pacho got the ancient text from the Macarios monastery in Egypt. Founded in the 6th century c.e. and located between Cairo and Alexandria in the Nitrian Valley, Macarios is one of the oldest Syrian monasteries in the world. The manuscript left the monastery in July but en route to the UK, Pacho made a stop over in Paris, probably selling other manuscripts to the libraries there. He finally made it to the UK in November and promptly sold the text to the British Museum, which then turned it over to the British Library.

The Macarios Monastery manuscript was filed under the unpretentious name *British Library Manuscript Number 17,202*. It's written in Syriac, a Middle Eastern language related to Aramaic, the language spoken by Jesus and many of his contemporaries. Titled *A Volume of Records of Events Which Have Shaped the World*, it's a collection of writings—a kind of miniature library. It represents an anonymous 6th-century monk's attempt to preserve a record of events which, in his view, were earth-shattering in their import. As a result, he includes in his collection an account of the conversion of the Emperor Constantine to Christianity; an important church history that relates the debates over the person of Christ; the finding of key 1st-century Christian relics; and a proof of eternal life provided by the once-famous legend of the "Seven Sleepers of Ephesus."

All hot topics in his day . . . and for his community of believers.

One manuscript does not seem to fit this collection of ostensibly important writings. It is called *The Story of Joseph the Just and Aseneth his Wife*. It's this writing that concerns us here. This is our mysterious text, and it represents the focus of our investigation.

The Story of Joseph the Just and Aseneth his Wife did not originate with the 6th-century monk who preserved it. It was translated into Syriac, as an anonymous letter-writer who introduces the work tells us, from a much earlier Greek work—perhaps a century or more earlier. Even that previous document was most likely a copy of a still earlier work. It was copied, like the New Testament documents themselves, by generations of dedicated scribes who toiled to preserve this precious tale for future readers. The story this Syriac manuscript relates, therefore, stretches back in history—beyond the 4th and 3rd centuries— as far back as the 2nd or perhaps even the 1st century c.e.

Put differently, the story that *British Library Manuscript Number 17,202* tells may go as far back as Jesus' lifetime or shortly thereafter. It reaches back to the time when the canonical Gospels found in the New Testament were being written. We cannot be absolutely sure of its dating. Nor can we be sure of the dating of the Gospels themselves. In this regard, most scholars date the Gospel of Mark to around 70 c.e.; Matthew to the 80s; Luke to the 90s; and John from 90 onwards. These dates for original composition are based on historical reconstructions that take into account when their message would best fit the development of early Christianity within the wider context of the Roman world. There are no New Testament manuscripts dating from the 1st century—hence no originals. The earliest surviving complete copies of the Gospels date no earlier than the 4th century. In both cases—our manuscript and the canonical Gospels—we do not know who the author was. As in the Gospels, there are no dates given within our manuscript concerning its authorship. Nor are there datable originals with which to compare our copy. We only have copies of copies of copies, written centuries after the original, and the manuscript trail takes us back only so far. And yet, our manuscript roughly dates to the same time as our earliest copies of the Gospels—maybe even earlier.

While the document in question went by many names in the ancient world, scholars today refer to it as *Joseph and Aseneth*. The work is a curious one. For one thing, its name is terribly misleading. It was dubbed *Joseph and Aseneth* because it purports to be about the ancient Israelite patriarch Joseph and his obscure Egyptian wife, Aseneth. According to the Biblical Book of Genesis (chapters 37–50), these individuals lived some thirty-seven hundred years ago, a few generations after Abraham but long before Moses and 1,500 to 1,700 years before the birth of Jesus of Nazareth.

In contrast to the Biblical story of *Joseph and Aseneth*, the British Library manuscript tells a seemingly different story. It is a tale of love, sacred sex, politics, betrayal, and murder.

Pretty hot stuff, even by ancient standards.

In fact, there is very little in the manuscript that corresponds to the Biblical account of *Joseph and Aseneth*. It's not the same story at all. There are too many details within the writing which invite—even demand—that we move beyond its superficial layer to its underlying meaning; a secret history, if you will. In other words, we strongly suspect that the surface narrative is really a cover story for a much deeper message—one that makes eminent sense only in the context of the first days of Christianity.

2

WHAT DOES IT SAY? . . .
AND
WHAT DOES IT NOT SAY?

To review: the British Library's *Joseph and Aseneth* represents a very different story from the one found in the Book of Genesis. It seems to be using the names Joseph and Aseneth as ciphers, to tell us something very important, in a disguised fashion, about the history of two other individuals. In other words, hidden beneath the superficial narrative is a deeper, far more pressing message.

There are four episodes in our document. To clearly differentiate our commentary from the synopsis, we have separated out the latter and put it in different typeface. A complete translation of *Joseph and Aseneth* based on the original Syriac manuscript can be found as Appendix I.

Here, then, is *The Story of Joseph the Just and Aseneth his Wife*, the questions it raises, and the hidden history at which it hints.

Episode 1: The Meeting
First impressions. Joseph's prayer for Aseneth's transformation.

Synopsis

Joseph, the ancient Israelite patriarch, is in Egypt and approaches the city of Heliopolis. He sends messengers to Potiphar, a priest of Heliopolis and advisor to Pharaoh, indicating that he would like to have lunch with him. Potiphar has a beautiful daughter, Aseneth, an 18-year-old virgin who has shunned men. Joseph, too, is a virgin.

While Aseneth is an Egyptian, she is described as being "noble and glorious like Sarah, beautiful like Rebecca, and virtuous like Rachel" (1:5), the matriarchs of ancient Israel.

Potiphar's estate is described in detail. It includes a house and a lush garden. Most importantly, it contains a tall tower. Aseneth lives on the top floor of the tower. She occupies a suite with ten rooms, which are described in detail including a room devoted to a host of deities. She is attended by seven beautiful virgins. Potiphar's entire estate is enclosed with a wall and gates.

To greet Joseph, Aseneth puts on "garments of fine white linen and rubies" (3:6). She then places "a crown on her head and covered herself with bridal veils" (3:7). Her parents rejoice to see her "adorned like a Bride of God" (4:1). Potiphar describes Joseph as "the Powerful One of God" (3:4) and as "the savior" (4:7). He continues, telling Aseneth that Joseph "will be given to you as a bridegroom forever" (4:9).

Aseneth initially despises Joseph as a foreigner—"the son of a shepherd from Canaan" (4:11), she says dismissively—but when she sees him she quickly changes her mind. Joseph arrives in style in his golden chariot. He wears a white tunic and a purple robe and his head is adorned with a golden crown. Twelve golden rays of light "like the rays of the shining sun" (5:5) emanate from his head. There is a royal scepter in his left hand, a plant like an olive branch in his right. Aseneth quickly revises her first contemptuous impression. She says: "Now I see the sun shining from his chariot that has come to us" (6:2), adding that she hadn't realized that "Joseph was the Son of God" (6:3).

Joseph eats separately from the Egyptians (presumably because of Jewish dietary concerns). Aseneth greets Joseph, "Blessed one of God Most High, peace to you" (8:2). Joseph replies, "May the Lord, bringer of life to all things, bless you" (8:3). Joseph and Aseneth are proclaimed to be "brother" and "sister" (8:4 and 7:10).

Potiphar encourages them to kiss. As they are about to kiss, Joseph places his right hand between Aseneth's breasts and says, "It is not right for a man worshipping God, who blesses the living God and eats the blessed bread of life and drinks the blessed cup of immortality and incorruptibility and is anointed with the perfumed ointment of holiness, to have sexual relations and kiss a foreign woman who blesses dead, empty idols, and eats foul strangled food and drinks the libation of deceit and is anointed with the ointment of corruption" (8:6).

Aseneth is taken aback by this rejection. Seeing Aseneth's pain, Joseph is moved to prayer. In the name of the God who calls people from "darkness to light, from error to truth, and from death to life" (8:12) he beseeches Him to renew and transform Aseneth. He prays that she may eat the eternal bread of life, drink the blessed cup, be counted amongst God's people "and live forever" (8:14). With that said, Joseph leaves, promising to return in eight days.

If this story is really referring to the Biblical Joseph and Aseneth, right away we see problems with this text. In this account, Aseneth quickly moves to center stage, whereas the Bible makes Joseph the primary figure. In the Biblical narrative, Joseph is betrayed by his brothers and sold into slavery in Egypt. The Book of Genesis tells us that Joseph's brothers were jealous of their father's love for him. After all, as a sign of his affection, the patriarch Jacob had given his son Joseph a multi-colored coat. In the Biblical tale, after a series of trials including sexual temptation and imprisonment, Joseph works his way up to becoming the second most powerful person in Egypt next to Pharaoh. In the Book of Genesis, Pharaoh gives Joseph an Egyptian wife, Aseneth. She is the daughter of Potiphar, priest of On (Genesis 41:45). In this way, Joseph is married into an influential Egyptian priestly family. In time, they have two sons: Manasseh and Ephrem (Genesis 41:50–52).

That's all we ever hear of Aseneth in the Biblical text. No sooner is she mentioned than she disappears. All the Bible tells us is that Aseneth is the daughter of an Egyptian priest, she was given in marriage to Joseph, and she bore him two children. We are provided with absolutely no information about her appearance, beliefs, personality, values, or character. There is nothing that would indicate that she was a person of importance or that she played a vital role in human history.

Joseph and Aseneth, on the other hand, right away takes us into vastly different territory, one that is chaste and sensual at the same time. This Aseneth is an attractive woman with strong opinions of her own. She is a forceful personality and her perceptions of, and reactions to, Joseph are featured prominently in the narrative. Her parents respect her wishes. Although Aseneth is an Egyptian, she is described as having the virtues of the Israelite matriarchs—comparable to Sarah, Rebecca, and Rachel. Later Greek manuscripts heighten her "Jewishness": "and this [girl] had nothing similar to the virgins of the Egyptians, but she was in every respect similar to the daughters of the Hebrews."[1]

Why? Why the insistence upon her Jewish qualities? The Biblical Aseneth did not live among Israelites. Is our manuscript perhaps referring to a woman who did?

Moreover, in our document, Aseneth's father's impressive estate is described in detail: a house, a garden, walls, and, most importantly, a tower in which Aseneth lives. Do these seemingly irrelevant facts have a deeper significance?

After an initial hesitation, Aseneth is attracted to Joseph and is groomed to be "the Bride of God" (4:1). This is very strange language about an ordinary human wedding—if indeed that is what it's about. In the Bible, Joseph is a Hebrew, the forefather of two of the twelve Israelite tribes of the ancient world. In contrast, the language describing him in the *Joseph and Aseneth* manuscript is not Hebraic. It is not Jewish. In the Jewish tradition, no human would ever be described as "God" or a "Bride of God." In this text, "Aseneth is the divine bride, [and] Joseph is her groom."[2] If this were a Jewish text, this idea would be utter blasphemy.

As Erwin Goodenough has noted, "Christian traditions of the first centuries as taken from the Christian writers refer to the contemporary writings of not a single Jew."[3] In other words, seen from the Christian side, *Joseph and Aseneth* is unlikely to be a Jewish text. On the Jewish side, in Ross Shepard Kraemer's words, there is a total "absence of any knowledge of this Aseneth story in early Jewish sources."[4] But, if it's not Jewish, is it Christian?

The attempt to locate the people who wrote this text is crucial to understanding the manuscript. To make sense of the text, we need to understand the original community from which it sprang. So let's examine how Joseph is described in *Joseph and Aseneth*. For starters, Joseph's physical appearance is described in our manuscript in far more detail than in Genesis. Here he wears not the multi-colored coat of a Hebrew, nor the clothing of an Egyptian, but a white tunic and a purple robe, reminiscent of the attire of a Roman emperor. Furthermore, he is adorned with a crown, and twelve rays of light emanate from his head. He holds a scepter in his hand. These can hardly be accidental details. But what do they signify?

In this text, Joseph is Torah-observant (that is, he observes the laws in the Five Books of Moses) and serious about his religion. He is concerned about Aseneth's worship of idols—so much so that he refuses to kiss her and draws away from her. What are we to make of Joseph's refusal to kiss Aseneth prior to marriage? He seems to protest too much, and it's curious that kissing and sexual relations are mentioned at all. The Bible never mentions any intimacy between Joseph and Aseneth.

Moreover, Joseph's subsequent prayer for Aseneth's transformation is also odd. It is offered in the name of the God who calls people "from darkness to light, from error to truth, from death to life" (8:12). Joseph prays that she might be recreated, referring to her receiving "the eternal bread of life" and "the blessed cup" so that she might live forever (8:13–14). These phrases are nowhere to be found in the Hebrew Bible. Simply put, once again, they sound Christian, not Jewish.

There are a lot of remarkable details here. It sounds as if the writer is trying to tell us something very important and, perhaps, at the time of writing, something very dangerous. Perhaps that is why the original author of the manuscript tells the story using surrogates.

Episode 2: The Rebirth
A strange dreamlike sequence involving Aseneth in a tower.

After confessing her sins, she is visited by an angelic being who looks like Joseph. She eats honey and is swarmed by bees.

Synopsis
While Joseph is away, Aseneth weeps for a week, eats nothing and is unable to sleep. She puts on a black mourning garment. She tosses her

fine robes, jewelry, and golden crown out of the window. Similarly she throws all her idols, engravings, and images of Egyptian deities out of the window. She takes the offerings to the gods—food and libations—and throws these out the window too, for the wild dogs to consume. She spreads ashes around her room. All this lasts for seven days.

Finally, she prays to God. She confesses her sins: transgressing God's law and offering sacrifices to idols. She prays for deliverance from persecutors (foreshadowing later developments) knowing that "an old lion," "the father of the gods of Egypt" (12:12), will seek retribution for her abandonment of them. She asks for divine forgiveness for initially speaking poorly of Joseph: "[I] said evil, empty things against my lord Joseph because I did not know he was your son" (13:9). She sees the morning star and rejoices.

Then a man from heaven appears—someone "alike in every respect to Joseph in clothes and crown and royal scepter" (14:8) but whose face was like lightning and his eyes "like the splendor of the sun" (14:9). He orders her to take off her black robe and put on a new one along with a belt. She washes. The man from heaven informs her that today her name has been written in the Book of Life; that she is renewed, refashioned, and has been granted new life. She is, essentially, born again.

He also tells her that she will eat the bread of life, drink the cup of immortality, and be anointed with the ointment of incorruptibility. God has given Joseph to you, he says, adding that no longer will her name be Aseneth but "City of Refuge" (15:5). The man from heaven also tells her that all the nations shall take refuge in her—those who give their allegiance to God in repentance will find in her security. Repentance, the man from heaven explains, is the daughter of the Most High, the mother of virgins, who has prepared a "heavenly bridal chamber for those who love her" (15:7). God himself loves her and the angels respect her.

Aseneth offers the man from heaven bread and wine. He then asks for a honeycomb, which mysteriously appears in Aseneth's chamber; white as snow and smelling pleasantly like the spirit of life. He eats a piece of the comb and puts another piece into Aseneth's mouth, while tracing—in blood—the sign of the cross on the surface of the honeycomb. Suddenly, a multitude of bees flies up from the honeycomb. They totally envelop

Aseneth. Some good bees fly upwards to heaven; evil bees—i.e., those who wish to injure Aseneth—die but are brought back to life by the command of the heavenly man. The man from heaven then blesses her and her seven virgin attendants. With that, he disappears.

As the heavenly man recedes, Aseneth confesses that she "did not know that God from heaven appeared in my bed" (17:7).

Clearly, Aseneth is front and center. This is her story—her remarkable transformation—totally unlike anything found in the Bible.

The unexpected language also leaps off the page—Joseph is "God's son." No matter how much in love with him she is, why would Aseneth describe Joseph, the ancient Israelite patriarch, in such non-Torah terms? Again, this is Christian terminology. Simply put, there is nothing—absolutely nothing—like this in the Five Books of Moses. In the Book of Genesis, Joseph appears as an agent of God—strong, faithful, intelligent, focused, and pure. In a sense, he is, indeed, a savior-figure—he not only saves the Egyptians from starvation but also ensures the continuity of the Israelite people. But, in a Jewish text, he would never have been described as "God's son."

Moreover, what are we to make of the heavenly Joseph look-alike? This is an episode completely missing from the Biblical narrative. In our manuscript, Joseph is a spiritual being as well as an earthly figure. Put differently, he has many natures and assumes several forms. Furthermore, according to the manuscript, *Joseph and Aseneth*'s union is first celebrated in heaven, not on earth. This spiritual ceremony is interesting. Aseneth confesses her sins, is robed in a new garment, and then she washes—is all this symbolic of her new life? The angelic being tells her she will eat of the bread of life and drink from the cup of immortality, being anointed with the oil of incorruption. Kraemer states that the "ensuing dialogue between Aseneth and the angel is frustratingly esoteric."[5] It can be decoded, however, if we pay attention to what happens next. The angel literally puts a piece of honeycomb into Aseneth's mouth, all the while tracing in blood the sign of the cross across its surface. This is not so esoteric. Clearly, this is a kind of Christian Communion ceremony. At the same time, the whole thing is oddly erotic, since it represents the consummation of her marriage with Joseph's heavenly counterpart.

But what does this heavenly ceremony signify? How does it relate to the later earthly marriage? And why do the bees fly up from the honeycomb, encircling her and finally settling near her tower? In the entire corpus of the Hebrew Bible and Rabbinic tradition, there is nothing—absolutely nothing—like this story.

But if the story is Christian, not Jewish, and is referring to sex and marriage between a divinely chosen "Bride of God" and "God's son," can it be that this ancient document, last copied by Syriac monks some fifteen hundred years ago, is preserving a tradition hinted at in Christian texts but so far missing in the historical record?

The deciphering process requires us to look deeper.

Specifically, what are we to make of the odd designation of Aseneth as a "City of Refuge" (15:5 and later 19:4)? In what sense could Aseneth be a "City of Refuge"? Why is she called this? There are six cities of refuge mentioned in the Bible (Numbers 35:11–24; Deuteronomy 19:1–13). They represent safe havens for individuals charged with unintentional murder. Are the Biblical cities of refuge the intended reference here? What does our text have to do with serious crimes involving both slayers and avengers? Who would seek refuge in Aseneth? Who are they fleeing? What is their crime?

We know that within the Biblical tradition, naming is associated with creation and renaming with new creation. In Genesis, for example, the structural elements of the universe are named along with humans and animals. Later on, in the speeches of Isaiah (chapter 60, for instance), the prophet envisages a restored Israel freed from captivity in Babylon. He sees an exciting new social and political reality about to dawn on the world's stage. He urges the exiles to prepare for their triumphant march homeward—valleys shall be raised and mountains lowered so that their passage from Babylon back to Jerusalem will be an easy trek. Describing God as "your Redeemer, the Mighty One of Jacob" (Isaiah 60:16), the prophet becomes ecstatic as he proclaims that God will rename Jerusalem "the City of the Lord" (Isaiah 60:14); He will rename the walls "Salvation" (Isaiah 60:18); and its gates, He will rename "Praise" (Isaiah 60:18).

But what new creation is taking place in our story? In what way will all nations take refuge in Aseneth? After all, the Biblical Aseneth is neither a Bride of God nor a refuge to many people. The text itself seems to suggest an answer. The specific rituals involved in the strange heavenly ceremony—the centerpiece of our story—are very carefully depicted. The sequence is: confession, dressing, washing, offering bread and wine, eating, encirclement by bees, and a final blessing. What is the meaning of this mysterious and moving ceremony? It sounds highly liturgical.

But what liturgy?

To some extent this ritual is explained in *Joseph and Aseneth*. In other words, the text provides clues for its own decipherment. On a simple level, the ritual is about Aseneth's transformation into a suitable bride for Joseph and it seems to be built around a Communion-like ceremony. But many details elude us: the honeycomb, for instance, and the bees which encircle Aseneth and which end up near her tower. They appear just after the eating of the honey—almost as the climax of the ceremony—and just before the angelic being blesses Aseneth, the final element in this ritual. Why all this imagery of honey, honeycomb, and bees? These cannot be accidental details. What does this strange liturgy tell us about the two central figures—Joseph and Aseneth? Or the people they really represent?

Obviously, the decoding has to start with the cross. The symbolism of the cross—drawn in blood—seems quite explicit. This suggests that our story comes from Christian circles, not Jewish ones, as had been previously surmised by some scholars.[6] We also should not conclude that the presence of the cross is either a late interpolation into an early text, or proof that the text is no earlier than the 4th century, when the cross is assumed to have become a Christian symbol. The fact is that we have dozens of crosses from the 1st century in clearly Christian contexts. They are usually dismissed as arbitrary scratches or stonemasons' marks. For example, there are several crosses next to the name Jesus on ossuaries from 1st-century Jerusalem tombs.[7] At Bethsaida, in the Galilee, archaeologists Rami Arav and Richard Freund have discovered a 1st-century cross in situ.[8] There is also a clear cross in Herculaneum, a Roman city that was destroyed, along with Pompeii, by the eruption of Mount Vesuvius in the year 79 C.E. This would place Christian crosses firmly in the 1st century. As a result, some have dismissed the Herculaneum cross as the remains of a bookshelf.[9] But the best 1st-century Christian cross is from Pompeii, where a clear cross was found in a graffito in a courtyard. It has *VIV* inscribed at the top, probably short for the Latin *vivat*, meaning *live*.[10]

When the author of *Joseph and Aseneth* has the angelic being draw a cross in blood across the honeycomb, we sense that he is trying to convey something important to us. To that end, he may have embedded clues within his writing to prompt us to make connections to other people and other events. For example, the "bridal chamber" phrase immediately conjures up Gnosticism, a branch of early Christianity that reveled in mysticism and hidden codes. After the 4th century, when Trinitarian Christianity (that is, the idea that God is both one and three in the persons of the Father, the Son and the Holy Ghost) won exclusive imperial favor, Gnosticism was banned by the triumphant church and was accused, among other things, of indulging in secret ceremonies involving ritualized sex. Indeed, some Gnostic writings like the *Gospel of Philip* talk about a heavenly bridal chamber as a sacrament, that is, a holy ritual. The honeycomb ceremony in *Joseph and Aseneth* also feels sacramental—something akin to the Christian Communion service. Maybe it's preserving something historical and describing, in Gnostic terms, the first Communion ever held. Furthermore, Aseneth's report of the episode with the heavenly man as "God from heaven appeared in my bed" (17:7) is, to say the least, highly unusual and erotic. Again, the combination of *God* and *bed* in the same breath seems to suggest early Christian Gnosticism, as opposed to anything Jewish or Trinitarian.

The next episode in the *Joseph and Aseneth* manuscript focuses on the actual marriage and its consummation, resulting in children.

Episode 3: The Marriage

The wedding, the consummation, and the children.

Synopsis

Joseph returns from his trip and Aseneth dresses resplendently for her wedding—a glittering robe, a golden belt, bracelets, anklets, a precious necklace, and a crown of gold upon her head. She covers her head with a bridal veil and washes her face. The manager of her father's estate greets her by saying, "The Lord God of heaven truly chose you to be the bride of his first-born son" (18:13).

Aseneth meets Joseph and recounts to him her experiences with the heavenly visitor. They embrace for a long time and Aseneth receives from him the spirit of life, the spirit of wisdom and, finally, the spirit of truth. Aseneth insists on washing Joseph's feet. Joseph takes hold of Aseneth's right hand and kisses her on the head. Everyone who sees this is "amazed at her beauty" and they give "glory to God who gives life and raises the dead" (20:5). Aseneth's father announces that tomorrow the wedding will take place. Joseph stays in Potiphar's house but does not have sexual intercourse with Aseneth, noting "it is not right for a man who worships God to know his bride before the wedding" (20:8).

Pharaoh, the ruler, blesses Aseneth: "Blessed are you by the Lord God of Joseph, because he is the first-born of God, and you will be called the Daughter of God Most High" (21:3). They kiss. After seven days of celebration, Joseph engages in sexual intercourse with Aseneth. In time, they have two children.

As noted, no Jewish author would ever refer to an Israelite patriarch, or anyone else for that matter, as "the Son of God" (6:3). This is just not part of the Jewish landscape and was at the core of the rift between Judaism and Christianity some nineteen hundred years ago. In Judaism, God is one. "Hear, O Israel, the Lord is our God. The Lord is One" (Deuteronomy 6:4) is the central declaration of Jewish faith. To this day, an observant Jew proclaims this statement of faith once during daylight hours and once at night. If a Jew believes that he's about to die, he must endeavor to utter this statement as his dying words. Moreover, within Judaism, God does not have a divine family—no sons or daughters. Again, here we have the clear sense that this text comes from a Christian source for which having a plurality within the Godhead is not anathema.

But once again, we have to ask: to whom is the text referring? Clearly, it is not referring to the Joseph of history, the ancient Israelite patriarch.

We now note that the marriage described in our manuscript is literally made in heaven. There is a heavenly Joseph and an earthly Joseph. Only after Joseph and Aseneth are proclaimed as the "first-born son of God" and, most intriguingly, "daughter of the Lord" do the lovers kiss and have sexual relations. Only then is their marriage consummated and their union blessed with two children.

Curiously enough, the story doesn't end here. It's not a "happily ever after" account.

Episode 4: The Murder Plot

The conspiracy to abduct Aseneth, kill Joseph, and murder their children is foiled.

Synopsis

There are seven years of plenty. These come to an end and seven years of famine begin. Aseneth instigates a visit to Joseph's father, Jacob, and his family. Jacob is described by Aseneth as "like a god to me" (22:3), resplendent in his old age, with bright flashing eyes and the body of a mighty man. Joseph's brother Levi, described as a prophet who knows "the secrets of God" (22:14), informs Aseneth of her elevated status.

Seeing Aseneth's great beauty, Pharaoh's first-born son is jealous and desires her. He approaches Simon and Levi, both brothers of Joseph, trying to bribe them with great wealth if they would consent to forge an alliance with him. The plan is to kill Joseph and his children so he can marry Aseneth. They refuse. Pharaoh's son succeeds in recruiting Dan, Gad, Naphtali, and Asher (sons of Jacob with his two concubines), however, and provides them with two thousand troops to help capture Aseneth, kill Joseph, and murder the children. Pharaoh's son also plans to murder his father, the Pharaoh.

The plot is foiled. Pharaoh's son is unable to kill his father. The loyal brothers of Joseph rescue Aseneth. The treasonous brothers throw themselves on Aseneth's mercy. She is forgiving, saying that it is wrong to repay evil with evil. Benjamin, another of Joseph's brothers who is accompanying Aseneth, takes a stone and hits Pharaoh's son in the left temple. He is about to finish him off when Aseneth intercedes, again saying that we must not repay evil for evil. They bandage up the wounded son of Pharaoh and take him to his father.

On the third day, however, Pharaoh's son dies from the wound.

And there the dramatic story abruptly ends: the plot is foiled. Again, the story is curious. Who are Joseph's enemies? Who is Pharaoh's son? Why does the son of the Pharaoh want to kill his father as well as Joseph, when he's trying to take Aseneth by force? Is Egypt really Egypt or is this, too, a surrogate for another major empire?

In the context of the Joseph story, the Bible, of course, does talk of seven years of plenty and seven years of famine. In fact, the story of the plenty and the famine is central to the Biblical tale. But here it is totally marginalized, overtaken by a character who doesn't appear in the Bible at all, that is, Pharaoh's son.

Also, in this story, Joseph disappears from the narrative. In the Bible, he is front and center and it is Aseneth who disappears.

In this story, the brothers divide along pro-Aseneth and anti-Aseneth factions. In the Bible, however, Aseneth is irrelevant to Joseph's brothers. To the degree that they are divided, the brothers are divided along Joseph lines. When Joseph is sold to Arab traders, there are some brothers who intercede on his behalf and others who are against him.

In contrast to our manuscript, in the Bible there is no plot, no battle, and no military victory. There is nothing like this in the Book of Genesis. Clearly, something other than the story of the Biblical Joseph and Aseneth is driving the narrative in this ancient manuscript.

3

WHAT DO WE KNOW ABOUT THE MANUSCRIPT?

1. It Records a World-Changing Event

We've already mentioned that the manuscript—*British Library Manuscript #17,202*, in which *Joseph and Aseneth* is found—forms part of a larger collection of writings. A Syriac-speaking Christian monk put the collection together around 570 C.E.[1] Since scholars don't know this monk's name, they refer to him by the awkward-sounding designation Pseudo-Zacharias Rhetor. In academic terms, Pseudo-Zacharias Rhetor means "not that Zacharias," not the Zacharias who was a famous orator. For convenience sake, we'll call this unnamed monk who preserved our copy of *Joseph and Aseneth* by the name Second Zacharias.

Second Zacharias gave his work a masterful title: *A Volume of Records of Events Which Have Shaped the World*. It was an ambitious project by any standard. It seems that Second Zacharias was a monk with a tremendous sense of history who believed that the ancient writings that he was including in his collection were of great importance and had to be preserved for posterity. And so he assembled them in one convenient place. As far as Second Zacharias was concerned, these are not documents that just describe random happenings: they are writings about events that transformed the world . . . his world.

Here's what Second Zacharias chose to include in this anthology of important ancient documents:

- A work by Sylvester, Bishop of Rome, relating to the conversion and Baptism of the Roman Emperor Constantine;

- A document related to finding the 1st-century relics of Stephen and Nicodemus, two important early followers of Jesus;

- A story of miracles, the Legend of the Seven Sleepers of Ephesus;

- An important church history penned by an eyewitness, the so-called real Zacharias Rhetor; and, central to our interests,

- A translation of the work he called "The Story of Joseph the Just and Aseneth his Wife."

Note that Second Zacharias didn't compose this latter writing. It's not something that originated with him in the 6th century. In his compilation, just before his section on "The Story of Joseph the Just and Aseneth his Wife," Second Zacharias tells us the origin of the translation that he's including in his collection. He appends a letter from some anonymous individual—likely a monk—to a man called Moses of Ingila. We know the latter from the historical record. In Appendix II, we have provided the first-ever translation of this letter to Moses of Ingila, which tells us how our manuscript came to be translated from ancient Greek into Syriac. In other words, in his collection of works, Second Zacharias tells us that he is preserving the Syriac translation, one initiated some years earlier at the behest of an anonymous writer. So what prompted the translation?

Around 550 c.e., the anonymous letter-writer tells us that he was in the library of the bishops of Beroea, in the town of Resh'aina located close to the Persian border, in the extreme eastern portion of the Roman Empire. There he found "a small, very old book written in Greek called 'of Aseneth'." He asks Moses of Ingila to translate this ancient writing from Greek into Syriac. When we read this previously untranslated almost fifteen-hundred-year-old letter, we were surprised to learn the anonymous letter-writer's motive for initiating this translation: he suspected that the manuscript contained a "hidden wisdom" and an "inner meaning." As a result, he asked Moses of Ingila to provide not only a translation, but also an explanation.

In his reply—which we've also translated and included in Appendix II—Moses of Ingila agrees to translate the Greek text. Furthermore, Moses confirms that, in his judgment, *Joseph and Aseneth* contains a hidden message, an "inner meaning." But he says that he "hesitate[s]" to speculate on what that meaning may be. To justify his silence, he quotes scripture: "the babbling mouth draws ruin near" (Proverbs 10:19)—something akin to "loose lips sink ships."

More than this, Moses of Ingila hints that dealing with the text's secrets may put his life in danger. To emphasize the danger, he again quotes scripture: "He who guards his mouth will preserve his life" (Proverbs 13:3). He reiterates that his response is driven by "fear" of revealing what God has concealed, again quoting scripture: "It is the glory of God to conceal things" (Proverbs 25:2). While acknowledging this divine prerogative, however, Moses of Ingila confirms that the document does contain a hidden meaning: it has to do, he says, with the Word becoming flesh—that is, it has something to do with Jesus. In his words: "For I have read the story from the old Greek book you sent to me, and there is inner meaning in it. In short, to tell the truth: our Lord, our God, the Word who, at the will of the father and by the power of the Holy Spirit of the Lord, took flesh, and [became human] and was united to the soul with its senses completely. . . ." and here the manuscript is deliberately cut by someone who wanted to forever obliterate what Moses of Ingila thought the encrypted meaning was.

From these letters we now know that the translator of the text into Syriac and the man who commissioned him both believed it had a secret meaning. At least one of them believed that the secret had something to do with Jesus. The latter also believed that revealing the secret could get you killed. What possible secret involving Christianity would make people living in the 6th century feel that their lives were in danger for having come into contact with this text?

We investigate further.

We now know that while the 6th-century Syriac manuscript included by Second Zacharias in his collection is the oldest surviving manuscript of this work, its origins go back to earlier times. On this point, it is important to note that it is not unusual to have a 4th-, 5th-, or 6th-century manuscript of an important early Christian text, even though the original must have been much older. For example, we don't have any 2nd- or 1st-century originals of the New Testament writings. The oldest surviving manuscripts of the Gospels date from the 4th century,[2] roughly the same time as *Joseph and Aseneth*. As with our manuscript, however, we know—or at least strongly suspect—that the earliest copies of the New Testament in existence were, in fact, composed much earlier. In other words, our text seems to be as old as the New Testament writings—or, perhaps, even older.[3]

To review—the context in which our work is located gives us vital information about its stature and perceived importance: *Joseph and Aseneth* is included in a series of writings Second Zacharias considered transformative. Recall that he was a 6th-century Christian monk and concerned about events that shaped the world as he knew it. Let's take a closer look at what he assembled for posterity.

One text relates to the relics of Stephen and Nicodemus. These are not obscure figures. Rather, these artifacts concern the very beginnings of the Christian Church. According to the New Testament Book of Acts, sometime in the 30s C.E. Stephen became the first Christian martyr (Acts 6:8–7:60). Stephen was a Hellenist, a Jew who spoke Greek and who had possibly also adopted non-Jewish or Gentile practices. He paid with his life for being a member of the early Jesus movement. For his part, Nicodemus was an influential Pharisee and a member of the supreme Jewish ruling council, the Sanhedrin. Along with Joseph of Arimathaea, another influential member of the Sanhedrin, Nicodemus prepared Jesus' body for burial (John 19:38–42).

Pairing Nicodemus and Stephen is very significant. One represents continuity with the Jewish tradition. The other represents the embrace of Hellenism (that is, Gentile culture and values). The alleged discovery of 1st-century relics pertaining to these two individuals—one of its first Jewish sympathizers and Christianity's first martyr—must have been sensational news to devout Christians of the 6th century. But is this why they were included in Second Zacharias' collection? On a very simple level, what do their lives teach us? Nicodemus kept his faith a secret, and he survived. Stephen was open about it, and he died.

Second Zacharias also included a work of political transformation in his anthology that had a profound impact upon the future of Christianity. This was an important writing about Constantine, the first Christian emperor. Without Constantine, Christianity might have remained a collection of disparate groups—persecuted minorities—fighting amongst themselves: Arians, Gnostics, Ebionites, and many others, as well as the so-called orthodox Christians who stemmed from Paul's teachings. Through Constantine's efforts, this latter form of Christianity emerged as the favored religion of the empire. Constantine's motivation? There are several possibilities, but seeing the sign of the cross in the sky before a crucial battle is the traditional story. Just sensing that the empire required a new, more robust faith to undergird its institutions is another possibility. At any rate, Constantine moved swiftly to reverse the anti-Christian policies of his predecessor, Diocletian. In the Edict of Milan in 313 C.E. he proclaimed tolerance for all religions throughout the empire, Christianity included. By 325 C.E., Christianity was the favored religion, and in that year Constantine assembled the historic Council of Nicea, which issued the defining creed of Christianity, the Nicene Creed. Henceforth, being a Christian meant subscribing to the statement of faith that Constantine created. Clearly, this was a defining moment for the Christian Church. It also defined who got to preserve their texts and their beliefs. This meant that one form of Christianity now had the muscle of the Roman emperor behind it. The others could choose to go the Stephen way and become martyrs, or take the path of Nicodemus and go underground.

One of the most interesting texts Second Zacharias included in his anthology deals with personal transformation. Should anyone doubt, here was proof positive of eternal life: The Legend of the Seven Sleepers of Ephesus. This legend constituted a key miracle narrative, one that was more up-to-date than the miracle stories of Jesus' own time. The text concerns Christian believers who were walled up in a cave during the persecutions of Emperor Decius around 250 C.E. Over a century later they were discovered . . . no, not dead as we might expect . . . but, remarkably, just sleeping. According to the story, they then awakened.[4] For Christians like Second Zacharias, this was proof that God preserves the faithful. Again, on a very simple level, it teaches that during times of persecution it's good to hide because the day will come when your beliefs—assumed dead—can see the light of day again.

Another text included in Second Zacharias' anthology relates to an important theological transformation that the church of his time was undergoing. The 5th and 6th centuries were remarkably fruitful in terms of theological development as Christians strove to thrash out the correct formulation of Jesus' identity. In those days, one set of issues concerned what Christian theologians call "the person of Christ"—was he really, truly, and fully human? If he was, then perhaps he had a wife and children. Or was he wholly divine and only appeared to be human? Or was he, perhaps, part human and part divine?

If the latter, a divine-human, then how should certain puzzling New Testament texts be explained? Two key passages are at stake. Jesus' Baptism by John, for instance, would imply sinfulness on the part of Jesus, since John's Baptism was for the remission of sin. Was Jesus sinful? Similarly, Jesus' suffering and death upon the cross—did he really die? If Jesus were solely divine, the crucifixion would be a sham execution and sacrifice of his human avatar. If Jesus were partly divine, then only one part of him died. After all, by definition, God cannot die. In the alternative, if Jesus were fully human, are we speaking about human sacrifice here? All these seemingly arcane questions are actually connected to Jesus' relationship to God—was he God? Or was he, while divine, in some way subordinate to God? Was he, perhaps, an angelic being—quasi-divine, as it were?

This debate is preserved in the *Church History* composed by the real Zacharias Rhetor. This original Zacharias was a Christian born in Gaza who subsequently practiced law in Constantinople before becoming the Bishop of Mytilene. In his day, the original Zacharias participated in some of the most important Christian councils of the 5th century. Out of these experiences, Zacharias wrote a *Church History* still consulted by scholars today. It's because of the prominence given to this history in Second Zacharias' compilation that the anonymous monk was given the scholarly nickname of *Pseudo-Zacharias Rhetor.*

The *Church History* of the real Zacharias Rhetor covers the crucial period between 451 and 491 C.E., outlining the struggles of the church to express the doctrine of Christ in precise theological terms. Zacharias seems to have leaned toward monophysite Christianity, meaning the belief in Jesus' *mono* or *single* nature. But this doctrine did not win out. The theological and power-politics debate led to the doctrine of the Trinity, the view that Jesus is fully divine and fully human, and that God is to be spoken of as three-in-one: Father, Son, and Spirit. Put differently, Zacharias' history records the victory of one version of Christianity over all others. It also explains why the texts of the losers had to be encoded.

As can be readily seen, all the writings included in *A Volume of Records of Events Which Have Shaped the World* pertain to Christian transformation. All, that is, except—on the surface—*Joseph and Aseneth*, which seems to stand out as an anomaly in this collection. More than this, all the texts seem to point to the need to hide one's beliefs from the empowered authorities, if one's beliefs do not jibe with their official versions.

Why did Second Zacharias include *Joseph and Aseneth*? The simple answer is that it, too, must be a Christian text. Meaning, the only reason why he would include it in a collection of texts dealing exclusively with Christian history and theology is because it is not a Jewish exegesis on Joseph, but a Christian exposition on Joseph. But why include an encoded Christian text? The other manuscripts in this anthology, especially original Zacharias' *Church History*, provide the answer. At the time of Second Zacharias' compilation, one form of Christianity had triumphed over the others. If it were to survive, any text that diverged from the official line would have had to be either hidden or encoded.

Let us elaborate. The 4th and 5th centuries were truly dangerous times. Christians with differing views—their churches, writings, and leaders—were often persecuted or suppressed by the faction that had won. One example of this was Athanasius' Festal Letter of 367 C.E., circulated to all the churches and monasteries under his supervision. In this document, he outlined the twenty-seven authoritative books that he believed should make up the New Testament. Athanasius was the highly influential bishop of Alexandria, Egypt, one of the most important Christian centers of the ancient Roman world. Over the course of the next fifty years, other bishops agreed with Athanasius' selection of authoritative books. As a result, his letter had the honor of defining the set of writings that would eventually constitute the New Testament.

But by defining what was in, Athanasius' letter also defined what was out. By identifying twenty-seven authoritative texts, his letter excluded Gospels and letters that other communities of Christians considered authoritative. His letter excluded texts that certain Christian communities used in their worship services and in formulating their doctrines. Basically, these other sets of authoritative writings from other Christian communities—those not on Athanasius' privileged list—were now consigned to the fire.

If you were a monk who did not agree with Athanasius, and if you were not prepared to give up your holy scripture just because some powerful bishops decided to exclude them, what did you do? What were your options? Basically, you only had two: physically hide your scriptures, or alter them slightly so that they can be hidden in plain sight.

Unbeknownst to Athanasius, for example, a group of monks under his authority in Egypt buried some of their library codices in jars and placed these in caves near Nag Hammadi. Like the Seven Sleepers, these hidden manuscripts—once thought dead—came back to life. They were found in 1945 and now provide us with some fifty Christian writings that we did not have previously because Athanasius designated them as unacceptable. The Nag Hammadi writings include the *Gospel of Thomas*, the *Gospel of Philip*, the *Dialogue of the Savior*, and the *Gospel of Truth*—all-important texts read, discussed, preserved, and transmitted by a segment of early Christianity.[5] From these texts we know that the monks who buried them may have pretended to be orthodox but were, actually, preserving dissenting opinions—just as Second Zacharias does with *Joseph and Aseneth*.

So why did our monk choose to include *Joseph and Aseneth* in his remarkable collection of Christian texts? What is the world-changing event to which this manuscript is hinting? What are its secrets?

2. It's Written in Syriac, an Ancient Christian Language

The oldest version of *Joseph and Aseneth* is written in Syriac. If we could figure out when the original story was composed, clearly, this would help us decode the historical context it's referring to.

Syriac, along with Greek and Latin, was one of the three major languages used by ancient Christians. In fact, Syriac Christianity preserved traditions and beliefs that were unique to its culture. Not infrequently, Syriac Christians in the eastern Roman Empire and beyond saw matters differently from Christians in the western portion of the empire. Many Syriac Christians, for instance, refused to honor the title given to Mary, mother of Jesus, at a church council in 431 C.E. That council—the Council of Ephesus—acclaimed Mary as *theotokos*, that is, Greek for "God-bearer" or "Mother of God."

Many Syriac Christians preferred a more modest theology, one that would speak of Mary as the mother of Jesus' humanity. For them, the phrase *Mother of God* sounded blasphemous if not utterly impossible, a view shared later on in history by Protestant Christianity. The Syriac Christians didn't win this battle. To this day, the most popular prayer in millions of Christian homes goes as follows: "Holy Mary, Mother of God, pray for us sinners now and at the hour of our death." This prayer to Mary to intercede with her son probably surpasses the number of daily recitals of the Lord's Prayer.

Syriac is a dialect of Aramaic, the language spoken by Jesus and his early disciples. It is written from right to left, like Hebrew and Arabic. Reading the Gospels in Syriac is the closest we can come today to the sound and nuances of the original words uttered by Jesus. For centuries, many Christians in the eastern Roman Empire used Syriac in their liturgy, gospels, hymns, and theological writings. In its heyday, from the 3rd through the 7th centuries, Syriac-speaking Christianity rivaled Greek and Latin-speaking Christianity in size, stretching from modern-day Turkey, Lebanon, Syria, Iraq, Iran, and Afghanistan into regions of India and even, eventually, Mongolia and China. While suffering from assimilation after the Islamic conquests of much of its historic territory, several Syriac-speaking churches still survive today, including the Syriac Orthodox Church and the Assyrian Church of the East (Nestorian).

Syriac Christianity represents an important religious tradition, little known in Protestant and Catholic North America and Europe today. It preserves texts and writings not widely distributed in the West. The Syriac Christians were closer in thought and spirit to their Jewish counterparts living in the same geographical areas. They were also less dismissive of the Old Testament than their Western counterparts. For example, well-known Syriac leaders such as the church father Aphrahat, who lived in the late 3rd century C.E., engaged in dialogue with Jewish leaders. Also, a prominent early 4th-century composer, Ephrem the Syrian, wrote thousands of hymns as teaching vehicles, often on Old Testament themes.

Syriac Christianity traces its origins to a letter that it claims was written to Jesus in the late 20s C.E. by King Abgar V of Edessa in what is now southeastern Turkey. In that letter, the ailing Abgar begged Jesus to come and heal him. In exchange, he offered Jesus sanctuary from those who would seek to kill him. This incidentally underscores that, during the time of his activism, it was well known that Jesus' life was threatened. According to the traditions of the Syriac Christians, although Jesus did not flee to Edessa, he did take the time to dictate a personal response to King Abgar. In this letter, he assured the King that an emissary would be sent to heal him, but only after his own death and resurrection.

Modern scholars think this correspondence is mythical, but that was not the perception in the early church. Eusebius, the influential 4th-century church historian, thought that the letters were genuine (*Ecclesiastical History*, Book 1, Chapter 13). He tells us that the originals were stored in the Archives of Edessa, and he conveniently provides a translation of these Syriac documents. He also says that Jesus kept his promise to King Abgar. Eusebius relates that after Jesus' ascension, Judas Thomas, one of Jesus' original disciples, sent Thaddeus (also known as Addai), an intimate of the group, to heal Abgar.

According to these traditions, therefore, Jesus kept his promise to King Abgar. But what about King Abgar's promise to provide Jesus with refuge? In the Eastern tradition a king never went back on his word—recall, for example, the Book of Esther and the edicts of the Persian ruler. If the Kingdom of Edessa preserved what it believed was King Abgar's promise of refuge for Jesus, how did its inhabitants believe that the promise had been kept? Is it possible that after Jesus' crucifixion, this kingdom provided refuge for his biological family? Or perhaps in return for curing King Abgar, the kingdom provided refuge for Jesus' "theological" descendants, that is, his "true" church? Perhaps Syriac-speaking monks saw it as their duty to preserve texts banned by the Western church—to give them refuge, so to speak. In any event, the Kingdom of Edessa was one of the earliest kingdoms to convert to Christianity.

This reinforces the question: whatever the connection between Syriac Christianity and *Joseph and Aseneth*, what does its preservation among this particular group of Christians tell us about the meaning of the text?

3. It Was a Popular Story

Although the text is now virtually unknown, numerous manuscripts of *Joseph and Aseneth* have come down to us from antiquity. These are all later than the Syriac one. Not a single one was transmitted by Jews. It should be noted that Greek, Armenian, Slavonic, and Romanian manuscripts survive *only* in Christian contexts,[6] nowhere else. But, as this manuscript's legacy indicates, the text was preserved primarily in Eastern Christian circles—Syriac, Armenian, and Greek Christian traditions. Moreover, regardless of the textual family to which they belong, more than half of the Greek manuscripts of *Joseph and Aseneth* also contain another work called *The Life of Joseph*. This work is associated with the great 4th-century Syrian Christian hymnist Ephrem. Although *The*

Life of Joseph does deal with the Biblical Joseph, there is no question that it is a Christian retelling of the story. Because of this, Kraemer concludes that "the composition of Aseneth by a Christian is inherently plausible."[7]

Joseph and Aseneth only entered western Christianity very, very late, in the 13th century; and from that time onwards a number of Latin copies were made. For the most part, scholars have ignored the Syriac manuscript. While several English translations of *Joseph and Aseneth* are available, all of these are based on later Greek manuscripts. Until now, except for the Latin version, there has been no translation based on the Syriac text.

Moreover, the manuscripts vary considerably—some are longer than others.[8] It's hard to tell if the original was a simple text elaborated on by later copyists, or if the original was longer and was edited down by later censors.[9] The Syriac manuscript in the British Library belongs to one of the longer versions of the story.

The sheer number of surviving manuscripts and variants, therefore, makes clear that this was at one time a popular story. It's possible that *Joseph and Aseneth* changed and expanded over the centuries to suit different occasions and audience interests, and to put down in writing what had previously been understood. This is not unusual. Texts composed during the early Christian period were not treated as the unalterable or inerrant word of God. The author of the Gospel of Matthew, for example, felt perfectly free to correct the Gospel of Mark.[10] The author of the Gospel of Luke also altered Mark. Consider, for example, how Luke handles Jesus' Baptism. Mark confidently has Jesus baptized by John (Mark 1:9). Writing some twenty years later than Mark, Luke senses a theological problem. Namely, John the Baptizer's Baptism was for the remission of sin. So Jesus being baptized by him might suggest that Jesus was a sinful human being. As a result, Luke fudges the account. He notes that John had been arrested and then mentions that Jesus was baptized, but he doesn't indicate how or by whom (Luke 3:15–21). Put simply, New Testament manuscripts were altered in the process of transmission so as to bring their point of view into conformity with the growing theology of the early church.[11]

Manuscript variation is also not foreign to the Christian Biblical tradition. Various endings to the Gospel of Mark are well known to scholars, and many editions of the New Testament include both a shorter and a longer ending. There's even an entirely different version that scholars refer to as *Secret Mark*, a document Morton Smith claimed to have found in the Mar Saba Monastery in the Judaean desert.[12]

The Gospel of Matthew also existed in several forms in the early church. The Ebionites, an early Jewish/Christian group, for instance, used a version of Matthew that did not include any reference to a virgin birth, believing that Jesus had a natural birth like any other human. Another version of the Gospel of Matthew, based on a different manuscript tradition, has recently come to light. It was preserved in Jewish circles and was found in the writings of the 14th-century Jewish philosopher Shem-Tob ben-Isaac ben-Shaprut.[13]

These kinds of variations are not unique to New Testament texts. For example, the Greek or Septuagint version of the Book of Esther is considerably longer than the Hebrew account: it makes the character of Esther less idealized and more human than the Hebrew version. Likewise, the Septuagint version of the Book of Daniel contains passages not found in the Hebrew Bible (e.g., the Prayer of Azariah in the furnace, the story of Susanna, and Bel and the Dragon).

So textual variants are not at all unknown when it comes to influential Biblical writings. But these variations always serve some kind of theological agenda. What theological agenda is *Joseph and Aseneth* serving? What Christian story is it refining? Furthermore, what accounts for the extraordinary popularity of the *Joseph and Aseneth* tale?

To sum up: what we now know about the manuscript heightens the intrigue. It's ensconced in an anthology of writings that relate to world-transforming events. It was preserved by an ancient Christian community, one that used a language very similar to that spoken by Jesus and his followers. And it was exceedingly popular.

If it were just a story about two figures from ancient Jewish history, why would successive generations of Christians have read, treasured, translated, expanded, and preserved this writing? No other figure from the Hebrew Bible received such popularization at Christian hands—not Abraham, not Moses, not David, not Ezra. Just Joseph. Why him alone of all the available figures? And why Aseneth, about whom the Bible is relatively silent? Why her?

Is it, perhaps, because *Joseph and Aseneth* is an extremely good ancient yarn . . . or is there more to the story?

4

WHEN WAS IT WRITTEN?

The Manuscript Trail

So far we have noted that around 550 C.E., Moses of Ingila made the Syriac translation of *Joseph and Aseneth* included in Second Zacharias' compilation. An anonymous individual had come across a very ancient Greek manuscript in a library and had sent it to Moses for translation. That individual's covering letter and Moses' reply and translation are included in Second Zacharias' compilation some twenty years later. It is evident he was being very careful to establish this writing's lineage—and history—so far as he knew it.

But here our trail ends. How ancient was the Greek manuscript that Moses used for his Syriac translation? Was it a 5th-century, 4th-century, or perhaps even a 3rd-century document? What, moreover, was its lineage? Was the earlier Greek version itself a copy of an older Hebrew, Aramaic, or even Greek manuscript? And, if so, how far back in time does this copying and recopying process extend?

We'd really like to know when *Joseph and Aseneth* was originally composed. After all, if it can be dated to the time of Jesus, maybe it preserves not only a forgotten theology, but also a lost history penned by the people who knew him.

A manuscript trail—back to an existing 4th-century version with tantalizing possibilities of even earlier manuscripts—is not at all uncommon in the study of early church writings. As we've seen, very rarely do earlier manuscripts exist, even for such foundational Christian writings as the Gospels and Paul's letters that most scholars agree date from the 1st century. Just because the earliest existing copies of these documents come from the 4th century, no one argues that they were first written in that century. Given what we know of the Roman Empire at the time, and the likely course of Christian theological development, most scholars attempt to find a niche for the Gospels within earlier Christianity when Christian writings could logically have first been written.[1]

The same is true of the Dead Sea Scrolls, which in addition to the community's own sectarian writings also preserved the oldest known manuscripts of virtually all of the books of the Hebrew Bible. Based on this find, we can now trace most of the books of the Hebrew Bible to at least the 1st century B.C.E. But this doesn't mean that this is when they were first composed. The presumption for both the Christian Scriptures and the Hebrew Bible is that the existing manuscripts represent copies of copies of copies of much earlier writings.

The key point is that the date for the initial composition of an ancient writing cannot be established solely on the basis of manuscript lineage. Evidence of when a document was originally composed is circumstantial. It's essentially an argument from fit—that is, the congruence between that about which the text speaks and the historical circumstances we think it addresses. In an attempt to date the composition of a text, scholars also use quotations by earlier ancient authors.

For assistance in dating the composition of *Joseph and Aseneth*, therefore, we turned to the few scholars who have examined this text over the past century. For various reasons, but primarily because the main characters seem to be the Hebrew patriarch Joseph and his wife, Aseneth, most of these scholars believe that the author of *Joseph and Aseneth* is likely Jewish and that the text should be placed in a Jewish context. Some, like Ross Shepard Kraemer and Rivka Nir, however, believe that the work is Christian in origin, not Jewish.[2] Surprisingly, as we shall soon see, we discovered that many date its original composition to early Christian times—1st century C.E. In other words, according to many of the scholars who studied the text, our manuscript may very well have been written when Jesus, Mary the Magdalene, and Jesus' disciples were still alive.

A 1st-Century Origin?

There are a number of ancient writings relating to the Hebrew Bible or Christian Old Testament that were not included in any Bible—Jewish or Christian. These works were influential in their day, at least in some circles; but for some reason, they were not deemed by religious authorities to be sufficiently meritorious to be canonized as sacred scripture. Scholars call this literature *Apocrypha* or *Pseudepigrapha*. Many of these writings were produced—close to the 1st century C.E.—by apocalyptically-minded individuals, devout people who were convinced that the end of the present age was at hand. These collections include such important ancient writings as the *Book of Enoch*, *Jubilees*, the *Psalms of Solomon*, and other writings attributed to notable figures such as the prophet Ezra, Adam, Jacob, and Moses.

Apocryphal and pseudepigraphal texts have been collected in recent years by H. F. D. Sparks and by James H. Charlesworth.[3] The latter, for instance, has assembled over sixty such pseudepigraphal writings, and both his book and Sparks' contain translations as well as useful introductions to each work. Interestingly, *Joseph and Aseneth* is present in both collections. The inclusion of this document in a group of apocryphal or pseudepigraphal writings indicates that these compilers think it originated in early or even pre-Christian times.

In the late 19th century, one of the earliest scholars to examine *Joseph and Aseneth*, Pierre Batiffol, at first dated the writing to the 5th century C.E., surmising that it was based on a legend originating in the 4th century. Later on, however, he changed his mind, re-dating it to the 1st century C.E. This dating seems to have stuck with later 20th-century scholars.[4] A French scholar, Marc Philonenko, for instance, dated it to around 100 C.E.[5] In 1985, Christoph Burchard—who translated *Joseph and Aseneth* in Charlesworth's compilation from a variety of later Greek manuscripts—contended that the writing originated either in the 1st century B.C.E. or the 1st century C.E.[6] In 1996, Gideon Bohak placed the origin of the work even earlier than all others, dating it to the time of the Maccabean revolt in the 2nd century B.C.E.[7]

Summarizing scholarly opinion in the mid-1980s, Burchard notes that "none has put the book much after A.D. 200, and some have placed it as early as the second century B.C."[8] More recently, however, Ross Shepard Kraemer arrived at a different date. She concludes: "the cumulative evidence overwhelmingly places our Aseneth no earlier than the third or fourth century C.E."[9]

So all the scholars are clear that *Joseph and Aseneth* represents a very ancient text, the origins of which go well beyond the 6th-century Syriac manuscript in our possession. But how far back is a question open to debate. Many think the

1st century c.e. is likely—that is, during early Christian times, perhaps dating to Jesus' lifetime, or some time right after his crucifixion.

For our part, we believe that there are several indications within the text itself that favor an early dating—to the 100s or even earlier. Like other scholars, our arguments are circumstantial, so they're open to the charge of being speculative. But circumstantial evidence is still better than none at all. Let's turn to it now.

First, we note the imagery of the bridal chamber in the scenes where Aseneth shares her bed, so to speak, with the angelic Joseph. In our text, this idea is central to understanding the union between the transformed Aseneth and the heavenly Joseph. Gilles Quispel has suggested that a heavenly journey resulting in a meeting with a cosmic twin can be found in some forms of early Jewish mysticism. Perhaps here we have a missing link between early heretical Jewish mysticism, Jewish Christianity, and Gnosticism.[10] In any event, sharing a bed with Joseph's heavenly twin is not an accidental feature of the *Joseph and Aseneth* story. It tells us a lot about how this marriage was understood theologically by the people who preserved this text. Later, we'll discuss in detail the significance of this powerful imagery. In the meantime, we draw your attention to the fact that for at least one influential form of early Christianity—Valentinian Gnosticism—the ceremony of the *bridal chamber* constituted one of their most sacred rituals, having to do with the real meaning of human redemption. The leader of this movement, Valentinus, lived during the first half of the 2nd century, from approximately 100 to 160 c.e. Interestingly, he almost became bishop of Rome, the Pope.[11]

Gnosticism derives its name from *gnosis*, the Greek word for knowledge. Pagans, Jews, and Christians all had esoteric knowledge streams in their respective religions. These represented an attempt to glean hidden knowledge from the various traditions. Christian Gnosticism was a form of Christian mysticism. Within this tradition, there were various teachers and various schools. According to Jonathan Hill, "some of the most important Christian teachers of the 2nd century are thought to have been Gnostics."[12] Within Gnosticism, Valentinians formed one of the major groups. For them, the bridal chamber was at the center of their theology.

Since *Joseph and Aseneth* uses bridal chamber imagery to convey the inner meaning of the sacred union between Joseph and Aseneth, we are inclined to posit the heyday of this writing no later than the 2nd century, when this kind of theology was vigorous and widespread. After all, by the 3rd century, Valentinian Christianity had dwindled and by the 4th century it had virtually disappeared.

In fact, our document likely comes from the 1st century. While *Joseph and Aseneth* uses bridal-chamber imagery for interpreting the significance of the marriage, it interestingly does not set forth a bridal-chamber ritual or sacrament for its followers. That is, the manuscript is content to report on the marriage using bridal-chamber symbolism. But it stops there. It does not go on to institutionalize this unique event as a ritual, as a way in which faithful followers could memorialize, celebrate, or participate in its meaning. This gap between reporting and ritualizing is significant. Judaism, for instance, doesn't just report on the Exodus from Egypt, it ritualizes it in the annual commemoration of Passover. Paul, moreover, didn't just report Jesus' death. By the mid-50s, he had memorialized that unique event in his Eucharistic ceremony so that his followers could participate in the body and blood of the Christ. In this way, they could vicariously experience Jesus' suffering on the cross. Likewise, by the 80s, in the *Didache*, the Jesus Movement members in Jerusalem—later called Ebionites—developed their own version of the Friday night Jewish prayers, celebrating the life and teachings of Jesus.

By way of contrast, the community for whom *Joseph and Aseneth* was a key writing had not yet created a ritual around it. There is no mention in the text that readers of this writing should participate in some rite that would perpetuate that unique event, namely Jesus' marriage to Mary the Magdalene. So, we suggest, this points to an early dating for our manuscript, likely sometime in the 1st century C.E., during the interval between when the marriage was reported and when the event became ritualized in the bridal chamber sacrament.

So the work probably already existed in the 2nd century. But that doesn't mean that it originated then. The story, as we have it now, likely grew somewhat in the telling. Just because it contains Valentinian Gnostic imagery doesn't mean that the writing as a whole was composed in Valentinian circles. The nucleus of the tale, and the ideas it represents, may have existed earlier, receiving Valentinian coloring in the 2nd century.

Second, as we will soon see, it seems that the text is referring to an actual community, a hitherto unknown form of early Christianity that sprang from Jesus himself and survived among his earliest Gentile followers.[13] This group may represent the missing link between Jesus and Gnostic Christianity which emerges full-blown on the historical scene in the 2nd century, its origins unknown. Put differently, scholars have no idea what led to the creation of Christian Gnosticism, which seems to appear on the historical scene fully formed in the 2nd century. Gnosticism's origins are a mystery to scholars of early Christianity. How did it come to be? In *Joseph and Aseneth*, we may indeed have discovered the roots of Gnostic Christianity.

Many Pauline traditionalists like to dismiss the Gnostics. For example, as Bernard Green condescendingly writes, "Lost gospels, secret teaching, hidden mysteries: these all sound intoxicating to the modern reader but when the myths are written out in cold prose they sound banal and absurd."[14] This is obviously not an objective assessment. This is Green's theology. As we will show, these "banal" myths may be better grounded in history than the canonical Gospels.

At any rate, the earliest Christian community constitutes the natural environment in which the text itself could have been composed—perhaps in northern Israel, or what is today Syria or southeastern Turkey—right where our manuscript was preserved.

Third, there is no indication in our text of any preoccupation with the stature of Joseph other than to indicate that he is both human and angelic—that is, divine. Whoever Joseph represents, if it is a Christian text, the writer does not betray any preoccupation with such theological matters as the incarnation of God, the person of Christ, or the relationship of the Son to God the Father. These so-called Trinitarian disputes were characteristic of the 3rd and 4th centuries. Because our text is not concerned with these subtleties, we suspect that its composition would have had to occur prior to these times.

Fourth, a 2nd-century or earlier dating would fit what we know of other writings produced during this era. By the time of the 2nd century, Christians were attempting to fill in the historical gaps. Many undoubtedly asked: What was Jesus' young life like? And so we get tales like the *Infancy Gospel of Thomas*, telling us of Jesus' boyhood adventures. Others asked: Why was Mary, Jesus' mother, so special? Why was she chosen to be the "God-bearer"? And so we have the *Infancy Gospel of James*, which tells us of Mary's own immaculate conception and her very special upbringing, first in her own home and then in the Jerusalem Temple under the guidance of the priests. Still others wanted to know: What was Paul's real message? And so we have *The Acts of Thecla*, tracing Paul's ascetic preaching in a place called Iconium and examining his impact upon an impressionable teenage girl called Thecla. Others asked: Who was Thomas and where did he go after the crucifixion? Hence *The Acts of Judas Thomas* was produced, which traces his route through Syria into India.

In other words, the 2nd century was a rich time for supplementing what we know from the Gospel writings, to satisfy early Christian curiosity concerning details about which the canonical texts are silent. All or some of these texts may have been based on more or less historical material. In any event, the 2nd century represents an excellent environment in which *Joseph and Aseneth* could have developed from an earlier story set in Jesus' lifetime. This is all-important. Put simply, the evidence suggests that *Joseph and Aseneth* is not some late work of fiction, but an early writing preserving some kind of encoded history.

Taken together, it is clear from the scholarly literature that it is not outlandish to date the text—at least the nucleus of the text—to the time of Jesus or shortly thereafter. More than this, many of the scholars contend that *Joseph and Aseneth* dates to a time earlier than our earliest Gospels. In other words, we are on solid scholarly ground when we suggest that the work is both early and Christian.

5

IS THERE MORE TO THIS STORY
THAN MEETS THE EYE?

Before we proceed to the inner meaning of the text, let's remember that encoding secrets in the body of a Christian text is not something invented in 21st-century Hollywood thrillers. Even the Apostle Paul describes his insights into Jesus' message as a "revelation of the mystery that was kept secret for long ages" (1 Corinthians 2:7). The Greek word *mysterion* means *secret*.[1] So finding an esoteric, secret level to a Christian text is as old as Christianity itself.

Recently, however, scholars have given up on identifying secret or esoteric Christian texts. In Kraemer's words, any "texts that lack explicit Christian identifiers . . . are now uniformly classified as Jewish." When these texts exhibit minor Christian features (e.g., a cross drawn in blood across a honeycomb), "such features are generally considered the results of Christian interpolation" (i.e., later Christian insertions into early Jewish texts). The result of all this "is that any anonymous or pseudonymous parabiblical text that does not scream Christian at us is almost certain to be labeled Jewish . . . thus greatly reducing the chances that we will ever identify a Christian parabiblical composition that lacks explicit Christian features."[2] In other words, what this scholar is saying in very scholarly terms is that the game is rigged. The rules are that if it doesn't scream "Christian" at us, it's not Christian. And since—by definition—secret or esoteric texts don't scream anything at us, they will never be labeled for what they actually are—that is, esoteric Christian texts. Kraemer goes on to say "I cannot think of a single, parabiblical narrative like Aseneth."[3] In other words, it's unique and we have to be open to that uniqueness. To that end, Kraemer speculates that maybe the author of *Joseph and Aseneth* "was both Jewish *and* Christian."[4] If Kraemer is right on this point, the author of *Joseph and Aseneth* may be a member of the original group surrounding Jesus. This would situate the story in the 1st century.

We are aware that the secret history embedded in *Joseph and Aseneth* will arouse much controversy. Therefore, for the sake of caution, before we move on, let's review for a moment why we think that the story that this text tells isn't just an elaboration on the Biblical tale of Joseph and his wife Aseneth. In other words, why do we think that there is more to *Joseph and Aseneth* than the surface meaning? Here are the clues that motivated us to investigate this manuscript further.

Clue #1: The story in our manuscript is simply not the story found in Genesis.

Joseph and Aseneth describes Aseneth in great detail—her personality, her family home, her ten-room tower, and her first impressions of Joseph. In our manuscript, it's her story. In contrast, the Biblical account which it purportedly comments on hardly mentions her name. In the Book of Genesis, it's his story.

Joseph and Aseneth tells of an extensive love story between a Joseph and an Aseneth. Both are described in detail: they are pure, virginal, and committed to each other. In contrast, the Biblical account has no such story.

Joseph and Aseneth focuses prominently on Joseph's and Aseneth's physical relationship—touching, kissing, and, eventually, sexual relations. In contrast, the Bible makes no mention of any of this.

Joseph and Aseneth relates a mystical union between Aseneth and a Joseph-like angel. There is also a strange Communion-like rite that involves eating a honeycomb. In contrast, the Bible makes no mention of these mysterious rituals. In fact, in the Biblical text, honey is explicitly excluded from the list of substances that can be brought as a sacrificial offering to God (Leviticus 2:11).

In *Joseph and Aseneth*, Joseph is described as the "Son of God" (6:3). Aseneth is described as the "Bride of God" (4:1). The text also uses phrases such as the "cup of immortality" and the "oil of incorruption." This is language that is completely foreign to the Book of Genesis where the original Joseph and Aseneth are introduced.

Joseph and Aseneth talks of a threat on Joseph's life and those of his two sons. It also describes a plot to abduct his wife, Aseneth. This has absolutely nothing to do with the Biblical narrative.

Even from an initial superficial glance, it is not difficult to see that the narrative in the *Joseph and Aseneth* manuscript is not the story of the Biblical Joseph and Aseneth. It's not even an elaboration on it. It's a different tale altogether. *Joseph and Aseneth* simply uses these names for some mysterious and as yet undiscovered reason. What we do know is that Second Zacharias considered the story of the relationship between this *Joseph* and this *Aseneth* of world-shaping importance.

Clue #2: Something other than the Biblical account drives the narrative in *Joseph and Aseneth.*

The account of Joseph and his wife Aseneth in the Book of Genesis is not dictating the imagery and the language of our manuscript. In contrast to the Biblical text, there is no mention here of Joseph's dreams, of his incarceration, of his release, of his reunion with his brothers and father, etc. There is not one thing that drives the plot in the Bible that also drives the plot in our text. Something else is going on. But, at this point, we don't yet know what this something else is. We suspect that Joseph and Aseneth might be surrogates for other people— people much more germane to the lives of Christian monks than the Israelite Joseph or the Egyptian Aseneth.

Perhaps, we surmise, the story is historical, but it is about the life history of two individuals other than Joseph and Aseneth.

Our hunch is that this is a work of disguised history.

Clue #3: The manuscript is Christian, not Jewish.

Incredibly, when we set out to decipher the text, we found that up until Kraemer, the majority of 20th-century scholars have contended that the work was Jewish in origin. When we first began exploring the literature, this finding acted as a bombshell, stopping us right in our tracks . . . at least for a moment. As recently as 1996, Bohak was able to report that "current scholarship is almost unanimous in seeing *Joseph and Aseneth* as a Jewish work. Its protagonists are the Jewish patriarchs, its language and style are modeled on the Hebrew Bible (in its Greek translation), and it shows no familiarity with the New Testament or with typically Christian concepts and concerns."[5]

This statement floored us. Surely, anyone familiar with Judaism would immediately realize that the idea that this is a Jewish text is a nonstarter. There is no reference to the work in any Jewish writings, rabbinic or otherwise. Nor was it preserved in any Jewish context whatsoever. The language and content of this text have nothing to do with Judaism. Quite the opposite, the text involves concepts and titles that are anathema to Jews. *Joseph and Aseneth* is without a doubt Christian.

But let's quickly review the literature, looking this time at its likely place of origin, not its date of initial composition. Why did scholars latch on to the idea that its provenance was Jewish?

Since both Sparks and Charlesworth include *Joseph and Aseneth* in their collection of apocryphal or pseudepigraphal writings, they seem to think that the story has to do, in some way, with an elaboration on the Joseph story in the Book of Genesis. They seem to share the assumption, rife amongst scholars, that something having to do with the Biblical Joseph would, of course, have to be Jewish. The consensus opinion reflects the view that *Joseph and Aseneth* represents an elaboration upon the Book of Genesis' account of the ancient Israelite patriarch's relationship with Aseneth. These scholars call *Joseph and Aseneth* a *midrash*, a Jewish writing that fills in details missing from the original, providing a fuller story designed to satisfy the curious mind.

Building upon this assumption, scholars then looked for an appropriate historical fit. When, they asked, would an elaboration on the Biblical Joseph story have made sense within a Jewish context? The introductions provided in Sparks' and Charlesworth's translations of the later Greek text review the various interpretations of the manuscript. Thinking of its author as Jewish, some opined that the writer of *Joseph and Aseneth* could have been a member of a strict Jewish sect such as the Essenes, who lived in Israel, around the Dead Sea area. Or perhaps he was a member of the Essenes' Egyptian counterpart, the Therapeutae.

But on the face of it, these suggestions do not work. After all, both the Essenes and Therapeutae groups seem to have been strict Torah-observant sects. Although there are, indeed, indications of Torah-observance in the manuscript—for example, Joseph follows Jewish dietary laws; he seems to avoid meeting Aseneth on the Sabbath; and he's a monotheist rejecting pagan deities—the text as a whole does not reflect strict Jewish observance. Nor, like most of the books of the Hebrew Bible, is it advocating adherence to Torah. That's simply not its focus or its message.

Alternatively, some scholars conjectured that the purpose of the document was to explain how a Jewish Joseph could have married a non-Jewish Aseneth—what she would have had to do to become a suitable Jewish bride. Thus, they interpret the work as dealing with a conversion experience. And yet, other than her embrace of monotheism, there is nothing in Aseneth's behavior to suggest that she becomes Jewish. She does not convert. She simply embraces monotheism, throwing away her statues and votive offerings. We hear nothing about her taking on the obligations of the Torah or going through any ritual of conversion to Judaism. Her focus is on becoming the "Bride of God."

The simple fact is that in the text she's a non-Jew who remains a non-Jew. As we shall see, this gives us a vital clue as to who she really is.

Of course, we're not the first to notice that Aseneth does not convert. This led some scholars to alternative, but related, theories. For example, Marc Philonenko suggested that perhaps *Joseph and Aseneth* deals specifically with the question of interfaith marriages. Perhaps, he speculated, the author was an Egyptian Jew concerned with intermarriage. Sparks appears to agree. Yet Philonenko and Sparks advance this position in the absence of any historical evidence that interfaith marriages and conversions from Egyptian religion to Judaism was an issue that perplexed ancient Jewish leaders. Judaism is, after all, a religion noted for not encouraging conversion or, for that matter, interfaith marriages. *Joseph and Aseneth*—whatever it is about—is by no means a manual on how to convert, nor a guide for the intermarried. In addition, no Jewish conversion process, or interfaith marriage, requires a heavenly Holy Communion within the bridal chamber.

For his part, Bohak proposes a different historical fit altogether. He links the narrative to a now-forgotten Jewish temple in Egypt during the Maccabean period—over 150 years before Jesus, and some fifteen hundred years after Joseph.

What drives all these theories is the assumption that the author of *Joseph and Aseneth* must be Jewish, just because the lead character in the story is one of the Jewish patriarchs. Clearly, that assumption has taken scholars on a lengthy wild-goose chase and they have ended up with speculations that are demonstrably off the mark. They can't agree with each other and they really don't know what to make of the manuscript.

But we are not original in identifying *Joseph and Aseneth* as a Christian text. One of the few scholars to consider the possibility that the author of *Joseph and Aseneth* might not be Jewish was also one of the earliest to examine the document. In 1889, French scholar Pierre Batiffol published the first critical edition of *Joseph and Aseneth*. He presented it as a Christian composition.[6] In 1918, he was followed in the English language by E. W. Brooks, who contended "that the book in its present shape is the work of a Christian writer will be at once recognized by any reader."[7] References to the sacred bread and cup, he observed, are clear indications of a Eucharist-like ceremony. This important observation was lost to 20th-century *Joseph and Aseneth* scholarship, which generally ignored Brooks' translation and introduction. The resistance was partially theological. After all, if *Joseph and Aseneth* was Christian, then it was presenting a non-Pauline version of Christianity. We are so used to thinking inside Paul's theological box that we have almost lost the capacity to see a Christianity that predates or differs from Paul's. Writing against the idea that *Joseph and Aseneth* could be a Christian text, Randall Chesnutt states "there is in the conversion story in *Joseph and Aseneth* no Christ, no redeemer figure of any sort, no historical salvation event, no Baptism and no talk of such Christian Hauptbegriffe [key concepts] as faith, love, justification, salvation and Church."[8] Professor Chesnutt is wrong. There is all of that and more. His problem is that these "Christian *Hauptbegriffe*" are not packaged in Pauline terminology.

But we don't have to go all the way back to the early 20th century to find allies for our reading. As Batiffol and Brooks had done before her, Israeli scholar Rivka Nir stated categorically in the title of her 2012 publication that *Joseph and Aseneth* is a Christian book. She has also underlined the Christian character of the honeycomb ceremony, including the use of the cross.[9] Why, we wonder, did it take so long for somebody to notice the sign of the cross—written in blood, no less—across the honeycomb wafer? Surely that's a dead giveaway.

Finally, Ross Shepard Kraemer, arguably one of the top scholars on the subject today, concludes "the arguments for its Jewishness are largely without foundation. . . . In particular, a strong case can be made for Christian composition and redaction."[10] We agree.

The strong case is as follows: *Joseph and Aseneth* is not a Jewish work about conversion to Judaism or interfaith marriages. We have already catalogued significant differences between the Biblical Joseph and the Joseph of *Joseph and Aseneth*. We have also raised critical questions about the language and imagery in the text. All these sound Christian rather than Jewish. The divinization of Joseph as "Son of God" and the heavenly Communion rite make this all too evident.

Furthermore, the context in which the Syriac manuscript is lodged has to do with events that have shaped the Christian—not the Jewish—world. A Syriac-speaking individual chose to include this writing in his compilation of works because it addresses an important concern of his community. For the devout Christian whom we call Second Zacharias, *Joseph and Aseneth* is right up there with the conversion of the pagan Emperor Constantine to Christianity.

It's clear that Christians wouldn't have had any interest in preserving a story that had to do with purely Jewish matters. Christians would certainly not have been interested in the story of an obscure Jewish temple in Egypt, or conversion to Judaism, or the problems of Jewish/non-Jewish intermarriage. These topics would have had absolutely no appeal to the early Christian monks who copied, preserved, transmitted, and translated this manuscript.

As Kraemer points out, it was Christians—not Jews—who preserved *Joseph and Aseneth*. All surviving manuscripts—without exception—come from Christian sources. A Jewish authorship cannot account for the popularity and spread of this text exclusively in Christian circles. There is also not one shred of evidence that *Joseph and Aseneth* was ever read, transmitted, or even discussed by Jewish writers or leaders. Writing about non-canonical Christian texts in general, Robert Kraft states "when the evidence is clear that only Christians preserved the material, the Christianity of it is the given."[11]

When it comes to *Joseph and Aseneth*, therefore, Batiffol, Brooks, Kraemer, and Nir are right. The majority of scholars have been searching for the writer and meaning of *Joseph and Aseneth* in all the wrong places. We contend that the author must be Christian.

The all-important question is: if the work is Christian, what does its origin tell us about its meaning?

Clue #4: We're told it may contain a hidden meaning.
The anonymous letter-writer who commissioned the translation from Moses of Ingila in the 6th century requested him to do two things: translate the ancient Greek manuscript he had found in the episcopal library in Resh'aina into Syriac, and explain its inner meaning.[12] This was not a casual request. To ask for a text's inner meaning is to inquire about its hidden meaning. A secret meaning indicates that the superficial reading cannot be the real meaning. As we shall see, many early Christians thought that Biblical and related writings contained hidden levels of meaning. We'll discuss this approach to Biblical interpretation in due course.

In the British Library we have Moses of Ingila's translation from Greek into Syriac. Unfortunately, part of the manuscript is missing and we do not have his decoding of the text, if he ever wrote one. But we do have part of his response where he alludes to a concealed message that is dangerous to discuss publicly. That's a vital piece of evidence. Here we have two Christians in the 6th century—the anonymous letter-writer and Moses of Ingila—who clearly surmised that this writing contained more than just a literal story about two Old Testament characters.

We wonder why a century of scholarship would have missed this vital clue. We suspect that they simply ignored the Syriac text, concentrating only on later Greek editions. In this way, they missed the anonymous writer's letter and his references to "hidden meanings."

So, who is hiding behind Joseph?

Who is hiding behind Aseneth?

Why is the story encoded?

What heretical history might it be preserving?

PART II
DECODING THE MANUSCRIPT

6

WHAT'S THE MOST
IMPORTANT CLUE?

T he four clues we have identified for decoding the text suggest that perhaps scholars have been making what the philosopher Gilbert Ryle calls "a category mistake." By viewing the writing as a Judaic elaboration upon a Biblical story, they positioned it as an apocryphal, post-Biblical expansion of the Genesis narrative. That move blinded them to the possibility that the language and symbolism used within the story could represent a different genre—namely, a disguised historical narrative.

If *Joseph and Aseneth* is an encoded Christian text, we can now place it within a well-known literary tradition. Early Christians, after all, interpreted Biblical writings very differently from how scholars approach those writings today.

It is well known among scholars that in Eastern Christianity, where *Joseph and Aseneth* was preserved longest, the preferred method of textual interpretation was typology.[1] The major theological schools of Syriac Christianity—Antioch, Nisibis, and Edessa—specialized in seeing parallels between the Old Testament and the new Christian writings. Figures and events from the Old Testament were seen through the eye of Christian faith as types, that is, as foreshadows of later figures and events. In their view, characters in the Old Testament were prototypes of characters in the New Testament.

The methodology is somewhat familiar to readers of the New Testament. Paul, for instance, engages in typology in his letter to the Galatians (Galatians 4:21–31). There he chooses Sarah, the wife of Abraham, as a type for his followers. Sarah was "the free woman," Paul said, and she typifies those who have found freedom in Christ. Hagar, Sarah's slave, on the other hand, represents a type of those who remain locked in slavery. In Paul's opinion, Hagar typifies those Jewish people who remained bound to the Torah, which in his view represents slavery.

So, according to Paul, in reading the story of Abraham and his two significant relationships—Sarah and Hagar—we are not really reading about Abraham, his wife, and his concubine. Instead, we should be looking at the text through the eye of Christian faith. When we do, we realize that Sarah represents Christians and Hagar represents the Jewish people. In Paul's view, the former are superior to the latter.

The "eye of faith" is crucial to this analysis because no Jewish interpreter—and no Moslem one, for that matter—would see the narrative in this way. We are firmly on Christian ground here.

Typology really represents a theology of history: one earlier historical character, or event, prefigures a later one. More importantly, typology contends that the later historical event is really what was intended all along. The former was merely a foreshadowing—a kind of dress rehearsal—of what was yet to come. In Jonathan Hill's words: "a 'type' is an event or object of the past which somehow mirrors or foreshadows something in the future. Some Christians believed that much of the Jewish religion was a 'type' of Christ."[2]

Theologically, typological analysis presupposes the Christian conviction that events in the life of Jesus and the early church fulfill incidents described in the Old Testament. That is, it assumes the truth of the Christian message and then reads it backward into the literary tradition to create linkages between earlier and later narratives.

Before returning to our text, so as to become more familiar with this way of thinking, here are several more examples of typological interpretation at work. Early Christians saw the crossing of the Red Sea as a type of Christian Baptism—crossing the Red Sea typifying passage through water into salvation. Similarly, Jonah's time in the belly of a giant fish and his subsequent escape after three days was seen as a Jesus-type death. Jonah's escape was interpreted as a kind of resurrection. The belly of the fish was understood as a type of grave, or tomb.

The Biblical cities of refuge with their doors flung wide open to receive criminals were seen as stand-ins for Jesus himself, with his arms spread open on the cross to embrace all sinners. The Tower of Babel was a type of the true Tower, the real bridge to God, namely the church, with Jesus as the real architect or builder. Similarly, the Jerusalem Temple typified the church, the place wherein God's presence dwells. The giving of the Torah to the Israelite people through Moses on Mount Sinai represented a type of Sermon on the Mount. And so on.

Typological analysis goes even further. Not only does it contend that earlier characters represent later characters and earlier events represent later events, it contends that earlier writers didn't understand what they themselves were writing. Basically, it takes a Christian to explain a text that was written hundreds and sometimes thousands of years before the advent of Christianity. According to this view, the author of Genesis, for example, did not realize that in writing about Abraham's relationships with Sarah and Hagar he was really talking about the relationship between Christians and Jews thousands of years later. Nor did the author of the Book of Exodus understand that by talking about Moses and the Exodus he was really speaking about Jesus' redemption of humanity from sin. Unless, of course, the author of both Genesis and Exodus was God, who intended us to see the Christian reality in these Jewish texts. And that was probably the view of many—if not most—early Christians.

Typology, therefore, preserved the usefulness of the Old Testament for Christian purposes. By interpreting the Old Testament in this manner, a rich lexicon of meaning could be derived. Typological analysis yielded results that were exceptionally useful for the Christian Church: it unearthed a Christian narrative running throughout the Hebrew Scriptures. It was a methodology that bypassed its Jewish interpretation, supplanting Jewish history and Torah instruction with the message of the Christian Gospel.

In fact, typology makes the Old Testament out to be a Christian narrative. That's a remarkable tour de force!

There are many reasons why typology caught on. One has to do with the prevalence of what scholars call "Platonistic" or "neo-Platonistic" thinking that informed the culture of the time. Building upon Plato's contrast between the "World of Appearance" and the "World of Reality," Platonism argued that the material world, the world of change, was an illusion. Reality, according to the Platonists, lay beyond our senses in what only reason and insight could discover. Today, we emphasize trial and error, hypothesis and experiments—the *real* world. But for Plato, our world is the illusion, and the ideas behind it are the real world.

In the 1st century, educated people were influenced by these platonic ideas and distrusted observation. They didn't care about the commonplace opinions of the untutored masses, nor did they care about the ordinary meaning of texts. They wouldn't have cared about polls or surveys. The study of history, while engaged in by some authors, was also devalued because historical events were part of the transitory world of change. The real task, according to this group, was to find the deeper, spiritual meaning—the unchangeable, eternal truths— behind the ever-changing historical phenomena.

Typology fit nicely with the intellectual current of the times. It encouraged the practice of seeing deeper significance within the plain or literal meaning of the text. It also linked together different writings into one continuous narrative. Thus, connections were created between documents as different as Genesis, Exodus, and the Gospels, giving the impression that the Bible was one continuous narrative penned by God, leading to the creation of the church. For many early Christians these writings, Old and New, represented one consistent story of salvation through Christ.

Another reason for typology's success has to do with the value placed on the Old Testament. As we have noted, early Christians did not value the Hebrew Bible as a historical document. They weren't interested in the movement of the Jewish people through time, living the life of the Covenant with God and interpreting their historical experiences in this light. Today, we might think of the Old Testament as embracing the historic call to Abraham, the Exodus out of Egypt into the Promised Land, the rise of the great Israelite monarchy under Saul, David, and Solomon, and so forth. For Christians in antiquity, however, looking at the Old Testament in this fashion was wrong. It was looking at the "World of Appearance" and missing the "World of Reality." It was looking at the surface and missing the underlying hidden truths.

Even though typologists read a Christian narrative into a pre-existing Old Testament text, at least they were in favor of retaining the Old Testament. Many factions of early Christianity wanted to dispense with the Hebrew writings altogether. These Christians pointed out that Torah-observance is clearly the central message of the Old Testament. They were right. No passage in the Hebrew Bible can be read without being confronted with the obligation to observe Torah commandments as the divinely revealed laws of God.

Although it is clear that Jesus led the life of a Torah-observant Jew, following Paul and his letter to the Galatians, most Christians contended that they were "freed from the law"—exempt from such matters as keeping the Sabbath (which is enshrined in the Ten Commandments), circumcising male infants on the eighth day after birth, or following the dietary laws. Paul had said that it didn't matter what Christians ate—even meat obtained from temples dedicated to pagan deities was fit food (1 Corinthians 8:4). He ridiculed circumcision and prayed that the hands of circumcisers would slip so that they'd castrate themselves (Galatians 5:12). He is never depicted as preparing for the Sabbath. For Paul, now that Jesus had come, Christians were called to "freedom in Christ," not slavery in Torah (Galatians 5:1).

The idea of dispensing with the Old Testament was a natural consequence of this view, and the matter was actively discussed within 2nd-century Christianity. If Christians were no longer subject to Jewish law, the question naturally arose: Why retain and read texts whose central message was contrary to that view? Why expose converts and new Christians to these kinds of writings, only to have church leaders say that they don't believe these teachings are relevant in the post-Christ world? From this pedagogical and theological perspective, retaining the Old Testament would seem pointless . . . even counter-productive.

Marcion, a colorful 2nd-century figure, was a Christian leader who advocated getting rid of the Old Testament. A wealthy owner of a fleet of trading ships, he became a bishop and, in the 140s, wrote an influential work called *Antitheses*. This writing—only snippets of which survive—apparently contrasted the teachings of Jesus with those of the Old Testament. He did not like the God of the Old Testament, which he saw as a vengeful, wrathful God. In time, he postulated a God beyond God—a real God, the God of love. For Marcion, Jesus was not the Jewish Messiah prophesied in the Old Testament. For Marcion, the true God beyond the God of the Old Testament sent his emissary—Christ—to reveal the true nature of divinity to humanity. That task, Marcion thought, was the true mission of Christ. According to Marcion, Jesus was the emissary of the God that stood above the God of Israel. In this way, Marcion was one of the first to divorce Jesus from his historical context.

Although it was highly influential, Marcion's position did not win the day. Most Christians favored retaining the writings of the Old Testament. They were kept, as we have seen, because it gave the new religion an ancient pedigree and because, through typology, the older writings could be interpreted as anticipating Jesus and the church's message of salvation and eternal life. In a sense, typologists went one further than Marcion. Instead of rejecting the Hebrew Bible, they appropriated it.

Through typology, the new Christian movement created an ancient history for itself by retroactively usurping the Hebrew Bible for Christian purposes. Put another way, the majority of Christians took the growing library of Christian writings as authoritative and then read the message of Christian salvation back into the Old Testament. Essentially, it is reverse interpretation—here's what we believe about Christ, now let's see which of these ancient writings can be construed as referring to him.

In summary, typology represented a way of salvaging the relevance of the Old Testament for Christian ends. According to this view, the earlier writings depicted happenings that prefigured the events that were really intended, those that occurred in the Christian era. Thus, the Old would give way to the New, and appearance would give way to reality. Simply put, the Hebrew Bible had to be mined for Christian prototypes.

The Most Important Clue

We can now state without hesitation that the majority of scholars who examined *Joseph and Aseneth* overlooked the context in which the manuscript was preserved—namely, Eastern Christianity and its fondness for typological analysis. By trying to force *Joseph and Aseneth* into a Jewish world, scholars completely ignored the cultural environment in which the text was translated and transmitted. They have searched for interpretive clues in the wrong environment—trying to wedge the text into totally inappropriate historical contexts.

But when you look at the text without preconceptions, what is immediately clear is that *Joseph and Aseneth* represents a dramatic narrative replete with mysterious symbols and ceremonies that beg to be deciphered:

Joseph—Who is he really?
Aseneth—Who is she really?

Why is Aseneth depicted as living in a tower?

What does the heavenly ritual signify?

Who are Joseph and Aseneth's enemies?

If we can answer these questions in a consistent and historically accurate way, we will be well on our way to making sense of this puzzling—and tantalizing—manuscript. We will soon discover that Joseph, Aseneth, the tower, the honey, the bees, the mystical bridal chamber, Pharaoh, and Egypt can all be deciphered as representing a specific cast of characters from the 1st century.

Put simply, what we really have to hunt for is not the Joseph of Jewish history, but Joseph understood in Christian typological terms as a prototype of someone else.

To decipher the real identity of this Joseph, we have to look in the right place.

7

JOSEPH

If the Joseph of *Joseph and Aseneth* is not the Biblical Joseph, then who is he really? In Syriac Christianity, whom does Joseph stand for? Remarkably, we find that Syriac-speaking Christians did see Joseph as a type. In fact, in Syriac Christianity, Joseph is a surrogate for none other than Jesus himself. As Kristian Heal puts it, "Joseph was seen in early Syriac Christianity first and foremost as a type of Christ."[1]

We had already suspected that Joseph was seen as a prefiguration of Jesus, since both Joseph and Jesus are redemptive figures. Nonetheless, it was gratifying to find that early Christian leaders had understood the Joseph narrative as a story about Jesus. This also helped us discover why early Christians had an interest in Joseph: it really wasn't an interest in Joseph—it was an interest in Jesus.

Ephrem the Syrian

In the 4th century, Ephrem the Syrian was one of the most distinguished leaders in Syriac Christianity. He lived in Nisibis (modern-day Nusaybin) from approximately 306 to 373 c.e. Later, when the Romans ceded that city to the Persian Empire, he moved west, to Edessa (modern-day Sanliurfa). Today, both cities are in southeastern Turkey. Ephrem was a deacon and a member of a religious community called the Brothers of the Covenant. Like their female counterparts, the Sisters of the Covenant, the members of this religious community dedicated themselves to a life of service and devotion while abstaining from sexual activity and married life. Ephrem was Orthodox in his beliefs, and his bishop, Jacob of Nisibis, attended the highly influential Council of Nicea in 325 C.E., participating in the formulation of the authoritative statement of Christian faith, the Nicene Creed.

An extremely prolific Syriac writer, Ephrem wrote commentaries on individual Biblical writings, preached sermons, and composed many hymns. Over four hundred of these hymns survive. Because of his poetic eloquence, he was nicknamed *Harp of the Holy Spirit*. He used hymns not just as praise of God, but also primarily as an innovative teaching device. He used song to reinforce true belief, to encourage virginity, to urge periodic fasting, and—especially—to counter the opinions of those Christian groups he considered heretical. Other hymns were composed to celebrate particular events within the Christian liturgical year. For example, he penned hymns honoring the birth of Jesus or celebrating the adoration of the Magi at the feast of the Epiphany. These teaching hymns were exceptionally popular, and many were used in a liturgical context. A priest or deacon might chant portions of the hymn, and then the female choir would join in for the response or chorus.

Ephrem's sermons covered a wide range of topics—on Abraham and Isaac, on Jesus' suffering and death, and on repentance. His sermons abounded in types, and his penchant for typological analysis often creates difficulties for the modern reader not attuned to this interpretive maneuver. There is one sermon, however, that is especially relevant to our study. Remarkably, this sermon—"On Joseph the Most Virtuous"—not only survives but is readily available online.[2]

The opening lines of the sermon draw significant parallels between the life of Joseph, the Israelite patriarch, and that of Jesus. We don't know when Ephrem delivered this lengthy sermon, but his point is clear: Joseph is a type of Jesus, and the story about the Biblical Joseph is really about the Christian message.

Here are some of Ephrem's main comparisons:

- Joseph's brothers plotted to destroy him. Likewise, "the Jews," who were Jesus' "brothers," plotted against Jesus, saying "this is the heir, let us kill him and all will be ours."

- Joseph's brothers, while eating, sold Joseph; "The Jews," while partaking of the Passover meal, slew the Savior.

- Joseph went down into Egypt; Jesus descended into the land of the dead.

- Joseph resisted the power of Potiphar's wife; Jesus destroyed the power of death.

- Joseph saved his brothers; Jesus saved us all.

Incident by incident, Ephrem writes, there are significant parallels between Joseph and Jesus. In Ephrem's words, "and so truly a type he became of that future Coming of the Lord" (Joseph the Most Virtuous, 25:17). All this leads Ephrem to the conclusion: Joseph = Jesus.

From this perspective, when a Christian reads the story of Joseph in the Book of Genesis, he is really reading a story about Jesus. Joseph is simply a surrogate figure. What happened in Joseph's day was fulfilled in a deeper way in the life of Jesus. The latter's life, moreover, is the real meaning of the original story. The original was a foreshadowing of events that would take place more than fifteen hundred years after Joseph was laid to rest.

As can be seen in the writings of Ephrem, typology removes the Hebrew Bible from its historical context. On this view, there is no need to do archaeology to find evidence of Joseph in Egypt. Nor is there any point to engaging in historical research in an attempt to identify the particular Egyptian Pharaoh under whom Joseph served. Nor would it serve any purpose to place the story of the ancient Israelite patriarchs in the nomadic world of the Middle East prior to 1500 B.C.E. All this kind of interpretation—the sort modern scholars would undertake—would be utterly irrelevant for Ephrem and his community of believers.

The Syriac Christians regarded both segments of the Bible, the Old and New Testaments, as a unified whole. They believed that both Old and New Testaments affirmed the truth, not of a historical Joseph, but of the Christian faith. Ephrem would have expected informed members of his congregation to make the connections he made and to be able to read through the superficial story to its real underlying import. Simply put, when reading the Syriac text of *Joseph and Aseneth*, Ephrem's Syriac community would have substituted Jesus for Joseph.

Typological analysis demonstrates conclusively that neither Second Zacharias, who preserved *Joseph and Aseneth*, nor his intended audience would have had a scrap of interest in the ancient figure of Joseph. That story was useful and of significance only insofar as it revealed a truth about Jesus.

That was its real message.

Aphrahat

Ephrem was not alone in this view that Joseph is a type of Jesus. Another Syriac writer, Aphrahat, also treated Joseph as a Jesus figure. Aphrahat lived slightly before Ephrem, in the late 3rd and early 4th centuries C.E. (approximately 270–345 C.E.). Unlike Ephrem, who stayed within the Roman Empire, Aphrahat lived his life within the Persian Empire.

Aphrahat wrote a series of "Demonstrations" on various aspects of the Christian faith. Each *Demonstration* started with one of the letters of the 22-letter alphabet of the Syriac language. *Demonstration 21* was likely written in 344 C.E., toward the end of Aphrahat's life, and was perhaps not too distant from the time of Ephrem's sermon on the same topic. Like Ephrem's sermon, Aphrahat's work can also be found online.[3]

Aphrahat drew many more parallels than Ephrem did between Joseph and Jesus. Here are just some of them, especially the ones not mentioned by Ephrem:

- Joseph's father, Jacob, clothed him in a multi-colored robe; Jesus' father, God, clothed him with a physical body through the Virgin Mary.

- Joseph was his father's favorite; so, too, was Jesus the dearly beloved and only-begotten son of the Father.

- Joseph was persecuted by his brothers; Jesus was also persecuted by his brothers—his fellow Jews.

- Joseph saw visions and dreamed dreams; Jesus fulfilled visions and the predictions of the Prophets.

- Joseph was a shepherd; Jesus is the Chief Shepherd.

- Joseph's brothers threw him into a well, from which he was eventually rescued; Jesus' fellow Jews laid him in a tomb, from which he eventually rose.

- Joseph, at age thirty, stood before Pharaoh and became Lord over Egypt; Jesus, at age thirty, stood before John the Baptizer and was baptized. He became Lord of the world.

- Joseph nourished Egypt with bread; Jesus nourished the whole world with the bread of life.

- Joseph married Aseneth, the daughter of a non-Jewish "unclean" priest; Jesus "married" the church composed of non-Jewish, "unclean" pagans.

- Joseph died and was buried in Egypt, his bones eventually being transferred to Israel; Jesus died and was buried in Jerusalem, where his "Father raised him from the abode of the dead and took his body into heaven, uncorrupted" (*Demonstration* 21:9).

For Aphrahat, like Ephrem, Joseph = Jesus. The story of Joseph is really, in an earlier guise, the story of Jesus. Aphrahat, also like Ephrem, would have expected that educated members of his community would pick up on these parallels and so derive confirmation of the Christian message.

Typology, as can be readily seen, was the key that transformed the Old Testament into a Christian text. Through interpretive transferences, typology was the means by which people in Ephrem and Aphrahat's religious communities made the narratives of the Old Testament into the Christian story.

Narsai, the head of the school of Edessa and the founder of the theological School at Nisibis, followed Aphrahat's interpretive model. With respect to the Biblical Joseph, he states that "this wonderful story" is full of "symbols and types of the son of God" (N. 42:1–2). He goes on to say "the type of our Lord is depicted in the stories of Joseph and his brothers" (N. 43:17).[4]

Heal states that "for early Syriac writers such as Aphrahat and his younger contemporary Ephrem, typology was a central mode of expression." He also states that "we find, then, in the literature of this early period of Syriac Christianity one of the few examples of a 'genuinely Semitic-Christian literature'."[5] Heal proceeds to provide seven pages of "Syriac comparisons of Joseph and Jesus."[6] But the Syriacs were not alone. There were other early Christian theologians who drew the parallels between Joseph and Jesus.

Tertullian

Before Aphrahat, Ephrem, and Narsai, a late 2nd-century and early 3rd-century African Christian writer by the name of Tertullian (about 160 to 220 c.e.) tried to show how Jesus appears throughout the Old Testament. In his work *Against Marcion*—the Christian leader mentioned above who dismissed the value of the Old Testament—Tertullian sought to demonstrate the importance of these writings. Like others, Tertullian employed typology to discern the Christian message embedded in the historical narrative. In this way, Tertullian thought he could preserve the Old Testament for Christian purposes.

In particular, Tertullian devoted a chapter in his work *Against Marcion* to showing that the Old Testament presents "types of the death of Christ" (*Against Marcion*, Book III, chapter XVIII). Isaac, for instance, about to be sacrificed by his father as an offering to God, carries his own wood, just as Jesus carries the cross to his place of execution. Joseph likewise, Tertullian writes, "was a type of Christ" because he suffered persecution for the sake of his brothers, just as Jesus suffered on behalf of his fellow Jews and, indeed, all of humanity.

Tertullian goes further, noting a blessing Moses makes at the end of the Book of Deuteronomy. This blessing says that Joseph is "a firstborn bull—majesty is his! His horns are the horns of a wild ox; with them he gores the peoples, driving them to the ends of the earth" (Deuteronomy 33:17). The "horns of the wild ox" Tertullian interprets as a type of cross—the horizontal crossbeam reminiscent of the two horns of the ox. As he says, "the horns were the extremities of the cross." As for the line "driving the peoples to the ends of the earth," Tertullian equates this Biblical reference to Joseph as a description of Jesus' manner—i.e., pushing some people from earth to heaven and others to judgment.

Joseph Decoded

```
Step One
Joseph = Jesus
```

As has been made clear—and this is really not a matter of conjecture—in the Syriac Christian context, Joseph is a type of Jesus, that is, a *surrogate* in modern language. But *Joseph and Aseneth* goes a step further. As we have seen, the text does not relate the story of Joseph only to read Jesus into it. It actually seems to be relating the story of Jesus and using his surrogate Joseph to mask that fact. Once this is understood, we can begin to make sense of the messianic language in *Joseph and Aseneth*, especially the phrases *Son of God* and *savior*. Even in a Christian context, these titles would not apply to Joseph the ancient Israelite. They would, however, pertain to Jesus and to Jesus alone. The Christian religious terminology—"the bread of life," "the cup of life," "the oil of incorruptibility," "living forever," the honeycomb liturgy with its pronouncement that "this is the honeycomb of life and those who eat from it will not die but live forever"—these phrases begin to make sense within the historical context in which we will now see *Joseph and Aseneth*.

An Incredible First
Seen in this light, we begin to understand that *Joseph and Aseneth* is a Christian story—a Gospel, if you will—about Jesus. Not rumor. Not speculation.

When interpreted in the way that ancient Christians understood their sacred writings, this is absolutely the first written document that makes the personal life of Jesus apparent. After all, it tells the story of how Jesus met his wife, how they married, and how they had children. More than this, it goes into details of who she was and what happened in their lives after the marriage and before the crucifixion. It's surprising—perhaps shocking to some—but it presents a history that has thus far been hinted at but not otherwise known.

One scholar who got intriguingly close to this conclusion was the scholar priest Pierre Batiffol, the editor of the first modern edition of *Joseph and Aseneth*.[7] As Kraemer puts it, "In Batiffol's view, Joseph was an obvious type of Christ."[8] Batiffol couldn't figure out, however, whom Aseneth represented. In Kraemer's words, "the figure of Aseneth gave him a little more pause."[9] As a result, to once again quote Kraemer, Batiffol concluded that "the text grafted a symbolic interpretation of *Joseph and Aseneth* onto older Jewish stories about [their] marriage and that such symbolic interpretation could only have been Christian."[10] Put a different way, Batiffol believed that the Christian symbolism was grafted onto an earlier Jewish text. But how could the entire story of *Joseph and Aseneth*, as it appears in the text, be grafted? If you remove the symbolic grafted elements, you are left with no original text. What Batiffol missed is that the symbolic elements *are* the original story. The reason he missed this point is because he was typologically looking for Aseneth in all the wrong places—i.e., within Western Christian orthodoxy. Nonetheless, he concluded that Aseneth stands for virginity.[11] As we shall see, he wasn't far from the mark. He was just associating virginity with Jesus' mother, who does not correspond to the figure of Aseneth as presented in *Joseph and Aseneth*. He never thought that the virgin in the text might be a woman who the church has traditionally presented as a reformed whore.

Batiffol based his conclusion that the text was Christian on a strong argument for Joseph being Jesus, and a weak argument for Aseneth representing virginity. As a result, he was open to scholarly criticism and it was quick in coming. But he was on to something. What he couldn't figure out was the typology of Aseneth.

If Joseph is Jesus, who, then, is Aseneth?

8

ASENETH

For the same reasons that the Joseph of the manuscript cannot be the Joseph of the Book of Genesis, Aseneth cannot be the obscure Egyptian woman who married the Hebrew patriarch. The Genesis Aseneth would not have been of interest to early Christians. Remember, Marcion did not even care about the God of the Old Testament, never mind Aseneth.

So who is Aseneth? Let's recall what *Joseph and Aseneth* says about her. In our manuscript, Aseneth's beauty, her home, and her spiritual transformation are described in great detail. She lives in a tower (2:1–7). She is eighteen years old, tall, beautiful, and a graceful virgin who has kept herself away from men. She has a kind of Jewish soul locked inside a Gentile body, being "noble and glorious like Sarah, beautiful like Rebecca, and virtuous like Rachel" (1:5). In other words, she possesses all the outstanding qualities of the ancient Jewish matriarchs while being a Gentile. Aseneth is summoned by Joseph to move from darkness into light, from error into truth and from death to life. As she repents, she destroys her idols and embraces monotheism. She then undergoes a rebirthing experience, culminating in a honeycomb sacrament and a wedding. Yet she is not in any way a formal convert to Judaism. There is no sense in the text that she is now committed to the 613 Commandments of the Torah. For example, we don't suddenly see her changing her dietary requirements. Rather, after embracing monotheism, she is called a "City of Refuge" (15:5; 19:4) and is ready to be married—to become "the Bride of God" (4:1). All the while, she remains a Gentile. As we shall soon see, this is significant.

To really understand who Aseneth stands for, we need to make sense of the imagery associated with her: in the first place, the tower symbolism and also the term "City of Refuge," which becomes her proper name. What is already clear, however, is that the text is not talking about an obscure woman. It is pointing at someone truly significant—nothing less than the Bride of God.

What does this mean?

The identity of Aseneth must be decoded in the same way that we successfully decoded Joseph—that is, we have to go back to the environment in which the text was translated, preserved, and transmitted. Since the earliest version of *Joseph and Aseneth* is in Syriac, maybe once again the ancient writers of Syriac Christianity will set us on the right path.

Aseneth = Tower

In *Joseph and Aseneth*, the family home is adjoined by a tower. Aseneth occupies the upper story of ten rooms. Aseneth is literally the woman in the tower—she's the "Tower Lady," if you will. Each of her rooms is described as luxuriously appointed. Three are described in detail.

One room serves as a shrine with a gold ceiling. It is adorned with precious stones. Around the room are representations of the gods and goddesses that Aseneth worships. There, in that room, Aseneth prostrates herself to her idols and offers daily sacrifices. It's her chapel.

Her own bedchamber seems to have occupied the entire east side of the tower. It is described as a large room, with three windows looking out over the courtyard to the east and the street to the north, as well as to the south. Another room was a storeroom for all her personal possessions, her clothing and accessories, as well as ritual coverings for the idols. The remaining seven rooms were occupied by her personal attendants, seven virgins, all born on the same day as she was.

So, of what significance is the description of Aseneth as a tower lady? Using Syriac typological analysis, to whom does she correspond?

Mary the Magdalene = Tower

Since we have firmly set this story in a Christian context, we know of only one tower lady in Christian tradition, and she happens to be intimately associated with Jesus. She is none other than Mary the Magdalene.

As we shall now see, the reasons are straightforward and compelling. Scholars generally speculate that the term "Magdalene" refers to Mary's place of birth. According to this view, Mary hails from Magdala in the Galilee, a village just a few miles southwest of Capernaeum, where Jesus' headquarters were located during his Galilean activism. In other words, according to the prevailing scholarly opinion, she is Mary *from* Magdala.

The standard interpretation is only partially right. The problem with this interpretation of Mary the Magdalene's name is that in the New Testament, Mary is called Mary the Magdalene, not Mary Magdalene.[1] "The Magdalene" represents a title. It is not a surname or, for that matter, a place name. She is not, for instance, Mary of Magdala or Mary from the town of Magdala. She is Mary the Magdalene. What do we make of this?

Let's start at the beginning. *Migdal* in Hebrew (*Magdala* in Aramaic) means—of all things—*Tower*. Translated literally, Mary the Magdalene means Mary the Tower. Even if Mary the Magdalene's name does mean Mary from the town of Migdal, as the standard interpretation would have it, her name would mean Mary from Tower Town and, curiously, there are still remnants of a somewhat later tower in that ancient village on the shores of the Sea of Galilee. Either way, Mary the Magdalene is the only figure in Christian tradition identified with a tower.

So we have two tower ladies: Aseneth and Mary the Magdalene. Taken together with Joseph/Jesus' typology, Aseneth of the Tower in our manuscript is clearly Mary the Magdalene or "Mary the Tower" of the Gospels. Put simply, just as Joseph is a Syriac surrogate for Jesus, Aseneth is a Syriac surrogate for Mary the Magdalene.

Mary the Magdalene in the Canonical Gospels

But if that's the case, doesn't the parallel with the Gospels end there? After all, in *Joseph and Aseneth*, Aseneth, the Magdalene surrogate, is the focus of the story, a powerful figure and the bride of Joseph/Jesus. Does this imagery exist in a New Testament vacuum, or are there hints of her status in the Gospels themselves?

Again, let's start at the beginning. With respect to her being a powerful figure, the fact is that according to the Gospels, along with several other wealthy women, Mary the Magdalene financially supported Jesus' mission (Luke 8:2–3). This was no mean undertaking. It involved providing food, shelter, clothing, and travel costs for at least thirteen individuals—Jesus and his disciples—and their family members over a three-year period. Furthermore, Mary the Magdalene of the Gospels seems to have been with Jesus wherever he went. She was present during his last week in Jerusalem, and even at his crucifixion. As Ann Graham Brock points out, "Whenever the texts [i.e., the four canonical Gospels] refer to a group of women, they always name her first. More importantly . . . [she is] chosen to be the first witness of the resurrection."[2]

Given all this, perhaps the tower imagery in the canonical Gospels should also be understood metaphorically, not simply geographically. That is, perhaps her title in the Gospels doesn't simply refer to her hometown. Mary may have been called the Magdalene—the tower—because she was a towering figure or presence within early Christianity. If we look carefully at the plain meaning of the Gospels we see that, without a doubt, Mary the Magdalene is one of the most eminent persons associated with Jesus, if not the most important person in the group. The tower analogy, or nickname, would then testify to her exalted status among Jesus' earliest followers.[3]

With this in mind, let's remember that it was not unusual for members of Jesus' band to be given nicknames. In the Gospels, many of the key figures are given such names, and they don't refer to towns. For example, Peter's name is really Simon. He is called Peter because in Greek Peter literally means the Rock or "Rocky." The sons of Zebedee are nicknamed "Sons of Thunder." And Judas Iscariot is, most probably, Judas the Sicarius, that is, the Assassin or "Dagger Man." So, whether *the Magdalene* is a nickname referring to her place of birth or her status in the Jesus movement, in the Gospels, just as in our text, Mary the Magdalene is identified with a tower and perceived as a powerful figure.

As for Mary the Magdalene being the Bride of Jesus, here too there seems to be some synchronicity between *Joseph and Aseneth* and the Gospels. For example, in the Gospel of John, there is the so-called wedding at Cana (John 2:1) which some have identified with the wedding of Jesus to Mary the Magdalene.[4] That's the incident where, at his mother's insistence, Jesus turns water into wine. But if he's not the bridegroom, why does his mother expect him to supply the wine?[5]

To the careful reader, there is another incident recounted in the Gospel of John that powerfully indicates that Mary the Magdalene is, indeed, Jesus' bride. As John tells it, after the crucifixion and the Sabbath that followed, before dawn on Sunday, Mary the Magdalene goes to Jesus' tomb along with Jesus' mother and sister. What is she doing there with his next of kin? The Gospel of Mark tells us (Mark 16:1) that her intention was to "anoint" the body—that is, to prepare Jesus' naked body for final burial.

The above detail is of tremendous significance. Anointing Jesus' body means washing it and then rubbing it with various oils. Anointing a man who has been whipped and crucified is no easy task. The badly mutilated body has to be carefully and repeatedly scrubbed. Obviously, a mere follower of Jesus—a marginal follower as some would have it—would not be allowed to "anoint" the naked body of the deceased religious leader and get it ready for burial—especially if the follower is a woman! In Judaism, this was a task that was reserved only for the very closest relatives—certainly not a disciple, and not some marginal female from an extended entourage. Simply put, this important and overlooked detail strongly suggests that Mary the Magdalene was Jesus' wife. Otherwise, she had no business being there at all, much less touching Jesus' naked corpse. It's that simple.

Perhaps most tellingly, Mary the Magdalene was the first to see the risen Jesus and the first to speak with him. She was also the first to announce to the disciples, "I have seen the Lord" (John 20:1–18). Even before his own mother or, for that matter, his brothers and disciples, Jesus shows himself to Mary the Magdalene and reassures her that he will ascend to the Father.

The idea that Jesus would speak first with Mary the Magdalene and not Mary, his mother, represented a sore point within the early Christian community at the time when veneration of the latter was on the rise. Many, including Ephrem the Syrian, wished that Jesus had announced his heavenly birth to Mary, his mother, just as he had his earthly birth through her. That symmetry—Mary, the mother, present at both "births"—would have made sense, or so they thought. But, according to the Gospels, it was to Mary the Magdalene whom Jesus first chose to reveal himself. The choice is very revealing—this preference and word of comfort hint at the fact that she was his closest relative, not some marginal enthusiastic groupie.

Finally, another way orthodox Christians thought of Mary the Magdalene was as the bride mentioned in the Song of Songs. In the 2nd century, Cyril of Jerusalem said, "[When it is written], in the Song of Songs, 'on my bed I sought Him whom my soul loved' it is referring to the Magdalene."[6]

Mary the Magdalene in the Gnostic Gospels

The Gnostic Gospels are even more forthcoming than the canonical Gospels about the preeminent role of Mary the Magdalene and her personal relationship with Jesus. These early Christian texts, such as the *Gospel of Mary Magdalene*, are very clear that Mary the Magdalene is the person closest to Jesus. She is described in Greek as his *koinonos*, a term that can be translated as "companion," and, indeed, that is how it has mostly been translated. It can just as accurately be translated as "lover."

The 2nd-century *Gospel of Peter* makes it clear why Mary the Magdalene went to the tomb on the Sunday that she found it empty. She went there to do "the things which women are wont to do for those that die and for those that are *beloved* of them" (12:50, emphasis added).

If you think that citing a Gnostic non-canonical text is weak history, consider this: the earliest manuscripts of the canonical Gospels date no earlier—even in fragmentary form—than the earliest Gnostic texts (i.e., 2nd to 4th centuries). It's a scholarly guess that the canonical Gospels were initially composed in the late 1st century, but the manuscript trail ends well before then. Nonetheless, theological bullies treat the canonical writings as if they were the original, undisputed works. That helps them describe texts that they don't agree with as late and, as a consequence, heretical or inaccurate.

The fact is that according to an increasing number of historians, the view of Mary the Magdalene espoused in the Gnostic Gospels is more historically accurate than the image portrayed in the canonical Gospels. For example, with respect to the Gnostic *Gospel of Mary Magdalene*, one of the preeminent scholars on Gnosticism, Karen King, states: "Historians . . . have come more and more to understand [that] the Gospel of Mary's portrait [of the early church is] . . . in a number of respects more historically accurate than that of the master [canonical] story."[7] In fact, given its sudden appearance on the historical stage, it is impossible to explain the elaborate mythological system of Gnosticism if it's not based on history. The alternative is to attribute Gnosticism entirely to writers such as Valentinus—but, as Bernard Green states concerning Valentinian beliefs, ". . . how they could have elaborated into such a complex and rigid mythological form within the space of about twenty years still needs to be explained."[8]

The Gnostic *Gospel of Philip* tells the same story. There, it is explicitly said that "the companion of the [savior] is Mary of Magdala. The [savior loved] her more than [all] the disciples, [and he] kissed her often on her [mouth]."[9] According to Elaine Pagels, the term *companion* here is rendered as *syzygos* and "can suggest sexual intimacy."[10] King goes further. She states that in the *Gospel of Philip* both the terms *koinônos* and *hôtre* may refer to heterosexual intercourse. She concludes therefore that "the multivalent representation of Mary as Jesus' *koinônos* and *hôtre*, her link with the heavenly Sophia or Holy Spirit, as well as Jesus kissing her, all function as symbolic-paradigms for the salvation effected in the bridal chamber."[11] In other words, according to the *Gospel of Philip*, Jesus had a "real marital relationship with Mary Magdalene," and this relationship provided the paradigm for "the initiation ritual [known] as a bridal chamber."[12]

The Gnostic Gospels were revered by a large and influential segment of early Christianity—not some small cult or sect. Here, in these writings, Mary the Magdalene is not only the *koinonos* who is regularly and publicly kissed by Jesus, she is also his smartest disciple. According to Pagels, ". . . *every one of the recently discovered sources that mentioned Mary Magdalene* . . . picture Mary as one of Jesus' most trusted disciples. Some even revere her as his *foremost* disciple, Jesus' closest confidante. . . ."[13] She is the one who knows Jesus' true teachings and has the task of imparting her special knowledge to other disciples. We see this, for instance, in the *Gospel of Mary Magdalene* mentioned above. There, after the crucifixion, the disciples are disheartened and come to Mary the Magdalene, asking her: "How can we go to the Gentiles and preach the good news of the kingdom of the child of humanity? If they did not spare him, how will we be spared?"[14] Good question. First of all, notice that they come to her because she has expertise concerning the Gentiles. Second of all, she's clearly used to leadership. While Peter and the other disciples quiver, Mary takes charge, comforting all of them and handling their request to pass Jesus' secret teachings on to them. She is clearly the apostle to the apostles, the *apostola apostolorum*.

Mary the Magdalene's role within Gnosticism reflects an early understanding of her significance and her special connection to Jesus. In these non-canonical early Christian texts, Mary the Magdalene is the guardian and teacher of Jesus' authentic message. All this fits perfectly with the portrait of Aseneth, the tower lady in *Joseph and Aseneth*.

Mary the Magdalene as Priestess

But there is more. In the manuscript, before she meets Joseph, Aseneth is some kind of pagan priestess—attended to by seven virgins. This is suggestive. Was Mary the Magdalene a Gentile priestess before she met Jesus? After her transformation, did she represent a particular faction within the earliest Jesus movement?

If Mary the Magdalene was a priestess, she would have been a "Phoenician" one. "Phoenician" was, essentially, a Greek name for coastal Canaanites. The Canaanites were the pre-Hebrew people of the area. By the time of Jesus, they lived primarily in the area of modern Lebanon, just north of the Galilee. In fact, Jesus' ministry took place in the Galilee, a place of mixed Jewish and Phoenician/Canaanite culture. Allen Jones puts it very well when he states, "One tends to forget how close were the cultural relationships between and among the peoples of the Aegeo-Mediterranean area. The sea was a highway rather than a barrier."[15] Elaborating on this point, speaking specifically of Judaea, Morton Smith states that "the Semitic-speaking people of the land were by no means wholly Jewish. . . . Therefore, to picture Jesus' environment we have to reckon with a strong strain of native, Palestinian, Semitic paganism. Besides this, the country had long been influenced by Phoenician and Egyptian beliefs."[16] Recent excavations at Bethsaida[17]—home to as many as five of Jesus' twelve disciples—confirm the heterogeneity of the Galilean population in the 1st century C.E. Also, the discovery of what seems to be the town of Dalmanutha, described in the Gospel of Mark (8:10) as the place Jesus sailed to after miraculously feeding four thousand people by multiplying a few fish and loaves of bread, has unearthed architectural remains and pottery suggesting "that Jews and those following a polytheistic religion lived side by side in the community."[18] Dalmanutha was situated less than a mile from Magdala. In other words, the Galilee was a place of mixed Jewish and Phoenician people. It was a melting pot of various cultures, not purely Jewish by ethnicity or religion.

Jesus himself was no stranger to Phoenician culture. For example, in the Gospel of Mark (7:24–31), he takes an unexplained journey outside Jewish territory to the region of Tyre and Sidon—modern Lebanon. That is, he undertakes a journey to the middle of the Phoenician world. Why? According to the Gospels, there he has an interaction with an unnamed Gentile, a "Syro-Phoenician" woman (Mark 7:26) who seeks his help in healing her daughter. Can this be a canonical echo of the meeting that forms the heart of the *Joseph and Aseneth* narrative? Put differently, is the encounter between Jesus and the Syro-Phoenician woman an echo of the first meeting between Jesus and Mary the Magdalene?

To return to our text, Aseneth's tower in the manuscript is described as a kind of temple with an outer shrine and an inner Holy of Holies or "bridal chamber." This dual-chamber architecture parallels the temple in Jerusalem and the Phoenician temple in Tyre. This is not surprising. After all, Hiram King of Tyre helped King Solomon build the temple in Jerusalem (1 Kings 7:13; 2 Chronicles 4:11). More than this, Aseneth's shrine is described as having a gold ceiling exactly like the temples in Jerusalem and Tyre. In other words, the story in *Joseph and Aseneth* seems to clarify a detail that is only alluded to in the canonical Gospels, namely that Mary the Magdalene was not only a Syro-Phoenician woman but a Syro-Phoenician priestess.

But if Mary the Magdalene was, indeed, a Phoenician priestess until her encounter with Jesus of Nazareth, did she now convert to Judaism? Or, perhaps, did she convert her tower into a church for her Gentile followers?

What Typology Tells Us

In Syriac Christianity, the types all dovetail. Aseneth is equated with Mary the Magdalene, just as Joseph is equated with Jesus. Here's how Syriac Christians saw things:

1. Church = Tower

The tower imagery in *Joseph and Aseneth* and the match between Aseneth and Mary the Magdalene are no mere coincidences. Ephrem explicitly makes the identification of the tower with the church. Here's what he says:

> The Church, moreover, is the Tower
> The Tower which the many built
> Was a symbol, looking to the One:
> He came down and built on earth
> The Tower that leads up to heaven.[19]

Ephrem may be reminding us here that the ancients tried to reach God physically, by ascending ziggurats—terraced towers—to heaven. In contrast, the church represents a spiritual path to God. It is what "He who came down" wanted to build on earth.

But there's more to the story. How did the one who "came down" build the church? What were the means by which the church came to be? And here we make an amazing discovery: both Aseneth and Mary the Magdalene are explicitly interpreted in Syriac Christianity as surrogates for the church.

2. Aseneth = Church

Ephrem depicts Aseneth, our tower lady, as the type for the church. His Hymn 21 goes as follows:

> You [Ephraim] are the son of Aseneth, the daughter of a pagan priest;
> She is *the symbol of the church of the Gentiles.*[20]

Ephrem's hymn is telling us that Aseneth is "the daughter of a pagan priest." But if we are not talking about ancient Egypt then, in a Phoenician context, as Athalya Brenner reminds us, "the king was high priest of Ashtoreth and his daughter was *high priestess* of Ba'al."[21] If the equation between Aseneth and Mary the Magdalene is correct, beyond the church typology, Ephrem is telling us that Mary the Magdalene was both a Phoenician and a priestess.

Furthermore, the hymn explicitly tells us that after her transformation, Aseneth becomes the symbol of the church. Clearly, she is not the church—she is the *symbol* of the church. Meaning she's not an institution, she's an individual. But this has nothing to do with the obscure Aseneth in the Book of Genesis. We are in solid Christian territory here. He must be speaking about the tower lady that Aseneth, typologically speaking, represents. She is none other than Mary the Magdalene.

Hymn 21 gives us the name of the particular church community that Aseneth represents. It's the "Church of the Gentiles." What is this church? How does this community relate to our understanding of early Christianity?

Aphrahat too, in *Demonstration 21*, makes the same point and explicitly connects Joseph/Aseneth to Jesus/church:[22]

Joseph married the daughter of an unclean priest
And Jesus brought to himself the Church from the unclean Gentiles.

Simply put, this means that just as Joseph married Aseneth, the daughter of a non-Jewish priest, so, too, Jesus can be said to have married the Gentile Church. In other words, in Aphrahat's parallel, Joseph is Jesus and Aseneth—his Gentile bride—is the church. Writing in the 3rd century, Cyprian, leader of the church in Carthage, explicitly stated that the church was the "bride of Christ"—anyone who did not have the bride as a mother could not have God as the father.[23]

3. Mary the Magdalene = Church
But do either Ephrem or Aphrahat explicitly refer to Mary the Magdalene and relate her, like Aseneth, to Jesus' bride—that is, to the church?

Remarkably, Ephrem does just that.

In another passage of Hymn 21, Ephrem the Syrian writes the following about Mary the Magdalene:

> Let us call the Church itself "Mary."
> For it befits her to have two names.
> For to Simon, the Foundation,
> Mary was first to run,
> And like the Church brought him the good news
> And told him what she had seen
> That our Lord has risen and was raised up.[24]

Here, it's not the Virgin Mary but Mary the Magdalene—the first to run to Jesus' tomb—who is called the church. After all, Mary the Magdalene is the first to see the resurrection and the first to proclaim the essential Christian message, namely, that Jesus was raised from the dead. In other words, according to Ephrem, while Simon Peter may be the foundation of the church, Mary the Magdalene, like Aseneth, is the symbol for the church.

4. The Church of the Gentiles
Furthermore, both Mary the Magdalene and Aseneth are referred to by Ephrem as "the Church of the Gentiles." This strange terminology refers to those who

had been converted to Jesus' message but who remained non-Jews. Though they may formerly have been worshippers of many of the popular deities around the Mediterranean world—Mithras, Dionysus, Artemis, and so forth—these individuals remained non-Jewish but became attached to Jesus' movement. Hence, they were the Church of the Gentiles, as opposed to the Church of the Circumcised, the Jewish followers of Jesus.

Ephrem's description of Mary perfectly matches our manuscript's depiction of Aseneth. In *Joseph and Aseneth*, Aseneth is renamed City of Refuge. The angelic being who visits her in her suite tells us the reason for this. In her, many nations—not the House of Israel—will take refuge with the Lord God, and she will protect those people who trust in God. In other words, Aseneth becomes a kind of tower leading to heaven, sheltering the Gentile faithful. Her walls, it is predicted, will guard those who attach themselves to the Most High God.

As in Ephrem, *Joseph and Aseneth* tells us that Mary the Magdalene represented a group of faithful who become "attached"—but not necessarily converted—to the religion of the Most High God. Mary the Magdalene, therefore, was a symbol for a specific community of believers. For those people, she became a City of Refuge or, in Ephrem's words, a "Church of the Gentiles."

Interestingly, as noted above, in the Gnostic *Gospel of Mary Magdalene*, Jesus' disciples go to Mary the Magdalene to ask a question specifically related to the Church of the Gentiles: "How can we go to the Gentiles and preach the good news?" We also find backing for the idea that Mary the Magdalene was the leader of the Gentile followers of Jesus in a 2nd-century Greek text. There, a pagan philosopher named Celsus mentions a Christian group named after a woman named Mary, who is otherwise unidentified.[25] Clearly, in light of the new evidence, we are talking about Mary the Magdalene. More than this, as Stephen Shoemaker states, Celsus' group "bears some relation to the 'Nassenes' of Hippolytus' *Refutatio*, whose teachings were supposedly passed down from James the brother of the Lord through a woman named Mariamne."[26] This is a group of Gentiles, and Celsus' "Mary" is referred to by her Greek name "Mariamne," not some Hebrew or Aramaic version of her name. Not coincidentally, Mariamne, or Mariamene, is the exact Greek version of Mary that appears on an ossuary (bone box) in a 1st-century Jerusalem tomb next to the ossuary of a man named "Jesus, son of Joseph."[27] In other words, the portrayal of Mary the Magdalene in our text, as the leader of the Gentile Church, matches both the archaeological and textual evidence.

But what about the designation City of Refuge applied to Mary the Magdalene? In effect, in *Joseph and Aseneth*, Aseneth/Mary the Magdalene is renamed "Artemis." In Greek, the name Artemis means "safe and sound"—that is, the goddess who gives refuge. In the original Greek version of *Joseph and Aseneth*, there was probably a play on words here; she wasn't being renamed City of Refuge, she was being renamed Artemis.[28] As we shall see later, this is very significant.

Most interestingly, "City of Refuge" is a designation reserved for Jesus himself. There is an ancient Gnostic writing which talks about Jesus in exactly the same terms that *Joseph and Aseneth* uses to talk about Mary the Magdalene. In the 3rd-century *The Acts of Judas Thomas*, Jesus is called a "City of Refuge." We find this idea expressed in a prayer:

> Our Lord, Companion of his servants,
> Guide and Leader of those who believe in him,
> *City of Refuge* and Repose of the afflicted,
> Hope of the poor and Deliverer of the feeble. . . .[29]

The City of Refuge is obviously a code for Church of the Gentiles. What we learn from all this is that the Church of the Gentiles goes back beyond Paul to the earliest days of Christianity, and it seems to have been led by Mary the Magdalene. In Jane Schaberg's words: "I like to think of the Magdalene figure . . . as an actual person who lived and who, I think, has a better claim than Paul to being the founder of Christianity."[30] This Gentile Church was separate from the somewhat later congregations of the Christ that sprouted up throughout modern-day Turkey and Greece in the 40s and 50s under Paul's influence. The theology of Mary the Magdalene's Church of the Gentiles would have differed significantly, both from the "Christ congregations" of Paul—which were also Gentile in composition—and from the Jewish Jesus Movement, led by Jesus' brother James until his violent death in 62 C.E.

In light of our text, it now becomes clear that there must have been three distinctive forms of early Christianity, each differing somewhat from the others in beliefs and practices:

The Jesus Movement—Jesus' first Jewish followers under James in Jerusalem. Essentially, this was a Torah-observant Jewish group that saw Jesus as the anticipated fully human Messiah or redeemer.

The Church of the Gentiles—the community of Gentile followers of Jesus, stemming from Mary the Magdalene. This group paralleled the fully Jewish Jesus movement by preserving a more historical Jesus. At the same time, they seem to have introduced non-Jewish ideas into the movement—for example, the elevation of Jesus from a human Messiah to some kind of divine being or "Son of God," and likewise the elevation of Mary the Magdalene to some kind of "Bride of God."[31]

The Christ Movement—Paul's congregations, based on Paul's visions of the resurrected Christ. This movement diminished the statures of Mary the Magdalene, Jesus' family, and his earthly ministry. It worshipped the Christ figure as a dying-rising savior god-human and viewed Jesus' death as the gateway to salvation.

The first two movements would have arisen out of Jesus' intimate circle—Jews and Gentiles. Paul, who came on the scene in the mid-30s, spearheaded the Christ Movement a few years after Jesus' crucifixion. Simply put, as our text highlights, Paul seems to have had very little connection to the Jesus of history, his early Jewish followers, or the beginnings of the Gentile Jesus movement. Unlike Mary the Magdalene and James, Paul never met the Jesus who taught in the late 20s throughout the Galilee and in Jerusalem.

In time, a fourth movement developed, represented by Gnostic Christianity. This movement seems to have been related to the Church of the Gentiles in which Mary the Magdalene played such a prominent role.

We'll return to these divisions within early Christianity in a later chapter.

Putting It All Together

Here's what we have deciphered so far concerning the Aseneth character in *Joseph and Aseneth*:

Aseneth = Church = Tower
Mary the Magdalene = Church = Tower

Using methods employed by Syriac Christians, we've been able to establish the true identity of the Aseneth in our manuscript. The typological identifications reinforce one another: Aseneth and Mary the Magdalene are both Towers and types of the church. The logic is clear: Aseneth and Mary the Magdalene are identical, the former acting as a surrogate for the latter.

Aseneth Decoded

Step Two
Aseneth = Mary the Magdalene

The Shepherd of Hermas

There are other writings that build upon the same typology; for example, the influential 2nd-century writing *The Shepherd of Hermas*.[32] Irenaeus, the early church father living in what is today Lyon, France, considered this text scriptural, placing it on the same level as the material in the Bible. This writing is also included in the Muratorian Canon, an early list of authoritative Christian texts.

Attributed to Hermas, the brother of Pius, bishop of Rome (around 140–154), *The Shepherd of Hermas* contains mysterious visions, commandments and parables all dealing with ethical concerns and the need for repentance. Reading it in light of *Joseph and Aseneth*, we can see that they belong to the same genre. In *The Shepherd of Hermas*, an "eminent looking man," an emissary "sent from the most revered angel," the "shepherd to whom you have been entrusted"[33] reveals himself to Hermas, the hero of the story. The angel proceeds, god-like, to legislate commandments. The fourth commandment stresses that he is "in charge of repentance" and that "repentance is itself a form of understanding" (*The Shepherd of Hermas* 30, section IV, 2, verse 2).[34] This angelic message parallels the importance of repentance uttered by the angelic Joseph in the transformation of Aseneth.

More than this, when speaking of the church, many of the images used in *The Shepherd of Hermas* parallel those used in *Joseph and Aseneth*. In the third vision, for example, an elderly woman approaches Hermas. She shows him a tower. Addressing her as "Lady," Hermas inquires as to the significance of the tower. She responds, "The tower, which you see being built, is I, the church" (*The Shepherd of Hermas* 9, section III, 3, verse 3).[35] Here we explicitly see that the tower = the lady = the church.

Moreover, around the tower are seven women, reminiscent of the seven virgins who attend Aseneth in her tower.[36] They have different names which the "lady" indicates are Faith, Self-restraint, Simplicity, Knowledge, Innocence, Reverence, and Love. These represent seven steps in the spiritual process toward perfection, each one giving rise to the next. "Whoever," notes the Lady to Hermas, "serves as their slave and is able to adhere to their deeds will have a place to reside in the tower, along with the saints of God" (*The Shepherd of Hermas* 16, section III, 8, verse 8).[37] The tower, therefore, is the place of refuge: it represents the church where those who have been redeemed through repentance dwell.

In the fourth vision, Hermas recounts: "a young woman suddenly met me, clothed as if coming from a bridal chamber, dressed all in white and with white sandals, veiled down to her forehead. . . . From my earlier visions I knew that she was the church" (*The Shepherd of Hermas*, section 23, section IV, 2 verses 1, 2).[38] Again, here we see the same typology at work: the Church = the Bride = the Lady = the Tower. Also note the importance of the "bridal chamber" from which the "young woman" emerges. This woman, the Bride, is the one who can protect the faithful from a prophesied great beast, which Hermas interprets as a foreshadowing of a great affliction.

Thus, *Joseph and Aseneth* is not alone in using the typology of tower, Bride, and lady for the church. Nor is this symbolism just confined to the eastern Syriac-speaking Christianity and the North African writer Tertullian. According to most scholars, *The Shepherd of Hermas* originated within Rome, right in the center of the empire. It was disseminated widely, becoming one of the most popular writings within early Christianity.

In other words, the imagery we encounter in *Joseph and Aseneth* was commonplace in the 2nd and 3rd centuries around the Mediterranean Christian world, another argument for an early dating of our manuscript. In *Joseph and Aseneth* we are not dealing with isolated or idiosyncratic typology. Such discourse was rife throughout the empire.

In fact, there are at least three Aseneth-type legends in the Syriac church—all of them explicitly Christian, all of them dated to the 3rd and 4th century. They concern St. Barbara, St. Irene, and St. Christina. Like Aseneth, St. Barbara is extremely beautiful, lives in the Egyptian city of Heliopolis, has a rich pagan father, lives in a tower, destroys her idols, and turns toward God. Unlike Aseneth, she is described explicitly as a Christian, and when she is murdered for her faith, she is designated a martyr. Like Aseneth and Barbara, St. Irene is beautiful, has a powerful father, and lives in a tower. She has a life-altering conversion from paganism to Christianity. She dies at least twice, but is resurrected each time. She ends her life in the region of Ephesus, the home of the goddess Artemis. Finally, there is St. Christina. Like Aseneth, Barbara, and Irene, Christina is pagan, has a powerful father and lives in a tower. She is being groomed as a Phoenician pagan priestess when an angel, who converts her to Christianity, visits her. She cries a lot and is ultimately martyred.

There are only two main differences between Ascneth and the rest of these saintly and beautiful tower ladies. They are explicitly Christian, while Aseneth's theology is never described openly. More to the point, they are all celibate, while Aseneth is both sexually active and ultimately married. Kraemer puts it this way: "If the linchpin of the Aseneth tale is her marriage to Joseph, the linchpin of these martyrologies is the renunciation of marriage and the wrath such renunciation brings on women, together with its ultimate rewards."[39]

We think the marriage explains the cover-up. Meaning: Barbara, Irene, and Christina are explicitly called Christian because they are celibate. Aseneth's Christian past is masked because she is married.

Which story is the earlier? Clearly, *Joseph and Aseneth*. It is the only text where the religion of the female protagonist is kept ambiguous, and it is the only story that showcases a married woman. It would make no sense, given the Christian context where these texts were preserved, for a writer to model Aseneth on a celibate Christian woman and turn her into a married pagan heroine. On the other hand, it makes perfect sense—once the figure of Aseneth is transformed into various martyrs who are consistent with Pauline theology—that Barbara, Irene, and Christina are modeled on Aseneth. Basically, these three women are sanitized Pauline versions of Aseneth. In other words, what we are seeing is the historical process by which Mary the Magdalene was airbrushed out of history. First she is transformed into Aseneth, the Bride of God. Then she is transformed into the beautiful, celibate tower ladies and martyrs Barbara, Irene, and Christina.

What these three female Christian saints give us is a literary tradition—a genre. Given the similarities, there's absolutely no reason to pull Aseneth out of this tradition, except that our original tower lady does not die a martyr's death, is not Christian in the Pauline sense, and is very much married to someone called "the Son of God." Unless there was some kind of psychological need for Syrian Christians to invent beautiful tower ladies, there is a historical reality behind the Syriac mythology. Faced with these kinds of texts, Ann Graham Brock says "It is possible to make the sociological link between text and historical context."[40] In other words, if Aseneth stands behind the Syrian Christian martyrs Barbara, Irene, and Christina, who stands behind Aseneth? Historically speaking, whom is she covering for?

The Clincher

Let's go back to Hymn 21 of Ephrem the Syrian to see if the explicit equations between Aseneth, Mary the Magdalene, and the church can be made even more explicit. Here's what the hymn says:

> You [Ephraim] are the son of Aseneth, the daughter of a pagan priest;
> She [Aseneth] is the symbol of the Church of the Gentiles.
> She [Aseneth] loved Joseph, and Joseph's son . . .
> in truth, the Holy Church loved.
> She had many children by the Crucified,
> And every one of them is marked with the cross.[41]

Clearly, the above hymn cannot be read as referring to the Biblical Aseneth or Joseph, or Joseph's son as in the Book of Genesis. That would be absurd—the Aseneth of the Book of Genesis did not have "many children by the Crucified." If Aseneth is Mary the Magdalene, let's examine how the hymn would read, simply substituting Jesus for Joseph and Mary the Magdalene for Aseneth:

> Ephraim, you are the son of Mary the Magdalene,
> daughter of a pagan priest;
> Mary the Magdalene is the symbol of the Church of the Gentiles.
> She loved Jesus, and Jesus' son . . .
> in truth, the Holy Church loved.
> Mary the Magdalene had many children by the Crucified,
> And every one of them is marked with the cross.

In other words:

- Mary the Magdalene is the daughter of a non-Jewish priest.

- Mary the Magdalene is the symbol for the Church of the Gentiles.

- Mary the Magdalene loved Jesus.

- Mary the Magdalene had many children by Jesus.

- The children were all marked for death.

In light of *Joseph and Aseneth*, this is now the most natural reconstruction. The substitutions make sense. They show decisively that in Syriac Christianity, Aseneth is linked to Mary the Magdalene. She is the Bride of God and the mother of his children.

Some might argue that this passage can also be construed spiritually with Mary the Magdalene representing the Church of the Gentiles. Converts to her movement would represent her "children." On this reading, Aseneth/Mary the Magdalene is the church which had many metaphorical children by Jesus. All these children, therefore, are marked by the sign of the cross. Such a reading is obviously theologically motivated. It asks us to look beyond the plain language at metaphors that are not even hinted at. But, even if we accept this reading, the point is that, beyond a doubt, in Syriac Christianity, Aseneth is equated with Mary the Magdalene, who is then equated with an important branch of the Christian Church.

Having said this, with respect to metaphorical readings, the rule of thumb should be that they are perfectly legitimate ways to interpret a text, but not at the expense of ignoring the simple meaning of the words. In other words, it's all right to go deeper, as we have done with *Joseph and Aseneth*, but it's another thing to ignore the surface meaning altogether. In the instance of Ephrem's Hymn 21, it's very clear that a woman—here called Aseneth—is having "many children by the Crucified." The plain meaning cannot be ignored. In fact, it has to lead. As *Joseph and Aseneth* will soon make clear, the plain meaning points to real history. Meaning, the marriage and children were real.

9

ASENETH: HER STORY

The Meeting

Joseph and Aseneth opens with Joseph about to descend on the estate of Potiphar, Aseneth's father, a priest of Heliopolis in Egypt. The late-morning heat is overpowering, and Joseph and his retinue wish to stop to rest and enjoy refreshments.

Potiphar is overjoyed and immediately orders preparations for a feast. He and his wife take their daughter aside, explaining to her that Joseph, "the Powerful One of God" (3:4) and the ruler of all Egypt, is about to honor them by having lunch with them. He describes Joseph as a worshipper of God, a virgin, and a man of great wisdom. He calls him "the savior" (4:7). He adds that the "holy spirit of God" (4:8) is in him. Potiphar then informs Aseneth that he intends to give her to Joseph as a wife.

Aseneth's immediate reaction is one of "rage and indignation" (4:10). Why, she asks, should she be handed over like a prisoner to a person "who is not one of my people" (4:10)? She also wonders out loud about the rumor that Joseph "attempted adultery" with his master's wife (4:11).[1] Potiphar wisely decides to hold his tongue, knowing that his daughter would eventually calm down.

Joseph sends "twelve men ahead of him" (3:2) and then arrives in regal style, rich in royal and divine symbolism. The next chapter will probe the significance of these important details, for they tell us much about who Joseph is modeled on. For the moment, suffice it to say that this Joseph—like Jesus and unlike the

Biblical Joseph[2]—is surrounded by twelve men. Like Jesus, as depicted in count-less paintings, mosaics, and stained-glass windows, Joseph is here described as arriving on a chariot made of gold and pulled by white horses. Later editions of the text say that the horses were four in number. The text is also very clear that he is "clothed in beautiful white linen and wrapped in a purple cloak" (5:5). He wears a crown of gold and he holds a royal scepter. This is a classic depiction of the Greek god Helios, called Apollo by the Romans. Later, he is also called Sol Invictus, the "Unconquered Sun." At about the same time as the rise of Chris-tianity in the 2nd century, Sol Invictus became identified with the Persian Sun god Mithras and worshipped throughout the Roman Empire. The Egyptians called him Horus. The Phoenicians called him Ba'al. All these appellations were various names for the Sun god who drives his chariot across the heavens, dies and is resurrected every morning, remaining, that is, unconquered by dark-ness. Helios/Apollo was believed to have had twelve disciples represented by the twelve signs of the zodiac.

These symbols—the signs of the zodiac and the chariot—also meant some-thing in a Jewish context. Let's not forget, the original Jerusalem Church was essentially a Jewish affair. According to Rachel Elior, the writers of the Dead Sea Scrolls, for example—or at least some of them—were part of what would later become known as the "Merkavah" chariot tradition. This Jewish form of mys-ticism involved some kind of ascent to the heavenly throne, use of a solar—as opposed to a lunar—calendar, and, as in *Joseph and Aseneth*, the belief that an angelic priesthood would imminently appear. *Joseph and Aseneth*, therefore, appears to be consistent with the beliefs of an ideological minority within the Jewish spectrum. More important, however, is the manner in which these ideas were adopted by the non-Jewish Christian movement.[3]

The early Gentile Christian Church promoted Jesus–Apollo–Helios–Sol Invictus–Mithras symbolism and syncretism (fused religious symbols) so as to attract various peoples in the Roman Empire to the Christian fold. In fact, after the empire became Christian in the 4th century, only Jesus could be depicted with the symbolism once reserved for Apollo, Helios, Mithras, and Sol Invictus. It was illegal for anyone else—commoner or Caesar—to be portrayed in this way.

Identifying sun imagery with Jesus is not unique to our analysis. It's the norm. For example, right under St. Peter's Basilica in Rome, archaeologists have found a largely pagan cemetery dating to the 1st century. One of the most impressive tombs belongs to what has been identified as an early Christian family named Julii. How did archaeologists determine that the Julii family gave up paganism and became some of the earliest followers of Jesus? On the wall of the tomb, there is an image of Jonah and the whale (associated by early Christians with Jesus), a Good Shepherd (Christian iconography), and Jesus, depicted as the Sun god, riding on a chariot pulled by white horses.[4] Simply put, although there is precedent for some of these symbols in the Jewish and pagan traditions, the earliest Christian tomb in Rome—right under the Vatican—depicts Jesus in exactly the manner that he is portrayed in *Joseph and Aseneth*.

The mix of sun-god imagery, signs of the zodiac, and Jewish symbolism is a classic marker for the early Church of the Gentiles. In fact, churches of this kind have been unearthed in the very birthplace of the movement—in the Galilee. Because there is Jewish symbolism in the mosaics that have been excavated there, Israeli archaeologists have dubbed the ancient buildings that housed them "synagogues." But our contention is that the mosaics at Beit Alpha, Tiberias, Sepphoris,[5] etc. have been wrongly identified, in the same way that *Joseph and Aseneth* has been wrongly labeled as Jewish. Many scholars mistakenly assume that a Jewish symbol or character must mean a Jewish text or edifice. They disregard the fact that in the early stages of the development of the new religion, many Christian groups still had a distinctly Jewish flavor and used Jewish symbols. In the Galilean Beit Alpha, Tiberias, and Sepphoris houses of worship, for example, the depictions of Helios perfectly match the description of Joseph in our text, and they are both virtually identical to depictions of Jesus from the 1st century to this day. In other words, Joseph's grand entrance in our text is a classic depiction of Jesus as a Sun god. Commenting on this entrance, Nir states "Joseph is pictured as Helios, but he's also the prototype of Jesus Christ."[6]

We'll elaborate on Joseph/Jesus in the next chapter. Let's return to Aseneth's story, one that has been suppressed and ignored for centuries. What does it tell us? And what can we infer about Mary the Magdalene as a result?

Again, we let the text take the lead.

As the story unfolds, Aseneth catches a glimpse of Joseph from the upper window of her very tall tower and, seeing him in person, she is immediately taken with him. Her reaction is spiritual, physical, and sexual. When she sees him, her knees literally shake and "the joints of her hips were loosened" (6:1). She now regrets her former impetuous words. She says of Joseph/Jesus, "Now I see the sun shining from his chariot" (6:2). Putting her former arrogance aside, she states that she would be willing to be given to him, to "serve him forever" (6:7). Aseneth's physical reaction to Joseph is significant. In the Gospels "Jesus was expressly portrayed as a man who loved women, and whom women loved."[7] Also significant is the self-deprecation by the formerly arrogant Aseneth.

The encounter between Jesus and the Syro-Phoenician or Canaanite woman in the Gospel of Matthew (15:21–29) that we alluded to earlier seems to parallel Aseneth's first encounter with Joseph. Consider: in Matthew, when the Gentile woman asks Jesus to heal her dying daughter, Jesus tells her that he is only interested in healing Jews, that is, that he was sent only to the House of Israel. He compares his disciples to his "children" and compares the Syro-Phoenician woman to a dog. What's going on here? Either Jesus believes that all Gentiles are dogs, or there is something about this woman that connects her specifically with dogs. It's unlikely that Jesus believed all Gentiles were dogs. This does not fit with what he has to say about Samaritans, Romans, or other ethnic groups. So, clearly, there must be something about this particular woman that merits the designation of "dog." The incredible thing is that the woman doesn't argue. She agrees with this characterization. When she does, Jesus calls her a woman of faith and agrees to heal her daughter. Again, what's going on here?

To reiterate, Jesus calls the Syro-Phoenician woman in the Gospels a dog. Since she is female, it would be more correct to say "bitch." As it turns out, the bitch was a sacred animal for the goddess Artemis.[8] A recent discovery of hundreds of dog burials in Ashkelon, Israel, in a Phoenician/Canaanite religious context, sheds more light on the incident involving the Syro-Phoenician woman.[9] Specifically, it seems that dogs were not only sacred, but were used in Canaanite pagan rituals—hence Jesus' insult. For the dog appellation to make sense, the Syro-Phoenician woman must have been a Canaanite priestess involved in dog sacrifices. Jesus is insulting her by reminding her of her occupation. By agreeing with him, she is transformed. It is only then that he agrees to heal her daughter.

If we are right and Mary the Magdalene—a.k.a. Aseneth—is a Syro-Phoenician priestess, then her self-deprecation in the face of Joseph mirrors the Syro-Phoenician woman's self-deprecation in the face of Jesus. The passage in Matthew may be another echo of the relationship between Jesus and Mary the Magdalene preserved in the canonical Gospels.[10]

Her parents now bring Aseneth down from her suite high in the tower. For the first time, she meets Joseph face to face. Aseneth's father tells her to go and kiss Joseph. She immediately goes up to him. In later Greek versions of *Joseph and Aseneth*, in erotic detail, the text notes that "her breasts were already standing upright like handsome apples."[11] But Joseph rejects her. Having said this, it's a particular kind of rejection, a kind of erotic push–pull. The text says that he places his right hand on her chest between her two young breasts (8:5).[12]

As the saying goes, the devil is in the details. There is a rabbinic commentary in the Jerusalem Talmud which directly connects this breast-touching episode to Jesus. The Jerusalem Talmud was written during the 4th and 5th centuries. In this section, the rabbis are commenting on improper sexual relations involving someone named Gehazi. As it turns out, "Gehazi" is a code name for Jesus.[13] He is described in the Talmud as pushing a woman away in an inappropriate manner. Like Joseph in *Joseph and Aseneth*, he "placed his hand on the most magnificent of her beauties—between her breasts" (*Yebamot* 2:4).

In other words, in *Joseph and Aseneth* and in the Talmud we have stand-ins for Jesus and a description of the exact same scene: a pushing-away that involves the erotic placement of the hand between the breasts of the woman who is being rejected. Clearly, they are describing the exact same episode in Jesus and Mary the Magdalene's lives. But are there echoes of this scene in the Gospels themselves? In fact, Joseph's touch-me-not arm movement in *Joseph and Aseneth* corresponds to one of the most dramatic scenes in the Gospels, when Mary the Magdalene goes to Jesus' tomb only to find it empty. At that point, she despairs until she sees a gardener, who she identifies as Jesus. She then rushes toward him but is stopped dead in her tracks. Jesus puts up his hand and says "touch me not." In the Latin version of the Gospels, this line was translated as "*noli me tangere*" (John 20:17). It became one of the most famous lines of the Gospels, depicted in countless masterpieces (see, for example, Fra Angelico, Correggio, and Fra Bartolomeo). In other words, in the Talmud and in *Joseph and Aseneth* we have the exact same scene as in the Gospels, except that in these texts the woman is rushing toward a very much alive Jesus. In *Joseph and Aseneth*, the touch-me-not scene is not the end of the story as it is in the Gospels but, rather, it is the beginning.

As he's rejecting her, Joseph/Jesus says that it is not right for him to kiss Aseneth/Mary the Magdalene. After all, he's a person who worships the one true God. Joseph/Jesus says that while he blesses God, eats the bread of life, drinks the cup of immortality, and is anointed with the oil of incorruptibility, Aseneth/Mary the Magdalene is a woman who uses her mouth to bless idols, eat "strangled food," and drink the "libation of deceit" (8:6). Further, he says that she anoints herself with the "ointment of corruption" (8:6). Whatever these strange descriptions signify, they are all indicators of her commitment to—and, most probably, role in—the worship of false deities . . . and of Joseph/ Jesus' contempt for her religion.

Aseneth/Mary the Magdalene is naturally taken aback by this harsh and unexpected rejection. She weeps, and, as with the Syro-Phoenician woman in the Gospels, Joseph/Jesus takes pity on her. He puts his hand above her head and prays that she may be refashioned. He begins by invoking the God who calls all things from darkness into light, from error into truth, and from death into life. He prays that God will renew her, infusing her with His life so that she may eat of the bread of life, drink the cup of blessing, and, finally, that she may be prepared to enter into life eternal. Aseneth rejoices with Joseph's blessing and returns to her room in the tower. There she experiences a mixture of emotions: happiness, but also consternation and fear.

Aseneth's Transformation: Her Rebirth as the Bride of God
At this point in the narrative, we encounter a perplexing scene. After Joseph leaves, promising to return in eight days, Aseneth is left to ponder her future. What happens next represents an amazing transformation, one that is fundamentally sacramental and mystical in nature. It is described as a threefold sequence. First, there is true and heartfelt repentance—over a whole week. Then, there is an epiphany in which the true nature of Joseph is disclosed to her. Finally, it all culminates in nothing less than Holy Communion—the first Communion ever recorded. This remarkable experience results in Aseneth being refashioned. The text now tells us that she is no longer a worshipper of idols and is fit to become the Bride of God (4:1).

As described earlier, Aseneth's transformation involves an encounter with a heavenly Joseph look-alike. She eats a piece of a mysterious honeycomb from his hand, and she also witnesses the heavenly stranger making the sign of the cross on the honeycomb . . . in blood. Then, all of a sudden, seemingly out of nowhere, Aseneth is swarmed by bees, which end up settling near the tower. How are these strange symbols and events to be understood?

We should not forget that standing behind the figure of Aseneth is Mary the Magdalene. What then do these incidents tell us about her?

Pagan Priestess

To begin with, we need to make sense of the symbolism in the manuscript and then trace its implications for understanding Mary the Magdalene's relationship with Jesus. We don't have to go far to decode some of the symbols in the text—any local Catholic, Orthodox, or Anglican church will do. The reason is simple. As we shall see, the symbolism in our text is directly related to the rite variously called the Eucharist, Mass, or Holy Communion, the partaking of bread and wine for sacramental purposes.[14]

But we're getting ahead of ourselves. Let's pick up the story at the point that Joseph leaves Aseneth's courtyard. Immediately after, Aseneth weeps bitterly and mourns. She places ashes on the floor and dresses herself in a somber black tunic, the one she had worn, according to the narrative, when her brother had died. Here, too, there is an interesting parallel between Aseneth/Mary the Magdalene and the Syro-Phoenician/Canaanite woman in the Gospels. In our text, we meet Aseneth/Mary the Magdalene after she lost a brother. In the Gospels, we meet the Syro-Phoenician/Canaanite woman as her daughter lies dying. In our text, Joseph/Jesus comes after the fact. In the Gospels, Jesus performs a miracle and saves the girl. Are we dealing with history here and theology in the Gospels?

In any event, at this point in the story, Aseneth/Mary the Magdalene discards all the icons of her life up to that point, taking her best robe, for example, and throwing it out the window for the poor. But she doesn't stop there. She smashes into pieces the gold and silver images of her gods and goddesses. For good measure, she hurls them out the window. She then takes her dinner, including all the food and libations intended for her deities, and throws everything out the window—for the dogs to consume.

She cries so much that when morning comes, ". . . mud had formed from the multitude of tears from her eyes in the great weeping she had done" (10:17). She's a real crier, this Aseneth. She mixes her tears with ashes and turns them into mud.

If the evidence so far has not clinched the identification of Aseneth with Mary the Magdalene, this propensity for tearfulness should. After all, we must

not forget that the English word *maudlin*, meaning "tearfully or weakly emo-
tional," is an alteration of the word Magdalene, as in Mary the Magdalene. In
the Gospel of John (20:11), the writer states "Mary stayed outside the tomb
weeping," and then Jesus said to her "Woman, why are you weeping?" From that
time forward, Mary the Magdalene was identified with weeping. She's called the
weeper in poetry. In paintings, she is often represented with red and swollen eyes.

In any event, for seven days Aseneth mourns, eating nothing. All the symbols
of her earlier life are now gone. Clothing that is symbolic of her old self, precious
statues of deities, unholy food—all these have been jettisoned as she prepares
herself for an enhanced life and a new role.

In Biblical terms, throwing idols out the window of a tower for the dogs is
not connected on any level whatsoever with Egyptian religion, as in the superficial reading of *Joseph and Aseneth*. All these actions are explicitly connected
to Canaanite or Phoenician religion—and always to women. There is a famous
example of a Syro-Phoenician/Canaanite priestess—living in the area of the
Galilee—being tossed out the window of her tower to be eaten by dogs. The
priestess' name is Jezebel. Her story is told in the Biblical Books of Kings (1 Kings
19; 2 Kings 1–9). To summarize that narrative: Jezebel is a coastal Canaanite, a
member of a nation that scholars like to call "Phoenician" or "Syro-Phoenician."
According to the Bible, she marries Ahab, King of Israel. She then attempts to
wipe out the religion of the God of Israel and substitute it with the worship of
Ba'al, the Phoenician or Canaanite Sun god. As punishment, she is tossed out
her window and the dogs devour her body. Clearly, what we have in the *Joseph
and Aseneth* text is an apologetic for another "King of the Jews" who marries a
Phoenician woman—Jesus. In this instance, however, we are told that the Phoenician woman in question repented. Rather than meriting a Jezebel-style death,
Mary the Magdalene/Aseneth is forgiven because she does not fight the God of
Israel. On the contrary, she tosses the deities that she had once worshipped out
the window . . . to the dogs. Obviously, dogs are more interested in flesh and
blood than gold and silver, but the point of the story is to tell the reader that
Mary the Magdalene is not another Jezebel, she is the anti-Jezebel.[15]

And what of the window? It may surprise many, but the "woman in the
window" motif is very well-known from near-eastern archaeology.[16] One
example is a Phoenician image found carved in wood, ivory, and bone.[17]
Although its precise meaning has been lost, it seems to connote some kind of

Syro-Phoenician ritual. Clearly, it is no accident that Jezebel, who tried to impose the rituals of "the woman in the window" on Biblical Israel, gets tossed out the window. And clearly, it is no accident that Mary the Magdalene/Aseneth tosses the idols that Jezebel worshipped out the window.

More than this, "the woman in the window" was probably a Canaanite/Phoenician priestess. Her presence at the window probably served the same function as the Pope's appearance in the Vatican window, or on his balcony in St. Peter's Square. This parallel couldn't be clearer in the *Joseph and Aseneth* text. When Joseph/Jesus first appears, Aseneth "went up the tower, entered her bedchamber and stood to the side of the large window facing east so she could look at Joseph as he entered her father's house" (5:2).[18] For his part, Joseph also notices this appearance at the window. As the text puts it, "Joseph looked at the tower and said 'Remove the young woman who is observing from the window'" (7:2). He is obviously uncomfortable with a pagan priestess observing him, and he wants her removed from that role.

To reiterate, it seems very important to the author of *Joseph and Aseneth* that everyone understands that Aseneth/Mary the Magdalene is not another Jezebel. While the latter made war on the God of the Hebrews, the former embraces Him. While Jezebel murdered his prophets, Aseneth marries one. While Jezebel stays the woman in the window to the gruesome end, Aseneth is removed from the window. What the story is clearly telling us is that in preparation for marrying Jesus, the "King of Israel," Mary the Magdalene—unlike Jezebel—renounced her native gods and fed them to the dogs.

The reference to Aseneth's seven attendant priestesses is also suggestive. The Gospels of Mark (16:9) and Luke (8:2) tell us that Jesus cast out seven demons from Mary the Magdalene. This has been variously interpreted as Jesus curing Mary of seven vices, including an obsession with sex, or curing Mary of seven illnesses.[19] On the face of it, neither of these explanations makes any sense. Seven illnesses are a lot of illnesses, and there's no record or tradition of Mary being on her deathbed when she met Jesus. As for vices, this is a late tradition that started with Pope Gregory in the late 6th century, specifically associating Mary with prostitution. But *Joseph and Aseneth* may be providing us with the answer to Mary's seven-demons puzzle.

Aseneth has seven women attendants, co-priestesses. In the eyes of monotheist Jews and pagans of the time, these priestesses would have been seen as spirits—or, in Greek, *daimons*—demons who officiated with her in her tower. When, as a result of meeting Joseph, Aseneth rejects her gods, she also has no further use for her seven vestal virgins. They are dispensed with—in a sense, cast out or cast away. The seven-demons story in the canonical Gospels seems to be an echo of the story of the seven virgin priestesses in *Joseph and Aseneth*.

But what of the tower? What does it mean? As always, let's start with the facts. We know that Mary the Magdalene means Mary the Tower Lady, Mary of the Tower, or Mary from Tower Town. In every version, she is literally defined by a tower. We also know that in Jesus' time there was a town called Migdal, or Magdala, on the Sea of Galilee, right in the center of his area of operation. Archaeologically speaking, a tower, albeit a much later tower, has been excavated on the site and nowhere else in the Galilee. Furthermore, Magdala may have been associated with towers for millennia. In 2013, next to the land ruins of Magdala, archaeologists discovered submerged in the Sea of Galilee a monumental tower/pyramid whose precise function is still a mystery.[20] In other words, in the ancient world, a tower was linked with Magdala much as the Eiffel Tower is linked to Paris today. But what did the Syro-Phoenician tower that dominated Magdala's skyscape at the time of Jesus look like? Did it look like the tower described in *Joseph and Aseneth*?

The fact is that archaeologists have found one—and only one—intact Syro-Phoenician tower. This tower, which is presently in storage at the British Museum, was found in the 1850s in Carthage by archaeologist Nathan Davis.[21] It's a small version—likely a replica—of something that must have been much bigger. It is a kind of tourist version of the Eiffel Tower, not the tower itself. It dates to the 3rd or 4th century B.C.E. Carthage was a Syro-Phoenician colony in what is now Tunisia, a center that at one time vied with Rome for the domination of the Mediterranean.

The Carthaginians fought three wars with Rome, the so-called Punic Wars. After losing the last war, they were totally destroyed. Had they won, we'd all be speaking Semitic-based languages (e.g., Hebrew or Phoenician, a variant of Hebrew) instead of Latin-based languages. In any event, the same Mediterranean culture that colonized the port city of Carthage also settled the port town of Magdala. Here's the revelation—the tower found in Carthage perfectly corresponds to the tower described in our *Joseph and Aseneth* manuscript. It has three windows, not four—one in each direction as we would expect—and a single entrance that is not aligned with the windows. It is clearly not a military tower, having no military indicators whatsoever. The fact that a scale tower of this kind was found carved in stone indicates a ritual use for it, once again confirming the linkage between tower, religion, and the Phoenicians.

But why would Phoenicians that were primarily—but not exclusively—based in what is now Lebanon want to build a tower and a town on the shores of the Sea of Galilee? The answer is simple—money. The Phoenicians were the great merchants of the ancient world, and Magdala was the world's headquarters for the caviar of the ancient world—salted fish.[22] Cato the Elder (239–149 B.C.E.) complained that "a fish sells for more in Rome than a cow, and they sell a cask of smoked fish for a price that a hundred sheep plus one ox in the lead wouldn't bring."[23] In Greek, Magdala was called Taricheae, or "town of the fish salters." So it seems that what drew the Phoenicians to Magdala was the combination of readily available fish (from the Sea of Galilee) and salt (from the relatively close Dead Sea), and its location on the Via Maris, one of the main highways of the ancient world. The town of Magdala might have been a Phoenician merchant outpost dominated by a ritual tower, hence the name.

Significantly, Phoenician temples to Artemis were usually built on the shores of lakes and dedicated to Artemis Limnaia, meaning Lady of the Lake. So we can now infer that the temple that gave Magdala its name was probably dedicated to Artemis. Also, in a hymn dedicated to Artemis, the Greek poet Callimachus calls her "Watcher over roads and harbors."[24] Magdala's tower, on the Via Maris and overlooking the harbors of the Sea of Galilee, was perfectly positioned as a temple dedicated to Artemis.

Furthermore, Artemis' connection to lakes resulted in declaring freshwater fish as sacred to the goddess. Rose Lou Bengisu reports that Artemis worship seems originally to have been connected to a fish cult.[25] As a result, fish had to be associated with the founding of any temple. As Sorita d'Este reminds us, "[a] fish figured in the founding of the city of Ephesus where the largest and most famous temple of Artemis was located."[26] This explains the strange name that Magdala had in Aramaic: Migdal Nunia, or Fish Tower. This name has confounded scholars. We can now solve the mystery. The name does not refer to a pile of fish. It refers to the *founding* of the tower, meaning its dedication, as in Ephesus, to the goddess Artemis. The sacredness of the fish in the Artemis tradition may also explain why the fish became the earliest symbol of Christianity.

Taken together, therefore, the most recent archaeology, combined with a careful reading of *Joseph and Aseneth* and the Gospels, reveals that in Jesus' time the Galilee was not a backwater, not exclusively Jewish, and not populated solely by poor peasants and fishermen. Historically speaking, the Galilee was a cosmopolitan place where Jews, Romans, and Syro-Phoenicians, amongst others, mingled. Also, it was linked to the heart of the Roman Empire by roads and money. How did all this happen?

The Galilee had been part of an almost exclusively Israelite state until the invasion of the Assyrians in 760 B.C.E. At that time, the ten northern Israelite tribes—the so-called Lost Tribes of Israel—were exiled and the area was largely depopulated. In place of the Israelite tribes, the Assyrians brought people from the east and north, including many coastal Canaanites/Phoenicians who gravitated toward Israel as their original homeland. Six hundred years later, during the Maccabean revolt in the 160s B.C.E., Jewish nationalism won the day and the Canaanite/Phoenicians of the Galilee were given a choice: convert to Judaism, or leave. Most left, but the rest converted. The result of this uncharacteristic conversion program was to leave the area under-populated and dominated by people who were nominally Jewish, but still pagan beneath the surface.

By the time of King Herod the Great—a Roman puppet who lived just prior to the birth of Jesus—the Romans complained that their strategic highways in the area were the targets of constant brigandage. They gave Herod a choice: clean up the Galilee, or we will. Herod cleaned it up in part by forcibly populating it with southern Judaeans, and by creating brand-new towns for these relocated Jews—towns like Nazareth.[27]

As a result of all this, the Galilee was not a homogeneous place of orthodox Jewish peasants listening wide-eyed to local carpenter preachers. It was a place where non-Jewish[28] and Jewish populations were rubbing shoulders and coming up with syncretistic and revolutionary religious ideas.

This historical reality is reflected in the archaeological story being unearthed in places like Bethsaida. It also explains very nicely why a family that was originally from Bethlehem suddenly found itself in Nazareth of the Galilee. The repopulation of the Galilee created security on the roads and stability for people such as the Phoenician fish entrepreneurs of Magdala.

Given all this, strategic location and newfound stability literally converted fishermen into wealthy fish barons. More than this, the new money and the mix of Judaeans, pagan Phoenicians, Judeo-Phoenicians (forcibly converted by the Maccabees), and Hellenists who arrived in the wake of Herod and his Roman backers, created a cosmopolitan population the likes of which would never have been tolerated in the Judaean south. At Bethsaida, for example, archaeologists have discovered pagan places of worship[29] in the midst of Torah-observant Jews. Again, this kind of "multiculturalism" would never have been tolerated in Jerusalem.[30]

In any event, the real world that Jesus was born into was one that is accurately reflected in the *Joseph and Aseneth* manuscript, a world at odds with the images generated by Hollywood films. It was a place where Jewish nationalism— orthodox and messianic—interacted with Phoenician and Roman paganism. And there was no better example of this kind of syncretistic or mixed culture than Magdala—Mary's hometown. Magdala was a place of money. And this is perfectly consistent with the Christian Bible, which preserves the tradition that, at its inception, Mary the Magdalene helped finance the entire Jesus movement.

In sum, the description of the Tower Lady in the *Joseph and Aseneth* manuscript—that she is not Jewish, lives in a Phoenician tower, and is wealthy—seems to match the known facts about Mary the Magdalene. What we seem to have here is perfect synchronicity between text and archaeology.[31]

A Marriage Made in Heaven

By the eighth day of her spiritual rebirth, Aseneth is in a weakened state. She had been fasting and praying to God the entire time. Throughout, she confesses her sins . . . a litany of faults. Among other things, she admits to having transgressed the law of God; to having spoken evil things by worshipping idols; and to having spoken poorly of Joseph (that is, Jesus) (13:9 and earlier 6:3). She asks for pardon, especially for having spoken in haste and in ignorance. She had been told that Joseph/Jesus was just a peasant's son from Canaan, a man of lowly birth, well beneath her social status.[32] She had been misled. Having repented and confessed her sins, she now turns her life in a new direction. She literally becomes a new person.

Addressing God, Aseneth/Mary the Magdalene states that she had not realized that Joseph/Jesus was His "Son" (6:3, 6:5, 13:9). This then is her epiphany. She discerns that Joseph/Jesus is none other than the "Son of God" (6:3). This is not, of course, what we would call Jewish talk. It's Christian through and through. While Jews still await a Messiah, they do not imagine him to be a "Son of God." Only Christians combined the Jewish concept of a "Messiah"[33] with the Gentile concept of a "Son of God." For Jews, the Messiah is a human being, an anointed king of Israel and a powerful leader who will help God bring about world transformation. The messianic period in human history will be very different from the world we now experience. It will be a time of everlasting peace, when evil will be defeated and the righteous will be rewarded. It will be a time when God's Messiah, his "anointed one" from the line of David, will rule in Jerusalem and all people will come to worship the one true God.

Our manuscript reflects a very different perspective of messiahship than the traditional Jewish one. It reflects a view that has been associated with Christianity. Here, Joseph is described as God's "Son," but sometimes he seems to *be* God—Aseneth prays, "How can I hide myself from his presence so that Joseph, the Son of God, cannot see me? Where will I flee since every place is uncovered and spread out visibly before him?" (6:5). This is Christian terrain, wherein the divinity of Jesus represents an essential aspect of the belief in him. This "Son of God" is not the Messiah of Judaism.

Returning to the text, we note that in a more human vein, Aseneth gushes that Joseph is the most handsome, wisest, and strongest man who had ever lived. Humbly, she asks God that she be given to him as his servant, so that she might wash his feet and serve him as a slave for the rest of her life. Again, this section of the narrative is echoed in the Gospels where an unnamed woman, who has for centuries been identified with Mary the Magdalene, washes Jesus' feet and dries them with her hair (Luke 7:37 and John 12:3). Graydon Snyder sees this passage as revealing "the love connection between Jesus and this woman."[34]

The hair-drying in the Gospels is significant in another way. In Judaism, hair can change its status to *erva*, meaning nakedness.[35] This happens only after a woman has had sexual relations and not before. That's why to this day young, unmarried, orthodox Jewish girls do not cover their hair. But once a marriage has been consummated, the hair is considered "nakedness" and is covered as a sign of modesty and exclusivity to the husband. A grown Jewish woman would never dry the feet of a man with her hair, then or now. It would be tantamount to rubbing a private part against a man's body. However, once hair is cut, it loses all status as nakedness. For this reason, to this day, orthodox Jewish women can wear wigs made of natural human hair. In other words, hair that's been cut is not considered nakedness.

Given all this, if Mary the Magdalene did, indeed, wipe Jesus' feet with her hair, as the Gospels report, she must have cut it first. Even if she wasn't Jewish, she would have had to follow the local Galilean customs of modesty before drying a rabbi's feet. Once we understand this, we again discover in the Gospels a powerful symbolic subtext related to Artemis. In the *Orphic Hymn* to Artemis (36) the goddess is referred to as the one "with lovely hair." At coming-of-age ceremonies involving the goddess, girls would dedicate a lock of their hair to her. "It has been suggested that the lock of hair symbolized the virginity that the girl would be leaving behind."[36] Put simply, by understanding the social context of the hair-drying act we see that the Gospels preserve the very moment, as elaborated on in *Joseph and Aseneth*, when—using Artemisian symbolism—Mary the Magdalene declares her intention to wed Jesus.[37]

To get back to our text, the arrogant and impetuous Aseneth is now gone. She has experienced an immense epiphany—a deep disclosure or personal revelation. She now knows who Joseph really is: he is "God's son." Through repentance, a change in life, and true insight, she is now ready to undergo a unique and remarkable experience.

"When Aseneth stopped confessing to the Lord, behold, the morning star rose out of heaven to the east" (14:1). She is overjoyed, knowing that this star is the harbinger of a great day.

The symbolism is superb. There is a passage in the Book of Numbers that records one of the prophecies of the Gentile prophet Balaam, son of Beor (Numbers 24:15–19).[38] Early Christians, like many Jewish groups, believed that Balaam's prophecy was a description of the coming of the Messiah. In fact, it is the only passage in the Torah believed to refer to the coming of the Messiah. The relevant phrase goes, ". . . a star shall come out of Jacob, and a scepter shall rise out of Israel. . . ." At the outset of the movement, Christians interpreted this Biblical passage as referring to Jesus. In the Gospel of Matthew, for example, this tradition is preserved in the Star of Bethlehem narrative. In this view, it is Jesus who fulfills the prophecy of a star coming out of Jacob.

After Jesus, Josephus, the Jewish historian, applied the star prophecy to the Roman general Vespasian, who became emperor in 69 c.e. while in Judaea quelling a Jewish revolt. In 135 c.e., Rabbi Akiva applied the same prophecy to another messianic figure, Simon Bar Cosiba—who has come down to us by his nickname *Bar Kokhba*, that is, "Son of the Star." Bar Kokhba led an unsuccessful revolt against Rome and, like Jesus, ended up dead at Roman hands. In other words, *star* language is messianic language. And here, in *Joseph and Aseneth*, we have the star prophecy applied to Joseph—that is, Jesus. Not only that, the prophecy states that "a scepter shall rise out of Israel," and Joseph arrives on the scene carrying a scepter.

No sooner does the morning star appear to Aseneth/Mary the Magdalene than the sky opens up, revealing a burst of intense light. Clearly, she's about to undergo a kind of Baptism similar to that of Jesus. Notice the parallel. In Matthew 3:16–17, it states: "And when Jesus was baptized, immediately he went up from the water, and behold, the heavens were opened to him, and he saw the Spirit of God descending like a dove and coming to rest on him; and behold, a voice from heaven said, 'This is my beloved Son, with whom I am well pleased'."[39] When the heavens open up for Aseneth, she falls to the ground. As she does so, "a man from heaven" (14:4) appears and stands over her. He calls to her, "Aseneth." She is perplexed that anyone—especially a man—could gain access to her inner chamber. The heavenly figure calls her name a second time, and she responds. She looks up and sees a being like Joseph "in every respect" (14:8). He has a robe, a crown, and a royal scepter. As in the iconography of Jesus, the features of his head radiate light. Aseneth rises, and the heavenly Joseph look-alike asks her to take off her black tunic, to wash with "living water" (Baptism), and to put on a new robe (14:12–13). She does as she is told.

Being dressed in new clothing and washing is clearly symbolic of Aseneth's new life. Aseneth is now a different person, the new clothing being the outer expression of an inner transformation. But undressing in an apartment alone with a man, even a heavenly one, is an intimate act without parallel in the Hebrew or Christian Scriptures. It is an act that a woman reserves solely for her husband. And yet she undresses without even a hint of embarrassment. In other words, at this moment in the *Joseph and Aseneth* narrative we are told that after—and only after—she has renounced her pagan ways, Mary the Magdalene becomes Jesus' wife. In the Gospels, we encounter Mary the Magdalene after her transformation, after the seven demons had been driven away. All that remains of her previous life are echoes in episodes such as the Syro-Phoenician woman and the woman who washes Jesus' feet, kisses them, and dries them with her hair. But here, in *Joseph and Aseneth*, we have the full story prior to the transformation and including the rebirth.

The symbolism resonates on many levels. Washing, of course, is reminiscent of the rite of Baptism: the person immersed in water becomes cleansed from sins. But washing and stripping off old clothing is also the metaphor used in the Gnostic *Gospel of Thomas* as the necessary preparation for a new life. Saying 37 of this Gospel states:

Jesus said, "When you strip without being ashamed and you take your clothes and put them under your feet like little children and trample them, then [you] will see the child of the living one and you will not be afraid."[40]

Joseph and Aseneth obviously parallels the *Gospel of Thomas*.[41] After she puts on new clothes "without being ashamed," the supernatural figure addresses Aseneth/Mary the Magdalene, indicating that she is refashioned and given new life. In fact, she is now ready to eat the "bread of life" and drink the "cup of immortality" and "be anointed with the ointment of incorruptibility" (15:3).

At this point, the text explicitly tells us: "Behold, the Lord gave you to Joseph as a bride and he will be your bridegroom" (15:4). The text also tells us that from here on in she will be called "City of Refuge" (15:5), adding that many nations shall take refuge in her and that those who come to God through penitence will find security within her. Clearly, the text is not talking about the Aseneth of the Book of Genesis. That woman is a minor figure who disappeared from the world stage at least seventeen hundred years before *Joseph and Aseneth* was written. What we are being told—in very clear terms—is that Aseneth (that is, Mary the Magdalene) was perceived by her followers as a figure of Penitence, and a Daughter of God, who prepared "a heavenly bridal chamber for those who love her" (15:7). In Kraemer's words, the text describes a marriage that "enacts the divine union of the Son and Daughter of God."[42]

In Matthew, Jesus' Baptism is followed by the heavens opening up and a voice declaring Jesus to be the Son of God. Here, Mary the Magdalene's Baptism is followed by the heavens opening up and a heavenly, Jesus-like figure declaring that she is the Bride of God. The parallel couldn't be more explicit.

Aseneth is now immediately bidden to put on her wedding robe and jewelry, to make herself ready to become Joseph's bride. Strangely, she interrupts this process and asks the heavenly man to sit "upon the bed" (15:14) while she prepares food and wine for him. The heavenly figure accepts her offerings and requests that she also bring him a "honeycomb" (16:1), which he promises she will miraculously find in one of her rooms. The honeycomb is described as being "full of honey," as "white as snow," and smelling "of the spirit of life" (16:4).

On one level, the honeycomb—clearly—is like the manna provided by God in the wilderness for the Israelites. It gives life and sustains those who eat it. According to the Book of Exodus, the manna was white and tasted like wafers made with honey (Exodus 16:31). This manna became the type for the life-giving bread of the Christian Communion service and for Jesus himself as represented by this manna-like bread. As the Gospel of John says, "I am the living bread that came down from heaven. Whoever eats of this bread will live forever" (John 6:51). In one of his hymns, Ephrem the Syrian puts it this way:

> The Church has given us Living Bread
> In place of the unleavened bread which Egypt gave.[43]

For the early Christians and for Christians today, the life-giving bread is Jesus. It is also the consecrated bread used within the Eucharist, the Christian Communion, during which the bread becomes the "body of Christ Jesus." Today, Christians disagree on precisely how the bread becomes the body of Jesus: whether the transformation is symbolic, spiritual, or "transubstantiated," becoming, in this latter case, the actual "body of Christ." But, again, here we have a typological equation:

> Manna = Jesus as the "living bread"
> The living bread = Christ's body in the Eucharist

The First Holy Communion Ever

The narrative now turns to the honeycomb ceremony. The heavenly figure who, in a sense, has just shared her bed, places his hand above Aseneth's head and gives her a double blessing. First, he blesses her saying that the "secrets of the Lord" (16:11) have been revealed to her. She now knows something about the mysteries of God. Second, he says, "Blessed are those who attach themselves to the Lord God Most High in penance because, from this honeycomb, they will eat and live forever" (16:11). What is about to happen is of tremendous import—nothing less than a renewal of life and life everlasting.

Remarkably, this initiation ceremony parallels a fragment of *The Secret Gospel of Mark* discovered by Morton Smith in 1958 in the monastery library of Mar Saba, in the Judaean Desert. According to Smith, the fragment is a copy of a 2nd-century document that preserves a secret version of Mark in which Jesus teaches "the mystery of the Kingdom of God" to a youth "wearing a linen cloth over [his] naked [body]."[44]

In *Secret Mark*, the story seems to involve the resurrection of Lazarus, as described in the Gospel of John. But in *Secret Mark* there is no mention of the youth's name. As in *Joseph and Aseneth*, the story in *Secret Mark* involves Jesus arriving at the residence of "a certain woman, whose brother had died." This is exactly the situation in *Joseph and Aseneth*. In *Secret Mark*, Jesus touches the dead brother and brings him back to life. In *Joseph and Aseneth*, the story is structurally the same, but it is not the dead brother who is brought back to life: it is Aseneth—that is, Mary the Magdalene. The heavenly Joseph draws near to Aseneth and, as the Syriac manuscript says, "he stretched out his right hand and drew her head near" (16:10).[45] She is transformed from worshipping dead idols, and therefore being dead herself, to acquiring everlasting life—"renewed, reformed and revivified" (15:3). In a sense, it is she who is brought back to life, not the brother who is literally dead.

There are other narrative parallels. In *Secret Mark*, the moment the youth sees Jesus, he falls in love with him: ". . . the youth, looking upon him, loved him and began to beseech him that he might be with him." As we have seen, the youthful Aseneth goes through a similar process. In *Secret Mark*, the youth is rich. In *Joseph and Aseneth*, Aseneth is wealthy. In *Secret Mark*, after six days Jesus instructs the youth concerning what to do so as to be inducted into "the mystery of the Kingdom of God." In *Joseph and Aseneth*, on the seventh day (i.e., after six days) the heavenly Jesus figure instructs Aseneth into "the secret mysteries of the Most High." This is a perfect synchronicity, even when it comes to the number of days since, in *Secret Mark*, the youth is instructed on the night of the sixth day. Given that Jewish days begin the night before, at sundown, the two texts describe the same waiting period, seven days, before the initiation into the mysteries of the Kingdom of God begins. Once the initiation commences, in both cases it involves wearing a linen garment and engaging in some kind of sexuality.

Later Greek versions of *Joseph and Aseneth* make all this more explicit— and erotic—than does the Syriac: "And Aseneth stretched out her right hand

and put it on his knees [that is, the knees of the heavenly Joseph] and said to him, 'I beg you, Lord, sit down a little on this bed, because this bed is pure and undefiled, and a man or woman never sat on it. And I will set a table before you. . . .'" "Knees" here seems to be a euphemism for penis. The Syriac manuscript at 15:14 simply says, "sit a little upon the bed and I will set a table. . . ."[46]

In *Secret Mark*, Jesus interacts with a young man. Interestingly, in *Joseph and Aseneth*, Aseneth is described in the following manner: ". . . today you are a chaste virgin and your head is like that of a young man" (15:1).

Clearly, both texts are describing some kind of sexual initiation. This fits well into the Hellenized Galilean context where the Jesus movement was born. For the Greeks, in Michel Foucault's words, "truth and sex were linked . . . sex served as a medium for initiation into learning."[47] But here, the narratives are depicting an encounter with Jesus. In *Joseph and Aseneth*, we seem to have a more historical version, rooted in an upcoming marriage. In John and *Secret Mark*, the sister's rebirth is transferred to the dead brother. In *Joseph and Aseneth*, Jesus is not being intimate with a man who has risen from the dead, but with a beautiful young woman who had been spiritually dead and was now ready to become his bride.

Obviously, there are structural parallels between the two narratives. These parallels make clear that *Joseph and Aseneth*, like *Secret Mark*, fits within an esoteric Christian tradition that still resonates in the canonical Gospels.

Finally, let's look at the honeycomb. In the story, it is the food of eternal life made, the heavenly Joseph says, by bees from the Garden of Eden. Since bees were equated with souls, the honeycomb was the food of immortality.[48] It was said that angels eat of it. And those who partake of it with angels never die. As part of the ceremony, the heavenly man breaks off a piece of the honeycomb and in the quasi-erotic, quasi-spiritual language of the text he places it in Aseneth's mouth.[49] While doing this, he traces in blood the sign of the cross on the remaining piece of the honeycomb.

No one familiar with the Christian Eucharist would miss the significance of this ritual. Nearly seventeen hundred years ago, Ephrem the Syrian used the same imagery—of a finger tracing blood—to describe the Eucharist:

> See—your image is depicted
> In the *blood* of grapes

On the top of the bread,
And it is depicted on the heart
By the *finger* of love.[50]

Some fifty years after Ephrem, Theodore of Mopsuestia made the same point, "and with the bread he makes the sign of the cross over the blood, and with the blood over the bread."[51] Close to a hundred years ago, E. W. Brooks commented briefly on the parallels between the honeycomb scene in *Joseph and Aseneth* and the Anglican Eucharist. His astute observation was lost, however, because much of *Joseph and Aseneth* scholarship after Brooks misplaced the narrative within a Jewish context. But, as Brooks noted, this is clearly Holy Communion—truly Holy Communion—for it takes place within the heavenly bridal chamber presided over by an angelic figure and features the food of angels. The language of this mystical ceremony in *Joseph and Aseneth* precisely mirrors the four actions of the Christian Communion:[52]

1. Taking

In *Joseph and Aseneth*, Aseneth makes full repentance and then experiences a revelation concerning the true nature of Joseph, "God's son." This is similar to the spiritual movement in the first part of the Mass. The action moves through confession of sins, absolution, and then the reading of various scriptural lessons that culminate in the congregational response: "we believe." What ensues is the affirmation of the Creed of Christianity that relates Jesus both to the Godhead and to his role as God incarnate. Then and only then is the table (altar) prepared for the Communion. Aseneth too *takes*, or prepares, a table for the man from heaven. It is set with wine and a white honeycomb.

2. Giving Thanks

In stage two, Aseneth is blessed by the heavenly figure, who tells her that she has been privileged to have had the indescribable things of God revealed to her. He identifies the honeycomb as the food of eternal life. No one, he says, who eats of this food will die.

Again, this is perfectly reflected in the drama of the Christian Communion service. As the Eucharist moves toward the consecration of the elements, the bread and the wine, the people gather together along with angels and archangels to praise the holiness of God. Congregants pray to eat the flesh of Jesus and to drink his blood so that his body may cleanse their sinful bodies and their souls may be washed by his precious blood. To this day, congregants ask that Jesus may dwell in them and they in him. In receiving Communion—the consecrated bread, now the body of Jesus—the priest prays that it may preserve the bodies and souls of the participants in eternal life. The same with the wine.

3. Breaking
The heavenly man—the Joseph look-alike—takes the honeycomb and breaks it, just as the priest takes the bread and, lifting it up, breaks it for all to see.

4. Eating
The heavenly figure now eats a piece of the honeycomb, just as the priest does at Mass. Then he gives a piece to Aseneth, placing it in her mouth, just as priests do in parishes today and have done throughout history.

Simply put, unarguably, here we have the four central actions of the Christian Communion. But there's more. So as to drive the point home, the heavenly man makes the sign of the cross—in blood—on the remaining honeycomb (16:18–19). In the words of the text, "the path of the honey was now blood" (16:19). Could the Christian references be made any more explicit? It's astounding how anyone could mistake this for a Jewish text.

If the implications of this text haven't yet crystallized in our reader's mind, suffice it to say that what *Joseph and Aseneth* here documents is a Holy Communion celebrated by Jesus himself with Mary the Magdalene as the penitent communicant ready for a new life. Later, Paul would take up the idea of the Lord's Supper with enthusiasm. But he gives it a completely different spin. In Paul's version, Communion involves eating the bread—which represents Jesus' body—and drinking the wine—which represents his blood (1 Corinthians 10:16–17 and 1 Corinthians 11:23–26). As James Tabor has convincingly demonstrated, the originator of this idea is Paul, not Jesus and not Mark, the earliest Gospel.[53] In any event, the idea of eating your god's flesh and drinking his blood is not Jewish. It comes from Greek religious traditions in which the deity was symbolically consumed[54]—ritualized cannibalism.[55] Here, instead, *Joseph and Aseneth* describes an esoteric ceremony that takes place in a bridal chamber—on Aseneth/Mary the Magdalene's bed. She is now fit to be the Bride of God and, very shortly, the actual earthly marriage service begins.

If this still needs repeating, all this has nothing—absolutely nothing—to do with the Aseneth of ancient history. It has everything—absolutely everything—to do with Mary the Magdalene. It is, obviously, the story of the young Mary, a girl of eighteen, being prepared for marriage with Jesus. It's the story, clearly told and preserved by her followers, of Mary's intense personal transformation from pagan priestess into the Bride of God.

Remember, for those who believe that Jesus is God incarnate, every one of his actions and words have metaphysical implications. If Jesus chose Mary the Magdalene as his *koinonos*, his companion—the woman who shared his bridal chamber—this would have deeply impacted on the beliefs of his followers. More than this, if he was God and Mary the Magdalene was the Bride of God, was she a goddess? The answer to this question involves the honey and the bees.

Honey and Bees

Let's start with the honey. In fact, honey—as a symbol—is relatively easy to explain, at least in general terms. In the ancient world, honey possessed religious and medicinal value.[56] In ancient Greek, Egyptian, and Roman societies, for example, honey represented a valued offering to the gods and goddesses of the Mediterranean world. Writing in the 2nd century, the Roman writer Lucian has his hero in Menippus join some Chaldean mystics. This was their diet: "our food was nuts, our drink milk and a mixture of honey and milk."[57] Honey was a symbol of health and wellbeing.[58] According to 3rd-century Neoplatonist writer Porphyry, honey is "both cathartic and preservative." It is associated with death, mummification, and the whole preservation process. Likewise, one can "purify the tongue from all the defilement of evil with honey." It is, literally, the "food of the gods," and its sweetness is associated with "the pleasure arising from copulation." It can also draw "souls downward."[59] And it was always associated with religious ritual.

John Chadwick, who was the associate of Michael Ventris in deciphering the Minoan/Mycenaean linear B tablets, pointed out how important honey was in the life and religion of the Minoans and Mycenaeans. The main context in which honey appears in the now-deciphered linear B tablets is religious.[60] The Mycenaeans were not unique. Many groups clustered around ancient religious centers engaged in beekeeping. Indeed, honey is still honored in many societies around the eastern Mediterranean. It is often a companion to meals and festivities, especially in Turkey and Greece.

In addition, as Rivka Nir has pointed out, honey formed part of the Communion service in parts of the early church. She cites the testimony of Hippolytus, a late 2nd-century/early 3rd-century Christian writer living in Rome.[61] Hippolytus reports that in addition to the bread and wine, the celebrant blessed milk and honey mixed together. His contemporary Tertullian also mentions a ritual use of milk and honey by early Christians as part of the meal following Baptism and as part of the *agape* (or "love feast"), a Communion-like meal.[62] This rite was performed in order to fulfill God's promise that his people will come to a land flowing with "milk and honey." Here the metaphor for the land of Israel as the Promised Land is transposed to the church—the new Promised Land—and to the sacrament of Communion. Recently, physical evidence for the importance of honey to early Christians was discovered in Rome. Many of the tombs revealed in the Autoparco and Santa Rosa excavations at the Vatican had terra cotta pipes inserted into them so that relatives could feed the deceased by pouring wine, milk, or honey into the graves.[63]

Where Honey, Bees and the Tower Meet

But to crack the Mary the Magdalene Code, as depicted in *Joseph and Aseneth*, we need to understand honey not in general terms, but in the way it is portrayed in our text. We need to find a place in the ancient world where honey, bees, and a tower come together. As luck would have it, we found just such a place in Ephesus, western Turkey.

As noted in the Preface, we made this discovery in July 2008, when we were in Ephesus filming an episode on Paul for a documentary series on early Christianity. As the New Testament makes clear, Paul had used this city as his western headquarters for a number of years, just as he had previously used Antioch in the east. It was also here, in the Church of St. Mary, where the Council of Ephesus was held in 431 c.e. This was the council that decided that Mary, mother of Jesus, should be spoken of as *Mother of God*, a phrase that caused enormous problems for Syriac Christians whose view of the person of Jesus differed from the dominant Roman view. Today, tourists to Ephesus can visit what is alleged to be the home of Mary, mother of Jesus, who was said to have traveled to Ephesus after her son's crucifixion. Here, too, is the traditional burial place of John, one of Jesus' disciples, under the Basilica of St. John. For all these reasons, some sixteen hundred years ago Ephesus became a major Christian center.

As a result of centuries of silting, today Ephesus is a few miles inland from the shore. But in ancient times, Ephesus was an important seaport, the gateway to Greece, Italy, France, Spain, and the cities of North Africa. Ephesus in the first few centuries C.E. was also preeminently the city of Artemis. It was the epicenter for followers of this great Greek goddess who was one of the most widely worshipped deities throughout the world of early Christianity. Her temples were everywhere—throughout the regions that today we call Turkey, Greece, the Aegean, Crete, Italy, Sicily, Spain, the Ukraine, southern France, and even, as we subsequently found out, in Israel and Jordan. Today, in the Vatican, anyone heading toward the Sistine Chapel passes by one of the only Artemis statues excavated in Rome. Strabo mentions a center dedicated to the goddess Artemis in Massilia that boasted a replica of Artemis of Ephesus. There were two important temples to Artemis in Athens itself: one on the Acropolis; another one dedicated to Artemis Agrotera (Huntress) clustered near the ancient Ilissos River, along with a massive temple to Zeus her father and Apollo her twin brother. Another temple was located on the island of Delos, the religious capital of ancient Greece and the goddess' birthplace in the sacred grove of Zeus. Citing ancient records such as Pausanias, Sorita d'Este lists 116 sites known to have housed temples to Artemis.[64]

Artemis' popularity brought it into conflict with Judaism. This conflict is dramatically illustrated in the largest ancient synagogue discovered in the Jewish diaspora at Sardis, modern Turkey. Although the synagogue dates from the 4th century C.E., the site was developed at least two centuries earlier. The stylobate (an upper step supporting a column) in the synagogue's outer court reused a stele of Artemis, relief side downward, with her face defaced. It seems that even in the 4th century she was causing problems to the Jews of Sardis.[65]

The New Testament Book of Acts records an incident whereby Paul is run out of Ephesus by an Artemis follower. According to Acts, a man named Demetrius complained to civic authorities in Ephesus that, by introducing Christianity to the city, Paul was driving people away from Artemis worship. As a result, the goddess would be deprived of the preeminent position "that brought all Asia and the world to worship her" (Acts 19:27). Spurred by this allegation, the population of Ephesus chased Paul out of town. "Great is Artemis of the Ephesians," Ephesus' citizens shouted when they heard Demetrius raise his voice against Paul.

Demetrius wasn't kidding when he attacked Paul. The worship of Artemis represented an important multicultural religion . . . and a huge international business vital to the economy of many cities, especially Ephesus. But why was Demetrius worried? Was Paul such a great orator that he could singlehandedly undermine a religion that had been around for thousands of years? The pagan world was multicultural—at least it accepted a variety of deities—so what was Demetrius worked up about? There's only one explanation: the religion that Paul was espousing was too Artemis-like. The problem was not that the gospel that Paul was preaching was nothing like Artemis worship. The problem was that it was close enough that Demetrius feared that many Ephesians would defect.

In the 2nd century, Pausanias in his Description of Greece notes that *all* cities worshipped Artemis of Ephesus, and he gave a number of reasons: the renown of the Amazons who traditionally settled there; the immense size of the temple, which surpassed all other buildings in ancient Greece; as well as the prominence of the port itself, situated on the edge of the Aegean. Pilgrims and merchants descended upon the city by the thousands, and they needed accommodations, sacrificial offerings, food, travel arrangements, and, undoubtedly, souvenirs to show the folks back home. In Ephesus, Artemis' impressive temple, dating back to the 6th century B.C.E.—three times larger than the Parthenon—was rated one of the Seven Wonders of the Ancient World. It dazzled pilgrims with its beauty, and its white marble façade brilliantly reflected the sunlight. Today, only one of the original 127 columns remains standing. But one thing that does survive is a large statue of Artemis.

The statue of the virgin goddess is housed in the Ephesus Museum; it dates to the 1st century C.E. It is called "Great Artemis." The goddess stands erect, serenely and confidently facing her devotees. Her welcoming pose greeted travelers from distant lands entering the sacred precincts of her temple. Working on a documentary, we were allowed to get within one inch of this imposing sculpture, rather than the 15 to 20 feet minimum required of tourists. Also, we were able to see the rear side of the statue that visitors cannot see. As we inspected the detail on the statue, we began to notice things that made sense of the imagery of Aseneth/Mary the Magdalene.

To our surprise, we discovered that Aseneth—that is, Mary the Magdalene—is modeled on the goddess Artemis.

Consider these significant parallels.

1. The Tower

First, we immediately noted that Artemis, like Aseneth and Mary the Magdalene, is a Tower Lady. She literally wears a Tower on her head. This is no ordinary headdress. It's not a tiara. It's a symbol. The Artemis Tower has several layers, like a series of three deep round cakes each piled on top of the other. Each layer, front and back, features buildings and temples. The Tower is a representation of a city built upon her head. It's her city, complete with her sanctuaries and notable structures.

The Tower tells us something very important about this great moon goddess: Artemis is a protectress. Her temples are places of shelter. Her centers—like Ephesus—are cities of refuge. Aseneth, too, is said to be a City of Refuge. In other words, when we read *Joseph and Aseneth*, the focus should not be on the Biblical cities of refuge, as some scholars have suggested, but on Artemis. She provides shelter for her people through her temples: caring for them, protecting them, and nurturing them. This is her civic role.

2. Bees

Second, we were startled to see panels of bees on Artemis' apparel, literally clinging to her as the bees cling to Aseneth/Mary the Magdalene in *Joseph and Aseneth*. Why bees?

The initial and immediate impression was that Artemis is the Queen Bee and her temple is a beehive. This impression was quickly reinforced when we examined the terminology used to describe the priestesses of her temple. They were called *Melissai*—that is, bees. Her male priests were referred to as—some people may be surprised by this—*Essenes*, or king bees.[66] Furthermore, in order to serve in her temple, her priestesses were required to be *parthenoi* or "revered virgins." Pausanias described the king bees—the Essenes—as living in purity and celibacy. They did so for a year. What happened after that year, he fails to tell us. Presumably, they returned to normal civilian life, free to marry or, perhaps, free to resume their marriages.

We wondered at the term *Essenes*, for that reminded us of the Essenes within Israel, who are widely regarded as strict followers of a particular view of Torah. They seemed to have lived in the 1st century B.C.E. and 1st century C.E., by the shores of the Dead Sea. Were these "Essenes," who are presumed to be the authors of the now-famous Dead Sea Scrolls, priests of Artemis?

The etymology of the word *Essene*, when applied to the Dead Sea Scroll community, is hotly debated—does it mean practitioners of Torah? Or, perhaps, healers? Even in ancient times, it was not clear. The 1st-century Alexandrian Jewish philosopher Philo suggested that the origin of the name was to be found in Greek rather than in Hebrew: it is a variation of *ostiotes*, meaning holiness. If this is true, then out of the four main Jewish sects of the time, only the Essenes have a name rooted in Greek, not Hebrew. This would indicate that, from the beginning, the Essenes were part of a Jewish/non-Jewish world.[67] We suspect that the Essenes saw themselves as the king bees[68] of the Torah, the Hebrew counterparts to the priests of Artemis in Ephesus.

Let's take a closer look at these Essenes. The fact is that we are not sure that the Essenes wrote the Dead Sea Scrolls. The writers of the Dead Sea Scrolls referred to themselves as the "Sons of Tzadok," the *Yahad* (that is, the community), "the Way," or the "Sons of Light." Whether they wrote the Dead Sea Scrolls or not, we know for a fact that there was a group that some called Essenes living along the Dead Sea in the 1st century. The term does not appear in the Talmud; not once. The only people who referred to the Dead Sea sect as Essenes were Hellenized Jews such as Josephus and Gentiles such as the 1st-century Roman naturalist Pliny, both of whom wrote in Greek.[69] There must have been a reason for this designation. Josephus and Pliny, who were familiar with the Jewish and non-Jewish worlds, were likely aware of the broader connotations of the term "Essenes." John Kampen believes that they "detected similarities" between the Dead Sea Jews and "the 'Essenes' in the temple of Artemis at Ephesus" and decided to designate both groups with "the same appellation."[70] In other words, the reason the term is used to describe both a Jewish sect and the priests of Artemis is because there must have been a connection, ignored by the more mainstream Jews, between certain Jews in Jesus' time and the worshippers of Artemis.

Perhaps the word "Essenes," therefore, functioned as a generic description. As Allen H. Jones points out, the priests of Artemis and the Essenes by the Dead Sea functioned much in the same way.[71] For example, both were in charge of preparing for feasts and both used a solar calendar. More importantly, Pliny, and his contemporary Philo, noted that the Essenes who lived by the shores of the Dead Sea were beekeepers.[72] In his famous play *The Frogs*, the 5th century B.C.E. Greek playwright Aristophanes writes, "The bee-keepers are here and they will open the temple of Artemis."[73] Clearly, the beekeepers are also the Essene priests who have the keys to the temple. According to Jones, there wasn't a theological connection between the Israelite Essenes and the Artemis Essenes. Rather, it was a term describing superficial and accidental similarities between some Jews and some pagans. We think he's wrong. The fact is that, as Jones himself states, beekeeping in the ancient world was almost always connected with religion. For example, among the Minoans, "beekeeper" always carried with it a religious connotation.[74] It is unlikely that there were two religious orders living at the same time, both engaged in beekeeping, and both called "Essenes" that had nothing to do with each other. The reason people have kept them apart is because in retrospect we can't imagine ancient Jews being anything but orthodox in their practice. There's a simpler explanation, however, concerning the relationship between the two groups: the Jewish Essenes, like the early Jesus followers who wrote *Joseph and Aseneth*, were not altogether kosher Jews. They were believers in Artemis or some kind of Judaic-Artemesian religious hybrid.[75]

If this seems like a stretch, it's because we've been conditioned to ignore the plain meaning of terms in favor of whatever theory has become the received wisdom of an age. But the fact remains: in the 1st century, there was a group of Jews called Essenes and a group of Artemis worshippers also called by the same name. They must have been related.[76]

In other words, now that we understand from *Joseph and Aseneth* that Mary the Magdalene was regarded by some of the earliest followers of Jesus as the Bride of God and that they modeled her on the goddess Artemis, we can conclude that some of the people we call Essenes were followers of Jesus of Nazareth and Mary of Magdala. It seems that all along the earliest followers of Jesus may have been hiding in plain sight, obscured by the term "Essene."[77]

Here, then, we have the smoking gun. By connecting Mary the Magdalene to the Essenes of Artemis, what the *Joseph and Aseneth* manuscript demonstrates is that the marriage of Joseph and Aseneth—of Jesus and Mary the Magdalene—brought together Hebrews and Gentiles that saw themselves, or were seen by others, as Essenes.[78] Put a different way, from the inception of the movement, the followers of Jesus saw themselves as living in messianic times where both Jew and Gentile would soon be worshipping together. It seems that Paul did not invent Gentile Christianity: he hijacked the movement from the Bride of God and her Essene followers.

To return to our paradigm-shifting gospel, what exactly is the significance of bees and Artemis?

It turns out that in the Roman world, bees were taken as symbols of virginity because it was widely believed that they reproduced without sexual intercourse or any form of copulation—simply put, bees were the symbols of immaculate conception. Aristotle, for instance, in *Generation of Animals, Book III*, articulates this view. This was also the way in which bees were interpreted within early Christianity. In a work on the life of St. Ambrose, his birth around the year 340 C.E. was said to have been attended by a swarm of bees which flew about his cradle—some entering his mouth—before rising up and vanishing out of sight.[79] The author of the life of St. Ambrose interprets this swarming as a sign of Ambrose's lifelong virginity, future greatness, and eloquence. Think of the implications of the above: in *Joseph and Aseneth*, the virginal bees are connected with the wife, not the mother.

It seems that once Mary the wife was written out of history, Mary the mother was elevated to near-goddess status and retroactively declared a virgin. This was not an arbitrary process. As Ann Graham Brock and Robert Murray make clear with respect to the Syriac tradition, this was a conscious theological policy of replacing Mary the Magdalene with Mary the mother. It involved a "deliberate and systematic 'superimposition' of the Marys."[80] However, once we understand that in *Joseph and Aseneth* Mary the Magdalene is modeled on the virgin goddess Artemis,[81] we can get beyond the superimposition and realize that Jesus called his wife, not his mother, a Holy Virgin. Later, the mother was substituted for the daughter-in-law. In other words, it was Mary the Magdalene who was the original Virgin Mary.[82]

3. Bees and Breasts

While we were standing next to the statue of Artemis, we also noticed—how could one miss—a cluster of more than two dozen egg-shaped protuberances from Artemis' body. These are often interpreted as multiple breasts, an attribution, perhaps, of the goddess' fertility or, more likely, of her life-giving and life-sustaining functions. After all, she was the goddess who nurtured her people, saved them from harm, and brought them prosperity. As mentioned before, the fact is that they don't look like breasts, are situated in the wrong place on her body, and lack any suggestion of nipples.

As stated in the Preface, others have speculated that perhaps these unusual shapes represent bulls' testicles—testes from bulls sacrificed to Artemis, appended to her statue. This theory also doesn't make much sense. First, bulls' testes come in pairs and there are several isolated protrusions on Artemis' body. Second, if they were bulls' testes, they would be hung from her attire, not nurtured by her body.

When we saw the bees on Artemis' body, it struck us immediately that the mysterious protrusions are bee-related. Some might call them "cocoons," but this is not technically correct. They are "queen cells." Normal cells do not protrude and they are horizontal. In contrast, queen cells are vertical and protrude out of the comb in order to accommodate potential queens. They look exactly like the protrusions from Artemis' body. This process occurs when a queen dies, or at springtime during periods of plenty. Put simply, for a culture that prizes honey, queen cells represent renewal and plenty. More than this, they can represent the "resurrection" of the dead queen through her successors.

The swarming of Aseneth/Mary the Magdalene in our text is also very significant. Talking to beekeepers, we realized that bees swarm only when they are in transition between the mother hive and a new colony. What happens is that the breakaway swarm establishes a temporary colony in a tree. At its center, there is the breakaway queen from the hive. The swarming is the bees' way of protecting the new queen so that scouts can find a "city of refuge," so to speak—a new and permanent home. At this stage, the queen is transitioning from her virgin state to her mother state. In other words, *Joseph and Aseneth* may have been written at the very moment that the Jesus/ Mary the Magdalene followers were declaring their abandonment of the old hive, what Christians call the "Old Testament," and their establishment of a new hive or, more properly, a "New Testament." Once bees leave a hive, they establish a new signature smell. And once that occurs, there's no going back to the old hive.

For a society that venerated Artemis, the bee imagery signified healing, plenty, renewal, resurrection, virginity, and immortality. But there is one more thing. If the protrusions are, indeed, queen cells, then Artemis' body is the honeycomb. As stated, in *Joseph and Aseneth* what we are witnessing is the first-ever Communion ceremony between Aseneth (a.k.a. Mary the Magdalene) and the angel (a.k.a. Jesus). But take note, in this ceremony it is not *his* body that they are eating—it is *hers*.

Taken all together, it is obvious that Artemis is not multi-breasted nor is she proudly wearing bulls' testicles. She is the Queen Bee. Her attendants are bees. And her magnificent temple is the beehive. In our text, Mary the Magdalene seems to be fashioned in the image of this goddess.[83]

The equation of Mary the Magdalene with Artemis fits the religious context in which the first followers of Jesus and Mary the Magdalene lived. For example, a series of tablets were found at Knossos on Crete that depict large jars of honey being given as offerings to the gods. Another group of tablets are known as the *honey tablets* in which the name of Eleuthia, the goddess of childbirth, is mentioned. According to John Chadwick, "it is of some significance that she [Eleuthia] later became identified with Artemis, whose symbol at Ephesus was a bee."[84]

On the island of Thera, modern Santorini, 3,500-year-old pieces of jewelry have been found which depict a female head with a bee's body. Similar images have been found on the island of Rhodes at Kamiros. On Thera, coin-like bronze objects have been found on which there is a figure of a bee enclosed within a mysterious inscription that has not yet been deciphered. Hilda Ransome believes that these are all connected to the worship of Artemis and they have something to do with her "secret rites."[85]

Since Jesus has always been somehow associated with Mary the Magdalene, if we are right and Mary the Magdalene is modeled on Artemis, there should be some echo in the Gospels—however faint—of the connection between Jesus and Artemis, between Jesus and bees. And there is. Several times in the Synoptic Gospels (Matthew, Mark, and Luke)[86] Jesus is accused of engaging in forbidden magic, for example driving out demons in the name of "Baalzebub." What is the meaning of this term? Scholars are not sure. As we've noted above, Ba'al was a Canaanite god. His name is translated as *Lord*. *Zebub*, in Hebrew, signifies a moving, buzzing insect, most often identified with a fly. People translate *Baalzebub* as "Lord of the Flies," identifying this deity with the Canaanite Pantheon.

However, there is no extra-Biblical reference to such a god. In fact, in light of our text, we may now hypothesize that the Baalzebub reference in the Gospels may be a Jewish put-down of a god or a goddess that is associated with a flying insect.

But why the put-down? We can now answer that question. It seems that what we have in the Gospels is a play on his association with bees. According to Diane Apostolos-Cappadona, "Mary Magdalene as well as Mary of Nazareth are many times associated with the attributes and characteristics of previous goddesses."[87] If we are right, Mary the Magdalene was seen by her followers as the incarnation of a specific goddess—Artemis. Jesus, therefore, would have been associated with a bee goddess and, as the Gospels record, his opponents may well have charged him of heretically healing in her name. Put differently, since Artemis was associated by her Syro-Phoenician followers with bees, honey, and life, it seems that Jesus' Jewish opponents were accusing him of being associated with flies, darkness, and dung.[88]

Some might object that despite the parallels that we have drawn, no connection exists in the historical record between Artemis and the land of Israel, where Mary the Magdalene was from. Are they right? Was there a tradition of Artemis worship in the general area of ancient Israel? In fact, there was—a very long tradition.

The most incredible surviving monument to Artemis in this part of the world is her temple in Jerash/Gerasa. Jerash/Gerasa is in modern-day Jordan, across the Jordan River, not far from the Galilee. The structure that is found there today was dedicated around the end of the 1st century, but according to John Kampen, "the evidence suggests that a cult and temple to Artemis are not innovations introduced to Gerasa in 100 C.E. Nor was Artemis a rarity in Syro-Palestine in the first century."[89]

The most famous statue of Artemis found in Israel was discovered by an Italian team excavating at Caesarea in 1961.[90] Another statue was discovered in the area of Gadara across the Sea of Galilee from Magdala, Mary the Magdalene's hometown. A further connection is with the Nabataeans of Petra fame. Their kingdom, also in modern-day Jordan, reached its greatest heights during the reign of Aretas IV (9 B.C.E.–40 C.E.), who reigned during the time of Jesus and Mary the Magdalene. At the time, the Nabataeans worshipped Atargatis— the so-called Syrian goddess—who was clearly modeled on none other than Artemis.[91] Atargatis was a fertility goddess identified with dolphins[92] and fish.

She was a fish goddess. At Ashkelon, in modern Israel, she was described as half woman and half fish.[93] In other words, as with Artemis and early Christianity, the fish was sacred for the cult of Atargatis.

But how can it be that Artemis was so important in Biblical Israel, ancient Canaan, and yet is never mentioned in the Bible? The fact is that the Bible does mention Artemis. The Israelites were not immune to her theological charms. The reason we haven't noticed her is because she too has been hiding for millennia in plain sight. In the land of Canaan/Israel she was not called Artemis. The fact is that she had different names in different places. In Phrygia, she was called Rhea, in Egypt she was called Isis,[94] and in ancient Canaan/Israel she was called Asherah. In the Bible she is one of the most notable goddesses attracting wayward Israelites. For example, when the children of Israel are about to enter the Holy Land, God warns them not to engage in Asherah (i.e., Artemis) worship by designating sacred trees next to their holy altars as symbols of her presence: "You shall not plant for yourself an Asherah of any tree next to an altar of God, your God, that you make for yourself" (Deuteronomy 16:21). Clearly, some Israelites did not heed God's warning. In a place called Kuntillet 'Ajrud, in the Sinai Peninsula just outside modern-day Israel, a wall painting was found where Asherah/Artemis is described as the consort of the God of Israel himself.[95]

When the Babylonians destroyed Jerusalem in 587 B.C.E., some of the Judaean refugees confronted the prophet Jeremiah. They did not blame their misfortunes on their neglect of the God of Israel but, rather, of the goddess Asherah, "queen of heaven," in whose honor they had once baked special honey cakes and burned incense (Jeremiah 44:16–20).

Asherah worship seems to have involved some kind of ritual sex. The greatest theological challenge that Moses faced at the time of the Biblical Exodus occurred when a prince of the tribe of Simon, Zimri by name, engaged in ritual sex with Kosbi, a priestess of the Midianite version of Artemis, at the entrance of the Holy of Holies where the Ark of the Covenant was kept. Simply put, the theological challenge of Artemis to the God of Israel did not start with Jesus and Mary the Magdalene. Already, in Moses' time, Zimri and Kosbi were engaged in some kind of syncretic fusion of Judaism and Artemis worship. Perhaps they called themselves the "Son of God" and the "Bride of God." Whatever they were doing, it involved an attempt to join the Midianite and Israelite nations. More than this, it seems they used sex in a cultic manner, a ritual that scholars would later associate with Gnosticism. The Zimri/Kosbi episode ended when Pinchas, a relative of Moses, speared Zimri and Kosbi in flagrante delicto—in the act of copulation (Numbers 25:1–8). What all this means is that Artemis (a.k.a. Asherah) was already seducing Israelites as early as 1500 B.C.E.

But what of the Galilee in Jesus' time? The connection between the early Jesus movement and Artemis only makes sense if there was a long Galilean tradition of associating female goddesses with Artemis, or her Canaanite predecessor Asherah. Incredibly, in 2010, in the Beit She'an Valley in Israel, archaeologists discovered thirty intact, approximately 3,000-year-old bee-hives—part of a cluster of one to two hundred beehives—in the ruins of the ancient city of Rehov. The beehives date back to 900 B.C.E. Although some speculated that these beehives were part of a honey-making industry, the hypothesis makes no sense. The bees were found in the heart of an urban center. No community would want an estimated one million bees producing honey next to their windows. It seems that the bees served a cultic purpose. Incense burners were found next to the hives. More than this, the ceramic burners had small Artemis-like protrusions encircling the cultic stand—foreshadows of the Artemis queen-bee cells. The greatest surprise of all was the charred preservation of intact, millennia-old bees. This allowed scientists to examine the bees under a microscope. Shockingly, they were not of the local Syrian variety. They had been brought all the way from Turkey! It seems that they must have been Ephesian bees (i.e., bees from Ephesus)—holy bees. This places an Anatolian/Turkish bee cult next door to the Galilee nine hundred years before Jesus and Mary the Magdalene. Clearly, the iconography of Artemis was deeply ingrained in the Jesus-era Galilean psyche.[96]

There may be echoes in the Gospels of this Galilean Artemis connection. In a famous incident, an unnamed woman anoints Jesus' head with *nard*, perfume (Mark 14:3–9). The Jewish tradition was to anoint a king with oil, not perfume. Interestingly, Xenophon of Ephesus wrote a romance in which the main characters fall in love while participating in a festival for Artemis. In it he describes the members of the procession carrying torches, baskets, and perfumes for the sacrifice to the goddess.[97] So the perfume incident may be preserving a tradition whereby Mary the Magdalene anoints Jesus using the rites of a priestess of Artemis.

We see the Artemis connection again with respect to another of Jesus' followers. One of the most mysterious characters mentioned in the Gospels is a man named Alphaeus. It is not a Hebrew name unless it is related to the Hebrew *Halfi*, which means "changing." He appears five times in the New Testament.[98] We don't know who he is except that he's the father of two of the apostles—Levi/Matthew and James. So what is it about Alphaeus' background that connects him so powerfully to Jesus? And why are the Gospels so quiet about him? As it turns out, "there was a sacred precinct to Artemis Alpheiaia, meaning of the river Alpheios, at the village of Letrinoi near the outlet of the river in Elis in southern Greece."[99] According to Greek tradition, Artemis was the love object of Alphaeus. Pausanias relates that at Olympia the two divinities had one altar in common.[100] In other words, Alphaeus may be a theophoric name, that is to say, a name that embeds the name of the god in a personal name. It may point to a Galilean family that was already enmeshed in Artemis worship, or had a Canaanite/Phoenician background involving the goddess.[101] This may explain why—when Jesus and Mary the Magdalene were perceived by some of their followers as gods incarnate—two of Alphaeus' sons heeded the call and became part of the original twelve.

Finally, the Artemis-Judaism-early Christian connection may be illustrated dramatically by an archaeological find north of the Galilee in Dura Europos, a border outpost in modern-day Syria. There, archaeologists have uncovered a synagogue dating to the 2nd century. Right next to it was discovered the earliest house church ever unearthed. Surprisingly, various Hebrew texts were found in it. Clearly there were Jews worshipping in this church. There were also paintings in both the church and the synagogue. The latter are particularly spectacular. They depict various Biblical scenes such as the Exodus, Ezekiel's Vision, and King David. But there is something very strange about this "synagogue." First of all, why are there human images in a Jewish house of worship—a clear transgression of Biblical law? Second of all, in one scene, which depicts Pharaoh's daughter bathing in the Nile, the princess is rendered in the nude. What kind of synagogue is this that depicts Biblical princesses in the fashion of modern centerfolds? And why is the synagogue right next to what is probably a Judeo-Christian house church? The answer, once again, may involve Artemis.

Right next to the synagogue, a temple dedicated to Adonis and the Nabataean counterpart to Artemis, Atargatis, was also discovered. In the temple, there were nine small rooms similar to the prostitution rooms in Pompeii and pagan temple cells where cult prostitution was practiced. Recently, Edward Lipinski concluded that the rooms in the Dura Europos Atargatis/Artemis temple "may well have included the sexual services of women."[102] What all this means is that in the 2nd century you have celebrants of Artemis, early Christians and Jews right next to each other, worshipping together and seemingly involved in Artemis-related ritual sex.

Artemis and Apollo: Twins—Sister and Brother

There's another strange passage in Joseph and Aseneth in which Joseph and Aseneth are said to be not only husband and wife but also "brother and sister" (7:10; 8:1; 8:4). This obviously has nothing to do with the Biblical Joseph and Aseneth. But does it have anything to do with Jesus and Mary the Magdalene? How could they be both spouses and siblings?[103] The appellation sounds almost incestuous. Again, Artemis provides the answer for a problem raised by the Joseph and Aseneth text.

In Greek mythology, Artemis was the twin of none other than Apollo. They were sister and brother, the moon and the sun, paired forever. Both are children of Zeus—the supreme god—and his wife, Leto. While there are conflicting mythological accounts regarding the location of her birth, one version has Artemis born in the sacred lake on the island of Delos, the religious capital of ancient Greece. In other words, Apollo and Artemis are the son and daughter of god. As stated earlier, by early Christian times Apollo had become identified with Helios and Mithras, the Persian "son of god," whose birthday was December 25th.[104] All these Sun gods were then identified with Jesus. What Joseph and Aseneth is telling us is that the moon goddess was identified with his wife.[105]

Finally, if we're right and Aseneth/Mary the Magdalene is modeled on Artemis, this would make sense of why she is portrayed in Joseph and Aseneth as both Jesus' sister and his wife. In other words, the brother/sister, bridegroom/ bride terminology only makes sense if Aseneth/Mary the Magdalene is understood as Artemis, consort and sister of Jesus/Apollo/Helios.

Aseneth/Mary the Magdalene Decoded

> ### Step Three
> Mary the Magdalene (Aseneth) is modeled on the goddess Artemis

Mary the Magdalene as Goddess

In *Joseph and Aseneth*, the typology could not be clearer. The unknown author of this work has taken a figure well known within the cultural context of his 1st-century Syro-Phoenician audience and merged it with Mary the Magdalene so as to convey an important truth about her. What truth?

Just as Joseph is a prefiguration of Jesus, drawn from a Hebrew text, Artemis is a prefiguration of Mary the Magdalene, drawn from a Gentile myth. We should note that early Christians had no problem drawing on pagan myths as foreshadows of the life of Jesus. Writing in Rome in the 150s, Justin Martyr states that all rational pagans are retroactively Christians: "those who have lived rationally [*meta logou*] belonged to Christ even though they have been atheists such as Socrates, Heraclitus and those like them. . . ."[106]

From the point of view of the early Christians, therefore, in their story of Apollo and Artemis, the pagans had anticipated the arrival of the real divine pair—the children of the true God—Jesus and Mary the Magdalene.

When the symbolic language of *Joseph and Aseneth* is understood, it testifies to Mary the Magdalene's immense power and status in the early Jesus movement. For example, scourging was related to Artemis even before the birth of Jesus. The philosopher Apollonius of Tyana describes the ritual scourging that was done in honor of Artemis of Scythia: "The scourging would continue until blood was flowing freely and the blood from the wounds would be smeared on the altar, as prescribed by the oracle."[107] In Sparta, too, young men underwent severe scourging until the altar of Artemis was covered in blood.[108] In fact, the story of Jesus' scourging during his final moments before the crucifixion may be borrowed from Artemis/Mary the Magdalene–related rituals.

Also, Artemis was often called Artemis Soteira, Artemis the Savior.[109] By describing Mary the Magdalene in Artemisian language, *Joseph and Aseneth* is describing Mary the Magdalene as the goddess incarnate. In other words, what has always been suspected is now confirmed. Mary the Magdalene was not a peripheral follower or a reformed prostitute. She was a savior in her own right; Jesus' bride, his wife, his spiritual sister and . . . his co-deity.

Today, after two millennia of traditional Christian theology, describing Mary the Magdalene as a goddess seems strange. But, in the 1st century, it was understood that some people could be raised to the status of gods and goddesses. By a vote of the senate, the Romans regularly elevated emperors, along with their wives and sometimes their mothers, to the status of gods. For example, after her death, Livia Drusilla, wife of the emperor/god Augustus and mother of the emperor/god Tiberius, was posthumously turned into a goddess by the Emperor Claudius in 42 C.E., around a decade after the crucifixion of Jesus. Again, though this may seem strange to modern sensibilities, historically speaking, elevating a Gentile woman to the status of a pagan goddess is no stranger than elevating a Jewish rabbi to the status of a Roman god. Once the leap had been made in the minds of some of his followers that Jesus was God incarnate, his wife, like the wife of any ruler, would also have to be elevated to the status of a goddess.[110]

We're so removed from the reality of the early Jesus-and-Mary movement that we've lost touch with the historical context into which that community was born. For example, after the crucifixion, many early traditions link early Christians to Ephesus—Paul, John, Mary the mother of Jesus . . . and Mary the Magdalene, are all said to have gone to Ephesus, where Ephesian Artemis ruled. The author of *Joseph and Aseneth* is drawing on iconic imagery from Jewish and Gentile sources so as to speak to his Jewish and Gentile audiences. He's literally marrying the traditions of Rome, Ephesus, and Jerusalem. And all this prior to Rome becoming Christian, without so much as a hint of Paul's influence.

At any rate, in the early days before the crucifixion, equating a flesh-and-blood woman such as Mary the Magdalene with the goddess Artemis would have been a good move. It would have immediately associated her with a goddess who was a healer, protector, nurturer, and savior. Since it is an undisputed fact that Jesus became associated with Helios/Apollo, if Jesus and Mary the Magdalene were married, Mary had to be associated with Artemis.

In the 1st-century world of Jesus and Mary the Magdalene, the goddess Artemis was the only way to come to terms with any wife of Jesus. Describing Mary the Magdalene as a rabbi's wife would have meant nothing outside a Jewish context, and would have served to define her solely in relation to her male partner. Further, such an appellation would have been unthinkable for a group that already saw Jesus as a deity. Simply put, if he was a god, she had to be a goddess. If we've understood the text correctly, and Mary the Magdalene was a former priestess of Ba'al and Artemis, we now see that her transformation did not involve a total abandonment of Ba'al and Artemis for the sake of marrying a Jewish rabbi. Quite the contrary, she became Artemis when she married Ba'al/Helios/Apollo. In the process, she became the head of the newly founded Church of the Gentiles.

The author of *Joseph and Aseneth* is also telling us that just as the worshippers of Osiris, Mithras, and Dionysus (all dying-and-resurrecting gods) flocked to worship Jesus so, too, the worshippers of Artemis—the provider of shelter and everlasting life—flocked to the worship of Mary the Magdalene. In other words, to the Phoenicians/Canaanites of Tyre, Sidon, and Magdala, *Joseph and Aseneth* seems to have been a Gospel of the Church of Mary the Magdalene, the religious community of the first Gentiles who followed the teachings of Jesus as interpreted through the apostle Mary the Magdalene.

Archaeologically speaking, it is significant that in the controversial "Jesus family tomb" found in 1980 in Talpiot, east Jerusalem, close to the ossuary, or bone box, of a man called "Jesus son of Joseph," there was an ossuary inscribed in Greek that reads "Mary also known as Mara."[111] *Mara* is an Aramaic term used by Hebrews and Phoenicians/Canaanites. It can be translated as *master* or *lady*. It is the female equivalent of *lord*.

In the Israel Antiquities Authority (IAA) collection of more than a thousand ossuaries, there are only six that have the appellation *Mara* inscribed on them.[112] In the three instances where *Mara* is referring to a male, the epigraphers take the term to mean *master*.[113] In the three instances that *Mara* appears next to a woman's name, the term is not translated as the female equivalent of *master*, which is mistress, but is taken as a nickname for *Martha*.[114] This is patently absurd.[115] *Mara*, when applied to females, must mean the same thing as it does when applied to males. If it doesn't, no one has made an argument as to why not.

In the Ethiopic *Liber Requiei*, the earliest Christian text dealing with the Virgin Mary's death, *Mara* is used in one sense only: "our Master." Stephen Shoemaker, the translator of the text, states that the Ethiopic equivalent of *Mara* means "mistress" and "lady." But, for complete accuracy, he translates the word as "Master." Shoemaker states that he is using this word "in a neutered sense," meaning that "it should not be taken as suggesting the use of masculine forms."[116] Put simply, if we want to know what *Mara* means, we need to look no further than the *Liber Requiei*, where *Mara* refers to a woman and it means *master*.

If the Talpiot tomb is, indeed, the Jesus family tomb and one of the "Mary" ossuaries found in it belongs to Mary the Magdalene, then the "Mara" inscription on her ossuary means that she was called "lady" or "master." Significantly, in the original Syriac of *Joseph and Aseneth*, Mary the Magdalene is also referred to using the epithet "Mara" or "Lady" (10:7; 18:13; 28:2; 28:11).[117] But let's not forget the connection with Artemis. One of the appellations of Artemis is *Potnia Theron*. For example, this is the way she's referred to in Homer's *Iliad* (21:470). *Potnia* is a Mycenaean word, which can be translated as "lady" or "mistress."[118] In *The Greek Magical Papyri*, a collection of magical spells found in Egypt dating from the 2nd century B.C.E. to the 5th century C.E., Artemis is referred to as both *august virgin* and *mistress*.[119] Here again we have perfect synchronicity between the archaeology, the Artemis tradition, and our text.[120] When it comes to Mary the Magdalene, they are all telling the same story.

Now, again, it might seem far-fetched that a Jewish rabbi—a healer belonging to a Jewish religious elite—would marry a Gentile priestess, but this is only as a result of imposing later prejudices on earlier realities. The fact is that we have both historical and archaeological evidence for precisely the kind of union described in *Joseph and Aseneth*. Historically speaking, not long after Mary the Magdalene (around the end of the 1st century), Julia, a Herodian princess (a Jewish princess of the royal Herodian house), married a Roman senator and settled in Perga (modern Turkey), where she became a priestess of Artemis. Following in Julia's footsteps, her daughter, Plancia Magna, also became a high priestess of Artemis.[121]

But one does not have to go outside of the Holy Land to find such Artemis priestesses. For example, in 1989 three adjacent burial caves were found in Jerusalem's Kidron Valley in an area called Akeldama (i.e., the "field of blood"), traditionally associated with the place where Judas Iscariot hanged himself. The caves contained twenty-three ossuaries in total. Many of them had inscriptions on them. What the archaeology demonstrates is a totally syncretic family—some kind of mixed Jewish-Greek family that consisted of Jews, Gentiles, and converts. Incredibly, one ossuary has a bilingual inscription in Greek and Hebrew that reads *Jesus*. Next to it is an ossuary of a woman who is called *Kyria* in

Greek—this means *Mara* in Aramaic. And next to her there's an ossuary of a woman called by the very un-Jewish name of *Megiste*. She is identified as "the priestess."[122]

In case one thinks that this kind of archaeology is a complete anomaly, there is always the famous tomb of Jason found in 1995 in the fashionable Jerusalem district of Rehavia. Among the various images of ships and Greek names, there is a faded inscription written in Hebrew of a woman whose name is now illegible. But her title is not: it's "the priestess."[123]

It seems, therefore, that from the beginning, the Church of The Lady, Mary the Magdalene, would have involved a Gentile congregation distinct from the Gentile congregations of the Christ, later founded by Paul. Paul's group was founded on his mystical experience of the post-crucifixion Christ. In contrast, Mary the Magdalene's group seems to have been born out of an attempt to understand her earthly marriage to Jesus of Nazareth. This Gentile Church was based not on Paul's mystical experiences on the road to Damascus, but on Mary the Magdalene's experiences as the Bride of God.

Our reading of *Joseph and Aseneth* suggests, therefore, that Paul and subsequent Pauline Christians retroactively made Jesus celibate so they could write Jesus' wife out of their theology, while simultaneously taking over her Gentile Church. Margaret Starbird puts it this way: "In denying the role of the Sacred Bride, the church fathers in effect gave us a distorted view of Jesus. He became envisioned as a celibate god, seated on a celestial throne—the celibate son of a Virgin Mother."[124] *Joseph and Aseneth* did not have the luxury of writing people in and out of history. All the text could do is find theological meaning in the historical reality of Jesus' married life. In other words, the early Church of Mary the Magdalene could not leave Jesus' marital status ambiguous, as it is in the Gospels, because people knew the truth. Furthermore, once Jesus had been deified, his followers had no choice but to also regard the woman who shared the Son of God's bed as a goddess incarnate in her own right—the Lady: Mary the Magdalene.

It is interesting to note that just as virginity was later moved from Mary the Magdalene to Mary the mother, so too did the designation "Our Lady." In other words, Pauline Christians took Artemis' titles from Jesus' Bride and conferred them on Jesus' mother. In the process, they also made sure that the mother was totally desexualized. As the story was now told, she was born of an immaculate conception, gave birth through a virginal delivery, and stayed ever-virgin. Significantly, they did all this at the Council of Ephesus, where they started a tradition that the Virgin Mary relocated from Jerusalem to the center of Artemis worship in Ephesus. In this way, Jesus' mother forever replaced both Artemis and Mary the Magdalene.

In sum, a Church of Mary the Magdalene would have represented a group of congregations or assemblies who had been nurtured by Mary the Magdalene during her lifetime. They would have surely followed her version of the teachings and practices of her husband-rabbi, the divine-human Jesus. Of course, there are echoes of all this in the Gospels themselves: the wedding at Cana, where the bride and the groom are never identified; the incident with the Syro-Phoenician woman; the episode where Jesus' feet are washed by an unnamed woman who sensuously dries them with her hair; and the attempt by Mary the Magdalene to wash and anoint the dead body of Jesus.[125]

But is there any evidence that the Church of Mary the Magdalene survived beyond Jesus and Mary the Magdalene? In fact, there is. For example, there are early traditions surrounding an enigmatic figure called Simon Magus, that is "Simon the Magician" and his Syro-Phoenician wife, Helena. In Pauline Christianity, Simon is vilified as a bad guy and an opponent of both Peter and Paul. For example, in Acts 8:9–24 he is presented as a false convert to Christianity who confronts the apostle Paul. Simon is also called a heretic in several early 2nd-century writings by Irenaeus, Justin Martyr, and Hippolytus. In at least one text, echoing traditions about Jesus, Simon's mother is described as Jewish and his father as Roman.[126]

Simon Magus' story roughly parallels the story in *Joseph and Aseneth*—one generation of leadership later. It seems that Simon claimed to be Jesus reincarnated and, perhaps not coincidentally, Simon's wife, Helena, like Mary the Magdalene, is described by the church fathers as a former prostitute.[127] In other words, Simon and Helena seem to be carrying on the tradition established by Jesus and Mary the Magdalene, as described in *Joseph and Aseneth*. In Simon we have a half-Roman, half-Jewish miracle worker who has a Syro-Phoenician priestess as his consort or wife. So for those who think that the Jesus–Mary the Magdalene coupling has no historical or textual basis, in Simon and Helena we see a couple that perfectly fits what we would expect from the Church of Mary the Magdalene after the Magdalene's death. Justin Martyr called Simon's movement *Simonians*.[128] It carried on the tradition of the bridal chamber and is credited with starting Gnosticism.

It seems, therefore, that Simon Magus and his wife Helena stepped into the sandals, so to speak, of Jesus and Mary the Magdalene. They were so important that they could not be ignored by the church fathers but, as with all opponents of orthodoxy, they were dubbed heretics, magicians, and prostitutes.

Textually and historically, there are further echoes of the marriage of Jesus and Mary in the so-called Gnostic Christian communities where Mary the Magdalene is depicted as the apostle to the apostles, the most important follower of Jesus, his lifelong companion and his trusted confidante. In fact, the Gnostics may have been the immediate successors to the Church of Mary the Magdalene.

Taking all this together with our lost gospel, it is now clear that, at least for her followers, Mary the Magdalene played a major role—perhaps equal to Jesus—in the drama of human redemption.

10

JOSEPH: HIS STORY

The Sun God

As we have seen, investigating who the Joseph in our manuscript might be patterned after led us to the New Testament. Our reasoning is straightforward. Modeling was a problem not just for someone who wanted to write about Mary the Magdalene; it concerned Jesus as well. There are two levels to this argument. First, if someone is burning your books, you have to hide them or encode them. After the 4th-century victory of one form of Christianity over all others, the losers could give in, actively oppose the dominant stream, go underground, or hide in plain sight. We think we've demonstrated that, using the tools of typology, the author of *Joseph and Aseneth* decided to do the latter. Nonetheless, that only gets you half way. There's a second consideration. Hiding Jesus behind the Biblical Joseph allows your text to survive, but it does not dictate what you're going to say about him. There were a number of options. The depiction of Jesus could draw on actual history, Christian theology, Jewish theology, pagan mythology, and more. In other words, the author of *Joseph and Aseneth* had to do more than simply hide Jesus behind Joseph. If he was going to tell us who or what he thought Jesus really was, he had to elaborate on Joseph in ways that clearly had nothing to do with the story in Genesis. Presumably, he thought his readers would catch on.

In some ways, the authors of the New Testament Gospels were faced with a task similar to the author of *Joseph and Aseneth*: how best to represent Jesus in terms that their audience would grasp. To this end, they literally ransacked the Jewish and Roman worlds to find suitable models of famous individuals to whom Jesus could be compared. The four canonical Gospel writers appear to have given considerable thought to this question, and they arrived at different conclusions.

The author of the Gospel of Mark, for instance, positioned Jesus as a miracle worker, devoting about a third of his writing to such feats—healing people, feeding five thousand, and walking on water. He portrayed Jesus as a superior version of the great miracle workers of the Hebrew Bible, such as Elijah and Elisha—they were his role models. According to one scholar, whereas Elijah performed eight miracles and Elisha sixteen, Jesus got to twenty-four.[1] In other words, for Mark, Jesus was the greatest miracle worker of all time. That was his model and that's how he portrayed him.

In contrast, although they differ in details, the Gospels of Matthew and Luke both emphasize Jesus' virgin birth. This is not a Jewish concept. It is derived, however, from a common idea extremely familiar to people in the 1st century C.E. In that era—and this may surprise people not familiar with this history—Roman emperors claimed virgin/divine births. Similarly, founders of major religions such as Dionysus and Mithras were also regarded as the offspring of virgin births. All these individuals were said, like Jesus, to have had divine fathers and human mothers. Even the philosopher Plato, some said, had a virgin birth. In other words, to be somebody truly significant in the Roman world, an individual had to have had a virgin birth. Somehow, he had to have been fathered by a divine, not human, seed.

In religious terms, therefore, the virgin birth story doesn't make Jesus unique. In the Roman world, such births—when it came to rulers and religious founders—were commonplace.[2] Virgin birth was the price of entry, so to speak, into the ranks of the most notable. Hardly biology or history, this mythological narrative was a way of saying that Jesus—at the very least—was on a par with none other than the Roman emperors and the founders of the most popular religions of the time. It signaled to contemporary readers the immense importance the Gospel writers attached to his birth.

The Gospel of John goes in a different direction, modeling Jesus on the *Logos* or "the Word." The Logos is a Greek philosophical concept, a phrase denoting the expression of God. This represents something far beyond anything that Mark, Matthew, or Luke imagined. John makes it clear that, in his view, the Logos is not only "with God" but "*is* God" (John 1:1). From John's perspective, the abstract divine manifestation—the Word—became incarnate, that is, it took on human form. Thus, for John, Jesus is not merely a miracle worker or even a Son of God but—as many Roman emperors claimed about themselves—he is God who became flesh (John 1:14).

As these examples show, any writer setting out to write a Gospel such as *Joseph and Aseneth* would have had to shape his Jesus according to pre-existing concepts concerning messiahship and divinity.[3]

So what does the manuscript really tell us about Jesus? Who is he modeled after? Is there any hidden teaching or history to be gleaned from the text?

Jesus as the Roman Emperor

From the outset, the figure of Joseph as presented in *Joseph and Aseneth* is impressive. The symbolism is carefully crafted to reveal Joseph's true essence. In modern film parlance, it's a gradual build. Detail upon detail is disclosed so that we take in the true measure of the man. First of all, the Joseph figure in *Joseph and Aseneth* appears wearing a white tunic, a purple robe, and a golden crown with twelve precious stones. Above the crown there are golden rays. This isn't Egyptian dress, as a superficial reading might imply. This is undisputedly the garb of a Roman emperor—white tunic, purple robe. No one reading this text in the first centuries of the Common Era would have missed the point. Basically, what this encoded Gospel is telling us is that Jesus is the true ruler of the world. But there's more.

Though Joseph/Jesus first appears to Aseneth/Mary the Magdalene as a Roman emperor, the text tells us that he is more than a mere Roman ruler. He is the true king of Israel, God's anointed one. Instead of a crown of thorns, however, in *Joseph and Aseneth* Jesus is wearing a golden crown emblazoned with twelve stones, representing the twelve Tribes of Israel. Essentially, Jesus is depicted not only as a King, but also as a Jewish high priest (Exodus 28:1–31).

The Jewish high priesthood was made up of descendants of Aaron. The high priest wore a breastplate decorated with twelve stones representing the twelve tribes of Israel (Exodus 28:15–19). Until the Maccabees in 165 B.C.E., King and Priest were different people representing some kind of system of checks and balances. After the Maccabees, also known as the Hasmoneans, the two roles were collapsed into one. By wearing both the crown and the stones, Jesus is being represented as King and High Priest. In other words, he is depicted in Maccabean fashion as both Moses and Aaron. Of course, the twelve stones also represent Jesus' twelve disciples who were chosen to spread his message to the far-flung corners of the world.

Jesus as the True Vine
In the text, Joseph/Jesus carries a royal scepter as well as an olive branch. The latter is not simply a gesture of good will—extending the olive branch, so to speak. The olive tree is a code word for faithful Christians, those who persevere in spite of obstacles like persecution directed at them from fellow Christians. While it may sound somewhat strange to our ears today, the "olive" is none other than Jesus himself. Ephrem the Syrian, for example, explores the symbolism of the olive tree in one of his hymns:

> The prudent olive has no fear
> Of the cold which terrifies all
> Under the scourges of the freezing winter
> Its leaves stand fast, as though faithful.
> They are an image of the faithful
> Who persevere in *Christ the Olive*.[4]

So, once again, Ephrem's typology comes in handy: the Olive = Christ. The identification is apt. The olive is hardy and long-lasting and can withstand the rigors of many different hostile environments. It is an image that grows out of both a Roman as well as a Jewish environment. Cultures around the Mediterranean world grew the olive tree and it was a staple of trade and diet, then and now. It was emblematic of human existence and so presented a suitable image for Jesus. Remember, "Christ" means "Anointed one," the anointing consisting of having ritually pure olive oil poured over one's head as a symbol of divine election.

The image of the olive tree emerges from a specifically Jewish matrix. In this context, the vineyard—like the olive grove—also represents a central metaphor for God's people, those whom He carefully tends and nurtures—"For the vineyard of the Lord of Hosts is the House of Israel, and the people of Judah are his pleasant planting" (Isaiah 5: 7). When devastation threatens the Jewish people, the image used is that of the vineyard becoming desolate (Isaiah 5:5, 6). God prunes Israel, so to speak, cutting off shoots with pruning shears and hewing away the spreading branches (Isaiah 18:5). In this way, God forms the vine into any shape He desires. Disobedient Israel is referred to as a degenerate vineyard yielding "wild grapes" (Isaiah 5:2; Jeremiah 2:21). Conversely, the righteous are referred to as "the shoot that I [God] planted, the work of My hands" (Isaiah 60:21). The righteous are the shoot, or branch, of the vine that yields good fruit. The members of the Dead Sea Scroll community envisaged themselves as a new planting, in fact, "an everlasting plantation" (*Community Rule* 8).

From a Christian perspective, while Jesus was the olive, Jesus' followers saw themselves representing the "true vine" of Israel. This is the vine of righteousness, the branch of David, the shoot that God tends and cares for and which yields good fruit. In Hebrew, a branch or shoot is called a *Netzer* and, to this day, Hebrew speakers call Christians *Notzrim*, that is, the "followers of the shoot." In fact, the name Nazareth probably means "place of the branch," signifying the village to which a Bethlehem-based branch of a family claiming Davidic descent was transplanted at the time of Herod the Great. More than a mere emperor, the symbolism in *Joseph and Aseneth* makes it clear that, for his followers, Jesus is the fulfillment of Israel's hopes and dreams—even humanity's hopes and dreams. According to this view, the church is the place where God nurtures his people through good times as well as times of persecution. Ephrem's hymn, quoted above, goes on to say:

> In persecution the faithless have fallen like leaves
> Which do not abide on their trees;
> But Christians, hanging on Christ,
> Are like olive-leaves in winter,
> All of them planted wholly in him.[5]

According to this model, Jesus is the olive tree, the giver and sustainer of life, the reliable root from which many will grow and flourish. In other words, every single symbol associated with Joseph in our manuscript points to Jesus, and to Jesus alone.

Jesus as Helios the Sun God

Most importantly, as previously noted, in our text we find Joseph modeled on the Sun god—Helios—also known as Sol Invictus or Apollo. Indisputably, Joseph in *Joseph and Aseneth* is portrayed as a Sun god, with twelve rays of sunlight emanating from his crown (5:5). His chariot is also impressive: it's covered with gold and pulled by white horses—again a symbol of the sun whose movement across the sky was thought to be caused by mighty steeds pulling a magnificent celestial chariot (5:4).[6] By this point in the narrative, everyone should realize that this is not the Biblical Joseph who is paraded by Pharaoh through the streets on a chariot. It is Jesus depicted as Helios. In fact, Aseneth—facing east—welcomes Joseph with these words: "Now I see the sun shining from his chariot that has come to us, and its radiance lights up our home" (6:2). In other words, the Sun god has deigned to come down to earth, to court, marry, and eventually procreate with her.

In Christian terms, Jesus is equated with the sun's light, and this is part and parcel of the agenda of the early church in order to assert his divinity. Jesus is said to be the "Light of the World" (John 8:12). His followers "will have the light of life" (John 8:12). And when he was crucified, the Gospel of Luke tells us that "the sun's light failed" (23:45)—perhaps a reference to an actual eclipse, but metaphorically suggestive of the sun dying. In other words, in *Joseph and Aseneth*, Helios is clearly the prototype chosen to represent the power and significance of Jesus.

The choice is an interesting one, for Helios was the model for at least one Roman emperor and one major Roman religion. Julian, the 4th-century Roman emperor, composed a Hymn to Helios in praise of the power of the Sun god. There he proclaimed his allegiance to King Helios, describing him as the intellectual god, the source of all truth and goodness. For Julian, Helios was like Plato's Form of the Good. In *The Republic*, Plato had compared the highest "form," or foundational concept, to the sun which illumines both the World of Reality and the World of Appearance. Julian's attempt to reinvigorate ancient Graeco-Roman religion was not long-lasting. He was overshadowed by Christian emperors before and after him, and his brief foray into pagan revivalism earned him the nickname the *apostate*. For his efforts to resurrect sun worship, Julian was assassinated on the battlefield, allegedly by a Christian soldier. Before and after Julian, Helios imagery was applied by Christians not to a Sun god, but to a "son" god—to Jesus and Jesus alone.

A more robust and long-standing tradition of Helios can be found within Mithraism, a Roman religion of Persian origin. Mithraism was a strong competitor to Christianity in the first few centuries, and there are many similarities between the two faiths, Mithraism being the older of the two religions. In fact, it seems that Christians deliberately borrowed Mithraic images to bolster their religion and, essentially, to put Mithraism out of business. For example, Mithras was born in a cave. Jesus too is said to have been born in a cave-like grotto or manger. Like Jesus, Mithras had a divine father and a human mother. Also, he was worshipped in a ceremony of bread and wine during which his followers celebrated his victory over death. Central to Mithraic mythology was the sacrifice of the primordial bull whose spilled blood redeemed the world. The parallels to Christianity are obvious. In Christianity, it is Jesus himself who is the sacrifice and it is his blood that redeems the world. Most interesting for a modern audience, Mithras' birthday was December 25th, the time during which the days in the northern hemisphere become longer, representing the victory of light over darkness. As a result of all this, Mithras, too, came to be pictured as the Sun god—as Helios or as Sol Invictus, the Conquering Sun.

As can be seen from the above, early Christianity borrowed much of its imagery from Mithraism. In fact, there is an echo of the conflation of Mithras and Jesus in the story of the three wise men or Magi. The Magi were, after all, the priests of Mithras. In the Gospel of Matthew (2:1), when they show up in the manger of Bethlehem for the "adoration" of the divine child, what they are in fact doing is equating Mithras with Jesus. An ancient depiction of Mithras exists to this day underneath the Church of St. Prisca in Rome. Appropriately, the church was built over a huge mithraeum, a temple devoted to the worship of Mithras.

In *When Aseneth Met Joseph*, Ross Shepard Kraemer writes, "that Helios imagery is central to the tale of Aseneth is obvious from the outset of Joseph's actual appearance on the scene. . . ."[7] She also makes the point—just in passing, mind you—that Artemis was the moon goddess of those times.[8] All that remained for her to say is what we are saying now: by depicting Joseph/Jesus as Helios and Aseneth/Mary the Magdalene as Artemis, the manuscript in the British Library called *Joseph and Aseneth* reveals that for their earliest followers, the marriage of Jesus to Mary the Magdalene represented nothing less than the sacred union of the sun and the moon.

Helios and the Zodiac in Ancient Jewish "Synagogues"

If *Joseph and Aseneth* represents, in essence, a lost gospel in which Jesus is modeled after Helios and Mary the Magdalene is modeled after Artemis, why is there no physical evidence—for example, houses of worship—of the community for which this text would have been holy writ? Surprisingly, there is. At least six houses of worship excavated so far in the land of Israel have yielded 3rd- to 6th-century mosaic zodiac floors: Hammath Tiberias, Beit Alpha, Isfiya, Sussiya, Na'aran, and Sepphoris. At the center of the zodiacs, we have various depictions of Helios, sometimes riding his chariot. Because some of these mosaics also have "Jewish" imagery, such as a menorah/candelabra, a ram's horn/Shofar, and temple paraphernalia, these houses of worship have been categorized as "synagogues." Since Jews are forbidden by the Torah to depict "graven images"—that is to say, human figures or pagan gods—scholars have argued that these images don't mean anything—they are purely decorative. According to these scholars, the zodiacs and Helios are an ancient case of keeping up with the Joneses—since the non-Jews had mosaics, zodiacs, and Helios, the Jews had to have them too. One scholar who disagrees with this interpretation is the foremost expert on synagogue mosaics in the Galilee, Professor Rachel Hachlili. In her seminal book on the subject, *Ancient Synagogues—Archaeology and Art: New Discoveries and Current Research*, she writes that the community that created the mosaic "was not interested merely in a purely decorative design for its floors. There must have been something unique about this particular design . . . [it] had more than a merely decorative function."[9]

Professor Ross Shepard Kraemer agrees with Professor Hachlili. When writing about *Joseph and Aseneth*, Kraemer notes the similarities between, for example, the depiction of Joseph in the text and the depiction of Helios in the Galilean mosaics. She argues that these images could not be merely decorative. They must have religious significance.[10]

We think Kraemer is on to something very important. Maybe—just maybe—these Galilean buildings are not synagogues. Maybe they are something different. Perhaps they are the synagogues—or, more properly, churches—for Christians for whom *Joseph and Aseneth* was a sacred text.[11] After all, "Christian art was about conveying a message, often one that a casual viewer would not understand."[12] Perhaps here, in these mosaics, we have another secret code to be deciphered. And maybe, if we succeed in deciphering the mosaics, we will find the houses of worship of those followers of Jesus for whom Jesus' marriage, not his crucifixion, was the key event in his life.

Let's first consider Beit Alpha, which, as Kraemer notes, is the best-preserved of the mosaics. Beit Alpha is located in the northeast sector of Israel, in the Beit She'an Valley not far from the base of Mount Gilboa. Near the entranceway to this building there are two inscriptions. One in Aramaic says that the building was built during the reign of the Emperor Justinian (527 to 565 C.E.) with funds provided by local people. The other, in Greek, mentions two craftsmen by name.

The main floor of the sanctuary is divided into three areas of mosaics. Starting at the north end of the building, the entranceway, and moving south, we first encounter a Biblical scene: the near-sacrifice of Isaac by Abraham. It shows Abraham with a knife; he is about to kill Isaac on the pyre, but is prevented by the hand of an angel. There is a ram caught in a thicket. The figures are labeled in Hebrew.

As we move farther into the building, the next panel of mosaics that we encounter is the largest one. Surprisingly, it features Helios surrounded by the twelve figures of the zodiac, every one of them named in Hebrew. At each of the four corners of the panel is one of the four seasons. They are depicted as women with wings.

Finally, at the south end of the room, there is a mosaic of the Holy Ark of the Covenant, the *aron ha-brith* which once housed the Ten Commandments. The Ark is surrounded by menorahs (temple candelabras), birds, two lions, and various vessels used in temple worship. These include a *shofar* (ram's horn), a *lulav* (palm branch), *etrog* (a large citrus similar to a lemon), and an incense shovel. The building is aligned southwest, in the general direction of Jerusalem.

Because of the presence of Jewish images such as the sacrifice of Isaac and the Ark of the Covenant, many scholars have dubbed the building a "synagogue." They have ignored the many pagan images: Helios, the four seasons, the zodiac, and so on. In fact, by circular argument, Beit Alpha is called a synagogue because it is similar to the mosaic found in Tiberias, which in turn is called a synagogue because it reminds one of Beit Alpha.

Let's think outside the box for a moment and revisit the symbolism in the Beit Alpha mosaic.

Any investigation of the mosaic has to start with the impressive central panel. If we stand in front of this huge mosaic and look at the center circle, what we see is Helios. Remarkably, as Kraemer notes, it's exactly like the description of Joseph/Jesus depicted in *Joseph and Aseneth*. Helios is riding a chariot pulled by four white horses, two on either side. There are rays of light streaming out from above his head. There are some stars but not many—most are below Helios indicating that it is now dawn and Helios is ascending. Even the crescent-shaped moon appears to be waning, as it is positioned lower than Helios' head. Outside the inner circle are the twelve figures of the zodiac. Pisces is represented by two fish, for instance, and in Gemini the twins look conjoined. Faces are clearly depicted along with the conventional animals and insects that comprise the zodiac figures.

Why is Helios, a Sun god, here? A pagan divinity in what is ostensibly a Jewish synagogue? Why the zodiac? The Torah explicitly forbids the study of astrology: "and when you look up to the sky and behold the sun and the moon and the stars, the whole heavenly host, you must not be lured into bowing down to them or serving them . . ." (Deuteronomy 4:19). Some kind of astrology is, indeed, developed within mystical Judaism, but its study is regarded with suspicion and it certainly does not involve physical representations of pagan deities. So, why were these zodiacal images chosen to adorn what is supposed to be a Jewish place of prayer, where graven images are strictly forbidden? Here, at Beit Alpha, we have a strange mixture of Jewish and non-Jewish art. Why? And why do Helios and the zodiac dwarf in size the depictions from the Bible, even God's temple in Jerusalem?

If this is indeed a synagogue, this is truly a shocking scene.

As stated above, Beit Alpha is not the only place in which Helios and the zodiac are to be found. There's a similar mosaic in a building at Hammat Tiberias, located on the western shore of the Sea of Galilee, about two miles south of the city of Tiberias, not far from Magdala. As with Beit Alpha, Hammat Tiberias also has a representation of the Ark/temple, complete with two menorahs (candelabras), two rams' horns, and various plants. But here again we see a depiction of Helios riding across the sky, complete with a halo of light and rays streaming from his face. As we examine the mosaic, Helios is looking out toward his right. His right hand is raised, and in his left hand he holds the earth and a whip. He appears to be riding a chariot but the details here have been obliterated. Nine of the original twelve zodiac figures are distinguishable and, shockingly, they include nude depictions of youths. Oddly, Libra (the Scales) appears to be drawn as an uncircumcised male. In addition, some of the Hebrew inscriptions appear to have been purposely misspelled.

All this adds up to a monumental mystery. Again, why the figure of Helios and the zodiac in what is supposed to be a synagogue? Why the spelling errors—didn't someone have sufficient knowledge of Hebrew to instruct the mosaic-maker in proper spelling? And why, of all things, an uncircumcised naked male in what's supposed to be a Jewish house of worship?[13]

Another representation of the sun and the zodiac within what appears to be a 5th- or 6th-century synagogue can be found at ancient Sepphoris—"the orna-ment of the Galilee," in Josephus' apt description. This impressive Hellenistic city is just a few miles north of Nazareth. Jesus could have seen this city from any hill next to Nazareth. Perhaps he and his father, a contractor, were engaged in building projects in this magnificent Roman center that is now gradually being excavated.

One building at Sepphoris is relevant to our investigations. It, too, is said to be a synagogue. And, as you might have guessed by now, it includes various mosaic depictions, some of which represent Biblical scenes. One mosaic illus-trates the near-sacrifice of Isaac. Another badly damaged one has been described by scholars as a depiction of the visit of angels to Sarah, Abraham's wife. There are also menorahs, shofars, and other items used in temple sacrifice. In addition, there is a panel with the name "Aaron" beside it, probably referring to Moses' brother, the priest.

The main mosaic in this building, however, is the sun-and-zodiac panel. Human figures are present in each of the panels, and the month that corresponds to the zodiac name is depicted. Thus for Scorpio, not only is there a scorpion but also a man, the Hebrew name for Scorpio ('akrav) and the Hebrew name of the month (Cheshvan). Portions of the zodiac, however, are no longer observable. In the center of the zodiac there is—of course—the Sun god. Here there is no human figure for Helios. Rather, he is represented simply as the sun, accompa-nied by a moon and a star.

As we've noted, identification of these sites as "synagogues" results from contradictory and circular reasoning. Since there are Jewish religious symbols here, scholars reason, these must be synagogues. But we can just as easily say that since there are pagan images here, these must be pagan places of worship. In fact, on the simplest level, the latter statement makes more sense because paganism does not preclude the use of Jewish symbols, but Judaism absolutely forbids the use of pagan symbols.

So what are the possible explanations for these strange mosaics which broadly correspond to our text?

Let's look at the synagogue option again: one possibility is that these represent synagogues of highly assimilated Jews who, forgetting the Biblical injunctions to shun pagan practices, make the Sun god the central image within their houses of worship. That is, of course, possible, but it would represent a very high degree of assimilation and, essentially, the abandonment of basic Torah prohibitions. If the people worshipping in these synagogues are Jewish, they don't practice any Judaism that is attested to in any text.

The other option is that these are pagan houses of worship, but by the time some of these were built—the 6th century—Christianity had already been firmly ensconced for hundreds of years. This kind of paganism would simply not have been tolerated. Also, we have no record of a Judaized paganism flourishing in Israel from the 3rd to 6th centuries.

But perhaps there's another way to look at the Biblical scenes depicted in the mosaics. If we reconsider these scenes, we come to the same realization that we arrived at when decoding *Joseph and Aseneth*. Simply put, these images are consistent with Christian, not Jewish, iconography.

Let's look at the panel on Sarah and the angels. In the Book of Genesis (18:10), Sarah is visited by angels who tell her that she will give birth to Isaac. In Christian theology, this episode is a foreshadowing—a type—of the annunciation to Mary that she would give birth to Jesus.[14] As for the mosaic of the temple, this too can be understood in a Christian context. After all, Jesus predicted that the temple would be destroyed and that he would rebuild it in three days (John 2:19). Orthodox Christian theology has interpreted Jesus' reference to the temple as a reference to his own physical body and the reference to three days as a veiled prediction of his own resurrection. But it seems that the earliest followers of Jesus did not understand Jesus' prediction metaphorically. They understood it literally. And they waited for the Second Coming so as to see the rebuilding of the Temple of God.

Alternatively, some Christians began to think of the church and even its members as the new temple. The First Letter of Peter, for example, urges members to be "built into a spiritual house, to be a holy priesthood, to offer spiritual sacrifices acceptable to God through Jesus Christ" (1 Peter 2:5). Ephrem the Syrian composed a hymn comparing the church to the tabernacle Moses built in the wilderness, the forerunner and pattern on which the First and Second Temples were constructed. The hymn goes as follows:

> Moses built a tabernacle
> In the desert for the Godhead;
> Because He dwelt not in their hearts,
> He shall dwell in the Holy of Holies.
> For the Gentiles the Church was built,
> A gathering for prayers.[15]

We suggest that Kraemer was on to something when she linked the figure of Helios in *Joseph and Aseneth*—it's the cover art of her book—with the so-called synagogues in northern Israel. In Kraemer's words, "one might wonder whether it is precisely the association of Christ with Helios and of Joseph with Christ that could ground the representation of Joseph as Helios." By not pursuing the insight, she remained just one step away from the explicit identification of Helios with Joseph and the latter with Jesus in *Joseph and Aseneth*.[16]

Unlike Kraemer, archaeologists were thrown off by the so-called Jewish symbols in the mosaic and mislabeled the buildings as synagogues. What they forgot is that many early Christians were Jews, and that early Christianity appropriated Jewish symbols such as the temple for its own agenda. In fact, all the Biblical depictions in the mosaics are Old Testament scenes that were used to serve a Jesus narrative at the beginning of the Christian movement.

In light of all this, the depiction of the near-sacrifice of Isaac can now be seen as a Christian representation of Jesus in the role of the sacrificial offering. He is the ram in the thicket, offered to God as a sacrifice for human sin: that is, as "the lamb of God."

If you think that looking at the sacrifice of Isaac as a metaphor for the crucifixion of Jesus is the product of an imagination gone wild, think again. There are many examples that establish Isaac as a "type" for Jesus in early Christianity.[17] From this perspective, both were sons of a righteous father, and both were descendants of Abraham. Both were offered in sacrifice in the same geographic area (i.e., in the Holy Land). And both carried the material on which they were to be offered to God—wood in Isaac's case, and a wooden cross in the case of Jesus—to the place of the intended sacrifice. Moreover, Isaac's ordeal lasted three days before he was restored whole to his father and the Gospels report that Jesus rose from the dead after three days, before he was restored to *his* father. Scholars all agree that early Christians saw in the story of Isaac a foreshadowing of the sacrifice that Jesus willingly made on behalf of all humanity.

Most recently, the Vatican announced the use of laser technology to reveal a previously unseen painting in the Christian catacombs in Rome. One of the images is considered to be the earliest image of St. Paul ever found. Right next to it, restorers discovered a panel depicting the sacrifice of Isaac.[18]

Seen in this light, the mosaics discovered at Sepphoris depict the annunciation[19] (Sarah/angel), the crucifixion (Abraham/Isaac), the resurrection (the "reborn" sun), and the future temple of God—to be rebuilt after the Second Coming. In other words, the so-called Helios synagogues in Israel seem to be Christian places of worship. We might call them "Christian synagogues," or Judeo-Christian synagogues. They are mosaic parallels to our *Joseph and Aseneth* manuscript.

We are not saying that we know for sure that the Gospel that became *Joseph and Aseneth* was read in these houses of worship. What we are saying is that the manuscript and the mosaics belong to the same cultural and religious milieu, and that they reflect similar theologies. The fact is that the depictions of Helios in these buildings are exactly like the depiction of Helios in *Joseph and Aseneth*. As in our manuscript, these mosaics feature Jesus as the central figure, imaged as the Sun god. It seems, therefore, that the people who worshipped in these buildings belonged to some kind of early Christian sect, such as the one for whom *Joseph and Aseneth* was a sacred text. The mosaic and the text use almost the same iconography. This is actually the *only* explanation that makes sense of pagan symbols, such as Helios and the zodiac, being intermingled with traditional Jewish icons.

The Secrets of the Mosaics

What all this means is that *Joseph and Aseneth* has led us to a community of early Jesus followers that had been lost to history. This insight, in turn, has made us realize that the houses of worship of this community have already been discovered. But now that we know who created the Galilee's mosaic floors, what secrets are these mosaics willing to share with us?

It's in the iconography—explicit and implicit—that the key to the secret code embedded in the mosaics can be found. The ultimate clues are the spelling errors or, more precisely, the incorrect renderings of Hebrew letters that occur in the Hammat Tiberias zodiac in the word *fish*.

Before the cross became the symbol of Christianity, the sign of the fish served that purpose. In the singular, the Hebrew word for fish is *dag*. In the plural, it is *dagim*. It's the plural that appears in the zodiac mosaic at Hammat Tiberias—but with a twist. And this is significant. The letter "g" in *dagim* is the Hebrew letter *gimel*. In the Hammat Tiberias mosaic, the letter gimel in the word *dagim* is rendered as its mirror image.

In other words, at Hammat Tiberias, in the one image of the mosaic that can be explicitly linked to Christianity, we are invited to flip the entire zodiac, so to speak. We are invited to look for a deeper meaning than the surface meaning. Simply put, you can look at the fish in the mosaic and think they are Jewish, written incorrectly by a person who does not know how to make a *gimel*, as the majority of scholars have so far concluded—or you can focus on the only symbol of Christianity on the mosaic floor and flip the imagery as it invites you to: you can extract the Helios out of Judaism and place it in the Christian context where it belongs.

But even if one doesn't accept the use of Helios and the encoded fish in Hammat Tiberias as early Christian, there is no argument about the mosaic at Megiddo (the place the New Testament calls Armageddon). The mosaic here was found in the earliest confirmed church ever excavated in Israel. In this context, we have a 3rd-century inscription that explicitly refers to Jesus as a god. At its center, the mosaic has two fish that are virtually identical to the ones in Hammat Tiberias. Both, for example, are positioned head to tail.[20] In the catacombs in Rome, the earliest Christian symbol is a *single* fish identified with *ICHTHYS*, which means *fish* in Greek. The letters are presumed to be an acronym for "Jesus Christ, the Son of God, Savior." But in Israel the symbol in all the zodiacs that have survived, and in the church at Megiddo, are *two* fish, not one. In Margaret Starbird's words, "this discovery [Megiddo church mosaic] confirms that early Christians honored the zodiac symbol for Pisces long before they chose to identify themselves with the cross . . . I have long asserted that Mary Magdalene represented that 'other fish'."[21]

The Artemis tradition supports Starbird's conclusion. As is well known, Jesus is associated with fishing. In one instance, he tells his disciples, who have failed to catch any fish, where to cast their nets (John 21:6). In another instance, he finds a coin in a fish's mouth (Matthew 17:27). He famously feeds a multitude with two fish (Matthew 14:16–19). Then, when he recruits two of his disciples, he tells them that he will make them "fishers of men" (Matthew 4:19), meaning that they should put down their nets, follow him, and cast a wider net, one aimed at recruiting people to their movement. It shouldn't surprise us, therefore, that Artemis was a huntress of fish and had the title Diktynna—"Artemis of the nets."[22] So it seems that the two fish that fed the five thousand were Jesus and Mary the Magdalene, and that the two fish at Megiddo commemorated that miracle for their followers.

Lest anyone think we are seeing Jesus and Mary the Magdalene where there are only fish, consider this: in the ruins of the monastery of "Lady Mary" (that is, Mary the "Mara" at Tel Istaba, which was first excavated in the autumn of 1930 near Beit She'an in the lower Galilee), archaeologists discovered a calendar mosaic in the shape of the Galilean zodiacs with which we have become familiar. The disc does not have zodiacal signs but, rather, twelve males representing the various months and Jesus' twelve disciples.

The Tel Istaba mosaic is off the beaten track. The site is behind a shopping plaza in a locked and fenced-off area. There is not a single sign indicating the identity of the place. Even the people working in the shopping plaza are not aware of the existence of Tel Istaba behind their parking lot. In fact, for the sake of "preservation," the mosaic has been literally covered up.

It is very hard to track down any information whatsoever on Tel Istaba. After much digging we learned that a group from the University of Pennsylvania, led by archaeologist Gerald Milne Fitzgerald, excavated the place in 1930. He published his findings in 1939,[23] and there have hardly been any articles on the site since then.[24] At the time, the area was part of British-mandate Palestine. To protect Tel Istaba, the British built a protective wall with a corrugated tin roof on top of it. The roof has since disappeared, and rain is damaging the ancient monastery. In 2013, the Israel Antiquities Authority (IAA) undertook some minimal preservation work and temporarily re-exposed the mosaic. We immediately drove to the location.

Though the roof has fallen off, the metal structure is still standing, making the overall effect somewhat surreal. The mosaic is really quite big and impressive. Archaeologist Gaby Mazor, until recently the director of the Beit She'an excavations, told us that Tel Istaba sits just outside of the ancient city of Beit She'an. The area boasts three archaeological sites, dating to the 6th century: the monastery that houses the mosaic, another monastery, and a Samaritan synagogue. The Samaritan synagogue also had a disc mosaic in it, but no human figures, no zodiac, and certainly no gods and goddesses. It did, however, have some images of the Jerusalem Temple. Because Israeli archaeologists believe that temple images can only be found in Jewish contexts, the Samaritan synagogue mosaic has been removed and is now part of the Israel Museum collection. Take note: mosaics that fit the accepted wisdom are put on display, while those that don't are covered up with earth and left to the elements.

The Samaritan synagogue is totally inaccessible now, as is the second monastery. One of the mysteries of nearby Beit She'an (a.k.a. Scythopolis) is that, unlike other cities in the Decapolis (the ten Gentile cities leagued together in the land of Israel and modern-day Jordan), no churches or cathedrals were found in the city itself. All the churches that have been found are part of monasteries at the edges of the city. Kiya Maria (the monastery of "our lady" at Tel Istaba) is only a few meters from the Beit She'an city wall. Dr. Mazor also told us that there was a tower near the Tel, which formed part of the city wall. Some scholars speculate that the monastery was built there because a monk named Elias, named in the mosaic inscriptions, had practiced solitude in the tower.[25]

Put simply, at Tel Istaba we have a monastery linked to a "tower" and a "lady," in an undisputed Christian context. As in the other Galilean mosaics, at the center of the Tel Istaba mosaic you have the image of a Sun god. All around, there are twelve men depicting the months of the year. Since the context is Christian, here Helios undoubtedly represents Jesus and the twelve men are his first disciples. A similar image, with Jesus at its center and the apostles in a circle around him, appears on a mosaic in an Arian baptistry of the 5th or 6th century from Ravenna, Italy.[26] But there is something different in the Tel Istaba mosaic. Something that differentiates it from all other Christian art—next to the god there is a goddess.

Dr. Mazor, reflecting the prevailing view of Israeli archaeologists, has no opinion on the god and goddess at the center of the Tel Istaba mosaic, except to say that the calendar was decorative. According to Mazor, the reason that nearly identical images appear in a church and in the so-called synagogues is because both sites were drawing on Hellenistic culture.[27] Again, they are just decorative.

They don't mean anything. People put them in their houses of worship to express their Hellenistic culture and nothing more. But this idea makes no sense whatsoever. The fact is that if people go to great expense and effort to put images in their places of worship, these must mean something to them. Also, one of the Ten Commandments is: "you shall not make for yourselves idols, nor shall you set up for yourselves an image or a sacred pillar, nor shall you place a figured stone in your land to bow down to it; for I am the Lord your God" (Leviticus 26:1). This is hardly an endorsement of pagan gods in your houses of worship. In other words, Jews would never put such a mosaic in their synagogue for merely decorative reasons, and Christians would not draw on the same images for no reason at all. So who are the figures at the center of the calendar? If the male is Jesus depicted as Helios, who is the woman?

The monastery is called *Our Lady Mary*. From the inscriptions, it's clear that the name is not referring to Jesus' mother. Rather, a monk named Elias dedicates the inscription to "the lady Mary" who, he says, "founded this church."[28] The excavator of Tel Istaba, G. M. Fitzgerald, interpreted "founded" as "paid for." Meaning, according to the original excavators, the monastery is named after a 6th-century lady who paid for the construction of the church. But the inscription says "founded," not "paid for." More than this, the monk Elias says that "the lady" is buried with her son "Maximus," which means, the "greatest," under a stone with a wreath and a cross on it.[29] The Pennsylvania University team found such a grave and removed two skulls from it.[30] Curiously, although there is a cemetery outside the monastery, the lady and her descendants were buried in the church itself. More than this, Stephanie Hagan notes, "The location of a burial near the altar is highly unusual for a Byzantine church: interments were typically only allowed in the nave or the narthex, away from the sanctuary."[31] In other words, these people were interred in an unusual place. Not only this, but the burials seem to have been very controversial because Elias curses anyone who opposes our lady or her descendants being buried in the church.[32] Clearly, this has nothing to do with a rich lady who paid for the mosaics. It has everything to do with a controversial foundress of a movement.

One way to read the inscription on the Tel Istaba mosaic is that the builders of the church and monastery transferred Mary the Magdalene's bones from her original resting place and—over the objections of her opponents—buried them in the monastery. This would mean that Mary the Magdalene and some of Jesus' descendants were buried in this early Christian site. But whatever the identity of the Mary who was buried in the church, the fact is that there is a woman at the center of the mosaic, next to Jesus.[33] Clearly, she is none other than Mary the Magdalene depicted as the Moon goddess, the Bride of God. Put simply, this is the only mosaic that is clearly in a Christian context and in a house of worship that depicts Jesus with a female partner. It is a perfect depiction in stone of the theology of *Joseph and Aseneth*. If we're right, this is the only depiction—anywhere—of Jesus and Mary the Magdalene as a divine couple.

Why the curses and the code? Why did the builders of the monastery have to keep the "holy couple" a secret? The answer is simple: as Orthodox Christianity won the day, it forced congregations that espoused a "heretical" Christian theology to go underground. Otherwise, the price exacted was heavy indeed. Consider the case of Hypatia of Alexandria. She was born around 355 C.E., she was the teacher of at least two bishops of the Christian church, and she was a confidante of the Christian prefect of Alexandria. She was renowned in her world as a teacher and philosopher. She was also a Gnostic. For her beliefs, she was murdered by the order of Cyril, the patriarch of the Alexandrian Church, but not before she was stripped, beaten, dragged through the streets of the city, and finally burned. According to tradition, a lot of this took place in the local church.[34] So if you didn't want to end up like Hypatia, you kept your traditions encoded or oral. You did not commit them to writing. As Kathleen McGowan puts it, much of Mary the Magdalene's story has been passed on ". . . as oral traditions and have been preserved in highly protected environments by those who have feared repercussions . . . the ancient followers of Mary Magdalene, known as the Cathars . . . were hunted down by the medieval church, brutally tortured and executed in the most horrific ways. Over a million people were massacred in the south of France for their 'heretical' belief in the role of Mary Magdalene as the wife of Jesus and subsequently as the true spiritual founder of Christianity in the Western world."[35]

Given all this, if you wanted to commit your theology to writing, under the circumstances, you had to know how to hide it in plain sight. Those Jesus followers who had a different story to tell learned to use pagan and Jewish imagery to tell their version of the Christian narrative. They had to learn to keep secrets, even while preserving their traditions. They had to learn to write books like *Joseph and Aseneth* and to pray in churches that looked like synagogues.

Interestingly, it seems that Jesus also had to speak in code about Mary the Magdalene in his own lifetime, and that an echo of this is preserved in the Gospels themselves. At one point, the scribes and Pharisees approach Jesus, asking for a "sign." Jesus then makes reference to the "Sign of Jonah." He says to his audience that someone greater than Jonah is present, referring to himself. The reference to the Sign of Jonah is, more or less, common knowledge, but what follows is typically ignored. Immediately, in the same breath, so to speak, Jesus makes another statement: "the Queen of the South will rise up at the judgment with this generation and condemn it, because she came from the ends of the earth to listen to the wisdom of Solomon, and see, something greater than Solomon is here!" (Matthew 12:38–42). Since the Queen of the South is referred to in conjunction with King Solomon, she's identified as the African Queen of Sheba. In other words, Jesus himself is using typology. He is speaking in coded language referring to himself as greater than Solomon. But if that's the case, who is the Queen of the South? Who is Jesus' Sheba?

Building upon the portrait of the Queen of Sheba who visited Solomon (1 Kings 10:1–10), we can surmise that Jesus' Sheba is also a foreigner. According to the 1st-century Jewish historian Josephus, the Queen of Sheba is powerful and independently wealthy.[36] She's an intellectual—she quizzes, challenges, and tests Solomon with "hard questions," and she blesses him (1 Kings 10:9). The Bible notes that "King Solomon gave to the queen of Sheba every desire that she expressed" (1 Kings 10:13). Later legends associate the Queen of Sheba with Solomon's lover in the Song of Songs, and an Ethiopian tradition explicitly contends that they engaged in sexual relations and had a child together.

We suggest that Jesus' Sheba is none other than Mary the Magdalene. The portrait fits: Mary the Magdalene is a wealthy woman, non-Jewish, a person with a mind of her own, and the one who is closest to Jesus. By referring to himself as greater than Solomon, Jesus is also saying that his consort is greater than Sheba. By speaking in code, he is saying to his audience: "you don't know who we are. You don't see us for what we represent. And my female counterpart will judge you."

Finally, lest anyone conclude that we are seeing secrets where none exist, consider this: the only so-called "synagogue" in which the zodiac is referenced, but not depicted, is in Ein Gedi, on the shores of the Dead Sea, close to where the Dead Sea Scrolls were discovered. It is here where the proto-Christian Essenes used to live. At this location, the mosaic does not depict the zodiac but references it in a long text. Right under the inscription there is an ancient curse, a Judeo-Aramaic inscription warning inhabitants against "revealing the town's secret."[37] If these were ordinary synagogues, there would be no secret to keep. But there is a secret, and we've deciphered it.

11

THE GREATEST WEDDING
OF ALL TIME

N ow that we have analyzed both the Jesus and Mary the Magdalene figures in our manuscript, we have to deal with the fact that, according to the text, they got married. By this point in our narrative, the idea of Jesus being married should no longer seem far-fetched. As stated, for a Jew then, as now, fulfilling the first Biblical commandment—"be fruitful and multiply" (Genesis 1:28)—was seen as a righteous obligation, not a flight of fancy. Jesus must have taken this Biblical commandment at least as seriously as do all other Torah-observant Jews.

Let's put it differently. As previously noted, an unmarried Jesus would have been absolutely scandalous to his contemporaries. A celibate Jesus—not a married one—is what people of his era would have found shocking. His unmarried status—if it were true—would have invited considerable comment and nasty gossip. An unmarried son? Now that's something that would have called for an explanation. Was he being disobedient to the expressed will of God? Was he feeble-minded? Did he belong to some strange ascetic cult? Was he, perhaps, physically incapacitated in some way? Or was he not so inclined? What explanation would fit?

In the mid-second decade of our era, roughly 15 C.E., Jesus would have been approximately twenty years old, just the right age for marriage. At the time, males married between the ages of fifteen and twenty; females even younger. Jesus' mother, Mary, for instance, would have been a young teenager when she married Joseph. A 2nd-century Christian document, *The Infancy Gospel of James*, says Mary was as old as sixteen but could have easily been fourteen or fifteen. Yes, Mary the mother of Jesus was a young teenager, not the mature twenty-something so often found in later Christian representations of the Madonna and child.

The year 15 C.E., therefore, is an approximate date that makes sense for Jesus' wedding. Is there any echo of this status in the canonical Gospels? In fact, besides the wedding at Cana and Mary the Magdalene's desire to anoint Jesus' naked corpse, Jesus' marriage is hinted to at least two more times in the Gospels. Matthew 22:1–14 contains the "Parable of the Wedding Feast." The story imagines what would happen if a king were to throw a wedding feast for his son. According to the parable, some invitees refuse to attend the wedding, offering excuses, while others make light of the invitation and return to work. The king is obviously a surrogate for God and the son for Jesus. The Gospel— that is, the "Good News"—is that God's son is getting married. The message to the faithful is: don't refuse to come to the greatest wedding of all time. Theologically speaking, for some of Jesus' earliest followers, it is this wedding that opens up the kingdom to everyone.

The Book of Revelation 19:6–9 also depicts a marriage. It is the marriage of the Lamb, that is, Jesus, to a bride described in Aseneth-type imagery as "clothed with fine linen, bright and pure." Here, the Book of Revelation specifically blesses those who are invited to the metaphysical party, the marriage feast.

A Challenging New Image of Jesus: Jesus the Family Man

The *Joseph and Aseneth* manuscript is forcing us to reassess the marriage-related passages in the Gospels. More than this, it is obliging us to rethink what we know about the historical Jesus and the historical Mary the Magdalene. For example, Christians today typically think of Jesus as asexual. According to this view, he wasn't married, didn't have children, and did not enjoy family time with his relatives. He wasn't like us, with sexual feelings and passions. He wasn't beset by all the conflicting emotions that being part of an extended family entails—happiness, sorrows, hurts, hopes, dreams, successes and failures. Jesus isn't depicted as grieving over the loss of close relatives, nor is he up all night, anxious over a child with an unexplained fever or pain. He is not portrayed as sharing in the successes of friends or commiserating with those who have suffered tragedy in their lives. While he is a teacher, a healer, and a debater, we don't see Jesus caught in a web of social and familial relationships—Jesus as husband, father, uncle, brother, or son-in-law does not exist. In fact, in Matthew 12:48, when some of his followers say that his mother and brothers have come to speak to him, Jesus explicitly rejects his biological family. He rudely dismisses them, saying to his followers: "'Who is my mother and who are my brothers?' And pointing to his disciples, he said, 'Here are my mother and my brothers! For whoever does the will of my Father in heaven is my brother and sister and mother'."

As a result of the victory of Pauline Christianity over all the other forms that once existed, the conventional picture is that Jesus is God incarnate, a being far removed from our way of existing in the world, curiously detached from what ordinary people experience and feel. As Meyer puts it, "This prominent Christian focus on Jesus as a dying and rising savior . . . seems to minimize or even ignore the life of the historical Jesus . . . in whose name and memory Christianity was founded."[1]

For Christians—and even non-Christians accustomed to thinking in theological terms—facts associated with the historical Jesus seem blasphemous. He was—wasn't he?—the son of God, God in human form, a divinity, the savior of all humanity, the redeemer, the second person of the Trinity. To think of such a unique being as experiencing sexual urges—let alone satisfying them—seems outrageous.

But it wasn't outrageous to all, most, or even many early Christians. Once deciphered, *Joseph and Aseneth* provides solid, textual evidence that Jesus had an active sexual life, was a family man—a father, a brother, an uncle, and a real husband. And this outraged no one.

Our exploration now takes an interesting turn, right into the very heart of what Jesus' marriage to Mary the Magdalene signified for his earliest followers.

Many Unanswered Questions
Clearly, if they did marry, Jesus' marriage to Mary the Magdalene would have been no ordinary wedding. It raises many interesting questions. First, what would this marriage have meant to Jesus? Second, why Mary the Magdalene?

Moreover, what did Jesus' marriage mean to his original followers? What authority would "Mrs. Jesus" have had among Jesus' early followers? And if he was married, did Jesus' marriage threaten anybody, as the *Joseph and Aseneth* text implies? Although these questions seem unanswerable, reading our manuscript in light of the known history provides all the answers.

What Do We Really Know of Jesus' Life?

A wedding around 15 C.E. would help fill in some of the missing gaps in Jesus' life. But before we get to the wedding, let's start at the beginning. As already noted in passing, his name wasn't *Jesus*. Nobody ever called him that. He wouldn't have turned around in a crowd if anyone had shouted out, "Jesus, Jesus." *Jesus* is an Anglicized rendition of the Greek version of his Hebrew name. His name, in Hebrew, was *Yeshua*, which can be translated into English as *Joshua* or *Jesus*. According to the Gospel of Matthew, Yeshua/Jesus was born just before the death of Herod the Great in the year 4 B.C.E.—say 6 or 5 B.C.E. But that birth date is uncertain, for the Gospel of Luke dates it some ten years later, around 6 C.E. when a historically verifiable tax census took place. The tax census seems to match the story in the Gospels concerning a census that causes Joseph and a pregnant Mary to leave Nazareth and end up in a Bethlehem manger. According to the Gospels, Jesus had four brothers. The "brothers" are mentioned in the Gospels of Matthew (13:55) and Mark (6:3). They were younger, older, or not full brothers at all.

In Luke 2:21 we are told that Jesus, following the requirements of Torah, was circumcised on the eighth day after his birth. We are also told that his parents underwent the Jewish ceremony—still practiced today—for the Redemption of the Firstborn.[2] According to this ceremony, in gratitude to God for not killing the firstborn males of Israel at the time of the Biblical Exodus, Jewish parents "redeem," or symbolically buy back, their firstborn male children for the price of a silver coin.[3] To this day, friends gather, food is served, and a silver coin is given to a descendant of a temple priest—usually a man named *Cohen* (priest), in a kind of exchange for the infant. The fact that Luke 2:21 tells us that Jesus' parents redeemed him from the temple priests tells us that Jesus was the firstborn male of Mary.

We also know from Luke that Jesus' family trekked annually from Nazareth up to Jerusalem to observe the festival of Passover (Luke 2:41–51). This represented a major commitment on the part of Mary and Joseph, Jesus' parents. In those days, this pilgrimage took at least two weeks and involved serious travel expenses and loss of income. In other words, from his circumcision to his redemption to the annual pilgrimage, the Gospels paint a picture of Jesus' family as Torah-observant Jews.[4] They were what we would call today an Orthodox Jewish family. But what about Jesus? What do we know about his youth?

As it turns out, one of the few incidents we hear of regarding his youth is an episode involving Jesus discussing Torah with temple teachers, when he was only twelve years old. As the story goes, during the Passover pilgrimage, Jesus lagged behind his family, spending time discussing fine points of Torah law with temple authorities (Luke 2:41–52). In other words, the only thing the Gospels choose to tell us about Jesus' youth is that he was precocious in Torah studies.

After that, silence reigns within the canonical Gospels until the late 20s C.E. when Jesus begins his mission. It's a rather thin resume. Think about it, isn't it amazing that from the time Jesus was eight days old—when he was circumcised—until he's in his early thirties, we know nothing about him except for one incident on the steps of the Holy Temple? Obviously, there is much to learn about this thirty-year period of silence.

If we know so little about Jesus, how could we possibly hope to learn anything about Mary the Magdalene? The canonical Gospels are, fortunately, not the only Christian source of information about Mary the Magdalene. We also have the so-called Gnostic Gospels. As we are beginning to see, these play an important role in helping to uncover the reality that Jesus and Mary the Magdalene were married. They also help explain what the wedding of Jesus and Mary the Magdalene meant to their loyal followers. On this point, we need to reiterate that the contents of the New Testament were decided upon in the 4th century C.E. This occurred, as we have noted, as the result of a letter circulated by Archbishop Athanasius of Alexandria, Egypt, to his churches and monasteries. In it, he outlined what was scripture and what was not. He had literally hundreds of existing texts from which to choose. In time, other bishops "agreed" with Athanasius' list, and this became the "New" Testament. This set of writings reflects the ideology of the winning party, the group within early Christianity favored by the Roman emperor Constantine. It is by no means an impartial set of writings and certainly not reflective of the range of early Christian positions.

Historically speaking, we must go outside the canonical Gospels to reconstruct
Jesus and Mary the Magdalene's life.

The Wedding

Dan Brown notwithstanding, if we base ourselves on *Joseph and Aseneth* and
Gnostic movements such as the Valentinians, Jesus and Mary the Magdalene
were married. In these texts, that's a fact.[5] In the canonical Gospels, the strongest
arguments for their marriage have to do with Mary's presence at the crucifixion
and at the burial. According to all the Gospels, Mary the Magdalene—along with
some women in Jesus' family—was present at the crucifixion. If she wasn't his
wife, why was she there? More than this, according to three of the four canonical
Gospels, after the crucifixion she goes to anoint (wash) his naked corpse to
prepare him for burial. As stated earlier, if she wasn't his wife, how could she
presume to touch his naked body? In the context of 1st-century Judaism, in the
absence of menfolk, only family could get close to the corpse.

So it seems that sometime, probably around 15 C.E., when Jesus would
have been twenty and Mary the Magdalene around eighteen, they must have
married. Likely, they got married in the Galilee where they were both living,
perhaps at Cana where the only wedding recorded in the Gospels takes place.
It must have been—like all weddings—a joyous occasion, no doubt attended
by everyone in the village. His mother would have been there. So, too, his four
brothers—Ya'akov (Jacob or James as we usually refer to him in English), Yosé
(or Joseph), Simon, and Judah—as well as his two sisters (Matthew 13:55). The
names of the sisters are not mentioned in the New Testament, but early Christian
tradition refers to them as Mary and Salome. Joseph, Jesus' father, probably
was not there: he seems to have died by the time of Jesus' marriage. In fact,
Joseph is not mentioned in any records after the pilgrimage to Jerusalem for
Passover when Jesus was only twelve. Were mother Mary's parents—Anna and
Joachim—in attendance? Maybe his cousin John the Baptizer came for the
celebration? If they were still alive in the year 15 C.E., maybe John's parents—
Elizabeth and Zechariah (Luke 1:40)—were also present.

And what of Mary the Magdalene? Were her parents there? Any siblings?
Other relatives?

Unfortunately, until now, we didn't know the answers to these intriguing
questions. They seem to have been purposely written out of the Gospels. But

Joseph and Aseneth tells us that Mary the Magdalene's parents were there and that the wedding was a big one. According to the text, Aseneth—a.k.a. Mary the Magdalene—prepared for her wedding carefully, donning her finest robe and golden boots. She adorned herself with a band around her waist, filled with precious gems. She wore golden bracelets around her wrists and an expensive necklace around her neck. She put a golden crown on her head and covered her face with a veil. She looked at herself in a basin of reflected water and saw that her face was radiant, like the sun, and that her eyes were like the morning star (18:5–10). She was now ready to meet Jesus, her groom.

According to our manuscript, after Joseph/Jesus entered her father's estate, Aseneth/Mary the Magdalene insists on washing his feet. As we have said, an echo of this incident is present in the Gospels. In Luke, the woman is anonymous. She appears with an alabaster jar; she weeps, kisses Jesus' feet, and washes them. She then dries his feet with her hair (Luke 7:37, 38).[6] This story is also related in John (11:2), where the woman is identified as "Mary of Bethany." In the Catholic tradition, at least from the 6th century, Mary of Bethany is identified with Mary the Magdalene.[7] Timothy Freke and Peter Gandy write, "In the Gospel of Luke, Mary wipes her hair on Jesus' feet. According to Jewish law, only a husband was allowed to see a woman's hair unbound and if a woman let down her hair in front of another man, this was a sign of impropriety and grounds for mandatory divorce. . . ."[8] Interestingly, in *Joseph and Aseneth*, Aseneth/Mary the Magdalene does not kiss Joseph's/Jesus' feet. On the contrary, it is he who kisses her right hand. She, in turn, kisses his head. As we saw earlier, in *Joseph and Aseneth*, Jesus refuses to let Mary the Magdalene cross an intimacy line before marriage. It seems that this version of the story is earlier. It is more consistent with 1st-century Jewish norms than are the canonical Gospels where the two share intimacies not appropriate for an unmarried couple. In the Gospels, therefore, the story seems to be a leftover from a real-life event that occurred right before their marriage. In fact, it seems that the only reason this story survived in the canonical texts is because it was so important. In *Joseph and Aseneth*, it is immediately after this foot-washing ritual that the main protagonists are ready to be married.

Though Jesus and Mary the Magdalene were now betrothed, the *Joseph and Aseneth* text explicitly tells us that they waited before engaging in sexual relations (21:1). In Judaism, then and now, marriage is a two-step process: first a betrothal, then a marriage. Today, the two ceremonies are performed practically at the same time. In the 1st century, however, there was a long time—sometimes years—between betrothal and marriage.

The *Joseph and Aseneth* manuscript goes out of its way to tell us that Mary the Magdalene did not have sexual relations with her husband after the betrothal and before the marriage. This is an all-important clue. What the text is telling us is that this wedding is taking place not in Egypt, as the surface story suggests, nor in Judaea as our reading would imply, but specifically in the Galilee. To understand why, one has to understand 1st- and 2nd-century Judaean marriage practices. According to Rivka Nir, the northern Galileans differed from the southern Judaeans with regard to their attitude toward sex in the period between betrothal and wedding: "there seems to be a regional division, with Judaea allowing such practice and Galilee forbidding any sexual contact until after the wedding."[9] In the Babylonian Talmud, Rabbi Yehudah states that from the "first, in Judaea, they would leave the bride and the groom alone for one hour before the chuppa [wedding ceremony], so that his heart may become crude with her. But in the Galilee they did not do so."[10] In other words, the wedding described in *Joseph and Aseneth* is a Galilean wedding, and the only wedding described in the Gospels takes place in the Galilee in a town called Cana, just outside of Nazareth.

But why would the text go out of its way to make this point? Is it simply to tell us that Jesus and Mary the Magdalene were not promiscuous like the Judaeans? Or is it because the issue of sex *after* betrothal but *before* the wedding ceremony was a touchy subject in the family? After all, the Gospel of Matthew tells us that Joseph was going to refuse to marry Mary, Jesus' mother, when he found out that she was pregnant *after* their betrothal and *before* their marriage (1:19). It took an act of divine intervention to get him to go through with the marriage. By insisting on the fact that Jesus and Mary the Magdalene did not have sex until marriage, is *Joseph and Aseneth* telling us that Jesus' relations with his wife were unlike his mother's relations with her husband?

According to the text, Jesus and Mary the Magdalene didn't have to wait long to consummate the marriage. The wedding took place the day after the betrothal. In the manuscript, "Pharaoh"—the ruler—is astonished at Aseneth's beauty and he blesses her. Restored to its original form, replacing Joseph with Jesus, the blessing reads: "Blessed are you by the Lord God of Jesus because he is the firstborn of God and you will be called the Daughter of God Most High and the bride of Jesus now and forever" (21:3). If our reconstruction is right, here we have the actual blessing conferred at Jesus' wedding on his bride. Put differently, as a result of our deciphered document we have not only textual proof of Jesus' marriage to Mary the Magdalene, but also a verbatim rendition of the blessing conferred on his bride.

The wedding ceremony commences. Pharaoh takes golden crowns and places them on the bride and groom. Even today in Eastern Orthodox Christian weddings, the officiant places crowns on the heads of those about to be married. Remarkably, in another historical echo of that long-ago wedding, the names of *Joseph and Aseneth* are invoked twice within the Orthodox Christian wedding liturgy.[11]

The wedding celebrations lasted a week. Only then did Joseph/Jesus have sexual relations with Aseneth/Mary the Magdalene.[12] They had, in time, two children.[13]

The detailed descriptions in *Joseph and Aseneth* give us unique insight into the marriage of Jesus and Mary the Magdalene. Obviously, for Jesus' followers, this wedding represented the union of the "Son of God" (6:3; 6:5; 13:9; 23:10) to the "Daughter of God Most High" (21:3). According to this text—ignored for millennia—it was a marriage made in heaven, a gala affair, and a weeklong celebration of rejoicing. Family members met and greeted each other, relatives caught up with each other's doings, and there would have been endless parties to attend throughout the village. Since the Gospel of John gives us the only description of a wedding attended by Jesus and his family, let's revisit the Wedding at Cana and see if it is consistent with the marriage described in *Joseph and Aseneth*.

In the first place, we should note that Cana is just a few miles northwest of Nazareth. Strangely, John doesn't tell us who's getting married. He leaves that all-important fact out. But he does tell us that when the wedding party runs short of wine, Jesus performs a miracle, changing water into wine. If it's not his wedding, why does he play the role of wine provider? If it's not his wedding, why aren't we told whose wedding it is? If it's not his wedding, why does his mother insist that it's Jesus' responsibility to supply wine to the guests?

In any respect, it must have been someone important for Jesus and his family to attend and for Jesus to supply the wine. Furthermore, notice the amount of wine Jesus generates: we know from archaeology that each of the six stone vessels that were involved in the water-into-wine miracle held some twenty or thirty gallons of liquid—that's 120 to 180 gallons of wine! Assuming that only (or primarily) males indulged—a good assumption, given women's roles at the time—and that (on average) each drinker had the equivalent of half a bottle of wine, there would have been over twenty-five hundred guests at this wedding. This is nothing less than a royal wedding, or the wedding of someone whose followers believed was the "Son of God."

What Did the Wedding of Jesus and Mary the Magdalene Signify to Early Christians?

Gnostic Christianity

What were the theological implications of Jesus' marriage to Mary the Magdalene? To understand the meaning of such a wedding for Jesus' followers, we have to turn to an alternate form of Christianity, namely Gnostic Christianity. *Gnosis* is the Greek word for "knowledge" or "insight." The Gnostics were those Christians who did not follow what came to be known as "orthodox" or "catholic" Christianity. While it is clear that the mainstream church did not pursue issues related to Jesus and marriage and downplayed Mary the Magdalene (by the 6th century she had become a reformed whore), for the Gnostics it was Jesus' marriage to Mary the Magdalene that made all the difference in the world. It was in fact, from their point of view, the basis for human salvation. This may strike some of us as strange, for this message contrasts sharply with the more familiar message of Paul who focused on "Christ's passion"—that is, on Jesus' suffering and death. Put differently, in the early phases of Christianity Jesus' followers had at least two brands of Christianity to choose from—Gnosticism and Paulism. For the first, Jesus' marriage and sex life were the central events of his ministry; for the second, it was Jesus' asceticism and suffering, his death and resurrection that were key.[14]

Paul was born in Anatolia in what is now Turkey. He's known as Paul of Tarsus, a city in south-central Turkey some twelve miles inland from the Mediterranean Sea. He was born Saul. He was Jewish. His family may have originated in the Galilee.[15] According to the Book of Acts (18:3), the family business was tent-making. Since there was little recreational camping in those days, their main client must have been the Roman army. Paul's family suspiciously moved out of the Galilee to Tarsus right after the Jewish Revolt that took place around Jesus' birth and Herod the Great's death. Were they fleeing for their lives from Jewish revolutionaries who saw them as collaborators with Rome? Is that what forced the relocation? It would make sense, since Paul seems very confused about his Jewish identity, sometimes asserting it with pride and sometimes vehemently opposing his own traditions.

Paul was also a Roman citizen. This reinforces the idea that he was supplying tents to the Roman army. Roman citizenship would also not have endeared Paul and his family to the revolutionaries. This is important because it shows that Paul came from what we would call today an assimilated Jewish family. They were Hellenized, and they probably regarded Jewish revolutionary groups as fanatics. We know from the Book of Acts that Paul was initially in the employ of the temple priesthood, which itself was appointed by the Roman authorities. In other words, although he grew up in Tarsus, at some point he moved to Jerusalem and worked as an enforcer of Roman power. By his own admission, he regarded the early followers of Jesus, the people who actually knew Jesus, as troublemakers. He persecuted them and was present when at least one of Jesus' followers was stoned to death.[16] While he had never met the historical Jesus, at some point, this self-described enforcer had a vision of the resurrected Christ and became a follower, rather than an enemy of Jesus. Trouble was that his version of Jesus' teaching did not jibe with that of Jesus' original followers, the ones who knew him best and who had followed him throughout his mission. It seems that some wanted to kill Paul—likely Torah-observant members among Jesus' first followers[17]—and he needed Roman protection to save his life.

Unperturbed, Paul continued to spread his version of Christianity with great zeal and success. Around 64 C.E. he disappears from history. Some argue that he was caught up in anti-Christian persecutions that followed the great fire of Rome that, according to the Roman historian Tacitus, the Emperor Nero blamed on the followers of Jesus.[18] Others argue that he had all along been a Roman spy and was now taken in out of the cold.[19] Either way, Paul disappears, leaving behind Pauline groups. These differed from Jesus' first followers in terms of origins, teachings, and practices.[20] Two years later, Judaea revolts against Roman rule and four years after that, Judaea, Jerusalem, and the House of God (the Temple of Jerusalem) all go up in flames, torched by the future Roman emperors Vespasian and Titus. With the destruction of the Jerusalem Church, the headquarters of the movement that grew around Jesus, Pauline Christianity moves to the fore. Also, with the destruction of Judaean independence and the diminishment of Jewish power, non-Jewish Christianity takes over from the original movement. In this way, Pauline theology eclipses whatever the original followers of Jesus actually believed.[21]

As a result of this Pauline victory, we tend to regard Pauline groups as historical and movements such as the Gnostics as marginal and unhistorical.[22] The reality is probably the exact opposite. After all, Gnosticism seems to have grown out of the original Jewish mystics who followed Jesus, and Christian orthodoxy seems to have grown out of the Gentile groups that originated with Paul. The first group more or less preserved historical teachings. The second group—including its founder Paul—had no knowledge of the historical Jesus and based themselves on ideas that were supposedly revealed mystically to Paul after Jesus' crucifixion, teachings that seem at odds with what the Jesus of history taught and practiced.

Theologically, Paul taught that we should all participate in the suffering and death of Christ, the hope being that we, like Jesus, might be raised from the dead. Identification with and participation in Jesus' death—and, hopefully, in his resurrection—was virtually the only aspect of Jesus that Paul was interested in. He wasn't interested in his life, ministry, or teachings. He rarely quotes Jesus. The Gnostics, however, thought that Jesus' death had no significance. None at all. They focused on his life, vitality, sexuality, and, most significantly, the marriage through which they believed he linked heaven and earth. Whatever the truth, the fact is that the Gnostics attempted to theologize history while the Pauline Christians attempted to historicize theology. Put simply, for those who actually knew Jesus, the challenge was to find theological meaning in his life. For those who did not know Jesus, the challenge was to find historical justification for their theology. In other words, if you based your Christianity on post-crucifixion revelations, the challenge was to find historical justification for your ideas. But if you actually knew Jesus, if you broke bread with him and, say, his wife, you would have to find meaning in the fact that he ate like the rest of us and was married.

Gnostics kept themselves separate from the Pauline Christians, the—"Congregations of the Christ," as they came to be known. While for Paul's followers Jesus was a god, for the Gnostics he was a guide and a teacher sent from the one true God to enlighten humanity and to act as a catalyst for spiritual growth, maturity, and redemption. In the earliest "Dormition" traditions—those Gnostic traditions related to the death of the Virgin Mary—Jesus is identified as a Great Angel. The text puts special emphasis on "secret and often soteriological [i.e., salvation] knowledge, and [on] a common Gnostic creation myth."[23] Meaning, according to the Gnostics, Jesus wasn't just a teacher but a teacher of esoteric or hidden knowledge. Sometimes the Gnostics refer to Jesus as Son of God, but it is not always clear whether they meant a literal son, or an enlightened being whose task it was to turn all of us into children of God.

Despite the fact that the church tried to wipe out the Gnostics by marginalizing them, ridiculing them, killing them, and burning their books, we know a lot about Gnosticism today primarily as a result of the discovery of Gnostic texts and gospels in Nag Hammadi, Egypt in 1945. Gnostics living in the 4th century C.E. had buried these books so as to avoid the fires of orthodoxy.

Among the newly discovered texts, there are fifty-two intriguing new writings, including Gospels attributed to Thomas, Philip, Mary the Magdalene, and even Jesus himself. The manuscripts also include secret books ascribed to James and John. None of these writings provide a narrative structure similar to the canonical Gospels. The Gnostic Gospels are either sayings or long discourses—no story component. Basically, they cared about Jesus' teaching, not his ministry. In the 4th century, none of their writings were included in the New Testament, but it is simply a historical fact that they represented an important branch of early Christianity.

From a Gnostic point of view, since Jesus was the "Son of God" (i.e., the long-awaited Messiah or "anointed one"), every move he made was laden with cosmic significance. This isn't hard to understand. Some measure of this perspective is preserved, for example, in the Catholic Communion, which is based on the Last Supper. In other words, Catholics believe that when one takes Communion, the wine that one consumes is miraculously transformed into Jesus' blood and the wafer into his body. The point of the matter is that a meal shared by Jesus with his disciples takes on cosmic proportions because, well, he's Jesus. If sharing a meal can be significant, how much more so is sharing his bed?

Simply put, for Gnostic Christians, especially a group called Valentinians, after their 2nd-century leader Valentinus (c. 100–c. 160),[24] it wasn't the Last

Supper or the crucifixion that was the most significant episode in Jesus' life, but his marriage to Mary the Magdalene.

The Gnostic View of Redemption

As stated, to understand the meaning of the marriage of Jesus of Nazareth to Mary the Magdalene for their earliest followers, we have to mine Gnosticism in light of *Joseph and Aseneth*.

Gnostic cosmology is based on the idea that a fundamental rift exists within the universe. In the Gnostic writing *The Secret Book (or Apocryphon) of John*, Jesus discloses to his disciple, John, how creation actually took place.[25] In so doing, he provides John with a creation story that differs markedly from the Book of Genesis.

According to this view, the one true God—the Perfect One—is described as an invisible Spirit, greater than what we might think of as the God of the Hebrew Bible. The Perfect One is absolutely complete, illimitable, unfathomable, immeasurable, eternal, unutterable and unnamable, a being much greater than anything that is in existence, not a part of space or time, the source of all mercy and knowledge, the head of all worlds who sustains the universe through goodness. This creative being, the mother-father of all, is a perfect "dyad" of male-female. It is this dyad that created a series of primordial entities. The Gnostics called the first such entity "Barbelo," which is an image of the "perfect Spirit," the one who precedes all that there is.[26] Then, a series of further creations or "aeons"—male-female emanations from the Perfect One—took place. The complex details need not detain us. Eventually, an entity called "Sophia," the Heavenly Wisdom, is fashioned.

And this is where all the trouble begins.

Sophia decides to go it alone—to act on her own, without any male involvement. As *The Secret Book of John* puts it, "She wanted to bring forth something like herself, without the consent of the spirit, who had not given approval, without her partner and without his consideration."[27] Out of this great desire she creates a child, one called *Yaldabaoth*. In Hebrew, this name means "she gave birth" (i.e., she created), "by means of the sign." Yaldabaoth turns out to be the one whom we normally call God; that is, the God of the Bible. According to the Gnostics, he is not the *real* God who created all that there is, but a much lesser being—Yaldabaoth. This god is described by the Gnostics as jealous, wicked, and ignorant because he/she himself/herself does not know that there is a greater spiritual power than itself. This god does not know who he/she is or where he/she came from. It is this limited being who creates humanity. As a result, we humans are far removed from the true source of life and goodness which is the Perfect One. Put differently, Yaldabaoth simply botched creation. As the *Gospel of Thomas* says, "Whoever has come to know the world has just discovered a carcass" (Saying 56).[28]

According to this view, creation went from bad to worse. The greatest flaw was caused by the wayward Sophia who gave birth to supernatural entities without benefit of male assistance.[29] According to the Gnostics, this rebellion by Sophia destroyed the balance of the universe, which they viewed as a dyad of male and female primordial principles. An echo of this idea can also be found in the 2nd-century Talmud, the most important text of Judaism outside of the Bible. In the Talmud, there is a *midrash* or elaboration on the Bible stating that prior to Eve, Adam had a wife called Lilith. Lilith rebelled against Adam's rule, so to speak. Specifically, when engaged in sexual relations, she insisted on being on top. For her transgressions, she was banned from the Garden of Eden. This takes place prior to the creation of Eve.[30] In other words, in the Talmud, we also find some kind of cosmological imbalance created when the sexual harmony between male and female principles is disrupted.[31]

Valentinus was arguably the greatest Christian Gnostic teacher. He lived and taught at the beginning of the 2nd century. Following his teachings, the Valentinian Gnostics believed that Jesus left the Pleroma, or the heavenly realm, for the sole purpose of taking up residence with Sophia.[32] In other words, meeting Mary the Magdalene was not incidental to his mission. It was central. The divine Jesus became incarnate so that he could find and mate with the wayward divine Sophia and in so doing re-harmonize the universe. Put simply, the redemption of the cosmos depended on the sexual life of the incarnate Jesus and the incarnate Mary the Magdalene/Sophia. In a sense, for their followers, Jesus and Mary the Magdalene were living cherubim. Cherubim are the angelic figures that kept guard over the Ark of the Covenant. Various rabbinic traditions portray them "as if their bodies were 'intertwined with one another,' possibly alluding to sexual intimacy."[33]

According to the Valentinians, accompanying Jesus on his earthly mission were his angels, a special group of spiritual beings. When she first encountered

Jesus, Sophia—like Aseneth—immediately wanted to embrace him. In a Valentinian text called *Excerpts of Theodotus*, when Sophia saw Jesus she ran up to him, rejoiced, and worshipped him. But when she saw the male angels who were sent out with him, "she was abashed and put on a veil" (section 44). This is a direct parallel with Aseneth's reactions in *Joseph and Aseneth*. Furthermore, as in our *Joseph and Aseneth*, in the *Excerpts of Theodotus* Jesus does not return Sophia's initial embrace.

Also, in Valentinian theology as in *Joseph and Aseneth* there are double marriages: heavenly and earthly. Angels literally sit on the marriage bed. Why? Because in their own marriages Valentinians tried to emulate the holy couple. If they succeeded, they believed that they—like Aseneth—drew angels into their bedrooms. In April DeConick's words, "if the married couple had drawn the spirit, or angel, it joins with them during sexual relations."[34] DeConick summarizes the Valentinian ideas this way: "the Valentinians believed that sex was more than a physical activity with physical consequences. The thoughts of the sexual partners either raised intercourse to sacred heights or drew it down to the depths of sin."[35]

How does Valentinian theology match up with *Joseph and Aseneth*? Put simply, every aspect of Valentinian Gnosticism is reflected in our text. Aseneth first rejects Jesus, then comes running to embrace him. Jesus first rejects Aseneth, then embraces her. Aseneth's transformation, the celestial sex with a Jesus look-alike angel, the veil, the garments—everything in our text accords with Valentinian theology.

In this theology, it was the task of the "Christ," the new Adam, to return Lilith (or Aseneth or Sophia) to her rightful place at his side. In this way, he would return humanity to the Garden of Eden and the eternal life for which we were all destined. In Kraemer's words, "Aseneth and the angelic double of Joseph reverse the primordial sin of Eve and Adam."[36]

Redemption, from this perspective, is only possible by the union of the male and the female on both the spiritual and physical level. That's what the Gnostics looked for: marriage and the joining of the male to the female, in heaven and on earth. According to them, this was the only route to overcoming original sin—not Adam's, but Sophia's.

If all this sounds strange, keep in mind that sex as sinful is a post-Pauline concept. Prior to Paul, at least in the so-called pagan world, sex was redemptive.

In many societies, for example, in ancient Egypt as in Mesopotamia generally, the fertility of the seasons depended on the fecundity of the royal couple. Given that the ancient Egyptians perceived their rulers as divine beings, they believed that the physical relations between them had spiritual and metaphysical implications. In other words, the sex of divine kings and queens was different from everyone else's sex. Because they were divine and human at the same time, their act of procreation was a metaphor for creation itself. In this sense, therefore, Egyptian-based Christian Gnosticism was drawing on millennia—we reiterate: millennia—of Egyptian tradition. So it is not surprising that they viewed Jesus not merely as a prophet or messiah but, literally, as a god. It is also not surprising that they would have viewed his consort as a goddess.

From this it would follow that the most intimate activity between the god and the goddess is also the most important. Practically speaking, Gnosticism stressed the need to elevate the physical to the spiritual, the world of matter to the world of spirit. This is exactly the opposite of what became the orthodox Christian doctrine of the incarnation. According to orthodox or Pauline Christianity, spirit became matter, the divine Logos became enfleshed. For the Gnostics, it was the other way around: flesh had to become spirit. That's why Pauline Christianity celebrates asceticism and the Gnostics celebrated sex.[37]

As we have seen, *Joseph and Aseneth* reads like a Valentinian manuscript. More precisely, we believe it is a Valentinian Gospel. Since it may precede Valentinus, we may refer to it as a proto-Valentinian text. To arrive at this conclusion, one simply has to look at other Valentinian texts. The most important of these is the *Gospel of Philip*. This Gospel was most likely composed in Syria during the 2nd century. The original language was probably Greek.[38] In other words, the *Gospel of Philip* is roughly situated in the same time and place as *Joseph and Aseneth*. According to Marvin Meyer, "a major theme in the Gospel of Philip is the nature of the sacraments, especially the sacrament of the bridal chamber."[39] This Gospel lists five sacraments—Baptism, chrism (anointment), the Eucharist, redemption, and the bridal chamber—calling each a "mystery." The highest mystery is the last one—the "bridal chamber"—which the Gospel calls the "Holy of Holies." What happens in the Holy of Holies is only for the select few: "go into your chamber and shut the door behind you, and pray to your Father who is in secret."[40] In other words, according to the *Gospel of Philip*, the greatest lesson that Jesus taught humanity is not how to die and live again, but how to have sacred sex. This teaching, however, was only for the few because "if a marriage is open to the public, it has become prostitution, and the bride plays the harlot" (82.10).[41]

This was explosive material even in the 2nd century. In the *Gospel of Thomas*, the disciple Thomas is aware that Jesus' secret teaching, if made public, would be regarded as sacrilegious by the Christian masses. As a result, he advocates an esoteric approach to Jesus' message. Otherwise, he says, "If I tell you one of the sayings he spoke to me, you will pick up rocks and stone me" (Saying 13).[42] Another Gnostic text, the *Book of Baruch*, opens with an oath: "I swear by the Good, who is over all, to keep these mysteries and to tell them to no one."[43] In *The Round Dance of the Cross*, the reader is told "if you have seen what I do, keep quiet about my mysteries."[44] Clearly, this theology was not meant for everyone.

The secret teaching was not intended to be salacious, although its practitioners were accused of salacious acts. According to the church fathers, Valentinian Gnosticism deteriorated into orgiastic celebrations akin to pagan rituals such as those practiced by the Dionysians. Most Valentinians, however, upheld Pauline principles, at least in public. They only followed Valentinian rites in private. In fact, the elect among the Valentinians did not believe that the average Christian should become aware of the greatest mysteries. According to the Valentinians, average Christians should rely on good works and faith as their ticket to heaven. For the initiated, however, for those who understood that the highest level of spirituality involves the spiritualization of sex, a hidden teaching was available. This teaching involved the Valentinian sacrament of the bridal chamber.

For the Valentinians, this sacrament operated on several levels. In its most basic form, it involved sexual intercourse as an act of worship—but it was undertaken not only in a physical or carnal sense, but in a spiritual sense as well. In its Valentinian context, the act represents the full union of the male with the female. As the Gnostic writing *Exegesis on the Soul* says, once they have sexual relations, a man and a woman become a single life. In a sense, the couple symbolically becomes the original creation of God, the original human that, as we have already noted, was both male and female prior to the separation (Genesis 1:27). In this sense, holy sex is the means of healing not only the rift created between the sexes but also the alienation of humanity from God.

By definition, a sacrament is a rite in which an outer physical expression conveys an inner spiritual truth. This means that there *must* be the physical element present. For example, a Baptism isn't a Baptism without water. Similarly, a Eucharist isn't a Communion without actual bread and wine. There is no sacrament of Ordination without a physical laying on of hands. Similarly, if the bridal chamber is to be a sacrament, then it must by definition have a physical component, namely, real sexual intercourse. The point to all these sacraments, however, is that the rite is more than physical: a spiritual connection is conveyed in and through the physical representation. A Baptism isn't just water; a Eucharist isn't just bread and wine; the Bridal Chamber isn't just physical sex.

For the Valentinians then, the reenactment of the sacramental rite of the bridal chamber was a mystery that involved actual sexual relations. Perhaps one can try to relegate Valentinians and their views to the Christian margins. People have done this successfully for almost two thousand years. But were the Gnostics really at the margins? Let's take, for instance, the earliest traditions related to the death of the Virgin Mary. According to Stephen Shoemaker, they probably have "a Gnostic origin." Why has this been forgotten? Because the Pauline Christians who preserved these traditions felt the need to sanitize the earlier texts. Reading these texts, Shoemaker detects "an editorial cleansing that is quite evident in the earliest transmission of these legends."[45] Another obstacle to getting at the Valentinians and other Gnostics is that their traditions—to the degree that they have been preserved—have not been translated into English and, in some cases, not into any modern language. But the Gnostics in general, and the Valentinians in particular, were not marginal. Consider this: one of the earliest—if not the earliest—Christian inscriptions found in Rome dates to the 2nd century.[46] It is not Pauline. Rather, it is Valentinian and explicitly talks about the "brothers of the bridal chamber" who "carry the torches" so as to glorify "the Son."[47] Like *Joseph and Aseneth*, this earliest of Christian inscriptions is written in code. According to Snyder, the Christian character of the text "would have been clear to insiders but not glaringly obvious to someone unfamiliar with the theology of the group who commissioned [it]."[48] Like *Joseph and Aseneth*, the inscription throws readers off by using so-called "pagan" vocabulary and concepts. But again, like *Joseph and Aseneth*, the language of the text makes "the most sense under a Christian interpretation."[49] In other words, it is a Christian poem that employs conventions of pagan poetry to throw the uninitiated off course.[50]

Since scholars do not like to explore the possibility of Christian inscriptions and sacred sex, they interpret Valentinian theology as metaphorical,[51] or they don't see the sex at all. With respect to this particular inscription, scholars are divided between those who see it as a Baptismal Valentinian inscription and those who see it as Valentinian funeral poetry.[52] But let's look at what it actually says:

> To my bath, the brothers of the bridal chamber carry the torches,
> [here] in our halls, they hunger for the [true] banquets,
> even while praising the Father and glorifying the Son.
> There [with the Father and the Son] is the only spring and source
> of truth.[53]

Here we have a fraternity of brothers carrying torches and escorting someone from a bath to a bedroom, consummating the true banquet in the bridal chamber, all the while praising the Father and glorifying the Son. In any event, scholars agree that this inscription most probably originated not in a cemetery but in a villa[54] and that it is Valentinian.

In other words, we can argue whether Valentinian Gnosticism was marginal or not. We can also debate whether it preserves an authentic history. We can even argue whether or not *Joseph and Aseneth* is a Valentinian text. But the idea that the Valentinians believed what we've described above is a historical fact confirmed in text and archaeology.

The sacrament of the bridal chamber represented the culmination of the spiritual process. According to the Gnostics, it was the only means by which redemption could be truly achieved. As a result, they participated in the redemptive act, as a sacrament: human sexual intercourse, spiritually undertaken, mimicking the actions of the Savior. It was a powerful message.

The Gnostic view of sacred sex as a Christian sacrament was not born in a vacuum. As stated, there was an Egyptian precedent: namely, in ancient Egypt the welfare of the state depended on the sex life of the rulers. More than this, for the Egyptians, the very idea of the afterlife was associated with sacred sex. The myth of Isis and Osiris was central to this belief. According to the story, Isis and Osiris were brother and sister, husband and wife. Their jealous brother Seth murdered Osiris, tearing the body into fourteen pieces, which he scattered throughout their kingdom. After a long search, Isis located all but her lover's penis. She reassembled her brother/husband, turned herself into a hawk, and then hovered over the crotch of her dead mate. Using the flapping of her wings, she literally resurrected his penis. She then lowered herself onto his organ, received his seed, and gave birth to Horus—the son of god—from whom all pharaohs claimed descent.[55] In other words, sacred sex, resurrection, and the afterlife were part and parcel of the cultural–theological landscape into which Christian Gnosticism was born.

There was even a Midianite precedent for sacred sex that is mentioned in the Bible with respect to the heresy of Zimri and Kosbi, who copulated before the Ark of the Covenant (Numbers 25). This was not a mere act of exhibitionism. According to the Bible, it represented a theological challenge to Torah-based Judaism. For their part, the Greeks had Dionysus. Like Jesus, he was a dying-and-resurrecting god, and like the Gnostic version of Jesus, he drove his followers—especially women called *maenads*—into sexual frenzy.

Paul came from Phrygia, an area of modern-day Turkey that worshipped Attis, not Dionysus. Like Dionysus and Jesus, Attis is a dying-and-resurrecting god. He is called "the Good Shepherd," and the earliest depictions of him show him with a sheep across his shoulders. These are all images that were later incorporated into the iconography of Pauline Christianity. Attis too had a great love in his life, Cybele. But they did not engage in sacred sex. On the contrary, on his wedding night, Attis castrated himself in a moment of madness and ecstasy. Attis is Cybele's honey-man. He is bee-like. Basically, he is a male bee (drone) whose sexual organs are torn off after copulating with the queen.[56] The Latin poet Catullus, writing in the 1st century B.C.E., put it this way, "exalted by amorous rage, his mind gone, he cut off his testicles with a sharp flint."[57] Attis' priests, the Galli, would imitate their god by driving themselves into a holy frenzy, emasculating themselves, and offering their penises as holy sacrifices.[58] In this context, to honor their gods men made themselves females. In contrast, in Gnosticism, Jesus makes the female male. In a sense, one can say that Jesus and Mary the Magdalene created a syncretic cult that combined elements of Jewish, Artemisian, and Dionysian mysticism that involved the *hieros gamos*—sacred sex. The 3rd-century C.E. philosopher Porphyry presents "Jesus as a great teacher who after his death had been wrongly proclaimed a god by his followers. In this view, Jesus was a pious pagan."[59] At the very least, he was a Jew with an attraction to religious syncretism.

For his part, Paul took over this movement but substituted sacred castration for sacred sex. Paul did not insist on literal emasculation, although the church father Origen did just that. Rather, as we see later with the Roman Catholic priesthood, Paul advocated abstinence and celibacy instead of sex and procreation. There was one group, the Naassene Gnostics, that incorporated this idea into their mysticism. Hippolytus states that the Naassenes did not become Galli physically but spiritually: "they only perform the functions of those who are castrated" by abstaining from sexual intercourse.[60] In the 2nd century, Clement of Alexandria argued that the central purpose of Jesus' mission in the world was to end carnal procreation.[61] Basically, the orthodox critique of Valentinian sexuality came from individuals who had adopted a Christian Attisism, as articulated by Paul.

Tertullian, an important church father writing at the end of the 1st century and beginning of the 2nd century, for example, explicitly criticized the Gnostics for what, in his view, was participation in sordid sexual practices.[62] But the Valentinians countered that they were not engaged in anything distasteful. Quite the contrary, they were unapologetic. From their point of view, they were celebrating the mystery of divine love: "Love [never says] it owns something, [though] it owns [everything]. Love does not [say, 'This is mine'] or 'That is mine,' but rather, '[All that is mine] is yours'."[63] Paul's famous "love is patient, love is kind" teaching (1 Corinthians 13:4–7), which is so incongruous with the rest of his theology, can now be seen as a desexualized echo of Valentinian beliefs. And these in turn seem to be rooted in some kind of historical experience, namely, the marriage of Jesus and Mary the Magdalene.

Over and over in Valentinian texts, Mary the Magdalene—sometimes called Sophia—is portrayed, like Aseneth, weeping, repenting, and being redeemed through her relationship with her holy partner. For example, in *The Secret Book of John* it is written that when Sophia repented, she did so "with many tears."[64] It is also said that "the whole realm of fullness heard her prayer of repentance." And it is further said that "the holy spirit *poured upon her* some of the fullness of all."[65] In a Valentinian context, it is clear that what is meant by "poured upon her," etc., is basically the sexual act between Jesus and Mary the Magdalene. It is now also clear that the marriage of Jesus and Sophia in *The Secret Book of John* is the same as the marriage of Joseph and Aseneth in *Joseph and Aseneth*. Both represent a theology that teased meaning out of an actual marriage between Jesus and Mary the Magdalene.

Marriage was central to the Valentinians. It was not simply a compromise with man's carnal nature, as in Pauline Christianity. Rather, it was a celebration of the most hidden aspects of the act of creation. Concerning marriage, the *Gospel of Philip* states: "No [one can] know when [a husband] and wife have sex except these two, for marriage is a mystery for those married. If defiled marriage is hidden, how much more is undefiled marriage a true mystery."[66] In other words, if ordinary marriage is private, how much more so is the sacred marriage between Jesus and Mary the Magdalene. But if one wants to aspire to the highest mystery, one needs to learn that sex in this undefiled marriage "is not fleshly but pure. It belongs not to desire but to will. It belongs not to darkness or night but to the day and the light."[67]

Valentinian Christians believed that their teachers had powers that the rest of us don't. For example, they believed that a true master of Jesus-inspired sexual techniques could impregnate his soul mate without intercourse. After all, "the perfect conceive and give birth through a kiss."[68] For people who believed this, there was no end to virgin births.

Despite this, the Valentinians rejected Jesus' virgin birth as taught by Pauline Christianity. They pointed out that in the Hebrew tradition, "the holy spirit" is called the *shekhina* and is feminine. They therefore mocked orthodox Christians, stating "some said Mary became pregnant by the holy spirit. They are wrong and do not know what they are saying. When did a woman ever get pregnant by a woman?"[69]

For the Valentinians, virginity is a state of mind, not biology. It is part and parcel of a theology of sacred sex. The *Joseph and Aseneth* text literally calls Aseneth/Mary the Magdalene a *virgin*. Not only that, it's clear from the manuscript that her status as virgin was part of her divine role. Like Artemis, despite sharing a bed with the Son of God, Mary the Magdalene remained a virgin. How is this possible? It's possible because she is a goddess and he is a god. When you sleep with a god, you don't lose your virginity. If this is true, we come to the realization that the original Virgin Mary was Jesus' wife, not his mother.[70]

In this respect, in the *Gospel of Philip*, the Valentinians say that "three women always walked with the master: Mary his mother, [his] sister, and Mary of Magdala, who is called his companion (*koinonos*)."[71] As stated, the word *koinonos* can be translated as *lover*. In this sense, at the highest level, mother, sister,[72] and bride all teach the unity of love. They are all virgins because none of them are defiled. But it was Mary the Magdalene who was Jesus' soul mate. Again, according to the *Gospel of Philip*, when the disciples became jealous of Jesus' relationship with Mary the Magdalene, he rebuked them, saying "Why do I not love you like her? If a blind person and one who can see are both in darkness, they are the same. When the light comes, one who can see will see the light, and the blind person will stay in darkness."[73] Clearly for Jesus, his relationship with Mary the Magdalene was all about the "light." Those who did not understand were left in "darkness."

This bond between bridegroom and bride is the mystery of marriage. According to the Valentinians, the existence of the world depends on this mystery and the "power of intercourse"[74] that is related to it. When people are outside marriage, their power is corrupted. According to the *Gospel of Philip*, "When foolish females see a man by himself, they jump on him, fondle him, and pollute him. Likewise, when foolish males see a beautiful woman by herself, they seduce and violate her in order to pollute her. But when they see a husband and wife together, the females cannot make advances on the man and the males cannot make advances on the woman. So also if the image and the angel are joined, none can dare to make advances on the male or the female."[75] As in *Joseph and Aseneth*, the *Gospel of Philip* celebrates the coming together on the bridal bed of the male, the female, and "the angel"—that is, the physical is literally transposed into the spiritual when male, female, and the heavenly realm are brought into perfect balance.

The canonical Gospel of John calls Jesus *the Word*. In contrast, the *Gospel of Philip* encourages each one of us to become *the Word*, and promises that "if you become Word, Word will have intercourse with you."[76] When that happens, death is overcome. "When Eve was in Adam, there was no death. When she was separated from him, death came. If [she] enters into him again and he embraces [her], death will cease to be."[77] In this sense, Jesus is the new Adam and Mary the Magdalene is the new Eve—as a new integrated entity, they repair the rift created when God's paradise was destroyed and sin and death entered the world.[78] Together, they show us the way to immortality.

For the Valentinians, "redemption is in the bridal chamber."[79] As in *Joseph and Aseneth*, the bridal chamber is defined as the holy of holies. Notice the parallels between the Jerusalem *temple* in the *Gospel of Philip* and the *tower* in *Joseph and Aseneth*. The descriptions are almost identical: "There were three structures for sacrifice in Jerusalem. One opened to the west and was called the holy place; a second opened to the south and was called the holy of the holy; the third opened to the east and was called the holy of holies, where only the high priest could enter."[80] The author of the *Gospel of Philip* decodes the architecture of the sacred temple in terms of the Gnostic sacraments, "the holy place is baptism; the holy of the holy is redemption; the holy of holies is the bridal chamber."[81]

But there is actually a triple code at work. On the one hand, Aseneth's dwelling at the top of her tower is a clear metaphor for the temple. On another hand, there is clear sexual imagery here with Aseneth's bedchamber representing the Holy of Holies inside the temple. There is a third level, however, that would not have been lost on *Joseph and Aseneth*'s 1st- or 2nd-century readers. In the rabbinic use of the word *chamber*, besides the commonplace meaning, the term can take on a specific connotation. In Peter Schafer's words, "In halakhic [rabbinic law] terminology, *heder* [chamber] signifies the innermost part of the female genitals, that is the uterus followed by the 'aliyyah (literally 'attic' = the vagina) and the *prozdor* (literally 'vestibule' = the vulva)."[82] So when Aseneth sits on her bed, dripping honey from her mouth, with the man angel next to her in her innermost bedchamber, the metaphor for Valentinians—and not only Valentinians—would have been clear. Aseneth's body is the temple containing the Holy of Holies. It is within that sacred space that redemption occurs, spiritually and physically. Her body—her womb—is the bridal chamber. So Mary is truly the Magdalene: she is Tower, Temple, and Holy of Holies. In sum, DeConick asks, "how important was sex to the Valentinians?" And she answers, "the coming of the final day and the redemption of God depended on it."[83]

When we enter the world of Valentinian Gnosticism, we enter a philosophical space very different from the one we are used to. For example, Gnostics had a very different idea of sin from the one the West has inherited from orthodox Christianity. In Marvin Meyer's words, "I believe that among the Gnostics, sin was not the basic human problem; ignorance was . . . you may call something sin but . . . there really isn't any ultimate thing out there called sin."[84] Whatever sin might have meant for them, it certainly did not mean sex.

The church father Epiphanius of Salamis seems to have infiltrated a Gnostic sect around 335 c.e. In his attack on this "heresy," he has left us a graphic account of Gnostic rituals, which included considerable foreplay and sexual intercourse. Tellingly, after 730 ritual copulations, the adept declares, "I am Christ."[85] They also seem to have had a gospel related to Mary the Magdalene that has not yet been discovered. It was called *The Questions of Mary*. In it, Jesus, like Adam, has a woman ripped from his side. Since he is God, he rips her out of his own side and proceeds to have intercourse with her. He does all this as a way of instructing Mary the Magdalene in the secrets of their theology.[86]

Of course, the Valentinians were well aware that their teachings could be misconstrued in inappropriate ways. Their solution for this problem was to keep their rituals secret and to encode their sacred texts. In their words: "If marriage is exposed, it has become prostitution, and the bride plays the harlot not only if she is impregnated by another man but even if she slips out of her bedchamber and is seen. Let her show herself only to her father and her mother, the friend of the bridegroom, and the attendants of the bridegroom. They are allowed to enter the bridal chamber every day. But let the others yearn just to hear her voice and enjoy the fragrance of her ointment, and let them feed like dogs on the crumbs that fall from the table."[87]

Here we have the cipher for *Joseph and Aseneth*. According to the Gnostics, had *Joseph and Aseneth* explicitly described the relationship between Jesus and Mary the Magdalene, it would have turned that relationship into a kind of prostitution. It would have cheapened the entire theology.[88] So, as Jesus initially taught the Syro-Phoenician woman, those at a lower level have to be satisfied with the crumbs that fall from the table—for the dogs. They cannot engage in the sacrament of the bridal chamber. But for those limited few described in the *Gospel of Philip* and in *Joseph and Aseneth*—the bridegroom, the bride, the father, the mother, the friend (the angel), and the attendants—they will get to "enter the bridal chamber every day." They will participate in life everlasting. The *Gospel of Philip* is clearly the companion text to *Joseph and Aseneth*. It couldn't be any clearer. It couldn't fit any better.

Again, we realize that all this may sound strange to the modern ear, but it was not so for many early Christians. They simply had to come to terms with the consequences of worshipping a man-god, and this was true for both the Pauline Christians and the Gnostics. Unlike the Pauline Christians, who focused on the significance of Jesus' death, Gnostic Christians reflected on the sacramental meaning of the most intimate aspects of his marriage.

But it's not only about sex and marriage. Thinking through what the humanity of Jesus meant, they speculated on the implications of his humanity when it came to everything—food and waste, for example. In this respect, Valentinus writes that Jesus "ate and drank in a unique way, without excreting solids."[89] In other words, since we know from the Gospels that Jesus ate, the question arises, did he defecate? The Valentinians' answer was a resounding "no"! According to this view, Jesus' body was so perfect that it did not create waste. Similarly, he was so perfect that he could have sex, in a sense, without having sex. His partner would literally not lose her virginity and his arousal would be triggered by spiritual, not carnal, desires.[90]

But if Gnosticism—an ancient version of Christianity that is at least as old as the Pauline version—explicitly states that Jesus was married to Sophia and that Mary the Magdalene was his consort, why have scholars ignored this ancient attestation to the marriage? The answer is simple—theology. People don't want a married Jesus, so they reduce Gnosticism to mythology and elevate the canonical Gospels to history. In part, the orthodox camp of scholars and theologians was able to do this because Gnosticism is expressed mostly in sayings, not in narrative gospels. But now, in *Joseph and Aseneth*, we finally have a Gnostic text that is a narrative. It seems to provide us with the historical circumstances that gave rise to Valentinian theology.

Unlike other Gnostic texts, *Joseph and Aseneth* is not a series of fragments: it is an encoded Gospel with a beginning, middle, and end. Instead of thinking of Valentinian Gnosticism as a mythology shopping for a god and finding one in Jesus, we can now see that the followers of Jesus and Mary the Magdalene created a theology in order to explain the most intimate aspect of their relationship—their sex life.

As with the wedding at Cana, the redemptive powers of their bridal chamber are echoed in the canonical Gospels themselves. In Mark 2:18–20, some Pharisees wonder why, while everyone is fasting according to Torah law, the disciples of Jesus do not fast. Jesus' answer is that "While the bridegroom is with them, the attendants of the bridegroom cannot fast, can they? So long as they have the bridegroom with them, they cannot fast. But the days will come when the bridegroom is taken away from them, and then they will fast in that day."

Notice Jesus' description of himself as a bridegroom. Notice also the implications of his status as bridegroom. His activity in the bridal chamber nullifies

Torah law! As long as his followers (the attendants of the bridegroom) are with him, and as long as he continues to be a "bridegroom," the attendants do not need to join the Torah-abiding community in their fast. In these circumstances, they are exempted from the law. In other words, the sacrament of the bridal chamber is the new Sinai: sacred sex supersedes the revelation at Mount Sinai. The old law continues to be in force for the ones who don't attend to the bridegroom; but, for the ones who do, a New Testament has now been revealed.

Jesus' nullification of Torah law, specifically as it concerns sexual relations, is hinted at in one of the most famous chapters of Jesus' life, the Last Supper. Prior to this Last Supper, Jesus told his disciples that when outsiders were listening he had to speak in parables (Mark 4:11), but for insiders he had a different rule: ". . . when he was alone with his own disciples, he *explained everything*" (Mark 4:34, emphasis added). The Last Supper was an occasion when the inner circle was around the table, but others were hosting it. Meaning, there were outsiders present. By his own rules, Jesus had to speak in code. It is at this moment that he starts talking about sex in semi-coded terms. We say "semi-coded" because he is surprisingly explicit. After all, he compares the bread on the table to his own body. We can theologize all we want, but the fact is that Jesus suddenly shifts the conversation from bread to his own body. But what is he telling us about his body and sexual relations? The answer to that question is in the blood. Jesus proceeds to talk about the wine on the table, comparing it to blood: "This cup is the new covenant in my blood, which is poured out for you" (Luke 22:20). What can this possibly mean?

Traditionally, many Christian groups have understood these actions as the prototypes for the Eucharist. Meaning, during the Last Supper, Jesus instructs his disciples in some kind of ritualized cannibalism. By some miracle—"transmutation"—those who ingest the bread (called "the host," because it "hosts" the body of Christ) and drink the wine are actually tasting Jesus' flesh and drinking his blood.

Two points have to be made concerning the traditional Christian interpretation. First, it is entirely alien to Jewish tradition. Let's remember, as far as we know, all the disciples at the Last Supper were Jews. It would never occur to them that they are being instructed with respect to some kind of new and kosher cannibalism. In its cultural and religious context, this interpretation is simply a nonstarter. This kind of interpretation has its origin in pagan theology, not

Jewish theology. For example, in the 2nd century c.e., Achilles Tatius of Alexandria composed a tale about the god Dionysus and his great gift to humanity: "the blood of the grape." That is, wine. He goes on to call wine "blood so sweet."[91] Furthermore, the wild immortal female followers of Dionysus—the Maenads—were rumored to devour the raw flesh of an animal in their "feast of flesh." As Marvin Meyer states, the "participants believed they were consuming the god himself."[92] While pagan writings are rife with this kind of fare, there is nothing like this in any Jewish writings. As another example, the 1st-century Roman poet Lucan wrote of a witch who devoted herself to some kind of underworld cult. When the witch turned to her deity for help, she referred to her cannibalism as a merit for which she should be rewarded: "If I call on you with a mouth sufficiently evil and polluted, if I never sing these hymns without having eaten human flesh . . . grant [my] prayer."[93]

In the ancient world, Christians were often accused of cannibalism. This is usually interpreted as a pagan misunderstanding of the Eucharist, but the charges of cannibalism and infanticide related to orgies were varied and numerous. As Andrew McGowan states, "Christians became for a time the ancient cannibals par excellence."[94]

Our point is not to enter into a discussion of whether some early Christians did or did not engage in actual cannibalism. Our point is that the interpretation given to the Last Supper by various Christian groups has absolutely nothing to do with the historical context of the Last Supper and everything to do with various pagan myths, theologies, and rituals. So let's return for a moment to the Last Supper—which we take as an actual historical event. Jesus refers to the wine as his blood and the drinking of it as marking a "new covenant." If he's not referring to some kind of cannibalism, or cannibalism by transmutation, what is Jesus talking about?

One way to look at the scene is that Jesus is nullifying the Mosaic kosher laws (i.e., the laws involving kosher and un-kosher food). According to the Torah, Jews may not partake of other humans nor, in fact, drink the blood of any animals. To this day, therefore, kosher meat involves a process of salting which removes blood from animal flesh. These kosher laws derive from the Biblical statement "You are not to eat the blood of any flesh, for the life of all flesh is its blood; whoever eats it shall be cut off" (Leviticus 17:14). Is this what it's all about? Is Jesus merely allowing his disciples to put juicy steaks on the grill? Is he advocating for rare roast beef? Steak tartare? Is this how his statement would have been understood by the people around the table at the Last Supper? Obviously not.

In fact, the prohibition against drinking blood is specifically carried over from the Hebrew Bible to the Christian New Testament. At the so-called First Jerusalem Council, James, the brother of Jesus, makes the prohibition against drinking blood one of the very few rules that Gentiles wanting to become followers of Jesus must still adhere to: "And so my [James'] judgment is that we should not make it difficult for the Gentiles who are turning to God. Instead, we should write and tell them to abstain from eating food offered to idols . . . from eating the meat of strangled animals, and from consuming blood" (Acts 15:19–20). So if Jesus' new covenant of blood is not referring to cannibalism, or the consumption of blood, what is this new divinely sanctioned deal all about?

The answer is simple. It has been all but forgotten, obfuscated by thousands of years of Pauline theology. The issue of blood—in the Jewish context—refers first and foremost to laws relating to matters of "family purity." These laws are now unfamiliar to most Christians who, not observing Torah, pass over the purity laws of Leviticus as if they did not exist. Some background is required.

Jewish family purity laws are a subsection of purity laws in general. Purity, in its Biblical context, has been misunderstood as relating to issues of *clean* and *unclean*. In reality, it's another matter altogether. Generally speaking, one is *pure* when coming into contact with *life-giving* forces and *impure* when coming into contact with *death* (or the vacuum created by the departure of life-giving forces from a place that they once occupied). The blood of animals is a good example. Since blood is perceived as the life blood of existence, when we kill an animal, Biblically speaking, we must not partake of what the Bible identifies as the substance that had carried the life force of the now-dead creature. Similarly, and more importantly, the presence of blood makes a woman impure to her husband, because menstrual blood represents the loss of the capacity to create life. This means that during her cycle, when a woman goes through a period of fertility, there is a life force in her. Then, when the woman's egg is eliminated, there is a loss of that life-giving potential. As a result, until she ovulates again, she's considered impure to her husband. The ancients may not have understood the precise mechanics of ovulation, but they did understand fertility periods.

Put simply, a Torah-observant Jew, then and now, does not touch his wife during her menstrual cycle. In fact, so important is this rule that the rabbis have added another week after menstruation has stopped to the Biblical "no touch" period . . . just to be sure. Once a woman is pure, she can immerse herself in a mikveh (a ritual pool), becoming sexually available to her spouse.

In its historical context, for the people around the table at the Last Supper, the immediate impact of Jesus' statement about blood would have had nothing to do with cannibalism or barbecues and everything to do with sex. This shouldn't surprise us because, for early Christians, "eating and sex alike were closely associated with the sin of Adam and Eve in Genesis 3; [Adam and Eve] sinned when they ate the forbidden fruit, and upon being cast out of Eden, they slept together and had children."[95] Seen in this light, we now realize that a theologically motivated scribe probably tampered with the depiction of the Last Supper in the Gospels. Originally, this is what Jesus probably said: "this is *my* body, this is *her* blood." But even if he said what the Gospels say he says—"this is *my* body, this is *my* blood"—what he seems to be doing is "appropriating" the blood and annulling its impure status. By doing so, he is eliminating the sexual "off" period observed by Torah-abiding men and women. He's announcing that there is no more impurity now that the bridegroom has arrived. Practically speaking, the implication of Jesus' statement for his followers would have been that men and women can have sexual relations at *all* times.

The issue of a woman's menstrual blood is not peripheral to the birth of Christianity. It may sound odd to non-Jews today to be talking about female menstruation in the context of the Last Supper, but we have to remember that non-Jews were not sitting around the table at the Last Supper. Everyone in the room was Jewish except, as it seems, Jesus' companion, Mary the Magdalene. For these people, menstrual blood was more important than death on the cross.

Let's also remember that central to Pauline theology is the idea that Jesus is the "sacrificial lamb." Meaning, Jesus is sacrificed on the cross to remove the sins of the world. But the idea of a "sin offering" is not original with Paul. It is Biblical. Until 70 C.E., for some thousand years, every day, animals were sacrificed in the temple of Jerusalem to atone for sins. Paul's innovation was to substitute Jesus—a human being—for the animal sin offering. Was Paul right? At the Last Supper, was Jesus really prophesying that he would annul the Biblical laws by dying? Or was he saying that he had already annulled them by living? When Jesus tasted the wine and referred to blood, was he referring to his own blood on the cross, or was he making a comment about sexual purity involving menstrual blood?

In Judaism, the only animal sacrifice associated with death and resurrection is the sacrifice of the "red cow" (Numbers 19:1–13).[96] This is a Biblical mystery referring to a cow that has a reddish color. The cow is burned in its entirety on the sacrificial altar and its ashes are then mixed with water, which has the power to purify individuals who have come into contact with death. The required redness of the cow seems to be connected to blood.[97] In fact, the elixir created by mixing the ashes of the sacrificed red cow with water is called *mei niddah* in Biblical Hebrew. This is usually translated as waters of "separation." But as Hyam Maccoby has pointed out, it can also be translated as "waters of menstruation."[98]

In the ancient world, menstrual blood was associated with virgin birth. To qualify for the sacrifice, the Biblical red cow had to be a virgin. Furthermore, according to Griselda Pollock, "[m]any peoples believed that fetuses are formed from menstrual blood which later becomes the milk that nourishe[s] the born baby."[99] In other words, in the ancient world, menstrual blood was associated with virginity and—through fetuses forming out of blood—virginal conception. In Judaism, by associating menstrual blood with the sacrifice of the red cow, the Bible desexualized the issue. It moved people away from actual menstrual blood and involved them with "waters of menstruation" created from the ashes of the red cow. At the Last Supper, Jesus re-sexualized the blood by taking it out of its temple context. In this way, he challenged the Biblical laws of purification in front of an audience that understood exactly what he was talking about.

Put simply: seen in its historical context, it's obvious that at the Last Supper Jesus could not have been referring to the wine on the table as his *own* blood. By referring to the wine as blood and then drinking it, what Jesus was saying was that the *mei niddah* (i.e., the menstrual blood symbolized by the ashes of the red cow) were no longer needed. By drinking her *mei niddah* at the Last Supper, he was saying that the real instrument for overcoming the impurity of death was his wife Mary the Magdalene. Gnostically speaking, for his original followers, it seems that it was not his suffering on the cross that overcame death, but the bridal chamber he shared with Mary the Magdalene, even during her menstrual period. This is not theoretical. This is exactly how some early Christians understood Jesus. In fact, they went further. Not only did they have sex during a woman's menstrual period, they ate the menstrual blood just to make the point. We know of these people from the attacks on them. In the late 4th century C.E., Epiphanius, Bishop of Salamis in modern-day Cyprus, wrote against a group that called themselves Nicolaitans. He accuses them of eating the blood of menstruation.[100] Later, a group that Epiphanius calls Borborites, who were descended from the Nicolaitans, was also accused of strange sexual sacraments, some of which included smearing their hands with menstrual blood.[101]

Put differently, if sacred sex is the vehicle of the ascent to heaven, by putting aside periods of menstruation-related impurity, Jesus makes this ascent available all the time. Compare Jesus' type of ascent to the rabbinic tradition where you have, for example, Rabbi Nehunya son of Haqanah, a mystic who ascends to heaven while remaining physically present among his fellow rabbis. His body never leaves the room but his spirit does. To bring him back down to earth, the rabbis employ menstrual blood "to bring him [Nehunya] back, the rabbis put a rag on his knees that has been in contact with a miniscule amount of female impurity."[102] In contrast to the rabbis, as stated above, what Jesus is saying is that there is no more female impurity. He purifies it for all time when he drinks the "blood" at the Last Supper. From this perspective, heaven is available all the time and nothing can bring the true mystic down to earth.

It may very well be that Jesus' annulment of family purity laws was not unique to him. It seems that around that time, other religious leaders were also disregarding Torah laws governing sexual relations. For example, in the *Damascus Document*, found among the Dead Sea Scrolls, there is a passage that has never been completely understood. Here, the author describes the Jerusalem leadership of his time as utterly and completely sexually corrupted. "[T]hey *relished* the customs of fornication," says the writer. He also charges that they "threw off *all* restraint" and, as in our reading of the Last Supper, he connects this type of lewd activity with a Biblical passage concerning wine: "their wine is venom of serpents, the cruel poison of vipers."[103]

Based on the sources, therefore, it seems that at the Last Supper Jesus was referring not to his blood, but to Mary the Magdalene's blood. He's not making a statement about kosher cannibalism, but about kosher sex. As attested to by many writers in the Roman world, some followers took his sacred sex formula to heart; but, as the *Damascus Document* demonstrates, others saw the ideas surrounding the wine of the Last Supper as the venom of vipers.

It took the lost gospel of *Joseph and Aseneth* to bring this theology into clear focus. Make no mistake about it: this is not simply about sexual liberation. It's a different model of redemption. In this scenario, salvation is not brought about through Jesus' death but through his life-giving marriage, sexual relations, and offspring. It is a union that brings the entire universe back into a primordial harmony. The bridal chamber—not Holy Communion, the Mass, or the Eucharist—is the rite whereby his first followers partook in this process of redemption. This is the key element that has been obscured for almost two millennia by the Pauline interpretation of Jesus' words at the Last Supper.

The implications are staggering. If, indeed, followers of Jesus felt—as Paul explicitly states—that Jesus liberated them from the Mosaic law, then what scholars have called a libertine or freewheeling tradition ensues.[104] Basically, what this means is that the line between sacred sex and outright prostitution in the early Jesus movement was very thin indeed. Again, if you think this is far-fetched, consider this: the most consistent charge against Christians and heretic Christians in ancient times was that they engaged in depraved sexual acts.[105] That's what the pagans said. That's what the Jews said. That's what the church fathers said of the heretics. And that's what the Gospels record.

In Mark 6:1, for example, it is said that Jesus' neighbors in his hometown of Nazareth were scandalized by his behavior. In contrast to his cousin John the Baptizer, Jesus was accused of being gluttonous and a drunkard (Matthew 11:19). More than this, people didn't like the company he kept, specifically "publicans" (that is, Hellenized collaborators with the Roman regime) and "prostitutes" (Mark 2:16). Scholars often say that the sin of publicans was tax collection, as if this was the only issue of importance for 1st-century Jews in Judaea. But Jews were far more concerned with issues of purity than taxation. The Hellenized world was a world where homosexuality and bisexuality were common and acceptable, especially in the upper classes. Accusing Jesus of hanging out with publicans and prostitutes is accusing him of hanging out with two groups of people whose sexual practices are disapproved by the Torah.

This theme of Jesus and prostitution is echoed in the Talmud where the only saying of Jesus that is recorded is his legal opinion that the wages of a prostitute, if donated to the holy temple in Jerusalem, could be used for building the toilet of a high priest (*Bavli Avodah Zarah* 16b–17a).[106] In his *Dialogue with Trypho*, the 2nd-century Christian apologist Justin Martyr defends Christians against charges that they are involved in "godless and lawless and unholy things," which include the practice of all-night orgies and incestuous intercourse (108.3).[107] At the end of the 1st century, a Christian prophetess in Thyatira, modern Turkey, encouraged fellow Christians to engage in sacred sexual acts with her (Revelation 2:18–26). Graffiti found in Carthage dating to a little before 197 C.E. shows a figure with donkey ears and a hoof carrying a book and wrapped in a toga. The accompanying inscription reads "the god of the Christians [is] a donkey who beds [with his worshippers]."[108] Minucius Felix, a Christian apologist writing in approximately 200 C.E., repeats a pagan accusation against Christians: "they recognize each other by secret signs and objects, and love each other almost before they meet. Among them religion constantly joins with itself, as it were, a sort of lust, and they commonly call each other brothers and sisters, so that even ordinary debauchery may be made incest by the use of the sacred name" (*Octavius* 9.2).[109]

These attacks don't only come from outside the original Jesus movement. They don't just come from people who misunderstand what truly goes on among Christians. These charges come from inside the movement as well. In 1909, the famous Syriac scholar J. Rendel Harris made an astounding discovery. He discovered forty-two *Odes of Solomon*, which he described as "an early Christian hymnbook." In fact, what he discovered was *the earliest* Christian hymnbook. Like *Joseph and Aseneth*, it emerged out of a Syriac milieu, and, like *Joseph and Aseneth*, it never mentions Jesus while constantly referring to him. Specialists agree that the collection of odes is Christian. Some believe an Essene-turned-Christian composed them, others believe that a Judeo-Christian, or an early Gnostic, wrote them. As James Charlesworth puts it, "the odes seem to have been composed when Judaism, Gnostic ideas . . . and belief in Jesus' messianic stature are mixing easily."[110] The texts are dated to 125 C.E., but they may be earlier. They are called proto-Gnostic[111] by Charlesworth because, like most scholars, he doesn't want to move Gnosticism into the 1st century. Essentially, if Gnosticism is kept in the 2nd century, it can be relegated to myth. But if it appears in the 1st century, it may be recording history. What history?

Although Charlesworth hints at a possible connection between the *Odes of Solomon* and *Joseph and Aseneth*,[112] the first to draw attention to the similarities is Kraemer. For example, regarding *Ode* 13, "Behold, the Lord is our mirror," she notes, "this hymn corresponds quite nicely to Aseneth's use of the water basin as a mirror."[113] Elsewhere, she draws attention to the similarities between sun imagery in *Joseph and Aseneth*'s description of Joseph and the *Odes*. For example, *Ode* 15 states "He is my sun, and his rays rouse me." In Kraemer's words, "as Christ here is the sun whose light dispels darkness from before the soul's face, so Joseph is Helios, whose light dispels darkness before Aseneth."[114] She concludes that "both Aseneth and the Odes could easily be at home in the same community."[115] But what community? Did the Syrian Christian community originate these stories? Or is it preserving tales told by the first group of Jesus followers: the people who knew him?

Upon a closer reading, we see that the *Odes of Solomon* witness the very issues that we have been talking about: Jesus' sexual theology and the danger of prostituting it. Jesus' teaching is described in exactly the same language as *Joseph and Aseneth*, complete with honeycomb, bees, and offspring. Specifically, Jesus is described as "the son of God,"[116] riding "a chariot."[117] There is a woman in the story who is associated with bees and has children: "As honey drips from the honeycomb of bees, And milk flows from the woman who loves her children, So also is my hope upon you, O my God."[118] Jesus' relationship with his lover— i.e., the one the Gnostic gospels identify with Mary the Magdalene/Sophia—is described in terms that are both carnal and metaphysical: "for I should not have known to love the Lord, if He had not loved me continuously. I have been united (to Him), because the lover has found the Beloved."[119]

Despite the elevated sexual theology, the author witnesses to the fact that sacred sex doesn't always stay sacred. False teachers who imitate the rites of the bridal chamber lead followers astray and pull them into prostitution. For example, *Ode* 38 rails against someone called "the Corrupter" who turned the bridal chamber into a den of prostitution: "And they *imitate* the Beloved and His Bride, And they cause the world to err and *corrupt* it." The writer goes on to describe a drunken orgy in the name of the Christ: "And they invite many to the wedding feast, and cause them to drink the wine of their intoxications. So they cause them to vomit up their wisdom and their knowledge, and make them senseless."[120]

What all this demonstrates is that there was *something* in the original Jesus and Mary the Magdalene movement that contemporary and later critics repeatedly associated with sexual excesses. That *something*, in Morton Smith's words, must have started with Jesus: "whatever else Jesus may or may not have done, he unquestionably started the process that became Christianity."[121] Therefore, we have to take very seriously the fact that the common feature of all the early anti-Christian accusations have to do with sexual practices mixed with religious rites. In Smith's words, they are "only explicable from a tradition based on observation of Jesus himself."[122]

But for Jesus to engage in anything like the sexual practices attributed to his followers, there must have been some Biblical source text that he could cite to defend his actions. Put differently, since most of Jesus' earliest followers were Jews, even if their view of Jesus and Mary the Magdalene was influenced by Syro-Phoenician (Canaanite), Artemis-based religious ideas, you would expect to find some Biblical Jewish text that would justify their beliefs concerning this couple. If for their earliest followers Jesus and Mary the Magdalene were co-partners in "messiahship," there should be a prophetic Hebrew text that they would have used to rationalize their movement. More than this, the descriptions of Jesus and Mary the Magdalene in our manuscript—including the rites of sacred sex—would have to be modeled to some extent on a Hebrew text in order to give them scriptural sanction. In fact, there is such a text, and we are led to it by the Christian Bible. The Epistle to the Hebrews, traditionally written by Paul or, more likely, by a contemporary who was influenced by him, is dated to some time between Jesus' crucifixion and the destruction of the Temple (70 C.E.), meaning it is one of the earliest Christian writings. In this text (Hebrews 1:8–9), the author is referring to Jesus as messiah, and he references Psalm 45 as a proof text. Here is how the King James translation renders the Psalm: "But unto the Son he saith, Thy throne, O God, is for ever and ever: a sceptre of righteousness is the sceptre of thy kingdom; Thou hast loved righteousness, and hated iniquity; therefore God, even thy God, hath anointed thee with the oil of gladness above thy fellows."

So the earliest Christians used Psalm 45 as a proof text for Jesus' messiahship, even as a justification for calling Jesus both "Son" and "God." In Jewish tradition, Psalm 45 is not a reference to Jesus, though it is taken as a prophetic description of the messiah yet to come.

In other words, both traditions agree that Psalm 45 is describing King Messiah. So if Jesus' apostles used this text to understand Jesus, what would they have gleaned from it? Does it refer to a sacred marriage? Sacred sex? Would they have found a way to wrap their minds around the fact that their leader had taken up with a former pagan priestess?

In fact, Psalm 45 would have provided them with all they needed to celebrate the messiah's bridal chamber. The Psalm is so explicit that it is never translated properly. Here is what it says in the original Hebrew: verse 3 describes the coming messiah as "more beautiful than human beings" (i.e., he is not a mere mortal). Then, in the lines referenced in Hebrews, it describes him as a warrior for truth and righteousness. Like Joseph in our manuscript, who appears riding a chariot and carrying a scepter, verse 5 describes the messiah as "riding" to victory, and verse 7 describes him carrying the "sceptre of royalty." More than this, it states that "God is your throne" or "Your throne, O God, is for eternity." Meaning, the messiah is a godlike figure subservient only to God on High, but superior to humans. Verse 8 states that God has "anointed" the chosen one with the "oil of gladness."

Now that the poet has described the crowning of King Messiah, he goes on to the controversial, overlooked, and mistranslated passages. In verse 9, the messiah is prepared for the bridal chamber by being anointed with perfumes: "myrrh, aloes and cassia." It then states that "from ivory chambers many will gladden you." Who are these "many?" Verse 10 states, "daughters of kings will come to you." During this bridal-chamber ceremony, the messiah is not alone. Rather, to his right is his "consort." The Hebrew word is *shegal*. This is often translated as "queen." But *mishgal* means "sexual intercourse." So the literal translation is either "sexual partner," "wife," or "consort." "Consort" is a more appropriate appellation for the woman standing at the messiah's right hand, because she is then described as wearing *ketem offir*. This is often translated as "golden settings," or "golden jewelry," but Offir is a place, and *ketem offir* should be translated as "the mark of Offir," which is synonymous with a kind of gold that was used in the building of the temple. So, to the right hand of the messiah, who is visited by daughters of kings whose purpose is to gladden him, stands his consort arrayed in the gold of the temple.

At this point, verse 11, the Psalmist addresses this woman: "Hear, O daughter, and see, and incline your ear." What is she supposed to hear? The Psalmist is explicit: "Forget your people and your father's house." In other words, the messiah's consort is not destined to be Jewish. What people does she belong to? Verse 13 tells us that she is a "daughter of Tyre," meaning she is a Syro-Phoenician woman. Once this Syro-Phoenician woman becomes the consort or wife of the messiah, verse 12 tells her that "the king will lust after your beauty, for he is your Lord and you shall bow down to him." By bowing down to him, however, she elevates herself above everyone else, specifically the temple priesthood. Verse 13 tells us that at the afternoon sacrifices, the people's elite will "supplicate before your countenance." Meaning, by sharing King Messiah's bed, this former Syro-Phoenician priestess, a daughter of a king, will be elevated above everyone but the messiah. Verse 14 tells us that she will share her "honor" only with the king. Verse 15 tells us that she will also make available to him "her virgin attendants." The ceremony is consummated with "gladness and joy" in the "chamber of the King." The Psalm concludes by telling us that the sons who will result from this ritual will "replace" (in Hebrew *tachat ihiu*) the Davidic royal line and will be appointed "princes in all the land." The last line states that "your name will be remembered in all generations" and that "nations will praise you forever more."

Psalm 45 is the Jewish source code of the earliest followers of Jesus and Mary the Magdalene. Of course, it can be and has been read in different ways. But the simplest reading would have provided Jesus' earliest followers with what they were looking for: the job description for the messiah. His job was not to die on a cross. Rather, his job was to replace the traditional temple priesthood, establish a new royal/priestly line, and find a Tyrean princess willing to abandon her father's house and her religion. Thereafter, their mission was to establish a new covenant by consummating their relationship in the royal bridal chamber. Psalm 45 demonstrates that *Joseph and Aseneth* did not emerge out of a theological vacuum: it was firmly rooted in the Galilean Judeo-Phoenician context of the 1st century.

All these references to sacred sex and fornication led Henry Chadwick to speculate that behind it all there must be a lost gospel of some kind: "an apocryphal work . . . the mother of their [Gnostic] licentiousness."[123] Now, finally, we have the text Chadwick was looking for: a gospel that makes sense, from the inside, of the actions that gave rise to the various accusations—namely, sacred sex based on Jesus' union with Mary the Magdalene, a former priestess of Artemis.

Marriage as Redemptive

When we leave the orbit of Pauline Christianity, we enter a vastly different conceptual environment. As we have seen, *Joseph and Aseneth* finds its natural home in Valentinian Gnosticism. In fact, it seems to describe the situation that gave rise to that Gnosticism. It is similar to such important writings as the *Gospel of Philip*, the *Gospel of Mary*, and *The Secret Book of John*. The focus, concepts, and intellectual landscape of all these texts mirror each other.

With *Joseph and Aseneth* and Valentinian Gnosticism, the emphasis is on life, happiness, and redemption—not suffering, death, and salvation through participation in Christ's "passion." In Gnosticism, the focus is on celebrating vitality and offspring. The most holy act is the sacrament of the bridal chamber—that is, sacred sex. According to this view, the "aeon" Jesus (i.e., the enlightened Jesus) fulfilled his task not when he became a human and not when he was crucified, but when he met, married, and had sexual intercourse with Mary the Magdalene. In this way, he returned the wayward Sophia to her proper home. As the *Gospel of Philip* (63:33) states, "Sophia . . . is the mother of the angels and the companion of the [savior]. The [savior loved] Mary of Magdala more than [all the disciples], [and he] kissed her often. . . ."[124] More than this, both in the Gospel of John and the Gnostic *Gospel of Philip*, Jesus is described as the "Word." Here is how the *Gospel of Philip* describes it:

> Humans have sex with humans, horses have sex with horses, donkeys have sex with donkeys. Members of a species have sex with members of the same species. So also the spirit has intercourse with spirit, word mingles with word, light mingles [with light] . . . if [you] become human, [a human] will love you. If you become [spirit], spirit will unite with you. If you become word, word will have intercourse with you.[125]

Since Jesus is the "Word," who is he having "intercourse" with? Clearly it has to be someone on the same level as him. If he is a god made flesh—"in the beginning there was the Word . . . and the Word became flesh" (John 1:1–15)—the *Gospel of Philip* is alluding to a goddess also made flesh. Here is an explicit reference to the idea: "if you become Word, Word will have intercourse with you." Notice the Gnostic philosophy: as you ascend spiritually, you also ascend physically. Remember, it is only after Aseneth/Mary the Magdalene's repentance that the angel comes to her bed.

Put differently, according to Valentinian Gnostics, when Jesus married Mary the Magdalene, he literally re-harmonized the cosmos. In a sense, their union returned humanity to a pre-exile-from-paradise state. In the Garden of Eden, Adam and Eve were blameless and shameless. They were not even aware of their nakedness until after Eve ate of the forbidden fruit. Prior to this act of disobedience, there was no tension between the physical and the spiritual. In a sense, by mating, Jesus (the new Adam) and Mary the Magdalene (the new Eve) re-opened the door to paradise: "Adam came from two virgins, the spirit and the virgin earth. Christ was born of a virgin to correct the fall that occurred in the beginning."[126]

Historically speaking, it's now clear that the matrimonial home of Jesus and Mary the Magdalene was no ordinary home. For their followers, it was a temple. Their bedchamber was no ordinary bedchamber: "The bedchamber is . . . the holy of holy."[127] The road to salvation ran literally through their bedroom. In the words of the *Gospel of Philip*, "if someone becomes an attendant of the bridal chamber, that person will receive the light."[128]

In the Hellenized world that Jesus was born into, these kinds of ideas were not strange or novel. In some sense, they were mainstream. For example, the followers of Dionysus acknowledged the god's presence in a phallus concealed in a baby basket. One who was possessed by the god would feel this power by getting high on wine or some other drug or by becoming sexually aroused. Such a person "became one with Dionysos."[129] In other words, one could become one with the god through a ritual involving sacred sex.

When it comes to Jesus and Mary the Magdalene, we have to remember that according to their Gnostic followers, Jesus and Mary the Magdalene were no ordinary human beings. Valentinus argued that one of Jesus' defining characteristics was his self-control in all things. We can imagine what this means sexually. In fact, according to Valentinus, Jesus' "power of self-control was so great that even the food inside him was not corrupted."[130] For the Gnostics, Jesus and Mary the Magdalene were gods who had been spirit and were now flesh. The *Gospel of Philip* explicitly states "when we were Hebrews we were orphans . . . but when we became Christians we had a father *and a mother*."[131] The father and mother were Jesus and Mary the Magdalene. At this point, it is clear that there are simply no other candidates for these historical roles.

From the Valentinian point of view, when Jesus and Mary the Magdalene had intercourse, the physical and spiritual were no longer divided and all divisions disappeared. By imitating them, their followers participated fully in all that the holy couple had to offer. In a sense, they also became "Christs"—i.e., anointed ones. Basically, Paul substituted suffering for sex, but left the theological infra-structure intact. To become infused with the "Christ-Spirit," one had to suffer rather than procreate . . . but the end result was the same: "you have received the spirit of Son-ship. When we cry, 'Abba Father,' it is the Spirit itself bearing witness with our spirit that we are children of God, and if children then heirs, heirs of God and co-heirs with Christ, *provided we suffer with him* in order that we may also be glorified with him" (Romans 8:15–17).[132] In contrast, according to the Gnostics, the way to be "glorified with Christ" was not to be an ascetic who suffers like Jesus, but to find a mate and make love in the manner that Jesus and Mary the Magdalene made love. For the Gnostics, the bed, not the cross, was the ultimate symbol of redemption.[133]

Some of this sacred sex theology may have been retained as a memory in the view that Magdala was a licentious city,[134] and in the church's tradition that Mary the Magdalene was a prostitute.[135] Ours seems to be the best explanation for these traditions, since there is absolutely nothing in the Christian Bible that identifies Mary the Magdalene as a prostitute. Put differently, in the words of Nancy Qualls-Corbett, "Although clouded in confusion from Biblical scripture, I think and feel that Mary Magdalene was endowed with the selfsame attributes as the sacred prostitute."[136]

Although somewhat distorted, the original Gnosticism is even echoed in Paul's strange androgyny theology of the sexes. For example, in his letter to the Galatians, Paul states: "You are all sons of God through faith in Christ Jesus, for all of you who were baptized into Christ have clothed yourselves with Christ. There is neither Jew nor Greek, slave nor free, male nor female, for you are all one in Christ Jesus" (3:26–28). Consider what this means in a sexual context. This statement is anathema to any Torah-observant Jew where the emphasis is on holy separation (i.e., separating kosher from un-kosher, weekdays from the Sabbath, purity from impurity, etc.). With respect to male and female differ-ences, the Torah explicitly forbids a man to dress like a woman or vice versa (Deuteronomy 22:5). Meaning, in the Jewish world that Jesus and Paul were born into, men are supposed to be men and women are supposed to be women. But here is Paul proudly proclaiming that in Jesus there is neither male nor female. The Gnostics agreed. In the *Gospel of Thomas*, like Paul, Jesus states:

"When you make male and female into a single one, so that the male will not be male nor the female be female . . . then you enter [the Kingdom]."[137]

In fact, bisexuality and androgyny seem to run throughout the Gnostic texts. As another example, at one point, Peter attacks Jesus' relationship with Mary the Magdalene, arguing that "women are not worthy" of eternal life. To which Jesus responds, "I shall guide her to make her male, so that she too may become a living spirit resembling you males. For every female who makes herself male will enter Heaven's Kingdom."[138] Once again, this strengthens the parallel between Mary the Magdalene and Artemis, who is called in the Orphic hymns (36) "of manly form." Clearly, there is a vision of androgyny here—of male and female becoming one.

Of course, it will be argued that all this is metaphor. But in a Gnostic context, it can't be. For the Gnostics, the sex was real. After all, their model was not a celibate Paul, but a married Jesus. It all seems rooted in a syncretic theology of sex that evolved as a response to a real-life marriage between Jesus and a former priestess of Artemis.

To be clear, for their followers, Jesus' marriage to Mary the Magdalene healed the rift dividing male from female and humanity from God. According to the Gnostics, once the holy marriage took place, believers now had the ability to be made whole. This was a vision of a restored humanity returning to its primordial state.

The reason all this had to be a secret doctrine, or at least a doctrine revealed in stages to its adherents, is that—obviously—it can easily be misunderstood. Gnostics were aware of the potential for licentiousness built into their theology. So they opted for secrecy and secret codes: "If marriage is exposed, it has become prostitution, and the bride plays the harlot. . . ."[139] In other words, not everyone would understand the holiness of sacred sex. Not everyone would understand that when participating in this kind of Holy Communion you don't lose your virginity but, in a sense, you gain it. You move from a state of sin into a state of innocence.

From a Gnostic point of view, therefore, Mary the Magdalene was the original mother of the Church of the Gentiles, the original Virgin Mary. From this point of view, even though she had sexual relations and offspring, she was permanently in a state of spiritual purity. She was called "the mother of the virgins" (15:7). More than this, in *Joseph and Aseneth*, Mary the Magdalene becomes the shelter for those who turn to God in repentance. In effect, she was equated with repentance, and as such she was elevated to the status of "Daughter of God" (15:6). She was the necessary other half of the Jesus equation. The Gnostics would have never conceived of Jesus as celibate. They would have regarded such an idea as the height of foolishness. From their perspective, the fundamental rupture in the universe was the separation of Sophia from her mate. A celibate Jesus would have been a contradiction in terms. It would have perpetuated everything that is wrong in the world. His mission, so to speak, was not to go it alone but to correct the fact that she had. It was his God-ordained task to return her to her rightful place in the community of those spiritual beings that the Gnostics called *aeons*.

Seen in the Gnostic light, Mary the Magdalene is a co-redemptrix (that is, she is a co-redeemer of humanity) for, without her, Jesus could not have wrought salvation. According to this view, death is not conquered by Jesus' resurrection, but by the new Eve's sex life with the new Adam: "When Eve was in Adam, there was no death. When she was separated from him, death came. If [she] enters into him again and he embraces [her], death will cease to be."[140]

For at least some of their original followers, after he was gone, the possibility of redemption continued only through her. This is the logical consequence of the idea that Jesus was not a metaphysical solo act but, rather, one half of a holy dyad. To understand how this theology expresses itself after the crucifixion, we must revisit the central story of orthodox Christianity (i.e., the empty tomb) and re-examine it in light of our newfound gospel.

After the crucifixion, the discovery of the empty tomb signals Jesus' resurrection. This is the central event on which the church is based. Nothing is more important. It's as simple as that. But what actually happened, and how can we understand it in light of the Gnosticism revealed in our text?

According to the Gospels, it is none other than Mary the Magdalene who discovers the empty tomb on the Sunday after the crucifixion (John 20:1–18; Luke 24:1–12; Matthew 28:1–10; Mark 16:1–8). Put simply, the entire religion depends on her report.[141] When it comes to that report, however, the message becomes confusing and contradictory. In one scenario, Luke admits that no one believed her and her female companions: "they believed them not" (24:11). In another version, there is a "gardener" outside the tomb that Mary somehow identifies with Jesus. In several versions, there are angels involved. In one version, Peter and someone called "the beloved disciple" run a foot race to the tomb to see if it is, indeed, empty. What all these have in common is an attempt to diminish Mary the Magdalene's role in the central event of Christianity. Suddenly, it's not just Mary the Magdalene and the empty tomb—the gardener is involved, Peter is involved, the mysterious beloved disciple is involved, angels are involved, other women are involved, et cetera. In fact, so frustrated were orthodox Christians that the empty tomb was discovered by Mary the Magdalene and not by the Virgin Mary that, by the 7th century, they rewrote the story and substituted the mother for the wife.

This latter tradition appears in *The Life of the Virgin*, written by Maximus the Confessor, one of the most important theologians of the early Byzantine period. In this work, Maximus takes the classic description of Mary the Magdalene as a weeper and transforms it into a description of the Virgin Mother. His description of the mother is practically identical to the description of Aseneth, a.k.a. Mary the Magdalene, in our text, including the creation of tear puddles on the ground: "She stretched forth her hands, beat her breast, and groaned from the depths of her heart, and she endured her torments and drenched the earth with her tears."[142] Maximus then says that since the "immaculate mother was inseparable from the tomb [of the Lord] . . . she received the good news of the Resurrection before everyone else."[143] This blatant contradiction of the Gospels reflects a need to disassociate the resurrection from Mary the Magdalene. Why?

Let's look at the typology again and the Gnostic symbolism provided by our lost—now found—gospel. Joseph is Jesus. Aseneth is Mary the Magdalene. More than this, Joseph is Mithras/Helios/Apollo/Sol Invictus, and Mary the Magdalene is Ashera/Great Goddess/Artemis. What is the symbology associated with each? As we've seen "Artemis is a bee."[144] Joseph is a bull. Deuteronomy 33:17 calls him a "firstborn bull" and says "his horns are the horns of a wild ox." In the Roman pagan world, a parallel tradition is reflected in the stories associated with the Sun god Helios Mithras. The central event on which this mystery-religion was based involved the slaying of the primordial bull and the redemption of the world through his blood. The followers of Mithras had a Communion-like meal where the initiates ate bread and drank from a cup of water mixed with wine. It seems that these elements were "symbolic of the body and blood of the bull."[145]

The bull on the one hand and the bee on the other were associated in the minds of the ancients with one unique, singular phenomenon: resurrection. But the resurrection only works if they are *both* involved. This is the way Marija Gimbutas puts it: "the idea of a 'life in death' in this singularly interesting concept is expressed by the belief that the life of the bull passed into that of the bees."[146] One of the earliest writers to mention the bull-born bee is Antigonos of Karystos, about 250 B.C.E., who says: "In Egypt if you bury the ox in certain places, so that only his horns project above the ground and then saw them off, they say that bees fly out; *for the ox putrefies and is resolved into bees.*"[147]

The language of the Gospels follows the resurrection formula described by Antigonos to the letter. Namely, Jesus is buried in a tomb according to the rules of flesh putrefaction and bone reinterment. The idea is that "the ox putrefies and is resolved into bees." If he is the ox and she is the bee, then the story of the empty tomb describes the process whereby *he became her.* Those who rejected Mary the Magdalene kept the story *of* the resurrection but dismissed the vessel *for* the resurrection. They wrote other people into the event and effectively diminished her role in the whole affair.

But if we use the typology of *Joseph and Aseneth*—he is Joseph the ox and she is Artemis the bee—and place it back into its historical context, we realize that in the resurrection language of the time, the ox didn't rise out of the grave . . . he survived through the bee. Using the symbolic syntax of *Joseph and Aseneth*, we have come to realize that *the resurrected Jesus is Mary the Magdalene.*

We haven't invented the above idea. It emerges from the historical context itself and survives for centuries. For example, from the 2nd century there was a movement in Phrygia, modern Turkey, known as Montanism. A man named Montanus and two women named Priscilla and Maximilla led it. One of these "Christian prophets" had a "famous vision of Christ in female form."[148] In fact, from the 4th century onward, a tradition developed in Christian art that involved "representing Jesus as quite feminine with long hair, wide hips and even breasts."[149] Basically, Jesus came to be depicted as Mary the Magdalene.

12

JESUS AND A GENTILE

H aving explored the theological implications of the marriage of Jesus to
Mary the Magdalene, let us now return to the text and see what other
historical facts we can glean from the material. In *Joseph and Aseneth*, Aseneth
is a non-Jew. While she is transformed, she is not converted to Judaism. Dispensing with her worship of many gods and goddesses, she does come to believe
in one God and so becomes a monotheist. And she does marry a Jew. But that's
all. There's no indication that Aseneth takes upon herself any of the practices
of Judaism—nor is there any evidence that Joseph insists on her doing so. She
doesn't undergo any rite of becoming Jewish. We don't see her immersing in a
mikvah (a Jewish Baptismal pool), preparing for the Sabbath, following kosher
dietary laws, or observing Jewish festivals. She remains a non-Jew.

This suggests that Mary the Magdalene—like Aseneth—was a non-Jew and,
more importantly, stayed a non-Jew. This piece of information is very surprising,
since it implies that Jesus—a 1st-century Jewish rabbi (remember, he is called
rabbi in the Gospels[1])—married a Gentile. Does this make sense in light of any
of the known historical sources concerning Jesus?

God-Fearers
Scholars have long known that in the 1st century, many Gentiles were attracted
to and converted to Judaism. In the 1st century, according to Josephus, there

was not a town in the Roman Empire where some Gentiles did not observe the Sabbath, along with other Jewish practices such as lighting lamps and fasting.[2] Onkelos, for example, one of the greatest Torah scholars of all time (c. 35 c.e.–120 c.e.), is reported to have been a nephew of the Roman emperor Titus.[3] Beside the converts—and this may come as a surprise to most people—many Gentiles participated in synagogue activities. These non-Jews were called "God-fearers" or "Fearers of Heaven."[4] God-fearers were non-Jews who found some aspects of Judaism appealing. Remember, up to the late 1st century there was no Christianity, and until the 7th century there was no Islam. In other words, for centuries, if you rejected paganism, Judaism was the only monotheistic game in town. And many Gentiles were attracted by Judaism's uncompromising monotheism. Yet, while these people were attracted to the ethical provisions of Torah, many of them were not interested in adopting the dietary laws or Sabbath observances that went with them. Put differently, while many non-Jews accepted the norms of ethical monotheism—e.g., all humans are created in God's image—they shied away from becoming full converts to Judaism.[5] For adult Gentile males, one major impediment to full conversion was circumcision. Understandably for adults, this option is never an appealing procedure, but it was especially unappealing given 1st-century medical practices. Also, circumcision was totally inconsistent with the Hellenistic view of the human body as a temple.

For the Jews, the God-fearers were useful allies during difficult times—a group that could be counted on to help mitigate non-Jewish anger and hostility. According to Bernard Green, these people were like "a buttress from the outside rather than like a pillar from within."[6] Synagogue inscriptions refer to God-fearers as major donors to various building projects. For example, inscriptions in the Jewish synagogue at Aphrodisias, Turkey, reveal that the contributors to the synagogue in ancient times were 55% Jews, 2% converts and 43% *theosebeis* (God-fearers).[7] In the port of Ostia, north of Rome, a synagogue was excavated that reveals that there were almost as many God-fearers attending that synagogue as Jews.[8] Recently, Mark Fairchild identified what could be the earliest known synagogue at Çatiören, Turkey, ancient Cilicia—Paul country. Besides drawings of a menorah and a lulav (palm branch), he found an inscription that seems to be referring to Gentiles or God-fearers who were "Sabbath keepers" and obeyed "the Sabbath God."[9] The historian Josephus states that Jews around the world donated to the upkeep of the Temple in Jerusalem. Significantly, he adds that God-fearers contributed as well.[10] Put simply, Gentile God-fearers were an important constituency at the time of Jesus, his brother James, and, later, Paul.[11] In fact, after his vision of the risen Christ, it seems Paul targeted these God-fearers when setting up Christian congregations throughout the Jewish Diaspora. Paul's first stop in any new community was always the synagogues.[12] It is doubtful that he was trying to recruit Jews to his brand of Christianity. It is more likely that he was targeting these God-fearers, those Gentiles who had already bought into monotheism but not into Judaism's 613 Commandments. It would have been an easy sell. Basically, what Paul was saying to them was: if you are attracted to the God of Israel but not the Laws of Israel, why be second-class citizens in the synagogue when, in my church, you can be the "New Israel"? Selling monotheism without circumcision, kosher laws, and Sabbath observance worked. In Ostia, for example, we find the remains of an early church just a few yards from the synagogue. It seems that many God-fearers here preferred the New Testament to the Old, so they left the synagogue and established their own house of worship. Not unnaturally, Paul aroused the ire of synagogue officials when he detached this important constituency from their membership. In effect, Paul was not only poaching members but also removing a valued buffer—Gentiles who were sympathetic to Judaism in the midst of a predominantly anti-Jewish world.

Given the role of God-fearers in Jewish life at the time of Jesus and prior to Paul, can it be that Jesus married one of these Gentiles? Can it be that Mary the Magdalene was one of these God-fearers? This would explain a lot. In fact, it would explain the unique theology of *Joseph and Aseneth*, arising out of a Jewish/God-fearing Gentile context. Kraemer speculates that the text may have been written by a God-fearer and that "[t]his theory has the advantage of accounting for Aseneth's affinities with numerous ancient traditions and for some of its peculiar, almost chameleon-like, qualities."[13] If this is the case, what does it tell us about early Christianity? And what does it tell us about the historical Jesus?

To answer these questions, we need to investigate the circumstances of Jesus' birth.

The Virgin Birth

In Judaism, marriage is restrained by birth status. For example, to this day, a Cohen—that is, a priest—cannot marry a convert or a widow. What was Jesus' birth status? And what does this convey about his marriage possibilities? The fact is that, since antiquity, questions have been raised about the circumstances of Jesus' birth.

The Gospel of Mark, the earliest Gospel, doesn't say anything about Jesus' birth, preferring to start his account with John the Baptizer and Jesus beginning their missions. Having said this, there is a curious incident in Mark. At one point, some townspeople refer to Jesus as "the son of Mary" (6:3). In Morton Smith's words, "In Semitic usage, to refer to a man as the son of his mother was to indicate that his father's identity was uncertain."[14] Paul only says that Jesus was "born of a woman" (Galatians 4:4). For his part, Matthew 1:1 begins with an odd genealogy listing four women in Jesus' family tree. They are Tamar, Rachab, Ruth, and Bathsheba. All four women were involved in what appeared to be un-kosher relationships.[15] Tamar pretended to be a Canaanite prostitute priestess (*kedesha*) so as to seduce her father-in-law Judah (Genesis 38:1–30). She lived prior to the revelation at Mount Sinai; before there was Judaism as such. At the time of the Biblical Exodus, Rachab ran some kind of inn or cultic Canaanite prostitution house in Jericho (Joshua 2:3). Ruth was a Moabite (Ruth 1:4), technically forbidden to Jews (Deuteronomy 23:3).[16] More than this, according to Talmudic tradition, she was a princess (*Ruth R. ii.9*), which automatically would have made her a pagan priestess. After she was widowed, she followed her mother-in-law, Naomi, to the land of Israel and seduced Naomi's kinsman Boaz (Ruth 3:14). Although we don't know Bathsheba's ethnic origins, we suspect she is not an Israelite. She was married to a Hittite general in King David's army and, after the King famously saw her bathing on a rooftop, she ended up married to David. Since her first husband was not a Jew and her name can be read as *daughter of the oath*, Bathsheba may very well have been a convert (2 Samuel 11:3). Notice all four women were not Jewish, and all of them were involved in some kind of sexual affair, often in a cultic context. Most importantly, the messianic line was established out of all four. Clearly, in writing this genealogy, Matthew is providing us with an apologetic for Jesus' birth. Namely, the messianic line is shrouded in mystery. Out of seemingly illicit sexual relationships comes the Savior of the world. In other words, the long historical march to the final apocalypse and the Kingdom of God is sometimes strewn with some less-than-kosher sex.

But this is not all.

The Gospels depict Joseph—the Virgin Mary's husband—as not believing Mary's virgin birth story until he receives divine revelation himself (Matthew 1:1–22). Presumably, the other people in the village who did not receive divine revelation continued to think that Mary was with child from a man to whom she was not betrothed. The point being that if we take the Gospel of Matthew at face value, he's telling us four things concerning Jesus' birth: first, his mother was impregnated by the Holy Spirit; second, everyone including her husband thought that she had been impregnated by another man; third, her husband was eventually convinced otherwise by divine revelation; fourth, though it didn't look good to anyone else, the Messiah's birth had been heralded by four relationships that were, on the surface, improper.

From the point of view of Christian theology, all this is irrelevant since, at the end of the day, Jesus' birth was miraculous. Meaning, Joseph's suspicions, Jesus' strange pedigree, et cetera are all irrelevant since Jesus' birth was the result of a virginal conception and a virgin birth. These doctrines, first put forward by the Gospels of Matthew and Luke and then elaborated upon in the later *Infancy Gospel of James*, assert that Mary, mother of Jesus, who was a teenage girl at the time, became pregnant through the activity of God's Holy Spirit.

More than this, according to some forms of Christian theology, there were no obvious signs of pregnancy when it came to Jesus: no distension of Mary's uterus and no disruption to her hymen. Rarely in Christian art do we encounter a depiction of a pregnant Madonna, and for good reason: according to some ancient sources, she did not "show." The rather lurid *Infancy Gospel of James* goes so far as to depict a midwife reaching into Mary's vagina to check the status of her hymen . . . such was the thoroughness of the ancient church fathers and writers to make sure that Mary was perceived as a virgin, before and after Jesus' birth. Incidentally, this particular text was enormously popular and could have easily become part of the New Testament scripture.[17]

Furthermore, as the theology developed, Mary herself was said to have had a special birth. After all, she was the carrier of God's humanity. Remember, in ancient times, women were viewed as vessels. They contributed nothing to the human being that they gave birth to, other than being the "container," so to speak, for the germination of the male seed. DNA and ova had not yet been discovered. To become a holy "vessel," Mary herself had to be holy. So, for some Christians whose faith includes the doctrine of the Immaculate Conception,

Mary's own birth by her mother Anna is depicted as taking place without the assistance of Mary's father, Joachim. Presumably, Anna was also impregnated with divine seed.[18]

Shielding Jesus and his mother, Mary, from anything sexual seems to have been a special preoccupation with early church writers, as if virginity, asceticism, and avoidance of anything sexual were vitally important for purity. When it came to the orthodox Christian view of Jesus' birth, there was a virtual obsession with sexual purity and the avoidance of contamination brought about as a result of sexual intercourse. This culminated in the view of the philosopher Augustine (end of 4th century, beginning of 5th) that the fault/sin of Adam—that is, the whole reason why human beings are mortal—is transmitted biologically in the male sperm.

Many Christians have—and still do—interpret these birth doctrines of Jesus and his mother Mary as biological and historical. Put simply, Mary and Jesus were literally the product of virgin births. Most scholars, however, hold that these birth narratives represent, at best, a way of speaking, not a historical record.

As it turns out, Roman emperors such as Augustus and founders of competing religions such as Dionysus and Mithras also had virgin births. Proclaiming that Jesus had a virginal birth was a way of saying that Jesus was a celebrity, a god, and on the same plane as these illustrious figures. Furthermore, in the transformation of the Jesus of history into the Christ of Pauline Christianity, Jesus was distanced from his Judaism, taking on more and more pagan traits. In this light, he could not be anything less than the Roman–Persian man–god Mithras, for example. But virgin birth in this sense was more of a literary device, not a report concerning an actual historical occurrence.

Even as a literary conceit, the idea of an actual virgin birth has always posed problems for many readers of the New Testament. For one thing, there are differences in the birth narratives in the Gospels and, for that matter, in the *Infancy Gospel of James*. The latter states that the birth occurred in a cave in Bethlehem—and that's what the historic Church of the Nativity seems to be saying: that he was not born in a manger or a stable as in the earlier writings but, rather, in a cave under the church. The Gospel of Luke has Jesus' family traveling from Bethlehem to Jerusalem for Jesus' circumcision, as per tradition, on the 8th day following his birth. The Gospel of Matthew, on the other hand, has the family fleeing to Egypt to avoid the wrath of Herod the Great. There are wise men—Magi or astrologers—in Matthew's account; there are shepherds in Luke's version. Furthermore, the dating of Jesus' birth also differs from source to source: prior to the death of Herod the Great in 4 B.C.E. (Gospel of Matthew) or during a census almost a decade later (Gospel of Luke).

Most problematic for the virgin-birth theory—besides the fact that normally virgins don't give birth—is the well-recognized problem that the Gospel of Matthew misapplies a passage from the Hebrew prophet Isaiah concerning a "young" woman giving birth. Searching for a Biblical passage that could be interpreted as being "fulfilled" in the birth of Jesus, the author of the Gospel of Matthew quotes from the Greek version of Isaiah. That version wrongly translates the original Hebrew word *alma* as virgin. This is the only instance of *alma* being translated as "virgin." In all other instances, *alma* is translated as "young woman." The original Hebrew line in Isaiah states that a *young woman*, not a virgin, will give birth to the redeemer (7:14). In other words, the entire virgin-birth narrative may be the result of a mistranslation from Hebrew to Greek.

Problems about the Jesus birth narratives multiply. This story undercuts the whole point of the genealogies relating to Jesus, which trace his ancestry back through his father Joseph to King David, to Abraham (Matthew) and to Adam (Luke). All those genealogies attempt to show that Jesus was a descendant of King David. After all, that was a precondition for the Jewish Messiah. He had to be a descendant of David. But a virgin birth cuts the bond between Jesus and his ancestors by removing Joseph—the genealogical link—from the scene. Simply put, the virgin birth story renders the genealogies pointless and undermines the claim that Jesus is a biological descendant of King David.

A virgin birth, moreover, makes Jesus a divine-human, a hybrid of sorts, and this then poses all sorts of complex theological problems. For instance, Jesus was baptized by his cousin John the Baptizer. But John's baptizing water ritual was for the express purpose of attaining forgiveness of sins. Was the divine-human Jesus in need of such forgiveness? If so, what was his sin? If he didn't need forgiveness, then what was the point of this procedure?

Also, the virgin birth poses problems for understanding Jesus' death: did Jesus actually die? Did only part of him die, the human part, leaving the divine portion intact (since, by definition, God cannot die)? Did all of Jesus suffer, or only his human part? These questions are not academic, at least not for the early church.

Most people today prefer to skip over the story of the virgin birth, even though it is mentioned in the Nicene Creed as part of official Christian theology. Probably, in the West at least, many prefer to think of Jesus as the child of Mary and Joseph, born of a normal human birth. They think of the virgin birth as representing some kind of Christmas-type spin on Jesus' importance. This idea accords with recent scholarship. According to many scholars, Jesus' virgin birth is a fiction far removed from the historical Jesus—a story designed to convey the message that Jesus was exceptionally important on the world's stage.

In light of our findings that Jesus was modeled on Helios, we should note that what the virgin-birth narrative does demonstrate is that very early on, within fifty or sixty years of his death, Jesus was already being imaged by his followers in ways that Gentiles around the Mediterranean world would easily have understood. A virgin birth was not part of Jewish culture but very much an element of Roman civic and religious mythology. The depiction of Jesus as Helios and Mary the Magdalene as Artemis is consistent with this early trend to move Jesus out of his Jewish matrix into mainstream Roman culture.

But what of the Jewish context that Jesus was born into? The reason we dwell on the problems surrounding his birth is that if Jesus was perceived as having been born of an adulterous relationship, his status under Jewish law would have been as a *mamzer* (one born of an illicit relationship) and he would not have been allowed to marry a fellow Jew.

It's important to remember what *mamzer* means under Jewish law. It does not mean bastard, a child born outside of wedlock. A *mamzer* in Jewish law refers to a child born as a result of an illicit sexual union. As Bruce Chilton clearly puts it in *Rabbi Jesus*, "the fundamental issue [in Jewish law] was not sex before marriage (which was broadly tolerated) but sex with a wrong person, someone other than your husband."[19] According to this criterion, even if we accept the Christian tradition that God the Father miraculously impregnated Mary, practically speaking, the outcome for Jesus would have been the same. Since you cannot prove a virginal conception, Mary's child would have been regarded as a *mamzer*—even if God were the father. Put simply, if Jesus' father was not Mary's husband, Jesus would have been treated as a *mamzer*.

Jesus as *Mamzer*

As it turns out, a virgin birth is not the only ancient account of how Jesus came to be born. There are several other versions.

Above, we saw that an analysis of the Gospels—e.g., Matthew's genealogy—leads to the conclusion that Jesus' birth may have been suspect. This idea is bolstered by sources outside of the Gospels. For example, there is an ancient tradition preserved in the Talmud—the 2nd-century rabbinic code—hinting that Jesus was a *mamzer.* In one place in the Talmud the text refers to a young woman named Mary who engaged in an adulterous union with a person called Pantera. It does not say, however, that this liaison resulted in the birth of Jesus, just that Mary and Pantera had an affair.[20] Elsewhere in the Talmud, it explicitly relates this affair to the birth of a child. There, Jesus is called *ben Pantera*, that is, son of Pantera.[21]

In the late 2nd century, a Greek philosopher by the name of Celsus also attacked what he regarded as the foundations of Christianity.[22] Celsus contended that a man named Panthera made Mary pregnant. Celsus specifies that this individual was a Roman soldier. This charge is specific with respect to the name of Jesus' father and his occupation.[23] In the final analysis, what the Talmudic and pagan sources point to represents an alternate explanation for Jesus' birth, namely, that he was the result of an illicit union between Mary and a Roman soldier named Panthera or Pantera. Amazingly, in 1859 in Germany, archaeologists found a tombstone of a Roman soldier who had served in the Holy Land around the time of Jesus' birth. His name was Tiberius Iulius Abdes Pantera.[24]

As shocking as this story might be to modern Christian sensibility, the idea that Jesus could have been born as a result of a union between Mary and a soldier named Pantera is not unlikely. Although neither the Gospels nor the Talmud nor Celsus suggest this, Mary's pregnancy might have been the result of a rape. In 1st-century Galilee, this would not have been unusual. At the time of Jesus' birth (and Herod's death), there was a massive revolt in the land of Israel led by three messianic figures who were—like Jesus—called "good shepherds" by their followers.[25] Josephus tells us the names of all three leaders: Simon in Peraea, an area in modern Jordan where John the Baptizer met his end; Athronges in the Jerusalem area; and, finally, Judah, close to Jesus' home in the Galilee.[26] When the revolt was put down, hundreds, perhaps thousands, of children were born as a result of the violence of the Roman victory. In other words, Jesus was not born into a pastoral setting populated by wise men and shepherds. He was born in the midst of revolution where death, crucifixion, and rape were commonplace.

Jesus could also have been born as a result of a love match between a Roman soldier and a very young innocent, naïve Jewish girl. The fact is that many Roman soldiers serving in the area were not Roman. While most officers were indeed Roman, many soldiers were Phoenician (Semitic Canaanites) or even Jews. Interestingly, the Pantera tombstone in Germany calls him *Abdes* or slave in Hebrew/Phoenician.[27] This clue allows us to recreate his biography. The tombstone tells us that he died in 40 c.e., after forty years of service. Meaning, he entered the Roman army around the time that Jesus was born.

If Pantera started his military career as a slave, he would have been freed, as was the custom, after twenty-five years of service. His adopted name Tiberius tells us that he became a free man during the reign of Emperor Tiberius. It was in the early 30s, during the reign of this same emperor, that Jesus was crucified—approximately seven years after Pantera's status had changed from captive to free man. Is it possible that Pantera was a Jewish revolutionary enslaved as a result of the revolt that took place at the same time as Jesus' birth? Is it possible that he was transferred from the area of Judaea to Germany just prior to being granted freedom? Of course it is. When Roman soldiers were freed, they were given land, but it was Roman policy to free them far away from their homeland so that they wouldn't become powerful among their own people. Is it possible, therefore, that while Pantera was serving Rome in Germany, the Roman army was crucifying his son in Jerusalem? The chronology makes sense.

Whatever the historical reconstruction, what is certain is that there's a certain ambiguity in the sources about Jesus' birth status. To comprehend why, we have to understand what exactly constitutes an adulterous relationship in Jesus' world. As stated, under rabbinic law, if a betrothed or married Jewish woman becomes pregnant from a Jew other than her husband, then the child is considered a *mamzer*. Surprisingly, if the father is a non-Jew, there is no negative social impact on the child's status. For instance, if a Gentile Roman soldier raped a married Jewish woman, the resulting child *would not* have been considered a *mamzer*. On the other hand, if the same woman had a consensual sexual relationship with a Roman soldier who happened to be Jewish, the child *would have* been considered a *mamzer*.[28] Put simply, adultery with a fellow Jew has a far greater negative impact on the child than adultery with a non-Jew.

Perhaps the rabbinic view concerning adultery results from the fact that a Jewish woman was not supposed to be sleeping with a Gentile under any circumstances. As a result, there are no laws governing what, in effect, should not have happened in the first place. In any event, it is better for a child resulting from an adulterous relationship if the father is a non-Jew. This way, he is not considered a *mamzer* and he can marry anyone he wants to when he reaches adulthood. On the other hand, if his community considers him a *mamzer*, he may not marry a Jewish woman under any circumstances.

If Jesus' biological father was both Jewish and a Roman soldier, that would have resulted in a confusing view of his birth status. Rumors would have surrounded him from birth and, practically speaking, no Jewish woman would have been available to him for marriage.

We can now get back to *Joseph and Aseneth*. When Aseneth is first smitten by Joseph, she states, "Is he not the son of a shepherd from Canaan?" (4:11). It's odd that she would be referring to Joseph's father as a Canaanite shepherd, or even as a shepherd from Canaan. The story doesn't require a reference to the Biblical Jacob at this point. And when he does appear, Jacob is referred to as being "like a god," not a shepherd (22:3).

But if Aseneth is Mary the Magdalene, perhaps the reference is serving another purpose. Perhaps she's talking about Jesus. In this case, what she's telling us can provide a tremendous insight into Jesus' psyche. Why? Because if his father was not Joseph—and that's what the canonical Gospels tell us—but a Roman soldier as reported by Celsus and the Talmud, then the only way Jesus could have defended himself from the charge of being a *mamzer* was to prove the *non-Jewishness* of his Roman father. It's hard for a modern audience to appreciate the social impact of the situation—the only way for Jesus to prove that he wasn't a *mamzer* was to publicly admit that his mother was guilty of adultery, with a non-Jew no less. That would have been tantamount to accusing her of being a prostitute. But his wife could defend him. In this light, it seems that Aseneth's casual remark about Jesus' Canaanite pedigree is a polemic against the rumor that Pantera was a Roman soldier of Jewish ethnicity.

If Jesus didn't publicly defend himself, however, that would have created a permanent ambiguity around him. This ambiguity is reflected, for example, in the Talmud where it hints at but never explicitly states that Jesus is a *mamzer*, while authoritative commentaries on the Talmud like Rashi and Maimonides say that he was. It's even reflected in the Gospels themselves, where Jesus is referred to by the unlikely reference to his mother and not his father: "Isn't this Mary's son?" (Mark 6:3).

Being regarded as a *mamzer* would have had serious implications for Jesus' life. In the first instance, he would have had to live with constant aspersions. This may account for his interest in those who had been marginalized by society: tax collectors, people who were possessed, the sick, and women. Most importantly, it would have limited his marriage options. Deuteronomy makes clear the dire consequences of being a *mamzer*—"those born of an illicit union shall not be admitted to the assembly of the Lord. Even to the tenth generation, none of their descendants shall be admitted to the assembly of the Lord" (Deuteronomy 23:2).

There was, however, one way that a *mamzer* could get around the *mamzer* marriage prohibitions and have children that were "admitted to the assembly of the Lord." In Jewish law, religious affiliation is passed down through the woman, so a *mamzer* like Jesus (who could not marry a Jewess) could marry a Gentile woman and have their Gentile children converted to Judaism. In other words, if Jesus was regarded as a *mamzer* and he still wanted a kosher Jewish family, he would have had to marry a non-Jew and convert their children to Judaism. Incredibly, the only metaphor for this type of situation is the honeybee. Because bees were considered virginal, their bodies were regarded as mere vessels for their offspring. As a result, in Judaism, honey is the only kosher food that is the product of an un-kosher animal. Put differently, Jesus' marriage to a Gentile makes sense if he were a *mamzer*, or perceived to be a *mamzer*. His wife would have been, so to speak, his queen bee. Although his fellow Jews would have regarded his wife with suspicion, their converted children would have been regarded as kosher. This situation is exactly what we find in *Joseph and Aseneth*.[29]

In this light, *Joseph and Aseneth*'s insistence that Mary the Magdalene was a non-Jew fits with the tradition that Jesus was suspected of being born of an illegitimate relationship. Further, its association of Mary the Magdalene with the queen bee Artemis is a fitting apologetic for why a Galilean rabbi would have had children with a priestess of Artemis. More than this, the portrayal of Aseneth/Mary the Magdalene as a pagan priestess fits the Gospel of Matthew's apologetic concerning women in Jesus' genealogy who, on the surface, appeared as pagan priestesses involved in illicit sex. In fact, *Joseph and Aseneth* seems to be telling us that Jesus' marriage to Mary the Magdalene is part of a divine plan: precisely because she was a Phoenician/Canaanite priestess, Mary the Magdalene's transformation could bring the non-Jewish world into the process of redemption and salvation. According to our text, when Mary the Magdalene turned her back on her pagan past, like the Biblical Ruth, she initiated a process whereby the Gentile world could be brought into the Kingdom of God.

But is this history, or is it theology? Is Mary the Magdalene a literary figure, or an actual historical person? Does the story of *Joseph and Aseneth* fit with what we know of 1st-century Galilee? Did Jesus even know Gentiles, never mind marry one of them?

First of all, despite quaint Hollywood images that, at the time of Jesus, the land of Israel was populated by Jews in sandals and bed sheets, there were tens of thousands of non-Jews living in the Galilee. The Galilee was a melting pot of Jews, Gentiles, and God-fearers as well as worshippers of Zeus, Artemis, Dionysus, and many other deities. Recall that Sepphoris, the luxurious Roman city that has been excavated and archaeologically restored with its opulent buildings and beautiful mosaics, was located right on the doorstep of Nazareth. But that wasn't the only Hellenistic or Gentile center. At the time of Jesus' birth, on the western shore of the Sea of Galilee, Herod Antipas—Herod the Great's son—erected a gleaming new Hellenistic city in honor of his patron, the Roman emperor, Tiberius. Of course, he called it Tiberias. In fact, to totally ingratiate himself with the emperor, Herod Antipas also founded a Galilean city in honor of Tiberius' mother, Livias. But these were not Gentile exceptions in the Galilee area. Just across the small freshwater lake called the Sea of Galilee, there was a confederation of ten—count them, ten—Gentile cities called the Decapolis. And to the north of the Galilee (modern-day Lebanon), the land was populated by coastal Canaanites more commonly called "Phoenicians." In other words, to live in the Galilee was to live in a Gentile-Jewish context, not a Jewish backwater.

Most interestingly, Magdala, the town usually connected to Mary the Magdalene, was in many ways a Gentile city, specifically Phoenician, and primarily engaged in the production of salted fish. Much of Magdala's products were sent to Tiberias just a few miles south, to Damascus to the northeast, and to Tyre and Sidon up the coast in Phoenician territory. From these commercial hubs and Mediterranean port cities, Magdala's salted fish would have made their way throughout the empire.

As a result of all this, many of Magdala's inhabitants were Gentiles. The proof is in the material culture found in Magdala and in Bethsaida, a related Galilean town engaged in the fishing industry. Specifically, the archaeology reveals coins, statues, altars, and so forth. that attest to the fact that the residents of these towns were both Jewish and Gentile. Magdala also had many links to Phoenicia just a few miles to the northwest, outside Jewish territory. Even Jesus visited Phoenicia—the regions of Tyre and Sidon—on a mysterious trip to a specific house that is never identified by the Gospel writers. Curiously, this was a visit he wanted no one to know about, and no explanation for this silence is ever given in Christian tradition (Mark 7:24). Was he meeting his in-laws there? Or possibly his biological father, Pantera, who may have been stationed there? After all, Pantera's tombstone in Germany says that he was "from Sidon."

No matter how we answer these questions, Jesus clearly would have been aware of Gentiles. Even if his father was not a Gentile, he would have encountered non-Jews wherever he went and, very likely, there were even Gentile God-fearers in the synagogue in Capernaeum, his main headquarters. So perhaps a suspected *mamzer* living in the Jerusalem area would have resigned himself to his fate and remained unmarried his entire life. In Judaism's heartland, there were fewer Gentiles around and, since they came as occupiers, the interface with them was often hostile. But in the Galilee, the situation was different. The opportunities to do business with Gentiles, develop similar religious ideas, and even marry them were everywhere. Based on the evidence, the suggestion in *Joseph and Aseneth* that Jesus' wife was a Gentile makes sense.

In sum, we didn't expect to find a text that describes Mary the Magdalene as Jesus' wife. Nor did we expect that she would turn out to be a reformed Canaanite/Phoenician priestess. But when we evaluated the startling information conveyed in *Joseph and Aseneth* and compared it to the Gospels, the Talmud, pagan/Greco-Roman texts, and the archaeological and historical data, we found a perfect fit. The new information gleaned from *Joseph and Aseneth* about Mary the Magdalene allows us to bring this woman out of the historical shadows and to discover the human being behind the myth.

What Do We Know about Mary the Magdalene?
From the canonical Gospels, we don't know how and when Jesus and Mary the Magdalene met. In the Gospels, we are simply told that she accompanied

Jesus wherever he went and that she was wealthy, helping to underwrite the considerable costs of his activities. Maybe she had investments in some of the fish-processing plants in Magdala. Maybe her father was a salted-fish baron. Perhaps she had inherited money. Whatever the case, as the Gospels and *Joseph and Aseneth* illustrate, she was drawn to Jesus.

Mary the Magdalene was with Jesus when he died. She witnessed his suffering upon the cross, and she was the one who went to claim his body on that fateful Sunday morning, so as to prepare it for proper burial.[30] Deep in mourning and stunned by the empty tomb, she is called the first witness to the resurrection, as it states in Mark: "He first appeared to Mary the Magdalene" (16:9). Take note, according to the canonical Gospels, it is the Magdalene—not Jesus' mother, nor his siblings, nor his disciples—who is "the first witness." Mary the Magdalene was, in every sense, Jesus' closest companion. As the Gnostic Gospels tell us, she was the first apostle. A later Christian tradition says that after Jesus' death, she went to Ephesus. But *Joseph and Aseneth* seems to suggest otherwise. It seems to be telling us that she stayed in the Jerusalem area to the end.

Someone might ask: if, as you say, Mary the Magdalene was so important to Jesus and to the evolving Christian theology, why doesn't the New Testament tell us more about her? Why are we only now hearing about her? Why has the Roman Catholic Church only recently reversed its age-old position that she was a reformed prostitute?[31]

In answer to these questions, we suggest that Mary the Magdalene was intentionally written out of the New Testament. In the words of Margaret Starbird, "I believe that the earliest Christian heresy was the denial of the bride."[32] Understanding *Joseph and Aseneth* as a lost gospel of the early Jesus movement allows us to revisit another early Christian text, *The Acts of Thomas*, and finally see it for what it is—a transition document between Jesus and Mary the Magdalene's theology of the bride and her chamber, and Paul's theology of Christian asceticism.

The Acts of Thomas tells the story of Thomas, the twin brother of Jesus (i.e., a Jesus look-alike), who goes to India as a slave and ends up attending the wedding of the King's only daughter. At the wedding, Thomas sings a strange hymn in his native Hebrew. In *Joseph and Aseneth* fashion, the hymn describes the bride, focusing on her garments, her head, her feet, her tongue, her neck, her fingers, her bridal chamber, her gaits, and her bridesmaids. In other words, like the Syriac version of Aseneth, *The Acts of Thomas* draws from the Biblical Song of Songs to describe the would-be bride in overtly erotic terms. But it does so only to subvert the eros. In *The Acts of Thomas*, the bride is quickly transformed into a metaphor for the church. Here we have a veritable snapshot of the moment when a real-life woman is transformed into a church and a real-life wedding is transformed into a theology of abstinence. In other words, you marry the church, not each other.

In *The Acts of Thomas*, Jesus appears in the bridal chamber in the form of Thomas and persuades the bride and groom not to consummate their marriage. The day after the wedding night, the would-be lover–bride sits unveiled and announces that she has no need for the veil because she has given up on sex: "I'm no longer ashamed or abashed since the work of shame and bashfulness has been removed from me."[33] Commenting on this, Kraemer states, "Here, as in Aseneth 15.1, where the angelic figure instructs Aseneth to remove her head covering, sexuality and covering are clearly linked."[34] But there is a difference. As Kraemer notes, in *The Acts of Thomas*, "the unveiled woman is 'asexual'."[35] Meaning, *The Acts of Thomas* subverts the theology of *Joseph and Aseneth*. Whereas in *Joseph and Aseneth* the Jesus look-alike angel sits on Aseneth's bed and prepares her for marriage and intercourse with Joseph, in *The Acts of Thomas* the Jesus look-alike, Thomas, sits on the bridal bed and persuades the newlyweds to abstain from sex. Kraemer is intrigued by the fact that in *The Acts of Thomas* the newly converted couple express their devotion to Jesus "by sexual abstinence," and in *Joseph and Aseneth* the convert to monotheism expresses her devotion to Joseph "through sexual love, fidelity and childbearing." She concludes by stating that, in contrast to *The Acts of Thomas*, "Aseneth's message is clearly that sexuality and marriage are good and divinely ordained."[36]

But how do the two contradictory messages relate to each other? We have seen that *Joseph and Aseneth* is preserving a real-life relationship between Jesus and Mary the Magdalene. We now see that *The Acts of Thomas* records the moment that real history was transformed into a new theology. Put differently, Jesus is transformed from a husband and a lover into a ghost that visits bridal chambers so as to persuade newlyweds not to consummate their vows.

How did the original theology get forgotten?

First, we need to recall that the documents that make up the New Testament weren't decided upon until the late 4th century and that they represent a very careful culling of early Christian writings. The simple fact is that only those texts that supported the theological position of the faction favored by the Roman emperors were selected for inclusion. The writings used by all other Christian groups—the Gnostic Christians and the Ebionites, for instance—were omitted. Within Gnostic Christianity, as already mentioned, Mary the Magdalene was accorded a preeminent role. Yet those writings were deliberately excluded.

Second, sexual activity was threatening to the early church fathers who interpreted the new religion as demanding an ascetic mode of life. Virginity and the renunciation of sexuality were prized. Paul had only allowed marriage for those who had lost all self-control (1 Corinthians 7:9). Moreover, the writings that eventually wound their way into the New Testament said nothing about Jesus being married. Oddly enough, there is no clear-cut support for marriage and family life in the New Testament. No "family values." Nor is there any healthy role model for marriage. It is always second best to celibacy and sexual abstinence—second best to becoming a eunuch for the Kingdom of God.[37]

A third reason has to do with power struggles within the early church, specifically the success of Paul's version of Christianity over the beliefs held by Jesus' first followers. Paul's Christ-centered, non-Torah-observant, pro-Roman movement garnered huge support from Gentiles eager for a faith-based—not Torah-based—salvation. Paul's religion met their needs. It didn't involve Torah laws. It simply required faith in the Christ figure; a dying–rising god–human savior similar to Dionysus and Mithras. For Paul, salvation did not involve *mitzvoth*, the Torah-commanded "good works." In fact, Paul shied away from any suggestion that one could earn eternal life through good deeds. According to Paul, faith would ideally manifest itself in good works, but this was not essential. Everything was placed on faith . . . and faith alone.

Paul had help on his way to theological victory. Basically, the Romans took out his opponents. Paul's success and those of his followers in the 1st and 2nd centuries occurred at a time when Judaea was racked by wars against Rome— the Great Revolt from 66 to 70 C.E., and then the Bar Kochba revolt of 132 to 135 C.E. During these times, the leadership of all Jewish movements was vastly compromised and their people were dispersed. This dramatically affected Jesus' first followers because, in essence, with the destruction of Jerusalem, their power base was lost and their Jesus-inspired ideas were marginalized. In other words, history, politics, and theology all conspired to diminish the original followers of Jesus and their ideas. Paul's *Christ* eclipsed their *Jesus*, and they got written out of the narrative. For example, what do we know about Jesus' twelve disciples? Pretty much nothing. And if it was important to write Jesus' disciples out of history, it was even more important to diminish Mary the Magdalene. Why? Because Paul was reaching out to Gentiles and, as we now know, she was a Gentile. Not only that, she had been regarded by Jesus' earliest followers as the co-redemptrix of humanity, the Bride of God.

Based on the new evidence, let's try to understand what the Church of the Gentiles looked like before Paul got involved.

The Church of the Gentiles

After the crucifixion, Jesus' brother James led the Jesus Movement, the first Jewish followers of Jesus. According to Josephus, James was killed in a political struggle in the year 62 C.E. By this point, the original group was seriously compromised, losing first Jesus and then James. Four years later, the great Jewish Revolt began and four years after that, Jerusalem—headquarters for the Jesus Movement—was reduced to a smoldering heap of ash. Thousands were crucified, tens of thousands were taken into slavery, and, according to Josephus, hundreds of thousands died from starvation.

According to Christian tradition,[38] the early followers didn't just disappear. They regrouped under the leadership of another brother of Jesus, Simon (or Simeon), who, according to Christian tradition, was also crucified. The church father Eusebius records the names of fifteen leaders of the Jesus Movement down to the time of the Bar Kochba revolt in 132 C.E.: James, Simeon, Justus, Zaccheus, Tobias, Benjamin, John, Matthew, Philip, Seneca, Justus, Levi, Ephres, Joseph, and Judas. Eusebius says that they were all Jews—many of them must have been related to Jesus—and he adds that they "received the knowledge of Christ pure and unadulterated."[39] After the destruction of Judaea, Jesus' birthplace, the original followers lost their cohesiveness and were scattered to the ends of the earth. In time, we learn of a group called Ebionites and another called Nazarenes who appear to trace their lineage back to the early Jesus Movement in Jerusalem.

It may be a hard concept for someone raised in the Christian tradition to understand, but the original followers of Jesus were not Christians, at least not in the way that we understand Christianity today. Though the Roman Catholic

Church argues that there is an unbroken tradition from Jesus to Peter to the present-day Pope, historically speaking it seems clear that the early followers of Jesus had no inkling of the Christianity that caught on in the Roman Empire. Rather, they looked upon Jesus as a special human and as a teacher—a rabbi who had announced the Kingdom of God for which they had been patiently waiting.[40]

The early followers observed Torah, as Jesus himself seems to have done. They probably read a version of the Gospel of Matthew that did not include the virgin-birth narrative, and they rejected the letters of Paul. For them, Paul was a false teacher. According to Robert Eisenman, the two-thousand-year-old Dead Sea Scrolls discovered at Qumran in 1947 preserve their view of Paul in documents referring to a "spouter of lies."[41] Even if these documents refer to someone other than Paul, it's clear that the early followers of Jesus hated Paul. After all, by his own admission (Acts 26:4), Paul was a persecutor of Jesus' followers.[42] More than this, when he arrives in Jerusalem, after his vision of Christ, there is an attempt to lynch him. Only the timely intervention of the Roman army saves Paul from his fellow Jews (Acts 21:30–33). It's clear that the only ones who would have been aware of, or cared about, Paul's activities were the original Jesus followers.[43] It was they who wanted him dead.

In time, the churches that followed Paul would denounce these early Jesus groups as heretical. By the time of Constantine and the victory of this form of Christianity over all others, Eusebius has nothing but nasty words for the so-called Ebionites. He dismissed them with contempt, saying that the reason that they are called the "poor ones" is because they are feebleminded.[44] This represents an ironic twist of history. Simply put, the theology espoused by Jesus, his brother James, his brother Simon—all martyred at the hands of the Roman authorities or their lackeys—and the theology of their first followers was utterly rejected by the evolving church. The headquarters of the new Christ-centered religion moved from Jerusalem to Rome. Ironically, Paul's Church did not succeed among the people who knew Jesus, but among the very people who crucified him.

We are left with a question that the victorious Pauline church would have preferred that no one ever ask: what happened to the pre-Paul Church of the Gentiles? Meaning, what happened to the original followers of Jesus who were not Jewish? These people were unlike the first Jewish followers. For Jesus' later

Gentile followers, they would have been a theologically threatening group—a group to be written out of history. For the longest time, the cover-up worked. But given recent discoveries, we can try to reconnect with this long-forgotten movement. We can finally ask: What were their beliefs and practices? How significant were they numerically? Did Mary the Magdalene lead them after Jesus' execution? And what did they make of the religion developed in the 40s and 50s by Paul? We can't provide answers for all these questions, but our decoded gospel may finally provide some of the answers we are looking for.

Like Aseneth—that is, Mary the Magdalene—the original Church of the Gentiles probably did not follow all the laws of Torah. After all, they were Gentile God-fearers and not converts to Judaism. They likely followed the so-called Noahide laws. According to Judaism, these laws are incumbent upon all humanity, not just Jews. When Paul and James met in Jerusalem around the year 50 C.E., Paul was being criticized for allegedly encouraging Jews to abandon Torah law. Paul denied these charges and argued that he was just interested in bringing non-Jews to the movement. At this point, James insisted that individuals who wanted to follow Jesus and not convert to Judaism had to, nonetheless, keep the Torah's Noahide laws that included prohibitions against drinking blood, eating meat containing blood, and eating meat of animals not properly slain. James also insisted on respecting laws against fornication and idolatry.[45] In other words, the original Church of the Gentiles was asked by James, the brother of Jesus, to follow Torah law as it applies to non-Jews.[46] Paul later outmaneuvered James and created a Church of the Gentiles that followed none of the Torah laws and none of the laws prescribed by James.

But what happened to the Gentiles who wanted to follow Jesus in a non-Pauline manner? Did their movement survive the various wars between the Jewish people and Rome? Was it dispersed like James' Jewish Jesus movement? Again, we do not know the answers to these questions but we can now establish a textual connection between the original Gentile Church of Mary the Magdalene and Christian Gnosticism. Meaning, the pre-Paul Gentile church of Mary the Magdalene may not have disappeared. It may have simply morphed into what we now call Gnosticism.

One of the mysteries of early Christianity has to do with the rise of Christian Gnosticism. Until now, it seemed that this form of Christianity came out of nowhere. It suddenly pops up—fully realized—in Egypt, in the early 2nd century. But, clearly, Gnosticism didn't originate as a fully developed theology at the time of Valentinus, its greatest proponent.[47] The movement started earlier, in the 1st century.

The New Testament may be preserving a letter written to this Gentile Jesus movement by Jamesians who were critical of the path it was taking. It's called Second John. A John who is also called the "Elder" writes it. It is addressed to *"the lady chosen by God and to her children"* (emphasis added). After acknowledging that they share a common truth, John asks "the lady" (the *Mara*) to stay on message and to not drift from Jesus' original commands. He then calls someone the "antichrist." He calls this man's followers "deceivers." Second John may be speaking about Paul and his disciples who, he says, "have gone into the world" preaching a Christ which is different from the Jesus who had come "in the flesh"—different from the flesh-and-blood Jesus that the Mara and his earliest apostles knew.

Like so many touching on these secret teachings, the Elder is circumspect and cautious about committing too much to paper—"I do not want to use paper and ink"—and he tells "the lady" that he will visit so as to talk with her "face to face" (2 John 1–13).[48] Here we seem to have an inside look at the earliest days of the post-crucifixion Church of the Gentiles, led by Mary the Magdalene. Already, we see tension with both the Jamesians and with the followers of Paul. Clearly, with the destruction of Jerusalem, these followers of the lady developed their own texts and their own gospels, writings that would later be called Gnostic. What happened to these writings?

Some of the earliest texts of the Mary the Magdalene movement survived the fires of Christian orthodoxy and are now being unearthed. For example, parts of the Gnostic *Gospel of Thomas* appear to many scholars to have originated as early as the canonical Gospel of Mark, around 70 C.E. In other words, this Gnostic Gospel is as early as the earliest church-sanctioned Gospels or even earlier.[49] *The Gospel of Thomas* is a list of the sayings of Jesus, in seemingly random order. Some of the sayings are familiar to us from the canonical Gospels, but others are not.

The Gospel of Thomas contains no miracles, no indication of Jesus' movements from here to there, no Lord's Prayer, no Sermon on the Mount and—significantly—no birth stories and no account of his death. Jesus' birth and death are of no importance for the group for whom *The Gospel of Thomas* was Holy Scripture. All that matters to the author of this early Gospel were the teachings of Jesus—what he said and what he wanted people to internalize: namely, how humans were to mature and become fully realized beings. But where did this Gospel come from? And who were the Gnostics who cherished the theology represented by it? Since Egypt borders Israel and since only seventy or so years separate the crucifixion and the birth of Valentinus, the father of early Gnosticism for which *The Gospel of Thomas* was sacred text, it is safe to say that there must have been a direct link between at least some of the followers of Jesus and the earliest Gnostics.

It now seems that Mary the Magdalene's Church of the Gentiles is the missing link. It seems that what we know as Gnostic Christianity originated with the followers of the *Mara*, the *lady*—Mary the Magdalene.

Like the Jewish Jesus Movement in Jerusalem under James, the original Church of the Gentiles waited for the Kingdom of God to be made manifest upon earth, just as Jesus had promised. These Gentiles also expected to be part of the messianic kingdom, just as Jews would be. They further believed that Gentiles could become heirs to the promises of God to Abraham through membership in the Jesus movement. In their view, the movement was founded both spiritually and physically through the sacred union of the Jewish Jesus and the Gentile Mary the Magdalene. They were the ones chosen by God to undo the flaw that had bedeviled humanity. They were the ones who had restored wholeness, integrity, and harmony to the universe. As the Gospel of *Joseph and Aseneth* and the texts of the Valentinian Gnostics make clear, the Gentile followers of Mary the Magdalene believed that they would be saved through the actions of Jesus and Mary the Magdalene. Thus, according to the earliest Church of the Gentiles, redemption takes place not by participating in Jesus' death on the cross but by emulating his life in the matrimonial bed.

The people who regarded *Joseph and Aseneth* as Holy Scripture believed that flesh could become spirit, and that the disharmony of the universe—following the sin of Adam and Eve—could be overcome by a new Adam and a new Eve physically cleaving to each other and then, once again, becoming the primordial and androgynous "Son of Man." The Church of the Gentiles was a religion of life that celebrated vitality and encouraged its members to emulate Jesus not through celibacy but through Holy Communion understood as sacred sex. Harvard's Karen King recently stated that in contrast to Pauline Christians who celebrated celibacy, "there were early Christians . . . who could understand indeed that sexual union in marriage could be an imitation of God's creativity and generativity."[50] Clearly, the people who preserved *Joseph and Aseneth* were just such early Christians.

All this presents us with an alternative non-Pauline scenario of how Gentiles were incorporated into the promise of Abraham, namely, that through his seed all the families of the world would be blessed (Genesis 12:3). The contrast between Mary the Magdalene's Church of the Gentiles and Paul's Christ movement is stark. Early church fathers called the Gnostics lewd and accused them of engaging in abhorrent sex. Early Gnostics must have regarded those same church fathers as morbid and engaging in a cult of death.

In light of the evidence, we think it would be very hard for anyone to now argue that *Joseph and Aseneth* is not about Jesus and Mary the Magdalene. Also, in light of the total synchronicity between *Joseph and Aseneth* and Gnostic Christianity—especially as it was taught by Valentinians—we think there is no doubt that we are dealing with an early Gnostic text, or what some scholars might call a proto-Gnostic text. But is it history? Well, the fact is that unlike other Gnostic texts, *Joseph and Aseneth* is a narrative. Also, given its antiquity, it's at least as historical as the Gospels. More to the point is the last section of *Joseph and Aseneth*. While the first sections conform to Valentinian theology— the veil, the angel, the bridal chamber, and so forth—the last section seems to have no theological significance whatsoever. While the first sections are coded theology, the last section seems to be coded history.

But what long-forgotten episode in Jesus' career is it recounting? Incredibly, *Joseph and Aseneth* seems to be reporting that there was a plot hatched at the highest levels of Roman power to kill both Jesus and Mary the Magdalene.

13

THE PLOT: KILL JESUS,
ABDUCT MARY THE MAGDALENE,
AND MURDER THE KIDS

The final section of *Joseph and Aseneth* is remarkable. It tells us, in disguised fashion, of a hitherto-unknown plot against Jesus and his family. This was not his trial and execution by the Romans in Jerusalem around 30 C.E., for in our manuscript Jesus seems to survive the attempted assassination. No, the plot here refers to an incident that happened earlier in his life, perhaps as much as a decade before his death. As we shall see, the villain in the plot is someone the text calls "Pharaoh's son" and he, like the so-called "Pharaoh," remains unnamed.

Here's what *Joseph and Aseneth* tells us: "Pharaoh's son" covets Aseneth for her beauty and tries to bribe two of Joseph's brothers, Simon and Levi, to betray him. They defiantly refuse. "Pharaoh's son," however, manages to manipulate two other brothers, Dan and Gad, into cooperating with his evil scheme. He suggests to them that they have much to fear from their brother and that he will cut them off from their rightful inheritance, leaving them destitute. He also not-so-subtly threatens them, urging them to choose prosperity over death.

Together they hatch a plot. Now "Pharaoh's son" confides in Joseph's "brothers" that he plans to kill not only Joseph, but also his *own* father, the

Pharaoh. No reason is given for this—it just suddenly pops out in the narrative. Meanwhile, the traitorous brothers Dan and Gad inform "Pharaoh's son" that he will have an opportunity to seize Aseneth when she goes alone into the countryside to visit her estate. They suggest that "Pharaoh's son" ambush her and have his way with her. Meanwhile, they take it upon themselves to kill Joseph as he frets about Aseneth. For good effect before killing him, the brothers plan to murder Joseph's children before his eyes.

"Pharaoh's son" musters his supporters, but soon the plot begins to unravel. The son is prevented from killing his father by Pharaoh's guards, who deny him entrance into Pharaoh's chambers. Meanwhile, just as Dan and Gad had predicted, Aseneth leaves Joseph to visit their country estate. Joseph, described as a "savior," continues on his mission. On her way, Aseneth's chariot is ambushed and her protectors are killed, except for Benjamin (Joseph's favorite brother), who is in the chariot with her. He's eighteen years old and is described as "incredibly handsome" and "strong as a young lion." He succeeds in wounding "Pharaoh's son." The battle is won. Aseneth begs Joseph's other brothers and supporters not to kill "Pharaoh's son" or the brothers who had betrayed them, saying that it would not be right to repay evil with evil. However, on the third day following the battle, "Pharaoh's son" succumbs to his wounds. Pharaoh mourns his son's death, unaware of the son's attempt to kill him. After a long life, Pharaoh dies. And there the story ends abruptly.

Nothing more is said about Aseneth or the children or Joseph. In terms of a dramatic plot structure, we have a serious threat, an insidious betrayal from within the ranks, but eventually a successful outcome. Aseneth is not captured. Neither Joseph nor the children are killed. There's nothing about what happened subsequently: What did they do? Where did they go? When did they die? Where are they buried? What happened to the children?

Moreover, we once again notice that nothing in this account matches the Biblical story of Joseph. In that story, there is no estate and no "Pharaoh's son" who betrays his father and comes after Joseph and Aseneth. There's no battle and no wound. Whatever this story is about, as before, it has nothing to do with Joseph the Israelite patriarch of the Book of Genesis.

If we just peruse the broad outlines of the plot to kill Joseph and Aseneth— and contrast it to the Gospels—although there is much that is new, there's also much that sounds familiar. In the Gospels, there is a high-level plot to arrest and kill Jesus. According to the Gospels, it involves the highest levels of Roman authority in 1st-century Judaea. The Jewish High Priest Caiaphas; the ruler of the Galilee, Herod Antipas; the Roman procurator Pontius Pilate—are all involved. More than this, one of Jesus' disciples—that is, one of the band of brothers, the so-called "Judas"—betrays him. Not only that, Judas ends up committing suicide, either filled with remorse or anger at being double-crossed. So in the Gospels, as in *Joseph and Aseneth*, there are plots and counterplots that surround Jesus. These involve both his inner circle and the ruling authorities. Furthermore, in *Joseph and Aseneth* the son of Pharaoh is a central figure. Remember, in both Egyptian and Roman contexts the ruler literally represented a god. So in *Joseph and Aseneth* we have a "Son of God" who after three days dies of his wounds. In the Gospels, we have a "Son of God" who dies of his wounds and, after three days, is resurrected. They seem to be strange mirror images of each other. One is evil, is wounded, and after three days dies. The other is good, dies, and after three days lives again. So even before decoding the text, we are struck by the fact that *Joseph and Aseneth* continues to echo the Gospels, but with a twist. What secret is it telling us?

Surprising Questions

When we once again substitute Joseph with Jesus and Aseneth with Mary the Magdalene, we are immediately confronted with some entirely new and puzzling questions about their married life together.

What's this plot all about? When did it happen? Who was involved? Who wanted to kill Jesus early in his mission? What did he do that merited death in their eyes? Was it simply because his wife was incredibly beautiful?

We aren't explicitly told anything about this plot within the pages of the New Testament. But in a Gnostic dialogue called *Pistis Sophia* or *The Wisdom of Faith*, Mary does confide to Jesus that "Peter makes me hesitate; I am afraid of him because he hates the female race."[1] Interestingly, Margaret Starbird has connected Mary the Magdalene's disappearance from the canonical texts to historical circumstances in which she must have been in danger. In other words, Mary the Magdalene disappears from history because she had to disappear from her enemies. In Starbird's words, "My personal view is that the early church lost Mary Magdalene because her friends and family were trying so hard to protect her from perceived threats posed by Roman authorities . . . Mary Magdalene literally disappears. Paul's letters do not mention her, nor does the Book of Acts. What happened?"[2]

In the canonical Gospels, it is only at the end of Jesus' life that the anti-Jesus forces encircle him and the Romans put him to death just before Passover. Up until that point, everything seems to be relatively peaceful for him. He teaches, gathers huge crowds, heals, feeds people, and moves throughout northern Israel. Yet, as we shall see, within the canonical Gospels there are many clues that Jesus had influential enemies. It seems that early on, there were major plots against his life, and that he was acutely aware of them. Also, *Joseph and Aseneth* alludes to divisions within Jesus' ranks. What's all that about? It seems that some of his closest associates conspired with the political authorities to have him killed. What did they have against him?

According to the Gospels, Jesus was betrayed by one of his own. Why? What was Judas' motivation? Was Judas alone in wanting Jesus dead? Did Jesus disappoint in some way? According to the canonical Gospels, as Jesus entered Jerusalem, the crowds waved palm branches and cheered him. Then, within less than a week, they suddenly turned against him. What accounts for this amazing turnaround?

If "Pharaoh's son" corresponds to a historical personality, it would have to be the son of a ruler.[3] Does it make sense that a Roman emperor's son would even know about Jesus, much less want to kill him so as to force himself on his Syro-Phoenician wife? It hardly seems realistic. Why would such a powerful person be interested in them?

To answer these questions and retrieve the long-hidden history that our text records, we have to first figure out who the villain in *Joseph and Aseneth* is—a villain code-named *Pharaoh's son*.

The Political Jesus

First of all, Christmas plays to the contrary, the fact is that Jesus was a political figure and that he was seen as such by his contemporaries. His radical religious message—the Kingdom of God about to occur on earth—was a political bombshell. According to Jesus, there would soon emerge a new phase in world history, one dominated by a renewed Israel with its own king, from the restored Davidic monarchy. This new world order harkened back a thousand years earlier, to David's time, a period of history romanticized by later generations for its

British Library Manuscript Number 17,202: A Lost Gospel? *Photo credit: Associated Producers Ltd.*

Barrie Wilson with curator from British Library and multispectral imaging experts "x-raying" the ancient text. *Photo credit: Associated Producers Ltd.*

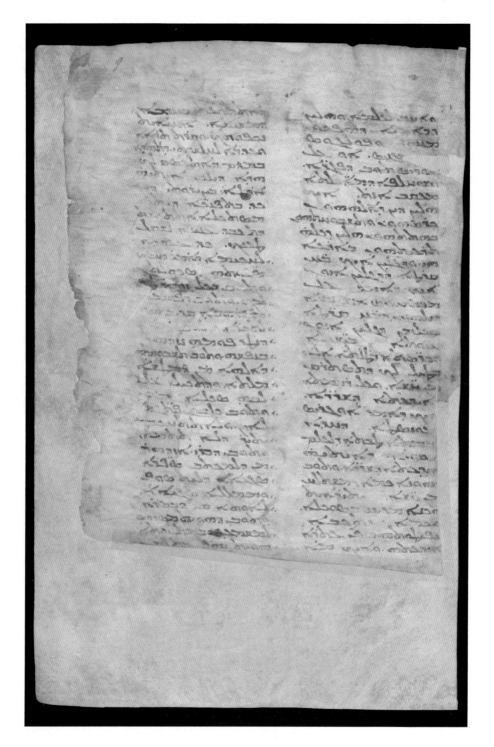

Cover letter on the Syriac edition. One can plainly see a straight cut censoring the text, where the translator was going to supply the "hidden meaning." *Photo credit: Associated Producers Ltd., multispectral image by Michael B. Toth and Bill Christens-Barry.*

ABOVE: Simcha and Barrie in front of the statue of the goddess Artemis, with tower on her head, in Ephesus, Turkey. *Photo credit: Associated Producers Ltd.* RIGHT: Notice the bees (collar) on Artemis' queen cells, formerly thought of as breasts. Roman age statue exhibited in the Viterbo Cathedral in Lazio, Italy. *Photo credit: trotalo/ Shutterstock.*

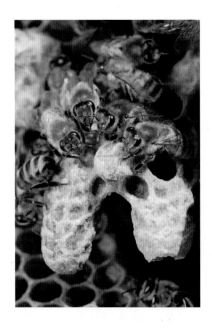

ABOVE LEFT: Bees tending to queen cells. *Photo credit: Eric Tourneret.* ABOVE RIGHT: Ruins of the Temple of Artemis at Ephesus. Formerly one of the Seven Wonders of the World. *Photo credit: Sailko, Creative Commons Attribution–Share Alike 3.0 Unported license.* BELOW: Beit Alpha "synagogue," complete with solar zodiac and image of god Helios riding his chariot (6th century c.e.). *Photo credit: Associated Producers Ltd.*

ABOVE: Simcha inspecting image of Helios in the center of zodiac at Hamat Tiberius, Galilee (4th century C.E.). *Photo credit: Associated Producers Ltd.* BELOW: Earliest Christian image in Rome (late 3rd to early 4th century C.E.): Jesus depicted as Helios. Julii family tomb, Vatican. *Photo credit: Simcha Jacobovici.*

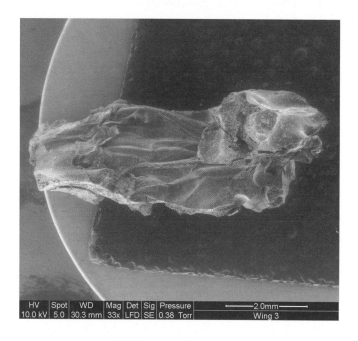

| HV | Spot | WD | Mag | Det | Sig | Pressure | ⊢———2.0mm———⊣ |
| 10.0 kV | 5.0 | 30.3 mm | 33x | LFD | SE | 0.38 Torr | Wing 3 |

ABOVE: Electron-microscope image of 3,000-year-old intact bee from Tel Rehov, Israel. *Photo credit: Dr. Vitaly Gutkin.* BELOW: 2,500-year old-dog burials related to Artemis/Asherah worship in Ashkelon, Israel. *Photo credit: Richard T. Nowitz/ CORBIS.*

ABOVE: Unusual "altar" found in a 1st-century "synagogue," at the edge of the ancient city of Magdala. *Photo credit: Israel Antiquitie/Chameleons Eye/Newscom.* LEFT: Arian Christian baptistry, late 5th century C.E., Ravenna, Italy. Jesus in central panel surrounded by the twelve apostles. *Photo credit: Baptistry of Ariani, Ravenna, Italy/ Giraudon/Bridgeman Images.*

ABOVE: Galilean mosaic, 6th century C.E. church of "Our Lady Mary," with Jesus as Helios and Mary the Magdalene as Artemis in the central panel. They are surrounded by the twelve apostles. *Photo credit: Associated Producers Ltd.* OPPOSITE PAGE: "Mr. and Mrs. Jesus" in the central panel in the church of "Our Lady Mary," Galilee, Israel. *Photo credit: Associated Producers Ltd.*

ABOVE: 18th century C.E., Dekoulou monastery, Mani Peninsula, Greece. Here Jesus is alone in the central panel. The apostles have been replaced by the signs of the zodiac. *Photo credit: Hercules Milas/Alamy.* BELOW: Jesus' father? Simcha inspecting Pantera's 1st-century C.E. tombstone, Bad Kreuznach Museum, Germany. Inscription on tombstone reads: "Tiberius Iulius Abdes Pantera from Sidon, aged 62 years. Served 40 years. Standard bearer of the first cohort of archers lies here." *Photo credit: Associated Producers Ltd.*

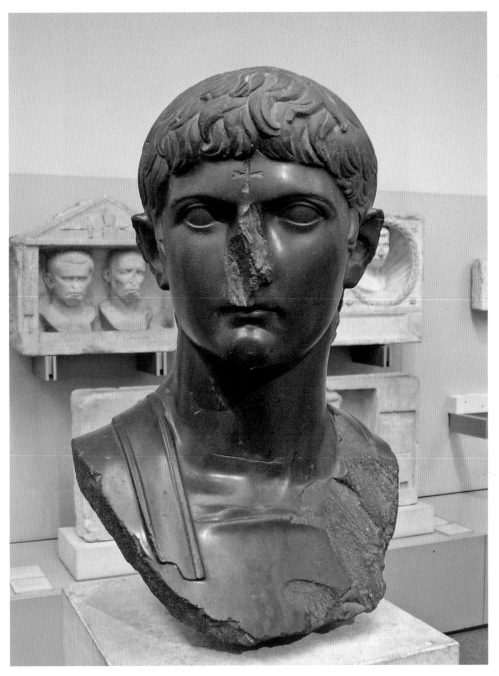

Germanicus, son of Tiberius (15 B.C.E.–19 C.E.). Is he the Roman code-named "Pharaoh's son" in our lost gospel? *Photo credit: Alun Salt, Creative Commons Attribution–Share Alike 2.0 Generic license.*

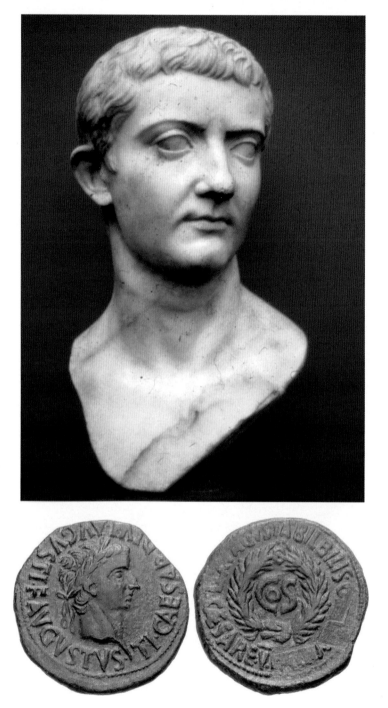

TOP: Emperor Tiberius (reigned 14–37 C.E.). Is he the ruler code-named "Pharaoh" in our lost gospel? *Photo credit: Public Domain, Wikimedia Commons.* BOTTOM: 1st-century C.E. image of Tiberius with Lucius Aelius Seianus' (Sejanus) name rubbed out ("damnatio") after his downfall. Did his demise precipitate Jesus' crucifixion? *Photo credit: Classical Numismatic Group, Inc., http://www.cngcoins.com.*

Sperlonga, Italy, site of Emperor Tiberius' palace. Sejanus rose to power after he saved Tiberius' life in 26 C.E. at this very spot. Was Sejanus Jesus' sponsor? *Photo credit: Associated Producers Ltd.*

ABOVE: Ivory depiction of "Woman at the Window," 9th-8th century B.C.E. Was Mary the Magdalene such a Phoenician/Canaanite priestess? *Photo credit: The Trustees of the British Museum/Art Resource, NY.* BELOW: Did Mary the "tower lady," i.e. the Magdalene, live in such a temple tower? Simcha with Jonathan N. Tubb, Middle East Keeper, The British Museum. *Photo credit: Associated Producers Ltd.*

ABOVE: "Jesus entering Jerusalem" (17th century C.E.) by Peter Paul Rubens. The palm fronds are associated with the Jewish holiday of Tabernacles, not Passover. *Photo credit: Erich Lessing/Art Resource, NY.* BELOW: *Noli me tangere* ("Touch me not"). As in Joseph and Aseneth, here Jesus pushes Mary the Magdalene away (John 20:17), his hand almost touching between her breasts. Painting by Franco Battista (16th century C.E.). *Photo credit: The Dayton Art Institute, Dayton, Ohio, USA/Museum purchase with funds provided by Mr. Robert Badenhop/Bridgeman Images.*

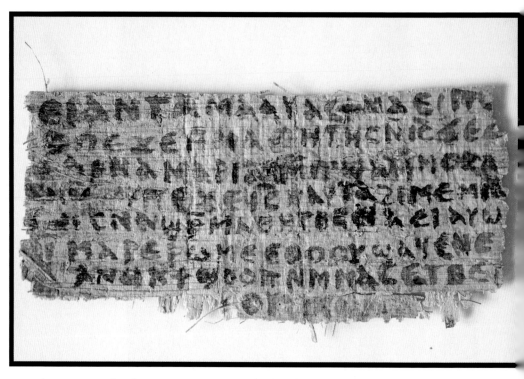

7th century C.E. Coptic papyrus. Here Jesus explicitly refers to someone—most probably Mary the Magdalene—as his "wife." *Photo credit: SIPA USA/Karen L. King/Harvard via Sipa/Newscom.*

splendor and glory. As an independent autonomous Torah-abiding Jewish state came into existence, the weight of Roman rule would be lifted. The occupying Roman troops, colonies of Roman citizens, and the much-hated and burdensome system of taxation would all be gone. Poverty would be eradicated and people would be able to enjoy life. According to Jesus, it was truly the time of a new deal.

Jesus' message resonated with the people to whom he spoke, and it tapped into the deep well of Jewish messianic hopes. After all, Jews believed then—as now—that in the messianic era, the world would experience peace and that the worship of the one God would become universal. As the prophets had prophesied: "And the Lord will become king over all the earth; on that day the Lord will be one and His name one" (Zechariah 14:9).

Jesus had talked about this message in covert terms, in parables. These metaphors were not just stories or teaching aids: they were how radical ideology disguised itself. Hiding the political overtones of his manifesto meant that Roman authorities on the fringes of his audience would not grasp the full implication of what he was saying. But, in time, they did. They correctly interpreted the true direction of his message and he was executed as a would-be "King of the Jews." If there is one thing we know about Jesus, it's that he was charged with sedition and crucified. Sedition was a political crime. It meant that he was found guilty of anti-Roman revolutionary activities. We also know that Jesus was crucified between two men that the Gospels call *lestes* in Greek. This is usually translated as *bandits* or *thieves*. But it rarely means that. In Josephus, for example, it always means *zealot* or *insurrectionist*.[4] Also, if Jesus thought of himself as the Messiah, he would have seen himself as a religious, political, and royal figure—the individual whom God anointed to be the Davidic monarch.

So the picture sketched in *Joseph and Aseneth*, of a political Jesus who finds himself in the middle of a conspiracy that reaches to the highest echelons of power and into his own inner circle, is not outrageous. In fact, it's consistent with what the Gospels themselves tell us of his betrayal, arrest, and execution.

There's another reason why Jesus was seen as political. His was a large entourage. We tend to think of Jesus acting alone—that's the way he's often depicted, speaking as an individual either to large crowds on a mountain or by the Sea of Galilee, or else privately to his immediate followers in a secluded area. This picture of the solo Jesus is grossly misleading. In addition to his own family—his own as well as those of his brothers and sisters—he had twelve *talmidim*, that is, students or disciples. Many if not all were like Simon Peter, married and with families.[5] Jesus also had another group about which we know very little. This group was called "the Seventy" (Luke 10:1–16—some ancient manuscripts say "the Seventy-two"). These were ambassadors that Jesus sent out to all parts of Israel, to awaken people to the coming political transformation.

Add up the numbers: four in his immediate family (himself, wife, and two children); six siblings; twelve disciples; seventy delegates. This totals ninety-two. Let's assume that most were married, many with children, and that there were parents and in-laws, brothers and sisters and their families, cousins, nephews and nieces, and we immediately have a large movement—all somewhat implicated in the idea that a new social reality was on the doorstep. The Romans would have perceived a large crowd like this as a provocation.

Furthermore, closely associated with Jesus' movement was the movement of his cousin—John the Baptizer. He, too, had disciples and he moved vast crowds to repentance and Baptism. All in all, these two related movements were part of a huge messianic mission designed to awaken the Jewish people to the new reality about to fundamentally shake up the world. As Josephus describes, these kinds of revival gatherings were tinderboxes, and any provocation could light the fires of rebellion.

Moreover, the Dead Sea Scrolls, discovered in 1947, also tell the story of a messianic figure who records similar attempts on his life ("violent men have sought my life"), and narrow escapes ("you have rescued the life of the poor one whom they plotted to destroy"), all seemingly connected with machinations surrounding the Holy Temple in Jerusalem ("[my] blood they planned to spill over the issue of your Temple service").[6]

Seen in his historical context, the politics surrounding Jesus in *Joseph and Aseneth* do not seem out of place. Furthermore, Jesus also promised that many would live to see the Kingdom.[7] It was coming that soon—a few weeks, perhaps several months, surely at worst a year or two down the road. His followers fully expected to be part of this changed landscape. The twelve disciples, in particular, were confident that they'd be the heads of the twelve restored tribes of Israel, political rulers under King Jesus in the messianic Kingdom of God.[8]

Given all this, was Jesus' movement just a local matter? A minor group located in the Galilee, always a sea of unrest? Or did it assume national importance, coming to the attention of the priestly and Roman authorities in

Jerusalem even prior to his arrival in the Jewish capital? And was it all somehow connected to the international scene, of importance even to political and military leaders in Rome itself?

As the Gospels make clear, Jesus' actions and words did come to the attention of the authorities . . . many with excellent connections to Rome.

All had reason to have him killed.

Jesus—Many Enemies

It was in many people's best interests to have Jesus out of the way. His teachings, practices, and popularity stood in the way of many agendas. Here's a brief survey of just some of the major players who had it in for Jesus:

The Pharisees

The Pharisees were the popular Jewish teachers of Torah, resident in towns and cities, close to people's daily life. They sought to build a bridge between Biblical injunctions and everyday practices. They came up with approaches concerning how to faithfully keep the commandments of God in the midst of difficult times, especially with Gentiles in control of the Judaean government and economy. The Biblical commandments were not always clear. What did the Torah mean by "observe the Sabbath and keep it holy"? The Pharisees interpreted the Torah and provided rules for its observance. How should kosher food be prepared? What kinds of interactions were permitted between Jews and Gentiles? What were the grounds for divorce? The Pharisees provided guidance on practical issues that touched people's lives. The great rabbinic sages Hillel and Shammai had lived and taught just before Jesus came on the scene. They, like the Teacher of Righteousness mentioned in the Dead Sea Scrolls, interpreted the law for the people.

In general, Pharisees were not as strict as the Essenes of the Dead Sea. Jesus sometimes chided Pharisees for being lax in their interpretations, seeking out loopholes. He objected, for instance, to Pharisees giving permission to individuals to donate money to the temple in order to wiggle out of support payments for aging parents, thus violating the commandment to honor your father and mother (Matthew 15:3–9). This circumvention of what Jesus took to be the straightforward meaning of Torah echoes the charge in the Dead Sea Scrolls that the Pharisees were "seekers after smooth things," that is, that they were too accommodating in their interpretations of Torah.

In the Gospel of Matthew, in his Sermon on the Mount, there too Jesus interpreted the Torah more rigorously than the Pharisees did—"For I tell you, unless your righteousness *exceeds* that of the scribes and Pharisees, you will never enter the kingdom of heaven" (Matthew 5:20, italics added). For people used to a Jesus who is anti-Torah, it's hard to think of him as a super-orthodox Jew. But remember, both his cousin John the Baptizer and his brother James were Nazirites: individuals who had taken a special vow of strict adherence to the Torah. For example, unlike mainstream Jews, Nazirites did not cut their hair and abstained from wine. In terms of strictness of Torah observance, initially at least, Jesus seems to have stood somewhere to the right of the Pharisees and to the left of the Essenes.

So far, it does not seem like the Pharisees are good candidates for Jesus' enemies as depicted in *Joseph and Aseneth*. But the picture we have of the Pharisees in the New Testament is ambivalent. Sometimes they are positioned as Jewish leaders who debated issues with Jesus. This is not necessarily a negative thing. Debate is not an uncommon Jewish pastime in those days or today. In a Jewish context, it simply represents a common search for the truth underlying a Biblical text. The schools of Hillel and Shammai, for example, had argued issues back and forth and disagreed on many topics. These differences are preserved rather than censored in the main text of rabbinic Judaism: the Talmud. A famous Dead Sea Scroll text dubbed *4QMMT* or just *MMT* outlines almost two dozen points of difference between their community and that of the elite Sadducee crowd.[9] In other words, modern sensibilities notwithstanding, depicting Pharisees debating Jesus is not necessarily putting them in a negative light.

At other times, the canonical Gospels depict the Pharisees not merely as debating partners but as outright enemies bent on killing Jesus. One instance of this occurs just after Jesus supposedly provides less-than-rigorous instructions on how to observe the Sabbath. The implication being that if Jesus was preaching a Gospel that involved breaking Sabbath laws, it is natural that the Pharisees would have wanted to kill him.[10] After all, the Book of Exodus says, "You shall keep the Sabbath, because it is holy for you; everyone who profanes it shall be put to death" (31:12–14). But by Jesus' time, in the 1st century, Jews were not put to death for less-than-rigorous Sabbath observances. That would have decimated the Jewish community. So it is unlikely that the Pharisees turned on Jesus for something like differences over Sabbath observance.

At other times in the Gospels, the Pharisees are spoken of as friends, warning Jesus of impending danger. In one instance, they let him know that Herod Antipas, the same ruler who had killed Jesus' cousin John the Baptizer, was now on the lookout for him (Luke 13:31). Interestingly, here, these sympathetic Pharisees are shown as go-betweens in the negotiations between Jesus and Herod. In other words, what we see in the depictions of the Pharisees is that alliances shifted; some Pharisees were plotting against Jesus, while others were warning him.

Could the Pharisees have been the instigators of a plot against Jesus and Mary the Magdalene? It's possible, but not very likely. Except for some theological differences on matters like Sabbath observance, there doesn't seem to be enough that divided them—hardly the stuff to motivate murder. Also, the ultra-religious Pharisees don't seem like the type of people who would want to rape Mary the Magdalene and kill her children. It's doubtful that they are the villains of *Joseph and Aseneth*.

The Essenes

Some Essenes might also have had an interest in killing Jesus. According to their *War Scroll* found at the Dead Sea and attributed to the Essenes, "the sons of light" were at war with all Jews who did not obey Torah according to the rigorous interpretation of their "Teacher of Righteousness." In effect, they were at war with the people they called the "sons of darkness," which at that point probably represented the majority of humanity. They held the view that while neighbors should be loved, enemies should be hated.[11] Even more than the Pharisees, they thought that correct Torah observance was a matter of ultimate concern. For them, the messianic era would not occur until Jews strictly observed the laws of Torah, forming a community of purity. In accordance with Isaiah, they went out into the desert, to prepare the Way of the Lord. From their own perspective, they were God's colony, the colony of the New Covenant or, if you will, the colony of the New Testament.

The Essenes might have been motivated to kill Jesus if they thought he was encouraging a mass following to get lax on the law. For them, nothing less than the future of the Jewish people and God's plans for humanity were at stake. They, far more than the Pharisees, had declared that God would wipe out the non-observers of Torah (those who had failed to enter into the New Covenant).

The *War Scroll* envisages them playing a major role in that apocalyptic battle under the leadership of two Messiahs, one priestly and one kingly.

Stereotypically, the writers of the Dead Sea Scrolls are seen as dropouts from society, living in Qumran on the shores of the Dead Sea. But Essenes were also found throughout Israel in many towns and villages and, though Qumran seems to have been their headquarters, it was only twenty miles east of Jerusalem, a day or day-and-a-half's walk from the capital. Jerusalem itself boasted an Essene quarter and an Essene gate. The only place outside of Qumran that Essene burials have been found is just outside Jerusalem in Beit Zafafa, near Talpiot.[12] As purists of the Torah law, they were very much aware of the activities of the temple priesthood and their masters, the Roman officials. Their Temple Scroll looks very much like a blueprint for a restored and purified temple. Anticipating that God would soon intervene in human affairs, they likely scrutinized world events to discern when and how God would act. They expected to be called into active service and to inherit the kingdom that God had promised to the truly faithful. So the Essenes were not some kind of proto-hippie community totally out of touch with the rest of Israel. They had both opportunity and motive to kill Jesus.

In spite of their perspective, there is no evidence of any direct connection between Jesus and the Essenes, no indications that they specifically had Jesus on their "hit list." The so-called false priests in Jerusalem (the high priest and Sadducees) as well as the so-called false teachers (the Pharisees) were much more on their radar. Moreover, they were preoccupied with plots against their own movement. Their Teacher of Righteousness—perhaps decades before Jesus— had to flee for his life.[13] Their Thanksgiving Psalms are riddled with perceived threats and opposition to them and their leaders.

So, could an Essene have been the villain of *Joseph and Aseneth*? Not likely. There is simply no evidence that they went after Jesus, and they certainly would have had no reason to go after his children.

The Zealots

The Zealots might have had good reason to want Jesus killed. Formed in the 1st decade of the Common Era, this faction was primarily political in focus. Hating foreign taxation and the colonizing efforts of the occupiers, Zealots were intensely anti-Roman. These extremists probably shared some of the messianic sentiments of the Essenes, looking forward to the day when the Romans would be gone from the land and they, the truly zealous, would be in control.

Jesus seems to have had an ambiguous relationship with the Zealots. On the one hand, he sometimes sounds like one. Matthew reports him saying "Do not think that I have come to bring peace to the earth; I have not come to bring peace, but a sword" (Matthew 10:34). In *The Gospel of Thomas*, Thomas states: "Jesus said, 'people think that I have come to impose peace on the world. They do not know that I have come to impose conflicts upon the earth: fire, sword, war'" (16:1–2).[14] These are strong indications that, at least at one point, Jesus subscribed to a revolutionary anti-Roman apocalyptic ideology. After all, one of his twelve disciples is called Simon Zealotes—i.e., Simon the Zealot (Luke 6:15 and Acts 1:13). Two disciples are nicknamed *Boanerges* or "Sons of Thunder" (James and John, sons of Zebedee), which may be an indication that they were fighters, not pacifists. And perhaps most shockingly, one of the twelve is called Judas Iscariot or, more correctly, Judah the Sicarius.[15] For those who don't know, the Sicarii were the most fanatical of the Zealot sects, named after their *sica* or short dagger. According to Josephus, they were basically assassins. Having all these people in his entourage would indicate some kind of affinity between Jesus, his followers, and the Zealots. The fact is that, in the end, Jesus is crucified between two Zealots, called *bandits* or *lestai* by the Gospels. Maybe he had abandoned their ideology by this point, but it seems that nobody told the Romans.

In any event, there is another side to Jesus. Luke reports that Jesus said "love your enemies, do good to those who hate you, bless those who curse you, pray for those who abuse you. If anyone strikes you on the cheek, offer the other also; and from anyone who takes away your coat do not withhold even your shirt" (Luke 6:27–29). Either this is a later attempt to present a non-Zealot Jesus to the world, or Jesus himself changed his mind about the efficacy of armed struggle. If the latter, this would go a long way to explain why someone like Judah the Sicarius (more familiarly, Judas Iscariot) would turn on him and why he might have made enemies in the Zealot/Sicarii camp.

A Zealot plot against Jesus, therefore, is not far-fetched. Judas may not have been the only one who harbored resentment against a teacher who, from his point of view, had failed to deliver on his promise of armed insurrection or the Kingdom of God.

But other than Judas acting directly against Jesus at the time of his trial, there is no evidence of any prior Zealot conspiracy to do him in. Although it would be tempting to identify Jesus' Zealot followers as the "brothers" who betray Joseph in *Joseph and Aseneth*, on the evidence it is unlikely that Zealots are those bad guys. If they did turn against Jesus, which the Gospels clearly state they did, it wasn't until after he left the Galilee and made his entrance into Jerusalem.[16]

Herod Antipas

A more likely candidate for the villain in *Joseph and Aseneth* is Herod Antipas, the Roman-appointed Jewish ruler of the Galilee. The Gospels explicitly tell us that Herod Antipas plotted to kill Jesus: "At that very hour some Pharisees came and said to him, 'Get away from here, for Herod [Antipas] wants to kill you'" (Luke 13:31). Here we have an incident that parallels events in *Joseph and Aseneth*, namely, a political leader at the highest levels of power was closely watching Jesus' movements and conspiring to kill him. For his part, Jesus seems to have a good sense of Herod Antipas. He calls him a "fox" (Luke 13:32), not that different from *Joseph and Aseneth* where Mary the Magdalene calls Pharaoh the "old lion" (12:12). Furthermore, by calling Herod a fox Jesus alludes to several problematic traits in Herod's character. One was that Herod was cunning or crafty. But there is also another meaning to "fox." The Talmud cryptically says that a lion's tail is worth more than a fox's head. In other words, Jesus' metaphor had political overtones. When the Emperor Tiberius died, Josephus writes that Agrippa—soon to be the Roman-appointed King of the Jews—was told that the "lion" had died.[17] In Talmudic terms, calling Herod Antipas a fox may have been a way of saying that Herod was a lackey of the lion, a mere puppet dependent upon the goodwill of Rome.

Herod Antipas had both the motive and the means to kill Jesus. As a son of Herod the Great, the hated ruler of Judaea, he might have been called "son of Pharaoh" in *Joseph and Aseneth*. More than this, as in our manuscript, Jesus seems aware of the threat against him by Herod and his supporters.[18] In other words, we have to take a closer look at Herod Antipas as a possible candidate for the villain in *Joseph and Aseneth*. To understand the threat that he posed to Jesus, we need to first understand the entire geography of the area and the political jurisdictions at the time of Jesus.

We tend to think of Jesus of Nazareth circulating around a place called Galilee until he makes his way to Jerusalem for his meeting with destiny. But the reality is that he was circulating in several jurisdictions with more than one local ruler. He had lots of opportunity to rub many of these people the wrong way.

Taking the Sea of Galilee as the fulcrum, we can detect seven different areas that played a role in Jesus' movements. The first area is the most famous—the Galilee. It represented the region to the west and to the northwest of the Sea of Galilee, in the hill country, and included such places as Tiberias, Nazareth, and Sepphoris. Many referred to it as "the Galilee of the Gentiles"[19] because of the presence of so many non-Jews there. To the west and to the north beyond the Galilee was the area called "Phoenicia" by the Greeks. This was an area inhabited by a non-Jewish, Canaanitish people, as well as Romans. To the northeast of the Sea of Galilee was Tetrarchy of Philip. This territory took in towns mentioned in the New Testament such as Bethsaida. Decapolis was southeast of the Sea of Galilee. East of the Jordan River and further south was Nabataean Peraea, spread out along the east side of the river down to the middle of the eastern shore of the Dead Sea. The area around Jerusalem and further south was Judaea. And between Judaea and the Galilee lay Samaria.[20]

This constellation of jurisdictions assumes importance when we learn that Jesus moved from the Galilee throughout this entire region. Each of the local rulers had his own political agenda and was concerned about how his actions locally would play out in Rome. Some undoubtedly felt threatened by Jesus and the considerable attention he was getting from huge crowds of common people. It was that political threat—and not any supposed religious revisionism on Jesus' part—that drew the ire of these local potentates. Implicit in Jesus' message was the replacement of Roman authority with a restored Davidic monarchy. Such a message would threaten everyone in civil authority. In other words, many local rulers had a lot to lose if Jesus was successful.

As stated, one of the most important of these local rulers was Herod Antipas, a man with huge aspirations. He was one of the sons of Herod the Great, that great builder and astute politician who had been King of the Jews from 37 B.C.E. until 4 B.C.E. Herod Antipas was educated in Rome. Upon the death of his father, he became ruler of two important provinces: Galilee and Peraea. If we monitor Jesus' movements, we notice that on many occasions Jesus seems to avoid Herod's territory, that is, Jesus frequently operated outside Galilee and Peraea. We find Jesus, for instance, on the east side of the Sea of Galilee, in Bethsaida in Gaulanitis; in Decapolis; in Phoenicia; or in Caesarea Philippi—all outside Herod Antipas' jurisdiction. In fact, Jesus never ventured into Herod's strongholds, Tiberias and Sepphoris, although these were the big cities in the area and the logical destinations for a young preacher. Harold W. Hoehner notes ten instances where Jesus changes his plans and withdraws from a particular territory, largely because of Herod Antipas.[21] Why? Was he afraid of Herod?

Perhaps he had intelligence at the highest levels of Herod Antipas' adminis-tration that would warn him when to avoid Herod's territory. Again, if this seems far-fetched, consider this: Herod's "steward," a position of high prominence, was a man named Chuza. In those days, the so-called steward was equivalent to the head of Homeland Security today. It was a position of intimate trust.[22] His job was not to lay out Herod Antipas' clothes in the morning. His task was to make sure Herod was still alive by nightfall. Incredibly, the Gospels tell us that Chuza's wife, Joanna, contributed financially to the support of Jesus' mission (Luke 8:3). In other words, one of Jesus' most important supporters, a woman, and a colleague of Mary the Magdalene, was married to the head of Herod Antipas' security service.[23]

So Jesus was very aware of Herod Antipas and his machinations. And there were many. Herod was bitterly disappointed that the Roman emperor, Augustus, had failed to grant him the title of King of the Jews. Instead, he was given the title of *tetrarch*, a much lesser honor and one that galled him throughout his life. Neither he nor his brothers who were granted other provinces in what was Herod the Great's domain were given the title *King*. That honor remained vacant from 4 B.C.E. until 41 C.E., when the Roman emperor Caligula made Agrippa I the King of the Jews. A grandson of Herod the Great, some believed him to be the Messiah.

But Herod Antipas was not just a would-be king. He was the head of a Hel-lenizing political movement—the Herodians.[24] These were Jews who adopted Greek culture, favored the Herodian dynasty and championed Herod Antipas' claim to the title King of the Jews. Likely, they wanted him to be king over the vast territory his father had ruled, an area reminiscent of the kingdom of David. Some Herodians may have also thought of Herod Antipas in messianic terms, as a viable candidate for creating a restored Israel free of Roman rule. The Herodians believed that the road to salvation lay with a bona fide King of the Jews and a policy of accommodation with the Romans. They believed that accommodation—not revolution—was the path to salvation. In Jesus' time, messianic claims were not unique, and they were almost always connected to political aspirations.

Herod Antipas was very much under the scrutiny of the Roman emperor at whose pleasure he served, and he, in turn, was careful to maintain good relationships with whoever happened to be in power in Rome. His was a sensitive position, however. The Galilee had been a hotbed of revolution early on in his career. In 4 B.C.E., even while he had been in Rome presenting his case before Emperor Augustus concerning why he should be crowned King of Jews, a political activist by the name of Judah son of Hezekiah had attacked the palace in Sepphoris, making off with money and weapons. The Roman governor of Syria responded with force, destroying the city and selling its inhabitants as slaves. Militants were hunted down and killed.

In time, Herod Antipas would rebuild Sepphoris, and when Tiberius became emperor in 14 C.E., Herod undertook the construction of a magnificent capital on the western shore of the Sea of Galilee, naming it Tiberias in the emperor's honor—a shrewd move.

Peraea, too, posed a challenge for Herod. This was a frontier state where the Roman Empire abutted the wealthy Nabataean Empire—of Petra fame—whose traders controlled the flow of goods east and west between the Mediterranean and the Indian Ocean—and, to some degree, north and south between Egypt and the Roman provinces beyond the Galilee. Herod Antipas' first wife had been the daughter of the Nabataean king, Aretas IV. Herod probably hoped that this political marriage would encourage peaceful relations between the two empires. But lust would trump politics in Herod's life. He divorced the Nabataean princess and married his niece Herodias, who also happened to be his brother's wife. This move precipitated external and internal conflict. Internally, the marriage to Herodias was the cause of fire-and-brimstone opposition from Jesus' cousin John the Baptizer. In response, Herod Antipas had John decapitated.[25] The Gospels tell us that Herod Antipas also had his eye on Jesus as a possible heir to John the Baptizer's movement (Matthew 14:2). Externally, war broke out with the neighboring Nabataeans, who did not take lightly Herod's divorce of their Nabataean princess. In this conflict, Antipas' army suffered a major defeat. At the time, some attributed his military disaster as divine punishment for what he had done to John.[26]

All in all, the world that Jesus moved in was not a simple one. He did not simply live "in the Galilee." His world was made up of a multiplicity of provinces, interests, personalities, and politics, where the local rulers were fighting each other and were on the lookout for any possible troublemakers. In this world, Herod Antipas was the big player.

To protect his status, Herod constantly followed politics in Rome. He had been educated there and knew the main players: Augustus, Tiberius, and the rising star Sejanus, who in time came to rival the emperor himself, until his sudden downfall in 31 c.e.[27] Herod didn't just know the very big players: to some degree he was a very big player himself. For example, during a mission undertaken at the behest of the emperor, Herod Antipas hosted an important reception on the banks of the Euphrates River, far from his domain. There he entertained Vitellius, the governor of Syria, and King Artabanus II of Parthia. Using his own communications network, he even succeeded in sending the emperor a report of this high-level, high-profile gathering well before Vitellius was able to do so.

In other words, in Jesus' time, the local players were not playing their game on the fringes of the empire. On the contrary, everyone had their own links to Rome—spies, informers, and message carriers. The empire was riddled with plots and subterfuge. Herod Antipas, like many others in sensitive positions, played these contacts well.

The final section in our lost gospel—the one dealing with the plot to murder Jesus and his children and rape and murder Mary the Magdalene, his wife— forces us to reassess our perception of the world in which Jesus and Mary the Magdalene lived. As it turns out, the picture painted by *Joseph and Aseneth* of plots and counterplots that reach the highest levels of power is closer to the historical reality than the images conjured up by television Christmas specials. Jesus and Mary the Magdalene must not be seen in the context of Galilean peasant life, but in the context of the politics of the Roman elite. In other words, we will need to examine the plot against Jesus and Mary the Magdalene as a conspiracy played out at the highest levels.

International Power Politics on the Stage of Northern Israel

Herodians are mentioned in the New Testament as being unfriendly toward Jesus. This makes sense. Jesus, from their perspective, was not only an upstart, but also a competitor for Herod Antipas' legitimate crown. As a consequence, in Mark 3:6 the Herodians are depicted as conspiring with the Pharisees to kill Jesus. This is in keeping with *Joseph and Aseneth*: namely, that the rulers were reaching into the ranks of people who were natural allies of a movement like Jesus' and turning them against him. In Mark 12:13, some Pharisees and Herodians come to Jesus with a trick question regarding the legitimacy of taxation, a potential trap since taxation was a litmus test of cooperation with the government. Revolutionaries opposed paying taxes. Collaborators supported paying them. Any way he answered, Jesus would alienate some constituency. But he proved to be an adept politician. He avoided the question, famously answering: "render unto Caesar what is Caesar's and to God what is God's."[28]

As can be seen, when we look at the historical texts more closely and at the Gospels more historically, we discover that before coming to Jerusalem, Jesus was already on the Herodian radar. Jesus, therefore, was not a bit player. On the contrary, he was part of the intrigue that accompanied Galilean politics at the highest levels. We want to reiterate this. It's hard for people accustomed to a depiction of Jesus as a Galilean peasant, far removed from the centers of power, to think of Jesus as a player. But the Gospels themselves tell us that he was—coming to the attention of rulers, high priests, and Roman governors. The Herodians, walking a fine line between their Roman masters and their alienated Jewish constituencies, would have been especially wary of Jesus and his entourage.

As a political party, the Herodians, like Herod Antipas himself, would have been suspicious of anyone promoting a Kingdom of God. After all, this was a code word for a regime change. The proclaimer of such a kingdom might very well have regarded himself as the future ruler of the new entity, thus challenging the privileged position of Herod Antipas and his supporters.

In an interesting episode, the Gospels tell the story that "Satan" tempted Jesus with worldly power (Matthew 4:1–11 and Luke 4:1–13). In Jewish thought, Satan is not a Lucifer-type figure. He has no power. In Hebrew, *Ha Satan* simply means an adversary, one who tempts people to go with their evil inclination. Is the story of Jesus' temptation, therefore, an allusion to a moment in Jesus' career when temporal power seemed attainable? If something like this actually happened, some political figure must have played the role of Satan. It's not a temptation if it's not real. And what, after all, do the Gospels say he was tempted with? Matthew and Luke are both very clear: political power, authority, an earthly kingdom. Whatever this means, at the very least it places Jesus in the push and pull of the politics of the area; and it records that he was tempted for at least forty days and forty nights, that is, for a significant amount of time. Put differently, according to the Gospels, Jesus' rejection of political power was not instantaneous.

Herod Antipas' downfall came in 39 C.E. It was the result of several factors. In part, it was rivalry with his nephew, Agrippa, who was destined to become what Antipas had always coveted, the King of the Jews. When Caligula became emperor in 37 C.E., he appointed Agrippa king—not tetrarch—over some of the jurisdictions east of the Sea of Galilee and Gaulanitis, and over what had previously been a tetrarchy. The title was impressive—here, finally, was a King of the Jews. Essentially, as Josephus makes clear, Agrippa was about to be declared Messiah by some of his followers—all with Rome's blessing.[29] In essence, the appointment of Agrippa as King of the Jews was a consequence of Rome getting into the "messiah game." Basically, the Romans decided to become proactive. Instead of waiting for revolutionary Jewish Messiahs to arise, they decided to appoint one of their own. Was the position of a Roman-sponsored messiahship offered to Jesus? Was *that* the temptation? Did Jesus reject what Agrippa later accepted?

In any event, the appointment of Herod Agrippa as King aroused the ire of Antipas' wife, Herodias. The situation was particularly galling because over the years she and her husband had helped Agrippa with funds and support. Moreover, she was of royal Hasmonean descent (i.e., Maccabean), and she saw Agrippa as a usurper. Sensing that the timing was right, she persuaded her husband, Herod Antipas, to head to Rome so as to once again press his case for kingship. Antipas failed on this mission. He was blindsided by Agrippa, who conspired against him and informed his friend, Emperor Caligula, that years before, Herod Antipas had been involved in a conspiracy against Rome.

Agrippa also maintained that Antipas was preparing a rebellion, having amassed a sizeable amount of weaponry—enough to field an army of some seventy thousand. Whether any of these charges were true or not, Agrippa was believed and Antipas and Herodias were sent into exile. Emperor Caligula handsomely rewarded Agrippa. He was given Antipas' estate as well as all his political jurisdictions.

Take note: when we first read in *Joseph and Aseneth* that Jesus and Mary the Magdalene were at the center of intrigue involving the highest levels of power, this seemed fantastic and not in keeping with our image of Jesus as a celibate, sandal-wearing Galilean peasant at the fringes of the Roman Empire. But when we put Jesus into his historical context, we see that King Agrippa himself charged that the man who ruled Galilee during Jesus' time—Herod Antipas—was involved in conspiracies that reached into the highest echelons of Roman society. This same Antipas was sufficiently aware of Jesus' family to arrest, imprison, and kill Jesus' cousin, John the Baptizer. In other words, there are no six degrees of separation here. Herod Antipas was suspicious of Jesus. Agrippa was suspicious of Antipas. And both had access to the emperor. It seems that very little separated Jesus from the emperor.[30]

Is Herod Antipas the villain we seek? There does seem to be some synchronicity. After all, he marries the daughter of the King of Nabataea, and *Joseph and Aseneth* does say that the daughter of the King of Moab (synonym for Nabataea) was intended for "Pharaoh's son." Like "Pharaoh's son," Herod is rumored to have plotted against Jesus, and this is not hard to imagine given the execution of John the Baptizer. Also, very much like "Pharaoh's son," Herod was a lusty individual, quickly putting aside his wife to marry a niece, Herodias, who was already married to his half-brother. Perhaps Herod Antipas also lusted after Mary the Magdalene. Since she lived in his jurisdiction, he certainly would have had occasion to notice her. Moreover, Herod Antipas had reason to fear a pretender to the throne of Israel; a man that some were already calling King of the Jews.

The problem with identifying Herod Antipas with "Pharaoh's son" in *Joseph and Aseneth* is that, in the text, "Pharaoh's son" is not married and Herod Antipas was famously married to Herodias. Also, in our story, "Pharaoh's son" dies suddenly at the hand of some relative or follower of Jesus. This was not Antipas' fate. As stated, he ended his life in exile.

But the Gospel of Luke notes something very interesting with respect to Herod Antipas. It states that on the day of Jesus' crucifixion, "Herod and Pilate became friends with each other; before this they had been enemies" (23:12). This is a strange statement. We are never told why they had been enemies, or the reasons for their reconciliation. Also, why would Jesus' crucifixion somehow lead to a friendship between Antipas, the Jewish tetrarch, and Pilate, the Roman procurator?

Incredibly, we can glean a lot of historical information from this one line in Luke . . . it all has to do with Agrippa's accusation against his uncle Antipas. Specifically, Agrippa charged that at the time of Jesus' crucifixion, Herod Antipas had conspired against the Emperor Tiberius. The alleged co-conspirator was a man named Sejanus.[31] As it turns out, Pilate—Antipas' newfound friend—was an appointee of Sejanus.[32] So perhaps there was a basis for Agrippa's accusation.

Perhaps the key to understanding the plot against Jesus and Mary the Magdalene in *Joseph and Aseneth* is the relationship between Antipas, the now-obscure Sejanus, and Pontius Pilate, his most infamous appointee and Roman ruler of Judaea.

Pontius Pilate

Pilate served as procurator of Judaea from the year 26 c.e. through to 36 c.e. and played a pivotal role in the trial of Jesus. The Gospels contend that Pilate found nothing in Jesus' teachings or actions that merited the death sentence. According to the Gospels, the issue for Pilate was essentially one of religious squabbling among Jews, with no political overtones. He seems disinterested or flip-floppy on the Jesus issue. Many have argued that the Gospels are simply lying about Pilate as a way of selling Christianity to the Romans. Meaning, by making Jews the bad guys of the story, the Gospels are whitewashing Pilate and the Romans he represented. According to this view, why would Jews demand the life of a fellow Jew (even if they disagreed with Jesus), and why would the bloodthirsty Pilate suddenly prevaricate? But if we take the Gospels at their word, there may be a surprising explanation for Pilate's behavior, once we fill out the story with the information provided by our lost gospel of *Joseph and Aseneth*.

According to the Gospels, as a result of intense pressure, Pilate half-heartedly relents and sends Jesus to the cross. According to John, Pilate decided to go against Jesus after two things happened. First, an unruly mob mobilized by the priests chanted for the release of an insurrectionist named Jesus Bar Abba. Second, Jesus' accusers raised a huge political red flag—Pilate would be "no friend of Caesar's" if he released Jesus, they said (19:12). This was an implicit threat that they would go behind Pilate's back and report his actions to Rome, directly to Emperor Tiberius. That was something Pilate seems to have greatly feared. Why? Why would a Roman procurator fear rumors spread by a conquered people?

On most occasions, Pilate appears to have been extremely antagonistic toward the Jewish people. That's the way he is portrayed in both Josephus and Philo, who have nothing but contempt for this allegedly brutal ruler.[33] In one instance, his troops carried an ensign with Caesar's image into Jerusalem, a clear provocation that resulted in a near-revolt. Another time, he utilized temple funds to pay for an aqueduct. This too aroused so much opposition that a rebellion broke out. Pilate quickly and violently put it down. On this occasion, he dressed his troops in civilian clothes and had them carry daggers under their garments. They then mixed with the crowds and butchered them. In other words, Pilate was a person who did not care a whit for Jewish sensitivities and who knowingly antagonized, provoked, and murdered Jews. How is it that in the case of Jesus, Pilate is depicted in the Gospels as going out of his way to treat Jesus with clemency? This seems curiously out of character . . . unless trying to absolve Jesus of a capital crime represented a calculated move on Pilate's part.

If Jesus' death occurred not in 30 c.e. but a little later, say in 31 c.e. as some have suggested, then Pilate may really not have known how to proceed with Jesus. In that year Pilate's mentor, Lucius Aelius Sejanus, fell from grace and from power overnight. One moment, he was de facto ruler of the empire, wielding power in the name of Tiberius; the next moment, he was dead.

Since Pilate was appointed by Sejanus, could it be that the Gospels are not lying about Pilate? Quite the contrary, could it be that they are correctly describing a moment of uncertainty that can actually be dated? Put differently, is it possible that Pilate's uncharacteristic leniency toward Jesus reflects a precise moment of historical uncertainty? Can it be that Pilate is wary of Jesus' connections? Can *Joseph and Aseneth* provide us with crucial information—missing in the Gospels—that can help us accurately reconstruct the events leading to Jesus' crucifixion?

14

THE VILLAIN

We have seen that the main political player in the Galilee during Jesus' entire life was a man named Herod Antipas. We have also seen that Jesus was intimately connected to him in many ways. According to the Gospel of Luke, they met face to face just prior to Jesus' crucifixion.[1] Luke tells us that, at the end of the day, it was Antipas who turned Jesus over to Pilate. Earlier in the story, Luke also reports that while Jesus was still in the Galilee, Antipas had conspired to kill him.[2] All this is in keeping with what we know of Antipas' character. After all, he is the man who arrested and executed Jesus' cousin, John the Baptizer. Interestingly, Antipas seems to change his mind about going after Jesus. Perhaps this change of heart had something to do with the fact that one of Jesus' main supporters was a woman named Joanna who was married to Herod Antipas' "steward"—that is, his chief of staff.[3] Perhaps also, for reasons that will become clear later, Jesus changed his message and became less of a threat to Antipas. Maybe that's why Joanna and her husband Chuza were able to get Antipas off Jesus' back. Ironically, it was a woman connected to Antipas, Herodias, who sealed John the Baptizer's fate, and it seems that it was a woman connected to Antipas, Joanna, who saved Jesus' life while he was still in the Galilee.

Herod Antipas played the game of politics very well. During extremely volatile times, he managed to rule the Galilee and Peraea for over forty-two years.

Not only that, when he finally went down, he managed to get himself exiled and not killed. Not bad, at a time when Roman emperors were being routinely murdered and poisoned, sometimes by their own families.

Antipas' demise seems to have been caused by two factors—his wife Herodias and his nephew Agrippa. Herodias was Antipas' niece and his brother Herod's former wife.[4] When she dumped Herod and married Antipas, Herodias was determined to trade upward. So she constantly pushed Antipas to get Rome to declare him King of the Jews,[5] instead of his more lowly title Tetrarch of Galilee and Peraea. After the death of Emperor Tiberius and his replacement with the infamous Caligula, she urged Antipas to once again raise the king issue in Rome—this time with the new emperor. It turned out to be a big mistake. Not only was Antipas not upgraded to king, he was removed from his position as Tetrarch and sent into permanent exile.

Herodias and Antipas had miscalculated the influence of Antipas' nephew, Herod Agrippa. The latter grew up in Rome with Caligula, so when Tiberius died and Caligula took over, Agrippa's stock went soaring. For his part, Agrippa had something of a strange relationship with his sister Bernice. A celebrated knockout, she had young men and emperors falling for her well into her late forties and early fifties. Her main interest, however, was coaching her brother Agrippa and sponsoring his career. When Caligula sought Agrippa's advice with respect to his uncle Antipas' desire to be declared king, Agrippa accused Antipas of having conspired against Emperor Tiberius six years earlier. According to Agrippa, Antipas' co-conspirator was a man named Sejanus. This accusation turned out to be Herod Antipas' undoing. So, who was Sejanus?

As it turns out, Sejanus was the de facto ruler of Rome at exactly the time that Jesus was gathering crowds in the Galilee and making his way to Jerusalem. More than this, Pontius Pilate, who would later send Jesus to the cross, was a personal appointee of Sejanus. In fact, until Pilate, Rome had appointed two rulers (a combination of governors and prefects) in the area: one sat in Jerusalem and the other in Syria. To strengthen Pilate's hand, however, Sejanus delayed sending anyone to Syria. In this way, he made sure that his man in Jerusalem would be stronger than any previous prefect.[6]

Since Antipas seems to have conspired with Sejanus around the same time that he stopped conspiring against Jesus, the fact that Sejanus was running the show while Jesus was on the move seems like an important lead. So let's retrace our steps and set up that singular historical moment when the trajectories of Sejanus; Sejanus' man in Jerusalem, Pilate; Herod Antipas; and Jesus converged. We'll start with the emperor who ruled just before Sejanus amassed his powers.

Augustus, Tiberius, and Sejanus

Gaius Julius Caesar Augustus (born Gaius Octavius Thurinus) is considered the first Roman emperor. He ruled from 27 B.C.E. until 14 C.E. His reign represented the transition of Rome from republic to full-fledged empire. It was a stable period. Augustus is credited with the so-called Pax Romana, a long period of enforced peace. He is also the first to seriously launch the so-called "Imperial Cult," in which the emperor was elevated from man to god. Augustus ruled at a time when the empire was seeking a new religion that would bind the different areas and peoples that it encompassed—hence the title Augustus, the "revered one." Upon his death in 14 C.E., the Senate declared Emperor Augustus a god.[7] This is no small point, especially when it comes to Judaea.

It is important to note, therefore, that for the first fifteen years of Jesus' life, the empire was ruled by Augustus, a *man* worshipped as a *god*. For Jesus' Jewish contemporaries, Augustus' claims were a provocation. The Jewish people were sure that the God of Israel would now send a divine emissary known as the "Anointed One." The Anointed One is called *Mashiach* in Hebrew (Messiah in English translation) and *Christos* in Greek (Christ in English translation). His divine mission was to liberate Judaea and the world from Roman idolatry, more precisely from the Imperial Cult: the worship of a man as a god. Jesus grew up during this specific period of Messianic expectations. But as Jesus was reaching manhood, Tiberius replaced Augustus.

Tiberius Julius Caesar Augustus succeeded Augustus as emperor in 14 C.E. and ruled until 37 C.E. He was one of Rome's greatest generals, conquering Pannonia, Dalmatia, Raetia, and temporarily Germania. He came to be remembered as an eccentric individual who often appeared disinterested in ruling. It was during his reign that Jesus was acclaimed by his followers as the long-awaited Messiah: the Anointed One. Jesus was crucified by the Roman army, which was nominally under Tiberius' command.

Tiberius wasn't supposed to have become emperor, but Augustus' two grandsons and presumed heirs died. Wanting to ensure a smooth transition of power, Augustus had to fashion a succession plan. In 4 C.E., around the time of Jesus' birth, Augustus "adopted" the 46-year-old Tiberius as son and heir. This adoption was a way of positioning Tiberius as the next emperor. But there was an important condition to the adoption: for his part, Tiberius had to "adopt" Augustus' nephew, Germanicus, as his son and heir, even though he was younger than Tiberius' own son, Drusus. Basically, Augustus' offer to Tiberius was, "I'll make you emperor if you make my nephew emperor after you."

After this arrangement, Tiberius' rise to power was meteoric. By the year 13 C.E., his authority was made equal to that of Augustus. When the latter died a year later, Tiberius was able to assume full imperial power without interruption or challenge.

As stated, Tiberius was an unusual emperor and in the 20s, in order to pursue his own personal hedonistic interests, he relinquished a considerable amount of power to a man named Sejanus. Sejanus was an ambitious soldier, and Tiberius appointed him commander of the Praetorian Guard, a position he held from 14 C.E. until his execution in 31 C.E. The Praetorian Guard was an influential military body that was created by Augustus to protect the imperial family. It expanded quickly from a group of bodyguards into a civic security force, protecting major sites and keeping the peace in the city of Rome. But despite its growth, Augustus had kept the unit decentralized. Once Sejanus took over, however, he moved quickly to consolidate the Guard into a central garrison. He also expanded the number of Guard cohorts (or divisions) from nine to twelve. At that point, it was clear to everyone but Tiberius, who was pursuing more worldly pleasures, that Sejanus was not going to be happy with limited power.

The transformation of the Praetorian Guard into a personal army—a force of approximately twelve thousand well-trained soldiers who reported directly to him—was Sejanus' first step in the pursuit of the crown. Step two was more complicated. It consisted of ruthlessly eliminating Tiberius' heirs. In 19 C.E., Tiberius' adopted son and heir, Germanicus, suddenly died under mysterious circumstances. Germanicus' wife, Agrippina, accused Sejanus of murder. Four years later, in 23 C.E., Tiberius' biological son, Drusus, also died a sudden but seemingly natural death. Much later, Tiberius would be told that Sejanus had had Drusus poisoned. Germanicus had been arrogant and therefore exposed. But it was not easy for Sejanus to get to Drusus. More than ever, after Germanicus' demise, Drusus was on the lookout for a possible assassination. But Sejanus was not to be thwarted. He succeeded in getting to Drusus by seducing Drusus' wife, Livilla. He then persuaded her to become his accomplice in murder.

With both Germanicus and Drusus out of the way, Sejanus' grand plan now involved a third step: insinuating himself into Tiberius' confidence. In this regard, he succeeded beyond his wildest dreams. In fact, it seemed as if there was divine intervention designed to make Sejanus look good. The story went like this: just after Drusus' murder, Sejanus found himself at a dinner party with Tiberius at the imperial villa in Sperlonga, about 75 miles south of Rome, on the Mediterranean coast. It was a place of sunshine and beaches where the emperor had one of his fancier villas, complete with a dining area on a man-made island, in front of a natural grotto. At the time, Sejanus was already very important—the head of the Praetorian Guard. But something happened at Sperlonga that would be very, very good for Sejanus. As the emperor was dining with his guests, some rocks came loose from on top of the grotto (maybe Sejanus even helped that process along). The giant rocks came falling down, crushing some of Tiberius' guests as they ate. Tiberius, however, was not hurt. Like a true bodyguard, Sejanus flung himself over the emperor, seemingly ready to die in his stead.[8] After this event, Sejanus became the emperor's most trusted adviser, his chief steward, so to speak. Tiberius now called him "my partner in my toils."

Still, not everything went Sejanus' way. In 25 C.E., with Livilla free of Drusus—at a time when Drusus' death was still perceived as natural—Sejanus petitioned the emperor for permission to marry the widow. The emperor refused, cautioning Sejanus not to overstep his rank. As a compromise, however, Tiberius suggested that Sejanus marry Livilla's daughter. By happily entertaining the idea, Sejanus now alienated Livilla, his lover and partner in murder. The latter vowed that Sejanus would never trade her in for a younger model, especially not her daughter. Despite the tensions, their partnership seems to have survived this episode.

After placating Livilla, Sejanus adopted a different tactic with Tiberius: isolation. In 26 C.E., he suggested that the emperor withdraw from Rome to the island of Capri, and Tiberius acquiesced. This was not out of character for Tiberius. Earlier in his life, he had abandoned a great military career for a stint of isolation on the island of Rhodes. Also, as ancient gossip had it, Tiberius possessed an insatiable sexual appetite for young girls and boys. A pleasure-palace in Capri allowed him to pursue his fantasies unfettered by officials in

Rome. In *The Twelve Caesars*, Suetonius describes these sordid pursuits in great detail—sex with young girls and boys, group sex, young children dressed up as nymphs cavorting in grottoes around the island for his voyeuristic pleasure, and so on.[9] This quasi-exile left day-to-day decisions in Sejanus' hands. The latter also controlled most of the information flow back and forth between Tiberius, the capital, and the Senate.

By 26 C.E., the year he appointed Pilate to represent him in Judaea, as Jesus was beginning to attract attention in the Galilee, Sejanus had become the real power in the empire, backed by the Praetorian Guard. His quest for power seemed tempered only by Tiberius' mother, Livia, a formidable player at the time. After her death in 29 C.E., however, Sejanus began a purge of opponents, eliminating all who stood in his way, senators included. Politicians and influential people throughout the empire lined up to declare their allegiance either to him or to Tiberius, and many who opted for the latter were executed. By the late 20s—at the same time as John the Baptizer and Jesus began to attract crowds—Sejanus was at the height of his powers and the de facto ruler of the entire Roman Empire. Incredibly, millions of Christians and most scholars have ignored all this when it comes to the Jesus story—as if it doesn't matter. But it does.

Sejanus did not sit aloof in Rome. He took an interest in the Middle East. As stated, in 26 C.E. he appointed none other than Pontius Pilate as his operative in Judaea. Pilate's policy of antagonizing the Jewish people likely played into Sejanus' long-range plans. Because he had not yet risen to the status of emperor, Sejanus loved creating tensions so as to make protagonists weak and dependent on him. It was probably then that Herod Antipas, sensing the changing fortunes in Rome, sided with Sejanus, just as Herod Agrippa later alleged.[10]

By 31 C.E., Sejanus felt that he was close to creating his own imperial dynasty. No doubt the fourth and final step of his plan was to eliminate Tiberius and assume the throne himself. By fall of that year, with Tiberius virtually exiled and opposing senators dead, Sejanus was well on the way to realizing his dream. Not much stood in his way.

But once again a woman played the critical role. Her name was Antonia, and she was mother of Livilla, the murderous widow of Drusus. The story goes that Apicata—Sejanus' spurned first wife—approached Antonia with information. She alleged that eight years earlier, a servant girl who had been in the employ of Drusus and Livilla had seen Livilla prepare the poison that killed Tiberius' son, Drusus. Obviously this was a serious charge. To get Tiberius out of his promise to Augustus that Germanicus would succeed him, it seems that Sejanus conspired with Tiberius to kill Germanicus. But according to Apicata, when it came to Drusus, Sejanus went behind Tiberius' back—killing his biological son without anyone but the conspirators knowing. It now seemed to Antonia that, together with her own daughter Livilla, Sejanus was about to make it three in a row—with Germanicus and Drusus out of the way, it was time to go after the emperor himself.

Antonia decided that enough was enough. Daughter or no daughter, Sejanus had to be stopped. So in a move that would influence the fate of Jesus and, as a consequence, the history of the world, she managed to smuggle a personal note to Tiberius, who was still ensconced on Capri playing sexual games with children. Upon reading Antonia's note, Tiberius kicked into action. He left Capri and returned to Rome. Through a ruse, he managed to get Sejanus into the Senate unprotected. Here, Tiberius had Sejanus condemned to death and summarily executed.

Several points should be noted: First, all this was going on while Jesus was purportedly healing the sick, turning water into wine, declaring the Kingdom of God, and getting ready to make his entrance into Jerusalem. Second, women were the key figures in most of these conspiracies. Finally, the world described above is perfectly mirrored in the plot to kill Jesus, Mary the Magdalene, and their children in *Joseph and Aseneth*. After all, *Joseph and Aseneth* describes an attempt to murder a "son of God," steal his wife, and murder his children. Basically, this is exactly what Sejanus was trying to do to the emperor. He killed Tiberius' children, seduced his daughter-in-law, and now he was going after the man-god himself.

We are not saying that *Joseph and Aseneth* is describing Sejanus' story as outlined above. Our point is that *Joseph and Aseneth* is describing the real-life world around Jesus in far more detail than the Gospels do. What seemed like fantasy is actually history, and what seems like history turns out to be carefully edited spin.

Again, let's look at *Joseph and Aseneth*. In this manuscript, it's Aseneth (Mary the Magdalene) who is front and center and it's Jesus who is in the background. In other words, it seems that *Joseph and Aseneth* is a document told from the point of view of one of the central women in the drama. Put differently, in

Joseph and Aseneth we not only have a rare document that takes us into a world of intrigue and betrayal, sex and murder conducted behind the scenes by people surrounding Jesus—it takes us into that world with a woman as our guide. Seen from this perspective, we can now see clearly that in Jesus' world it is the women who were often the main players—pushing their men toward that ultimate prize: divinely sanctioned rule.[11]

Let's take another look at the facts. Livilla conspired to kill her husband, marry Sejanus, and, together with him, make a grab for the imperial crown. Had they been successful, Sejanus would have been declared a god and she, as was sometimes the case, might have been elevated to the status of a goddess. Meanwhile, Herodias managed to get John the Baptizer executed and then pushed her husband, Antipas, to gamble everything for the title King of the Jews. At that same time, not to be outdone, Bernice, sister of Agrippa, was also pushing her brother—there were rumors that they were also lovers—to become King of the Jews. With this goal in mind, she reportedly bedded many of the power players in Rome and, in the end, succeeded: Agrippa was indeed declared King of the Jews. He was given a territory larger than Herod the Great's. Had he not died suddenly under mysterious circumstances, both his Jewish and Gentile followers might have declared him Messiah.[12]

As noted, *Joseph and Aseneth* perfectly reflects this period. But it adds something to the stories of intrigue in pursuit of power. It argues that Mary the Magdalene could have married a local political player, but she decided not to. She married a mystic and a healer, a magician and a miracle worker. He was, however, of royal lineage, and she backed him in his quest for the crown. In other words, she played the King of the Jews game. In this sense, Mary the Magdalene was one of the Messiah pushing girls, so to speak: Herodias had husband/uncle, Antipas; Bernice had brother/lover, Agrippa; while she had her Messiah/husband, Jesus.

Based on *Joseph and Aseneth*, we can imagine Mary the Magdalene conspiring with Joanna, wife of Chuza, surviving a near-assassination and making an alliance with Sejanus on behalf of her husband, Jesus. One can reject this scenario, but one thing is for sure: it is certainly true to the historical reality on the ground.

Herodias, her daughter Salome, Joanna, Livilla, Bernice, and Mary the Magdalene seem to be the unsung players who in the first decades of the 1st century were the main movers and shakers in the politics of Messiahship. Based on our newly deciphered text, it seems that Mary the Magdalene played the game well and, by the time her husband rode into Jerusalem, she must have secured assurances from Sejanus that even if Jesus caused a near-riot in the temple, he would not be touched. At first, he wasn't. But no one could have predicted that Antonia, the mother of Sejanus' mistress, Livilla, was about to intervene, causing Sejanus to go down—taking Jesus down with him.

Sejanus Close Up

Was Sejanus really that important to Jesus' life and death? The historical record is clear. Pilate and Antipas, two of the men who were principally responsible for the crucifixion of Jesus, were also intimate allies of Sejanus. This is not beside the point. It seems that these various stories somehow converged and, in the process, changed the world forever.

We are not the first to connect Sejanus and Jesus. Back in 1968, Paul Maier drew attention[13] to a strange report in the Gospel of John. John 19:12–15 records the Jewish high priests, which were led by the high priest Caiaphas, saying to Pilate: ". . . if you release this man [Jesus], you are no friend of the emperor." According to Maier, such a statement *only* makes sense after Sejanus' fall in 31 C.E. He is right. Pilate was Sejanus' man. After the fall of his mentor, he became vulnerable for the very first time since his arrival in Judaea. In Maier's words, the only time a Jewish high priest could have threatened his Roman boss was "at a time when Tiberius was prosecuting adherents of Sejanus . . . under the rubric of maiestas—treason to state and Emperor."[14]

Unfortunately, Maier goes further. He writes that since Sejanus was an anti-Semite (as attested to by Philo and Josephus), Jesus would not have dared to enter Jerusalem before his downfall. Meaning, Jesus must have come to Jerusalem *because* Sejanus had gone down. According to Maier, Jesus' plan backfired. By the time Jesus was arrested, Pilate was afraid to appear lenient toward a pretender to the Judaean throne, and Jesus' fate was sealed.

Maier's insight is that Sejanus' downfall is connected to Jesus' activities in the Galilee and his arrival in Jerusalem. But the problem with Maier's overall analysis is that it is contradictory. According to his view, Jesus went to Jerusalem after Sejanus' demise because he felt that it was now safe for him to be there. But Jesus miscalculated. Somehow, in the aftermath of Sejanus' downfall, Pilate felt vulnerable and turned out to be less than friendly. According to Maier's view, Sejanus' downfall makes things safer and more dangerous for Jesus at the same time. This simply doesn't work. If Jesus was afraid of Sejanus, why would he have gone to Jerusalem when Sejanus' man, Pilate, was still running things there?

Armed with the new information provided by *Joseph and Aseneth*, we can now see that though Maier is correct in connecting Sejanus to Jesus, he seriously underestimates the depth of that connection. Jesus didn't go to Jerusalem because Sejanus fell, he went to Jerusalem because Tiberius was about to fall. Sejanus' downfall did, indeed, affect Jesus. But it did not cause him to go to Jerusalem. It sent him to the cross.

Let's recapitulate the clues in this two-thousand-year-old mystery.

The detective work led us to Antipas, Antipas led us to Sejanus, and Sejanus led us to Pilate. Their interactions reached a climax at precisely the moment that Jesus rode his foal into Jerusalem. All this perfectly fits with *Joseph and Aseneth*, except that *Joseph and Aseneth* goes one step further. According to our text, Jesus, Mary the Magdalene, and Jesus' disciples are not passive observers. They are part and parcel of the intrigue—a plot involving someone code-named "Pharaoh's son." But who is this villain identified only as "Pharaoh's son?" Decoding his identity is key to making sense of this last section of *Joseph and Aseneth* . . . and also for understanding the power politics that led to Jesus' crucifixion.

Pharaoh's Son

Let's be precise. Since we've identified Joseph with Jesus and Aseneth with Mary the Magdalene, our entire reconstruction stands or falls on two things. "The Pharaoh" in *Joseph and Aseneth* must refer to a Roman emperor, and "Pharaoh's son" must refer to a biological son, an adopted son, or an intimate representative of the emperor's. We are obviously setting the bar quite high for ourselves. We are making our analysis of the plot to kill Jesus, Mary the Magdalene, and their children conditional on identifying the villain of the story: "Pharaoh's son." But what are the chances of identifying the son of a Roman emperor who is physically in the Galilee area during the height of Jesus' career? And even if we find such an individual, what are the odds that he would have had the opportunity and motive to penetrate Jesus' entourage and to conspire to kill Jesus, rape Mary, and murder their children? And even if we identify such an individual, what are the odds that he died in the Galilee area just as *Joseph and Aseneth* describes?

Here's the amazing thing about our text: *Joseph and Aseneth* leads us to not one, but two candidates for the role of "Pharaoh's son." As we've mentioned, Tiberius had two sons. Together with Livilla in 23 C.E., Sejanus killed Drusus, Tiberius' biological son. Earlier, in 19 C.E., Sejanus killed Germanicus, Tiberius' other son whom Augustus had forced him to adopt. Let's look at their stories more closely. One or the other of these two individuals has to be the villain.

Drusus

First of all, the identification of "Pharaoh" as Tiberius is solid. In fact, *Joseph and Aseneth* calls "Pharaoh," "the old lion." This fits perfectly with a story told by 1st-century historian Josephus concerning Tiberius: "Now Marsyas, Agrippa's freed-man, as soon as he heard of Tiberius's death, came running to him . . . and said, in the Hebrew tongue, 'The lion is dead.' Understanding his meaning, Agrippa became overjoyed at the news."[15]

It is interesting that the term *lion* for Tiberius seems to have been a code specific to the Jews. As in *Joseph and Aseneth*, Agrippa's servant does not mention Tiberius by name. Rather, *in the Hebrew tongue* he calls Tiberius *the lion*, and Agrippa immediately understands. In other words, both *Joseph and Aseneth* and Josephus use the exact same code word for Tiberius. So "Pharaoh" in *Joseph and Aseneth* is none other than the Roman emperor Tiberius.

But which son is "Pharaoh's son"? Whom can we identify?

Drusus is a very good candidate for this role. First, he is the biological son of Tiberius. Second, he dies in mysterious circumstances. Third, he is involved in plots and counter-plots that reach into the highest circles.

Drusus' story feels like *Joseph and Aseneth*. For example, in the manuscript, "Pharaoh's son" is called his "firstborn," which seems to be consistent with Drusus but not with Germanicus. Also, Germanicus never hung around Tiberius. He was always off fighting somewhere else. Drusus, on the other hand, stayed in Rome and probably visited his father's Capri pleasure-palace on numerous occasions. In *Joseph and Aseneth* there is an incident which vividly describes an aborted attempt by the son to murder the father. In 25:1 it states "Pharaoh's son rose in the night and went to his father to kill him with a blade but his father's guards prevented him from entering (the room)." It is easy to imagine young Drusus in Capri trying to sneak into his father's bedroom to do him in. The fact that it's his father's guards who thwart his plans is also consistent with the historical role of the Praetorian Guard. Furthermore, although the son plots against the father in *Joseph and Aseneth*, the father does not plot against the son. This suits Drusus. It seems that Tiberius may have plotted against Germanicus, but was taken aback by the murder of Drusus.

Drusus' relationship with his wife, Livilla, is also in keeping with his being "Pharaoh's son," the villain. In *Joseph and Aseneth*, the heir to the throne seems totally disinterested in anyone but Aseneth (a.k.a. Mary the Magdalene). In fact, his father asks him "why do you, the king and ruler of all the land, seek a wife beneath you?" (1:9). As we have seen, Drusus didn't have a very good relationship with his wife, Livilla. It is easy to understand why Drusus would be attracted to Mary the Magdalene while his woman was having sexual relations with Sejanus, becoming pregnant with Sejanus' twins and conspiring to murder her cuckolded husband.

When it comes to character here, too, the description of "Pharaoh's son" fits Drusus. Drusus was a drunk, a womanizer, and a regular patron at the local brothels. He also had a temper, once famously smashing Sejanus in the face. If he died a slow death at Sejanus' hands, he lived to regret that outburst. In any event, *Joseph and Aseneth* depicts "Pharaoh's son" as a scheming, spoiled, temperamental individual who alternates between bravado[16] and fear.[17] All this fits Drusus.

The main problem with identifying Drusus as "Pharaoh's son," however, is that we have no record of Drusus living or dying in the Middle East, as our manuscript clearly requires.

So we conclude that it is very likely that Drusus is not the "Pharaoh's son" of our lost gospel.

What, then, do we know about Germanicus?

Germanicus

As it turns out, we know for certain that Tiberius' adopted son, Germanicus, was in the vicinity of the Galilee during the time that Jesus was gaining followers there. Also, in a sense, he was Tiberius' firstborn. Although he was not the biological son of Tiberius, by virtue of the deal that had elevated Tiberius to the throne, Germanicus was in first position to take over from Tiberius. Legally speaking, by being the heir to the throne, he was the firstborn.

But did he have any interest in conspiring against his adoptive father, the Emperor Tiberius? On this score, too, Germanicus fits the bill.

Germanicus was a highly popular general, well beloved by the people. His campaigns in Germania were especially successful and, after the death of Emperor Augustus in 14 C.E., the troops under his command wanted to proclaim him emperor. He wisely turned down this premature acclamation, honoring Augustus' choice of Tiberius as his successor. At that time, instead of grabbing power, Germanicus took his soldiers into battle against a group of Germanic tribes, under their leader Arminius. A few years earlier, this same Arminius had successfully defied Roman rule and slaughtered thousands of Roman soldiers. Overstepping his authority, Germanicus took the battle across the Rhine River, which Tiberius had decreed as the outermost border for Roman rule. This would not be the only time Germanicus demonstrated disdain for his adoptive father's prerogatives.

Suspicious of Germanicus' growing popularity[18] and military might in 17 C.E., Tiberius recalled him to Rome under the pretext of honoring him with a full triumph. Five of his children accompanied Germanicus on his triumphal procession through the streets of Rome. The contrast between emperor and emperor's son was dramatic. There was Tiberius: the "old lion," an aging emperor, almost sixty. There, too, was Germanicus: the hero of the day, a highly decorated and popular military leader who had restored Roman pride on the northern frontier. And he was only thirty-two. With a roster of children on display, a dynasty seemed ensured.

Germanicus probably sensed that time was on his side and that it would not be long before he became emperor. At the time of his triumph, all of Rome must have thought so too. The onlookers included Sejanus, who immediately understood that he had a formidable rival with whom to contend.

In 18 C.E., Germanicus was made consul. Sejanus probably played no small role in this matter. The "promotion" was an opportunity to remove Germanicus from the center of power, and he was given a new command in the eastern part of the Roman Empire. There were problems in the East, especially in Parthia and Armenia. Also, the provinces of Syria and Judaea had petitioned for a reduction in taxation. As Tacitus puts it, "the commotion in the east was rather pleasing to Tiberius, as it was a pretext for withdrawing Germanicus from the legions which knew him well, and placing him over new provinces where he would be exposed both to treachery and to disasters."[19] As in *Joseph and Aseneth*'s depiction of "Pharaoh's son," treachery and disaster followed Germanicus everywhere he went.

Germanicus came to the East with the status of *maius imperium*, a position of power that exceeded the authority of every Roman governor or appointee in the area. In effect, this gave him virtual unlimited rule in the region, almost on par with the emperor himself. He was, in essence, co-emperor in all but name, and he was based in Antioch, just up the coast from the Galilee.

Rulers in the Middle East—Syria, Judaea, Galilee, Nabataea—would have been well aware of the implications of this appointment. Power had suddenly shifted: rather than reporting directly to the emperor, they would now be accountable to the emperor's son. As a result, it became important for Pilate's predecessor Valerius Gratus (15–26 C.E.) to ascertain Germanicus' policies and personal ambitions, and to align himself with them.

At precisely this moment in time—18 C.E.—Valerius appointed Caiaphas as high priest in Judaea, a term of office that lasted until 37 C.E. Obviously, this appointment would have been made with the new political reality in mind. In other words, the High Priest Caiaphas, the man that the Gospels accuse of arresting and trying Jesus, was appointed to his position precisely because our candidate for "Pharaoh's son"— the emperor's son, Germanicus—had arrived on the scene. To be appointed high priest by Valerius, Caiaphas must have been someone close to Valerius, someone the procurator thought he could count on. Caiaphas' appointment, therefore, would have connected him to Germanicus, not Sejanus. This should change the way we look at Jesus' confrontation with the authorities that ultimately had him crucified. When Jesus faced Caiaphas, Herod Antipas, and Pilate, he was facing a high priest who had been allied with Germanicus and two individuals implicated with Sejanus, the man who had Germanicus murdered.

In any event, in 18 C.E. Herod Antipas would also have taken note of Germanicus' arrival. During his lengthy forty-two year reign as tetrarch over the Galilee and Peraea (4 B.C.E.–39 C.E.), Herod Antipas saw many political masters come and go, and he outlasted them all. He didn't survive by ignoring their presence. In fact, after his arrival, all the political players in the area had to seek ways of ingratiating themselves to Germanicus.

But the political landscape was much more complicated than just cozying up to Germanicus and aligning one's policies with his objectives. At the same time as Germanicus was given enhanced imperial power, Tiberius created a new and complex political dynamic in the Middle East. Even as he "promoted" Germanicus, Tiberius removed Creticus Silanus, the governor of Syria, from his post. Silanus was a politician who had close ties to Germanicus. His removal was especially embarrassing for Germanicus, since Silanus' daughter was betrothed to Nero, Germanicus' oldest son. In Silanus' place, Tiberius appointed a strong opponent of Germanicus, Cneius Piso, whom Tacitus describes as a "man of violent temper, without an idea of obedience, with indeed a natural arrogance."[20] Piso was no fool. He understood that his mandate in the Middle East was to thwart the personal ambitions of Germanicus. But the animosity went much deeper—it involved their wives. Piso's wife, Plancina, hated Germanicus' wife, Agrippina. The hatreds, therefore, were political and personal and involved women. Once again, it seems that the political picture on the ground in Syria and Judaea was much closer to that in *Joseph and Aseneth* than to the accounts in any of the canonical Gospels. Intrigue, counter-intrigue, and shifting alliances were the order of the day. And in the midst of it all, as in our lost gospel, was an emperor's son.

In addition to Piso, Germanicus had to contend with Drusus, who was being groomed for power, closer to home. As Tiberius' natural son, he was a powerful rival. Then, too, there was Sejanus, who was beginning to make his moves on, and positioning himself as the head of, a well-trained army that reported solely to the emperor. It's entirely conceivable that in this web of intrigue, Germanicus began to think of how to rid himself of Tiberius before Tiberius got rid of him. Again, this is a perfect fit with *Joseph and Aseneth*, where "Pharaoh's son" wants the Pharaoh dead.

But let's take a closer look at our manuscript and see if we can bring the history into even sharper focus. According to our gospel, "Pharaoh's son" is foiled, and he dies in the area of the Galilee from wounds inflicted by one of Jesus' disciples. Did Germanicus die a gruesome death in the Syrian/Galilean area? Did he ever visit the area long enough to lust after Mary the Magdalene and hatch the plan described in *Joseph and Aseneth*?

Well, we know Germanicus traveled extensively throughout the Middle East. For one thing, he turned the regions of Cappadocia and Commagene in modern Turkey into Roman provinces. More specifically, according to Tacitus,[21] during his short-lived Middle Eastern career Germanicus attended a banquet hosted by Aretas IV, King of the Nabataeans.[22] Piso was there and took the occasion to insult his host as well as Germanicus. Herod Antipas was likely there because, at the time, he was probably still married to Aretas IV's daughter. Other local political and religious leaders must have been present as well—people like Chuza and Joanna.

From his base in Antioch, in order to get to Nabataea (modern-day Jordan), Germanicus would have had to travel along the Via Maris and then down the north-south highway that ran through Nabataea all the way to Egypt. These highways crossed at one specific spot: a town called Magdala, Mary the Magdalene's hometown. Incredibly, the highway intersection has recently been excavated and can be seen at the site.

Soon after visiting Nabataea, Germanicus visited Egypt, a country under the emperor's personal control. Entry for anyone who held the rank of senator or higher required the emperor's permission. Germanicus didn't ask for or receive permission to enter Egypt. Ostensibly, Germanicus went for sightseeing purposes, visiting the pyramids, Thebes, the great stone statues of Memnon and traveling as far south as Elephantine and Syene. But he also took the occasion to boost his popularity with the people, moving freely amongst them without soldiers as bodyguards. In particular, he reduced the price of corn by opening up the grain warehouses to help relieve a local famine—again, without the emperor's explicit permission.

Reducing the price of corn, an act of seeming civility, displeased Tiberius immensely, for Rome counted on Egyptian grain warehouses to feed her own people. Germanicus' act was political. It won favor for him in Egypt and sowed the seeds of trouble for Tiberius in Rome. It directly undermined the emperor's power.

What was Germanicus' motivation in venturing into Egypt? Was he really just a tourist? That's one possibility. More likely, he was mobilizing public support for his bid for the emperorship. Perhaps it was a test to determine how the "old lion" (that is, the aging Tiberius) would respond to an upcoming challenge to his authority.

In any event, the trip to Egypt would have taken Germanicus right past Magdala, back and forth. In other words, between the trips to Nabataea and Egypt, Germanicus passed through Magdala at least four times in the space of about a year. The question arises: in the midst of all the politicking against Tiberius, Sejanus, Piso, and all, was Germanicus the type of individual to go after a local leader, simply to assert himself over his wife? Opportunity is one thing, but are the actions described in *Joseph and Aseneth* in character for Germanicus?

The fact is that, historically speaking, we know Germanicus took a special interest in women, especially local leaders' wives. For example, after capturing Thusnelda, wife of Arminius, the German tribal leader, he sequestered her in his tent. She was already pregnant with Arminius' child at the time, but that didn't stop Germanicus. Both she and her child were later featured as prized conquests in Germanicus' triumphal procession through Rome. In similar fashion, Germanicus could well have attempted to push Jesus aside in order to abduct Mary the Magdalene. It would be totally in keeping with Germanicus' character to want to do to Jesus, Mary, and their children what he had already done to Arminius, Thusnelda, and their child.

Old prejudices die hard. We can imagine people thinking: come now, Mary the Magdalene is the object of Germanicus' lust? Jesus, the object of his envy? Politically speaking, wasn't Jesus too much of a bit player to be taken seriously by an emperor's son? Wasn't Jesus a starry-eyed preacher who was not on any Roman leader's radar? Well, not really.

As we've seen, the small cauldron of Middle East politics featured people such as Piso in Syria and Aretas IV in Nabataea who counted big-time in their day but are now all but forgotten by history. As we have also seen, seduction and murder feature prominently not only in our text but in Germanicus' life or, more precisely, in his untimely death. Jesus was no less important in the Galilean context than Arminius in the German context. In fact, unrest in Judaea might have had more far-reaching consequences than in Germania, at the outer borders of the empire. Also, Jesus had royal pretensions and was gathering a following. We see that later, in the aftermath of his cousin John the Baptizer's death, Jesus becomes the obvious candidate to wear John the Baptizer's mantle.[23]

So if we compare Jesus and Arminius, we see that they had several things in common: both had attractive wives, and both could make trouble. Also, as Tacitus reports concerning Piso's later attempt on Germanicus' life, the Romans were obsessed with magic, and Jesus had a reputation of being a world-class magician. This is attested to in the Gospels, the Talmud, and pagan texts.

Put differently, the story in *Joseph and Aseneth* makes perfect sense in the Galilean context of the 1st century. By comparison, we know that the plot against John the Baptizer involved a ruler (Antipas), two women (Salome and Herodias), and a death (John's). Similarly, the plot against Jesus seems to have involved a ruler (Germanicus), a woman (Mary the Magdalene), and a death

(Germanicus'). Seen in this light, i.e., that Germanicus is "Pharaoh's son," it seems that Germanicus' downfall saved Jesus, Mary, and their children.

Lets take a closer look: with Tiberius as his mentor, Piso constantly fought with Germanicus, undermining his decisions, insulting him, and refusing to implement his orders. For his part, Germanicus was eventually able to sideline Piso, but not before discovering that Piso was trying to poison him, using a combination of magic and germs. Tacitus writes that within the floors and walls of his living quarters, Germanicus found disinterred bodies, incantations, and spells. Also, the name of Germanicus had been inscribed on magical tablets. The plot seems to have worked, because Germanicus immediately became ill and died in Antioch in 19 C.E.[24] There were rumors at the time that his body showed evidence of poison, but it's entirely possible that he died of wounds inflicted on him in the Galilee, as he returned to Antioch from his insubordination in Egypt.

Germanicus' wife, Agrippina, widely blamed Tiberius for her husband's death. Piso was also blamed and arrested for treason, but he allegedly committed suicide before he could tell his part of the story. It had been anticipated that there would be a trial and Piso would sing like a canary, but his untimely "suicide" made that impossible.

All in all, whereas the idea of an emperor's son conspiring against the emperor and against Jesus and his family may have seemed outlandish when we first raised it in reference to *Joseph and Aseneth*, we can now see that there was an emperor's son in the area at the time, that he must have traveled through the Galilee on his way to Egypt and Nabataea, that he was involved in political intrigues, that he had reason to want the emperor dead, and that he was killed in a wide-ranging conspiracy that reached into the highest circles of power.

The fact is that in the extensive cover-up that followed his murder, no one is exactly sure of what did Germanicus in. As in *Joseph and Aseneth*, he was involved in a battle with enemies both in Rome and in the area of Judaea—and he lost. It's entirely possible that poison did him in or maybe, as it says in *Joseph and Aseneth*, he was struck and died of his wounds after three days. Perhaps poison was the official story. Maybe *Joseph and Aseneth* is giving us the inside story on this two-thousand-year-old cover-up. We don't know. The entire affair is shrouded in intrigue and mystery with dead bodies literally all over the place. What we do know for certain, however, is that the *Joseph and Aseneth* text led us to search for an emperor's son who died in the Galilee area under mysterious circumstances. And we found Germanicus.

Germanicus, not Drusus, perfectly fits the role of the villain, "Pharaoh's son."

Germanicus' widow, Agrippina, was not as fortunate as Mary the Magdalene. With Sejanus amassing power and consolidating influence with—and over—the emperor in 29 c.e., Agrippina and two of her sons—the heirs to the throne—were arrested. Soon after, the two boys died. The boys were probably murdered or, like Piso, committed "suicide." In 33 c.e., exiled and broken—just after the crucifixion of Jesus—Agrippina succeeded in starving herself to death. Basically, Sejanus did to Agrippina what "Pharaoh's son" (Germanicus) wanted to do to Mary the Magdalene.

In *Joseph and Aseneth*, the story of "Pharaoh's son" serves no theological purpose whatsoever. Kraemer is convinced that this "part of the story . . . takes place in 'history' and narrates the deeds of 'historical' persons."[25] Our analysis has demonstrated that this part of the story describes the historical circumstances that led to the Mara (i.e., the lady, Mary the Magdalene) being saved from the clutches of a member of the ruling class. In other words, since it isn't myth, it must be history.

15

THE POWER POLITICS BEHIND
THE CRUCIFIXION

The identification of Germanicus as "Pharaoh's son" allows us to pinpoint a specific moment in time in the now-lost story of Jesus' missing years. It's a period of great reversals. If we're right, *Joseph and Aseneth* is telling us that by killing Germanicus, Sejanus saved Jesus, Mary, and their children. In fact, it seems that *Joseph and Aseneth* is a pro-Sejanus apologetic. In a sense, it justifies the murder of Germanicus' wife, Agrippina, and her children because it argues that unprovoked, Germanicus was going to do the exact same thing to Mary the Magdalene and her children. Seen in this way, *Joseph and Aseneth* puts Jesus and his entourage squarely in Sejanus' camp. If Germanicus is the evil "Pharaoh's son," Sejanus is the front man for the increasingly isolated Pharaoh. The "Pharaoh" reference, therefore, must be to Tiberius, who was represented—as far as the masses were concerned—by Sejanus. In any event, identifying Germanicus with "Pharaoh's son" allows us to place Jesus' entry into Jerusalem *after* the death of Germanicus (19 c.e.) and *before* the downfall of Sejanus (31 c.e.). Based on our deciphered text, we can now literally reconstruct the events leading to Jesus' crucifixion, almost to the day.

Ascent to Jerusalem
So what prompted Jesus and his cousin John to push their missions to a new level in the late 20s? The answer is as simple as it is largely overlooked: Sejanus.

At precisely the moment that John and Jesus were gathering crowds, Sejanus was making his power grab in Rome. This is simply a matter of historical fact.

With Germanicus and Drusus both dead, it would have occurred to a wily politician such as Herod Antipas that, if he played his cards right, maybe this rising star—Sejanus—could help realize his wife's lifelong ambition that he become King of the Jews. At the same time, if Germanicus had made a failed grab for Mary the Magdalene, from the point of view of Jesus, Mary the Magdalene, and the swelling number of their adherents, Sejanus would have also been perceived as an ally. Wasn't he the man who murdered their deadly nemesis? In other words, the shifting alliances would have suddenly put Antipas and Jesus on the same side only in the late twenties and early thirties.

For his part, in his bid to become emperor, Sejanus had no option but to look for allies—not just in the Senate but out in the various provinces of the Roman Empire. No doubt, as the appointment of Pilate demonstrates, Sejanus was looking for influential leaders and charismatic people who could stand up for him and support his claims. Perhaps Sejanus was recruiting allies who would even go into battle with him, should civil war break out. As we have seen in these machinations, Sejanus was not one to overlook women. It's easy to imagine, therefore, that he would have been happy to make an alliance with a wealthy Phoenician woman who had a charismatic pretender to the Judaean throne as a husband. Why is Livilla believable as the object of Sejanus' attentions and not Mary the Magdalene?

In retrospect, Sejanus must have appeared as a godsend not only to Jesus and his followers, but also to the Jewish people as a whole. Remember, after Augustus, Roman emperors like Tiberius were making claims of divinity, and here was a commoner, a soldier, killing the royals one by one. It was hard to root for Tiberius, the pedophile god-emperor in Capri. It was much easier to be taken in by Sejanus. Besides, Tiberius didn't need allies on the ground; Sejanus did. Suddenly, it must have occurred to Jesus, or at least to his wife, Mary the Magdalene, that the ascent of Sejanus could propel them onto the national or even international stage.

When Jesus' brothers taunted him—"If you really are doing such things as these, show yourself to the world" (John 7:4–5)—Mary the Magdalene must have agreed. But there was a problem: To "show" himself to the world, Jesus needed to go to Jerusalem. But Jerusalem was not safe for Jesus. The temple hierarchy (code-named "the Jews" in the Gospel of John[1]) that was appointed at the time of Germanicus "were looking for [Jesus] and asking, 'where is he?'" (John 7:11–12).

Germanicus' downfall and Sejanus' power grab would have allowed Jesus to shift his focus from the villages of the Galilee to the capital itself. Perhaps the time was now ripe for an autonomous Jewish state led by a miracle-working descendant of the House of David.[2]

Situating Jesus' departure from Galilee and entrance into Jerusalem at this particular time in Sejanus' career helps to make sense of a puzzling passage in Mark that says the Kingdom of God is "at hand" (Mark 1:15). Why "at hand," now, at this particular time in history? What's driving this specific agenda? The shift in power in Rome and the impact it had on shifting power balances within the Middle East would help explain Jesus' timetable.

The identification of "Pharaoh's son" as Germanicus provides us with the missing key player in the Jesus drama, namely Sejanus. Once he is reintroduced into the story, the social matrix and the web of relationships surrounding Jesus can be reconstructed with various degrees of certainty. Of course, some of this has to be speculative because it was a secret even in Jesus' day. Even Tiberius didn't know what Sejanus was up to. Had Antonia not tipped him off, Tiberius would have ended up like Germanicus and Drusus before him.[3] Having said this, the reintroduction of Sejanus into the story allows us to explain much more of the Gospels' narrative than has so far been possible.

Jesus' famous provocative riot on the Temple Mount, after his entry into Jerusalem, suddenly makes sense. We can now see that by his actions he's not challenging Pilate or Antipas, Sejanus' protégés. Rather, he's challenging Caiaphas, the Germanicus-friendly high priest who was appointed by Valerius. That's why, uncharacteristically, there is absolutely no Roman reaction to Jesus' provocation. None whatsoever. That's why no Roman troops stationed nearby in their barracks on the northwest side of the Temple Mount came out to arrest Jesus. While there is opposition from the priesthood, there is complete silence from the Roman authorities (Matthew 21:17; Luke 19:47). The flip-flop policy of Antipas with respect to Jesus also starts to make sense. Even the presence of someone like Joanna, married to Antipas' head of security, in Jesus' most intimate circle only makes sense in the context of this lost world of intrigue and counter-intrigue opened up by *Joseph and Aseneth*. Once we reintroduce Germanicus and Sejanus into the Jesus story, we can finally understand the dynamics that led to Jesus' arrival in Jerusalem and to the sudden reversal of his fortunes.

Reconstruction

It must have seemed at that unique moment in history that everything was possible. As a result, in the Galilee, Herodias was pushing Antipas to become King of the Jews. In Rome, Bernice was pushing Agrippa toward the same goal. And, with their move to Jerusalem, it now seems clear that Mary the Magdalene was sponsoring her own candidate for the prize.

These women were all playing the same game: marry a pretender to the throne, make him the protégé of someone who might become emperor, and then propel him to the top. It must have seemed at that particular moment that compromises were possible. The power in Rome was shifting: Tiberius was about to fall; Sejanus was about to take over. Here was an opportunity to make Jesus of Nazareth a Sejanus-sponsored Messiah. If Jesus bought into this strategy, this meant that he would enter Jerusalem sponsored by the most powerful Roman of the time, second only to the emperor. But there was a price—he would have to give up on the Davidic throne. In that sense, he would be reversing his previous position. Why would he do this? For very practical reasons, it seems. His cousin John the Baptizer had not compromised with Herod Antipas and ended up decapitated. Here was an opportunity to avoid death. But more than this, there was a bigger prize at hand: the temple. If Jesus became a Sejanus-sponsored Messiah, he would be liberating the temple from the lackey priesthood led by the High Priest Caiaphas.[4] Put differently, if Jesus played along with Herod Antipas, and if they both had Sejanus' backing, he would no longer be seeking political independence for Judaea. But his growing movement would relocate from the religious periphery to the center of Judaean religious life—the temple in Jerusalem, the House of God. Perhaps there was, after all, room at the top for two Kings of the Jews—one political and one religious.

Until the Hasmoneans (that is, the Maccabeans) fused the roles of high priest and king in 168 B.C.E., kingship and priesthood had been separate affairs in Israel. King and high priest were supposed to be different individuals. They acted as checks and balances on each other. According to the Zadokites (traditional temple priests), the Hasmoneans erred when they united the two functions and ousted the temple hierarchy. This led to corruption and the debasement of the House of God. Later, under Roman rule, the high priest became a lackey of Roman power, an appointee of an emperor claiming to be a god. Even the high priest's vestments were now held by the idolaters and were only "loaned" to the high priest on holidays. The Zadokite priests never forgave the Hasmoneans for uniting the two offices into one. By accommodating himself with Antipas and Sejanus, Jesus now had the opportunity to oust the discredited priests, to align himself with a Herodian King of the Jews, and to get the Romans to cut the Jewish people some slack. Also, from Jesus' point of view, accommodating himself with another Jewish king would not have been betrayal. In fact, for a few years prior to this, some Judaeans had begun to believe that the Jewish people were about to be redeemed not by one but by two individuals. There was a precedent for this—very close to home.

When Jesus was born, or perhaps when he was a child about ten years old (6 C.E.), an uprising took place right in the area of Nazareth. The revolt was put down with savage brutality by the Roman procurator, Varius.[5] Hundreds, perhaps thousands, of Galileans were crucified. This revolt seems to have been spearheaded by two men: a revolutionary called Judah the Galilean, and a priest named Zadok. It seems, therefore, that some twenty years prior to Jesus' movement, the idea of power-sharing between revolutionary leaders who divided temporal rule from temple service was already in the air.

In fact, at the same time, in the entourage of the followers of another would-be Messiah named Simon of Peraea, a new and revolutionary idea emerged. The idea was that there would soon appear not one but two Messiahs—a political Messiah of the House of David and a spiritual Messiah of the House of Joseph.[6] Many now understood salvation as a dyad: that two leaders instead of one would herald it. The Dead Sea Scroll community, for instance, embraced this idea: two Messiahs, one kingly, one priestly, both together helping to usher in God's rule on earth.

It seems that Jesus introduced an innovation into this emerging formula. By proclaiming that his kingdom was not of this world, Jesus was signaling that he was declaring war on the high priest, Caiaphas, but not on the Romans and not on Antipas, their temporal representative. More than this, perhaps by declaring liberty from the Torah's law, Jesus was about to institute a new priesthood, with himself as high priest. Let's remember that according to Paul, Jesus has been made the "high priest" bearing the sacrifice of his own blood into the heavenly temple.[7] Perhaps in light of the crucifixion Paul was reinterpreting a historical run for the high priesthood. Let's remember that Jesus was accused of plotting to destroy the temple (Mark 14:58 and parallel John 2:19).[8] Clearly, what was meant was not a physical destruction but a spiritual takeover. Maybe that's why Caiaphas, Annas, and the priesthood were so worked up against Jesus. Maybe the sign the Romans nailed to the cross should have read "High Priest of the Jews" instead of "King of the Jews" (Matthew 27:37, Mark 15:26, Luke 23:38, John 19:19). All this seems to explain why Herod Antipas did nothing to Jesus when he had a chance to kill him in the Galilee.

Put differently, it seems that Jesus didn't want to end up like his cousin John, served up on a Roman platter. Perhaps it was this calculated and pragmatic move by Jesus that led Peter to deny him and Judas Iscariot (i.e., Judas the Sicarius) to betray him. Remember, Judas the Sicarius was a member of a group that would end their trajectory committing mass suicide in the mountain fortress of Masada. From Judas' point of view, a Jesus decision to lead a Roman-sponsored Messianic movement with the limited goal of a temple takeover must have seemed like treason.[9]

We shouldn't be confused by Jesus' actions in the temple as a challenge to Roman power. By overturning the moneychangers' tables in the Temple of Jerusalem—the so-called "cleansing of the temple"—and by calling the temple "my Father's house," Jesus was signaling a regime change in the high priesthood, not the government. Mary the Magdalene and Joanna may have brokered a deal whereby Jesus and Herod Antipas were to join forces. They probably came to the conclusion that Sejanus would have an interest in making Jesus a spiritual King of the Jews while finally crowning Herod Antipas the political King of the Jews.

If you think the idea of a Roman-sponsored Messianic grab for power by Jesus is far-fetched, think again. For example, the Talmud states that "Jesus the Nazarene was . . . close to the [Roman] crown."[10] This is not a Talmudic throwaway. When it comes to Jesus, it's a Talmudic theme: Jesus of Nazareth was connected at the highest levels to the Roman authorities. Also, you should recall that within a few years of Jesus' death, Tiberius' successor, Caligula, made Herod Agrippa King of the Jews and, as Josephus relates, positioned him to be declared Messiah by the Jewish masses. In that sense, perhaps the time—or timing—really was "at hand." Perhaps Sejanus, Herod Antipas, and Jesus were planning to pull off what Caligula and Agrippa were to accomplish a few years later. As with Jesus, it all went terribly wrong with Agrippa.

Today, we recognize that the "kingdom" didn't materialize the way Jesus and his followers intended or his contemporary audience understood. Later generations recognized this too and engaged in revisionist history, saying that Jesus' Kingdom was not at all of this world, that it was a supernatural, heavenly kingdom. This view simply doesn't ring true. Such an otherworldly view would not have corresponded with any Jewish messianic expectations whatsoever, then and now. Nor does it fit with Jesus' own prayer that God's will should be fulfilled on earth as it is in heaven.

How could Jesus, the messianic claimant, have become a Roman ruler's ally? As stated, the strange story related in the Gospels—that Jesus resisted Satan's offer of an earthly kingdom and that he was only interested in a heavenly one—is probably an echo of something that actually happened.[11] This would seem to indicate that, at some point, Jesus relinquished his earlier Zealot ideology ("I come not to bring peace on earth but the sword") for what the Zealots would have regarded as collaborationist tactics ("Give unto Caesar what is Caesar's and unto God what is God's"). This tilt toward Rome would have confused his followers, even while it facilitated Jesus' entry into Jerusalem.

In effect, *Joseph and Aseneth* gives us the key to reconcile the different Jesuses presented in the Gospels. He didn't advocate for the Kingdom of God in opposition to the Kingdom of Earth. It's merely that he was willing to separate the two. He could lead the former, Herod Antipas could lead the latter, and Sejanus could bless them both. Why was Jesus willing to do this? For the purpose of gaining control of the temple and, as a result, accelerating the advent of the Kingdom of God on earth.[12]

Understanding that Jesus' entrance into Jerusalem took place with the backing of Sejanus not only explains the contradictory depictions of Jesus in the Gospels and the ambivalent response of the authorities, but it also explains the shifting response of his own entourage, i.e., Peter's denial and Judas' betrayal and suicide. It also explains the disappearance of his disciples during the crucial hours of the trial and crucifixion: they felt betrayed by their leader.

Some might argue that the disciples disappeared not because they felt betrayed by Jesus but because they were scared of Pilate. Not likely. As we have seen, Zealots and Sicarii surrounded Jesus. As a point of information, this is the way Josephus describes the Sicarii under torture: "The Romans could not get anyone of them to declare, or even seem to declare, that Caesar was their

Lord. On the contrary, they stayed true to their beliefs despite all the tortures they had to endure. It was as if they received these torments, even when they were set on fire, with bodies insensible to pain, and with souls that, in a sense, rejoiced under torture. But what was most astonishing to eyewitnesses was the courage of the children; for not one of the Sicarii children was so overcome by torments as to name Caesar as his or her lord."[13] Josephus was a sworn enemy of the Sicarii and the Zealots. His testimony with respect to their courage comes from an opponent, not a supporter. Given this, is it believable that Jesus' disciples abandoned him at the time of his crucifixion because they were afraid of the authorities? Clearly, something else was at play here. Let's examine Jesus' evolving ideology.

Jesus' Evolving Message

In the canonical Gospels, we have a schizophrenic presentation of Jesus. "Jesus One" seems to be a Zealot, that is, a revolutionary espousing a violent philosophy and surrounding himself with violent men. This Jesus is a member of a revolutionary family that keeps being hounded by the authorities. After all, Jesus is crucified and, later on, so is his brother Simon; his brother James is stoned to death in 62 C.E., and his cousin John is beheaded. Further, two of the twelve disciples, Simon and Judas, are members of revolutionary groups; the two people crucified on either side of him are revolutionaries, and Jesus himself insists that his closest associates carry concealed weapons.[14]

In contrast to "Jesus One," however, the Gospels also present another Jesus: "Jesus Two." This Jesus shuns earthly kingdoms, separates what is due to Caesar from what is due to God, advocates turning the other cheek, and, when they come to arrest him, calms his violent disciples by stating that "he who lives by the sword shall die by the sword."[15]

How does one reconcile these two very different Jesuses? Traditionally, Christians have done this in two ways: denial and revisionism. With respect to the first, the world simply has erased from its collective memory the Jesus who advocated violence and surrounded himself with armed men. With respect to the revisionism, the strategy is more complex. According to this view, Jesus' message was so far above everyone's head that his most intimate followers didn't understand him. They thought he was a revolutionary Messiah, but he wasn't. They thought his message was a Jewish one, but it wasn't. They only started to get it after his death and resurrection. According to this view, it's the message that Jesus espoused after his death that's the clearest of all because, after all, that's the message he gives to the only apostle who didn't meet him—Paul.

To make this interpretation stick, however, certain passages in the Gospels have to be ignored or altered. According to this view, Simon—who is called the Zealot in the Gospels—wasn't really a Zealot, he was a reformed Zealot; Judas the Sicarius wasn't really a member of the Sicarii, he was actually Judas *Ish Kariot* (i.e., Judas the man-about-town). As for the two revolutionaries crucified with Jesus, they weren't really *lestes* (Zealots), as they are called in the original Greek, they were mere thieves—never mind that theft was not punishable by crucifixion. If we make all these changes to the text, Jesus turns into a pacifist. In response to this theological spin, some, like S. G. F. Brandon,[16] have argued that the only real Jesus is the revolutionary one.

But why do we need to turn Jesus into a Zealot or a pacifist? Why does he have to be one or the other? Why can't there be ambivalence in his program? Why could it not have evolved and changed over time? After all, besides Jesus, the most famous Galilean of that era is Joseph Bar Matia, known to history as Josephus Flavius, the historian who basically rescued the entire history of that period from oblivion. What do we know about Josephus' life? How did he react to the complex choices that his contemporaries faced? Was he a revolutionary or a collaborator? Well, he was both.

We know from Josephus' own writings that he was a general, a revolutionary, and a collaborator. Once he was convinced of the futility of armed struggle, he cooperated with the Roman generals Vespasian and Titus, all the while believing that he was serving the best interests of the Jewish people. In other words, in Josephus we have a Judaean born around the time of Jesus' crucifixion, a contemporary of Paul, who in his own life embodied the ambiguity that was inherent in the opposition to Rome.

Josephus at first surrounded himself with Zealots so as to fight the Romans; then he abandoned the Zealots and cooperated with the Romans. By his own admission, his former followers now wanted to kill him. Meaning, in Josephus we have a latter-day Jesus—a complex individual with an evolving philosophy, shifting alliances, and an enduring conviction that he was doing the right thing.

By his own admission, Josephus was prepared to do anything in order to "cleanse the temple"—to keep it functioning properly according to the ancient rituals, safeguarding it from destruction.[17] Jesus seems to have been motivated by similar concerns. Remember, we only see him weeping once—not during the crucifixion, but when he foresees the destruction of the temple.[18] In any event, the idea of a revolutionary that ends up finding a royal patron is only far-fetched if you are unfamiliar with the history of the period.

It seems that, like Josephus, Jesus was in the anti-Roman camp until he found a Roman he could work with. As it turns out, things turned out well for Josephus but not for Jesus. Josephus allied himself with a Roman commander named Vespasian, who then became emperor. Jesus allied himself with a Roman commander named Sejanus, who was executed by the emperor. Had Vespasian been killed as a captured revolutionary general, Josephus, like Jesus, would have probably ended up crucified in Judaea—instead of retired in Rome.

The Dating Game

Our explanation of the events in Jerusalem during Jesus' entry into the city is based on new information gleaned from our lost gospel of *Joseph and Aseneth*. The new reconstruction of events is based on the idea that Germanicus is the historical person called "Pharaoh's son" in the text, and that Jesus cooperated with Sejanus, Germanicus' enemy. All of this, in turn, depends on Jesus making his entrance into the capital at the precise moment of Sejanus' downfall in 31 C.E. But scholars generally propose 30 C.E. as the date of the crucifixion, not 31 C.E. How solid is their date?

It is important to note, in the first instance, that no one really knows the precise date of Jesus' crucifixion—30, 31, and even 33 C.E. have been proposed by scholars. So which is it? By all accounts, including the Talmud, Jesus was crucified on Passover. It's generally believed that in the year Jesus was crucified, Passover fell on a Sabbath. It seems that in the year 30, Passover did indeed fall on a Sabbath. That's why most scholars prefer this date for the crucifixion. But the argument is hardly convincing.

Synchronizing holidays to precise days of the week is an imprecise exercise at best, especially when we are talking about events that occurred some two thousand years ago. Also, today the Jewish people use astronomy to calculate holidays, but when the temple stood in Jerusalem, eyewitness reports of the new moon trumped scientific calculations. A cloudy day changed everything. So it is very hard to be sure on what particular day of the week a given holiday fell at the time of Jesus. Let's re-examine the Gospels, therefore, and see if there are solid reasons to shift the popular notion that the crucifixion happened in 30 C.E. and move it some eighteen months forward to coincide with Sejanus' downfall.

When it comes to Jesus' triumphal entry into Jerusalem, we suspect that most people have some kind of version of *Jesus Christ Superstar* pop up in their heads when they imagine the event. According to this stereotypical view, after three years of preaching and healing in northern Israel, Jesus chose Passover to make his big move into the holy city. Surrounded by his disciples, Jesus came riding on a donkey or colt—sometimes white, sometimes not—while masses of people waved palm fronds at him and welcomed his arrival with songs called *Hosannas*.

To make sense of this scene, let's imagine that we are describing not Jesus' entry into Jerusalem, but the triumphant return of a high school basketball team to a small town in Anywhere, U.S.A. The team just won the state championship and, as their vehicles roll into town, crowds of people waving lit pumpkin lanterns and kids wearing masks meet them. Everyone joyfully takes up the chant, "Trick or treat! Trick or treat!" What season of the year is being described? Of course, anyone familiar with Halloween would immediately say that the championship was won in October. In this analogy, the normal expression that accompanies Halloween seems to have been taken up by the crowds as a victory chant.

But imagine for a moment that a newspaper describing the above event is discovered thousands of years from now. People might think that the pumpkins were carved as way of greeting the team, and that "trick or treat" had some kind of meaning related to their victory. With this story in mind, we can now return to Jesus' entry into Jerusalem, where crowds waving palm fronds and chanting *Hosannas* met him.

There are three great pilgrimage holidays during which Jews congregated in Jerusalem and offered sacrifices in its holy temple—Passover (*Pesach*), Tabernacles (*Sukkot*) and Pentecost (*Shavuot*). Roughly, Passover celebrates the Biblical Exodus, when the Jewish nation was freed from slavery in Egypt; Tabernacles celebrates God's providence during the wanderings in the desert; and Pentecost celebrates the receiving of the Five Books of Moses, or the Torah. During these holidays, thousands upon thousands of pilgrims descended on the ancient city. They came from all over the Roman Empire and beyond; from places like Parthia and even India.

If we take Jesus' entrance into Jerusalem at face value—as reported in the Gospels—there are serious issues of chronology in their account. For example, all four canonical Gospels state that he came during Passover, and yet, three of the four Gospels report that pilgrims carrying some kind of branches and singing *Hosannas* greeted him.[19] The Gospel of John is more specific.[20] It states that the crowds were carrying not any old branches, but palm fronds. Waving palm fronds and singing *Hosannas* are specific to the rituals connected with the holiday of Tabernacles (in Hebrew, *Sukkot*), not Passover. They are as much a part of Tabernacles as pumpkins are a part of Halloween.

Some might say that you can grab a palm frond anytime. They've obviously never tried climbing a palm tree and cutting a leaf off. The harvesting and distribution of palm fronds during Tabernacles was and is a difficult business. Also, even if we imagine an entrepreneurial Jesus supporter climbing up a palm tree and throwing down some leaves, this would still not accord with the *Hosanna*-singing crowds that the Gospels describe. *Hosannas*, then and now, are prayer rituals specific to the holiday of Tabernacles/*Sukkot*.

We suspect, therefore, that the Gospels collapsed the calendar, compressing into a number of days what actually took months. Meaning, if Jesus arrived in the city during Tabernacles, then he arrived in the fall. This holiday occurs around October/November. And if Jesus was tried and executed during Passover, then he was crucified in the spring, around March/April. In other words, he didn't just spend four days in Jerusalem, as the Gospels relate. Put differently, if we are to believe that the residents of Jerusalem were singing *Hosannas* when Jesus arrived and were about to celebrate Passover when he was crucified, he must have spent about six months in the city.

To return to our basketball example, if we say the team became state champs when children were trick-or-treating and lost the nationals by Christmas, there is no way to imagine that less than a week separated the first event from the last. There's no way around it. It's as simple as that. So how did the palm fronds and *Hosannas* end up in a story about Passover?

It is acknowledged by scholars that during its final redaction, the Gospel of John was overwritten with a theological spin in mind. It is also acknowledged that embedded in John are eyewitness sources that are thoroughly familiar with Jewish life. For example, John has the best information of all the Gospels when it comes to Jewish festivals and other customs. As a result, John's description of

Jesus' entry into Jerusalem is probably the most accurate. This is what he says: "The next day the great body of pilgrims, who had come to the festival, hearing that Jesus was on the way to Jerusalem, took palm branches and went out to meet him, shouting 'Hosanna!' Blessings on him who comes in the name of the Lord! God bless the King of Israel!"(John 2:12–14).

This perfectly describes the feast of Tabernacles. Earlier, John tells us that Jesus was approached in the Galilee: "As the Jewish feast of Tabernacles was close at hand, his brothers said to him 'you should leave this district and go into Judaea, so that your disciples there may see the great things you are doing.' Surely no one can hope to be in the public eye if he works in seclusion . . . Later, when his brothers had gone to the festival, he went up by himself, not publicly, but almost in secret" (John 7:2–10). So, according to John, Jesus does go to Jerusalem in October. He enters the city in "secret." Why the secrecy? Well, here, too, John provides us with the answer. He says that when Jesus entered Jerusalem, the authorities were "looking for him" (7:12). Also, "there was much whispering about him in the crowds" (7:12), not all of it good.

It is clear, therefore, that John's palm-waving, *Hosanna*-shouting crowds belong to this episode. After this, Jesus does not go back to the Galilee. By December, during the festival of Chanukah, John says, "It was winter [and] Jesus was walking in the Temple precincts" (10:22). Always the temple! He then crosses the Jordan, "to the place where John had been baptizing earlier" (10:40), and he "goes back to Bethany . . . just under two miles from Jerusalem" (11:18). He now meets up with Mary the Magdalene (11:22), and they re-enter Jerusalem for the final Passover.

It seems that later, a redactor concerned that John's chronology might contradict the Synoptic Gospels moves the Tabernacles palm-fronds episode and places it before Passover. This final redactor is not familiar with Jewish holidays. All he is concerned with is harmonizing the texts. To reiterate: when we move Jesus' *Hosanna*-accompanied entry out of the spring and put it back into the fall where it belongs, we see that Jesus spent six months in Jerusalem and its environs before his fortunes changed—not four days.

We hope this is clear. Our redacted Gospel of John has Jesus secretly coming to Jerusalem in the fall and then publicly—with palm-waving and *Hosannas*—in the spring. But the public acclamation really belongs to the fall entry. That means that the first pilgrimage was not an insignificant foray. It was the key move out of the Galilee and into Jerusalem, a move that would end up in Jesus' crucifixion.

Why would the Gospels want to compress half a year into four days? The answer is pretty obvious. If the crowd went from ecstatic support to hostility in less than a hundred hours, the Jewish masses are the villains. The message seems to be: "What a fickle people these Jews are!" They literally go from singing *Hosannas* to shouts of "crucify him" in a matter of hours (John 19:7–12).

So perhaps there is more to the Gospel's obfuscation of the chronology. This portrayal seems to be no slip of the pen. It gave rise to millennia of anti-Semitism, culminating in the Holocaust. After all, what kind of people are these who, when faced with God made flesh, turn from adoration to murder in less than a week?

On the other hand, if Jesus arrived in the fall and was executed in the spring, the responsibility for his death shifts from "the Jews" to the Roman authorities and, maybe, even to Jesus himself. Meaning, if a man loses popularity in a matter of hours, you ask: "what's wrong with the audience?" If a man loses popularity over half a year, you might ask: "what did he do wrong?" This last question may lead to an investigation of the historical circumstances of his demise. If it all takes place in a matter of days and hours, one falls back on psychology to explain everything and indeed, for millennia, the blame was put on the national character of the "perfidious Jews."[21] But if Jesus came in the fall and was executed in the spring, perhaps the deadly shift in popularity is not to be found in psychology but in politics.

Let's remember why we embarked on this dating game in the first place. It is crucial to our analysis that Jesus' entry into Jerusalem coincides with Sejanus' fall. Does it? Perfectly. As it turns out, Sejanus was executed on October 18, 31 C.E., right around the Jewish holiday of Tabernacles.

We can now reconstruct the last six months of Jesus' life. As hypothesized, Jesus came into Jerusalem in the fall during the Festival of Tabernacles/*Sukkot*, seemingly under Sejanus' protection. He presented himself as a threat to Caiaphas but not to Antipas, and focused his activity exclusively on the temple. In fact, the Gospel of Mark relates that Jesus effectively shut the temple down for a day, not allowing anyone to carry anything through its precincts.[22] He did all this without any intervention by the Roman garrison stationed in the Antonia fortress overlooking the temple. Clearly, the Sejanus connection was working.

Within days, however, Sejanus was executed. But it took weeks and months for that information to filter to Jerusalem. By Passover—that is, by spring of the year 32 c.e.—all of Sejanus' supporters, like Herod Antipas and Pilate, were on the defensive. Based on the sources, all we can say is that Jesus was crucified as Sabbath was approaching, while pilgrims were gathering for the upcoming Passover holiday. The year 32 c.e. fits much better with the available facts and with our lost gospel. In that year, it is calculated that Passover fell on the Sunday night right after Jesus' crucifixion. According to the Gospels, by Sunday morning Jesus' body was no longer in the tomb. A Sunday night Passover, therefore, provides his disciples with a very small window in which to act to remove the body from its temporary burial near the place of crucifixion to a permanent place of burial. They would have had 24 hours to do so, from Saturday night after the completion of the Sabbath to Sunday night, the beginning of Passover.

They say the devil is in the details, and there is one last character lurking in the shadows of Jesus' trial that we need to now look at. His presence seals the argument. His name is Annas, or Hanan in Hebrew. According to the Gospel of John and only that Gospel, Jesus was handed to Annas before he was handed to the High Priest Caiaphas.[23] As often happens with John, he seems to be preserving a tradition lost or suppressed in the other Gospels. Since the incident with Annas seems to serve no theological purpose, it must be historical. So who is Annas?

A Priest Called Annas

Quirinius, the Roman governor of Syria, appointed Annas high priest in 6 c.e., during the reign of Augustus. He was then deposed by Valerius Gratus at the beginning of Tiberius' reign. In other words, Annas was perceived as a leftover of the previous administration. As things sorted themselves out in Rome, what followed were a few years of short-lived high priests. Remember, the high priest under Roman occupation was a Roman appointee.

Then Germanicus showed up in 18 c.e., ostensibly representing his adoptive father, Tiberius. At this point, Valerius appointed a new high priest, the man called Caiaphas. By 19 c.e., Germanicus was dead and Valerius was out, replaced by Sejanus' man, Pilate. Caiaphas, a son-in-law of Annas, survived the changes in Rome and seemed to accommodate himself with Pilate. Things stayed this way until 31 c.e., when Sejanus was about to murder Tiberius and hand the title King of the Jews to Herod Antipas, Tetrarch of Galilee and Peraea. According to our reading, Antipas was also about to let Jesus "cleanse the temple" of Caiaphas, replacing the latter with a hand-picked high priest more responsive to the messianic aspirations of people like Jesus—maybe Jesus himself. After all, Jesus is referred to as a high priest in the Christian Bible: ". . . we have a great high priest who has passed through the heavens, Jesus, the Son of God" (Hebrews 4:14). Working toward this goal, Jesus showed up in Jerusalem in the fall of 31 C.E. during the Festival of Tabernacles and caused a riot in the temple. He was not arrested. Then, by Passover the following year, 32 C.E., he was tracked down and hauled before first the Jewish and then the Roman authorities.

In the midst of all this, Annas showed up as the man judging Jesus. Why? After all, if the year is 30, 31, 32, or even 33, Annas had not been high priest for over a decade. Why the comeback?

Annas' brief re-appearance on the stage of history at this particular point only makes sense after the demise of Sejanus and before it is clear what the consequences of his departure would be. His appearance in the story is a tip-off with respect to the year of the crucifixion. In the year 30, Sejanus was at the height of his power in Rome and Pilate was ruling with no governor sitting in Syria. There was no reason to trot out a retired high priest to preside over Jesus. But in the spring of 32 C.E., in the aftermath of Sejanus' death, no one wanted to take responsibility for the execution of a man who had some kind of protection from the previous administration. Annas' sudden appearance demonstrates that the temple administration was trying to find a high priest who was not tainted by association with either Sejanus or Germanicus. To this end, they were forced to reach back to a high priest who had presided at the time of Augustus. This action throws light not only on the timing of the arrest, but also on the importance of Jesus in the constellation of Roman–Judaean politics.

Analysts can't have it both ways: one can't look at Jesus as an itinerant Galilean peasant and accept the Gospels' narrative with respect to the crucifixion. If Jesus was not a local player with connections at the top, why was everyone so afraid to try or execute him? After all, Jesus is handled like a political hot potato. He is arrested at night and handed over to Annas, then to Caiaphas, then to Pilate, then to Antipas, then back to Caiaphas, then back to Pilate,[24] all in less than twenty-four hours. More than this, two high priests (past and present), a Tetrarch, and a procurator are involved in the execution of a man who the common wisdom would have us believe was nothing more than a Galilean miracle worker. This makes no sense.

The kind of judicial buck-passing that occurred with Jesus only makes sense when the man being tried is important to someone high up and when the chain of command is unclear. There is only one specific moment when Roman history fits the Gospel narrative: namely, after Sejanus' demise and before its consequences had been made clear in Jerusalem. When you take all this into account, ours is the only scenario that makes sense of all the events and people surrounding the trial and crucifixion of Jesus.

More than this, the dynamics repeat themselves in almost exactly the same way in 62 C.E. with regard to the trial and execution of Jesus' brother James.

Brother James

After the crucifixion, Jesus' brother Ya'akov in Hebrew—"Jacob" in English or "James" as he is mostly commonly referred to in Christian tradition—headed Jesus' movement in Jerusalem. It seems that James, like his brother, was also obsessed with the temple. Church father Jerome (342–420 C.E.)[25] tells us that James was called "camel knees" because he had developed scars on his kneecaps from spending so much time kneeling in the temple.[26]

James' temple-centered focus was not viewed kindly by the high priests of the time. But these high priests were regarded by the Pharisees, the Essenes, the Zealots, and the members of James' Jesus Movement as illegitimate collaborators with the Roman occupation. Hatred of the priesthood reached a fever pitch during this period. Consider the following story in Josephus: when rebellion broke out in 66 C.E., the Sicarii under the command of one called Simon arrested a high priest named Mathias. They then killed him. But not before they made him watch the slaughter of his three sons, all high priests themselves.[27] Clearly, many people hated the high priests.

For their part, the Romans enjoyed dividing and conquering. As long as a Jewish group did not advocate armed insurrection but merely created trouble for the Roman-appointed priesthood, the Romans left it alone. Such groups served Roman interests because they made the priesthood ever more dependent on Roman arms.

It seems that James' Jerusalem group found favor both with the masses and with the authorities because James focused his attention on the temple, not on the Roman occupation. As long as the Roman procurator Festus was alive, no harm came to James. But the minute Festus died, in the interregnum before the arrival of his replacement, Albinus, the High Priest Annas, son of the very Annas who had been involved in the trial of Jesus, moved against James.

After a quick trial on trumped-up charges, Annas had James stoned to death. On this occasion, the Pharisees intervened with the Roman authorities against the high priest and on behalf of James. A delegation was sent to Alexandria, Egypt to meet the new procurator before he arrived in Jerusalem. After their petition, the High Priest Annas was removed from his position. He had served only three months in office—just long enough to execute James.[28]

This story once again strengthens the idea that Jesus and, indeed, his entourage were players in 1st-century Judeo–Roman politics. A cursory examination of the historical facts reveals that Jesus was on the powerful Annas family's radar. The Annas who had James stoned was basically waiting for the opportunity to get rid of James, just as his father had gotten rid of Jesus. As Josephus relates, the stoning of James cost the younger Annas the high priesthood. This was a very high price to pay for getting rid of James, and yet Annas was willing to pay it. There seems to have been a family grudge involved. In any event, the stoning of James demonstrates that James too was a player—you don't lose the high priesthood for getting rid of just anybody. It also reveals that whatever else James was up to, it was not revolution against Rome. How do we know this? Because Josephus tells us that the Annas who brought down James became one of the leading figures in the Jewish revolt against the Romans. Together with Joseph, son of Gorion, he was elected to the supreme control of affairs in Jerusalem during the revolt. He died a violent death in the winter of 67–68 C.E.[29]

So here we have a clearly documented case whereby a brother of Jesus, the first leader of the Jerusalem Church after the crucifixion, enjoyed Roman protection until he was killed by a high priest who took advantage of a regime change to arrest, try, and execute him. In James' case, it was the death of Festus that precipitated the events that led to his violent end. We now know from the decoded *Joseph and Aseneth* text that it was the death of Sejanus that precipitated the downfall of James' brother Jesus.

In James' case, Annas played the game himself. He tried James for heresy and punished him in the only manner available to him: stoning. In Jesus' case, because the post-Sejanus situation was so unclear, Caiaphas made sure that Jesus would be turned over to Pilate, who tried him for sedition and had him killed in the only way, according to Roman law, a revolutionary could be killed: a public execution by crucifixion. The facts are clear. To use Robert Eisenman's words: "Who and whatever James was, so was Jesus."[30]

As stated, when the High Priest Caiaphas leaned over and whispered to Pilate that if he let Jesus go he would be perceived as "no friend to the emperor," the message was clear. If Pilate continued to sponsor a Sejanus protégé, it would be interpreted in Rome as if Pilate, like his mentor Sejanus, was no friend of Tiberius. As a result, Jesus, the man who had been groomed to wear a crown of gold, now wore a crown of thorns. Over his head, they nailed to the cross the title so coveted by Antipas, King of the Jews.

Aftermath

After the crucifixion, Antipas and Pilate became friends. There is only one reason why this would have happened. Having been aligned with Sejanus, they were in the same boat now. Both were vulnerable in the anti-Sejanus purges that followed Tiberius' return to politics. As it turns out, Pilate survived for a while and was then removed and exiled in 36 C.E. Church father and historian Eusebius reports a tradition that he killed himself. As with Piso, after Germanicus' death, Pilate knew too much. He had to be forced to "commit suicide." In the year 39 C.E., Antipas was removed to a life of exile in Gaul. Herodias accompanied him. Like Mary the Magdalene at the cross, she must have finally realized that her husband was never going to be King of the Jews.

From the grave, Sejanus did offer Jesus one last favor. When Joseph of Arimathaea, a Jesus follower and member of the pro-Roman Jewish elite, asked for Jesus' body after he expired on the cross, Pilate allowed it.[31] In the post-Sejanus era, he could no longer provide Jesus with Roman protection, but he could save the body of the Sejanus-connected Messiah from the garbage heap reserved for crucified rebels. This was not what Jesus and Mary the Magdalene had anticipated when they entered Jerusalem some six months earlier.

Neither Jews nor Romans gave up on the idea of an emperor-sponsored Messiah. The dreams of a restored Judaic monarchy were realized just a few years later when Caligula rewarded his friend Agrippa with both the crown and the title. So Germanicus' son, Caligula, did what Sejanus and Tiberius could not do: choose a king *and* a Messiah for the Jewish people. At that point, history intervened. Like so many players in this drama, Agrippa suddenly died from a mysterious illness. Perhaps he was poisoned. On his deathbed, he attributed his disease to divine punishment for the arrogance he demonstrated when he basked in the crowd's chants of "Messiah." His lament somehow echoed Jesus' own cry, recorded in the Gospel of Mark: "Eli, Eli lama sabachtani?"[32] My Lord, my Lord, why have You forsaken me?

Although the political constellation changed after the destruction of Jerusalem in 70 C.E., the fact is that Jesus' family continued to be on the radar at the highest levels of Roman power. In other words, these people were not simply a group of shepherds, carpenters, or fishermen. The church father Eusebius tells us that in the 70s, the Roman emperor Vespasian ordered a hunt for all the family of King David (i.e., Jesus' family).[33] In the mid-80s, the Emperor Domitian interrogated two of Jesus' nephews or great-nephews, perhaps the sons of Jesus' brother Judas.[34] Around 106 C.E., the Emperor Trajan crucified Simeon, another relative of Jesus, who had succeeded James as the leader of the Jesus Movement.[35] As these accounts demonstrate, three Roman emperors—Vespasian, Domitian, Trajan—went after any individual who was related to Jesus. This illustrates in dramatic fashion that Jesus and his family represented a political threat and were treated as such at the highest levels of the empire. While other messianic claimants such as Judas the Galilean and Simon of Peraea were killed by lesser Roman officials, only with Jesus and his family did the Roman emperors, in the midst of running a vast complex empire, take the time to hunt down his descendants. It seems that until the Great Revolt in 66 C.E., the Jesus Movement was seen as a potential ally of Rome. After the destruction of Jerusalem in 70 C.E., it had outlived its usefulness.

But in a curious reversal of history, almost three hundred years after the crucifixion, Jesus would come back in a different form; not as enemy of Rome but as its deity. He made his comeback not in Jerusalem but in Rome.

It was in 312 C.E. that the Emperor Constantine became aligned with Pauline Christianity and the historical Jesus was eclipsed by Pauline theology. The relationship between Jesus and Mary the Magdalene was no longer important. In fact, she was airbrushed from history, and by the 7th century she was commonly portrayed as a weeping former prostitute. More than this, Jesus' life was no longer that important to the narrative. Following Paul, the new theology celebrated Jesus' death and resurrection. Only those Gospels that reflected this new theology were allowed to survive.

But now, at last, *Joseph and Aseneth* gives us a glimpse into a story untainted by later Roman theology. We finally have a document that was slated for the fire, but is now seeing the light of day.

PART III
IMPLICATIONS

16

CONCLUSION

I t's hard to think of a greater interpretive disaster than what happened to *Joseph and Aseneth*. This ancient text has been known for over a hundred years, but it was misnamed—as if it were about two figures from the Hebrew Bible. All this despite the fact that nothing in the manuscript fits with the Biblical story. *Joseph and Aseneth* was simply slotted into the wrong historical context. It was then subjected to modern literary criticism, ignoring the way in which such texts were written and the context in which they were produced, transmitted, read, and valued. No wonder people who have previously examined this text came away bewildered. It's a text that begs for accurate deciphering.

Western readers may be surprised that some texts require decoding and are not up-front with their meanings. In today's democratic societies, we are open with our opinions. But this is not how ancient writers—or even modern writers living under tyrannies—understood their texts.

The Dead Sea Scrolls community, for instance—that strict Jewish sect at the turn of the Common Era—understood the Hebrew Bible as coded language. Also, like *Joseph and Aseneth*, they did not call people by name. Thus we know of a "Teacher of Righteousness," a "Wicked Priest," and a "Liar," but we don't know who these people were. Like Jesus, the Teacher of Righteousness deciphered mysteries and expected God to intervene in human history to bring about the messianic era. The Teacher was sure it was coming soon since, in his judgment, he and his followers were living in the worst period in human history. Surely, they thought, God had to act swiftly. They expected, therefore, the eradication of all the unrighteous and the long-awaited moment when the righteous would be crowned with eternal life and the messianic Davidic king would rule upon his throne forever.

Likewise, as we have seen, Christians in antiquity did not regard the Bible as a historical account of the movement of the Jewish people through time. For them, the intended audience of these writings had come into being only after messianic times when these former events could be properly understood. Paul, for instance, talked about how Jewish leaders misunderstood their own writings—"Indeed, to this very day whenever Moses is read, a veil lies over their [the Jewish leaders'] minds; but when one turns to the Lord, the veil is removed" (2 Corinthians 3:16). The task, as far as all these writers were concerned, was to penetrate the veil: to see in these ancient Jewish writings events that pre-figured—albeit dimly—the real meaning which could only be understood in light of what Jesus had accomplished. The upshot of this view is that, for the early Christians, the Old Testament isn't really a collection of Jewish writings but a coded Christian text, one that recounts in coded form the whole drama of divine salvation through the "Christ."

In decoding *Joseph and Aseneth*, therefore, we haven't followed new-age techniques. On the contrary, we have used interpretive techniques that were current at the beginning of what would later be called Christianity. Doing so has opened up a wealth of detail only hinted at in ancient Christian sources.

Many Different Forms of Early Christianity

Christianity as we know it now only emerged in the 4th century thanks to the efforts of such Roman emperors as Constantine and, later, Theodosius who established it as the official religion of the Roman Empire. By "Christianity," however, these pagan emperors meant that faction that subscribed to the so-called Nicene Creed. Until then, there were many different groups vying for the mantle of "Christianity." It's difficult to speak of these various movements as Christian in any modern sense. Some scholars have created hybrid categories—e.g., "Jewish Christianity" or "Christian Judaism"—to talk about these early Jesus followers. But these are clearly anachronistic, applying modern words to ancient movements. Some early groups were clearly within the Jewish family, and some weren't. After the pagans got involved, the original Jewish movements were marginalized, condemned, and driven underground. So there are really two Christian worlds: the world of the winners (Paul's followers, which includes all the official Christian groups today) and the world of the losers (those who were banned, burned, ostracized, and driven underground). It's from the world of the losers that *Joseph and Aseneth* emerges. It's their views that it records. To the degree that we care about the birth of Christianity, we should try to reach beyond Pauline theology and make contact with these early Christian views. Paul may have won the theological battle, but it's the banned texts that may be preserving a more accurate history. So, who were the earliest Jesus followers?

Scholars have identified a wide swath of early Christian movements: there was James' Torah-observant Jewish Jesus Movement in Jerusalem and the Gnostics in Alexandria. In time, the "Jamesians" likely morphed into groups known to historians as Ebionites or Nazarenes. These disappeared from Western history around the 6th or 7th century. In Arabia, Islam likely absorbed them.[1] As well, there were probably groups associated with the apostles Thomas and John. Syriac Christianity began early on in Antioch, Syria and places farther east. Then there seems to have been a group we know very little about. It is called "Q" by scholars, for lack of more accurate information. For its part, Paul's Christ Movement thrived especially in Rome. It became highly successful in its ability to recruit Gentiles, at first mostly from the God-fearer segment of Judaized pagans and later, more generally, from monotheistic pagans (i.e., pagans who stressed one god above the others). It is largely from Paul's teachings and those of his successors that the Nicene Christianity we know today emerged.

Based on the textual evidence, Morton Smith has his own approach to the post-crucifixion Jesus movements and early churches. First, there were the legalists: those Torah-observant Jews who saw Jesus as a human messiah and yet remained loyal to the Judaic law. Then there were Jesus' brothers, who accepted Jesus as some kind of divine figure only after his crucifixion. In Smith's words: "none of the gospels represents them [Jesus' brothers] as part of his following. We may suppose that they came into the movement after his death; as members of the family of an alleged pretender to the throne, they were involved in his disaster whether they liked it or not. The probability therefore is that James (like the other converts made since Jesus' death) had never received Jesus' initiation. His succession to leadership of the Jerusalem church will have marked the triumph of the converts over Jesus' early circle."[2] Like Paul, James' authority was supported by a story that he had seen the risen Christ (1 Corinthians 15:7). Unlike scholars such as Robert Eisenman, who see James as a totally "kosher" Jew obedient to the Mosaic law, Smith believes that the James movement gave "the appearance of obeying the law"[3] while being "liberated" from it. In other words, for the Jamesians there was one law for the inner circle and another for the outer one. Third, there was Paul's movement—according to Paul there was "no need to appear to obey the [Mosaic] law unless apparent disobedience of it would lead you into danger or your fellow Christians into sin."[4] Fourth, Smith contends that there was, perhaps, "a mediating position" represented by Peter and Barnabas, "who felt no obligation to preserve appearances . . . but wanted to keep on good terms with James."[5] According to Smith, the idea of being "liberated" from the law while appearing to obey it "practically presupposes that the doctrine about the liberty of those in the kingdom will be kept *secret*."[6] This applies equally to James, Paul, and more extreme libertine groups. Therefore, "the libertinism, usually scandalous and occasionally criminal, was *concealed*."[7] What all these groups have in common is an element of secrecy with regard to their beliefs and practices. There were likely dozens of other Jesus-related communities about which we know nothing today. *Joseph and Aseneth* has now given us great insight into one of these communities—an important community, as it turns out—likely the very movement that was hijacked by Paul.

It's now also clear that all around the Roman Empire and places outside of it such as Parthia, there existed yet another early Christian community. This one was not part of the Jewish community. It was a pre-Paul Church of the Gentiles, a group founded by Mary the Magdalene. This community had a separate and earlier origin than Paul's more famous Gentile movement, being rooted in the teachings of Jesus and the woman they called the Mara (the lady), who was none other than Jesus' wife, the mother of his children, the feminine principle of his theology—Sophia/Artemis made flesh.

As we have seen, the idea that Jesus' teachings attracted Gentiles is not unexpected. According to our now-deciphered text, Mary the Magdalene was a Gentile. The canonical Gospels tell us that Jesus spent time in non-Jewish territory: as a youth in Egypt, most probably Alexandria, and later in Tyre and Sidon in particular. The Galilee, moreover, was a hotbed of Gentile activity—major highways crossed through the territory. In the north, they led to Europe on one side and Parthia on the other. In the south, they led to Egypt and Africa beyond. Beginning in 721 B.C.E., the Galilee was heavily colonized by non-Jewish peoples. Finally, the Romans established major colonies and cultural centers in such Galilean cities as Sepphoris and Tiberias. No wonder it was called "Galilee of the Nations" (Isaiah 9:2) or "Galilee of the Gentiles" (Matthew 4:15). Apparently, out of these Gentiles emerged the Church of the Gentiles as a parallel movement to James' orthodox—or orthodox-seeming—Jewish version of Christianity.

This hitherto-unknown community, moreover, helps to explain the origins of Gnosticism well before it flowered in the 2nd century. Gnosticism's theology of redemption through sacred sex is consistent with a syncretic Judeo/Gentile Galilean Jesus movement. Its acceptance of sexuality, the important role of women, and the meaning of the sacrament of the bridal chamber is consistent with a Gentile movement surrounding a married Jesus.

The existence of this Galilean Gentile community may also explain some anomalous structures found in northern Israel: the so-called synagogues at Beit Alpha, Hammat Tiberias, and Sepphoris with their zodiac depictions and images of Helios. Like the church of "Lady Mary" at Tel Istaba, these may represent synagogue churches, or houses of Christian worship for the 4th-century descendants of the early Church of the Gentiles.

The existence of a Mary-the-Magdalene–led Church of the Gentiles can also explain why *Joseph and Aseneth* was dutifully copied by monks for nearly two thousand years in places like Serbia, Greece, Armenia, Romania, and even Ethiopia. Moreover, it explains how, driven underground, this Gnostic version of Christianity—based on a historical marriage and an original libertine theology—survived as a sort of historical rumor. But, from time to time, it did surface in paintings, songs, novels, and poetry.

One of the most dramatic examples of the above phenomenon is the so-called "Bride of Christ" movement that sprang out of nowhere across Europe of the Middle Ages. This phenomenon has only recently become the subject of scholarly studies.[8] It began in the 13th century, coincidentally about the same time as *Joseph and Aseneth* was translated from Greek into a more accessible Latin.[9] The text seems to have had an almost immediate impact. Around 1260 C.E., it became even more popular when Vincent of Beauvais produced an abbreviated version of it.

Suddenly, women in places like the UK, Sweden, Italy, Hungary, Germany, France, and Holland started to have mystical relations with Jesus, often consummated with a marriage ceremony. These women, and sometimes men, were considered to be married to Christ.[10] The phenomenon lasted for hundreds of years, up to the 16th century. The people involved engaged in secret mystical acts, often violent and more often sexual. For example, *The Book of Margery Kempe*[11] describes physical love and marriage between Jesus and Margery Kempe, a married laywoman. Kempe was born in 1373 in Norfolk, England. Hers is said to be the first autobiography in the English language. Essentially, she became a medieval version of Mary the Magdalene as depicted in *Joseph and Aseneth*, complete with fasting, weeping, and mystical experiences of love and marriage with Jesus. She called herself a "Bride of Christ." Where did she get this, if not from *Joseph and Aseneth*? In her book, in *Joseph and Aseneth* fashion, Jesus reassures Margery that she's worthy to be his wife: "you know well that I treat you like a husband should his wedded wife . . . they may go to bed together without any shame . . . when you are in your bed, take me to yourself as your wedded husband, your beloved darling, as your sweet son because I want to be loved as a son should be loved by his mother and desire that you love me, daughter, as a good wife owes her love to her husband."[12] As in 2nd-century Gnosticism, notice that the lovers are variously called *mother, son, daughter, wife,* and *husband*. For her part, all of Margery's love was focused on "the manhood of Christ."[13]

It is important to note that this phenomenon is cross-European: it's not concentrated in one place. For example, the Prussian-born Dorothea von Montau was a contemporary of Margery. She too was called a "Bride of Christ." In that capacity, she had a vision in which "the Lord immediately wounded her with many arrows of love and ignited her with hot, burning love."[14] In the vision, Jesus revealed to her that he had "pulled" her away from her husband and "possessed her." In some kind of altered state, she had sex with Jesus. Despite her married status, she knew that she was doing no wrong because Jesus blessed their sex as a "service of love for Christ." Like Mary the Magdalene in our *Aseneth* text, Dorothea wept a lot, shedding many "sweet tears."[15] On her "wedding day" in Rome, Jesus promised Dorothea that he would lead her into the "paradise of passion and desire and into my secret chamber." Once there, she was shown the "secrets" of Jesus' heart.[16]

Katharina Tucher was also German and also lived in the late 14th century.[17] In her visions, she describes the same themes that are elaborated in Aseneth's transformation from pagan priestess to "Bride of God." Specifically, like Aseneth, Katharina sees an angel and, as with Aseneth, he gives her something to eat. With Katharina, it's not a honeycomb but some kind of drink which the angel calls his "precious treasure." Once she swallows this "precious treasure"—as with the honeycomb in *Joseph and Aseneth*—Katharina gets the gift of eternal life. Of course, like Aseneth (the stand-in for Mary the Magdalene), Katharina is a weeper, especially when she gets to drink the blood of salvation from Jesus' wound.[18] If that's not enough, in one vision, she holds a small cross in her hand, presumably praying over it, with Jesus' body close to her mouth. At that point, Katharina's connection with Mary the Magdalene is made explicit. Jesus tells her "you should not kiss me on my mouth. You are not worthy of this, only my mother is. Take yourself to the foot of the cross and join Mary [the] Magdalene."[19]

In all these instances, as in *Joseph and Aseneth*, and in contrast with the canonical Gospels, it's the bride, not Jesus, who is front and center. With time, the sex between them gets ever more explicit. In a 14th-century text called *Christos und die Minnende Seele* (*CMS*), "Jesus strips, beats, starves and mentally dominates the soul,"[20] depicted as a woman. In Rabia Gregory's words, "the [*CMS*] manuscript displays the female body in ways evocative of modern pornography."[21] In this instance, Jesus' love is tough love. The relationship is alternately violent, exhibitionist, and erotic.[22] At one point, for example, the feminine soul shouts to Jesus, "you hit me so hard I can no longer bear it."[23] At this point, the female soul finds redemption in this submissive love. All this reaches a climax when Jesus offers her "a kiss of mystery." When their lips touch, he fully reveals himself and they accomplish mystical union.[24] In fact, consistent with Mary the Magdalene being at the center of the Gnostic narrative, in this text it is the woman who is crucified, and it is Jesus who stands at the foot of the cross.[25]

One man who became a "Bride of Christ" was Heinrich Seuse, born around 1300 in Germany. Seuse went so far as to crucify himself in an effort to "surrender" himself to Christ, becoming "lovable" in the process.[26] It is difficult to ascertain whether the participation of men in mystical union with Jesus was a medieval innovation or a reflection of early Gnostic practices. Morton Smith has argued that the gospels themselves preserve hints of secret ceremonies involving homosexual acts: for example, when they come to arrest Jesus, a young man wearing a linen cloth over his naked body runs away from the scene (Mark 14:51–52). There is no hint of homosexuality, however, in *Joseph and Aseneth*. But there is the idea of sacred sex consummated in the bridal chamber.

It seems that in many places *Joseph-and-Aseneth*–type Gnosticism was removed from the realm of the here and now and projected into the hereafter where the "brides" could reunite with the "groom." For example, in 1423, Sister Eefce Neghels asked to strip naked on her deathbed. "A naked bridegroom wants to have a naked bride," she said. From the good nun's perspective, "taking her clothes off just before death signified the purity of her soul and her eagerness to please her waiting bridegroom."[27] The death of Lisbeth van Delft, a nun at Diepenveen, Holland, is also recorded in sexual, Valentinian-like terms: "in the year of our Lord 1423 she went to her bridegroom to enjoy him, face to face for all eternity."[28] Not all nuns at the Diepenveen convent waited for the moment of death to unite with the divine bridegroom. For example, when one nun was having trouble falling asleep, a sister showed her "how to lie on the chest of our dear Lord and suckle his bottomless love and mercy."[29] These examples are not unique. When introducing the experiences of 13th-century Flemish mystic Hadewijch of Brabant, Carolyn Walker Bynum warns readers that "this meeting with God reads like a description of a sexual orgasm."[30]

In Italy, another 14th-century "Bride of Christ," Catherine of Siena, sums it all up by stating that one does not marry Christ with a ring made of gold or silver "but with a ring of Christ's foreskin, given in the circumcision and accompanied by pain and the shedding of blood."[31]

Scholars have suggested that all these texts and experiences are related and that they espouse "a mystical agenda of some sort."[32] We agree. *Joseph and Aseneth* provides us with the key to understanding the agenda. Some might say that we have not shown a cause–effect relationship between the publication of *Joseph and Aseneth* in the 13th century and the beginnings of the "Bride of Christ" phenomenon. Perhaps not. After all, we're talking about secret traditions. But it's quite a coincidence that just as a text that we claim depicts the marriage and sacred sex between Jesus and Mary the Magdalene is translated into Latin, we suddenly have women all over Europe having mystical sex with their Savior. How else does one explain this phenomenon? The fact is that this kind of Christian Gnosticism does not appear full-blown out of nowhere. It has to be learned somehow. Since the church suppressed Gnosticism and the Nag Hammadi finds were centuries into the future, the only candidate for the source of medieval Gnosticism is *Joseph and Aseneth*. But how do we know that

Joseph and Aseneth was read then the way we propose it should be read today? The fact is that on this point we have a textual smoking gun.

In the 1400s, an English poem titled *The Storie of Asneth* suddenly appeared. An anonymous writer penned it at the request of some wellborn English lady. There is only one manuscript copy of this poem in existence. It was found in the collection of Lord Ellesmere at Bridgewater House, Westminster, London. Today, the manuscript is housed in the Huntington Library. Russell Peck brought it to light only recently.[33] Peck observes that the first page contains several names, all of them women. "One is struck," he says, "by the prominence of women in the history of the manuscript's ownership."[34] He also points out that "the middle English poem is rich in Christian typology . . . much of the typology may be traced back to the original Alexandrian Greek version of the 2nd century."[35] Peck continues by stating that in the poem "Joseph is Christ-like."[36] In fact, as in the Syriac, in the *Joseph and Aseneth* poem Joseph is explicitly called "the Savior."[37]

While Peck doesn't make the association of Aseneth with Mary the Magdalene, he explicitly states that Aseneth is depicted according to the conventions of Christian iconography and symbolism. In his mind, Aseneth is "adorned with Marian imagery." He concludes, therefore, that the poem's version of Aseneth is typologically identified with the Virgin Mary. But she can't possibly be identified with Jesus' mother because, as he admits, she is identified with "the bride in the Song of Songs." Jesus didn't marry his mother. The mother, therefore, can't be the bride of the story. Put simply, if Aseneth is not Mary the mother, she must be Mary the wife: Mary the Magdalene.

In any event, what is important for our investigation is that at the very beginning of the 15th century, we suddenly have a Christological English poem based on the Latin version of *Joseph and Aseneth*. And this version circulates mainly among women. Not only that, it seems to have involved a secret tradition and seems to have been part of a medieval phenomenon involving mostly women and some men[38] becoming Brides of Christ.[39]

Put differently, we now know that we are not the first to read *Joseph and Aseneth* as a Christian narrative. We now have a 15th-century English poem that reads it the same way. If people were interpreting the story and its bridal-chamber implications in Jesus-related ways, this goes a long way toward demonstrating that our lost gospel—more accurately: secret gospel—was somehow involved in rekindling in Europe the kind of Gnosticism that flourished in the Middle East between the 2nd and 4th centuries. What this teaches us is that for two millennia, the tradition of Jesus' sacred marriage to Mary the Magdalene survived in various underground forms and even managed to surface from time to time.

A Fully Human Jesus

Joseph and Aseneth represents an important early church writing, hidden away for centuries, that tells the story—in coded form—of the betrothal, spiritual Communion, and actual marriage of Jesus to Mary the Magdalene. It confirms what lies just beneath the surface of the canonical Gospels and makes explicit what the Gnostic writings celebrate.

Part of what it tells us about Jesus is familiar to us. This text celebrates the divinity of Jesus (e.g., he is "Son of God"). Yet it introduces concepts that are less familiar to most people today. Mary the Magdalene, for instance, is depicted as the "Bride of God." The union of Jesus with Mary the Magdalene, moreover, takes place on a heavenly plane as well as an earthly one.

What is also unfamiliar is the portrait of a married Jesus and what this entails. Simply put, it clearly affirms the full humanity of Jesus, his masculinity and his sexuality. More than that, this ancient text promotes the union between Jesus and Mary the Magdalene as the way in which God acts in history so as to redeem the world. From the point of view of the text, Jesus and Mary the Magdalene's bedroom is God's way of redeeming humanity. Our lost gospel does all this by celebrating Jesus and Mary the Magdalene's life—especially as it was consummated in their "bridal chamber"—as opposed to Jesus' suffering upon the cross, death, and third-day resurrection.

For many people, thinking of Jesus as married, having sexual relations, and bringing up children is problematic. It's the stuff of fiction. But if that isn't enough, the *Joseph and Aseneth* text now asks them to go beyond this by postulating that for Jesus' early followers, salvation involved the understanding and imitation of the sexual life of Jesus and Mary the Magdalene.

In a sense, believing that Jesus was married and had children is the easy part. The idea of a celibate Jesus is totally foreign to the Jewish world into which he was born. The fact is that it is incumbent on Jewish males to observe the first Biblical commandment—be fruitful and multiply. It is also a given in Judaism that the long-awaited *messiah*—Hebrew for the "anointed one" of God, *Christ* in Greek—will marry and sire a family. It's to be expected. For example, a hundred years after Jesus, there was a Messiah claimant named Simon, whose followers called him Bar Kochba or "The Son of the Star." He was no flash in the pan. On the contrary, he had the backing of the greatest rabbi of all time, Akiva, and it took the Emperor Hadrian and the might of the Roman Empire three years to put down his revolt. We know for a fact that Bar Kochba had a wife. In the context of history, thinking of Jesus as having a wife and children is no different than thinking of Bar Kochba as having a family. In the context of 1st-century Judaea, it would be scandalous to think otherwise.

A married Jesus is not an idea that should disturb anyone thinking in non-Pauline terms. What may be disturbing is the theology that grew up around it. But that's another matter. In our world, however, people's initial reactions are conditioned by Pauline theology. As a result, God the Father impregnating a Jewish teen named Mary so as to give birth to himself seems all right, but God the Son impregnating another Mary, known as the Magdalene, seems heretical.

More than this, we are used to a non-political Jesus, one whose kingdom is not of this earth. Our lost gospel, however, reveals a very different kind of Jesus: one involved in the messiah machinations of his time, allied with a Roman anti-Semite named Sejanus and making a power grab for the temple with the backing of his Gentile Syro-Phoenician wife. In *Joseph and Aseneth* we seem to have a Gnostic gospel grounded in history that fills in many of the missing pieces of the early Jesus movement. It also explains several historical phenomena, such as Paul's movement and Gnosticism, that otherwise seem inexplicable.

We believe that *Joseph and Aseneth* evolved from a 1st-century gospel recording the real-life events involving Jesus and Mary the Magdalene, through Gnostic Christianity, into the Greek writing that the anonymous monk came across in the library of the bishops of Aleppo. There were various cultural reasons along the way that would account for the need to encode its message: Roman persecution and, later on, Orthodox Christian persecution bent on squelching anything to do with Jesus' family and humanity.

But our gospel survived and, though it tells a very different story from the canonical Gospels, it is not incompatible with them. In fact, echoes of *Joseph and Aseneth* (e.g., Mary the Magdalene as a Syro-Phoenician and a wife) can be heard in the canonical Gospels themselves. Put differently, *Joseph and Aseneth* forces us to reassess enigmatic passages in the Gospels and understand them in a new way—but not only the Gospels.

In light of *Joseph and Aseneth*, many unintelligible texts can now come into sharp focus. For example, among the various Gnostic texts found at Nag Hammadi, there was a previously lost gospel. Its composition is very early, perhaps dating to just a few years after the crucifixion—scholars estimate somewhere between 40 C.E. and 140 C.E. Unlike the canonical Gospels and *Joseph and Aseneth*, this gospel is not a narrative. It is simply a series of statements attributed to Jesus. Stylistically, it gives the impression of notes taken during a series of sermons. Saying 61 records an exchange between a female disciple named Salome and Jesus. Here Jesus seems to allude to his sacred marriage with Mary the Magdalene and the fact that he is destined to abandon the bridal chamber by dying. He also seems to have been less than monogamous. He explicitly states that the way to celebrate the wholeness, or oneness, of God is to unite sexually with his son. This is what the gospel states: "Jesus said: Two will rest upon a bed; one will die, the other will live. Salome said: Who are you, O man? Who gave you birth? *You have mounted my bed* and eaten from my table. Jesus said to her: I am he who is equal to the One that sent me; I am empowered by my Father. [Salome said:] I am your disciple. [Jesus said to her:] Therefore I say: If *He is made whole*, He will be full of light, but if He is divided, He will be full of darkness."[40]

An incredible poem was also found in the Nag Hammadi collection. It gives us a glimpse of the power and charisma of Mary the Magdalene. We believe that it preserves an actual sermon delivered by her. It's called *The Thunder, Perfect Mind*. It quotes a female savior-figure sermonizing in a series of paradoxical statements. In the sermon, the speaker identifies herself much as Jesus identifies himself. For example, Jesus calls himself "the alpha and the omega"—i.e., the first and the last (Revelation 22:13)—and she identifies herself using the very same words—"I am first and the last." She then goes on to say, "I am the honored one and the scorned one. I am the whore and the holy one. I am the wife and the virgin."[41] Without a decoded *Joseph and Aseneth*, we would not be able to recognize the Magdalene's voice in this sermon. With a decoded *Joseph and Aseneth*, the words jump out at us as a perfect match with what we have gleaned as the voice of Jesus' wife and partner.

It's now time to review the revelations, study them, debate them and arrive at a new understanding. This will not be an easy process. We are used to Jesus being the "superstar" of the story. All the Gospels revolve around him as he talks in riddles, heals, performs miracles, is tried, crucified, and resurrected. But in our lost gospel, he is a more marginal figure. His greatest accomplishment is to win the favors of an aristocratic priestess of Artemis, Mary the Magdalene. It is she that became the "city of refuge" for many of their followers. In this text, it is she who is the superstar. It is she who became the link between the Church of the Hebrews and the Church of the Gentiles. More than this, it is she that, after the crucifixion, may have represented the resurrected Jesus himself, and it is her bedroom that became the holy of holies of a religion that claims over a billion followers today.

17

POSTSCRIPT

While we were working on this book, an incredible discovery that impacts on our Bride of God gospel made front pages around the world. It was the discovery of a papyrus fragment, probably dated to the 4th century, of a Coptic gospel in which Jesus refers to someone as his "wife"—most probably Mary the Magdalene. It's instructive to look at the reaction to this revelation, because it probably foreshadows what awaits our book.

Let's take a step back. Until now, one of the main objections to our thesis would have been that there is not a shred of textual evidence from antiquity linking Jesus to marriage. As we have shown, this is not true. The canonical Gospels hint at this marriage, at least one Nag Hammadi Gospel and various other Coptic fragments found in Egypt are explicit about it, and there is even archaeology (e.g., the Jesus Family Tomb) that is consistent with a married Jesus. The only way there is no evidence is if you keep ignoring the evidence. Nonetheless, the mantra has always been the same: there is no early incontrovertible textual evidence of a marriage between Jesus and anyone.

Then, on September 18, 2012, everything changed. At the 10th International Congress of Coptic Studies, hosted by the Vatican's Institutum Patristicum Augustinianum in Rome, Karen King, the Hollis Professor of Divinity at Harvard Divinity School, announced the existence of an ancient text with four earth-shattering Coptic words inscribed on them, which in translation read: "Jesus said to them, my wife." The words written in Coptic, a language of ancient Egyptian Christians, are on a papyrus fragment of about one and a half inches by three inches. While King tentatively dated the papyrus to the 4th century, she said that it may be preserving 2nd-century traditions. Meaning, it was even closer to the time of Jesus than originally thought. The complete text is as follows:

Translation—side 1

1] not [to] me. My mother gave to me li[fe . . .

2] The disciples said to Jesus, .[

3] deny. Mary is n[ot] worthy of it [

4] . . . Jesus said to them, My wife . . .[

5] . . . she will be able to be my disciple . . .[

6] Let wicked people swell up . . .[

7] As for me, I dwell with her in order to. [

8] an image [

On the back it says:

Translation—side 2

1] my moth[er

2] three [

3] . . . [

4] forth which . . .[

5] (illegible ink traces)

6] (illegible ink traces)[1]

When we look closely at the text, we see that lines #2 and #3 of side #1 are reminiscent of the Gnostic *Gospel of Mary,* where Peter expresses hostility against Mary the Magdalene. There, he states, "did he really speak with a woman in private without our knowledge? Should we all turn and listen to her? Did he prefer her to us?"[2] In *The Gospel of Thomas* (114), Peter is also hostile to Mary the Magdalene. There, he states, "Mary should leave us, for females are not worthy of life."[3] In this instance, Peter is probably not saying that Mary should die, but that she is not worthy of immortality. For his part, Jesus comes to Mary the Magdalene's defense saying, "I shall guide her to make her male." What he's really saying is that he shall elevate her so that she too becomes worthy of becoming "a living spirit."[4] In *The Gospel of Philip*, the disciples also oppose Mary the Magdalene. They bluntly ask Jesus, "why do you love her more than all of us?" Again Jesus comes to her defense, comparing her to light in the midst of darkness.[5]

Put simply, when we look at the content of the Jesus Wife papyrus, we see that it fits perfectly within a Gnostic context. More than this, like the Gnostic gospels, the papyrus was found in Egypt. Like the Gnostic gospels, it survived in Coptic. But, as we have said, there is a big difference between the previously discovered Gnostic gospels and the newly published Jesus Wife papyrus. In *The Gospel of Philip*, for example, Mary the Magdalene is called Jesus' *koinonos*, which *can* be translated as *wife* but also as *companion*. Those who have been denying that Jesus had a wife have preferred, obviously, the "companion" translation. In the most recent find, however, Jesus not only states that he dwells (lives) with the Magdalene, but the word he uses to describe her is the Coptic word *taàime*, which can *only* mean *wife*.

Karen King understood the potency of this discovery. An anonymous, private collector had approached her, and her first reaction was to ignore the document as a possible fake. But the collector also had two letters from the late 1970s or early 80s. One was written by Free University of Berlin Egyptologist Peter Munro (who died in 2008), and the other was penned by his colleague at the university, Egyptologist Gerhard Fecht (who died in 2006). Fecht states, in an unsigned letter that forms part of this collection, that the papyrus is the "sole example" of a text in which Jesus uses direct speech with reference to having a "wife." Fecht was also of the opinion that this could be evidence for a possible historical marriage. The two scholars authenticated the find. And yet, both Munro and Fecht went to their graves without publicizing their discovery. Why? Perhaps they feared personal attacks from theological bullies who would attempt to delegitimize them and their find.[6]

Armed with the fragment and the letters, King decided not to ignore the papyrus. Rather, she involved a leading papyrologist from Princeton University, Anne Marie Luijendijk, another leading papyrologist from New York University, Roger Bagnall, and Ariel Shisha-Halevy, a professor of linguistics at the Hebrew University in Jerusalem and a leading expert on the Coptic language.

All three world-class academics authenticated the find. In other words, by this point, counting King, Munro, and Fecht, we had six international experts declaring the find "kosher."

When she satisfied herself that the text was real and important, King decided to reveal her find at a very prestigious congress sponsored by the Vatican and to submit a paper on the find to the prestigious *Harvard Theological Review* (*HTR*) for a January 2013 issue. The story immediately hit front pages around the world. King was very careful to say that although the text was important, it did not throw any light on the historical Jesus, coming as it did centuries after the crucifixion. She said that all it shows is that there were groups that maintained that Jesus was married and groups that maintained that he was not. According to King, all this was theology. To avoid controversy, she stated that neither of these positions is historical. Obviously, this is a logical impossibility. One of these positions must be historical. Jesus was either married or not married.

King's disclaimers aside, the reaction was vicious and one-sided. King's reputation and the reputation of her colleagues did not help. Within days, the text was declared a forgery by a chorus of scholars. The Vatican dismissed the papyrus without examining it, and Internet bloggers with degrees from various Christian institutions manned their computer stations night and day to spread the good word that the inscription was no good. Suddenly, nobody was talking about the implications of Jesus' marriage. Nobody was talking about the uniqueness of the find. Rather, they were talking about the angles of Coptic letters and discussing who might have forged them.

Fortunately for King, nobody was suggesting that *she* had forged the papyrus, as they had with Morton Smith when he found *Secret Mark*. Everyone agreed that she was not a forger. Rather, according to this view, she was a naïve scholar who got duped by a money-starved, very clever, anonymous forger. We don't want to go into detail with respect to the forgery allegations. Suffice it to say that they never made any sense. Who is the forger? How did he make money when the object was never sold? If it's a fake, why were six world-class scholars authenticating it? What was wrong with their analysis?

The most interesting aspect of the forgery charge was that the forgery supposedly took place in the late 1990s or early 21st century. This would make the forger not only a world-class deceiver but a time traveler. Otherwise, how did

Munro and Fecht see this document at least twenty years before it was produced? No one addressed this little matter. In fact, there wasn't much interest in the content of the papyrus at all. As with the Jesus Family Tomb, it's incredible how people can just ignore findings that are not consistent with their dogmas. Anyway, the damage was done. Professor Karen King and her colleagues disappeared from the debate for over a year and a half. The papyrus was tainted by the controversy. As a result, the Smithsonian Channel, which was poised to broadcast a documentary on the subject, cancelled the airdate, and the *HTR* withdrew King's article from its publication schedule. The issue dropped off the public radar. The historical Jesus and his wife were pushed back into the shadows. A new find was delegitimized.

Then an amazing thing happened. Professor King stepped back into the limelight. She hadn't been wasting her time. She had recruited a veritable dream team of scientists to check the papyrus from every angle. After nearly two years of studies, the verdict was finally in, the documentary aired, and the long-awaited paper by Professor King was published. The conclusion: "the scientific testing completed thus far consistently provides positive evidence of the antiquity of the papyrus and ink, including radiocarbon, spectroscopic, and oxidation characteristics, with no evidence of modern fabrication."[7] There was no doubt about it: the papyrus was authentic.

All this didn't stop the nay-sayers. They now claimed that the Jesus Wife papyrus was found in the same collection as another papyrus that they deem a forgery. According to this logic, the Jesus Wife papyrus is a forgery by implication. Once again, Professor King retreated from the academic battlefield. She had presented the facts; she could not deal with the spin.

But this heartbreaking scenario is not new. It's part of an ongoing campaign to keep the Jesus of history away from the Jesus of theology. As you read this, we're sure that the theological bloggers are at their stations doing their best to delegitimize, marginalize, and ridicule our find. But consider this: the fact is that when we started writing this book, there was no explicit reference to a wife of Jesus in any early Christian text. Now, as a result of Professor King's find, there is.

To understand how myth becomes fact and fact becomes controversy, we have to look for a moment at how Christian orthodoxy mobilizes to delegitimize new discoveries because it will explain some of the inevitable reactions to our thesis. Morton Smith put it this way: "few public figures from the Greco-Roman world are so well documented, but none is so widely disputed [as Jesus]. This suggests that there's something strange about the documents or about the scholars who have studied them, or both." He goes on to state, "most of the scholars have not been historians, but theologians determined to make the documents justify their own theological position."[8] In other words, there is much talk about Jesus, but very little clarity. Why?

Jesus of Nazareth is arguably the most famous individual to ever have lived, and yet we hardly have any original insights from him. Over a billion people worship him as God and, except for a few parables about mustard seeds[9] and such, we have nothing from him. No philosophy, no theology, no legal doctrine. What's more, from the little we have, we can draw totally contradictory conclusions. In Matthew, as quoted before, he states, "do not suppose that I have come to bring peace to the earth. I did not come to bring peace, but a sword" (Matthew 10:34). Later in the Gospels, Jesus states, "If anyone slaps you on the right cheek, turn to them the other cheek also" (Matthew 5:39). Which is it? Is Jesus a warrior or a pacifist? The fact is that nobody knows. There seems to be a policy to fudge Jesus' teachings and his short life. Was he for or against paying taxes? This is an important issue because it would define if he was a warrior or a pacifist (was he willing to stand up to the Roman regime or give in to it?). His famous line "render unto Caesar what is Caesar's and to God what is God's" (Matthew 22:21) leaves us as confused today as it left people confused in his own day.

Was Jesus an orthodox rabbi, or a paganizing libertine? In one place he states, "Do not think that I have come to abolish the Law or the Prophets; I have not come to abolish them but to fulfill them." By fulfilling the laws, he seems to suggest that they have come to an end. He then fudges the message by stating, "I tell you the truth, until heaven and earth disappear, not the smallest letter, not the least stroke of a pen, will by any means disappear from the Law until everything is accomplished" (Matthew 5:17–18). What does he mean by "until everything is accomplished"? According to the church, everything was accomplished and therefore the Mosaic law does not apply. But if he came to destroy it (i.e., no Sabbath observance, no kosher observance, no circumcision, etc.), why did Jesus say "not the smallest letter . . . will by any means disappear from the law?" Some early followers of Jesus such as James and his community, the Ebionites and, at times, the Apostle Peter, held on to the Mosaic law. Others, like Paul, jettisoned the law. Which teaching was closer to the historical Jesus?

Until now, it seemed that we would never know. After all, one group of Jesus followers managed to become the official religion of the Roman Empire, and they had a policy of murdering their opposition and burning their books. That's why we only hear the official voices. The book-burning policy was explicitly articulated. In 333 C.E., for example, the Emperor Constantine issued the following edict against Arius, a leader of the early church: ". . . if any book written by Arius be found, it is to be consigned to the fire, so that not only his corrupt teachings may vanish, but no memory of him at all may remain."[10] This policy of destroying all versions of Christianity except one almost worked.

But a funny thing happened on the way to historical oblivion: some books survived. Some were hidden in jars; others were hidden in plain sight. Only the names were changed to protect the innocent. After two thousand years, they are starting to come to light. More than this, with the rebirth of the Jewish state in 1948 and the 1967 reunification of Jerusalem as the capital of modern Israel, bulldozers engaged in building the new country have smashed into hundreds of archaeological sites just below the surface. Suddenly, we have access to the bones, bone boxes, inscriptions and, now, writings of those first followers of Jesus. We are finally in a position to begin to retrieve the history behind the theology. And in the midst of all this, we find what appears to be an actual Gnostic narrative—a veritable lost gospel—telling the story of the Bride of God. Our gospel tells her story and it's a very, very different story from the one we are used to. It's a story of love and marriage, interfaith coupling, sacred sex, power grabs, plots and counterplots, children, and a theology that is both secret and public—thus accounting for two thousand years of built-in contradictions surrounding the person of Jesus.

It is important to note what is new and what is not new in our study. We say that *Joseph and Aseneth* may very well date to Jesus' time, in the 1st century. From a scholarly point of view, this is an acceptable statement. It's not even new. In fact, there are scholars like Gideon Bohak who believe this story dates to the 1st century *before* Jesus. The dates range from the 1st century B.C.E. to the 4th century C.E. Anywhere in there is acceptable from the point of view of mainstream scholarship. The Talmudic scholar Victor Aptowitzer, in 1924, conjectured that there was a now-lost Hebrew version of *Joseph and Aseneth* that was originally written in the land of Israel. This would coincide with the idea that the text originates in a place preserving the very first traditions associated with Jesus and his movement. Kraemer, too, has no problem with Aptowitzer's suggestions, stating, "the land of Israel . . . is not an impossible choice" for the origin of the text.[11] So our lost gospel may very well have originated in Israel as far back as the 1st century—the time of Jesus and Mary the Magdalene.

We say that this is a Christian text. The monks who dutifully copied our manuscript for hundreds and hundreds of years also believed that this story was an important Christian story. As for the scholars, the idea that *Joseph and Aseneth* is a Christian text has a proud tradition, ranging from Pierre Batiffol at the end of the 19th century to Rivka Nir at the beginning of the 21st century. Even Professor Richard Bauckham, a New Testament scholar and member of the Doctrine Commission of the Church of England, who is bound to have theological problems with our decoding of *Joseph and Aseneth*, states that "I strongly suspect that *Joseph and Asenath* is not a Jewish work, at least not in the form we have it, but a Christian work with allegorical meaning."[12]

We say that the Joseph figure in the text can be identified with Jesus. Again, it's not unique to us to link the Joseph of our text with the Jesus of the Gospels. From Batiffol through Brooks to Kraemer and Nir, this is a totally acceptable point of view. So what's new? The novelty of our interpretation involves identifying Aseneth with Mary the Magdalene. This is not to say that no one previously had given Aseneth a Christian interpretation. Even Ephrem in the 4th century gave her a similar interpretation. But the majority of scholars who read Aseneth typologically identify her with the church, rather than a real-life female. In this reading, Jesus marries the church, not Mary the Magdalene. But does this make any sense? After all, our text says that Joseph and Aseneth had "intercourse" and children resulted from this union. Traditionally, this kind of language is interpreted as a reference to the many proselytes to the Christian faith. Does this really make sense? Would anyone refer to conversions being the consequence of *intercourse*? More than this, what do we make of the entire last chapter of *Joseph and Aseneth* where "Pharaoh's son" wants to rape Aseneth and kill her children? Is this too a metaphor concerning the Church? Clearly, once we read the text typologically, if Joseph is a human being it makes sense to say that Aseneth is also a human being—not an institution. Basically, if Joseph is Jesus, Aseneth must be Mary the Magdalene. The text was probably encoded some time after the 4th-century victory of Pauline Christianity over all other forms of Christian belief.

As for the idea that this text is encoded, again, we didn't invent this notion—nor, for that matter, did Dan Brown. We've now translated the letter of the anonymous man who commissioned the Syriac version of the text 1,460 years ago. In his letter, this man clearly states that the reason he wants the text translated is because of the "secret messages" embedded in it. For his part, the ancient translator also agrees that there are encoded teachings in this text. He adds that these teachings are very dangerous. But that's not all. By definition, Gnostic texts are encoded. Theologically, they involve portraying historical characters in mythological terms. It is a genre, and it is a genre that is consistent with our newly rediscovered text. More than this, Syriac texts are also encoded. They use typology. We did not invent Syriac typology. In this tradition, Ephrem and Aphrahat explicitly tell us that Joseph is a stand-in for Jesus. So encoding heretical texts is a fact of life in the ancient world. It is not an unknown phenomenon. What we've done is restore this gospel to its original form.

And what do we learn? When we read the lost gospel in the way it was meant to be read, we see that the idea that Jesus and Mary the Magdalene were married is not a modern invention. It is at least as old as Valentinian Gnosticism and, as it now appears, older. It is echoed in many passages in the canonical Gospels themselves. Furthermore, when we uncover a sexual theology in our manuscript, this too is not original. It is at least as old as Gnosticism and it is echoed in the texts of pagans such as Celsus and in the Rabbinic literature as well. Even the church fathers attest to the fact that some of the earliest followers of Jesus turned his life into a theology of sexuality.

With the New Testament's silence regarding Jesus' marital status—especially Paul's failure to mention a non-married Jesus when arguing for the celibacy of his followers—various Coptic papyri, Gnostic gospels, assorted archaeology, and our manuscript showing he was married, the burden of proof now switches to those who'd deny Jesus' marriage. Show us a text that says he was *not* married. We now have a narrative that confirms what has been rumored for millennia: namely, that Jesus and Mary the Magdalene were married and that they had children. Gnostic Christianity kept this tradition alive. It was then preserved in the Syriac church and brought back to life with the rediscovery of the Syriac *Joseph and Aseneth*. We now have a very different Jesus than the one depicted by Pauline Christianity and a very, very different Mary the Magdalene.

Once we see Mary the Magdalene for who she is—once we stop reading Christian texts through the eyes of Pauline orthodoxy—a whole new world opens up. Suddenly, we realize that Mary the Magdalene was Jesus' wife and that she was not Jewish. We further realize that she was the original Virgin Mary and the original "lady" (as in "our lady"), not Jesus' mother. More than this, because of the suspected adultery, it was probably Mary the mother who was the object of scorn, no doubt called a prostitute behind her back. It seems that Pauline orthodoxy simply switched titles, calling the mother a virgin and the wife a prostitute.

We also realize that the Gentile church does not start with Paul, but with Mary the Magdalene. Suddenly we realize that Gnosticism does not begin with Valentinus, but with Jesus himself. We realize that the founders of Christianity were Jesus and Mary the Magdalene, not Paul. They taught a message that grew out of the margins of Judaism and blended with the margins of Artemis worship. It was this syncretic fusion that swept the Roman Empire. But it was a dangerous theology. It was adopted by Rome only after it was emasculated. Pauline Christianity took Mary the Magdalene out of the story and the sex out of the theology. In David Friedman's words, Christianity became "a culture where the virgin symbolized all that was pure, the penis stood for all that was evil. What defined Mary's sanctity was her lack of contact with a penis."[13] Put differently, Christianity became the official religion of the Roman empire only after the sexuality that was central to Jesus and Mary the Magdalene's "ministry" was removed and substituted with Paul's Attis-based asceticism.

Finally, when it comes to the plots and counterplots involving Jesus, Mary, and the ruling regime, this is not a story. It is reconstructed history that fits nicely with what we already know from the historical record. For example, Josephus relates that Jesus' brother, James, fell victim to a plot: he relates that a high priest named Hanan (in English, another Annas) used the transition between one Roman governor and another to murder James. In the aftermath, James' allies lobbied the new governor and Hanan was ousted from his position. In other words, what we read in *Joseph and Aseneth* with respect to Jesus, we also find in Josephus with respect to James.[14]

When we read the ancient story of *Joseph and Aseneth*, if we substitute Jesus for Joseph, Mary the Magdalene for Aseneth, and then go one step further and substitute Germanicus for "Pharaoh's son," a lost gospel emerges whose voice has not been heard in nearly two thousand years. This gospel provides us with hitherto-suppressed information. As a result of our lost gospel, we can now begin the process of understanding the impact that Jesus and Mary the Magdalene had on events that led up to the destruction of Jerusalem only thirty-eight years after the crucifixion.

Of course there is room for legitimate debate concerning our research and conclusions. But we know what happened in the past when scholars and journalists presented facts that did not support Pauline Christian dogma. Immediately those individuals who masquerade as disinterested scholars, while taking oaths to defend their churches and their theologies, reached for their keyboards and started a campaign whose goal was to discredit the new findings and the people who brought them to the world.

With respect to our book, sadly if the past is an indicator, most of the commentators and bloggers won't respond to the hundreds of facts enumerated in these pages. Rather, they will start a campaign to discredit the find by discrediting the authors. Some have already attacked this book before it was completed. But we take comfort from the fact that when it comes to personal attacks on the discoverers of inconvenient truths, we are in good company. Similar attacks were faced by earlier challengers of Pauline Christian doctrine, including Eleazer Sukenik (identifier of the Dead Sea Scrolls), Morton Smith (arguably the greatest New Testament scholar who ever lived), and Bellarmino Bagatti (the legendary Franciscan archaeologist). But all these campaigns aside, nothing will change the truth.

We have now restored *British Library Manuscript Number 17,202* to what it was prior to the victory of Pauline Christianity. It provides us with some missing links in Jesus' life. As well, it has filled in some historical lacunae in the period between the demise of the Jesus movement and the appearance of Gnosticism; between the Gentile church surrounding Jesus and the Gentile church that grew up around Paul. Now we even have the exact date of the crucifixion and the historical timetable leading up to it. What are the implications of all this? The short answer is that we now have a decoded manuscript—at least as authoritative as the canonical Gospels—that provides us with suppressed historical facts about one of the most important individuals who ever walked the face of our planet. It's as simple as that.

What we do with this information is another matter.

APPENDICES
THE LOST GOSPEL

Joseph and Aseneth and accompanying letters

Translated from the Syriac
by Dr. Tony Burke

with commentary
by Simcha Jacobovici and Barrie Wilson

APPENDIX I

JOSEPH AND ASENETH
TRANSLATED FROM THE SYRIAC

What follows is the first-ever translation of *Joseph and Aseneth* from Syriac into English. In order to read deteriorated words and see words that may have been deliberately smudged or covered up, high-tech state-of-the-art digital imaging was employed.

We secured permission from the British Library to engage the services of one of the world's leading digital-imaging specialists in ancient manuscripts: R. B. Toth Associates of Oakton, Virginia. The text was painstakingly scanned and analyzed by Dr. William A. Christens-Barry and the company's president, Michael Toth. They used a variety of imaging techniques including infrared photography. Thirteen images were made of each page in order to see through the smudged and damaged portions of the manuscript to the underlying text. This CSI-like technological analysis allowed us to make some significant break-through discoveries.

Before we discuss the high-tech revelations, let's revisit the facts surrounding the text that we present here for the first time. As we have seen, around 570 C.E., an individual whom scholars call Pseudo-Zacharias Rhetor made a compilation of writings in an ancient language called Syriac. He titled his mini-library—his personal encyclopedia, if you will—*A Volume of Records of Events that Have Shaped the World*. In this all-important compilation, he included the Syriac document that we are presenting here for the first time in a modern translation.

Pseudo-Zacharias Rhetor also included in his collection two letters that were in his possession. They served as a kind of preface, introduction, or cover letters to the document. Along with our translation, we are also providing the first-ever translations of these letters from the Syriac (Appendix II).

These letters demonstrate that Moses of Ingila—a scholar who lived over fourteen hundred years ago—translated the manuscript from Greek into Syriac. He had been asked to do so by an anonymous individual who had found a very ancient Greek copy of this work in a library in Resh'aina. It was a memorial library in that city for the bishops of the House of Beroea (modern-day Aleppo in northern Syria). So, the document we are presenting here is over fourteen hundred years old and is itself a translation of a much older text. Given that we believe that it is a lost gospel, it's all-important that the text may reach back to the time of Jesus or shortly thereafter.

The Syriac translation is preserved as *Manuscript 17,202* in the British Library, and it represents the oldest extant copy of this work in any language. According to William Wright, this manuscript was incorporated into the British Library collection in 1847.[1] It came from the library of the convent of St. Mary Deipara (St. Mary of the Syrians) in Egypt. A certain Moses the Nisibene from Baghdad had given many of the manuscripts in St. Mary Deipara to the convent in 932 C.E.

Manuscript 17,202 was transcribed by J. P. N. Land in 1870. He copied the document, letter by letter, from the Syriac manuscript in the British Library and published it in *Anecdota Syriaca*, vol. 3. Land's transcription represents the basis for our translation. However, as a result of the digital imaging process to which the manuscript was subjected, we have reintroduced several words and a line mistakenly omitted by Land. We also have made some corrections suggested from the Latin translation of the Syriac made by Gustav Oppenheim in *Fabula Josephi et Asenethae Apocrypha* (1886) and from our own first-hand examination of the manuscript at the British Library.

---

1   William Wright, *Catalogue of the Syriac Manuscripts in the British Museum Acquired Since the Year 1838* (London: British Museum, 1870), i–xxxiv.

There is an omission in the Syriac manuscript corresponding to *Joseph and Aseneth*, chapters 13:12–16:3. These have been translated from later Greek manuscripts edited by Marc Philonenko in *Joseph et Aséneth: Introduction texte critique traduction et notes* and reinserted in our text.

Dr. Tony Burke, Associate Professor, Humanities and Program Coordinator, Religious Studies, York University, Toronto made our translation. He was assisted by Slavomir Čéplö, Comenius University, Slovakia. So as not to bias the translation, Dr. Burke undertook this task without knowing the interpretation that we had arrived at.

Along with Land's 1870 transcription, Dr. Burke used black-and-white photographs of the Syriac manuscript in the possession of the British Library. When these were made is not known. When we examined the original document in the British Library, while most of the original pages were relatively clear, there was evidence of manuscript deterioration, indistinct lettering, some smudges, and what appear as deliberate attempts to cover some words. In addition, there were missing pages. One particular page was suspicious. In the letter that immediately precedes *Joseph and Aseneth*, Moses of Ingila tells us that the text contains a "hidden meaning." He says that he has to be careful when discussing it since the topic is dangerous. Then, just as he begins to reveal its secret, there is a cut line in the manuscript. The concluding portion of his letter is missing, as is the first chapter of *Joseph and Aseneth*, which had been on the reverse side of the deleted section of the letter.

Historical sleuthing has revealed that there were two types of censorship in the transmission of this text—omission and destruction. The first occurred in the 12th century, when a copy (*British Library Manuscript #7190*) was made of our 6th-century edition of *Joseph and Aseneth* (*British Library Manuscript #17,202*). Since the copy includes all the chapters of *Joseph and Aseneth*, we now know that the cut line had not occurred before the 12th century. And since the cover letters are not part of the copied text, we now also know that the 12th-century copyist chose to omit the two covering letters from his translation, likely not wanting to tip off his readers that the *Joseph and Aseneth* text contained a hidden meaning.

But did the 12th-century copyist decide to destroy the 6th-century cover letters? We can't be sure. But the fact is that our earlier text is missing the first chapter. Meaning sometime after the 12th century, someone decided that the

Moses of Ingila letter was too dangerous to ignore. Maybe it was the 12th-century copyist, or maybe someone who came after him. But whoever it was cut the bottom of the letter and with it the first chapter of the text in the 6th-century edition. Fortunately, we were able to retrieve the missing first chapter from the later edition.

The digital-imaging technology has now restored the original manuscript. For the first time in centuries, we can now see the writing as its author penned it. In particular, we can now discern portions of the manuscript that neither Land (in the mid-1860s) nor we could see with the naked eye.

All of this enables us to make sense of indistinct areas in the manuscript, simply worn down by time and handling over the centuries. Using these advanced techniques, we were also able to uncover the original lettering behind several smudges. More importantly, digital imaging revealed that a number of different inks and different colors were used in the smudged areas, as well as in other parts of the text. Overall, the most significant discovery was that the covering letter by Moses of Ingila was, as our visual inspection had suggested, deliberately cut. This cut line was subjected to intensive digital imaging and processing. By means of this technology, we could now discern that the cut line went right through a line of the text—right through the Syriac script—clearly indicating that this was an act of censorship. It was as if someone did not want readers of *Joseph and Aseneth* to think that it contained a hidden meaning and deleted the interpretive key. Put differently, some fourteen hundred years ago, Moses of Ingila was silenced and his secret history was censored. In a sense, our book is an attempt to restore Moses' lost interpretation.

Besides the act of restoration—and we are certain that we now have the basis for an accurate reconstruction of the original Syriac text—it is not our purpose here to compare this oldest existing version of *Joseph and Aseneth* with later versions of the same story in Greek, Latin, and other languages. However, we cannot help but notice that this earliest account tells the story in a more straightforward manner than later versions reflected in Burchard and Cook's translations. Our manuscript lacks many of the embellishments that a tale over the years would be expected to attract. The story likely grew over the centuries, just as the narrative about Jesus did. It is not our purpose here, however, to trace the possible evolution of the *Joseph and Aseneth* narrative.

In addition to the ecclesiastical circle in which it was preserved and transmitted, the language, symbolism, and events portrayed in this writing all point to a Christian context for making sense of the narrative. As the exchange of letters between Moses of Ingila and the anonymous individual who asked him for a Syriac translation from an ancient Greek manuscript reveals, and as our decoding above indicates, the story cannot be about the ancient Biblical figure Joseph and his little-known wife Aseneth. They represent stand-ins—surrogates or types—for two other figures of much greater interest to Christians. They are none other than Jesus and Mary the Magdalene.

Significantly, paralleling our text, Stephen Shoemaker notes that the "earliest extant Dormition [Mary's death] narrative . . . first appears in several Syriac fragments that were copied near the end of the 5th century."[2] Shoemaker says that it's not clear which Mary is described in this earliest tradition (is it the Virgin Mary or Mary the Magdalene?). He quotes Deirdre Good, who has suggested that we are dealing with a "composite identity": mother, sister, and companion. He goes on to say that, again, as with our text, it is "evident that the Syriac version has been translated from an earlier Greek narrative." Finally, he says that the depictions of Mary in the Dormition narratives bear "classically 'Gnostic' themes."[3] In other words, Syriac traditions usually associated with the Virgin Mary may actually be Gnostic, like our text, and dealing with Mary the Magdalene. This provides a wider context for our manuscript.

In our ancient manuscript, the story does not focus on Jesus' death, resurrection, and ascension or on Mother Mary's death or ascension but, as we have seen, on Mary the Magdalene's marriage to Jesus. From the perspective of the author of *Joseph and Aseneth*, it is this event which is most important, not any post-death ascension. Further, in our text Mary the Magdalene also represents the Church of the Gentiles. As a result, this writing takes on an overtly anti-Pauline stance. After all, Paul and his followers touted Paul as "the apostle to the Gentiles." We now know that there were already several rival Gentile movements as early as the confrontation between Paul and Mary. This text represents one such rival group.

---

2   Shoemaker, in Jones, op. cit., 6.

3   Ibid., 7. See also Stephen J. Shoemaker, *The Ancient Traditions of the Virgin Mary's Dormition and Assumption* (Oxford University Press, 2006).

When correctly positioned and interpreted using early Christian methodology, *Joseph and Aseneth* is revealed as a work of disguised history. It is important to realize that in our decipherment of the text, we have not employed modern means of interpretation but rather made use of techniques actually used by early Christians. The latter saw parallels between people and events in what they called the "Old Testament" and people and events in the Christian narrative. While this may seem strange to us today, setting up typological parallels was commonplace within the early church. Our discussion in the preceding chapters provides us with the necessary tools to understand the manuscript as early Christians would have understood it.

According to our analysis, this neglected and misunderstood text constitutes the first written evidence that Jesus was married to Mary the Magdalene, that they engaged in sexual relations, that they had children together, and that there was a hitherto unknown plot against the family. It also provides us with an alternative Christianity that may be historically closer to Jesus, Mary, and their original followers.

Words missing from the Syriac that are needed to make sense in English are indicated with parentheses such as this: (and); errors in the manuscript are indicated with angle brackets like this: <and>. We provide commentary and footnotes to explain the text. There is no standard division of verses for the text. While we have retained the traditional chapter numbering, the verse divisions are our own.

Translation © Associated Producers Ltd.

⬦

[THE STORY] OF ASENETH

Commonly called the story of
Joseph the Just and Aseneth his Wife[4]

Episode 1: The Meeting

First impressions. Joseph's prayer for Aseneth's transformation.

1.

1 In the first year of the seven years of plenty, on the fifth day of the second month, Pharaoh sent Joseph to go around the entire land of Egypt.[5] **2** In the fourth month of the first year Joseph came to the borders of the region of On—called Heliopolis in Greek—where he was gathering wheat. He gathered the crops of that region like the sand of the sea. **3** In that city there was a man, one of the magistrates and nobles of the Pharaoh. This man was very wealthy, wise, and gentle. He was a counselor of Pharaoh. His name was Potiphar,[6] a priest of the city of On.

4 He had a daughter who was lovely in appearance and a virgin. She was eighteen years old and her beauty (surpassed) that of all the virgins of the land, all the daughters of the people.

---

4   This is the way the title has come down to us in various later editions and how it's known in academia. Significantly, in our Syriac manuscript—the earliest available edition of this work—the title is simply *Of Aseneth*, i.e., The Story of Aseneth. Meaning, this is her story; Joseph/Jesus is not even mentioned in the title.

5   The story of Joseph can be found in the Book of Genesis, chapters 37–50. Few details in *Joseph and Aseneth* match those presented in the Biblical account. Its purpose is not to retell the Biblical story or to elaborate on its details. It's the telling of *another* story under the guise of such figures as Joseph, Aseneth, and "Pharaoh's son." The date presented here may correspond to a specific date in Tiberius' reign as Roman emperor.

6   The Book of Genesis calls Aseneth's father "Potiphera" (Genesis 41:45, 50 and 46:20). The man called "Potiphar" is an official in Pharaoh's court who buys Joseph from Midianite traders, to whom Joseph had been sold by his brothers. It is this Potiphar's wife who unsuccessfully attempts to seduce Joseph, her Hebrew slave (Genesis 39:1–20). The Syriac text here calls Aseneth's father *Potiphar*, as opposed to *Potiphera*. We could have corrected this, but we left it as is. In some traditions, the two are one and the same, creating irony that Joseph resisted the mother and married the daughter.

5 She was noble and glorious like Sarah, beautiful like Rebecca, and virtuous like Rachel.[7] Her name was Aseneth.[8]

6 News of her beauty spread throughout the land. All the nobles, magistrates, sons[9] of the king, and all the powerful youth wanted her. Thus war and disputes broke out among them because of her.

7 Pharaoh's firstborn son heard about her,[10] and he asked his father to give her to him from among the women.

8 He said (to his father), "Give me Aseneth, the daughter of Potiphar, the priest of On, as a wife."

---

7   The Genesis story makes no point about Aseneth's virginity or beauty. So while a Gentile (a non-Jew) and a daughter of Gentiles, this Aseneth possesses many of the traits associated with Israelite matriarchs. Later Greek manuscripts add that she was "quite unlike Egyptian girls but in every way *like* the daughters of the Hebrews." There may have been good reasons for heightening Aseneth's Jewish traits. If Aseneth is Mary the Magdalene and she is head of the Church of the Gentiles, she needed to be acceptable to *both* of Jesus' original constituencies. Note also the title of "virgin" that surpasses all other virgins is associated with Mary the Magdalene, not Jesus' mother.

8   Thus Aseneth, only briefly mentioned in the Book of Genesis (41:45, 50), achieves tremendous prominence in this story. Who she is, where she lives, what she thinks of Joseph, the transformative process she undergoes, the threat upon her life—all this assumes center stage in this document. It is very much her story.

    In the Syriac text, Aseneth's name is presented as Asyeth. We retain here the traditional spelling of the character's name.

9   Remember, Tiberius had two sons: Drusus and Germanicus. So this line is consistent with "Pharaoh" being, typologically, Tiberius.

10 Note that, at this point, he merely "heard" of her. This is consistent with Germanicus being in the general area of Phoenicia but not, at first, in the Galilee.

11 Notice Pharaoh calls his son "king" of all the land, not the *son* of a king. This is consistent with Germanicus' status upon being sent to the Middle East. The "King of Moab" here may refer to Aretas IV King of Nabataea, ancient Moab. He was, indeed, a regional player and he did marry off his daughter(s) for political purposes. But in later Greek additions to *Joseph and Aseneth*, this "King of Moab" is called by the Hebrew name "Joachim" and his daughter is referred to as "very beautiful" (1:13–14 in H. F. D. Sparks, ed., op cit., 473–503). So, given his Hebrew name, this "King of Moab" is not Nabataean, but Jewish. Perhaps he is both.

    During the time of Jesus, was there a part-Jewish, part-Nabataean "King of Moab?" In fact, there was—Herod Antipas. He was a descendant of Nabataean converts to Judaism. By Roman decree, he ruled the area of Galilee and Peraea, the latter being ancient Amon and Moab. Since Jews at the time saw the Herods as usurpers, it would be a fitting dig to call him a "King of Moab." It would suggest to the readers of *Joseph and Aseneth* that the Herods were foreigners from an area traditionally hostile to Israel. But by also calling him by his heretofore unknown Hebrew name "Joachim," the Greek editor of *Joseph and Aseneth* is telling his readers that he is not referring to a proper Nabataean, but a Jew of Nabataean descent.

9 Pharaoh answered him, "Why do you, the king and ruler of all the land, seek a wife beneath you? Look, the daughter of the king of Moab is virtuous and fitting for you."[11]

2.

1 Aseneth was proud, boastful, and treated all men with contempt. No man had ever known her. There was a <great>, very tall tower[12] attached to her father's house. At the top of (the tower) was a large dwelling place[13] and in it were ten bedchambers.[14]

Did Herod Antipas have a beautiful daughter who might have been a fit for Germanicus? In fact, his stepdaughter, Salome, is one of the most infamous beauties of history; the seductress who is alleged to have danced a particularly erotic dance at Antipas' birthday, and then asked for the head of John the Baptizer, Jesus' cousin. According to the Gospels, she did this because John refused to respond to her advances. The problem with Salome being the daughter of the King of Moab of this text is that she's assumed to have been born in 14 C.E. which would have made her only five years old at the time Germanicus arrived in the Middle East (19 C.E.). Did Antipas have other daughters? We don't know. He was already in his mid-twenties when he came to power in 4 C.E., and we don't know how many times he was wed. So by the time Germanicus came in 19 C.E., he may very well have had a biological daughter who was in her teens—an older half-sister to Salome. It seems that in our text, "Pharaoh" is recommending that Germanicus set his sights on this unknown daughter.

12   Notice the importance of the tower and its detailed description. This is Aseneth's domain in her father's magnificent estate. The Syriac word for *tower* in this oldest text is *migdala*. Aseneth is right away associated with the Hebrew cognate word *migdal*. She lives in a migdal. Like Mary the Magdalene, she is "Mary of the Tower." Both are tower ladies. In fact, as late as the 13th century, in a collection of saints' lives written by a Dominican called Jacobus de Voragine and titled *The Golden Legend*, Mary the Magdalene is still identified as an heiress who lives in a castle. See Joan Acocella, op. cit., 42.

13   For Aseneth's "dwelling place," the Syriac has the word *one* here, i.e., above this house there was *one* large, etc. Since this *one* has ten rooms in it, it could not itself be a room. The Greek has "upper room with ten bedchambers" but that creates rooms within a room. Some might translate this Syriac word as *apartment*, but that seems oddly modern and conjures up images of penthouse suites. *Dwelling place*, therefore, seems most accurate and most consistent with what comes after.

14   The reference to a *dwelling place* and *bedchambers* utilizes the language of Jewish mysticism of the 1st century, specifically what scholars call Merkavah and Hekhalot literature. As Schafer puts it, "there can be no doubt that 'chambers' (*hadarim*) frequently refer to the heavenly palaces so characteristic of Merkavah mysticism." Peter Schafer, *The Origins of Jewish Mysticism* (Princeton University Press, 2009), 199. See especially footnote 114.

2 The first chamber was splendid and beautifully adorned with a variety of precious stones. Its ceiling was overlaid with gold. On its walls were set up all the gods of the Egyptians in silver and gold. She worshipped all of them—Aseneth served them and prepared libations for them daily.[15]

3 In the second chamber were gold, silver, and valuable, precious stones, and all the ornaments of idols and the garments of Aseneth's virginity.[16] **4** There was a third chamber of her house. In it were all sorts of things, and all the good foods of the land. **5** In the remaining seven chambers lived individually seven virgins,[17] who served Aseneth.[18] They were born on the same day and year and they were beautiful in appearance. They appeared like the stars of heaven. No man had known them nor had any youth spoken to them.

6 There were three windows in the bedchamber of Aseneth in an atrium. One of them was large and faced a courtyard, looking to the east; a second turned to the south; and the third looked to the north to a street where you could watch passersby.[19]

7 Beneath the eastern window was placed a bed made entirely of gold. It was covered with Egyptian coverings spun of gold, along with purple,

---

15 Clearly, this "Mary of the Tower" is a pagan priestess living in the upper apartments of some kind of temple.

16 As with Artemis, the virginity is not a matter of sexual preference or modesty, but part and parcel of her religious calling.

17 Kraemer says that this is clearly an allusion to Isaiah 4:1 that speaks of the arrival of the messiah and of "seven women" who will take "hold of one man." In Kraemer's words, "the seven companions whom the angel blesses at Aseneth's behest may allude to the seven women [in Isaiah]." Meaning, it may be that just as Jesus surrounded himself with twelve men, representing the twelve tribes of Israel, Mary the Magdalene surrounded herself with seven virgins representing the seven women in Isaiah's Prophecy of Time. (Kraemer, op. cit., 36.)

18 Seven rooms and seven virgins serving the priestess. They are all part and parcel of her pagan ministry. A 1st- to 2nd-century gold Roman ring, encasing a red jasper cameo, depicts a bee in the mouth of a lion surrounded by seven stars (see France Cumont, *The Mysteries of Mithra* [Dover Publications, 1956], 185, fig. 42). This is reminiscent of Aseneth surrounded by her seven attendants. The ring clearly has magical purposes. It may be associated with Mithras, but the bee is more appropriate to Artemis. For example, in the 1st century B.C.E., Hyginus, a Latin author, says that The Pleiades constellation originated as seven daughters of Atlas who were companions to Artemis (*Astronomica* 2.21. See also *The Pleiades in Mythology*, Pleiade Associates [Bristol, United Kingdom, 2012].).

We think that the above is why the Gospels tell us that Jesus drove *seven* "daemons" out of Mary the Magdalene. The disappearance, later in the text, of these seven "guardians," i.e., the virgins attending Aseneth, is reminiscent of the seven spirits who leave Mary the Magdalene (Luke 8:2). The word used in Luke 8:2 in relation to the spirit that leaves Mary the Magdalene is not "demon" but "daemon." *Daemon* in Greek is a neutral word. It means scarlet and fine white linen. **8** In this (bed) Aseneth slept; no man ever sat on it.[20]

9 A great courtyard encircled this house. The wall encircling the court-yard was built of hewn stone.[21] There were four gates overlaid with iron in the courtyard; and these were guarded by eighteen armed young men. **10** Clinging to (the walls of) the courtyard were a variety of trees of summer-ripened fruit. On the right side of the courtyard was a spring of fresh water and, underneath the spring, a pool for the fresh water. From this (pool) a river issued forth and flowed through the middle of the courtyard and watered all those trees.

3.

1 In the first year of the seven years of plenty, on the eighteenth of the fourth month, Joseph arrived at the storehouse of the city of On. He was gathering and storing up the crops of the seven years of plenty. **2** As he drew near to the city of On, he sent twelve men ahead of him[22] to Potiphar the priest and said, "I shall come to you at noon,[23] at meal-time, and I shall rest from the heat of noon in your home."

---

a spiritual force, something like an angel, but much more limited in scope. It can mean a guardian spirit or a protector. In English Bibles, *daemon* is usually translated negatively as a demon, suggesting that Mary the Magdalene suffered from a serious medical condition. This is highly misleading. Luke 8:2 could simply mean that seven pagan attendants, or guardians, had left Mary the Magdalene because of Jesus. Interestingly, one of the Gnostic texts tells us that Jesus had seven women as well as twelve males among his disciples. This may be an echo of Mary the Magdalene's seven "daemons," before Jesus drove them out. On the latter point, see Joan Acocella, op. cit., 48.

19   The only known Phoenician tower—excavated in Carthage and currently in the British Museum—conforms perfectly with this description, including the three-window (as opposed to the four-window) design.

20   Clearly, this has to do with ritual purity. Not only is she a virgin, but no man ever *sat* on her bed. Male priests in the Jerusalem Temple, for example, could be defiled and rendered impure by nighttime emissions. Once they were so defiled, the process by which they regained purity was very complicated. Here we see that Aseneth is the subject of spiritual and ritual purity.

21   The temple in Jerusalem was built of hewn stones.

22   Twelve is a significant number, representing the twelve tribes of Israel, who in turn represented the twelve signs of the zodiac and the twelve months of the year. Jesus' twelve disciples also represented the twelve tribes of Israel. In the messianic kingdom, with Jesus as ruler of the restored Israel, the twelve disciples expected to be princes of the twelve tribes. There is nothing like this detail in the Biblical account of Joseph, nor is there any narrative concerning Joseph coming to Potiphar's estate and meeting Aseneth. Again, these details provide the careful reader with clues that more is intended than simply an elaboration on the Biblical Joseph story.

23   High noon is when the Sun god, Helios, is at his highest.

3 Potiphar heard and was joyously happy, saying "Blessed is the God of Joseph, who considered my home worthy of my lord Joseph."[24] **4** Potiphar called the manager of his home and said to him, "Be ready and prepare a great supper[25] in my house, because today Joseph, the Powerful One of God, will come to us."[26]

5 Aseneth heard that her father and mother had come from the village and she rejoiced and said, "Look, my father and mother have come from their estate." **6** Aseneth quickly put on her garments of fine white linen and rubies, clothing woven of gold. She placed bracelets and anklets on her hands and feet, and <wreathed> necklaces on her neck that were (made) of valuable, precious stones and pearls of many colors. On them the names and images of the many gods of the Egyptians were written and engraved on all the sides. **7** She placed a crown on her head and covered herself with bridal veils.[27]

4.

1 Quickly, she descended from her bedchamber and came to her father and mother. She greeted and kissed them. Potiphar and his wife were joyously happy with their daughter. They saw her adorned like a Bride of God.[28] **2** They brought forth all the fruit and various things they had brought with them from

---

24   Potiphar, the pagan priest, is here blessing the God of Israel on account of *my lord* Joseph.

25   It seems Joseph/Jesus is willing to eat food prepared by a non-Jew. This is very significant in terms of Jesus' stance toward the dietary laws.

26   This can also be translated as "the mighty one of God." In any event, compare this to Jesus described as "the Holy one of God" in Mark 1:24.

27   This description foreshadows the marriage. Also, it clearly involves the garments of a priestess, and the "bridal veil" corresponds to Gnosticism generally and to Valentinian Gnosticism in particular.

28   Very quickly the theme of marriage is introduced. First, Aseneth gets dressed as if for a wedding. Then the text uses terminology that no commentary on the Hebrew Bible would use—"Bride of God." This term would be repugnant to Jewish thought. God is one in the Hebrew tradition—he has no spouse, no female counterpart—as the *Shema*—the central tenet of Judaism—says, "Hear, O Israel, the Lord is our God, the Lord is one" (Deuteronomy 6:4).

     But our text is moving away from Judaism. Here, Mary the Magdalene is front and center and we are already told a lot about her: she is a Gentile, beautiful, a virgin, a priestess, the daughter of a priest, and she's about to become the Bride of God incarnate.

the village and gave (them) to Aseneth their daughter. Their daughter rejoiced at these things and was delighted.

3 Potiphar called out to Aseneth, "My daughter." And she replied, "Here I am, my lord." **4** He said to her, "Sit near us and listen to what I shall say to you." **5** Aseneth sat beside the two of them. Potiphar took his daughter Aseneth's right hand, kissed it and said to her, "My daughter." **6** And she answered, "Speak, my lord and father."

7 He said, "Today Joseph, the Man of God, has come to us. He is the magistrate of all the land of Egypt, because king Pharaoh put him in charge over all the land. He is the Savior. He bestows life in crops and food to all the land so that it may not be destroyed in the coming famine. **8** Joseph worships God; he is noble and gentle and a virgin as you are today. Joseph is a man great in wisdom and much knowledge because the Holy Spirit of God is in him and the Lord's grace is with him. **9** Therefore, come, my daughter, and I shall give you to him as a wife and you will be a bride to him. And he will be given to you as a bridegroom forever."[29]

10 When Aseneth heard her father's words, she fell on her face in reverence.[30] In rage and indignation she quarreled with her father, saying, "Why does my lord and father say such words? Would you give me to a man who is a captive

---

29   Notice what is said about Joseph. Clearly he is a stand-in for Jesus. He is called a "Man of God," a "Savior" who "bestows life," who is great in wisdom and in him the "Holy Spirit" resides. He is to be her bridegroom for time eternal. Aseneth, who clearly has a mind of her own, does not yet see the true identity of Joseph. As in Valentinian Gnosticism she—at first—rejects the aeon, or god, chosen for her. Also, in the gospels, Jesus refers to himself as the "bridegroom" in order to defend his disciples from the charge that they are disregarding Mosaic Law, by not fasting on a fast day: "Can you make the guests of the bridegroom fast while he is with them?" (Luke 5:34; see also Mark 2:19 and Matthew 9:15).

30   At this point, later Greek manuscripts have a very different description of events. Instead of Aseneth falling on her face in reverence, the sentence reads: "plenty of red sweat poured over her face" (C. Burchard, translation in James H. Charlesworth, op. cit., 207). This heightens the connection with Jesus, for in Luke 22:44, Jesus, in the Garden of Gethsemane, before his arrest and trial, prays so intensely that "his sweat became like great drops of blood falling down on the ground." Here, Aseneth—like Jesus in the Gospels—sweats blood at the news that she is to become Joseph's (Jesus') bride. We are indebted to David Mirsch, who comments on this linkage in his book *The Open Tomb: Why and How Jesus Faked His Death and Resurrection* (Booklocker, 2011), 192.

and a fugitive? Who was sold and is not one of my people? **11** Is he not the son of a shepherd[31] from Canaan? He was arrested when he attempted adultery with his mistress, and his lord put him in a dark prison. Pharaoh brought him out of the prison to interpret a dream to him like the old women of Egypt. **12** No, my parents, I will not be joined in marriage to this man. Nor will I be denied the firstborn of Pharaoh because he is the ruler and king of all Egypt."[32]

13 Potiphar had a heavy spirit and was afraid about what he might say to Aseneth because of what she had said to him boastfully in impudence.

5.

1 One of the young servants ran to Potiphar and said, "Behold, Joseph has come and he is approaching the entrance." **2** When Aseneth heard about Joseph<'s arrival>, she fled, removing herself from her father and mother. She went up the tower, entered her bedchamber, and stood to the side of the large window facing east so she could look at Joseph as he entered her father's house.[33]

3 Potiphar, his wife, and his entire household went out to meet Joseph. **4** They opened the east gates of the courtyard. Joseph entered, borne on the chariot of Pharaoh's second-in-command. The chariot was yoked with white horses and made entirely of pure gold.[34] **5** And Joseph was clothed in

---

31   So far Jesus has been called *Savior, Man of God*, etc., but not *shepherd* or the *son of a shepherd*. And yet the earliest depictions of Jesus are not on a cross but as the Good Shepherd with a sheep across his shoulders. The image is borrowed from the Phrygian (modern-day Turkey) Attis; the shepherd who fell in love with Cybele, a goddess. Attis' marriage to Cybele ended in tragedy as Attis was emasculated at the wedding feast. And yet, after he dies, he is resurrected. Early Christian commentators called Attis worship a "devilish counterfeit" of Jesus, designed by Satan to confound Christian believers. See Maria Grazia Lancallotti, *Attis: Between Myth and History: King, Priest and God* (Brill, 2002), 142. Clearly, Jesus was associated with Attis in both Orthodox Christianity and here. This may also be a reference to a biological father, the Sidonian Pantera, mentioned in the Talmud and by Celsus (see discussion in chapter 12).

32   The suggestion is that Mary the Magdalene had an initial interest in Germanicus. The attraction was not one-way.

33   Aseneth is in the Migdal, in her *bedroom*, the inner sanctum, facing east in the direction of the rising sun.

34   Later Greek manuscripts say that there were four horses, but the Syriac here lacks that numerical detail. Later, four horses are specified when the angel, i.e., the Joseph look-alike, rides his chariot to heaven (17:6). In any event, the image is clearly Helios as depicted in numerous temples and mithraeums. After a time, this depiction becomes associated with Jesus and no one else.

beautiful white linen and wrapped in a purple cloak woven with gold. On his head was a crown of gold with twelve seals and precious stones.[35] Above the twelve stones were twelve golden rays like the rays of the shining sun. **6** In his left hand he held a royal scepter. In his right hand was a blossoming plant like an olive branch that was rich with olives.[36]

7 When Joseph entered the courtyard, the gates of the courtyard were closed because the guards of the gates diligently closed the gates to keep out strangers. **8** Potiphar, his wife, and their household—all except for Aseneth their daughter—approached and bowed upon the ground to Joseph. Joseph came down from the chariot and stretched out his right hand to them.

6.

1 Aseneth looked at Joseph and lamented greatly, grieving to herself. Her knees shook, and the joints of her hips were loosened, and she became weak and listless. She was very afraid, groaned bitterly, and wept. She said in her heart,

2 "What shall I do, miserable and weak as I am? Because my foreign counselors[37] have deceived me, when they said to me that this Joseph, who has come, is the son of a shepherd of Canaan. Now I see the sun shining from his chariot that has come to us, and its radiance lights up our home. **3** But I, presumptuous

---

35 The twelve stones clearly reflect the twelve tribes of Israel. It would make no sense for the Biblical Joseph to wear these stones in his crown, since the tribes had not yet been established during his tenure in Egypt. At that stage, Joseph was part of a family that had not yet grown into a tribal confederation. In contrast, the Messiah is prophesied to lead the twelve tribes of Israel (Ezekiel 37:16). In other words, the description of Joseph does not fit the Biblical Joseph but the messianic claimant, Jesus of Nazareth (see Revelation 7:7–9 where the "lamb," i.e., Jesus, is at the head of the twelve tribes of Israel who have "seals" on them). For the same reason that the author of *Joseph and Aseneth* places twelve stones and twelve seals in the crown of Joseph, Jesus surrounds himself with twelve disciples, i.e., each representing a tribe of Israel.

36 Joseph enters Potiphar's estate from the east, from the direction of the sun. Notice how he is described—he wears a garment of white and purple; light rays emanate from his crown; he holds a scepter in one hand and an olive branch rich in olives in the other. These important symbols—his garments, light rays, scepter, olive branch—details not found at all in the Biblical account—help us understand who Joseph really represents: he is both god and ruler.

In the Jewish tradition, there is only one prophecy related to the coming of the Messiah in the Torah. It appears in Numbers 24:17: ". . . there shall come a Star out of Jacob, and a Sceptre shall rise out of Israel. . . ." Here Joseph is holding the scepter identifying himself as messiah.

37 Having "foreign counselors" is consistent with Mary the Magdalene's status as a princess and a priestess of Artemis. There's nothing to suggest that the Aseneth of Genesis had foreign counselors.

and stupid, treated him with contempt and spoke of him foolishly because I did not know Joseph was the Son of God.[38]

4 For who among humans shines with such beauty? It is surpassing the splendid appearances of the sons of the earth.[39] And what womb of (human) flesh gives birth to a radiance of light as splendid as this?[40]

I am weak and foolish, and I spoke stupidly to my father. **5** And now where can I go? How can I hide myself from his presence so that Joseph, the Son of God, cannot see me?[41] Where will I flee, since every place is uncovered and spread out visibly before him, because of the light that shines in him? **6** Now have pity on me, Lord God of Joseph,[42] because, like a fool, I spoke in ignorance.

7 Indeed, now let my father give me to Joseph as a wife and I shall serve him forever."[43]

7.

1 Joseph entered the house of Potiphar and sat upon the throne. They washed his feet and prepared before him his own table, for Joseph did not eat with the Egyptians because he abhorred this.[44]

---

38   Again, notice the terminology. It can't get more explicit. Joseph is described here as "the Son of God."

39   Here Aseneth is suggesting that Joseph is more than human. He surpasses human beings. "Son of" phraseology simply denotes that what is being talked about is of the same *kind* as what follows, i.e., *Sons of the earth* is a Semitic expression that simply means *humans*, just as *Son of man* means a *human being*; *Sons of Israel* denotes *Israelites*; and *Son of God* signifies a *divine being.*

40   The implication here is that Joseph is so extraordinary that his birth had to have been something special, not the usual kind of human birth but, rather, one that would befit a divine being. Clearly, by the time of the Gospels of Matthew and Luke in the late 1st century c.e. there were discussions as to the manner of Jesus' birth. They are the first writings to contain a virginal conception and virgin birth narrative, something not mentioned by either Paul or Mark earlier. This holy "womb" discussion places the text just prior to the virgin-birth narrative.

41   Here is another Son of God reference. Joseph is described as all-seeing, as omniscient as God. "How can I hide?" Aseneth asks. She has now discerned that Joseph is no ordinary human being, not merely the son of a Canaanite—something the astute reader of this text would now begin to appreciate through the language and symbolism associated with Joseph. Every place is uncovered and spread out visibly before him, she says. The two main characters described here clearly represent surrogates for two other individuals. By this point, the reader has grasped who they really are and the significance of the wedding that is likely to transpire.

42   She now turns her back on her gods and addresses the "Lord God of Joseph" for the first time.

43   For the first time, she now wants to be his "wife."

2 And Joseph looked at the tower and said, "Remove the young woman who is observing from the window.[45] She gazes impudently." For Joseph was on guard and did not let any woman approach him or have sexual relations with him. **3** Many daughters of princes and rulers were eagerly sent to him. They spoke softly to him so that they might be intimate with him because of the godly beauty that shone splendidly in his appearance. **4** He rejected their envoys and messengers and cast them out angrily because, Joseph said, "I will not sin before the Lord God of my father Israel." **5** He remembered again the teachings of his father Jacob who had commanded him and the rest of his sons: "keep yourselves from foreign women because sexual intercourse with them is destruction and ruin."[46] **6** That is why Joseph said, "Let her leave this house. Send away the young woman who observes from the window of the tower."

7 Potiphar said, "My Lord, the young woman you see in the tower is not a foreign woman but our daughter, a virgin who rejects all men and foreign husbands. No one has ever cleaved to her. No one has seen her except for you today. **8** If you wish she may come to bow and greet your nobility, because our daughter is your sister."[47]

---

44 Joseph now seems to be observing the Jewish dietary laws, a strange detail since the Biblical Joseph predated the giving of Torah to Moses some centuries later. In the Book of Genesis, it's the Egyptians who won't eat with the Hebrews. This provides strong evidence both for the view that this narrative is not about the Biblical Joseph and also for how the community around this document understood Jesus and his Torah-observance. Unlike Paul, who rejected Torah observance (see Galatians 3), this group, like those clustered around the Gospel of Matthew and Jesus' first followers under James in Jerusalem, seems to be ambivalent toward kosher laws. On the one hand, the food is prepared in an un-kosher kitchen; on the other hand, he is separating himself during the meal. This ambivalence parallels the ambiguity in the Gospels with respect to Jesus' commitment to Jewish dietary laws.

45 The woman-in-the-window-motif is a Phoenician priestess/Canaanite motif having to do with Ba'al. See discussion in chapter 9.

46 Again, it is clear that Mary the Magdalene is a "foreign woman" and that, once the obstacles are overcome, "sexual intercourse" is the desired result.

47 Here Potiphar calls Aseneth Joseph's "sister"; in 4:9 above he calls her Joseph's "wife." This is consistent with early Christianity, specifically the Valentinians. One of the earliest Christian funeral poems discovered in Rome, "the Flavia Sophe" inscription, records a husband referring to his wife as "sister, spouse, my Sophe anointed in the baths of Christ." It seems this Sophe was baptized by having "entered the bridal chamber." She then died, but her husband believed that on some level she continued to live: "She perished and she lives, she sees truly incorruptible light. She lives to those who are alive." The inscription was discovered on mile three on the Via Latina, probably within a mile or so of the earliest Christian inscription discussed above. See Gregory Snyder, op. cit., 173–174. See also Peter Lampe, *From Paul to Valentinus* (Fortress Press, 2003), 308. The "sister" description here is consistent with Gnostic texts where a love partner is called a "brother" or "sister," i.e., where sex has risen above lust.

9 Joseph rejoiced very much that Potiphar said she was a virgin. And Joseph thought, "If she is a virgin, she is holy.[48] She rejects all foreign men and will not harass me." **10** Joseph said to Potiphar and his household, "If she is your daughter and a virgin on good evidence, let her come, because she is my kinswoman and I shall embrace her; from this day she is like a sister."[49]

8.

1 Aseneth's mother went up the tower, brought Aseneth (down) and stood her before Joseph. Potiphar said to his daughter Aseneth, "Come near, adore and kiss your brother, because he is a virgin like you today and he rejects foreign women just as you reject foreign men."

2 Aseneth said to Joseph, "Blessed one of God Most High, peace to you." **3** And Joseph said, "May the Lord, bringer of life to all things, bless you."[50]

4 Potiphar said to his daughter, "Approach and kiss your brother."[51] **5** But when Aseneth approached, Joseph extended his right hand and placed it on her chest between her two young breasts.[52] **6** Joseph said, "It is not right for a man worshiping God, who blesses the living God and eats the blessed bread of life and drinks the blessed cup of immortality and incorruptibility and is anointed with the perfumed ointment of holiness, to have sexual relations and kiss a foreign woman, who blesses dead, empty idols, and eats foul strangled food and drinks

---

48   Notice how Aseneth is described. Not only is she eighteen years old and the daughter of a prominent priest, she is also a virgin, someone who has been sheltered by her parents from male contact, nothing less than a Bride-to-be of God and, moreover, she is said to be *holy* (a word missing from later Greek manuscripts). Joseph embraces her as a "kinswoman," someone, as we find out in the next chapter, who will become worthy of intimacy, who is his kin and who worships the living God. Again, there is nothing like this in the Biblical account, where Joseph is clearly an Israelite and Aseneth an Egyptian. Here Joseph has been described in supernatural terms and Aseneth has been singled out as holy—both are fit for each other and both are more than human.

49   The *mystai*, i.e., the initiates of Dionysus—a dying and resurrecting son of god born on December 25—celebrated their mysteries, which involved sexual acts, as "brothers and sisters in spirit." (Marvin W. Meyer, op cit., 9.)

50   Here, Joseph/Jesus is called both a "virgin" and a "brother" and, lest we forget, "blessed one of God Most High."

51   In his letter to the Romans, Paul calls Christians "brothers" and encourages them to "greet one another with a holy kiss" (Romans 16:16).

52   This is Gnostic sex at its most characteristic. On the one hand, Joseph/Jesus pushes Aseneth/Mary the Magdalene away. On the other hand, he does so in a highly erotic way by placing

the libation of deceit and is anointed with the ointment of corruption.[53] **7** But a man who worships God kisses the sister of his mother and a sister of the same tribe and family, and his wife. Intimacy is for those who, like him and his kin,[54] worship the living God."

8 And Joseph added, "Nor is it right for a woman who worships God to kiss a foreign man because this is foul and rejected before the living God."

9 Aseneth heard these words of Joseph and she lamented and grieved greatly. She groaned and gazed at Joseph. When she opened her eyes, she was astounded. And (her eyes) were so full of tears, they could not be seen.[55] **10** Joseph looked at her and saw her (crying) and had mercy on her. Joseph groaned also because he was gentle and innocent and merciful. **11** He worshipped God, lifted up his right hand, placed it upon her head and said,

12 "Lord God Most High of my father Israel,

The mighty one of Jacob

Who gave life to all (things),

The one who called (them) from darkness to light,

From error to truth,

From death to life,

Bless this virgin,

13 Renew her in spirit.

---

his hand "between her two young breasts." The rabbis describe the same scene in the Jerusalem Talmud (*Yebamot* 2:4). While the Gnostics celebrated this kind of push-pull sexuality, the rabbis condemned it. They compare Jesus to a certain "Gehazi," the prophet Elisha's corrupt servant (2 Kings 5:27). They also describe Gehazi's unsuccessful attempt to resurrect a woman's dead child. Again, this seems to be a critique of Jesus. According to the Babylonian Talmud (Sanhedrin 90a, 107b), like Jesus, Gehazi forfeited his place in the world to come. (See Peter Schäfer, *Jesus in the Talmud* [Princeton University Press, 2009], 34.) Since the rabbis are describing a scene straight out of *Joseph and Aseneth*, they must have been aware of this text as early as the 4th century, i.e., some two hundred years before our *Joseph and Aseneth* manuscript was written.

53 Again, note the descriptors of Joseph—he is a person who eats the bread of life, drinks the cup of immortality, and is anointed with the oil of holiness. Aseneth is taken aback because she is not ready yet for intimacy with such a person. She must undergo a divine transformation. See also Lawrence M. Wills who translates the *cup of immortality* as the *cup of resurrection*. (Lawrence M. Wills, *Ancient Jewish Novels*, 130.)

54 Notice that when he rejects her he contrasts her to tribe, family, and kin. Meaning, she's not of the tribe.

55 This connects Aseneth with Mary the Magdalene and the weeping-woman imagery. She is such a crier that you literally can't see her eyes.

Create her again mysteriously[56] by your right hand.

Give her life,

Let her eat the eternal bread of life,

And drink the blessed cup.

14 Let her be counted among your people and your inheritance,

She, who you chose from the beginning.[57]

Let her enter your holy rest

And live forever."[58]

Episode 2: The Rebirth

A strange dream-like sequence involving Aseneth in a tower.

After confessing her sins, she is visited by an angelic being who looks like Joseph.

She eats honey and is swarmed by bees.

9.

1 Aseneth rejoiced greatly in the blessing of Joseph. Immediately, she returned to her tower bedchamber,[59] alone as she was accustomed to. She fell down on her bed, anxious in her spirit and in grief because she was seized by joy, grief, and great

---

56 Note the emphasis on "mystery." Also note that at the time there were several religions called *mystery religions* that involved secret initiations, rituals, and beliefs. They were especially prevalent in the Roman army.

57 In the Greek text, this line appears at 8:14. There, Joseph blesses Aseneth and calls her "she whom you chose *before* she was conceived" (emphasis added). Commenting on this line, Kraemer states, "the notion that Aseneth was chosen by God before her birth clearly puts her into an elite class that includes only male figures . . ." (Kraemer, op. cit., 25). These figures include prophets such as Samuel, Jeremiah, Isaac, and Samson. Once again it's clear that the text cannot be referring to a minor Biblical character such as Aseneth. Clearly, the text is referring to a "daughter of God," a "Bride of God"—an exceptional woman who was chosen in the womb in the way that male prophets such as Isaiah were chosen. Aseneth had no followers. Mary the Magdalene obviously did. Compare John 17:5 where Jesus says, "And now, O Father, glorify me with your own self, with the glory which I had with you *before the world was*" (emphasis added).

58 In this moving prayer, Joseph asks God to transform Aseneth; teach her, prepare her to receive the eternal bread of life and drink from the cup of immortality, to be counted as part of God's people and to receive eternal life. She is to be fashioned by God into one with whom he can share intimacy. And then she will live forever.

59 *The Tower*, that is, *the Migdal* or *the Magdalene*, is the central image of Aseneth in the story and it is often directly connected to the inner sanctum, the holy of holies, that is, her tower bedroom.

fear—trembling with the knowledge of all the words she had heard Joseph say in the name of God Most High. **2** She wept greatly, loud and bitter. She sat up and repented of the worship of the gods whom she had served. She despised and rejected all of them. She loathed and rebuked them. She waited for evening to come.

3 But Joseph ate, drank, and said to his servants along with those who attended to him, "Prepare the chariot and yoke the horses," he said, "for I must leave immediately and go around the land." **4** Potiphar said to Joseph, "Wait, stay with us and rest again." **5** Joseph said, "I must go immediately because it is the first day on which God created everything on the face of the land. But after eight days I shall return to you here and rest."[60]

10.

1 Potiphar said <to> his household, "We, too, will go to our estate."

2 Aseneth remained alone with the seven virgins of her own age. But she was sad and wept until the sun set, not eating bread or drinking water. Night came and everyone in her home fell asleep.[61] In her solitude, she remained awake and attentive, thinking and weeping. She beat her breast and was in fear and trembling.[62] **3** She rose from her bed and, grieving, went down the stairs. She came to the mill, and the grinders and their children were sleeping.[63]

---

60 In all sol-related—that is, sun-related—religions and cults, evening represents the victory of dark over light, while dawn represents Sol Invictus, the all-conquering sun, the *victorious* sun, the *resurrected* sun. The sun is always represented as riding on his horse-drawn chariot, often with rays protruding from his crown. Sunday is the day of the "sun." In Judaism, it is the sixth day, the Sabbath that is celebrated as a holy day—the day on which God ceased from His creation. Here, paradoxically, a Torah reason is given for the shift from a Jewish to a pagan day of worship. Joseph/Jesus is portrayed as a Sun god. He leaves on a Sunday and he returns on a Sunday, but the reason he gives for all this is Judaic: ". . . because it is the first day in which God created everything. . . ." The text is literally written at *the* syncretistic moment when Judeo-Christianity is born.

61 Aseneth—Mary the Magdalene—is constantly associated with weeping, tower, bedroom, virginity, seven attending virgins, and now—as the drama progresses—with nightfall.

62 "Fear and trembling," which is also the title of Sören Kierkegaard's famous work of philosophy, came from Philippians 2:12. It is the hallmark of the Gentile God-fearers who have come to worship the God of the Torah without converting to Judaism.

63 The mill is an image not found in later Greek manuscripts, which refer to a structure near the gate, perhaps a gatehouse. There seems to be a reference here to the story of Ruth, a Moabite (and a princess, according to Jewish tradition) who rejected her gods and began to worship the God of Israel. According to the story, Ruth went to the threshing floor where grain was milled (Ruth 3). There, she met Boaz and, through him, helped establish the messianic line, her son (Obed) being the grandfather of King David. The suggestion may be that Aseneth is, like Ruth, an outsider who is essential to the messianic lineage.

4 She took down the curtain from the window and threw ashes on it. She <went back> up to her bedchamber and put (the curtain) on the floor.[64] **5** She shut the doors securely and also (fastened) the bolt.[65] She sighed greatly, groaning and weeping bitterly.

6 One of the virgins—her companion who was her foster sister and therefore, more than the others, was kin to her—heard the noise and woke up the six other companions. And they came together to the door. **7** They noticed her weeping and (heard) the sound of Aseneth's groans and sighs. They called to her, "Why are you sad, my lady?[66] Open (the door) to us so we might come in and see."[67]

8 But Aseneth did not open to them, saying, "My head hurts and I am in my bed. It is better for me to be alone that I might be in silence with myself and not in conversation. Also, all my limbs are weak and I am not strong enough to

---

64 Curtain imagery is very important in Christianity, especially early Christianity. Recall that in the canonical Gospels it is written that when Jesus was crucified, the curtain of the temple was torn in two, from top to bottom (Matthew 27:51). The curtain separated the people from the Holy of Holies. Taking it down and putting ashes on it is, essentially, an act of mourning for a religious phase that has passed. This may be a literary foreshadowing of the destruction of the Jerusalem Temple predicted by Jesus (Mark 13:1–4). Meaning, the text may have been written after the destruction, but describing events that took place before it. These actions, i.e., taking the curtain down and throwing ashes on it, inaugurate a new stage in the spiritual life of the early Christians.

65 By bolting the door, she alerts the reader that any man who ends up in her bed—who succeeds in entering the bolted room—must be otherworldly. An echo of Jesus' wall-passing prowess can be heard in John 20:26, where he shows himself to his disciples inside a bolted room after the crucifixion.

66 *My lady* or *my mistress* (in English) is *Mara* in the Syriac original, the female equivalent of *my lord* or *my master*. In this connection, it is interesting to note that in the so-called Jesus Family Tomb in Talpiot, Jerusalem, an ossuary was discovered (#80/500) which has inscribed on it, in Greek, "Mariamne [i.e., Mary] also known as Mara." See *The Jesus Family Tomb*, 76, 102, and the photograph of the ossuary on page 109. If *Mariamne* is to be identified with Mary the Magdalene, as the *Acts of Philip* explicitly does, then Mary the Magdalene was called Lord/Master, i.e., Lady/Mistress. See *The Jesus Family Tomb*, chapter 6. It is significant that this is the *only* time in the text that she is addressed by her attendants, i.e., followers, and they call her "Mara," as on the ossuary. This represents quite a coincidence for those who would want to argue against the identification of the "Mara" in the tomb *and* the "Mara" in this text with Mary the Magdalene.

Also, there is a 5th-century Christian codex preserving "dormition" traditions, i.e., traditions that involve the death of the Virgin Mary, that uses the term *Mara*, i.e., the *lady*

rise <and> open. Return immediately to your bedchambers and go to sleep as usual and leave me." They obeyed Aseneth and returned.

9 Afterwards, she rose quietly and entered her bedchamber where her things were lying. She opened a chest and brought out a black mourning garment which was hers from (the time) when her little brother died.[68] **10** She took the garment of mourning and closed the door securely.[69]

11 Aseneth promptly took off the garments of her joy and her virginity[70] and removed the ornaments from her. She loosened the gold chain from her hips. The crown of gold she took from her head. She removed the bracelets and anklets. **12** She gathered them together and threw them out the window, which faced north.

13 All the gods, idols, engravings, and images she let fall from where she had them set up and threw them from her window.

---

to describe Mary. As in *Joseph and Aseneth*, Jesus is represented as a Great Angel. As in *Joseph and Aseneth*, he is talking to someone called *My Lady Mary*. In this tradition the *Mara* is identified with Jesus' mother, instead of his wife. By this point in the evolution of Christianity, the substitution is complete. See Stephen J. Shoemaker, *Ancient Traditions*, op. cit., 194.

Artemis too was called "lady." Homer referred to her as *Potniatheron*, i.e., "lady" or "mistress." See Homer, *The Iliad*, XXI.470.

67 It is significant that the seven priestesses want to be part of this process—"open the door to us so we might come in and see"—but Aseneth keeps the door closed. Somehow these seven would obstruct the transformation. Again, this seems strangely consistent with the seven "daemons" that Jesus reportedly drove out from Mary the Magdalene.

68 In the Latin tradition, Mary of Bethany is identified with Mary the Magdalene. She's also identified with a woman in John 11:1–2 whose brother Lazarus dies and is raised by Jesus. Interestingly (another synchronicity), in our text too, Mary the Magdalene's brother dies. Here he is not raised from the dead. In *Secret Mark*, Jesus spends the night with Lazarus teaching him "the mystery of the kingdom of God" (Smith, op. cit., 15–16). In *Joseph and Aseneth*, Jesus takes the dead boy's sister for a wife.

69 Again, the door is closed securely. She must go through a process of mourning alone, prior to becoming the Bride of God.

70 She is setting aside her theologically based virginity. She is literally sacrificing it on the altar of her new god. Significantly, she does not set it aside for the God of Israel until, as the text says, she meets the "Son of God." With respect to her virginity, Kraemer hints at possible allusions to Mary (op. cit., 296), but she does not say which Mary. Clearly, it cannot be the mom, given that later the text explicitly has Aseneth having intercourse with Joseph (21:10). Is Kraemer hinting at Mary the Magdalene?

14 And the sacrifice and the libation from their altar, and all the food for their preparation she also hurled from her window, throwing them down to the wild dogs to eat because, she said in her heart, "It is better not to give this unclean food to dogs of the house to eat, but to wild dogs."[71]

15 Afterwards she lifted the ashes from the curtain and threw them on the floor of her bedchamber. She put sackcloth on her hips and loosened the braids in her hair. She sprinkled and spread out the ashes. **16** She beat her breasts with her hands and wept bitterly, throwing the ashes onto the floor of her home all night. **17** Morning appeared and behold, mud had formed from the multitude of tears from her eyes in the great weeping she had done. **18** And again she lay on the ashes until evening. **19** This Aseneth did for seven days. She ate no bread and drank no water those seven days of penance and suffering of the soul and her humiliation.

11.

1 At the dawn of the eighth day, she heard the sound of the birds of heaven and dogs barking at those passing by (on) the road. Aseneth raised her head from the ashes because she was weak and weary from her remorseful penance, fasting, and abstinence. **2** After (performing) the blessing on her knees, she rose and lifted her eyes up to heaven. She shook off the ashes from her hair, still crying and beating her chest. **3** She went to the window facing east and sat and lowered her head on to her knees. Her mouth was closed out of abstinence, having had little to eat in seven days of suffering.

With her mouth still closed after seven days, she said in her heart:[72]

---

71   Throwing the idols and all the equipment connected with idolatrous worship to the dogs is a clear reference to Jezebel. Jezebel, like Mary the Magdalene, is a Phoenician queen. She was married to Ahab, a King of Israel. Jezebel and her husband encouraged idol worship. In that story, he followed her in her idolatrous ways. Eventually, Hebrew monotheists threw her out the window of her tower to the dogs below. The story ends with the dogs consuming her (2 Kings 9:36). In the Book of Revelation, Jezebel is the personification of the church in Thyatira which engaged in fornication (often a metaphor for apostasy) and which permitted the eating of food sacrificed to idols (Revelation 2:19–29). At the Jerusalem Council, James banned the eating of food sacrificed to idols (Acts 15:29). Paul, however, permitted his followers to consume such food (1 Corinthians 8:1–13). Perhaps all this is alluded to here.

       In our text, Aseneth explicitly puts away pagan practices. She is the anti-Jezebel. In 2 Kings, Jezebel is thrown out the window to the dogs; here it is the idols that go out the tower window to the dogs. In 2 Kings, Jezebel led a king of Israel into apostasy. Here, a king of the Jews leads Mary the Magdalene into monotheism.

72   This prayer takes us into Aseneth's/Mary the Magdalene's innermost thoughts as she sums up her situation and rejects the gods of idolatry. At first she does not have the courage

4 "What shall I do?

Where shall I go?

To whom shall I flee?

And what shall I say?

I, a virgin and an orphan, abandoned and desolate,

5 Everyone despises and hates me,

(even) my father and mother,[73]

(because) now I hate the gods. I rejected, destroyed, and removed (them)

so that they might be trampled by the feet of man.

6 My mother, father, and my family said, 'Aseneth is not our daughter,

for she destroyed the gods and rejected them.'[74]

And the rest of men, the ones I rejected who desired me, hate me.[75]

They will rejoice on account of my humiliation.

7 But the Lord God Most High and Powerful of the wise Joseph

hates those who worship empty idols

because He is a jealous and frightening God

to those who worship foreign gods made by the hands of man.

8 Because I too am defiled—I worshipped and poured libations to them,

and served and ate from their sacrifices,

I do not have the confidence, my Lord, to call on the Lord God Most High

of Heaven.

9 But because I heard the God of the Hebrews is a true God,

merciful and compassionate, long-suffering, with great grace and truth,

---

to call upon the Lord Most High. But remembering that he is a forgiving, merciful God, she summons her strength and finally in verse 17 she "invokes the Holy Name of God the merciful." The metaphors are many. For example, the dogs barking remind the reader of the day after the Biblical Exodus, since the Torah tells us that no dogs barked during the Exodus (Exodus 11:7). Furthermore, the praying on one's knees establishes Christian worship in that position very early on, as is also evidenced in the kneeling altar in front of a cross found in Herculaneum, dated by its destruction in the eruption of Vesuvius no later than 79 C.E.

73 It's interesting that Aseneth knows she risks parental rejection because of her abandonment of her deities; hence she is not only a virgin but also a possible orphan.

74 Aseneth/Mary the Magdalene is quoting an initial rejection by her parents that is not depicted here.

75 This may refer to Germanicus who seemed to covet her and to whose advances she was initially open. It may be that Germanicus became aware of Jesus only after Mary the Magdalene turned her attention to him.

10 and (because) He forgives sins and is incorruptible, and abundantly turns away His anger,

and does not awaken all of His rage in the time when people—humiliated—call to Him,[76]

11 I venture to turn to Him

and take refuge with Him[77]

and confess my sins and my transgressions to Him.

12 And in prayer I will approach Him

so perhaps, seeing the humiliation of His servant,

He will have mercy on me

13 because He is the father of orphans

and protector of the weak,

and savior of the poor.[78]

14 I will speak and call out to Him."

15 Aseneth rose to the eastern window and she lifted up her hands to Heaven. But she was afraid to open her mouth and speak to God Most High and remember His holy name and call out. Again she repented. She sat to the side of the east window, and was striking her face. Beating her chest with her hands, she said in her heart without opening her mouth:

16 "I am weak, an orphan and lonely.

My mouth is defiled from the sacrifices

and the emptiness of the gods of the Egyptians, my people.[79]

17 And now in these tears of mine and in the ashes and dust of my own humiliation

---

76 This is reminiscent of the description of the attributes of God outlined in Exodus 34:6,7—"Lord, Lord, a God merciful and gracious, slow to anger and abounding in steadfast love and faithfulness, keeping steadfast love for the thousandth generation, forgiving iniquity and transgression and sin."

77 God is her refuge and she is the "refuge" to the nations.

78 As in the Gospels, the message is initially directed to the outcasts: "orphans . . . weak . . . poor."

79 This follows the Greek text. In the Syriac, *sacrifices* is singular and the blessings of the gods are called *emptiness*.

80 God is not only a forgiver, but also a healer.

on account of my sin offerings <and> the penance I made,

I venture to open my mouth and invoke the Holy Name of God the merciful.

18 And if the Lord becomes angry with me, He will chastise me today.

And He will take hold of me,

and if He strikes me, He will heal me again."[80]

12.

1 And she gazed up at Heaven and then, opening her mouth, she said,[81]

2 "Lord God of the ages and their Creator, and (the one who) gave life, who shone light on and brought forth everything invisible[82]

who created the entire world from nothing

3 who lifted up Heaven

and set again its foundations on the back of the wind

and founded the land upon the waters,

4 who set great stones on the abyss of water

and the stones did not sink

but they were carried like leaves.

5 They are living stones

and they obey you, Lord,

and keep your commandments

and do not transgress

because you spoke, Lord, and by your word[83] everything comes to life and exists.

---

81 Here Aseneth prays out loud. She asks for forgiveness for not knowing the true God and for thinking poorly of Joseph, not realizing that he was "God's son." She asks for protection from vengeful Egyptian deities. She thinks of God as a father who lovingly embraces his children. She concludes by beseeching God to grant her eternal life. There are no such prayers of Aseneth in the Biblical account.

82 The emphasis is on the hidden.

83 Cf. John 1:1 ("In the beginning was the Word, and the Word was with God, and the Word was God. He was in the beginning with God. All things came into being through Him, and without Him not one thing came into being."). See also Genesis 1, where God speaks and what he says is brought into being.

6 With you I will take refuge

and, calling out wailing,[84]

I will pour out <my prayer> before you

and confess my sins and transgressions.

7 Pity me, Lord,

who has sinned so much against you

and I have done evil things before you,

I have angered <you> and done wickedness

and spoke evil things that are not right to speak.

8 My mouth is unclean and <polluted> from the sacrifices to idols and the libations for the gods of the Egyptians

which I committed in my error.[85]

And I served and worshipped them.

I am not worthy to open my mouth to you, Lord.

9 I, Aseneth, the daughter of Potiphar the priest,

who, for some time, has been honored as a virgin and queen,

proud and prosperous surpassing all women.[86]

But now I am an orphan and desolated and abandoned by all the people.

10 I take refuge with you

---

84 According to the *Exegesis on the Soul*, another Nag Hammadi Gnostic document, the soul prostitutes herself with many lovers, experiences remorse, and "weeps before the Father." At this point she repents and "is immediately cleansed of the external pollution which was pressed upon it . . . that is her baptism." Having been so cleansed, she yearns for her true love: "from heaven the Father sent her [a] man who is her brother, the firstborn. Then the bridegroom came to the bride . . . she cleansed herself in the bridal chamber . . . she sat in waiting for the true bridegroom . . . but then the bridegroom, according to the Father's will, came down into her bridal chamber, which was prepared." (*Exegesis on the Soul* 131.27–132.26, quoted in Gregory Snyder, "A Second-Century Christian Inscription from the Via Latina," *Journal of Early Christian Studies*, Volume 19, Number 2 [Summer 2011]: 182–183.) Clearly, this is a perfect parallel to Aseneth's weeping, repentance, and preparation for her marriage with the heavenly "bridegroom."

85 Luke describes Mary the Magdalene as a person "from whom seven demons had gone out" (Luke 8:2). Perhaps this represents an oblique reference to her putting away her worship of foreign gods and goddesses. For this she is forgiven—and healed—by God.

86 Again, notice the descriptions of Aseneth: virgin, queen, proud, prosperous. She is a wealthy, royal figure. Mary the Magdalene, too, was wealthy. She, along with several other women (the former daemons?) underwrote the mission of Jesus and his followers (the twelve disciples; the seventy ambassadors; and others) over a three-year period—not an inconsiderable sum (Luke 8:2,3).

and I call out to you.

Save me before I am captured by my persecutors;[87]

11 like a little child who is terrified and flees to his father,

who stretches out his hands and receives him

and lifts him up from the ground

and embraces him at his breast.

And the child puts a hand on his father's neck,

and takes hold of his strength and is relieved from his fear

and rests on him.

But his father rejoices at the impetuosity of his son's childhood.[88]

12 And therefore you, Lord, stretch out your hands

and lift me up from the ground

because, behold, a wild animal, an old lion, persecutes me

because he is the father of the gods of Egypt.[89]

13 And now I hate the idols

because they are his children,

and I have thrown them all away and destroyed and removed them from me.

And indeed he is angry at me and persecutes me.

14 Save me from his hands, Lord.

---

87 A veiled reference to enemies; Germanicus' allies? Her former Canaanite/Phoenician followers?

88 In Gnosticism, the enhanced female is "like a man" (spiritually that is). Here, the daughter is compared to "the boy," i.e., to a son.

89 Who is this "old lion," the one who represents "the father of the gods?" There are several possibilities. One possibility is that the lion is Satan. The devil—or adversary—is described in 1 Peter 5:8 as a roaring lion who roams the earth, seeking someone to devour. In this case, the lion represents the spiritual force of deception, the one who stands behind false religion. It is so used in Revelation 2:9–11 describing "the synagogue of Satan"—specifically citing those groups who say that they are Jews and are not. Note, however, that Satan is not described as an "old" lion.

 Another possibility is that this phrase refers to an historical figure, an aging ruler or emperor. Given the references to "persecutors" above, it is unlikely that these are metaphors. They seem to be a cabal of people surrounding Germanicus. If that is the case, the "old lion" represents the Emperor Tiberius, under whose reign Jesus and Mary the Magdalene lived. As emperor, Tiberius represented the head of the Imperial Cult. He was literally "the father of the gods" of Rome, the sponsor of pagan religion in the empire. Also, Tiberius' nickname was *the lion*. When he died, it was said that "the lion is dead" (Josephus, *Antiquities*, Book 18, section 10).

And pull me from between his teeth.

And let him not snatch me again[90]

and corrupt me

and cast me into the flame of fire,

where I will sink again into the flame and be shrouded in darkness.

15 And, hurled into Sheol,[91]

I will descend to the bottom of the pit

and the dragon[92] of old will swallow me forever,

destroying me eternally.

16 No, save me, Lord

before all of this comes to me.

Save me, Lord,

the desolate one,

because my father and mother abandoned me[93]

and renounced me for rejecting the gods.

17 Today I am an orphan and miserable.

You alone are my hope, Lord,

father of orphans,

comforter of the weak,

and savior of the persecuted.

18 Have mercy on me, Lord,

an orphan, miserable, and abandoned

because you are a good father and kind.

19 And, again, who is equal to you and approaches your mercy like you?

---

90 Had Tiberius snatched and corrupted her before? Is that how Germanicus knew of her?

91 The Hebrew term for what Christians would later call "hell," that is, the netherworld.

92 This is significant. The Book of Jonah states that Jonah was swallowed by "a large fish" (Jonah 1:17), usually identified with a whale. In the Gospels, Jesus talks of the "Sign of Jonah"—"For just as Jonah was three days and three nights in the belly of the sea monster, so for three days and three nights the Son of Man will be in the heart of the earth" (Matthew 12:40). Early Christians in the catacombs of Rome depicted Jesus' resurrection as Jonah emerging alive from the belly of a dragon, not a fish. In other words, here Aseneth/Mary the Magdalene is making an explicit early Christian analogy stating that

And indeed who in your image is long-suffering and merciful?

20 For, behold, all the gifts of my father, Potiphar,

given to me as an inheritance, are empty and transient;

for a gift of your inheritance, Lord, is eternal and incorruptible."

13.

1 "I turn to you in my desolation, Lord.

Have mercy on me.

See my wickedness and naïveté, Lord,

<and> have pity on me,

because I departed from everything

and took refuge with you.

2 All earthly things I left

and fled to you.

And in sackcloth and ashes—

abandoned and stripped of royal power[94]

as well as the beauty of my <colorful> and varied adornment—

I put on a black mourning garment

without my splendid, beautiful ornaments.

3 I prepared my bedchambers,[95]

and the crown on my head and chain of gold on my hips

(I set) on the floor.

In the ashes I prostrated myself

and covered myself with sackcloth.

4 My mouth longed for delicacies and food

---

if the lord rejects her, she will lose life-everlasting and the primordial "dragon" will swallow her "forever."

93   In the Book of Genesis, Aseneth's parents do not abandon her. Or, at least, no mention is made of such a thing. In *Joseph and Aseneth*, there is no mention of Aseneth being "abandoned" by her parents. Quite the contrary, they are very supportive. Here we seem to have a biographical insight into the reaction of Mary the Magdalene's Phoenician parents when she abandoned her deities and followed Jesus.

94   Again, a hint that we are talking about someone—unlike the Biblical Aseneth—who is of royalty.

95   Once again, the Gnostic theme of sacrificed virginity in the bridal chamber.

and yet I fasted, enduring seven days

and I refrained from the food.

5 And also the ashes became mud from my tears

like a broad street.

I gave my supper of all things to the wild dogs.[96]

6 And behold, for seven days and seven nights

I did not eat bread nor drink water

until my tongue cleaved to my throat,

and my mouth smelled like a tomb,[97]

and my lips dried up like a potsherd,

and the appearance of my face was changed,

and my eyes grew weak from crying,

and my strength withdrew from me.

7 And the gods for whom I labored before in ignorance,

I rejected and threw away,

allowing them to be trampled by men and snatched away.

And I left the objects of gold and silver

and removed them from before my face.

8 And to you, Lord my God, I have fled.

But you, save me,

because in error I sinned against you,

---

96   She's given up eating animals sacrificed to idols, as per James' instruction in Acts 21:25.

97   Clearly this is a significant but ambiguous statement. Smelling like a tomb is an appropriate metaphor in 1st-century Jerusalem because that's when secondary burial—the type described in the canonical Gospels involving the burial of Jesus—i.e., washing, shrouding, laying out in a tomb (rather than in the ground)—was in vogue in the city. This practice involved placing bodies in burial caves and reinterring them after the flesh had decomposed. Mary the Magdalene is the first to report the missing body of Jesus when she goes to the tomb he was buried in. People practicing this type of "secondary burial" would enter these tombs, where there were shrouded cadavers in various stages of decomposition. "My mouth smelled like a tomb," therefore, is a very strong attack on her previous words and beliefs. It also shows her familiarity with secondary burial, a practice limited to Jerusalem and the Galilee between 30 B.C.E. and 70 C.E., when Jerusalem was destroyed by the Romans. This, too, speaks to an early date for our manuscript.

98   As this passage makes very clear, she now recognizes that Joseph/Jesus is God's "son," not the son of a shepherd from Canaan. Along with her personal transformation, Aseneth has undergone a process of insight—what Gnostic Christians called *gnosis*. The reference to Joseph/Jesus as the son of a Canaanite is also very significant.

99   A reference to Jesus' divine origin.

I, a virgin, a stray and a child,

9 who said evil, empty things against my lord Joseph

because I did not know he was your son.[98]

My people told me

that he was the son of a shepherd from Canaan.

10 And I believed them

and fell into error

and treated him with contempt.

11 For who among humans will give birth to such grace,[99]

wisdom, virtue, and strength?

Lord, I commit him to you, because I love him above myself.

12 Preserve him in the wisdom . . .[100]

. . . of your grace

and entrust me to him for a slave-girl,

that I will wash his feet[101]

and I will serve him

and be a slave to him forever."[102]

14.

1 When Aseneth stopped confessing to the Lord, behold, the morning star rose out of heaven to the east.[103] **2** Aseneth saw it and rejoiced and said,

---

100 Pages corresponding to chapters 13:12 to 16:3 are missing from the Syriac manuscript. This section has been translated from later Greek manuscripts.

101 Echo of the famous Gospel scene where an unnamed woman, usually identified with Mary the Magdalene, washes Jesus' feet and then dries them with her hair.

102 While Aseneth has turned away from the worship of pagan deities and embraced the worship of the one true God, she has not converted to any religion, e.g., to Judaism or, for that matter, to Christianity. There is no undertaking of Torah observance (Judaism) nor is there a Baptism (Christianity). Aseneth is like the God-fearers, a Gentile who worships God but who does not assume the obligations of Torah.

103 Likely a reference to the "Star prophecy" in Numbers—"a star shall come out of Jacob . . ." (Numbers 24:17), an event that heralds the advent or arrival of the Messiah. The star of Bethlehem narrative is based on this prophecy, i.e., according to the gospel of Matthew (2:9), a star heralded the birth of Jesus. In Matthew, the star is seen "in the east"; here too it is referred to as a "morning star," i.e., it is seen in the east. This goes together with the references to the scepter that Joseph is carrying when he first appears on the scene (5:6), to the scepter that the angelic version of Joseph carries (14:8 and 16:27), and to the scepter that Aseneth takes in her hand prior to marrying Joseph. Altogether, they are meant to fulfill the prophecy of Numbers 24:17. See especially 18:8 where Mary the Magdalene is holding the scepter, i.e., she is a partner in messiahship.

"So the Lord God listened to me, because this star is a messenger and a herald of the light of the great day."

3 And behold, near the morning star, heaven was torn apart[104] and an ineffable light shone. **4** Aseneth fell upon her face on the ashes.

A man from heaven[105] came to her and stood over her head. He called to her, "Aseneth." **5** And she said, "Who calls me? Because the door of my chamber is shut and the tower is high. How is it possible for him to have come into my chamber?"[106]

6 And the man called to her a second time and said, "Aseneth, Aseneth." And she said, "Here I am, Lord. Tell me who you are."[107] **7** The man said, "I am a commander of the house of the Lord and commander-in-chief of all the army of the Most High. Stand on your feet and I shall speak to you."

8 She raised her eyes, looked and beheld a man alike in every respect to

---

104   The "heaven was torn apart" line that is here associated with Aseneth (Mary the Magdalene), seems to be echoing the same kind of event in the canonical Gospels. There it is associated with Jesus' transformation when he is baptized by his cousin, John the Baptizer: "And just as he was coming up out of the water, he saw the heaven torn apart . . ." (Mark 1:9). After the "heaven was torn apart," both Jesus and Mary the Magdalene are ready to assume their metaphysical duties.

105   Compare this to Jesus' appearances in the form of an angel to the Virgin Mary in the Gnostic texts, e.g., "One day sometime after the Savior's ascension, a Great Angel, the Great Cherub of Light, appears to Mary and hands her a book of 'mysteries,' containing all the secrets of creation . . . the Great Angel discloses that he is in fact the Savior himself." (Stephen J. Shoemaker, op. cit., in Jones, 5.) Shoemaker's description is a summary from the *Liber Requiei*, an early account of Mary's departure from this world. Originally, before she was replaced by Jesus' mother, this idea might have referred to Mary the Magdalene.
    Compare also with the Enoch tradition that gives rise to apocalyptic movements such as the Jesus movement. In the so-called *Similitudes* or *Parables of Enoch* (1 *En*. 37–71), dated by most scholars to the late 1st century B.C.E. or even to early 1st century C.E. Judaea, i.e., the time of Jesus' "ministry," Enoch has a vision of a Son of Man or Elect One whose "face was full of graciousness, like one of the angels." The language in *Joseph and Aseneth* can be easily described as Enochite. This is one more indication that we are looking at one of the earliest—if not the earliest—gospels, one that still preserves its Enochite, pre-Gnostic origins.

106   Again, the emphasis is on shut or bolted rooms, as evidence that the man she is about to have sex with is the heavenly avatar of Joseph/Jesus. This man, like Jesus (John 20:19 and 20:26), is able to pass through locked doors.

107   Aseneth (Mary the Magdalene) is addressed like a prophet, most notably Abraham, i.e., the call of her name and her response. See Genesis 22:1 for a comparison.

108   This angel looks like Joseph (Jesus) in "every respect." Historically speaking, let's not forget that one of Jesus' disciples was called Thomas, in Hebrew *the twin*. According to Islam, it was

Joseph[108] in clothes and crown and royal scepter,[109] **9** but his face was like lightning, and his eyes like the splendor of the sun, and the hair of his head like a flame of fire, and his hands and feet like inflamed iron. **10** Aseneth saw and fell upon her face at his feet in great fear and trembling.

11 The (heavenly) man said to her, "Take courage, Aseneth, and do not fear, but stand upon your feet and I shall speak to you." **12** Aseneth stood, and the man said to her, "Take off the black garment which you have put on, (remove) the sackcloth from your hips, shake off the ashes from your head, and wash your face with living water. **13** Put on a new, untouched robe and gird your hips with the splendid double belt of your virginity. **14** And again come to me and I shall speak to you the words that I have been sent to (tell) you."

15 Aseneth went into her chamber[110] where the chests (containing) her

---

this man who looked like Jesus in every respect who was crucified instead of Jesus (Qur'an 4:157). Whoever Mary the Magdalene sees, the fact that she believes that he is an angelic version of Jesus is consistent with what we know of Jesus' followers at the time. The pagan writer Celsus states that Jesus was ranked by his followers among the angels. (See Morton Smith, op. cit., 60 and 66.) Also, this was not unique to Jesus. The *angelification* of Enoch is reported in Jewish works of about Jesus' time. In the pagan world, too, some began to regard their gods not as deities but as "angels" (ibid., 121). Interestingly, in the name of God, Aseneth/Mary the Magdalene gives up her pagan gods by throwing them out her tower's window. Almost immediately, through the same window, the man from heaven appears. In other words, this former pagan priestess can only really relate to an invisible God via an all-too-visible man. What we see here is what Smith calls, in reference to the earliest layer of gospel material, a "combination of theoretical monotheism with practical polytheism" (op. cit., 126).

109 The heavenly man is a Joseph look-alike in terms of his clothing, crown, and royal scepter, but his face, eyes, hair, hands, and feet are resplendent in light. These are Messianic terms. The Star and Scepter prophecy in Numbers (24:17) references a scepter, right after the star—"a star shall come out of Jacob, and a scepter shall rise out of Israel."

110 After the Virgin Mary takes the place of Mary the Magdalene in the Christian tradition, this exact scene finds its way into the earliest Greek Dormition narrative by St. John the Theologian. In this text, as the Virgin Mary was about to die, she went "into her secret, inner room." Here, she "undressed, she took water and washed and she put on different garments while blessing." Clearly, this is not a woman who is preparing herself for death. Clearly, this is a perfect parallel to the above scene in *Joseph and Aseneth*. In the narrative of St. John the Theologian, after Mary washes and puts on her finery, she says to an "angel" who "became as light" and "ascended into the heavens," "I bless you because you gave me a measure of virility for the parts of your body, and [because] I had been found worthy of the kiss of your bridal chamber" (Shoemaker, *Ancient Traditions*, op. cit., 356–357). Unless the Virgin was having sex with the angelic aspect of her son, this is referring to Mary the Magdalene speaking in Valentinian language to her bridegroom Jesus.

garments and accessories[111] were (located), and opened her box. She took out the fine new clothes, removed the black clothes, and put on new and splendid ones. **16** She loosened the rope and sackcloth from her waist and put on the splendid double belt of her virginity—one belt about her waist and one upon her breast. **17** And she shook off the ashes from her head and washed her face with pure water and covered her head with a beautiful and splendid veil.[112]

15.

1 And she came near the (heavenly) man.[113] Seeing her, the man said to her,

---

111 Literally, chests of her adornment. Interestingly, though she seems to be going into a different room, she doesn't seem to be hiding from the heavenly man as she undresses and dresses.

112 Aseneth has now shed her old self, symbolized by her old clothing, and adorned herself with a new dress, symbolic of her new life. Being re-clothed is a common image in the latter chapters of the book of the Hebrew prophet Isaiah, indicating the transformation of the people of Israel, e.g., "for he [God] has clothed me with the garments of salvation, he has covered me with the robe of righteousness, as a bridegroom decks himself with a garland, and as a bride adorns herself with her jewels" (Isaiah 61:10). It is also prevalent in Gnostic Christianity as a symbol for personal transformation—new clothing represents "the garments of life," as the *Dialogue of the Savior* puts it (19:11). Aseneth has repented and confessed her sins and is now ready for the next step: marriage. But here we encounter a surprise. As we are about to see in chapter 16, there is a heavenly marriage prior to the earthly one. And, being born again, so to speak, Aseneth is renamed "City of Refuge."

113 Notice that she is not afraid of him. After she made herself beautiful, she "came near to the (heavenly) man."

114 Removal of the veil implies both intimacy and marriage.

115 This line—"Like that of a young man"—is very revealing. Women becoming like men—that is, fully human—represents a common theme in Gnostic Christianity. In *The Gospel of Mary Magdalene*, for instance, Mary says to the grieving disciples that Jesus has prepared them all for their mission, i.e., to go among nonbelievers so as to announce the Gospel of the Kingdom. She adds that Jesus turned them all into men, that is, that Jesus has made all of them fully human. In fact, as chief of the apostles, Mary the Magdalene has herself become fully human and is no longer singularly gendered. In *The Gospel of Thomas* (saying 114), for example, Jesus responds to Peter, who was critical of Mary the Magdalene, saying, "I shall guide her to make her male, so that she too may become a living spirit resembling you males. For every female who makes herself male, will enter Heaven's Kingdom."

116 Here, Kraemer points out the differences between the short and long Greek versions of the text. Sometimes these are subtle but quite significant. In the short version, Aseneth is described as a "holy virgin" at this point. This is absent in the Syriac text. It seems that the redactor of the Greek version knows that Aseneth is a stand-in for Mary the Magdalene and ascribes to her, not to the mother, the title of holy virgin. (See Kraemer, op. cit., 60.)

"Remove the veil from your head,[114] for today you are a chaste virgin and your head is like that of a young man."[115] **2** And she removed it from her head. The man said to her, "Take courage, Aseneth. For behold, the Lord heard the words of your confession.

3 Take courage,[116] Aseneth. Behold, your name[117] was written in the Book of Life.[118] You will be renewed, reformed, and revivified. You will eat the bread of life, drink the cup of immortality, and be anointed with the ointment of incorruptibility.[119]

4 Take courage, Aseneth. Behold, the Lord gave you to Joseph as a bride

---

117 By stating that Aseneth's (Mary the Magdalene's) name is written in the Book of Life, a comparison is being made between Mary the Magdalene and God, whose name is unutterable. It seems that it was precisely this elevation of humans to divinity status—by using divine names to refer to humans—that upset the Jews of Judaea during the activism of Jesus and Mary the Magdalene. It seems that not only did Jesus heal in his own and/or God's name, but that others healed by substituting Jesus' name for God's name (see Mark 9:38). Clearly, the people were not upset with the healing; they were scandalized by references to *the* Name.

118 This is reminiscent of the *Apocalypse of Zephaniah* which most probably dates to the end of the 1st century C.E. Like *Joseph and Aseneth*, it is a syncretic Jewish/Christian work. In it, in the afterlife, "a great angel" announces to Zephaniah, "you will now cross over the crossing place. For your name is written in the Book of the Living" (9:2). Quoted in Peter Schafer, *The Origins of Jewish Mysticism* (Princeton University Press, 2009), 102. Also, in the famous War Scroll from Qumran, the holy ones "are listed with God and his angels in the Book of Life" (Schafer, ibid., 120. See 1QM, XII, 1–5).

119 The *Apocalypse of Peter*, a Gnostic work, refers to "those companions" who achieve redemption by means of "the wedding of incorruptibility" (*Apocalypse of Peter*, 79.3–7). Also, this is reminiscent of the fact that some opponents of Jesus negatively compared his feeding of four or five thousand to Moses who fed all the Israelites in the wilderness. As a result, John (6:26–58) gave up on numerical superiority: "made the feeding a symbol of the Eucharist, and argued that Jesus was greater because the bread he gave was not corruptible, but was the bread of life, his own body" (Morton Smith, op. cit., 161). All this perfectly mirrors the language above.
    It is interesting to note that John the Baptizer sustained himself on a diet of locusts and honey, the latter representing "incorruptibility" and "immortality," i.e., the two terms employed above. There is a sepulchral inscription that talks about the deceased as being in a "sweet sleep" and "lying in honey," i.e., honey is associated with incorruptibility. See Jane Harrison, *Prolegomena to the Study of Greek Religion* (New York: Meridian Books, 1960), 595. Finally, Kraemer states that the ointment referred to in the text may be "associated with sexuality and marriage" (Ibid., 74).

and he will be your bridegroom.[120] **5** No longer will you be called Aseneth, but your name will be 'City of Refuge,'[121] for with you all the nations will take refuge and many people will be sheltered under your wing, and in your wall will be kept safe the ones attached to God through repentance.[122] **6** For Repentance is the Daughter of God Most High[123] and intercedes with the Most High on your behalf at all times and on behalf of all those who repent, for he is the father of Repentance. **7** She is the mother of the virgins[124] and beseeches him at all times about the ones who repent, for she has prepared a heavenly bridal chamber[125] for those who love her, and she will serve them forever. **8** And Repentance is very good—a chaste virgin, holy and gentle. God Most High[126] loves her and all the angels respect her.

---

120 As this "annunciation" to Aseneth makes clear, this is a marriage made in heaven, not an earthly one arranged by her father and the Pharaoh. It is the Lord God who gives Aseneth to Joseph. There is no such episode in the Biblical account of Joseph and Aseneth, but it is clearly consistent with Jesus and Mary the Magdalene. Interestingly, using Joseph and Aseneth as a cipher, we can now see how echoes of this marriage have been preserved in various Christian texts. For example, in the Ethiopic *Liber Requiei*, the earliest surviving narrative of the Virgin Mary's death, Peter says to the Virgin, as she lies on her deathbed, ". . . you will enter into marriage and moreover you will enter and rest with the bridegroom." Clearly, this would be an odd thing to say to Jesus' mother, i.e., that she's about to marry her son. What we have here is language that perfectly mirrors the language of *Joseph and Aseneth*. It is a leftover fragment referring to the wife, not the mother. See Shoemaker, *Ancient Traditions*, op. cit., 321.

121 *Migdals* or towers, part of temple precincts, were places of refuge. Here we have a reference that can be understood as an allusion to Mary the Magdalene's name. In other words, the text literally tells us that once its esoteric meaning is understood, Aseneth "will no longer . . . be called Aseneth," but Magdala, i.e., City of Refuge. Kraemer also senses that behind this designation is a Jesus-related woman. The "female figure who comes to mind as efficacious intermediary between the heavenly and the divine is Mary, the mother of Jesus" (Kraemer, op. cit., 154). What this text makes clear, however, is that the designation "virgin" and the role of heavenly intermediary originally belonged to the bride, not the mother.

122 She is the refuge of a specific group of people—not Jews, nor Gentiles—they are "the ones attached to God through repentance," namely, the Gentile God-fearers. More than this, here we have a key name change. Meaning, it is not just us who argue that behind the name "Aseneth" there is another person—the text itself argues this. As part of the renaming of Aseneth, the angel explains that she is now called a "City of Refuge," whose walls shelter those attached to her through repentance. In a sense, he renames her Repentance. The angel (Jesus) in his aeonic/angelic form, calls "Repentance" the "Daughter of God the Most High." This passage is key. According to Valentinian Gnosticism, Sophia is an "emanation" (an aeon) or a divine being that brings about the ruptured universe we live in when she breaks off with her partner "the Christ." If Jesus is "the Christ" and Mary the Magdalene is "Sophia," the

9 And behold, I am going away to Joseph and I shall speak to him concerning you, and he will come to you today and see you and rejoice over you and he will be your bridegroom.

10 Finally, hear me, Aseneth, and put on the robe of marriage—the old, first robe you put away in your chamber—and put on all your choice adornment and adorn yourself like a bride and prepare for his meeting. **11** For behold, he is coming to you today; he will see you and rejoice."[127]

12 And when the man finished speaking to Aseneth, she was joyously happy and fell at his feet and said to him, **13** "Blessed be the Lord God, the one who sent you to rescue me from the darkness and lead me into the light, and blessed be his name forever. **14** I will speak now, Lord, if I have found favor before you.

---

only way, as we have stated, for the universe to be rectified is through their marriage. She must return to her bridal chamber in the immaterial world or *Pleroma*. She can only do this when she repents her original sin of going it alone without her divine partner. At this point in Aseneth's (Mary the Magadalene's) transformation, she is ready to become the Bride of God *because* she has repented. Through her repentance, the universe will be redeemed. Through her repentance, others will repent. She has literally become Sophia the repentant or Repentance itself. In this way, she has become the mother of all virgins and the daughter of God.

123   If anyone continues to think of the figure described here as the Biblical Aseneth, he/she has to contend with the fact that Aseneth is now elevated to nothing less than the Daughter of God. It couldn't be any clearer. From the point of view of this gospel and the people who believed in it—the Son of God was wed to the Daughter of God. Mary the Magdalene is here put on a near equal footing—as the moon is to the sun, or Artemis to Apollo—with Jesus.

124   Here it is crystal clear that the original "Mother Mary" or "Virgin Mary" was the wife, not the mother. Mary the Magdalene is here called "the mother of the virgins." In other words, "mother," "virgin," "lady," "mistress," i.e., all the designations later applied to Jesus' mother, are used in this text to describe Jesus' bride.

125   The major sacrament of Valentinian Gnostic Christianity in the early 2nd century was that of the bridal chamber. According to *The Gospel of Philip*, redemption takes place in the bridal chamber. The reference to "a heavenly bridal chamber" is very clear.

126   In the short Greek version, after "God the Most High" the word *Father* is added, i.e., God's maleness is emphasized, his *fatherhood*. See Kraemer op. cit., 61. Insertions such as this provide us with a glimpse into the precise moments when texts that emphasized Mary the Magdalene morph into male-oriented narratives.

127   The text is explicit that she is about to become a bride. But before consummating the earthly marriage, like the Gnostics, she consummates the heavenly one. Namely, Aseneth/Mary the Magdalene invites the heavenly Joseph/Jesus to "sit a little upon the bed." This is the same bed that no man had ever touched.

Sit a little upon the bed and I shall set a table[128] and you will eat bread and I shall bring you good wine,[129] the fragrance of which (goes) up to heaven, and you will drink and you will go your way."[130]

16.

1 The man said to her, "Bring me also a honeycomb."[131] **2** Aseneth answered, "Lord, let me send to my estate and I shall bring you a honey-comb."[132] **3** But the man said to her, "Go into your chamber and you will find a honeycomb."[133]

4 Aseneth entered her inner chamber and found a large honeycomb full of honey. It was white as snow and was lying on a table. Its honey was like small drops of dew from heaven and it smelled like the pleasant smell of the spirit of life.[134] **5** Aseneth wondered and said in her heart, "How did

---

128 See "the magical papyri anticipate that the god will come to the magician's house and share his *table* and even his *bed*" (Morton Smith, op. cit., 124, emphasis added). The "magician" in this case visits the house of his bride-to-be. The emphasis on the "table" involves both magic and sacrifice. The table is a kind of altar.

129 Notice that she puts before the angel the two foods that Jesus will comment on during the Last Supper: bread and wine. The angel, however, takes the matter a step further; he introduces the honeycomb.

130 Setting the table with bread and wine represents the beginning of the Communion-like ceremony in the heavenly bridal chamber in which Aseneth partakes of the food of eternal life. The *taking of bread and wine* and placing them on a table along with the subsequent actions—*giving thanks* (the blessing over Aseneth), *breaking* (the honeycomb), and *eating* (the honeycomb)—mirror the central actions of the Christian Eucharist (Mass, Divine Liturgy, Holy Communion). There is no such incident involving a heavenly Joseph look-alike or a heavenly Communion rite in the Biblical account of Joseph and Aseneth. It is, once again, clear that it's Jesus and Mary the Magdalene that we are speaking of here.

   Also, in the early church, the Sacrament of Baptism was immediately followed by Communion. This custom is still observed today among the Christian Copts of Egypt. During those early Communions, the "newborn in Christ" drank a mixture of milk and honey. See Jones, op. cit., 67. See also Harrison, op. cit., 508–509.

   Some magical papyri found in Egypt among a collection of magical texts dating from the 2nd century B.C.E. to the 5th century C.E. are of Christian origin. They instruct worshippers to "take the honey with the milk [and] drink it before the rising of the sun." In this way, they will partake of "something that is divine" (Harrison, op. cit., 595). In light of this text, if we identify Joseph with Helios/Jesus, i.e., the rising sun, it makes perfect sense for Aseneth (Mary the Magdalene) to partake of the honey before Joseph's/Jesus' return. This way she partakes of the divine, even before his arrival.

131 Magical papyri found in Egypt and stories of magicians from the ancient world speak of daemons making food appear. Meaning, this scene is consistent with magical traditions.

this honeycomb come from this man's mouth? Its smell is like the pleasant smell of his mouth."[135]

6 Aseneth took the honeycomb and brought it to the man. She put it on the table set up in front of him. **7** The man said to her, "How is it that you said 'the honeycomb is not in my bedchamber?' Behold, you have brought a wonderful honeycomb." **8** Aseneth was afraid and said, "Lord, there was never a honeycomb in my inner chamber[136] but you spoke and it happened. And it came from your mouth and it smelled like the smell of your mouth." **9** The man rejoiced at the understanding of Aseneth.[137] And he called her to him.

10 He stretched out his right hand and drew her head near. Aseneth was afraid because sparks of fire were coming out of his hand like from inflamed iron. **11** The man rejoiced to see her afraid, and he said, "Blessed are you, Aseneth, for the secrets of the Lord have been revealed to you.[138] Blessed are

---

132 Aseneth believes that there is no honeycomb in the tower. Interestingly, there would have been no honey in the Jerusalem Temple. It was forbidden (Leviticus 2:11). Yet, here, the angel allows it. He tells her where to look: not in the pantry, but in her bedroom. And there it is! In other words, the angel is overruling Biblical law. He is taking Aseneth into the inner sanctum of the tower, where the forbidden becomes permissible.

133 The Syriac text now resumes.

134 Notice the use of the sense of smell. Earlier, it was associated with the "smell of the tomb" (13:6). Here, the smell is associated with the "spirit of life." The intent, it seems, is to contrast a version of Christianity that smells "like the pleasant smell of the spirit of life" and is consecrated in sacred sex, and Pauline Christianity that smells "like a tomb" and celebrates death and resurrection. In any event, what is being contrasted is a form of religiosity that celebrates life and a form that is associated with death.

135 His mouth is contrasted with her mouth cited above.

136 The "inner chamber" corresponds to the Gnostic Holy of Holies, that is, the bridal chamber.

137 Again, what is it that Aseneth has understood? At one point her mouth "smelled like a tomb" (13:6); now the honeycomb smells like the scent of the heavenly man's mouth, the one who is "the spirit of life" (16:4). Thus, the contrast is between the religion of death represented by Aseneth's worship of false deities and the religion of life into which she is entering. As stated above, the contrast in early Christianity is also between Gnosticism and Pauline Christianity.

138 The language used here with regard to Aseneth is classic Gnosticism with regard to Mary the Magdalene. In the *Dialogue of the Savior*, Mary the Magdalene is spoken of as the woman "who fully understood" (20:2), the one whom Jesus himself said has come "to reveal the greatness of the revealer" (24:2). She is the one on whom the other apostles rely for the teachings of Jesus that they had not heard (*Gospel of Mary Magdalene* 6:2). Implicit in this is the claim that Jesus conveyed to Mary the Magdalene—alone—teachings he did not communicate to other disciples. In other words, he conveyed the secrets encoded in our text.

those who attach themselves to the Lord God Most High in penance because, from this honeycomb, they will eat and live forever.[139] **12** Because this is the spirit of life, for it was made by swarms of bees from the paradise of the Living God of Eden, from the dew of the rose of life in paradise, from which the angels of God eat and from which all the elect of God and the sons of the Most High eat. For this is the honeycomb of life and those who eat from it will not die but live forever."[140]

13 The man stretched out his right hand and took a little piece from the honeycomb and ate; the rest he put in Aseneth's mouth.[141] **14** The man

---

139   Why honeycomb for this Communion rite? The manna that the Israelites ate in the wilderness tasted like honey (Exodus 16:31) and is described as "the bread that the Lord has given you to eat" (Exodus 16:15). Jesus himself is said to be "the living bread that came down from heaven. Whoever eats of this bread will live forever" (John 6:51). Meaning, Jesus is compared to manna, which in turn is compared to honey. Also, since honey had been used throughout the Middle East to prevent bodies from decaying, it came to be associated with immortality. In the Egyptian context, the body was preserved by the honey, and the soul took the form of a bee (see Allen H. Jones, op. cit., 69–71). On one level, therefore, Communion with Jesus and participation in eternal life is what is conveyed through the symbol of the honeycomb. On another level, if the protrusions from her body are queen cells, then Artemis is the honeycomb. The honeycomb, therefore, is the only symbol that stands for both the bridegroom and the bride, i.e., Jesus and Mary the Magdalene.

   According to Luke (24:41) after the resurrection, Jesus appears to his disciples, who give him two kinds of food to eat that are laden with symbolism: fish and a honeycomb. This is Luke's description of a supper after the Last Supper, i.e., after Jesus' death and resurrection. So here, too, the honeycomb represents immortality. Curiously, "honeycomb" is included in the King James version but omitted in most modern translations. There is no mention of a honeycomb in the Greek version of the New Testament, but the Latin includes it. Clearly, some of the ancient authorities were uncomfortable with this echo of Artemisian theology surviving in the canonical Gospels themselves. In other words, the "fish," i.e., Jesus, survives the editorial process. The "honeycomb," i.e., Mary the Magdalene, is made to disappear. See also Jones, op. cit., 111.

140   The bees, honeycomb, the tower, and the City of Refuge all indicate that Aseneth (Mary the Magdalene) is modeled on the goddess Artemis. See chapters above for a full deciphering of these rich symbols.

141   In the *Acts of Philip* (14.7), the earliest version of which is a 4th-century Gnostic manuscript found in a monastery on Mt. Athos, Mary the Magdalene is explicitly identified. There she is called by one of the Greek versions of her name, Mariamne. When her "brother" Philip wants to cure a man from blindness, he imitates Jesus and uses saliva (Mark 8:22–26). But Philip does not use his own saliva. In a move clearly paralleling our text, he dips his finger into Mariamne's mouth, extracting *her* saliva for the healing. This episode was considered too shocking for the readers of the *Acts of Philip*. In François Bovon's words, "like the Evangelists Matthew and Luke, who considered Mark's episode too shocking to accept, a reader has torn away the folio between folios 87 and 88" and the end of the episode has been lost. See F. Bovon, "Mary Magdalene in the Acts of Philip," in Jones, op. cit., 81.

said to Aseneth, "So now you have eaten the bread of life and drunk the cup of life and have been anointed with the ointment of incorruptibility.[142] From today and this time forward, your flesh[143] will spring up blossoms of life from the <ground> of the Most High and your bones will grow strong again like the cedars of paradise.[144] **15** Unwavering strength will strengthen you, and your youth will remain forever and not see old age,[145] and your beauty will not fail forever. **16** You will be a mother of cities[146]—one with a strong city wall—with whom they will take refuge in the name of the Lord God, king of the ages."

Kraemer points out that this scene in *Joseph and Aseneth* is "an inversion of Genesis 2:3. There, of course, a woman eats the fruit of mortality and shares it with her husband. Here a masculine figure (a double of Aseneth's future husband, Joseph) eats the food of immortality and then gives some to the woman" (Kraemer, op. cit., 65). More than this, the inversion returns sex to its original innocent form. By placing the honey in her mouth while sitting on her bed, the angelic Joseph (a.k.a. the Son of God), the new Adam, reverses the sin of the original Adam and returns man to a state before Eve was seduced by the snake.

Finally, through the erotic union of placing honey in her mouth, both the angel and Aseneth are elevated. There is an echo here of the episode whereby God makes the prophet Ezekiel (Ezekiel 1:28–3:15) eat a scroll on which God has written all that He wants transmitted to the people of Israel. The scroll is put into Ezekiel's mouth by a "hand that was sent forth toward me." By placing the honey in Aseneth's (Mary the Magdalene's) mouth, Joseph (Jesus) elevates her to the level of prophecy and himself to the level of divinity.

142 Again, the emphasis is on the idea that this is a religion of life, not one that celebrates death—e.g., certain pagan cults and, as far as the author of this lost gospel is concerned, Pauline Christianity. The scene is highly erotic as he puts honey "in Aseneth's mouth" while sitting on the bed that up to this point had represented her virginity.

143 In Gnostic fashion, her flesh now becomes spiritualized, instead of her spirit becoming incarnate.

144 Charlesworth points out that in the *Odes* and in the Songs of Solomon 14, the righteous are described as trees planted in the Garden of Eden. The angel now promises that Aseneth's bones will one day grow like "cedars of paradise," i.e., she will achieve immortality. Here we may have an insight into secondary burial, practiced in Jerusalem at the time of Jesus, whereby bones were put into ossuaries after the flesh decomposed. Clearly, the ones performing the burial were expecting that the bones of the deceased will one day regenerate as cedars in the Garden of Eden.

145 The language here echoes Jesus' promise that the messianic era will dawn *before* his generation dies out: "But truly I tell you, there are some standing here who will not taste death before they see the kingdom of God" (Luke 9:27).

146 Here, Mary the Magdalene is again being called a holy mother, that is, a mother to all cities, in addition to a virgin—titles later applied to Mary, mother of Jesus.

17 He stretched out his right hand, and the piece broken from the honeycomb was replenished and it became as it was before without him touching it.[147]

18 And he turned again and stretched his right hand to the honeycomb and touched it with his finger deliberately on its eastern side. And he drew the part to him <and the path of the honey was now blood>. And he turned again and stretched his right hand and, with his finger, he touched the western side of the comb. And where he touched it, the path of the honey was now blood.

19 And again he stretched his hand and, with his finger, touched the northern part of the comb. And he drew it to himself, and again the path of the honey was now blood. And he stretched his hand again and, with his finger, he touched it on the southern side of the honeycomb. And again, the path of the honey was now blood.[148]

20 Aseneth was standing on the left of the man, watching all that he was doing.

---

147   Sacred sex can return the bride to the status of a virgin. Here, the honeycomb, possibly representing her hymen, gets miraculously "replenished . . . as it was before." For a community that understood beekeeping, the miracle here is not that the honeycomb was "as before," but that it happened without him touching it. The ability to heal or return to a virginal condition is, as far as we know, unique to bees and honeycombs. Meaning, if a beekeeper puts his finger into a honeycomb so as to partake of the honey, and then returns the honeycomb to the hive, the bees will "heal" the honeycomb, so to speak, and return it to its original state.

148   By moving from east to west (v.18) and from north to south (v.19) across the honeycomb, the heavenly man has made the sign of the cross—in blood—on the Communion honeycomb. There is clearly no parallel within either the Hebrew Bible or within Judaism for this. This is unmistakably Christian symbolism. During the Last Supper Jesus states "this is my body and this . . . my blood." In the last clause, Mark and Matthew have "my blood of the covenant" (Mark 14:24 and Matthew 26:28). Paul and most manuscripts of Luke have "the new covenant in my blood" (Luke 22:20 and 1 Corinthians 11:25). Meaning this is an explicit reference to the new covenant of Christianity. Furthermore, what is being changed into blood is the honey that has thus far represented the consummation of Mary the Magdalene's marriage to the heavenly figure. If the honey is a metaphor for sex, the blood is a metaphor for menstruation—a state of impurity in Judaism. By having Mary the Magdalene eat it, the writer of this gospel is indicating that the Torah laws concerning impurity have been superseded by the heavenly figure, i.e., Jesus. In any event, the cross—in blood—could not be made clearer as a Christian symbol.

   The sign of the cross on the honeycomb may also represent a later attempt by some redactor to convert Magdalene symbols into Pauline ones. As we have seen, the honey represents sexuality. In contrast, one of the pillars of Pauline theology is the forgiveness of sin through the blood of Christ (see James D. Tabor, *Paul and Jesus: How the Apostle Transformed Christianity*, 24). The statement that the "honey was now blood" may reflect a power struggle, i.e., a moment in time when the Church of the Gentiles was shifting from Magdalenism to Paulinism.

21 And the man said to the honeycomb, "Come, and see at once the great swarms of bees from the cells of the honeycomb." **22** And the cells were innumerable, a great multitude, and from all the house they appeared and were alive—a multitude of multitudes, a thousand thousands of bees, white as snow and their wings like the color of purple and jacinth and scarlet and fine white linen spun in gold.[149] A crown of gold (was) on each of their heads. Their stings were sharp, though they were injuring no one. **23** They circled around and seized Aseneth and clung to her[150] from her feet to her head. <More> bees were chosen—great bees like queen (bees). They came from the fragments which the man had broken off from the honeycomb. **24** They took hold of Aseneth's face and on her lips[151] made an image of the honeycomb set before the man. And it was full of very much honey. They all gathered and ate from the honey of the honeycomb on Aseneth's mouth.[152]

25 And the man said to those bees, "Go to your places." **26** The multitude of them rose and flew and went toward heaven.[153] Those who wished to injure Aseneth fell to the ground and died. **27** And the man stretched out the scepter

---

149 Gideon Bohak sees the colors of the bees as related to the colors of Jewish priestly garments (Bohak, op. cit., 11–12). He may be right. These colors may be related to Jesus and Mary the Magdalene's role in establishing a new Jerusalem Temple, or they may be related to Mary the Magdalene's standing as a priestess in the Temple of Artemis, or both.

150 Here we see Aseneth explicitly depicted as Artemis. If Jesus is Apollo/Helios, then his sister is none other than Apollo's twin, Artemis. As we discussed above, for their followers, if Jesus was—so to speak—the *real* Apollo, his consort had to be the *real* Artemis. That is, if he is a god incarnate she, too, is no ordinary human being, but a goddess; in the words of our text a "daughter of the Lord" (21:3). This explains why the Pauline Christians had to get rid of her. Simply put, she couldn't simply be a wife in the way, say, the disciples had wives. Once you have a god-man, either he stays celibate or you're into a pantheon (see the theology of Osiris, for example): God the Father, God the Son, and God the Daughter/sister/wife.

151 In the cultural context of the Mediterranean, bees on lips symbolize wise words. Pausanias tells the story of how the poet Pindar became tired and lay down to rest. Bees swarmed him, plastering his lips with wax. This accounted for Pindar's career as a poet. Cited in Jones, op. cit., 68.

152 Again, highly erotic and consistent with what the church fathers say about the Gnostics, namely, that they partake of sex including group sex. Notice that they *all* ate from the honey of "Aseneth's mouth."

153 Swarms of bees were associated with prophecy in the pagan world. For example, when the ancient Boeotians from central Greece went to the priestess at Delphi to instruct them, a swarm of bees appeared and one of the Boeotian envoys followed them in order to divine the future. See Jones, op. cit., 78.

in his hand to the dead bees and said to them, "Rise you also, and go to your places in the courtyard near Aseneth's tower. Settle on and remain on the fruit trees."[154]

17.

1 The man said to Aseneth, "Do you see these (things), Aseneth?" And she replied, "I see, my Lord." **2** The man said to her, "So it will be with all the words I spoke to you today."[155]

3 Again the man stretched out his hand and touched the fragment of the honeycomb and fire went up from the table and consumed the comb. It did not damage the table <nor did it catch fire>. The smell of burning from the honeycomb pleasantly blew throughout the entire house from the inner chamber of Aseneth.[156]

4 Then Aseneth said to the man, "My Lord, with me are seven virgins who are the same age as I am with the same upbringing and I love them like my sisters. I shall call them to you and you will bless them as you did

---

154   Here, the Joseph/Jesus look-alike from heaven, holding the messianic scepter, performs a minor miracle of resurrection by raising the dead bees with the words "rise you also." The good bees, so to speak, fly toward heaven. Those who wished to ignore Aseneth/Mary the Magdalene get a second chance on earth.

  Kraemer points out that in the Greek text the raising of the bees employs "the same verb used in Christian texts to designate resurrection from the dead" (Kraemer, op. cit., 67). She also points out that so far "scholars have been singularly unsuccessful in their attempts to decode" this passage (ibid.). In Ephrem, as in Aseneth, bees appear as symbols of the raising of the dead (see Kraemer, op. cit., 70 and Robert Murray, *Symbols of Church and Kingdom: A Study in Early Syriac Tradition* [Cambridge University Press, 1975], 292).

155   The raising of one set of bees to heaven and another from the dead is a kind of foreshadowing for what Christians now call the "Rapture" and the resurrection of the dead. "See this?" says the heavenly man; "I see, my Lord" says Aseneth/Mary the Magdalene. At which point he promises "so it will be with all the words I spoke to you today."

156   Again, the consummation of marriage is a sacrifice accepted by heaven. The heavenly fire is reminiscent of the heavenly fire that consumes Elijah's offering when confronting the priests of Ba'al (1 Kings 18:36–40). In that story, the Hebrew prophet Elijah confronts Jezebel's priests. They are defeated when a heavenly fire consumes his offering but not theirs, at which point they are slaughtered. Here it is the anti-Jezebel's offering that is accepted. Notice the sequence of this most sacred and mysterious rite: first, Aseneth/Mary the Magdalene repents; second, "the secrets of the lord [are] revealed" to her; third, she participates in a secret rite on her bed, in the innermost chamber of her tower/temple, that involves both marriage and

me." **5** The man said, "Call them." Aseneth called the seven virgins and stood (them) before him. The man said to them, "May the Lord God Most High bless you. You will be the seven pillars in the City of Refuge and all the daughters of the house of the Village of Refuge who you choose shall enter and upon you they shall rest forever."[157]

6 The man said to Aseneth, "Now take the table." When Aseneth took the table, the man changed before her. And she looked and, behold, a chariot of four horses going toward heaven to the east.[158] The appearance of the chariot was shining and burning like fire, and the appearance of the horses was like lightning. And the man was standing on the chariot.[159]

7 Aseneth said, "Truly I am foolish and presumptuous (because) I spoke these things and said a man came into my bedchamber. I did not know that God from heaven appeared in my bed.[160] Now, behold, he is returning to heaven." Aseneth said, "Have pity on your handmaiden (because) I spoke my words in ignorance."

resurrection; fourth, the fragrance from this activity "blew throughout" the entire house from the "inner chamber of Aseneth." What we have here is the long-lost theology of the original Gnostic followers of the holy dyad, the *aeons*, Jesus and Mary the Magdalene. This is nothing less than *their* Kabbalah.

157 The seven pagan demons are now transformed into seven pillars of the New Church.

158 He rises heavenward like Helios or, in the Jewish tradition, like Elijah. Also, in Jewish mysticism, the secret rites are called the secrets of the *Merkavah*, i.e., the chariot. Mastering their meaning is akin to riding the chariot heavenward. Finally, angels participating in rituals that link heavenly and earthly worship is characteristic of Qumran literature, i.e., the Dead Sea Scrolls. Meaning early Christians have been linked to the Essenes and here we have an episode—angel/human contact—that is very reminiscent of the Essene paradigm. See Elior, op. cit., 59.

159 As we've seen, the image of a being standing in a chariot, drawn by four horses, complete with rays streaming from his head, appears in mosaics in places of worship in northern Israel. For a discussion of these synagogues/churches, see chapters 9 and especially 10 in this book.

160 This represents an explicit acknowledgement of the depth of the intimacy experienced by Aseneth in the heavenly bridal chamber. Simply put, it all comes down to "a man came into my bedroom . . . God from heaven appeared in my bed." If it was not clear by now, this has nothing to do with Joseph and everything to do with Jesus. Not only that, here too we see how Pauline theology substituted the mother for the wife. In Orthodox Christianity, it is Mary, Jesus' mother, who is the mother of all virgins, who is visited by God in her bedchamber and who remains a perpetual virgin even after conceiving and giving birth. Here it is the wife who shares "God's bed."

Episode 3: The Marriage

The wedding, the consummation, and the children.

18.

1 As she was considering these things in her heart, a young man from Potiphar<'s staff> came and announced to the household, "Behold, the Man of God,[161] Joseph, is coming. His herald is standing at the gate of the courtyard."

2 Aseneth called her "foster father"[162]—the manager of her father's house—and said to him, "Make ready and prepare the house, and prepare a great dinner because Joseph, the Powerful One of God, is coming to us today." **3** But her foster father looked at her. Her face was sad from the suffering of her seven-day penitence. He grieved over it and wept. He took her right hand, kissed it, and said to her, "My daughter, what is this sadness in your face?" **4** She said to him, "My head hurts very much and sleep has been taken from me." And her foster father went immediately and made ready the house and dinner.

5 Aseneth remembered the (heavenly) man and his words. Immediately, she entered her second bedchamber, the place of her "chests of adornments" (that is, the one containing her garments and accessories). She opened them and brought out her first, glittering robe and put it on. **6** She girded herself with

---

161 Interestingly, not everyone calls Joseph/Jesus "Son of God." Sometime he is called "Man of God" or "Powerful One of God," etc.

162 "Foster father" appears to be a Syriac term of endearment. Aseneth is speaking of the manager or trusted senior servant of her father's estate who, in that capacity, would act in some ways like a father figure to her while running the household. She is not saying that the manager is her father or that her real father has somehow abandoned her.

163 She once again readies herself for a royal marriage, attiring herself as a queen. Her biological father is noticeable by his absence, as her "foster father" takes over. This seems to reflect a time when Mary the Magdalene's biological father, priest, and king "abandoned" her, before becoming reconciled to the marriage. At this point, she's about to become a Bride of God. She too holds a scepter in her hand. She's about to be elevated to the status of a co-messiah.

164 For a spiritual man, Joseph/Jesus seems to be into a woman's looks. This synchronizes with the Talmudic tradition that Jesus' teacher, Rabbi Yehoshua b. Perahya, broke with Jesus over the latter's comments concerning the narrowness of an innkeeper's eyes. See Peter Schafer, op. cit., 35.

165 She is now described in Jesus/Helios imagery complete with rays emanating from her face.

166 She's already holding her scepter and she is identified with the morning star. In other words, she is becoming co-regent in messiahship by fulfilling the star and scepter prophesy of Numbers 24:17.

a chain of gold on her hips. **7** She placed bracelets on her hands, anklets on her feet, and on her neck she put a wreathed necklace (inlayed with) various abundant, precious stones, and on her head a crown of gold. All of her clothes were devoid of adornments. And on the front of her crown were rubies and six costly stones.

8 On her head (she placed) a bridal veil. She took a scepter in her hand.[163] Then she remembered the words her foster father said to her, that the appearance of her face had darkened and become sad. And she groaned and became very distraught. Aseneth said, "When Joseph sees me so, he will treat me with contempt."[164] **9** She told one of her virgin companions to bring her clean water from the spring. And she put (it) in the basin. **10** As she lowered (herself) to wash, she saw her face was like rays of the sun,[165] and her eyes like the morning star rising,[166] and her cheeks like fields of the Most High, red like the blood of a son of man.[167] Her lips (were) like the rose of life plucked from its stalk;[168] her teeth like armed men prepared for battle; the hair of her head, like the vine of the paradise of God, abundant in fruit; her neck, like the islands of rest for the angels of heaven; and her breasts, like the mountains of love of the Most High.

11 Aseneth saw herself in the water and was amazed at her appearance.[169] Out of joy, she did not wash her face, saying, "Perhaps I will wash off this goodly

---

167 Whereas in Pauline Christianity during Communion, wine is transformed into Jesus' blood and is connected to his death and resurrection, here the reference to blood is both redemptive *and* sexual. This time it refers to her cheeks. This entire passage is a kind of Judeo-Christian Song of Songs referring to Mary the Magdalene's cheeks, lips, teeth, hair, neck, and breasts. See Kraemer: "perhaps this [passage] constitutes an intentional further recasting of Aseneth in the person of the beloved bride . . . for an author for whom Song of Songs was, indeed, the description of God's bride" (Kraemer, op. cit., 72).

168 The phrase "rose of life plucked from its stalk" seems to be the key to rosettes found all over Second Temple ossuaries in the Jerusalem area, including the so-called Jesus Family Tomb. It's a symbol of death (plucked from its stalk) and immortality (rose of life). Here, again, it is sexualized, referring to Aseneth's/Mary the Magdalene's *lips*.

169 Compare the Gnostic *Exegesis on the Soul* where it states that after repentance the soul "becomes young again . . . praising the Father and her brother by whom she was rescued. Thus it is by being born again that the soul will be saved" (*Exegesis on the Soul*, 134.6–15 quoted in Gregory Snyder, op. cit., 183). In the footnote, Snyder states that "reflecting the androgyne myth, this 'brother' who rescues the soul is in fact the soul's original partner" (p. 184). The androgyne theme is also in *Joseph and Aseneth* where Joseph/Jesus and Aseneth/ Mary the Magdalene play the roles of both siblings and spouses.

beauty." **12** Her foster father joined her again, to tell her that everything had been made ready. But when he saw her, he was terrified and could not find his speech. He was very afraid and fell before her feet. **13** Then at last he said, "My lady,[170] what is this appearance of virtue and marvelous beauty of the gods? The Lord God of heaven truly chose you to be the bride of his firstborn son."[171]

19.

1 A young man came and said to Aseneth, "Behold, Joseph is at the entrance of the courtyard." Running, Aseneth descended the steps with her seven virgin companions to meet Joseph and stood at the entrance of the house. Joseph entered the courtyard and they closed the gates and all the strangers remained outside.

2 Aseneth went out and rushed to meet Joseph. Joseph saw her and was amazed also at her beauty. He said to her, "Who are you? Quickly, tell me."

3 She answered him, "I am your maidservant and handmaiden, Aseneth, who has cast from me the idols and treated the gods with contempt and rejected them. Today, a man came to me from heaven and he gave me the bread of life—and I ate—and a cup of blessing—and I drank. **4** (The heavenly man)

---

170 The Syriac word is *Mara*, which is the female equivalent of *Mar, lord, owner, Master, prince.* So *Mara* is a term of utmost respect, denoting a woman of exalted stature, a *lady, governess, princess* or *saint.* In the Talpiot tomb associated with the Jesus Family Tomb, the woman called *Mariamene* is also called *Mara.* On ossuary #8 in the Rahmani catalogue of ossuaries, the word *Mara* is translated as *master.* On ossuary #327, *Mara* is translated as *Lord, Master.* And, on ossuary #560, *Mari* is translated as *Masters.* Recently, using a robotic camera, Simcha Jacobovici and his colleagues discovered the word *Mara* on an ossuary in an unexcavated tomb 60 meters from the Jesus Family Tomb. Close by, in this tomb, there is an ossuary with a cross on one side and the image of a big fish spewing out a stick figure on another side. Inscribed on the fish's head is the Hebrew word *Yonah* (Jonah in English). The "Sign of Jonah" is the earliest Biblical symbol of emerging Christianity. It stands for Jesus. Can it be that the *Jonah ossuary* is celebrating the bridegroom, while the *Mara ossuary* is celebrating the bride? See James D. Tabor and Simcha Jacobovici, *The Jesus Discovery,* op. cit., 67–68, 73–103, and 112–116. For the inscription see http://jamestabor.com/2013/09/13/can-you-read-jonah-in-hebrew/.

171 Like her father, Aseneth's foster father, i.e., the manager of Potiphar's estate, knows that she is to be the "bride" of "God's firstborn son." The text simply cannot be clearer about the main characters of this story.

said to me, 'I shall give you to Joseph as a bride: he will be a bridegroom to you forever.' He added, 'You will no longer be called Aseneth but you will be called the "City of Refuge."'[172] The people will flee and take refuge with you, and the families, tribes, and nations with God Most High.'[173] **5** He said to me, 'I shall go also to Joseph and speak to him these words concerning you.' Now you know, my Lord, whether a man has come to you and spoken to you concerning me."

6 Joseph said to Aseneth, "Blessed are you by God Most High. Blessed be your name forever, because the Lord God set your walls on high, for your walls are of living diamond (i.e., impenetrable) because the sons of the living God will dwell in the City of Refuge where the Lord God will rule over them forever. **7** Because this man who came to you today said to me also these words concerning you. And now, come to me, chaste virgin.[174] Why do you stand so far (from me)?"

8 Joseph stretched out his hands and, by a wink of his eyes,[175] he called Aseneth. Aseneth also stretched out her hands, ran to Joseph, fell on his neck and embraced it. They came alive in the spirit <and> embraced each other. **9** Joseph kissed Aseneth and gave to her the spirit of life. He kissed her a second time and gave her the spirit of wisdom. And he kissed her a third time and gave her the spirit of truth.

---

172 There is another possible allusion here that would have resonated with a Jewish or Judeo-Christian audience of the day. Specifically, there is a Jewish tradition that the Aseneth of Genesis is the product of the rape of Dinah (Gen. 34), daughter of Jacob, by Schechem, prince of the Canaanite city of Schechem, (Pirke De-Rabbi Eliezer, chap. 38). At the same time, there is a Christian tradition calling Jesus a City of Refuge (*Acts of Thomas*, Act 1, Chapter 10). In *Joseph and Aseneth* the epitaph is used with reference to her, not him. Can it be that there is a transposition taking place here? Meaning, normally Jesus is associated with a City of Refuge, and Aseneth is associated with a rape. Can it be that the author of *Joseph and Aseneth* is switching the roles? By associating her with a City of Refuge, is he associating Jesus with a rape, as opposed to a virgin birth?

173 This is reminiscent of the promise of God to Abraham that through him "all the families of the earth shall be blessed" (Genesis 12:3). Similarly, through Aseneth, all the families of the earth will find shelter. Her future role is more than simply being the Bride of God, i.e., God's son, Jesus. She will not simply bear and bring up children. Rather, while he is the Messiah of the Jewish people, she is the Savior of the Gentiles.

174 Originally, it was Mary the Magdalene who was called the virgin.

175 The author is literally winking at us when he calls Mary the Magdalene "Aseneth." Here, understood in a Jewish context, they are not behaving in a chaste manner; she wraps herself around his neck, they embrace, he kisses her, and then he gives her "the spirit of life" between kisses. All this in front of an audience of seven virgins!

20.

1 They squeezed each other's hands and embraced each other.[176] Aseneth said to Joseph, "Come, my Lord, and enter our house. Because, my Lord, I have prepared a great dinner in our house." They took each other by their hands, and she brought him to her house and sat him upon her father's throne.[177]

2 She brought water to wash his feet.[178] Joseph said, "Let one of the virgins come and wash my feet." **3** But Aseneth replied, "No, my Lord. Why should one of these maidservants wash your feet, my Lord? Rather I, (your) maidservant and handmaiden, will wash the feet of my Lord because your feet are my feet, your hands my hands, and your soul my soul."[179] And she urged him (to honor her request) and washed his feet. Joseph pondered her hands, which were like the hands of life, and her fingers, like the fingers of a skilled and esteemed scribe.

4 Afterwards, Joseph took hold of her right hand and kissed her on the head.[180] And she sat on his right side.

5 Her father, mother, and her family came from their estate. They saw Aseneth as if her appearance was of light and her beauty like the beauty of heaven. They saw her sitting with Joseph and dressed in a wedding garment. They were amazed at her beauty and gave glory to God who gives life and raises the dead.[181] After this, they ate and drank.

6 Potiphar said to Joseph, "Tomorrow I shall call the noblemen and the magistrates of the land of Egypt and have a marriage feast and you will take

---

176 Joseph is no ordinary man. As they embrace in this act of betrothal, he imparts to Aseneth three great gifts: the spirit of life, the spirit of wisdom, and the spirit of truth.

177 He is explicitly enthroned, becoming literally the King of the Jews.

178 As per the famous scene in the gospels where a woman, alleged to be Mary the Magdalene, washes Jesus' feet and then dries them with her hair. See Luke 7:38.

179 In Gnostic fashion, it is not spirit that becomes flesh, but vice versa. Namely, the sequence runs from feet (closest to ground) to hands (creativity) to soul.

180 Almost the exact wording as *The Gospel of Philip* (63:34) where it says that Jesus used to kiss Mary the Magdalene "often on her [mouth or head]"; the word is missing.

181 Aseneth's fears of parental rejection—because of her abandonment of their religion—do not materialize or, at least, there is reconciliation after an initial rejection. Her parents come around to the view of God as giving life and *raising the dead*. While they acknowledge the power of God, there is no suggestion that they—or Aseneth for that matter—convert to Judaism or Christianity. They merely adopt the belief in one God who gives life, including eternal life. The model is that of the Gentile God-fearer. Note that resurrection of the dead

Aseneth as a wife." **7** Joseph replied,[182] "Tomorrow I shall return to Pharaoh, the king, because he is like my father and has appointed me magistrate over the land. I shall speak to him concerning Aseneth. He will give her to me from (amongst) the women." Potiphar said, "Go in peace."

8 Joseph stayed that day with Potiphar but did not know Aseneth because, Joseph said, "It is not right for a man who worships God to know his bride before the wedding."[183]

21.

1 Joseph said to Pharaoh, "Give me as a wife the daughter of Potiphar, priest of On." **2** Pharaoh said to Joseph, "Behold, she was destined for you long ago and before God." **3** Pharaoh summoned Potiphar who brought Aseneth. (Pharaoh) was amazed at her beauty. He said, "Blessed are you by the Lord God of Joseph, because he is the firstborn of God, and you will be called the Daughter of God Most High[184] and the bride of Joseph now and forever."

4 Pharaoh approached Joseph and Aseneth and he placed on them crowns of gold that had been kept in his house from long ago. Pharaoh stood Aseneth on the right side of Joseph. **5** Putting his hand on their heads, he blessed them and said, "May the Lord God Most High bless you. May he bless and glorify you forever." **6** Then Pharaoh turned them to each other and they kissed each other.

---

has been added to the mix of ideas associated with Joseph/Jesus in this text—along with crosses of blood and titles such as Son of God.

182　If our typological understanding is correct, based on this text, Jesus seems to have a relationship with the Roman emperor Tiberius. If this sounds unlikely, remember that according to Jewish tradition, Onkelos, one of the greatest rabbis ever, was a Roman convert and nephew of the Emperor Nero. Furthermore, the redactor of the Talmud, Yehuda HaNasi—who, like Jesus, lived in the Galilee—is said to have been a close friend of the Emperor Antoninus Pius.

183　He doth protest too much.

184　Again, the titles clearly belong to a long-suppressed version of Christianity. Jesus is called "the firstborn of God" which is different from "Son of God" as an exclusive title. Meaning, we are all children of God but he is the favorite, the firstborn, the herald of a new step forward in the relationship between humanity and God. Mary the Magdalene is called "the daughter of the Lord." Clearly, she has almost equal status with "the son." See also Kraemer, who comments that in this passage "Aseneth becomes divinized and daughter of God. What Aseneth acquires [is] both immortality and infallible knowledge" (Kraemer, op. cit., 269).

7 After this, Pharaoh gave a wedding feast—a great dinner and a great banquet—for seven days. **8** He called all the chiefs of Egypt and all the kings of the nations and proclaimed to the whole land of Egypt that every man who does work for the seven days of the wedding of Joseph and Aseneth shall die.[185]

9 Afterwards Joseph had intercourse with Aseneth.[186] And Aseneth conceived from Joseph and gave birth to Manasseh and his brother Ephraim in Joseph's house.[187]

10 (This is the) hymn of thanksgiving of Aseneth to God, the Most High:[188]

11 "I have sinned much before you, Lord,

I, Aseneth, daughter of Potiphar, priest of On, city of the sun,

who oversees everything.

12 I have sinned and done evil things before you.

I was resting in my father's house,

but (was) proud and boastful.

13 I sinned before you, Lord.

I worshipped gods without number.

I ate their sacrifices and drank their libation.

14 I did not know the Lord God of Heaven,

and I did not believe in the Most High of life.

15 But I trusted in the glory of my riches and in my beauty.

---

185 "Pharaoh" here acts as Pontifex Maximus which, of course, was the title and role of a Roman emperor such as Tiberius; but he seems more intimately involved in blessing this union than Tiberius would have been—even if he was aware of it. More likely, it is Sejanus who is playing the de facto role of "Pharaoh" here, with Germanicus playing the role of "son of Pharaoh."

186 In the Syriac, literally: "went into."

187 After the wedding feast, Joseph and Aseneth engage in sexual intercourse and, in time, two sons are born: Ephraim and Manasseh. There is no such rich detail regarding the betrothal and wedding—nor any prayers by Aseneth—in the Biblical story of Joseph and Aseneth. With respect to Jesus and Mary the Magdalene, we can't even be sure of what the real names of their progeny were—Ephraim and Manasseh are likely code names. What is clear, however, is that "Joseph went into Aseneth." In other words, both Jesus and Mary the Magdalene lost their status of virgins and they sired at least two children. The Jesus Family Tomb in Talpiot has an ossuary in it marked with the name "Judah, son of Jesus."

I was proud and boastful.

16 I treated with contempt every man who was before me

and those who desired me.

17 I have sinned much before you, Lord.

And I spoke foolishly about you in vanity

and I said in my pride,

'There is no ruler of the earth who has aroused me,

but I shall be the bride of the firstborn of the king of Egypt.'[189]

18 Until Joseph, the Powerful One of God, came.

He pulled me down from my stronghold

and emptied me of my pride and weakened me of my strengths.

19 And by his beauty he caught me,[190]

and by his wisdom he grasped me like a fish on a hook,[191]

and by his spirit he has made me a servant for life,

and by his strength he has strengthened me

and drawn me near to God,

the chief and Lord of the ages.

20 And in my hands, the chief of the hosts of the Most High

has <given> to me the bread of life

and the cup of wisdom.

And I became his bride forever and ever."[192]

---

188 This title is written in red ink in the Syriac manuscript, suggesting that the hymn was of some importance, perhaps even that it may have once circulated independently of the text. Note also that it largely repeats material from chapters 11 and 12 and appears here in an unusual location (after the birth of Aseneth's sons).

189 The *firstborn* of the ruler of the land, i.e., Germanicus, is contrasted with the *firstborn* of the ruler of the universe.

190 Her first reaction is physical. Here wisdom follows beauty, not the other way around.

191 Being grasped like a fish on a hook is reminiscent of Jesus calling Simon, Peter, and Andrew to the task of discipleship so as to become "fishers of people" (Matthew 4:19).

192 Mary the Magdalene is the "bride" of the "Son of God"—"forever and ever." This line is not in a book of fiction. Here it appears in one of the earliest Christian texts ever discovered.

Episode 4: The Murder Plot

The conspiracy to abduct Aseneth, kill Joseph, and murder their children is foiled.

22.

1 And it happened after this: the seven years of plenty passed and the seven years of famine approached the land. **2** Jacob heard about Joseph, his son. On the twenty-first day of the second month of the second year of the famine, Israel departed and came to Egypt with all those born in his home and they dwelled in the land of Goshen.[193]

3 Aseneth said to Joseph, "I shall go and see your father Israel; he is like a god to me."[194] **4** Joseph replied, "You will see my father with me." **5** Joseph and Aseneth came to Goshen[195] and met the brothers of Joseph. They bowed to them with their faces upon the ground. **6** They went to Jacob, who was sitting on his bed, comfortable in his old age.[196]

7 Aseneth saw him and was amazed because Jacob was beautiful in appearance. His old age was surpassing the beauty of handsome young men, his head was white as snow, his hair was thick like an Ethiopian's, the end of his beard came down white upon his chest, his eyes were bright and flashing, his cheeks and shoulders and arms were firm like the appearance of an angel, and his thighs

---

193 These numbers: 7 and 7; 21, 2 and 2 seem to signify something in Gnostic Kabbalism. They are not arbitrary, but we have not cracked their code.

194 Aseneth/Mary the Magdalene gives us a key to deciphering the text. Namely, from her point of view, there are people around us who are the incarnations of energies and attributes that pagans falsely deified and represented in gold and silver. Once the idols are jettisoned, however, one can understand how both Holy Scriptures as well as pagan philosophies and theologies *anticipated* these special individuals. Simply put, these individuals are *like* gods. Therefore, Father Israel is "like a god," Jesus is the "firstborn of God" and "like the sun," and Mary the Magdalene is "daughter of the Lord," like Artemis, the holy virgin, sister and ultimately Bride of God. In other words, the reference to Jacob being like a god gives us an insight into early Christianity and its synchronicity with monotheistic paganism. Basically, they deified individuals while claiming that this deification did not detract from their monotheism.

195 Biblically speaking, there was no trip by Aseneth to Goshen. Joseph goes to his father with his two sons, without Aseneth (Genesis 47:28–50:26). Also, there is a Talmudic tradition that says Joseph allowed the mummification of Jacob/Israel because Israel was a *tzadik* (i.e., a righteous person or saint), and that the bodies of *tzadikim* are not corrupted after death. Fearing that the Egyptians would discover this and worship Israel as a god, Joseph allows

and his shins (were) like (those of) a mighty man. Jacob was like a man who had wrestled with God. **8** Aseneth saw him and was shocked. And she bowed with her face upon the ground. Jacob said to Joseph, "Is this my daughter-in-law, your wife? Blessed are you by God Most High."[197]

9 Jacob called her to him, blessed and kissed her. Aseneth stretched out her hands and embraced Jacob by the neck and hung herself from it off the ground, like someone who returns from war to his home after a long time. **10** After this they ate and drank. Then Joseph and Aseneth rose and went to their home.

11 They were accompanied only by the sons of Leah and the brothers of Joseph. But the sons of Bilhah and Zilpah, the handmaids of Leah and Rachel, did not accompany them because they were afraid as they remembered their earlier deceit.[198]

12 Levi[199] was traveling on the right side of Aseneth, holding her hand, and Joseph (held) her left hand. **13** Aseneth loved Levi more than all the brothers of Joseph, because he was close to the Living God. **14** The man was a prophet and prudent—his eyes were open and he was familiar with the words written in the books of Heaven, written by the finger of God. He knew the secrets of God, which had been revealed to him. He made known to Aseneth the secrets

them to mummify his father so as to avoid potential idolatry. Here, in opposition to Joseph's wishes, Aseneth worships Israel "like a god." Again, we are clearly in Gnostic territory.

196   In the Biblical story, he is not "comfortable." He is on his death bed.

197   Again, the emphasis is on physical beauty and health being the product of spirit. In this text, the flesh can be made spirit.

198   In the Biblical account, the brothers generally—not just those whose mothers were Bilhah and Zilpah—were involved in the plot to sell Joseph to traders passing by (Genesis 37). This text reflects a different understanding, i.e., that only the sons of the handmaidens Bilhah and Zilpah were involved. It seems to be referring not to the story of Genesis, but to differences among the disciples of Jesus.

199   Levi is here introduced as the "brother" for whom Aseneth/Mary the Magdalene has a "surpassing" love. Interestingly, in the Gnostic *Gospel of Mary Magdalene*, it is Levi who protects Mary the Magdalene from the other disciples, especially Peter. The canonical Gospels identify Levi with Matthew. In the Jesus Family Tomb, one of the inscribed ossuaries reads *Matia*, i.e., Matthew. Can it be that in the post-crucifixion period Levi took Jesus' place as Mary the Magdalene's husband? In the ancient Jewish context, a brother marrying his dead brother's widow is normative.

his mind knew—her place of rest on high, her eternal, impenetrable walls, and her foundations planted firmly upon a rock of stone long ago in the seventh heaven.[200]

23.

1 And it happened at the time when Joseph and Aseneth were passing by, that Pharaoh's firstborn saw Aseneth and Joseph from afar. Seeing Aseneth, he was jealous and desired her. He groaned and was troubled by her beauty, saying, "Why is this so?"[201]

2 Pharaoh's son[202] sent messengers and called Simeon and Levi to him.[203] The men came together and stood before him. Pharaoh's firstborn said to them, "I know you are powerful men surpassing all men on earth,[204] and that by your hands you laid waste to the city of Shechem, and by these two spears you killed three thousand fighting men. **3** Behold, today I shall become entirely your companion and friend and I shall give you gold, silver, much wealth and great, valuable inheritances. But I ask one thing of you—which you may do for me, my friends, because Joseph your brother despises me and treats me with contempt because he took Aseneth, my wife, who was rightly due to me long ago. **4** Now, come swear an oath to me and I shall make war on Joseph your brother and slay him with my own spear. **5** And Aseneth will be a wife to me, and you will be brothers and faithful friends.

---

200 Levi is Joseph's brother to whom she is closest. She loves him, and later Greek manuscripts add that he, too, loved her very much. Levi knows the "secrets of God" and has revealed to Aseneth her true spiritual identity. She is not just an ordinary woman, but a central figure in the drama of redemption—ensconced for all eternity in the seventh or highest heaven, closest to God. In fact, she is the "rock," probably *Petros* in the original Greek from which the Syriac is the oldest translation. She is literally the *real* Peter. In the *Gospel of Mary Magdalene*, Levi protects Mary the Magdalene from Andrew and Peter. Peter initially refuses to believe that what she teaches them are the authentic sayings of Jesus. There, Levi notes that Jesus loved Mary the Magdalene more than all the disciples and made her "worthy."

201 Again, the beauty theme.

202 The identity of "Pharaoh's son" is discussed in the previous chapters. Because we have located the context of this text in Roman times, specifically at the time of Jesus and Mary the Magdalene, "Pharaoh's son" would have to be related to the Roman emperor Tiberius, the Pharaoh who reigned from 14 to 37 C.E. As stated, the candidate who best fits the bill is Germanicus.

203 According to the Biblical account, Jacob had two wives, Leah and Rachel. Simon and Levi were two of the seven children Jacob had with Leah. Joseph and Benjamin were the only two children

But if you hesitate and delay and reject this thing, behold the point of my spear is drawn before you."

6 When he said this, he flashed his spear and showed its point. When the men—Simeon and Levi—heard these insolent words spoken by Pharaoh's first-born, they were very shocked. **7** Simeon was daring and angry and considered drawing his blade quickly to strike the firstborn of Pharaoh because he spoke harshly and impudently. **8** Levi, perceiving the intention of the heart of Simeon (because he was a prophet and soothsayer, and his eyes were open), trod on the foot of Simeon, signaling him to be silent and to calm his anger. **9** He said to Simeon privately, "Why are you angry and raging at this man? We are worshippers of God; it is not right to us to return evil for evil."[205]

10 Levi said to Pharaoh's son openly and peacefully, not in rage, "Why do you speak, our Lord, these words to us men who worship God? Our father is near and beloved of the Most High. Our brother Joseph is like a son of God[206] and the firstborn. **11** How could we do this evil thing and <sin> against God, and before our father Israel and our brother Joseph? **12** Now, hear my words: it is not right for any man who worships God to injure any man in any way. If a man harms a man who worships God, (with) the sword in his hand (the first man) will take vengeance on his rival. **13** Keep yourself from considering these things about our brother Joseph, lest you fall on the blade of the spear in our hands."

Jacob had with Rachel. This seems to be a coded reference to the attempt by "Pharaoh's son" to divide and conquer Jesus' disciples by appealing to their diverse tribal loyalties.

204   The tradition of Simon and Levi having superhuman strength is Talmudic.

205   In the canonical Gospels, it is Peter who draws the sword, angrily cutting off the ear of one of the high priest's men who had come to arrest Jesus. There, it is Jesus who calms Peter down, saying, "for all who take the sword will perish by the sword" (Matthew 26:52). Peter is not the birth name of the disciple who draws the sword. It is a nickname given by Jesus to the disciple named Simon. As in the canonical Gospels, here too we have a conspiracy and a representative of authority. Here too it is Simon/Peter who wishes to draw his "blade." Here, however, it is Levi, not Jesus, who calms Simon/Peter down by saying "it is not right for us to return evil for evil." Not returning evil for evil represents an important ethical principle in this work. In the New Testament, parallels to this phrase can be found in Romans 12:17 ("Do not repay anyone evil for evil") and 1 Peter 3:9 ("Do not repay evil for evil or abuse for abuse; but, on the contrary, repay with a blessing"). Is Levi, not Jesus, the source for this material? Is the "Pharaoh's son" conspiracy conflated in the canonical Gospels with the later Judas conspiracy?

206   Notice, Levi uses the *like* word. "Like a son of God," not *the* son of God. This is a different theology from what emerges later as Pauline Christianity.

14 And they showed their blades and said, "Look at these sharp spears. By these two blades we avenged the shame of Dinah our sister from the sons of Shechem."[207] **15** Pharaoh's son saw and was much afraid. He trembled and fell out of fear upon the ground before the feet of Simeon and Levi. **16** Levi stretched out his hand and raised him and said to him, "Rise and do not be afraid. But again, turn from your evils and do not plot[208] against Joseph, our brother."

And Simeon and Levi departed from the presence of Pharaoh's son.

24.

1 (Pharaoh's son) was troubled and in great anguish because of Aseneth's beauty. **2** His servants said to him, "Behold, the sons of Bilhah and Zilpah—the handmaidens of Leah and Rachel, the wives of Jacob—they are <jealous> and hate Joseph and Aseneth. They will listen to your counsel and do your will."[209]

3 He again sent messengers to them[210] and summoned them to him—the son of Pharaoh—in the night. They came and stood before him and he said to them, "You are brave and powerful men." **4** Dan and Gad, the oldest brothers,

---

207 In Genesis, Dinah had been raped. Here, "Pharaoh's son" threatens to do the same to Mary the Magdalene. Here, Simon/Peter and Matthew/Levi warn him that if he doesn't back off he will end up dead. This provides us with the motivation for the alliance between the early Jesus movement and Sejanus against Germanicus.

208 Here the "plot" is explicitly mentioned.

209 According to the Biblical text, Jacob had children with Bilhah (Rachel's handmaiden or servant) and with Zilpah (Leah's handmaiden). Dan and Naphtali were the children Jacob had with Bilhah; Gad and Asher, with Zilpah. Thus, these four sons of Jacob were, in a sense, once removed from the core family grouping consisting of the children of Leah and Rachel. Our text chooses to stress these four sons and the fact that they were alienated from Joseph (Jesus). This is different from the story in Genesis, where all the brothers conspire against Joseph, not just four.

"Pharaoh's son" knows of the complex loyalties in Jesus' family. He seeks to take advantage of a rift amongst the brothers. With respect to Jesus, as above, the canonical Gospels write about four brothers (James/Jacob, Simon, Judah, Yose/Joseph). Various traditions of Christianity interpret these "brothers" in different ways. According to the Orthodox Church, they are half-siblings from a previous marriage of Joseph's (mother Mary's husband). According to Catholics, they are "cousins." According to Protestants, they are full siblings born *after* the virgin birth. There is also some confusion in the Gospels with respect to mother Mary and Mary Clophas' wife, who seems to have children with exactly the same names as Mary, mother of Jesus. All this has led James Tabor to suggest that after Joseph's death, Mary, mother of Jesus married Joseph's brother "Clophas," also called "Alpheus." That would mean that Mary was the mother of all Jesus' siblings—by different fathers.

The picture that emerges from our deciphered text does not agree with Tabor's hypothesis. The half brothers are half brothers by virtue of having different mothers, not different fathers.

said to him, "Lord, speak because your servants will hear and do your will." **5** Pharaoh's son was joyously happy and he said to his servants, "Stand back a little, because I have a secret word[211] (to say) to these men." **6** And they all withdrew.

7 Pharaoh's son said (to Dan and Gad): "Behold, life and death are before me. Choose life because you are powerful men and will not die like women. But you are brave and seek vengeance from your enemies. **8** Because I heard Joseph your brother say to Pharaoh, 'The sons of Bilhah and Zilpah are my servants and, out of deceit and jealousy, they sold <me>. When the time comes to grieve for my father, I shall take vengeance on them and remove them from the earth, lest these sons of maidservants receive the inheritance with the freeborn sons.' **9** Pharaoh praised him and said to him, 'It is right to revenge this great, long-ago suffering. When the time comes, I shall help you in your revenge'."[212]

10 When the men heard these words they were shaken and much grieved. They said to Pharaoh's son, "We beseech you, lord, help us." **11** And he said to them "I shall help you provided that you obey me." **12** The men replied,

---

The family might have looked like this: Joseph/Clophas/Alpheus are all one and the same person. He had at least four male children and perhaps two female children with a woman named Mary. This Mary had a sister, also called Mary, who had originally been betrothed to Joseph but who became unavailable to him when she got pregnant with someone else's child, allegedly, a Roman soldier's child (see *Shabbat* 104b MS. Munich 95 in Schafer, op. cit., 16). Although Joseph raised all the children, he did not have relations with Mary, Jesus' mother. In *Joseph and Aseneth*, Mary, Jesus' mother, is compared to Rachel and Mary the mother of Jesus' half brothers is compared to Leah. In effect, by pointing out that there may be different mothers involved with the brothers of Jesus, the confusion about Jesus' family can now begin to be resolved.

210 As the text makes clear, the four brothers of the handmaidens appear before "Pharaoh's son." As stated above, Jesus also had four brothers, possibly half brothers. Christian tradition says that some of them had ambivalent feelings about Jesus. James, for example, only became a follower *after* the crucifixion. In the canonical Gospels, Jesus is sometimes hostile to his family (Mark 3:32–35). At one point, it seems that the family regards Jesus as mentally unstable (Mark 3:21).

211 The theme of secrecy continues in this text. Levi knew secret wisdom and he taught it to Mary the Magdalene. Here it is Germanicus—i.e., "Pharaoh's son"—who has a "secret word" to impart. He puts everyone not in the know at arm's length.

212 "Pharaoh's son" claims that Joseph (i.e., Jesus) was planning revenge against his brothers and involving Pharaoh in the plot. This, of course, would violate the central ethical principle of this work, i.e., not to repay evil for evil. Basically, "Pharaoh's son" must be lying about what Joseph and Pharaoh said to each other about seeking revenge. He is simply trying to divide and conquer.

"Behold, we stand before you as your servants. Speak, and by us your will shall be done." **13** Pharaoh's son said, "Behold, today I shall kill my father Pharaoh because he loved Joseph like a father. Instead of him, I shall reign. And you will slay Joseph your brother. Then once more, as is my desire, Aseneth will be my wife."

14 The men promised to do this and said, "We heard Joseph say to Aseneth, 'Go tomorrow to our estate because it is vintage season.' And he gave her six hundred men powerful in battle and fifty advance guards. **15** Now, we shall speak and our lord will listen and give us men in battle." **16** He gave them two thousand men, five hundred men for each of the four (brothers).[213] And he appointed them as chiefs of the five hundred.

17 Dan and Gad said, "We shall go by night and hide in the thicket of reeds in the valley. You take fifty archers and go before us and we shall rise from the ambush of the thicket and kill the six hundred men who are with her. When she is fleeing on the chariot, come upon her and do to her as you will. And after, when Joseph is grieving on account of Aseneth, we shall kill him and we shall slay his two sons before his eyes."[214]

18 Pharaoh's son rejoiced when he heard these words. He sent them from before him with two thousand armed men. **19** They came to the

---

213 There are *four* brothers of Joseph in the conspiracy. As stated, this corresponds to Jesus, not Joseph. Perhaps this refers to four of the twelve disciples.

214 The plot here is very specific. It has absolutely nothing to do with the text in Genesis, nor does it have anything to do with any Midrash or historical circumstances outside the Second Temple period. Furthermore, it serves absolutely no theological purpose. Clearly, what the text is telling us is that there was a plot against Jesus, his wife, and his family that involved the highest levels of the ruling regime in the Galilee. The plot involved a conspiracy, betrayal in the inner circle, an ambush, troops, and the deadly intent to kill the father and the children and abduct the wife. If this seems like fiction, remember that *all* four canonical Gospels describe a plot hatched at the highest levels of Judaean/Roman rule including the Jewish High Priest Caiaphas, the Roman Governor Pilate, and the local ruler Herod Antipas. There was also, according to the Gospels, a clear betrayal in the inner circle (Judas) and a partial betrayal (Peter). The plot ended with the crucifixion of Jesus and the temporary disbanding of his followers. According to the historian Josephus, a similar plot did James in, and another similar plot brought down the anonymous "Teacher of Righteousness" mentioned in the Dead Sea Scrolls as the leader of the group that produced some of those texts, possibly the Essenes. In other words, the plot described in *Joseph and Aseneth* is not far-fetched. It is consistent with similar events described in the New Testament and in other sources of the time.

valley and laid in wait in the thicket of reeds. They were divided into five hundred men on one side and five hundred on the other,[215] leaving a passage in the middle.[216]

25.

1 Pharaoh's son rose in the night and went to his father to kill him with a blade, but his father's guards[217] prevented him from entering (the room). They said to him, "What do you command, Lord?" **2** And he replied, "I wish to see my father because I am going to (harvest) the vintage of the planting of my vineyard." **3** And the guards[218] said to him, "Your father is vexed with a pain in his head this night and desires quiet. He commanded that no man awaken him, not even his firstborn."

4 Running, Pharaoh's son returned and took with him fifty archers, according to the counsel of Dan and Gad, and going ahead, he hid in the place. **5** <Naphtali> and Asher, the younger brothers of Dan and Gad, said (to their brothers), "Why are you again intending evil to Israel your father and to Joseph your brother, whom, behold, the Lord is guarding like the pupil of his eye? Did you not sell[219] him earlier? Behold, he rules over the land—he is the magistrate—and he gave grain from the provisions,

---

215 The Syriac text only accounts for the location of half of the two thousand armed men, five hundred on each side of the road Aseneth will travel. Where the other two groups of five hundred are stationed is not mentioned.

216 So here's the plan: "Pharaoh's son" will kill his father. Then "Pharaoh's son," assisted by the conspirators, will ambush Aseneth's retinue, killing the six hundred guards who are protecting her. Aseneth will be turned over to "Pharaoh's son" to do to her whatever he wishes. The conspirators will then kill the two children—Ephraim and Manasseh—before Joseph's eyes, and then kill him. There is nothing like this in the Biblical account of Joseph. However, in the Gnostic *Gospel of Philip*, there is a sense "of some sort of jealousy on the part of the other disciples" when it comes to Mary the Magdalene. See Ann Graham Brock, *Mary Magdalene, the First Apostle: The Struggle for Authority* (Harvard University Press, 2004), 90.

217 Since Sejanus was the head of the Praetorian Guard, the above is consistent with the idea that Sejanus' murder of Germanicus was a well timed rescue of the emperor from the machinations of Germanicus.

218 Those who guarded Emperor Tiberius were the Praetorian Guards, who eventually came to be controlled by the real power in Rome, Sejanus.

219 The idea that Jesus was sold, like Joseph, comes up in the canonical Gospels with Judas and the thirty pieces of silver (Matthew 27:3).

redeeming and saving many.[220] **6** Now, if you should attempt to do evil to him, he will climb up to heaven and send fire at you[221] and it will consume you because the angels of God are fighting for him and they are helping him."[222]

7 And Dan and Gad were angry and said to them, "If we don't (fight), we will die like women."

26.

1 Aseneth awoke at dawn and said to Joseph, "I will go to the vineyard in our estate, like you said, but I am afraid in my heart to part from you."

2 Joseph said to her, "Take courage and do not be afraid. I will go quickly and the Lord is with you and will guard you like the pupil of his eye and from an act of evil. **3** I will go to prepare the gift of life-giving provisions and abundant food; otherwise many in the land will perish." **4** Then Aseneth went on her way and Joseph turned back on his way.[223]

5 Aseneth and the six hundred men with her approached the valley. <Pharaoh's> men rose from the ambush and they joined <in battle> with Aseneth's men, killing them as well as her fifty advance guards. Aseneth fled on her chariot.

6 Levi made known the treachery to his brothers, the sons of Leah.[224] They placed the blades of their swords on their thighs, picked up their shields, put them on their arms, took their spears in their right hand and immediately pursued. Hastening, they came up to Aseneth.

7 As she was fleeing, behold, Pharaoh's son met her along with the fifty

---

220 "Redeeming and saving many" is clearly language associated with Jesus. For example, when John the Baptizer's disciples come to Jesus, he sends them back, asking them to tell John that "The blind receive sight, the lame walk, those who have leprosy are cleansed, the deaf hear, the dead are raised" (Luke 7:22), i.e., he is redeeming and saving many.

221 Clearly this is not something that the Joseph of Genesis could do. Climbing up to heaven and sending fire is something that only a god incarnate could do.

222 It's strange that these misgivings on the part of Naphtali and Asher should appear in the text at this point, since the negotiations have already concluded and the plan is already in progress. These caveats would make more sense during the negotiations between the conspirators and "Pharaoh's son." At any rate, nothing comes of these qualms and the plot proceeds with the four brothers in cahoots with "Pharaoh's son" against Joseph/Jesus, Aseneth/Mary the Magdalene, and their two sons.

horsemen who were with him. **8** Aseneth saw him and was afraid and trembled greatly. She called on the name of the Lord God Most High.

27.

1 But Benjamin[225] was with her in the chariot. Benjamin was a beautiful boy who worshipped God and was very courageous. **2** He came down from the chariot and gathered some smooth round stones from the valley and filled his hands. Not wavering, he courageously threw them at Pharaoh's son. He struck him on his left temple and wounded him greatly. **3** Pharaoh's son fell on the ground. **4** Then Benjamin ran and went up on a high rock and said to the driver of Aseneth's chariot, "Pass me stones from the valley." **5** And he gave him forty-eight stones.[226] He killed each of the forty-eight men joining Pharaoh's son.

6 The sons of Leah—Reuben, Simeon, Levi, Judah, Issachar, Zebulun—pursued the men who had ambushed them in the thicket of reeds in the valley. (The sons of Leah) fell on them all of a sudden and killed them all.

7 Their brothers, Dan and Gad—the sons of Bilhah and Zilpah—fled from them saying, "We are dying by our brothers and Pharaoh's son lives, afflicted with a deadly wound by Benjamin. **8** Now come, let us kill Aseneth and our brother Benjamin. Then we shall flee and take refuge in the thicket of reeds in the valley." **9** They came, their swords drawn and wet with blood.

But Aseneth saw them and said, **10** "Lord, who has given me life from death and said 'Your soul will live forever,' rescue me and save me from the blade of these deceitful men." **11** When they heard the prayer of Aseneth, the blades fell from their hands in dust upon the ground.

---

223 Our gospel does not record their reunion after the murder plot. This provides a textual *terminus ad quem*, i.e., a no-later-than date for the composition of the original manuscript. That is to say, if Germanicus is "Pharaoh's son" and he died in October, 19 C.E., then the original *Joseph and Aseneth* text was written *after* Germanicus died and *before* Jesus was crucified in the spring of 32 C.E., making it the earliest account from the first followers of Jesus and Mary the Magdalene.

224 The loyal disciples intervene.

225 In Genesis, Benjamin is the son of Israel by Rachel, as was Joseph. Thus, he is Joseph's full, younger brother, his closest sibling. Here he is entrusted with Aseneth's (i.e., Mary the Magdalene's) care. If Joseph is Jesus, then who is Benjamin? Benjamin is a somewhat mysterious figure here. In the Gospels, the mysterious figure is the unnamed "beloved disciple" who is entrusted with Mother Mary's care (John 19:25). Perhaps Benjamin is the unnamed beloved disciple of the Gospels and he was caring for Jesus' wife, not mother.

226 The number should be fifty (see 24:17; 25:4; 26:5).

28.

1 When they saw this, the sons of Bilhah and Zilpah were very afraid. They trembled and said, "Truly the Lord is fighting us on behalf of Aseneth." **2** They fell on the ground, bowed, and said to Aseneth, "Have mercy on us and pardon us, your servants, because you are our lady,[227] the queen.[228] **3** We committed evil against you and the Lord repaid us according to our deeds. **4** Now we pray to you: have mercy on us and save us from the hands of <our> brothers because already those avengers of the insult (done to you) have prepared their blades against us."

5 Aseneth said to them, "Take courage and do not fear from your brothers because they are worshippers of God and are respected by every man. Return to the thicket in the valley until I (can) calm their anger concerning you because you have increased your evils through boldness but the Lord will judge between me and you." **6** Dan and his brother fled to the thicket.

7 Behold, the sons of Leah came running like young stags. **8** Aseneth got down to meet them. Weeping, she took them by the hand and they fell and prostrated themselves on the ground. They wept greatly and searched for the sons of Bilhah and Zilpah, their brothers.

9 Aseneth said to them, "I pray you, leave them and do not return evil for evil. The Lord, who saved me from them and threw their blades on the ground and melted them like wax as if consumed before a fire, will treat me well on account of (how I treat) them. **10** It is enough that the Lord has fought against them. So spare them, because they are your brothers and sons of Israel your father."[229]

11 Simeon[230] said to her, "Why does our Lady[231] speak well concerning her enemies? Do not do so. Let us slay and destroy them by this blade because they were first to act deceitfully against us, against Israel our father and

---

227 Syriac *Mara*. This term *lady* is used in an early Christian context in the *Shepherd of Hermas*. Originally written in Greek, the text is the longest work to survive from the first hundred years of the Christian church. It was regarded by many Christians as canonical scripture. As in *Joseph and Aseneth*, Hermas' love object is referred to as a *sister, goddess,* and *lady.* See Bart D. Ehrman, *Lost Scriptures: Books that Did Not Make It into the New Testament* (Oxford University Press, 2005), 252–253. As in this text, there is also the idea of wife/sister: ". . . your wife, who is about to become your sister." Ibid., 254.

twice against Joseph our brother. And against you, our lady, who commands us today."

12 Aseneth lifted up her hand, took hold of his beard, kissed him, and said to him, "No, our brother, do not return evil for evil. Give the Lord (the right) to punish our insult, for they are your brothers and kinsmen of your father. They have fled and withdrawn from your presence."

13 Levi approached her, took her right hand, and kissed it. She knew that by this, he wished to spare his brothers. They were nearby, hiding in the thicket of reeds in the valley. Levi was aware of this but did not make it known to his brothers, for he was afraid that, in their anger, they might slay and destroy them.

29.

1 Pharaoh's son rose from the ground and sat up. He spat blood from his mouth because the blood from the wound on his temple ran down to his mouth.[232] **2** Benjamin ran to him and drew Pharaoh's son's own blade because he did not have a sword. He wished to strike him in his chest.

3 Levi ran, took his hand, and said to him, "Do not do this, my <brother>, because we are men who worship the Most High. <It is not right> to return evil for evil <by> increasing the pain of (his enemy's) death, spilling blood on the ground, and opposing (him) until he is dead. **4** Now return the sword to its sheath and come help me. We shall bind up and heal the man's wound and he will live. Therefore, his father Pharaoh will be a friend to us like our father."

5 Levi lifted the son of Pharaoh, wiped the blood from his face, bound up his wound, and put him on his horse. He brought him and stood him before his father, Pharaoh. He told him all these things. **6** Pharaoh rose from his throne and prostrated himself upon the ground before Levi.

---

228 Again, royal status.

229 Consistent with "love your enemy" and "turn the other cheek" theology.

230 Simeon here is very much in keeping with Simon Peter of the Gospels, who is quick with the blade at Gethsemane (John 18:10).

231 Syriac *Mara*.

232 The description is very graphic. Very real. There is nothing theological about this scene.

7 On the third day, when the firstborn of Pharaoh died from the wound of the little boy Benjamin, Pharaoh mourned for him. He grew weak and died at 177 years old. He left the diadem to Joseph and (Joseph) ruled in Egypt forty-eight years. Joseph entrusted the diadem to the grandson of Pharaoh who was nursing when Pharaoh died. And Joseph was like a father of the boy in Egypt all the days of his life.[233]

(This is) the end of the story of Joseph and of Aseneth, the wife of Joseph, translated from Greek into Syriac.

---

233 The text ends suddenly. The forty-eight years of rule is not consistent with Tiberius but more so with Herod Antipas, who ruled the area in his name from 4 B.C.E. to 39 C.E., a total of forty-three years. The death of "Pharaoh's son" of his "wounds" after "three days" seems to awkwardly foreshadow or allude to another son of *the* ruler who died of his wounds but rose after three days. It seems that the story breaks off just after one plot is foiled and before the other succeeds. We are basically left with a gospel compiled between the rescue of Mary the Magdalene and the crucifixion of Jesus.

APPENDIX II

LETTER TO MOSES OF INGILA
AND HIS REPLY

S ometime around 550 C.E., an anonymous individual, probably a monk, discovered an ancient work in the library of Resh'aina, modern-day Syria. It was written in Greek, and he was so intrigued by it that he wrote a letter to Moses of Ingila—a scholar and translator—asking him to translate the manuscript from Greek to Syriac (Christian Aramaic).

This letter is of tremendous significance. It places the oldest extant copy of *Joseph and Aseneth* in context. This anonymous individual tells us that he suspects this work contains a hidden meaning: more precisely, "hidden wisdom" that is expressed in "riddles." Moses replies, confirming that it does indeed contain an inner meaning. "It is the glory of God to conceal things," he writes. He agrees to do the translation but admits that he is afraid. He is concerned that the nature of the truth revealed by the text may endanger them. He cautions that "the babbling mouth" can put their lives at risk, and reminds our anonymous writer that "he who restrains the lips is wise." While Moses of Ingila's full reply is no longer extant, what he says by way of reply points us in the direction of a Jesus decoding. It literally breaks off as he is speaking about "the Lord [who] took flesh." Moses of Ingila either translated or had the "old Greek book" translated from Greek into Syriac. It was this Syriac version that was included in Pseudo Zacharias Rhetor's compilation, *A Volume of Records of Events that Have Shaped the World.*

In the following letters, each addresses the other as "O Excellent One." The book from which the anonymous writer and Moses of Ingila quote extensively is called *The Book of the Wise* or *The Wise.* This may refer specifically to the *Book of Proverbs,* whose authorship is explicitly ascribed to Solomon, son of David, king of Israel (Proverbs 1:1). Or, since the writer quotes from a number of related works, *The Book of the Wise* may refer more generally to a compilation of writings comprising the Wisdom Literature of ancient Israel—Proverbs, Ecclesiastes, and *The Wisdom of Solomon,* as well as *Ecclesiasticus* (also known as *Sirach*). The latter two works are sometimes included in the Apocrypha, i.e., books sometimes excluded from the Biblical canon. These works are treated as canonical in a number of Christian faith traditions, including, presumably, the one to which this letter-writer and the recipient belong.

The overall theme is that it is important to act as a wise person would act and to search out hidden meaning—"It is the glory of God to conceal a matter, and the glory of a king to plumb a matter" (Proverbs 25:2). It is significant that the letter-writer positions *Joseph and Aseneth* within the genre of wisdom writings, as a work containing a hidden truth that requires investigation and insight.

For those who believe that writing in code happens only in Hollywood fiction, these 1,460-year-old letters will be a revelation. The writers speak almost entirely in code.

AN EXPLANATION OF
THE STORY OF ASENETH AND JOSEPH.

A letter concerning this to Moses of Ingila.

The Book of the Wise, O Excellent One, says, "One who speaks in his season is good,"[1] and "It is the glory of a king to investigate a thing."[2] "A word spoken is like an apple of gold in a setting of silver"[3] and "Those who seek counsel are wise."[4] "The Lord guides the wise and we and our words are in his hands"[5] and, furthermore, "The words[6] from a wise man's mouth are glory."[7] Therefore, scripture advises us, "Whatever your hand finds to do, do."[8]

And we who are concerned with investigating "the words of the wise and their riddles"[9] do well, for "The wise mind will understand the speech of the wise, and the ear that hears will be thankful,"[10] because "The wise man's mouth is sought in the assembly, and they ponder his speech <in> their minds."[11] "For a wise man does not ignore hidden wisdom; rather he searches <for it> intensely[12] and the one who prospers investigates everything."[13]

---

1   Proverbs 15:23. A modern translation of this passage puts it this way, "How good is a word rightly timed" (Jewish Publication Society translation).

2   Proverbs 25:2. The full context of this passage is, "It is the glory of God to conceal a matter, and the glory of a king to plumb a matter" (Jewish Publication Society translation).

3   Proverbs 25:11.

4   Proverbs 13:10.

5   *The Wisdom of Solomon* 7:15, 16.

6   The manuscript has *my words.*

7   Ecclesiastes 10:12.

8   Ecclesiastes 9:10.

9   Proverbs 1:6. Throughout the letter, the writer puts an emphasis on wisdom and the need to discern the meaning of riddles. This aptly characterizes the work at hand, *Joseph and Aseneth.* It cannot mean what it superficially seems to mean.

10   *Sirach* 3:29. The *Wisdom of Jesus, Son of Sirach,* is also called *Ecclesiasticus.*

11   *Sirach* 21:17.

12   Both Proverbs and *Sirach* emphasize that wisdom is hidden and requires searching: "If you seek it as you do silver, And search for it as for treasures, Then you will understand the fear of the Lord And attain knowledge of God" (Proverbs 2:4, 5. Jewish Publication Society translation). Here the letter-writer suggests by this allusion that *Joseph and Aseneth* contains hidden wisdom that the wise person should investigate. (See also *Sirach* 20:30, 31).

13   *Sirach* 34:9.

380 SIMCHA JACOBOVICI AND BARRIE WILSON

Paul, moreover, made known that "All scripture written in the spirit is useful for teaching, for reproof, for correction, and for training in righteousness."[14]

Indeed, now that I understand these (sayings), I am writing the truth to you, dear sir. Henceforth, I ask that my request to you be granted for the sake of those in the flock in need of what is spiritually useful from you.[15]

For in the library in the city of Resh'aina established in memory of the bishops descended from "the house of Beroea,"[16] I was accompanied by a young man, a relative of these bishops, by the name of Mar Abda, whom I love in our Lord and has been a close friend of mine from childhood.

I found (there, in that library) a small, very old book written in Greek called "Of Aseneth."[17] I read the story by myself and I do not understand the inner meaning, because this language is difficult and strange to me.[18] For this reason I sent it you, dear sir, so that you will translate it for me into Syriac—the entire story—and that you will, in some measure, explain to me its inner meaning, so that the Lord may give knowledge, because "All wisdom is from the Lord and he gives his spirit to all men as he wishes."[19]

And (may) my request be filled quickly, so you may be recognized by those from above,[20] and so you may fulfill the command of the Lord who said, "Give to he who begs from you, and do not refuse he who seeks from you."[21]

Therefore I ask that this (translation into Syriac and explanation of the hidden meaning) be written and sent to me. Then, when meditating on it, I can

---

14   2 Timothy 3:16.

15   It is interesting that the letter-writer is a teacher and wants an elucidation of the meaning of this work, as well as a translation, so that he might better communicate its message to his students.

16   Ancient Beroea is Aleppo in northwest Syria. The library was in Resh'aina, but it was dedicated to the memory of the bishops of Beroea. Perhaps some calamity had befallen these bishops.

17   In other words, the Syriac translation we have from the 6th century C.E. rests on an earlier "very old book written in Greek." That's as far back as we can trace the manuscript tradition.

18   Note the mention of its "inner meaning."

19   *Sirach* 1:1, 9–10.

20   It is unclear what the letter-writer means by this. Who are "those from above"? They could refer to God and/or the heavenly host. Or they could mean his religious superiors. At any rate, having witnesses interested in the material puts an added onus on Moses of Ingila to comply with his request. He has already put pressure on him by quoting scriptural injunctions to seek out wisdom, as well as words from Jesus encouraging his followers to honor requests.

praise the works of the Lord[22] and the care of your fellowship, which is helpful to your brother in Christ—"just like a city receives help from its fortress,"[23] and is highly regarded by its <neighbor>, as he is himself, according to the word of Scripture.[24]

(MOSES OF INGILA'S) RESPONSE TO THE LETTER

Praise the care of God, who (watches) over all as well as over your diligence, which is not like the generation of others who abandoned virtues and training, who waste their days in vain, and who are busy with distractions and the vanities of the world and spiritual anguish—like Demas, who abandoned the skillful Paul and loved the world,[25] and those who were in Asia who turned away from him, including Phygelus <and Her>mogenes.[26] Nor (are you like those) who are concerned also with the foolishness of the flesh, who seek out a variety of foods, like the ones whose "gods are the belly, and their glory is in their shame; the ones whose minds are entirely on earthly things."[27] They lie like the sons of Crete, who lie as their own prophet Miksinidis[28] said, "The sons of Crete always lie, evil brutes and lazy bellies."[29] But you are not lazy, (for) you have been liberated from passions on account of love (and) knowledge of truth.

---

21   Matthew 5:42.

22   The anonymous writer seems to realize that the Joseph of the text is really "the Lord."

23   The Syriac word for *fortress* is *Chesnah*. It plays off the word *Migdal*. The fortress and the tower go together to give the city "life according to the text of Scripture." See also Proverbs 18:19.

24   Leviticus 19:18; Mark 12:31.

25   2 Timothy 4:10: ". . . for Demas, in love with this present world, has deserted me and gone to Thessalonica."

26   2 Timothy 1:15: "You are aware that all who are in Asia have turned away from me, including Phygelus and Hermogenes."

27   Philippians 3:19.

28   *Miksinidis* is a corruption of the name Epimenides, the author of *Cretica*.

29   Titus 1:12.

As Evagrius the Ascetic[30] said, "There abides one good thing in the world, and it is the knowledge of truth"; and again, "<Understand that> the more one is stripped of passions, the more one is acquainted with understanding; and the more he is diligent, the richer his knowledge." Your humility has burst forth in the love of Christ and called upon my unworthiness (to be) a teacher and helper, to lead you forward in this matter with which you struggle. This is an (endeavor) in which there is virtue.

But, recognizing my own shortcomings, <I>[31] truly hesitate to give an answer to relieve your burden, recalling *(the Book of) the Wise*[32] that says, "He who restrains the lips is intelligent;"[33] and again, "Above all else, guard your heart."[34] And again, "The babbling mouth draws ruin near;"[35] and again, "He who guards his mouth, will preserve his life";[36] and again, "It is the glory of God to conceal things;"[37] and moreover, "He who trusts in his own heart is a fool."[38] Furthermore, "All words are wearisome;"[39] "Do not be too zealous nor stupefied;"[40] and again, "My son, beware: of writing there is no end and much study is a weariness of the flesh."[41] Furthermore, "Be quick to hear (but) deliberate in writing; and if you have something to say, answer your neighbor; but if not, put <your hand> over <your mouth>."[42]

---

30 Evagrius Ponticus (345–399 C.E.).

31 The passage is somewhat unclear here. It reads "Truly my paucity, when recognized in the form of the self, hesitates to give answer. . . ." The sense is that Moses of Ingila hesitates to give the letter-writer an answer and in the following quotes a number of scriptural passages that urge caution.

32 Moses of Ingila also refers to "the Wise" presumably intending *The Book of the Wise*, and like the anonymous letter-writer, quotes from a number of works on wisdom.

33 Proverbs 10:19.

34 Proverbs 4:23.

35 Proverbs 10:14.

36 Proverbs 13:3.

37 Proverbs 25:2.

38 Proverbs 28:26.

39 Ecclesiastes 1:8.

40 Ecclesiastes 7:16, 17.

41 Ecclesiastes 12:12.

42 *Sirach* 5:11, 12.

Out of fear of these things (i.e., the cautionary words expressed above) I might have considered keeping silent if love had not compelled me and scripture not encouraged me, saying, "Give to he who begs from you."[43] Moreover, *(the Book of) the Wise* again commands, "Do not refuse to do good as much as it is in your hands to do; and, when you are able, do not say to your neighbor, '<Go> and come back again tomorrow and I will give to you';"[44] and, "the one who despises the word will be destroyed by it."[45] In addition, "He who despises his neighbor sins;"[46] (and), "The medicine of the tongue is <the tree of life>"[47] and the one who eats from its fruit is satisfied.[48] Also, "The joy of a man (is) the word of his mouth, and what is spoken in its season is good;"[49] and furthermore, "The one who recognizes the word will find prosperity."[50] Wisdom, humility, and knowledge are from the presence of the Lord. Love and the way of good deeds are in his company.[51]

<Evagrius the Ascetic> said, "The learned nature <demonstrates> knowledge, and likewise knowledge purifies the learned"; and also, "Everyone in creation is capable of the knowledge of God, but <he who> honors ignorance above this knowledge is justly called evil."

Scripture says, "Ask and it will be given you; knock and it will be opened to you"[52] as well as "Call and you will be answered."[53] Moreover,

---

43 Matthew 5:42.

44 Proverbs 3:27, 28.

45 Proverbs 13:13.

46 Proverbs 14:21.

47 Proverbs 15:4. A contemporary translation expresses the thought this way: "A healing tongue is a tree of life" (Jewish Publication Society translation).

48 Proverbs 18:20–21.

49 Proverbs 15:23. Again a contemporary translation puts it this way: "A ready response is a joy to a man, And how good is a word rightly timed" (Jewish Publication Society translation).

50 Proverbs 16:20.

51 Perhaps a reference to Proverbs 2:6–9: "For the Lord grants wisdom; Knowledge and discernment are by His decree. He reserves ability for the upright, And is a shield for those who live blamelessly, Guarding the paths of justice, Protecting the way of those loyal to him" (Jewish Publication Society translation). The final line of this column of text has been cut off.

52 Matthew 7:7.

53 Isaiah 58:9.

"If one who is lacking in wisdom asks from God, without hesitation it will be given to him."[54]

Therefore, O Excellent One, because of these things and the love which "does not ask for itself"[55] but for another, I am undertaking the fulfillment of your request.

For I have read the story from the old Greek book you sent to me, and there is inner meaning in it.[56] In short, to tell the truth: our Lord, our God, the Word who, at the will of the father and by the power of the Holy Spirit of the Lord, took flesh, and <became human> and was united to the soul with its senses completely . . . [The manuscript is deliberately cut off here.][57]

---

54   James 1:5.

55   1 Corinthians 13:5.

56   Thus Moses of Ingila confirms the anonymous letter writer's impression that *Joseph and Aseneth* contains an inner meaning.

57   The manuscript ends abruptly here. There is a straight cut across the page, right through a line of Syriac writing. This indicates that the section is missing not because of deterioration but because of censorship. Since the first page of the text is written on the back of the letter, and since the first page appears in a 12th-century edition, we know for a fact that the 12th-century copyist also had access to Moses of Ingila's letter. We suspect, therefore, that it was probably this second copyist who censored the text. Perhaps on the last page, Moses of Ingila disclosed his understanding of the hidden meaning contained in *Joseph and Aseneth*. Perhaps this was too heretical for the 12th-century copyist. As a result, Moses of Ingila's decoding was lost . . . until now.

ENDNOTES

PREFACE

1. Though people think her name was Mary Magdalene—that is, that Magdalene was her family name—the reality is that "the Magdalene" was a title, not a name. It may have served as a nickname but, literally translated from its original Hebrew/Greek, it means "Mary the tower lady."

2. B.C.E. stands for "before the common era;" C.E. stands for "common era." Many scholars prefer these neutral designations of time to the Christian abbreviations B.C. (Before Christ) and A.D. (*Anno Domini*, in the year of our Lord).

3. James D. Tabor, *Paul and Jesus: How the Apostle Transformed Christianity* (New York: Simon & Schuster, 2012), 44. For a discussion of the Didache, see also Barrie Wilson, *How Jesus Became Christian.* (New York: St. Martin's Press, 2008), 156–162.

4. Tabor, op. cit., 46.

5. The Hebrew Bible is called the Old Testament by Christians.

6. Quoted in Margaret Starbird, "Templars, Tombs and the Resurrection," *Sacred Union in Christianity* (blog), 19 May 2013, margaretstarbird.net/blog.html

7. Marvin W. Meyer, ed., *The Ancient Mysteries: A Sourcebook of Sacred Texts* (Philadelphia: University of Pennsylvania Press), 225.

8. Simcha experienced this kind of response when his film, *The Lost Tomb of Jesus*, and his book with Charles Pellegrino, *The Jesus Family Tomb*, came out in 2007 (New York: HarperOne). Basically, the film and book argue that a tomb found by archaeologists in 1980 in Talpiot, a suburb of Jerusalem, is the final resting place of Jesus and most of his family. Although many scholars supported the thesis, the idea of a Jesus-family tomb met with derision in many quarters. One year later, at an international conference sponsored by the Princeton Theological Seminary, fifty of the world's top scholars could not find one thing in the film or book that they could all agree to publicly criticize. The conference passed only one resolution—that the Talpiot tomb needs further study. And yet, because of theological considerations and personal attacks in the press, both the film and the book were buried. Somehow, suggesting that a tomb has been found in Jerusalem belonging to a 1st-century Jewish family—if that family belongs to Jesus of Nazareth—is regarded in the same vein as

suggesting that an alien landing site has been discovered. Nonetheless, Simcha's 2012 film *The Jesus Discovery/The Resurrection Tomb Mystery* and the publication with James Tabor of *The Jesus Discovery: The Resurrection Tomb that Reveals the Birth of Christianity* (New York: Simon and Schuster, 2012) have gone a long way toward strengthening the original thesis.

9.   That is, John the Baptist. We prefer to avoid this potentially misleading expression, as if John were a member of the Baptist Christian denomination.

10.   Diane Apostolos-Cappadona refers to the process by which these encoding conventions get codified as "communal memory." In the visual arts, for example, to this day, encoding a narrative is part and parcel of telling the story. In the words of Apostolos-Cappadona: "Over time, through artistic convention, recognizable codes developed: the Virgin Mary wears blue, Judas has red hair, Jesus appears in the center of *The Last Supper*, and Mary Magdalene is always seductively beautiful." Quoted in *Secrets of Mary Magdalene*, Dan Burnstein and Arne J. de Keijzer, eds. (New York: CDS Books, 2006), 254.

11.   We know very little about Moses of Ingila (sometimes spelled Inghila or Aggel). According to William Wright's *A Short History of Syriac Literature* (London: Adam and Charles Black, 1894), this Moses was a Monophysite Syriac Christian scholar who flourished around 550–570 C.E. (pp. 13–14). Wright further notes that this Moses translated *Joseph and Aseneth* from Greek into Syriac (ibid., 25) and also made a Syriac translation of Cyril of Alexandria's work entitled *Glaphyra* (ibid., 112).

12.   Although there was a 12th-century Latin version of the story, in modern times the Syriac manuscript was translated into Latin in 1886 by Gustav Oppenheim. This version may not be helpful to most readers of this book.

CHAPTER 2

1.   C. Burchard, translation, "Joseph and Aseneth," in James H. Charlesworth, *The Old Testament Pseudepigrapha*, volume 2 (New York: Doubleday, 1985), 203.

2.   Ross Shepard Kraemer, *When Aseneth Met Joseph* (New York: Oxford University Press, 1998), 22.

3.   Ibid., 226. See also Goodenough, *Jewish Symbols in the Greco-Roman Period* (Pantheon, 1953).

4.   Ibid., 228.

5.   Kraemer, op. cit., 37.

6.   Kraemer puts aside the scholarly near-consensus and states "the passage begins with a strange reference that led some earlier scholars to identify the text as Christian." Instead of elaborating on this idea, she states: "the significance of this symbol and, indeed, the entire following scene, is not explained" in any version of the text. See Kraemer, op. cit., 38.

7.   For crosses on ossuaries see L. Y. Rahmani, *A Catalogue of Jewish Ossuaries: In the Collections of the State of Israel* (Jerusalem: The Israel Antiquities Authority, 1994), 90 #56 (34.7753), 106 #114 (46.174), 223 #704 (80.503). In every instance, Rahmani tries to assure us that a cross is not a cross. For the most obvious cross of all, see Hannah M. Cotton, Leah Di Segni, et al., *Corpus Inscriptionum Iudaeae/Palaestinai, Volume I, Jerusalem.* (De Gruyter, 2010), 289 #263. The cross is carved on a 1st-century ossuary but because the authors don't believe that there are Christian crosses in the 1st century, they call it a "later addition." This conclusion is based on no evidence whatsoever.

8.   Mark Appold, "Bethsaida and a First-Century House Church?" in *Bethsaida: A City By the North Shore of the Sea of Galilee*, edited by Rami Arav and Richard Freund, volume two, *Bethsaida Excavations Project, Reports and Contextual Studies* (Trueman State University Press, 1999), 383.

9.   For the cross at Herculaneum see C. Giordano and I. Kahn, *The Jews in Pompeii, Herculaneum, Stabiae and in the Cities of Campania Felix*, Bardi Editor (2001), 30–32. Also, Professor A. Maiuri lectured on this discovery before the Pontifical Academy of Archaeology in Rome in November 1939. He came to the conclusion that it was a Christian cult place and that the cross had become a symbol of veneration for Christians by 79 C.E. when

Herculaneum was destroyed. See E. L. Sukenik, "The Earliest Records of Christianity," *American Journal of Archaeology*, vol. 51, no. 4 (Oct–Dec, 1947).

10. Francesco Paolo Maulucci, *Pompeii: I graffiti figurati* (Bastogi, 1993), 194. Also, a clear, very large Christian cross was found in a Pompeii bakery. See Maulucci, *Pompeii: Archaeological Guide to the Excavations of Pompeii with Itineraries, Plans and Reconstructions* (Carcavallo, 1987), 69. Like Cotton et al., Salvatore Nappo was so perturbed at seeing this cross where it shouldn't be that in his book on Pompeii he changed the cross to a pagan phallic symbol. S. Nappo, *Pompeii: A Guide to the Ancient City* (Barnes and Noble Books, 1998), 76. The idea, however, of pre-4th century Christian crosses is becoming a commonplace. Larry Hurtado, for example, sets the clock back to "as early as the mid/late 2nd century c.e." He argues that the Staurogram, that is, the superimposition of the Greek letters tau and rho to create "a monogram-like device . . . [representing] a crucified figure hanging on a cross," was well in use by the time of our earliest example of the Gospel of John on a papyrus, known as P66 (*Biblical Archaeology Review*, v. 39, no. 2 (March/April 2013): 49–52). Hurtado is right, but he seems unaware that a Christogram—the letters chi-rho referring to "Christ"—was found marked on an amphora at Pompeii, setting the clock on the Christogram back to the 1st century. See Maulucci, *Pompeii*, 191. See also Jacobovici, "Christians at Masada": simchajtv.com/christians-at-masada/. The idea that crosses are not Christian symbols before the 4th century is still widely held among Israeli archaeologists who are a few decades out of step with historians of early Christianity. As a result, all kinds of clear references to Christians in the 1st century are overlooked.

CHAPTER 3

1. This is *British Library Manuscript Number 17,202*.
2. Codices *Sinaiticus* and *Vaticanus*.
3. The dates are suggested by the text and Moses of Ingila's letter. Many of the scholars who have studied the text (e.g., M. Philonenko) allow for a 1st century c.e. composition. Some, like Gideon Bohak, date it even earlier; wrongly, we think.
4. The Cave of the Sleepers, by the way, can be visited in Ephesus, Turkey, even today.
5. *The Gospel of Mary [Magdalene]* was not part of the Nag Hammadi treasure of documents. It was discovered independently, in Cairo, in 1896. Because of its subject matter—the religious authority of Mary the Magdalene over the apostles—and its Gnostic origin, it was probably also subject to suppression by the faction of Christianity that won imperial favor in the 4th century.
6. See Ross Shepard Kraemer's excellent book, *When Aseneth Met Joseph* (New York: Oxford University Press, 1998). As Kraemer writes (on p. 6), "All our extant manuscripts of *Aseneth* are manifestly Christian (the earliest being seventh-century [sic] Syriac Christian), and we have no evidence that *Aseneth* was ever transmitted by Jews, or circulated by Jews, let alone composed by Jews." Note, however, that the Syriac manuscript dates from the 6th century.
7. Ibid., 24.
8. For a discussion of the textual history of *Joseph and Aseneth*, including shorter and longer versions, see Burchard's introduction in Charlesworth, op. cit., 180–181 and Kraemer, op. cit., Introduction.
9. The copy in the British Library was clearly censored. At least a page and a half were cut out by a 13th century copyist. See discussion in the Appendix.
10. For example, Mark confidently declares "Thus he [Jesus] declared all foods clean" (Mark 7:19). According to Mark, Jesus abolished *kashrut*, the Jewish dietary laws. Matthew's Gospel, however, omits this phrase (Matthew 15:17). For him, Jesus had not abolished the dietary laws and they were still in force. This represents a *major* difference in understanding Jesus' teachings and practices.
11. See Bart D. Ehrman, *Misquoting Jesus* (New York: HarperCollins, 2005), 90. As he notes: "There are more variations among our [New Testament] manuscripts than there are words in the New Testament."

12. Morton Smith, *The Secret Gospel: The Discovery and Interpretation of the Secret Gospel According to Mark*. Middleton, California: Dawn Horse Press, 2005. A translation of the secret ending to Mark's Gospel is found in that book on pp. 14–17. *The Secret Gospel* was originally published in 1973 by Harper & Row.

13. George Howard, *Hebrew Gospel of Matthew* (Macon, GA: The Mercer University Press, 1995).

CHAPTER 4

1. Scholars date the original writing of all the canonical Gospels to the 1st century. The assigned dates for original composition, however, are all speculative and are based on arguments from "fit," meaning we speculate as to which historical period they best fit into. We cannot prove that these were actually composed when scholars say they were. Even 2nd-century testimony is largely unhelpful. For instance, the church historian Eusebius tells us that Papias, in the late 2nd century, a man he describes as "very limited in his comprehension," stated that "Matthew composed his history in the Hebrew dialect" (*Ecclesiastical History*, Book 3, Chapter 39). Even if Papias means that Matthew composed his Gospel in Aramaic (not Hebrew), it likely does not apply to the Gospel we know of today as Matthew. Our Matthew makes several errors for someone allegedly familiar with either Aramaic or Hebrew. He does not know, for instance, the nature of parallelism in Hebrew poetry—he has Jesus entering Jerusalem awkwardly straddling *two* animals, a colt and a donkey, not just one animal as the Hebrew poetry would imply. Our Gospel of Matthew was probably composed initially in Greek and is not the document that Papias had in mind. Such 2nd-century testimony regarding 1st-century Gospel authorship is unreliable. Basically, dating *Joseph and Aseneth* is no more or less reliable than dating the Gospels.

2. Kraemer, op. cit. See also Rivka Nir's excellent recent book, *Joseph and Aseneth: A Christian Book* (Sheffield: Sheffield University Press, 2012).

3. H. F. D. Sparks, *The Apocryphal Old Testament* (Oxford: Clarendon Press, 1984), 465–503. James H. Charlesworth, op. cit., 177–247.

4. Charlesworth, op. cit., 187. For a recent discussion of the dating of *Joseph and Aseneth*, see Kraemer, op. cit., Chapter 8 ("The Dating of Aseneth Reconsidered").

5. Sparks (ed.), op. cit., 470.

6. Charlesworth, op. cit., 177 and 187–188.

7. Gideon Bohak, *Joseph and Aseneth and the Jewish Temple in Heliopolis* (Atlanta, GA: Scholars Press, 1996), xiii.

8. Charlesworth, op. cit., 187. For her part, Kraemer sums up recent scholarly opinions this way: "a scholarly consensus of sorts has emerged . . . most recent scholarly reference works describe *Aseneth* as a Jewish text written sometime between 100 B.C.E. and 135 C.E. . . ." Kraemer op. cit., 5.

9. Kraemer, op. cit, 237. In her earlier, partial translation of *Joseph and Aseneth* which she calls "*The Conversion and Marriage of Aseneth*" (1988), she dates the work to 1st century C.E.—Kraemer, *Maenads, Martyrs, Matrons, Monastics* (Philadelphia: Fortress Press, 1988), 263. Later, in her 1998 publication *When Aseneth Met Joseph*, she tentatively moves its date forward to the 3rd century. She does this in part because the text is not quoted in either Jewish or Christian sources during the first three centuries of our era. That lack of citation does not at all surprise us, however. As a Christian writing, it would not have appeared on a Jewish radar. As for Christian citations, we suspect that the work contains a secret teaching, an encoded message, one that mainstream Christianity would have vigorously disavowed. So here, too, a lack of citations is to be expected. It is not likely that surviving sources would have referred to this text any more than they do to other so-called dissident writings.

10. Alan F. Segal, *Two Powers in Heaven: Early Rabbinic Reports About Christianity and Gnosticism* (Leiden: E.J.Brill, 2002), 249 n. 17.

11. "It is clear that in the 140s and 150s Valentinus, as well as Marcion, was a prominent figure in Roman Christianity and that he led a group that had become separate from the main body of the church." Bernard Green, *Christianity in Ancient Rome: The First Three Centuries* (Edinburgh: T&T Clark, 2010), 74.

12. Jonathan Hill, *The Crucible of Christianity: The Forging of A World Faith* (Lion: 2010), 152.

13. "According to Han Drijvers, all the available evidence indicates that Syriac-speaking Christianity in northern Mesopotamia and eastern Syria was mainly of Gentile origin." Nir, op. cit., 179. Han Drijvers, "Syrian Christianity and Judaism," *in* Judith Lieu, John North, and Tessa Rajak (eds.), *The Jews among Pagans and Christians: In the Roman Empire* (London: Routledge, 1992), 134–46.

14. Green, op. cit., 75.

CHAPTER 5

1. See James D. Tabor, *Paul and Jesus: How the Apostle Transformed Christianity* (New York: Simon & Schuster, 2012), 108.

2. Kraemer, op. cit., 252.

3. Ibid.

4. Ibid. (emphasis added).

5. Bohak, op. cit., xiii.

6. Pierre Batiffol, "Le Livre de la Priere d'Aseneth" in *Studia patristica: etudes d'ancienne literature chretienne* (Paris: Leroux, 1889–90), 1–87.

7. E. W. Brooks, *Joseph and Asenath* (London: S.P.C.K., 1918), xi.

8. R. D. Chesnutt, "From Death to Life: Conversion in Joseph and Asenath." *Journal for the Study of the Pseudepigrapha*, Supplement Series, 16 (Sheffield: Sheffield Academic Press, 1995), 73.

9. Nir, op. cit., Chapter 1, especially pp. 39–48. Note that Nir also holds that Aseneth is a convert to Christianity.

10. Kraemer, op. cit., ix.

11. Robert A. Kraft, "Pseudepigrapha in Christianity" in John C. Reeves (ed.), *Tracing the Threads: Studies in the Vitality of Jewish Pseudepigrapha* (Atlanta, GA: Society of Biblical Literature, 1994), 75.

12. See Appendix II for a first-ever English translation of this letter to Moses of Ingila and his reply.

CHAPTER 6

1. Typology represents a different interpretive method to allegory.

Allegory is a theory of meaning. This method attributes a spiritual meaning to a passage, a deeper, truer meaning than the literal, superficial meaning. Thus the stages through which the Israelites left Egypt at the time of the Exodus to go to the Promised Land could be allegorically interpreted as stages in the soul's progression toward God. Allegorical interpretation was widely adopted in the ancient world, from Plato onward, and was favored in Alexandria and its school of Biblical interpretation.

Typology, however, represents a theory of history whereby one event or person is interpreted as really referring to a later event or person. Thus Moses leading the children out of Egypt into the Promised Land could be interpreted typologically, not as referring to the Exodus a thousand or more years B.C.E. but as representing Jesus leading humanity out of sin into the Kingdom of Heaven. So the earlier event (the Exodus) is interpreted typologically as a foreshadowing of a later event (Jesus' activity). For typologists, the actual later event is what the passage really signifies, not the earlier event. Typology was favored by Syriac Christianity in its exposition of the writings of the Hebrew Bible.

2. Hill, op. cit., 71.

CHAPTER 7

1. Kristian S. Heal, "Joseph as a Type of Christ in Syriac Literature," *Brigham Young University Studies* 41, no. 1 (2002): 29.
2. Archimandrite Ephrem (trans.), "Sermon on Joseph the Most Virtuous," last updated on 03 November 2008, anastasis.org.uk/on_joseph.htm.
3. Kevin Knight, ed., "Demonstration 21 (Of Persecution)," *New Advent*, newadvent.org/fathers/370121.htm
4. Quoted in Heal, op. cit., 32 and 48 n. 23.
5. Heal, op. cit., 38, and Sebastian P. Brock, "An Introduction to Syriac Studies," in *Horizons in Semitic Studies: Articles for the Student*, ed. John Herbert Eaton (University of Birmingham, 1980), 4.
6. Heal, op. cit., 39–45.
7. P. Batiffol, op. cit.
8. Kraemer, op. cit., 253. Kraemer also states that Joseph "in a Christian context is clearly a type of Christ, if not Christ himself." Ibid., 267.
9. Ibid.
10. Ibid., 253.
11. Quoted in Ibid.

CHAPTER 8

1. The Gospels refer to Mary the Magdalene in Greek as *"Maria hē Magdalēnē,"* that is "Mary the Magdalene." See Mark 15:40; Matthew 27:56; John 19:25; Mark 15:47; Matthew 27:61; Matthew 28:1; Mark 16:1; John 20:1; John 20:18. Similarly Luke 24:10 puts it *"hē Magdalēnē Maria,"* that is, "the Magdalene, Mary." Luke 8:1–3 says *"Maria hē kaloumenē Magdalēnē,"* that is, "Mary, the one called Magdalene." In all instances, Mary is spoken of as *"the* Magdalene," not as Mary Magdalene or Mary from Magdala. The Coptic *Gospel of Philip* also has Mary the Magdalene; "... and the consort of Christ is Mary the Magdalene [*Maria tē Magdalēnē*]."
2. Cited in Dan Burnstein and Arne J. de Keijzer, op. cit., 136.
3. Margaret Starbird perceptively relates Mary the Magdalene's title to a passage in the Hebrew prophet Micah. There, the prophet looks forward to Israel's glorious future and yearns for the restoration of the Davidic monarchy. In this context, Micah writes, "And you, O Migdal-eder [tower of the flock], outpost of fair Zion, it shall come to you: the former monarchy shall return—the kingship of Fair Jerusalem [alternate reading: House of Israel]" (Micah 4:8, Jewish Publication Society translation). See Margaret Starbird, *The Woman with the Alabaster Jar* (Rochester, VT: Bear and Co., 1993), 50.
4. See, for example, Starbird, op. cit., 55.
5. The parallels between Jesus and Dionysus are too many to enumerate. According to Pausanias, a Greek geographer who wrote in the 2nd century c.e., a miracle took place at a festival of Dionysus at Elis, Greece: "the priest brought empty jars into a shrine sacred to the god, and the next day the jars were miraculously filled with wine." See Marvin W. Meyer, ed., op. cit., 95. According to the Andrians, this miracle repeated itself every other year at their feast of Dionysus.
6. Quoted in Deirdre Good in Dan Burnstein and Arne J. de Keijzer, op. cit., 302–303.
7. Excerpted from Karen L. King, *The Gospel of Mary of Magdalene: Jesus and the First Woman Apostle* (Polebridge Press, 2003), cited in Dan Burnstein and Arne J. de Keijzer, op. cit., 105.
8. Green, op. cit., 77.
9. Marvin W. Meyer, *The Gnostic Gospels of Jesus* (New York: HarperCollins, 2005), 63.
10. *The Gospel of Philip* seems to indicate that, at least in the beginning, some of the disciples "were offended by this"—i.e., the intimacy between Jesus and Mary the Magdalene. Elaine Pagels in Dan Burnstein and Arne J. de Keijzer, op. cit., 6.

    Interestingly, the same mouth-to-mouth imagery we see in *The Gospel of Philip* occurs in Ephrem's writings. There he elaborates on the encounter in the temple described in Luke 2:36–38 between the infant Jesus and the prophetess Anna: "[she] embraced Him and put her mouth to his lips." (Quoted in Kraemer, op. cit., 65.) One wonders whether this Anna is a stand-in for Mary the Magdalene, given that kissing on the mouth is hardly consistent with embracing an infant.

11. Karen L. King, *The Place of the Gospel of Philip in the Context of Early Christian Claims about Jesus' Marital Status*, in "New Testament Studies," Cambridge University Press, 2013, p. 580.

12. Ibid, p. 576.

13. Quoted in Dan Burnstein and Arne J. de Keijzer, op. cit., 3, emphasis in the original.

14. Marvin W. Meyer, *The Gnostic Gospels of Jesus* (New York: HarperOne, 2005), 38.

15. Allen H. Jones, *Essenes: The Elect of Israel and the Priests of Artemis* (Lanham, MD: University Press of America, 1985), 65. The late Cyrus H. Gordon warned repeatedly that civilizations should not be compartmentalized simply because university departments are.

16. Morton Smith, *Jesus the Magician* (San Francisco: Harper & Row, 1978), 68.

17. Arav and Freund, op. cit. Note especially the article by Mark Appold, "Bethsaida and the First-Century House Church?" 373–396.

18. Owen Jarus, "Was Jesus Here? Biblical-era town Discovered along Sea of Galilee," *NBC News*, September 17, 2013, nbcnews.com/science/was-jesus-here-biblical-era-town-discovered-along-sea-galilee-4B11184418.

19. Robert Murray, trans., *Symbols of Church and Kingdom* (Cambridge: Cambridge University Press, 1975), 136.

20. Kathleen E. McVey, *Ephrem the Syrian: Hymns* (New York: Paulist Press, 1989), 353. Emphasis added.

21. Athalya Brenner, "The Israelite Woman: Social Role and Literary Type in Biblical Narrative," *Journal for the Study of the Old Testament* (1985), 24 (emphasis added).

22. Murray, op. cit., 136. In the 2nd-century text called *The Shepherd of Hermas*, a writing that was tremendously popular in the early centuries of Christianity, the church was also described as a tower. Bart D. Ehrman, *Lost Scriptures: Books That Did Not Make It into the New Testament* (New York: Oxford University Press, 2003), 251–279, especially Vision Three (III, 3, verses 1–5). *The Shepherd of Hermas* is discussed later in this chapter.

23. *De Unitate Ecclesia* 6–9. Green, op. cit., 155.

24. Murray, op. cit., 147.

25. Origen, *Cels.* 5.62 (Marcel Borret, ed., *Origene: Contre Celse* [5 vols.; SC 132, 136, 147, 150, 227; Paris: Cerf, 1967–76], 2:168–69 quoted in Stephen J. Shoemaker, "A Case of Mistaken Identity? Naming the Gnostic Mary" in Stanley F. Jones, ed., *"Which Mary? The Marys of Early Christian Tradition," Society of Biblical Literature, Symposium Series*, No. 19 (2002): 14.

26. Ibid., 14.

27. Simcha Jacobovici and Charles Pellegrino, *The Jesus Family Tomb* (New York: HarperSanFrancisco, 2007), 62, and James Tabor and Simcha Jacobovici, *The Jesus Discovery* (New York: Simon and Schuster, 2012), 96.

28. Rachel Lesser, "The Nature of Artemis Ephesia," *Hirundo: The McGill Journal of Classical Studies*, Volume IV (2005–2006), 46. Herodotus (*Historiae* 1.26 and Aelian *Var. Hist.* 3.26) reports that the sanctuary of Artemis in Ephesus was encompassed within the sacred space of the goddess, which was a protected place of refuge (Lesser, ibid., 47). Strabo (*Geographia* 14.1.23) reports how this sanctuary preserved its status as an asylum throughout its history (Lesser, ibid., 48).

29. Act 1, Chapter 10, translated by Murray, op. cit., 160. (Emphasis added.)

30. Cited in Dan Burnstein and Arne J. de Keijzer, op. cit., 171–172.

31. Daniel Boyarin argues that some of these ideas had already been introduced into the Judaic landscape prior to Jesus and that this is reflected in the Biblical Book of Daniel and the extrabiblical *Book of Enoch*. This may be, but they certainly were not mainstream or dominant views in the Second Temple Period. It is entirely possible, however, that some

Jews saw Jesus as an anticipated angelic-type messiah and that these early followers, along with like-minded Gentiles, mostly Phoenicians/Canaanites, formed the nucleus of what became the "Church of the Gentiles." See Daniel Boyarin, *The Jewish Gospels: The Story of the Jewish Christ* (New York: The New Press, 2012).

32. John C. O'Neill draws attention to the parallels between *Joseph and Aseneth* and *The Shepherd of Hermas* in his "What is Joseph and Aseneth About?" *Henoch*, vol. 16 (1994): 189–198.

33. Bart Ehrman, *Lost Scriptures*, 264.

34. Ibid., 267.

35. Ibid., 257.

36. According to the 2nd-century pagan author Celsus, the soul passes through seven heavenly gates, each associated with a planet. The planets, obviously, are astrologically connected to the birth dates of the seven virgins mentioned here. Clearly, these seven attendants are there to help the soul ascend to its highest potential. Origen, *Contra Celsum*, 6.22 quoted in Marvin W. Meyer, ed., *The Ancient Mysteries: A Sourcebook of Sacred Texts*, 209.

37. Ibid., 260.

38. Ibid., 263.

39. Kraemer, op. cit., 251. See also Sebastian P. Brock and Susan Ashbrook Harvey, *Holy Women of the Syrian Orient* (Berkeley: University of California Press, 1987), 7–12.

40. Ann Graham Brock, *Mary Magdalene, the First Apostle: The Struggle for Authority* (Cambridge, MA: Harvard University Press, 2004), 103–104.

41. McVey, op. cit., 353.

CHAPTER 9

1. In the story of Genesis, it is Potiphar's wife who attempts to seduce Joseph. Clearly, the Potiphar of this story is not the Potiphar of *that* story. Here Potiphar welcomes Joseph and wants to marry him to his daughter. Aseneth's reference to a rumored adultery has to do with a woman other than her mother. This is a dramatic difference that clearly demonstrates that the story in *Joseph and Aseneth* is not referring to the Biblical Joseph. But if this is the case, what rumor of "attempted adultery" surrounded Jesus? And is that rumor camouflaged in the text by referencing Joseph's episode with Potiphar's wife?

2. The patriarch Joseph is never depicted as surrounded by an entourage of twelve. In fact, since he's one of twelve brothers, at most only eleven could have surrounded him. In contrast, Jesus appointed twelve disciples to represent the twelve tribes of Israel, symbolic of Joseph and his eleven brothers.

3. Rachel Elior, *The Three Temples on the Emergence of Jewish Mysticism* (New York: Oxford, 2004), 61.

4. St. Peter's Basilica, Scavi, Tomb of Julii, Room M. See Pietro Zander, "The Necropolis Under St. Peter's Basilica in the Vatican" (Fabbrica di San Pietro in Vaticano, 2007), 99–100.

5. Six such mosaics have been found in total: Beit Alpha, Sepphoris, Tiberias, Na'aran, Sussiya, and Usifiyya. Also, a similar mosaic was found in Ein Gedi, minus the Helios, with the zodiac signs written instead of illustrated. See Walter Zanger, "Jewish Worship, Pagan Symbols: Zodiac Mosaics in Ancient Synagogues," *Biblical Archaeology Review*, published as e-features online (*Bar Magazine*, accessed March 2014, bib-arch.org/e-features/synagogue-zodiacs.asp). See also Rachel Hachlili, *Ancient Jewish Art and Archaeology in the Land of Israel* (Leiden: E.J. Brill, 1988), 347–365.

6. Nir, op. cit., 119.

7. James Carroll, "Who was Mary Magdalene?" in Dan Burnstein and Arne J. de Keijzer, op. cit., 29.

8. Lesser, op. cit., 45, and Sarah Iles Johnston, *Restless Dead* (Berkeley: University of California Press, 1999), 244.

9. Lawrence Stager, "Why Were Hundreds of Dogs Buried at Ashkelon?" *Biblical Archaeology Review*, published as e-feature online, July–Nov 2010, bib-arch.org/e-features/

dogs-buried-at-ashkelon.asp. Stager states: ". . . it was the Phoenicians, I believe, who were responsible for the dog burials at Ashkelon and who considered the dog a sacred animal."

10.   Another echo of the connection between the early Jesus movement and Syro-Phoenician religion may be found in the famous Gospel story of the "daemonics." According to the Gospels, Jesus exorcizes demons out of a daemonic or, in one version, daemonics (i.e., mad men) and proceeds to transfer these demons into a herd of pigs. The swine then go mad and jump off a cliff to their death in the waters below (see Matthew 7:6 and 8:31–32; Luke 8:32–33; Mark 5:11–16).

We have an interesting parallel in the 2nd-century writings of Claudius Aelianus (Aelian, *On the Characteristics of Animals* [Harvard University Press, 1958], 12.22 and 14.20), who tells the story of dogs in Rhokkha going mad and throwing themselves into the sea. Aelianus goes on to say that boys who were bitten by the daemonic dogs were taken to the Temple of Artemis for healing. See also Sorita d'Este, *Artemis* (London: Avalonia, 2012), 55. Besides the pigs (or boars) in the incident of the daemonics, Jesus is associated with fish. Interestingly, Ephesus, the center of Artemis worship, was also identified with pigs/boars and fish. According to Herodotus, the founding of Ephesus is associated with the place where a boar was killed, fulfilling the words of an oracle that "a fish and a boar will show you the way" (d'Este, op. cit., 75). In Acragas in Greek Sicily, coins were made depicting Artemis on one side and a wild boar on the reverse (*Diodorus Siculus* 22.5).

In other words, here we see that the specific iconography of pigs/boars, dogs, and fish all involve both early Christian and Syro-Phoenician beliefs.

11.   C. Burchard, translation in Charlesworth, op. cit., 211.

12.   This style of eroticized spirituality is a Gnostic marker. We will return to this later in the text.

13.   Peter Schäfer, *Jesus in the Talmud* (Princeton: Princeton University Press, 2007), 34.

14.   Also called the Sacrament of the Altar, Holy Communion is a reenactment of elements of the Last Supper.

15.   Paul picks up on this theme, but applies it to Christians who don't agree with him. For him, the dogs metaphor is no longer applied against Canaanite idolaters. Rather, it is against the circumcising Jewish followers of Jesus. In some of the last words penned by him, he states: "Look out for the dogs, look out for the evildoers, look out for those who mutilate the flesh. For we are the true circumcision . . ." (Philippians 3:2–3). See also James D. Tabor, *Paul and Jesus: How the Apostle Transformed Christianity*, 221.

16.   See, for example, Janet Howe Gaines, "How Bad Was Jezebel?" *Biblical Archaeology Review.* Published as an e-feature online, July–Nov 2010, bib-arch.org/e-features/how-bad-was-jezebel.asp.

17.   This example of an Egyptian-looking but nonetheless Phoenician representation of a woman at the window can be viewed at the British Museum website, britishmuseum.org/explore/highlights/highlight_objects/me/c/carved_ivory_depicting_a_woman.aspx.

18.   See also 2 Samuel 6:16 and 1 Chronicles 15:29. There Michal, daughter of King Saul and wife of King David, is depicted "looking through a window" at David as he dances before the Ark of the Covenant. At that moment, she "despises him in her heart." The Biblical author, in an attempt to criticize Michal, portrays her like a Phoenician priestess at the window. This is a powerful visual contrast to David, who is celebrating the Ark of the Covenant. In other words, if one is not aware of the significance of the "woman in the window," the visual juxtaposition is lost. But it is not a value-neutral detail. It is used to blame her for her actions, while defending David. Basically, by placing her at the window at this critical moment, the Biblical author reduces Michal's contempt for David to a form of idolatry.

19.   Pope Gregory I (pope 590–604), in a famous sermon on Mary the Magdalene given in Rome around 591, thought that *seven demons* meant every form of vice, i.e. total depravity, especially sexual. James Carroll provides a translation of a portion of his sermon in his "Who Was Mary Magdalene?" in Dan Burnstein and Arne J. de Keijzer, op. cit., 35. Modern scholars tend to construe the seven demons differently. In this regard, see Bruce Chilton,

"Possessed," *Mary Magdalene: A Biography* (New York: Doubleday, 2005) for a discussion of what constitutes a *daimon* in the Mediterranean world, as well as his chapter 3, "Secret Exorcism." The Talmud calls Magdala a place of "wealth and depravity." See John J. Rousseau and Rami Arav, *Jesus and His World: An Archaeological and Cultural Dictionary* (Minneapolis: Augsburg Fortress, 1988), 189.

20. Yediot Hachronot, *Musaf le Shabbat* (April 19, 2013), 18–19.

21. Carole Mendleson, "Catalogue of Punic Stelae in The British Museum," *The British Museum Occasional Paper* no. 98, Pu71.125324(57–12–18,37): 29–30 and 84.

22. John J. Rousseau and Rami Arav, op. cit., 94 and 189.

23. *Plutarch, The Parallel Lives, The Life of Cato the Elder*, Vol. II (Loeb Classical Library edition, 1914), 324.

24. Callimachus, Hymn 3 to Artemis.

25. Rose Lou Bengisu, "Lydian Mount Karios," in *Cybele, Attis and Related Cults*. Ed. Eugene N. Lane (New York: E. J. Brill, 1996), 10 n. 35.

26. d'Este, op. cit., 77–78.

27. Other towns include Capernaeum, Chorazin, Bethsaida, Nain, and Cana. Many Galilean sites were built earlier in the Hellenistic period but abandoned after the Hasmonean/Maccabean conquest in about 100 B.C.E. Herod then resettled them. "One hundred and seventy sites were recorded from the Roman period. As compared to the 106 Hellenistic sites, this is a rise of 60%." Rafael Frankel et al., "Settlement Dynamics and Regional Diversity in Ancient Upper Galilee" (Jerusalem: Israel Antiquities Authority, 2001), 110–111.

28. Sometimes this population is referred to as pagan. Some people feel that this is a derogatory term. They prefer the terms non-Jewish, Gentile, or Greco-Roman.

29. Recently, a temple of the Roman imperial cult was discovered. It was built by Phillip the son of Herod the Great.

30. For an overall archaeological understanding of this period, see John J. Rousseau and Rami Arav, op. cit.

31. Interestingly, Morton Smith anticipated this discovery. In one instance, he states: "Of course Jesus was a Jew, and so were all his disciples—*presumably.*" Op. cit., 147. (Emphasis added.) Meaning, Smith wasn't sure that all the disciples were Jewish. We now learn that at the very least, Mary the Magdalene was a Syro-Phoenician woman, probably a priestess.

32. There is a tradition in both pagan and rabbinic literature that Jesus was the son of a Roman soldier named Pantera. Most Roman soldiers were not Roman. The Roman army was made up of Roman officers commanding conquered peoples, usually serving in countries other than their birth. So it's entirely possible that Aseneth here is referring to rumors that Jesus was the son of a Canaanite peasant who had been serving in the Roman army. See James D. Tabor, *The Jesus Dynasty* (New York: Simon & Shuster, 2006), 64–72.

33. Literally, the Hebrew Messiah (*Mashiach*) translates into the *Anointed One*. In Greek, *Anointed One* translates as *Christos*, Christ in English. In other words, though many people think that Jesus Christ is a proper name, it translates as Jesus the Messiah. While both *Christos* and *Mashiach* are translated as Anointed One, they have different connotations. The *Christos* is a savior of humanity and, in the case of Jesus, a divine-human. A *Mashiach* is a human being.

34. Graydon Snyder, *Inculturation of the Jesus Tradition: The Impact of Jesus on Jewish and Roman Cultures* (Valley Forge, PA: Trinity Press International, 1999), 41.

35. See Ketubot 72a. See also Rabbi Yitzchak Yaakov Fuchs, *Salichot Bat Yisrael* (Jerusalem, 1983).

36. d'Este, op. cit., 66. See also Aphrodite Avagianou, *Sacred Marriage in the Rituals of Greek Religion* (1993), and Rush Rehm, *Marriage to Death: The Conflation of Wedding and Funeral Rituals in Greek Tragedy* (1994).

37. She does this using Artemisian rites: anointing with perfume/nard rather than oil.

38. In one of the great ironies of archaeology, the Archaeological Museum of Amman today houses a fragment of the Dead Sea Scrolls, written over two thousand years ago by Jewish

sectarians, which quotes this exact passage concerning the Balaam prophecy. On the same floor, just a few feet away, there is a non-Jewish inscription excavated in 1967 at Deir Alla in Jordan that preserves the exact same prophecy, from Balaam's point of view. In this instance, there is perfect synchronicity between the Bible and the historical record. See Andre Lemaire, "Fragments From the Book of Balaam Found at Deir Alla," *Biblical Archaeology Review* (Sept./Oct. 1985).

39.   Literally, the second half of the heavenly statement in Mark translates from the Greek as "my beloved, in you I take delight," which is closer to the erotic language of *Joseph and Aseneth*.

40.   Marvin W. Meyer, *The Gnostic Gospels of Jesus*, 14.

41.   Interestingly, *The Gospel of Thomas* only has six disciples, not twelve. Two of these are women, namely Mary the Magdalene and Salome, the latter being one of Mary the Magdalene's companions.

42.   Kraemer, op. cit., 21.

43.   Murray, op. cit., 78.

44.   Morton Smith, op. cit. The content of this now-lost fragment was so shocking that some accused the late Morton Smith of either sensationalizing an ancient forgery or else resorting to forgery himself. Smith was one of the most important and gifted scholars of his generation. In 1980, the authenticity of the fragment was given a strong vote of confidence when a group of four eminent scholars testified that they had seen and photographed the fragment in 1976. The four were David Flusser, Shlomo Pines, Archimandrite Meliton, and Guy G. Stroumsa. If there is any doubt remaining about the authenticity of Morton Smith's *Secret Mark*, the parallels with *Joseph and Aseneth* should dispel it. A translation of the secret ending to Mark's Gospel is found on pages 14–17 of Morton Smith's publication.

45.   Later Greek manuscripts make the touching much more explicit: the heavenly man stretched out his right hand "and grasped her head and shook her head with his right hand" (16:12–13). C. Burchard, translation in Charlesworth, op. cit., 228).

46.   *Joseph and Aseneth* 15:14. C. Burchard, translation in Charlesworth, op. cit., 228.

47.   Quoted in David Friedman, *A Mind of Its Own: A Cultural History of the Penis* (The Free Press, 2001), 24. See also Michel Foucault, *The History of Sexuality*, volumes 1 and 2 (Random House, 2012).

48.   Kraemer, op. cit., 170. The 1st century B.C.E. Roman poet Virgil compared bees to hovering spirits on the verge of reincarnation (Virgil, *Aeneid* 6:703–18). Also, it was believed that bees could not be defined as either masculine or feminine. This has interesting implications for the angel's description of Aseneth as androgynous (see Appendix 15.1), neither male nor female. Porphyry, a late-3rd-century anti-Christian Syrian writer, states that "the most blessed offspring come from the virginal soul and unmated intelligence" (quoted in Kraemer, op. cit., 172). Since the most blessed offspring come from virginal births, and since bees were considered virginal, it stands to reason, therefore, that honey was considered holy food.

49.   There may be an echo in the Talmud of the erotic use of honey. The Talmud records that eleven kinds of spices were used in the incense mixture for the temple. According to the Talmud, you could add a "minute amount of Jordan amber" to this mixture, but if the priest making the incense "placed honey into it, he invalidated it." Later, in the same discussion it says that Rabbi Bar Kappara taught that "had one put a kortov [1/20th of a fluid ounce, a minuscule amount] of honey into it, *no person could have resisted its scent.*" Why did they not mix honey into it? Because the Torah says (Leviticus 2:11) "for any leaven or any honey, you are not to burn from them a fire offering to God" (Talmud, kereisos 6a, yerushalmi yoma 4:5).

The Talmudic point seems to be that the Torah prohibits the use of honey in the incense offering because "no person could have resisted its scent." What does the Talmud mean by "resisted"? Resisted what? This seems to be a hint alluding to the use of honey in erotic pagan rituals. Along these lines, Jones describes "the near absence of bees" in the literature of the early Israelites, as a result of a "conviction that by including them they would be following heathen practices." See Jones, op. cit., 73.

Interestingly, the prophet Isaiah (7:15) prophesizes that Immanuel—i.e., the Messiah—shall come eating "butter and honey." This implies that while no ordinary man can withstand the seductive powers of honey, the future Messiah will be able to. Meaning, the connection between bees, honey, and the Jesus movement implied in the *Joseph and Aseneth* text may be partially due to this prophetic passage in Isaiah, which links honey and the Messiah.

50. Ephrem the Syrian (*HNat.* 16.7), quoted in Nir, op. cit., 90 (italics added).

51. Ibid., 89.

52. More recently Rivka Nir also points to these four central actions of the Eucharist. Nir, op. cit., 44–45. See also Gregory Dix, *The Shape of the Liturgy* (London, Dacre Press, 1945), 48.

53. See Tabor, op. cit., 144–151; Wilson, op. cit., 160–163.

54. Tabor, op. cit., 150. See also Preserved Smith, *A Short History of Christian Theopagy* (Chicago: Open Court, 1922).

55. As in *Joseph and Aseneth*, Ignatius, the early-2nd-century bishop of Antioch, believed that Communion represented immortality. For him, however, what had to be consumed was not the honeycomb—with its suggestions of sexuality—but the flesh of the celibate god. He condemns Christian groups who "do not confess that the Eucharist is the flesh of our Savior Jesus Christ" (*Smyrneans* 7). Quoted in Tabor, op. cit., 154. Justin, who lived in Rome around the same time, talks about the magical transmutation: the Communion meal, "from which our blood and flesh by transmutation are nourished, is the flesh and blood of that Jesus who was made flesh" (*Apology* 1.66). Quoted in ibid., 154.

56. "The gods of the ancient Greeks lived on top of Mount Olympus, feeding on nectar and ambrosia. Today, we do not know for certain what these foods were. They were produced by the bees and taken to the gods by winged doves." Luke Dixon, "Bees and Honey: Myth, Folklore and Traditions," in *Northern Bee Books* (UK, 2013), 15.

57. Quoted in Morton Smith, op. cit., 73–74.

58. Jones, op. cit., 67.

59. Quoted in Kraemer, op. cit., 170.

60. Jones, op. cit., 72.

61. Nir, op. cit., 43.

62. Thomas J. Heffeman, "Sacred Biography: Saints and Their Biographers in the Middle Ages," Oxford University Press, 1988, p. 209. Critics of the *agape* were concerned that sex usually followed the partaking of milk and honey in the ritual.

63. Green, op. cit., 176. In Rome, cremation gave way to inhumation (full-body burial) during the 2nd century. The Christian catacombs of Rome go back to at least the 3rd century. Even earlier, if the Vatican's claims for the tomb of Peter, under St. Peter's Cathedral, are accurate. See also: http://news.bbc.co.uk/2/hi/europe/6067020.stm.

64. d'Este, op. cit., 26–27.

65. Mark Wilson, *Biblical Turkey: A Guide to the Jewish and Christian Sites of Asia Minor* (Istanbul: Ege Yayinlari, 2012), 304.

66. Pausanias, *Description of Greece*, Arcadia 13, line 2 (*Essēnas*).

67. Jones, op. cit., 49.

68. Jones, op. cit., 61. See also the discussion in Geza Vermes, "The Etymology of Essenes," *Revue de Qumran*, 7 (June 1960).

69. Jones, op. cit., 105.

70. Ibid., 219.

71. Ibid., 113.

72. Jones, op. cit., 2–6. See Philo, *Hypothetica*, 11.9. See also Pliny, *Natural History*, Loeb Classical Library Edition, V. 73 (Cambridge: Harvard, 1969).

73. Aristophanes, *The Frogs*, line 1274.

74. Jones, op. cit., 52, and John Chadwick, *The Mycenaen World* (Cambridge: Cambridge University Press, 1976), 125–126.

75. This idea is supported by Pliny, who states that the Essenes have existed for "thousands" of years. Clearly, he could not have been simply referring to the sect described by Josephus that goes unmentioned in the Talmud. He must be harking back to an earlier Artemis/ Ashera Canaanite cult. See Pliny, op. cit.

76. In Jones' words, ". . . the name for the priests of Artemis and for [this] Jewish community was the same: 'Essenes'." Jones, op. cit., 20.

77. Robert Eisenman has long contended that the Essenes and Jesus' followers were one and the same. See Robert Eisenman, *The New Testament Code: The Cup of the Lord, The Damascus Covenant, The Blood of Christ* (London: Watkins Publishing, 2006), 4.

78. John Kampen, E. L. Hicks, J. B. Lightfoot, A.H. Jones, and others have argued that the name Essene "is derived from a group of functionaries in the cult of Artemis at Ephesus." John Kampen, "The Cult of Artemis and the Essenes in Syro-Palestine," in *Dead Sea Discoveries* vol. 10, no. 2 (2003): 205.

79. Jacobus de Voragine, "The Life of St. Ambrose," in *The Golden Legend or Lives of the Saints*, Volume 3. This bee-swarming was also said to have happened to the philosopher Plato at his birth.

80. Brock, op. cit., 131. See also Murray, op. cit., 329–330. In a Coptic fragment edited by Eugene Revillout, Mary the Magdalene is replaced by Mary the mother at the empty tomb. See Brock, op. cit., 134–135.

81. Homer called Artemis "Parthenon Aidoine," meaning "revered" or "holy" virgin (Hymn 27). The 4th century B.C.E. Greek poet Callimachus called her "Parthenos," meaning "virgin" (Hymn 3 to Artemis). Euripides called her "most virginal" (Hippolytus). d'Este states: "if we consider the development of the worship at Ephesus, when Artemis became the dominant goddess . . . the sacred virgin became preeminent not the sacred prostitute." See d'Este, op. cit., 64. So it seems that Mary the mother got the title of virgin and Mary the wife was left with the label of prostitute.

82. In the Gnostic *Pistis Sophia*, for example, the term *the blessed one*, later identified with Mary the mother, "explicitly refers to the Mary who is *not* the mother" (Brock, op. cit., 95, emphasis added). Ann Graham Brock traces a "crisis of authority" in the Gnostic Gospels, depicted as a competition between Peter and Mary the Magdalene. This is a first step toward the ultimate substitution of Mary the Magdalene with Mary the mother (ibid., 103). Brock surveys several texts including certain Syriac texts of Ephrem, the *Acta Thaddaei*, and the *Book of the Resurrection of Jesus Christ by Bartholomew the Apostle*. She concludes that in each of these narratives, "the figure of Mary Magdalene has been replaced by Mary the mother of Jesus" (ibid., 123). The idea that the daughter-in-law, not the mother, is the virgin may seem odd to those conditioned by the Pauline narrative, but in the ancient world it would have seemed strange to talk about the mother as the virgin. For example, in his history, written in the 5th century B.C.E., the Greek historian Herodotus states, "Every year the Athenians celebrate a festival in honor of the Mother and the Virgin" (*History*, Book 8.65). In Pauline Christianity, mother Mary *became* the Virgin, and the Virgin Mary the Magdalene was rebranded as a reformed prostitute.

83. Independent of our insight, in mid-2008, Maria Kasyan also noted the following: "To my opinion, the 'clusters' of the frontal decoration of these statues represent a group of bee cocoons, not of the ordinary working bees, but of the Queen (King)-bees, *i.e.* Essenes as priests of the Ephesian cult." Maria Kasyan, The Apocalyptic Scene In *The Apocryphal Story Joseph and Aseneth And Artemis of Ephesus* (Russia: Russian State University for the Humanities, 2008), REF: CJ/246. Available: ican2008.ul.pt/ICAN2008_pt/Programa/21_ July/CJ_246_Maria_Kasyan.pdf. As we have seen, Kasyan is essentially correct but, more accurately, we are not talking about *cocoons*. Rather, we are talking about queen-bee cells.

84. See Chadwick, op. cit., 125–126. One possible trajectory of this kind of earth-mother worship from Crete into Israel is the arrival of the Pelasgians—the Biblical Philistines— from the island of Crete (the Kaphtor of the Bible) into the land of Israel approximately 1200 B.C.E.

85. Hilda M. Ransome, *The Sacred Bee* (Boston: Houghton Mifflin, 1937), 59–60.

86. See Matthew 10:25, 12:24, 12:27; Mark 3:22; Luke 11:15, 11:18, 11:19.

87. Quoted in Dan Burnstein and Arne J. de Keijzer, op. cit., 83.

88. The Baalzebub play on words demonstrates that the bee references are early and also embedded in a Jewish context. Mainstream Judaism was objecting to the Jesus movement's usage of Artemis and bee imagery. This kind of play on words, involving Jesus and bees, is still echoed—hiding in plain sight—in the regular Jewish liturgy. For example, in the section called Hallel, which is recited during all Jewish holidays except Rosh Hashanah and Yom Kippur (the New Year and the Day of Atonement), the rabbis have included Psalm 118:10–14. Here, hostile nations are compared to bees that act much in the way of the bees in *Joseph and Aseneth*: "All the nations surround me; in the name of God I cut them down! They encircle me, they also surround me; in the name of God, I cut them down! They *encircle me like bees*, but they are extinguished as a fire does thorns; in the name of God I cut them down" (emphasis added). In light of this Psalm, some of the Jewish imagery in the section where Aseneth is encircled by bees becomes clear.

   In *Joseph and Aseneth*, it is the angel (Jesus) that rescues Aseneth (Mary the Magdalene). Meaning, in *Joseph and Aseneth*, salvation—Yeshua, in Hebrew—comes from Jesus. *Jesus*, after all, is simply the anglicized form of *Yeshua*.

   The rabbis seem aware of *Joseph and Aseneth*, or at least of this idea. In the Hallel liturgy, therefore, they quote Psalms where *salvation—Yeshua—*comes *only* from God. The Psalm states: "You pushed me hard that I might fall, but God assisted me! God is my might and my song, and He shall be a *Yeshua* [i.e., a salvation] for me."

   In other words, once we are sensitized to the symbols, what we see here are subtle dialogues and word plays whereby the early Christians claim that Jesus *is* salvation, and the Jews retort that salvation comes only from God (see *The Complete ArtScroll Siddur*, Mesorah Publications, 1990, 639). Bees are at the center of this polemic.

89. Kampen, op. cit., 209.

90. Ibid.

91. Ibid., N. 63, 215. It is noteworthy that, according to the Gospels, Jesus sailed to the land of the Gadarenes or Gerasenes (Mark 5:1; Luke 8:26; Matthew 8:28), variously identified with Jordan and southern Spain. According to Kampen, the identification of Artemis and Atargatis "grew with the spread of Nabataean trading interest throughout the [Roman] empire, especially in the east but also . . . as far west as Spain" (ibid., 215).

92. Interestingly, in the Jewish catacombs of Rome at Villa of Torlonia, an elaborate tomb has been found that features perfectly preserved wall paintings depicting the Temple in Jerusalem, menorahs (temple candelabra), and dolphins. Is this tomb archaeological evidence of the fusion (syncretism) of Jewish and Atargatis/Artemis symbolism? See rome.info/ancient/catacombs/.

93. Nelson Glueck, *Deities and Dolphins* (Farrar Straus & Giroux, 1965), 359, 381–82; Philip C. Hammond, *The Nabateans: Their History, Culture & Archaeology* (Coronet Books, 1973), 97; John Ferguson, *The Religions of the Roman Empire* (Cornell University Press, 1985), 19; and Ibid., 216.

94. It turns out that we are not the first to realize that Aseneth is modeled on a pagan deity. Marc Philonenko makes an argument that Aseneth is modeled on the Egyptian goddess Neith (Philonenko, *Joseph et Aseneth: Introduction, text critique, traduction et notes* [Brill Leiden, 1968], 61–79). Isis is a better fit. Philonenko also associates Aseneth with the Greek goddess Selene (ibid., 81). Selene is a good fit because she is the lover of Endymion, the shepherd king, who comes to be associated with Jesus, e.g., in the catacombs of Rome. In the catacombs, Endymion is depicted as the Biblical prophet Jonah, whose three days in the belly of the great fish is seen as a foreshadowing of Jesus' three days in the tomb, prior to resurrection.

95. See discussion of findings in Hershel Shanks, "The Persisting Uncertainties of Kuntillet 'Ajrud," *Biblical Archaeology Review* (November/December, 2012). See also Julia Fridman, "Archaeologists Discover: God's Wife?" *Haaretz*, September 15, 2013, haaretz.com/archaeology/.premium-1.547147.

96.   See Judy Siegel-Itzkovich, "Ancient Israelites Imported Honeybees From Turkey," *Jerusalem Post* (June 24, 2010). Also, in what must be one of the most incredible cultural echoes of the association of Mary the Magdalene and bees, in 2005, singer/songwriter Tori Amos came out with her hit album "The Bee Keeper." In her autobiography, *Tori Amos: Piece by Piece*, written in connection with the album, she has a chapter on Mary the Magdalene. Amos has done her homework and is more insightful than most scholars. Concerning bees she writes, "This feminine association of bees was known and honored in ancient times: priestesses of the goddess Artemis were called melissae, and Demeter was called 'the pure Mother Bee'." Concerning Mary the Magdalene she writes, "I realized that . . . she truly was the Lost Bride" (Tori Amos and Ann Powers, *Tori Amos: Piece by Piece* [Broadway Books, 2005], cited in Dan Burnstein and Arne J. de Keijzer, op. cit., 271–275).

97.   Xenophon, *An Ephesian Tale* 1.1–3, quoted in Lesser, op. cit., 49.

98.   Luke 6:15; Mark 3:18 and 2:14; Matthew 10:3; Acts 1:13.

99.   d'Este, op. cit., 43–44. See also Strabo, *The Geography of Strabo* (Cambridge, MA: Harvard University Press, 1967), 8.3.12.

100.   Pausanias, *Descriptions of Greece*, 5.14.6.

101.   Since the name *Levi* is a priestly name in Judaism, Alphaeus' family must have Levitical background. Having said this, they could have been enmeshed with Canaanites through marriage and adopted a syncretic version of Judaism.

102.   Edward Lipinski, "Cult Prostitution in Ancient Israel?" in *Biblical Archaeology Review,* Jan/Feb 2014, volume 40, no. 1, pp. 54–55.

103.   The terms *brother* and *sister*, applied to husband and wife, occur in other apocryphal texts, for example in Greek Esther and Tobit. See Lawrence M. Wills, *Ancient Jewish Novels: An Anthology* (New York: Oxford University Press, 2002), 65. Famously, in the Book of Genesis, Abraham refers to his wife Sarah as his "sister." In Genesis, Abraham is fudging his relationship with Sarah so as to save his own life. In Esther and Tobit, the term seems to refer to a relationship defined by respect, rather than lust. In any event, none of these people have claims to divinity. In the context of gods, we have to turn to Apollo and Artemis. Later, Paul reveals that Peter took his wife with him on his various travels (1 Cor. 9:5). He calls Peter's spouse "a sister wife." According to Green, "[t]he term 'sister wife' probably means a wife who is a believer" (op. cit., 45). It can also mean a wife who is a believer and has achieved a certain level of spiritual/physical intimacy, achievable only by modeling oneself on Mary the Magdalene, the Artemis-like "sister–wife" of God.

104.   The oracles of Apollo were called Sibyls. They are also identified first with Jewish prophecies, packaged in pagan terms, and then with Christian prophecies. In other words, we have a whole corpus of material called Sibylline Oracles that are Apollo/Artemis-related that we know for a fact are grounded in the earliest Jewish strata of Christianity. This connection between early Christianity and the cult of Artemis has been largely ignored, but it clearly fits nicely with *Joseph and Aseneth*. See Jones, op. cit., 53.

105.   In fact, at the highest level, they merge into one. "So it may well be more accurate to consider the twin gods of Artemis and Apollo as being both solar, and both lunar," d'Este, op. cit., 102.

106.   *First Apology* 46.224, quoted in Green, op. cit., 85.

107.   *Life of Apollonius of Tyana* 6.20, quoted in d'Este, op. cit., 56.

108.   Pausanias, op. cit., 3.16.7.

109.   Pausanias, op. cit., 1.40.2, quoted in d'Este, op. cit.

110.   Cleopatra was the first ruler to identify herself with many different female deities throughout the empire that she ruled, first alongside Julius Caesar and then with Marc Antony. Augustus was the first to truly harness the rise of various religious and political movements in the Roman Empire by creating the Imperial Cult, the first large-scale acceptance of a man as a god in the West. Without Julius Caesar, Cleopatra, Antony, and Augustus, a deified Jesus and Mary the Magdalene would have made no sense in 1st-century

Judaea. With them, in the context of those times, it makes complete sense that Jesus and Mary the Magdalene would be deified, especially in opposition to the Imperial Roman Cult. See Robert Turcan, *Cults of the Roman Empire* (Wiley-Blackwell, 1997) and David Wray, *The Secret Roots of Christianity: Decoding Religious History with Symbols on Ancient Coins* (Numismatics & History, 2012).

111. See Jacobovici and Pellegrino, op. cit., 18–19. See also Tabor and Jacobovici, op. cit., 112–116.

112. L. Y. Rahmani, *A Catalogue of Jewish Ossuaries: In the Collections of the State of Israel* (The Israel Antiquities Authority, 1994). Ossuaries #8; #327; #560; #468; #701; #868.

113. Ibid., #8; #327; #560 (referring to two brothers).

114. Ibid., #468; #701; #868.

115. The first time a female's ossuary was discovered with the word *Mara* on it (Rahmani, #468), the inscription read "Martha, also known as Mara." Epigraphers then assumed that this Martha could not have been known as "the Master" or "the Lady," in the sense of a teacher, or leader. Therefore, they concluded that *Mara*—when it refers to a woman—must be a nickname for *Martha*. From that time on, any female called Mara is assumed to also be a Martha. Clearly, this is circular thinking and pure sexism. "Martha also known as Mara" means what it means when the term is applied to males: "Martha also known as the Lady," or the "Master."

116. Stephen J. Shoemaker, *Ancient Traditions of the Virgin Mary's Dormition and Assumption* (Oxford University Press, 2002), 345.

117. Also significantly, sixty meters from the Jesus Family Tomb, Simcha Jacobovici, James Tabor, and Rami Arav inserted a robotic arm mounted with a camera into a sealed Jesus-era tomb and discovered the word *Mara* written on one of the ossuaries. It seems that just as Jesus' followers invoked him on their monuments, Mary the Magdalene's followers invoked her on theirs. See *The Resurrection Tomb mystery/The Jesus Discovery* film (thejesusdiscovery.org) and *The Jesus Discovery: The Resurrection Tomb that Reveals the Birth of Christianity* (Simon & Shuster, 2012), 67–68.

118. Quoted in d'Este, op. cit., 61.

119. PGM IV: 2721–26.

120. As a powerful example of how these traditions survive and morph, we have the late-11th to early-12th century historical phenomenon, in the region of southern France (an area traditionally associated with Mary the Magdalene), of a movement called the Cult of Amor, or more popularly known as Courtly Love, popularized by the story of Arthur, Guinevere, Lancelot, and the Round Table. The practitioners celebrated a mysterious woman called "The Lady" and addressed her as *Domna*, a shortening of the Latin Domina, the feminine form of Lord or Master. They regarded the object of their love as a lady in whom—in Gnostic fashion—their highest spiritual and carnal desires intersected. It may very well be that the entire Arthurian cycle is a metaphorical retelling of *Joseph and Aseneth* with Joseph/Jesus represented by Arthur; Aseneth/Mary the Magdalene represented by Guinevere, and Levi/the disciple Levi represented by Lancelot. On the connection between courtly love and Mary the Magdalene, see, for example, "The deep psycho/spiritual impact that produced the cult of romantic love came not from Jesus, but from his consort and counterpart, Mary Magdalene." John Lamb Lash in Dan Burnstein and Arne J. de Keijzer, op. cit. 133.

121. David Parrish, ed., "Urbanism in Western Asia Minor: New Studies on Aphrodisias, Ephesos, Hierapolis, Pergamon, Perge and Xanthos," *Journal of Roman Archaeology Supplementary Series*, Number 45: 179. See also John D. Grainger, *Nerva and The Roman Succession Crisis of AD 96–99* (London: Routledge, 2004), xvi, Table 5A and Richard D. Sullivan, *Near Eastern Royalty and Rome, 100–30 BC* (University of Toronto Press, 1990), 291.

122. Hannah M. Cotton, ed., *Corpus Inscriptionum Iudaeae/Palaestinae, Volume I Jerusalem, Part 1, 1–704* (Berlin: De Gruyter, 2010), 309–334, especially ossuaries #295, #296, and

#297. There's also another *kyria* (ossuary #302) in the tomb. Jonathan Price states that this "can be a name or title" (p. 325). *Kyria*, as stated, is the Greek version of *Mara*. In other words, it is clear that this family—like the principles in the *Joseph and Aseneth* story—is combining Greek, Jewish, and Canaanite/Phoenician traditions. For example, Ossuary #296—meaning the kyria/Mara has a bronze coin for Charon, the underworld ferryman of Greek mythology, in it. Shockingly, there are also cremated remains (completely against Jewish law) in the same ossuary. Ossuary #293 has the very un-Jewish name *erotas* carved on it. Most significantly, it also has carved on its side a bucranium, an ox-head. This too is clearly not Jewish, since Jews of the 1st century did not create what the Torah calls "graven images." The bucranium is a well-known symbol of Artemis [p. 316, *fig.* 293.3(b)].

123. Hanna M. Cotton, op. cit., #396, 420. The inscription is in a formal Jewish script. Ada Yardeni and Jonathan Price, who worked on the inscription, state, "if the reading is correct, a priestess, whose name has not been deciphered, was buried in this tomb."

124. Quoted in Dan Burnstein and Arne J. de Keijzer, op. cit., 86.

125. *The Gospel of Peter* also states that Mary the Magdalene went to the tomb to do "what women are wont to do for those beloved of them who die" (12:50). Quoted in John Dominic Crossan, *The Cross That Spoke: The Origins of the Passion Narrative* (Harper & Row, 1988), 412.

126. *Clementine Recognitions*, Book 2.

127. Epiphanius, *Panarion*, 21.3.5.

128. James Hastings, *Dictionary of the Apostolic Church*, Vol. 2 (T & T Clark, 1912), 496.

CHAPTER 10

1. Wolfgang Roth, *Hebrew Gospel: Cracking the Code of Mark* (Oak Park, IL: Meyer Stone Books, 1988), 16, 17. Roth writes, "As Elisha extends by eight Elijah's eight miracles, so now Jesus extends by another eight Elisha's sixteen. It is interesting that Jesus does not double the number of Elisha's miracles; direct continuity with the scriptural model is sought, and in this manner Jesus' mission is conceptualized and legitimated."

2. Of course, Christian believers can claim that whereas all the others *claimed* a virgin birth, only Jesus actually *had* one. This is a matter of faith, but even such an argument serves our present point. Namely, Christians were—and are—perfectly comfortable arguing that the inauthentic claims that were made on behalf of pagan gods such as Helios foreshadowed the real thing.

3. Mary, mother of Jesus, was also modeled on figures that 1st-century readers would have immediately recognized. In paintings and sculpture, she is often depicted as holding Jesus on her lap. This was patterned after the well-known figure of the goddess Isis holding Horus on *her* lap. That image—a kind of brand—originally Egyptian, was familiar throughout the ancient Mediterranean world (see, for example, British Museum website: britishmuseum. org/explore/highlights/highlight_objects/aes/b/bronze_figure_of_isis__horus.aspx).

    At the time of Jesus, there was even a prominent temple of Isis in the heart of Rome itself. As a result, the Isis/Horus depiction of Mary/Jesus conveyed much about Mary's pre-eminent importance and that of her child. To a 1st-century audience, depicting Mary holding Jesus on her lap was iconographic shorthand. The message was that Mary and Jesus, like Isis and Horus, were divine beings.

4. Translated by Murray, op. cit., 112. (Italics added.)

5. Ibid. See also Aphrahat, in *Demonstration* 6, where he states:
    Let us be planted as vines in His vineyard,
    Who is the true Vine(yard).
    Let us be good vines,
    That we be not uprooted from that vineyard (ibid., 105).

6. As already noted, the detail that there are *four* horses is missing in the Syriac but present in later Greek manuscripts—presumably added just to drive the point home.

7.   Kraemer, op. cit., 156.

8.   Ibid., 157.

9.   Rachel Hachlili, *Ancient Synagogues—Archaeology and Art: New Discoveries and Current Research* (Brill, 2013), 388.

10.   Kraemer, op. cit., 302. "Given the prominence of Helios in the center-floor mosaics of Hammath Tiberias and other late antique synagogues, it seems hard to imagine that it had no religious significance."

11.   Some places of early Christian worship were called synagogues. See *Letter of James* 2:2 where the word synagogue is used instead of church.

12.   Jonathan Hill, op. cit., 106.

13.   Clearly, this is an abomination in a synagogue. Perhaps it should be looked at in light of *Secret Mark*.

14.   As noted above, some scholars, such as archaeologist Rachel Hachlili, believe that one of the Biblical scenes in the mosaic of Sepphoris is the matriarch Sarah being visited by angels (Rachel Hachlili, *Ancient Mosaic Pavements: Themes, Issues, and Trends; Selected Studies* [Brill Academic Publishers, 2009], 87). Hachlili's reasoning is a prime example of seeing what you want to see. By any measure, this part of the mosaic is damaged beyond recognition. What remains visible is the top of a shrouded head in a doorway, next to what seems to be one or two figures. Based on this scant evidence and the assumption that this is a synagogue, Hachlili turns to the 6th-century c.e. Arian Christian mosaics from the Church of San Vitale, Ravenna, Italy. There she finds an image of Sarah, veiled and standing in the doorway of a hut. As a result, she concludes (along with other scholars) that the scene at Sepphoris also depicts angels visiting Sarah as in the Book of Genesis.

      But Hachlili could have gone next door to the Church of Sant'Apollinare Nuovo, also in Ravenna. In the mosaics there, she would have also found a shrouded figure in a doorway. But this figure is not Sarah. It is Lazarus. The man standing next to him is none other than Jesus. Meaning, based on the evidence, the scene at Sepphoris can just as easily be depicting the raising of Lazarus as the Jewish matriarch Sarah.

      What this demonstrates is that if you're looking for synagogues, you'll find synagogues, even when the evidence is not there. In any event, if the damaged panel depicts a New Testament scene, then clearly this is a Christian house of worship. However, in this context, even the "annunciation" to Sarah is more consistent with a Christian understanding than a Jewish one, and the closest mosaic parallel is not in another synagogue but in a church in Ravenna, Italy.

15.   Translated by Murray, op. cit., 79.

16.   Kraemer, op. cit., 302 and 291.

17.   See for example, Graydon F. Snyder, *Ante-Pacem: Archaeological Evidence of Church Life Before Constantine* (Macon, GA: Mercer University Press, 2003), especially p. 100 where he states that, after Constantine, the sacrifice of Isaac "became a central element in Byzantine art."

18.   Nicole Winfield, *Lasers Uncover First Icons of Sts. Peter and Paul* (Associated Press, June 22, 2010).

19.   Conservatively, we've gone along with the common interpretation of this annunciation scene as depicting Sarah and the angels. We simply put it in a Christian context. But since sequentially it *follows* the sacrifice of Isaac (i.e., the crucifixion) and since it depicts a shrouded person standing in the doorway of what appears to be a tomb, the scene is most likely depicting Mary the Magdalene discovering the risen Christ as described in John 20:14–16.

20.   For pictures, see armageddonchurch.com.

21.   Dan Burstein and Arne J. de Keijzer, op. cit., 88–89. Also, one of the finds in the church at Megiddo was a table dedicated by a woman. Interestingly, as Bruce Chilton points out, "Jews

and non-Jews in Jesus' movement could eat fish together without raising the question of whether it was kosher, always an issue in cases where meat was involved." Quoted in Dan Burnstein and Arne J. de Keijzer, op. cit., 100. In the Catholic tradition, eating the wafer during Communion somehow translates into partaking of Jesus' body. Perhaps, as the table and mosaic at Megiddo might suggest, for the earliest followers the act of eating the fish translated into somehow partaking of *both* their bodies—the body of Jesus and the body of his wife, Mary the Magdalene. In fact, the earliest Christian art in Rome, dating back to the 3rd century, typically depicts a banquet scene where several figures typically dine on two fish. Scholars have speculated that this is some kind of messianic feast. But the symbolism of the two fish has eluded them. Robin Jensen has connected the meal to the Eucharist, but has not explained the presence of the second fish. We now know that some of the earliest followers were partaking of the bodies of Jesus and Mary the Magdalene and depicting them as fish. (See Robin Margaret Jensen, "Fish and Meal Scenes" in *Understanding Early Christian Art* [Routledge, 2000], 52–59).

22. Cited in d'Este, op. cit., 69.

23. G. M. Fitzgerald, "A Sixth Century Monastery At Beth-She'an (Scythopolis)," *Publications of the Palestine Section of the University Museum, University of Pennsylvania* (University of Pennsylvania Press, Philadelphia, 1939), 1–19.

24. Since the University of Pennsylvania sponsored the 1930 expedition and the artifacts were taken to its museum, *Expedition*, the publication of the Penn Museum, published two short articles in 1962 (Frances W. James [Fall]: 21–24) and in 2013 (Stephanie Hagan, Vol. 55, no. 1: 37–42). In late 2013, Rachel Hachlili's *Ancient Synagogues—Archaeology and Art: New Discoveries and Current Research* (Brill, 2013) came out, which includes Tel Istaba in this definitive work on synagogues, their archaeology, and art. See also R. Hachlili, *Ancient Mosaic Pavements* (Leiden: Brill, 2009).

25. Leah Di Segni, "Dated Greek Inscriptions from Palestine from the Roman and Byzantine Periods," Volume I, PhD Thesis, submitted to the Senate of the Hebrew University of Jerusalem, 1977, p. 405.

26. Jonathan Hill, op. cit., 182 and 193. The fact that this baptistry is Arian is very significant. Arian Christianity followed Arius, who disagreed with the Nicene Creed. Put simply, the Arian Christians did not agree with what became mainstream Christianity, i.e., that Jesus (the son) and God (the father) were made of the same "substance." Meaning, Arian Christians believed in the divinity of Jesus but made that divinity subservient to God. Arianism became a heresy after the Council of Nicea in 325. In other words, the mosaic in Tel Istaba has a parallel in a church mosaic in Ravenna. But it isn't any church mosaic. It's an Arian mosaic, which means that it is closer to the Judeo-Christian theology reflected in *Joseph and Aseneth* and in the other mosaics of the Galilee.

27. Stephanie Hagan, in "Time, Memory, and Mosaics at the Monastery of Lady Mary," *Expedition*, vol. 55, Number 1, p. 38, calls the mosaic "a hybrid Romano-Judeo-Christian iconography that appears to be unique to this city" (op. cit., 38). In other words, she sees that this has "Judeo-Christian" elements.

28. Leah Di Segni, op. cit., 410.

29. Ibid., 408. Can Maximus be a code name for Jesus or one of his sons? Interestingly, *The Golden Legend*, written by Jacobus de Voragine (1260), mentions that Peter entrusted Mary the Magdalene into the hands of Maximin and that, together, they made it to Marseilles, in Provence, France (vol 1. [Princeton, 1993]: 376).

30. Ibid., 409.

31. Stephanie Hagan, op. cit., 42.

32. Leah Di Segni, op. cit., 410.

33. There is a zodiac, but no apostles, on a mosaic in Sparta. At its center there is a depiction of a male and a female. This 4th-century mosaic seems to have been a kind of pagan precedent for the later 6th-century mosaic at Tel Istaba. By the 6th century, the pagan images had been appropriated and Christianized. See Rachel Hachlili, op. cit., 376–381. Interestingly,

Hachlili thinks that Helios is depicted as a female at Tel Istaba (p. 379), but this clearly can't be. The sun is always male. What throws Hachlili off is the fact that the male sun figure is somewhat androgynous. But this fits with Gnosticism. In fact, in the middle of the 2nd century a man named Montanus began prophesying and leading a new Christian group in what is now Turkey. Foremost among his followers were two women named Priscilla and Maximilla. They were collectively known as "the three." One of them "had a famous vision of Christ in female form." This early Christian sect, which survived until the 5th century, seems to have preserved the tradition that Jesus was resurrected as a woman, i.e., as Mary the Magdalene. See Jonathan Hill, op. cit., 148.

34. Maria Dzielska, *Hypatia of Alexandria (Revealing Antiquity)* (Cambridge, MA: Harvard University Press, 1996).
35. Cited in Dan Burnstein and Arne J. de Keijzer, op. cit., 288.
36. Josephus, *Jewish Antiquities*, 8.5.2.
37. See Rachel Hachlili, *Ancient Jewish Art and Archaeology in the Land of Israel* (Brill, 1988), plate 51. The few scholars who are aware of Sepphoris' flipped gimels and the "secret" of Ein Gedi have dismissed the first as a spelling error and the latter as referring to a secret formula for perfume production. Can anyone really believe that a community that spends an incredible amount of money on a mosaic for its house of worship cannot even get the spelling right? Alternatively, is it really credible that in a house of worship, curses are embedded in its mosaic floors against members who give up corporate secrets involving perfume production? Clearly, the "secret" of Ein Gedi is a secret involving religious beliefs. It's about faith, not business. And if we link this inscription to the Helios mosaics, and to the *Joseph and Aseneth* text, we are in a position to create a consistent narrative that explains the theological secret of the Ein Gedi community.

CHAPTER 11

1. Marvin W. Meyer, ed., *The Ancient Mysteries: A Sourcebook of Sacred Texts*, 253.
2. *Pidyon Ha-Ben* in Hebrew.
3. After all, God struck down the first-born males of Egypt.
4. The Torah is the Hebrew word for the Five Books of Moses.
5. As we saw with the Galilean synagogues, theology and circular reasoning often dictate the conclusions on these matters. For example, speaking at the Princeton Theological Seminary Conference on the Talpiot tomb, which took place in Jerusalem, January 13–16, 2008, April D. DeConick managed to conclude that the ultimate proof that Jesus and Mary the Magdalene were *not* married can be found in the Valentinian Gnostic tradition where it is explicitly said that they *were* married. This strange twist of logic was published in DeConick's paper "The Memorial Mary Meets the Historical Mary: The Many Faces of the Magdalene in Ancient Christianity," which forms part of James Charlesworth's proceedings of the conference (See James Charlesworth, "The Tomb of Jesus and His Family? Exploring Ancient Jewish Tombs Near Jerusalem's Walls" [Eerdmans, 2013], 267–290, especially p. 283). So what's the reasoning? According to DeConick, men at the time of Jesus were, by and large, married. Jesus was not. After the fact, the Valentinian Christians wanted to retroactively marry the celibate Jesus to someone . . . but to whom? They had to find an unmarried woman to retroactively marry him to. Enter Mary the Magdalene. She must have been the only lady "available for marriage" from Jesus' lifetime. She must have been single. Ergo, the fact that the Valentinian texts say that they were married proves that they were not. We respect DeConick tremendously, but on this point we have to respectfully disagree.

    According to the above reasoning, since the Gospels say that Jesus was crucified, he must not have been. After all, Simon (Jesus' brother) was crucified, and James (another brother) was stoned to death. The Gospels, therefore, must have wanted to crucify Jesus retroactively. He must have been the only member of the family retroactively "available," as it were, for Pauline theology to crucify. He must have been the only one who lived a long life.

Obviously, this kind of reasoning gets you nowhere. Suffice it to say that if the Valentinian tradition claims that Jesus and Mary the Magdalene were husband and wife, this is a piece of evidence in favor of—not against—the idea that they *were* married. Put differently, Michael Jordan's basketball skills may grow with the years, but that's because there really is a Michael Jordan. Fans don't willy-nilly make up a story and then find an unsuspecting player to attach it to. It's *history* that gets mythologized, not the other way around. Even Paul doesn't dare say that Jesus wasn't married.

On this point, Ann Graham Brock seems more reasonable. In her words, "If we had incontrovertible evidence that Jesus had been married, then Mary Magdalene would be the most likely candidate by a long shot." (Cited in Dan Burnstein and Arne J. de Keijzer, op. cit., 142.) Because it was born in America, where freedom of religion is assured, Mormonism is the only Christian religion that was able to openly embrace a belief that Jesus was married and had children.

6. See Margaret Starbird, *The Woman with the Alabaster Jar* (Rochester, VT: Bear & Company, 1993).

7. H. Pope, "St. Mary Magdalen" in *The Catholic Encyclopedia* (New York: Robert Appleton Company, 1910).

8. Cited in Dan Burnstein and Arne J. de Keijzer, op. cit., 162. See also Timothy Freke and Peter Gandy, *Jesus and the Lost Goddess: The Secret Teachings of the Original Christians* (New York: Three Rivers Press, 2002).

9. Nir, op. cit., 153.

10. *Tosefta Ket.* 1.4; *b. Ket.* 12a. Quoted in Nir, Ibid., 154.

11. One of the blessings from the Orthodox wedding service includes the following: "Bless them, O Lord our God, as Thou blessed Abraham and Sarah, Isaac and Rebecca, Jacob and all the Patriarchs, Joseph and Aseneth, Moses and Zipporah, Joachim and Anna, and Zachariah and Elizabeth."

12. The text is quite explicit: "Afterwards [i.e., after the wedding feast] Joseph had intercourse with Aseneth. And Aseneth conceived from Joseph and gave birth to Manasseh and his brother Ephraim in Joseph's house" (21:9).

13. Using typology, the authors of *Joseph and Aseneth* had no choice but to keep the names of the Biblical Joseph's children as code names for Jesus' actual children. Otherwise, there would have been no code to break and the text would have been explicitly about Jesus and Mary the Magdalene. Meaning, just as Joseph is a stand-in for Jesus, and Aseneth is a stand-in for Mary the Magdalene, Manasseh and Ephraim are stand-ins for Jesus and Mary the Magdalene's actual children.

14. According to Marvin W. Meyer, "all of modern Christianity is built on this New Testament concept [resurrection]. Yet, *The Gospel of Mary* and *The Gospel of Philip*, and the others we now know about and call either Gnostic Gospels or mystical gospels, don't have a crucifixion, blood atonement, or a resurrection. . . ." Quoted in Dan Burnstein and Arne J. de Keijzer, op. cit., 109.

15. Jerome Murphy-O'Connor notes that the Galilean ancestry of Paul was affirmed by Jerome. Jerome Murphy-O'Connor, *Paul His Story* (Oxford: Oxford University Press, 2004), 2, 240.

16. Acts 7:58. This is usually associated with the stoning of "St. Stephen." Robert Eisenman argues that that this event is an echo of the stoning of James, brother of Jesus.

17. Acts 22:26–30.

18. Tacitus, *Annals* XV, 37–41.

19. See Rose Mary Sheldon and Thijs Voskuilen, *Operation Messiah: St. Paul, Roman Intelligence and the Birth of Christianity* (Portland, OR: Mitchell Vallentine & Company, 2008).

20. For a discussion of these significant differences, see Barrie Wilson, *How Jesus Became Christian*, chapter 9. Paul's religion is a *new* religion, not that of Jesus or his first followers. See also James D. Tabor, *Paul and Jesus: How the Apostle Transformed Christianity* (Simon & Schuster, 2012).

21. For the demise of the Jesus movement (later known as Ebionites or Nazarenes), see Barrie Wilson, op. cit., chapter 11. See also Jeffrey J. Bütz, *The Secret Legacy of Jesus* (Rochester, VT: Inner Traditions, 2010).

22. Realizing that Gnosticism is historical after all, Moritz Friedländer tries to push it back before Christianity and root it in Alexandrian Judaism. See Alan F. Segal, op. cit., 15. The fact is that Christian Gnosticism is reacting to something in the Christian tradition, meaning something *somehow* connected to Jesus.

23. Stephen J. Shoemaker, *Ancient Traditions of the Virgin Mary's Dormition and Assumption* (Oxford University Press, 2002), 6.

24. Valentinus was a gifted, hard-working intellectual who was educated in Alexandria, Egypt and who moved to Rome in the mid-130s c.e. There, he established a school and almost succeeded in becoming bishop of Rome, i.e., the Pope.

25. For a translation of *The Secret Book of John*, see Marvin Meyer, *The Gnostic Gospels of Jesus*, 149–183.

26. Interestingly, according to *The Secret Book of John*, Barbelo forms a kind of trinity being called "the triple power, the androgynous one with three names." Marvin Meyer, op. cit., 154.

27. Marvin Meyer, op. cit., 159.

28. Ibid., 16.

29. See, for example: ". . . she wanted to bring forth something like herself . . . without her partner and without his consideration. The male did not give approval . . . nonetheless she gave birth . . . she had produced it without her partner," in *The Secret Book of John* in Marvin Meyer, op. cit., 159.

30. In later tradition, without male assistance, the wayward Lilith proceeded to give birth to demons, i.e., frustrated entities resulting from male ejaculations.

31. One interpretation of Genesis 1:27 understands the first human as a male–female unity (note the Hebrew has "male and female he created *him*"), that is a single entity. Only later (Genesis 2:21–23) was this composite being divided into two separate genders and an imbalance occurred within humanity. Interestingly, in the Hellenistic world, the idea of a primordial gender splitting from an original composite human being is echoed in Plato's dialogue, *The Symposium*. For Plato, love involves reuniting with the partner from whom we have been separated . . . and from coming to know the Form of the Good, what the Judeo-Christian tradition would call God.

32. Sometimes Sophia's *lower* aspects are called *Achamoth*. At other times she is Mary the Magdalene.

33. Elior, op. cit., 55.

34. DeConick, op. cit., 337.

35. Ibid., 341–42. Sacred sex reached its highest expression in the version of Gnosticism taught by Valentinus. Another major stream were the Carpocratians, followers of the early 2nd-century teacher Carpocrates, who was based in Alexandria. He "was said to have taught that sin was a means of salvation. Only by committing all possible actions could the soul satisfy the demands of the rulers of the world and so be permitted to go to the heavens, its true home." Morton Smith, op. cit., 13.

36. Kraemer, op. cit., 266.

37. It's interesting that Paul, by his own admission a formerly orthodox Jew (Acts 22:3), is very liberal when it comes to food and diet. Meaning, he frees Christians from the dietary laws of the Hebrew Bible, which the Christians now dubbed the "Old" Testament. When it comes to sex, however, Paul is very strict and uncompromising. Why? Because being liberal on Biblical dietary laws positions him as anti-Torah; being strict on sexual matters positions him as anti-Magdalene.

38. References to Syriac terms in *The Gospel of Philip* suggest an acquaintance with Syriac language and literature. See Marvin Meyer, op. cit., 54.

39. Ibid., 45.
40. Marvin W. Meyer, ed., *The Ancient Mysteries: A Sourcebook of Sacred Texts*, 236–237.
41. Quoted in Marvin W. Meyer, ibid., 240.
42. Ibid., 10.
43. Ibid., 267.
44. Ibid., 284.
45. Shoemaker, *Ancient Traditions*, op. cit., 7.
46. The exact find-site and the date of its excavation is unknown. Gregory Snyder follows Peter Lampe and others dating the inscription between 138 and 192 C.E. See Gregory H. Snyder, "A Second-Century Christian Inscription from the Via Latina," *Journal of Early Christian Studies*, Volume 19, Number 2 (Summer 2011): 157.
47. Ibid., 157–195.
48. Ibid., 166.
49. Ibid., 173.
50. Ibid., 176.
51. April DeConick argues that the bridal-chamber language in *The Gospel of Philip* is conceptual (*True Mysteries: Sacramentalism in* The Gospel of Philip *VC 55* [2001], 230). In contrast, Nicola Denzey Lewis maintains that, at least for some Gnostic groups, the sex ritual was real ("*Apolytrosis* as Ritual and Sacrament: Determining a Ritual Context for Death in Second-Century Marcosian Valentinianism," *JECS 17* [2009]: 550). Ibid., 177 N63.
52. Ibid., 192.
53. Translated by Snyder, ibid., 191.
54. Ibid., 193.
55. See David Friedman, *A Mind of Its Own: A Cultural History of the Penis* (The Free Press, 2001), 8.
56. See Hearth Moon Rising, "Invoking Animal Magic," Moon Books, 2013, p. 45. It seems that Paul substituted Mary the Magdalene, who was perceived as a queen bee by her followers, with a drone-like Jesus.
57. Poem 63 quoted in Marvin W. Meyer, ed., *The Ancient Mysteries: A Sourcebook of Sacred Texts*, 126.
58. Ibid., 114.
59. Hill, op. cit., 114.
60. Hippolytus, *Refutation of All Heresies*, 5.9.10, quoted in Marvin Meyer, op. cit., 147.
61. Clement of Alexandria, *Stromateis* III, 9.6.3.
62. See *De praescriptione hereticorum*.
63. *Gospel of Philip* in Marvin Meyer, op. cit., 78.
64. Meyer, op. cit., 163.
65. Ibid. (Emphasis added.)
66. Ibid., 82.
67. Ibid.
68. Ibid., 57.
69. Ibid., 53.
70. Interestingly, the transformation of Christianity from a movement celebrating Mary the Magdalene, fertile Bride of God, into a religion focused on God's mother and her virginity, is a historical replay of the transformation of Artemis from a "fertility goddess with the usual fertility sexual rites" into a deity defined by her purity and chastity. See Jones, op. cit., 116.
71. Ibid., 57.
72. We are referring here to the fact that Valentinians and *Joseph and Aseneth* refer to a bride and a groom as *brother* and *sister*. The idea was that sexual attraction should be grounded in non-carnal love.
73. Ibid., 63.
74. Ibid., 64.

75. Ibid., 65.
76. Ibid., 79.
77. Ibid., 68.
78. *New Eve* was a title later appropriated by Pauline Christians and applied to Mary, Jesus' mother.
79. Ibid., 69. In Greek, the Bridal Chamber is called a *nymphion*.
80. Ibid., 69. Note, too, that this description is not architecturally accurate of the Second Temple in Jerusalem, which did not open to the west or south—only to the east. But it does correspond to the main architectural sections of the temple precincts: the outer court of the Israelites, the inner court of the priests, and the innermost holy of holies into which only the high priest could enter on the Day of Atonement.
81. *The Gospel of Philip* is equating the believer's spiritual process through the sacraments of Baptism, Redemption, and the Bridal Chamber with these architectural features of the Second Temple, from the court of the laity into the sanctuary of the priests and then into the abode of God into which only the high priest could enter once a year to make atonement for sin. In the bridal chamber, just as the people are reconciled to God through the actions of the high priest, so, too, the believers are reconciled to each other and to God through this sacred marriage.
82. Peter Schäfer, *The Origins of Jewish Mysticism* (Princeton University Press, 2009), 200. See also Jerusalem Talmud Niddah 2:5 and Babylonian Talmud Niddah 17b.
83. Quoted in ibid., 46.
84. Quoted in Dan Burnstein and Arne J. de Keijzer, op. cit., 110.
85. *Panarion* 26:8.8.
86. *Panarion* 26:8.2–3.
87. Ibid., 83. Here we have a reversal of the Jesus story in Mark (7:24–37) and Matthew (15:21–28). In Mark and Matthew, Jesus compares his teaching to bread for his disciples and the Syro-Phoenician woman compares herself to a dog deserving some of the breadcrumbs that fall off the disciples' table. In the *Panarion*, in the Valentinian tradition, it is the "bride" who the people yearn for and, like "dogs," they are only entitled to "crumbs," i.e., her "voice" and the "fragrance of her ointment." In this tradition, the masses are the dogs and the Syro-Phoenician woman (Mary the Magdalene) is what they yearn for. The Gospels reversed the metaphors, comparing her to a dog.
88. See Smith, *Clement*, 257: ". . . libertinism, usually scandalous and occasionally criminal, was concealed. Consequently, scholars have neglected it." See also the famous Mishna in *Hagigah* 2:1: "forbidden sexual relations may not be expounded by two/three." Meaning, "Mishna Hagigah turns the subject[s] of forbidden sexual relations . . . into an esoteric discipline open only to a chosen elite of very few." Peter Schäfer, *The Origins of Jewish Mysticism* (Princeton: Princeton University Press, 2009), 182–183.
89. Valentinus' Letter to Agathopus, quoted in Clement of Alexandria, *Stromateis* 3.59.3. See Piotr Ashwin-Siejkowski, *Clement of Alexandria on Trial: The Evidence of "Heresy" From Photius' Bibliotheca* (Brill, 2010), 96.
90. Notions of promiscuity would, in theory, not apply to Jesus or any of his truly enlightened followers: "The Savior replied 'there is no such thing as sin . . . whoever has ears to hear should hear'" (*Gospel of Mary*, in Marvin Meyer, *The Gnostic Gospels of Jesus*, 37). Furthermore, in Galatians 3:28, Paul tells us that "there is neither male nor female in Christ Jesus." Judaism explicitly creates divisions between weekdays and the Sabbath, kosher and un-kosher, male and female. What would Paul's extreme rejection of Torah law imply in a Valentinian context? Given the role of sex in their theology, it might have led to a secret teaching, which does not differentiate between heterosexual and homosexual sex.
91. Achilles Tatius, *The Adventures of Leucippe and Clitophon*, Book 2.2–3 quoted in Marvin W. Meyer, ed., *The Ancient Mysteries: A Sourcebook of Sacred Texts* (University of Pennsylvania Press, 1987), 93.

92. Marvin W. Meyer, op. cit., 8.

93. Quoted in Morton Smith, op. cit., 52.

94. Andrew McGowan, "Eating People: Accusations of Cannibalism Against Christians in the Second Century," *Journal of Early Christian Studies*, 2:3 (The Johns Hopkins University Press, 1994): 413–442. Available: unimelb.academia.edu/AndrewMcGowan/ Papers/812380/Eating_People_Accusations_of_Cannibalism_Against_Christians_in_ the_Second_Century

95. Hill, op. cit., 96.

96. Hyam Maccoby, *Ritual and Morality: The Ritual Purity System and its Place in Judaism*, Cambridge University Press, 1999, p. 112. Maccoby calls the use of the red cow's ashes "a kind of resurrection." Meaning, while other sacrifices had to be completely destroyed after their time of sacrificing or eating had elapsed, the red cow survived in changed form through the waters of purification.

97. "The goddess Isis-Hathor in Egypt was a cow-goddess, often portrayed with a cow's head. Her appearance with her child Horus in a cow-byre was the inspiration of the Gospel story of Jesus' birth in a manger. In India, the cow was the holy animal who embodied the feminine principle, immune from normal slaughter for food, yet the most potent of sacrifices, whose death had cosmic significance." Ibid, p. 109. Isis is the Egyptian equivalent of Artemis.

98. Ibid, p. 110.

99. Griselda Pollock, "Sacred Cows: Wandering in Feminism, Psychoanalysis and Anthropology" in *The Sacred and the Feminine: Imagination and Sexual Difference* edited by Griselda Pollock and Victoria Turvey Sauron, I.B. Tauris, 2007, p. 36

100. *The Panarion of Epiphanius of Salamis*, book 1, sects 1–46, quoted in Peter Schäfer, *Jesus in the Talmud*, op. cit., 178.

101. Ibid., sect 26.

102. Peter Schäfer, *The Origins of Jewish Mysticism*, 95.

103. The Biblical passage in question is Deuteronomy 32:33. See CD8:4–12 quoted in Michael O. Wise, *The First Messiah* (New York: HarperSanFrancisco, 1999), 159. (Emphasis added.)

104. See Morton Smith, *Clement of Alexandria and a Secret Gospel of Mark* (Cambridge, MA: Harvard University Press, 1973), 254: "The libertine party or parties, whose tradition derived from Jesus himself, must have been widespread and influential."

105. Ibid., 262: ". . . libertine Christianity was widespread and ancient. It is attested in Ephesus . . . must have been important in Syria too."

106. Quoted in Peter Schäfer, *Jesus in the Talmud*, 42–43. It is significant, as Eldad Keynan has pointed out to us, that Jesus may be turning holiness on its head here. By saying that a prostitute's wages can be used for building a toilet for the High Priest, he's either saying that the holiest of men can enjoy the benefits of the most humiliated of women or, if the prostitute is, indeed, sacred, then her status is higher than the high priest's—she can help him deal with his carnal nature in the holiest precincts of the temple.

107. Quoted in Morton Smith, *Jesus the Magician*, 54. See also 1 Corinthians 5:1 where the Corinthians are arrogant concerning an illicit relationship being practiced in their church. Also see Smith, *Clement of Alexandria and a Secret Gospel of Mark*, 273. Concerning the Gnostic Carpocratians, Clement reports that they engage in orgiastic *agapai*, i.e., sacred sex.

108. Ibid., 62.

109. Quoted in Morton Smith, *Jesus the Magician*, 183. Footnote to p. 66.

110. James H. Charlesworth, trans., *The Earliest Christian Hymnbook, The Odes of Solomon* (Cascade Books, 2009), xxviii.

111. Ibid.

112. Ibid., 17 note E.

113. Kraemer, op. cit., 256.

114. Ibid., 257.

115. Ibid., 260.

410 | SIMCHA JACOBOVICI ᴀɴᴅ BARRIE WILSON

116. *Ode* 36, ibid., 105.
117. *Ode* 38, ibid., 109.
118. *Ode* 40, ibid., 116. See also *Ode* 30 where Jesus' truth is described as better than honey: "For more refreshing is its water ['the spring of the Lord'] than honey, And the honeycomb of bees cannot be compared with it; Because it flowed from the lips of the Lord, And it assumed a name from the heart of the Lord."
119. *Ode* 3, ibid., 3.
120. Verses 11–13, ibid., 111. (Emphasis added.)
121. Smith, *Jesus the Magician*, 5.
122. Ibid., 57.
123. Henry Chadwick, "Alexandrian Christianity," ed. H. Chadwick and J. Oulton (London, 1954), II.209.17ff. Quoted in Morton Smith, *Clement of Alexandria and a Secret Gospel of Mark*, 273.
124. Marvin W. Meyer, *Gnostic Gospels of Jesus: The Definitive Collection of Mystical Gospels and Secret Books About Jesus of Nazareth* (HarperCollins, 2005), 63 and 302, footnotes 62 and 63.
125. Ibid., 79.
126. Ibid., 71.
127. Ibid., 85.
128. Ibid., 86.
129. Marvin W. Meyer, ed., *The Ancient Mysteries: A Sourcebook of Sacred Texts*, 63. It is interesting that like Jesus Dionysus was seen as "a god incognito, disguised as a man." This line is from Euripides: *Bacchae*, Book 5. In the play, Dionysus is associated with wine that, in Artemisian fashion, "runs with the nectar of bees" (5.140). He claims that he is a son of god, but others claim that his mother "lied" (5.25–30). In other words his mother, a virgin, is accused of prostituting herself. Because of that offense, Dionysus seeks to "vindicate" her by driving women crazy, compelling them to engage in orgies "when the holy flute like honey plays" (5.160). In effect, in order to clear his mother's name, he uses orgiastic sex to turn women into veritable prostitutes.
130. Clement, *Stromata* 3.59.3, quoted in Green, op. cit., 79.
131. Marvin W. Meyer, *The Gnostic Gospels of Jesus*, 50. (Emphasis added.)
132. See Tabor, *Paul and Jesus*, 117. (Emphasis added.)
133. We suspect that if they were around today, the Gnostics would be wearing small gold beds, not crosses, as jewelry around their necks.
134. Joan Acocella, "The Saintly Sinner," in Dan Burnstein and Arne J. de Keijzer, op. cit., 40.
135. If she had been a priestess of Artemis prior to meeting Jesus, this might have involved temple prostitution or "sacred sex" with kings, princes, warriors, and religious leaders. This was called "sacred marriage," or *hieros gamos*. See Dan Burnstein and Arne J. de Keijzer, op. cit., 23.
136. Quoted in Dan Burnstein and Arne J. de Keijzer, op. cit., 77.
137. Marvin W. Meyer, *The Gnostic Gospels of Jesus*, 12. *Gospel of Thomas*, saying 22.
138. Ibid., 25. *Gospel of Thomas*, saying 114.
139. Ibid., 83.
140. Ibid., 68. Also, it is incredible to see how these ideas survive and remain true to their original form. For example, in his 1951 book *The Last Temptation of Christ*, Nikos Kazantzakis articulates an exceedingly accurate view of the Gnostic concept of the "bridal chamber" when he puts in Jesus' mouth: "Beloved wife, I never knew the world was so beautiful or the flesh so holy. It too is a daughter of God, a graceful sister of the soul. I never knew that the joys of the body were not sinful."
141. Maybe the disciples who did not like her reburied Jesus' body without involving her. She certainly had her enemies among his "brothers" (see for example, Peter complaining to Jesus about Mary: "my Lord, we are not able to suffer this woman," *Pistis Sophia* 1–3, quoted in Brock, *Mary Magdalene*, op. cit., 87). What they didn't expect, however, is what happened when Mary was confronted by the empty tomb.

142. Maximus, *The Life of The Virgin: Maximus the Confessor* (Yale University Press, 2012), Section 80, translated by Shoemaker, 107.

143. Maximus, op. cit., Section 92, Shoemaker, 119.

144. Marija Gimbutas, *The Goddesses and Gods of Old Europe: Myths and Cult Images* (University of California Press, 1974), 182.

145. Meyer, *Ancient Mysteries*, op. cit., 200.

146. Gimbutas, op. cit., 182.

147. Antigonos, *Hist. mir.* 19; quoted by Gimbutas, 181. (Emphasis added.)

148. Hill, op. cit., 148.

149. Ibid., 184.

CHAPTER 12

1. See, for example, Mark 9:5, Matthew 26:29, and John 1:49.

2. Josephus Flavius, *Against Apion* 2.282. See also Green, op. cit., 13.

3. See Babylonian Talmud *Gittin* 56b.

4. For a discussion about the role of God-fearers in the synagogues of Diaspora Judaism in the 1st century C.E., see John Dominic Crossan and Jonathan L. Reed, *In Search of Paul*, New York: HarperSanFrancisco, 2004, Chapter 1 ("Jewish Faith and Pagan Society").

5. See Green, op. cit., 13–14.

6. Green, op. cit., 13.

7. Crossan and Reed, op. cit., 24. See also Angelos Chaniotis, "Godfearers in the City of Love," *Biblical Archaeology Review* (May/June, 2010).

8. The synagogue seems to have had sections for males, females, and God-fearers. The God-fearers section is almost as big as the Jewish male section. See so-called Study Hall on the synagogue plan, available: pohick.org/sts/ostia.html.

9. See Mark R. Fairchild, "Turkey's Unexcavated Synagogues," *Biblical Archaeology Review* (July/August 2012): 40–41. The inscription has been dated to the Hellenistic period in 300–50 B.C.E., but not later than the Augustan period from 27 B.C.E. to 14 C.E. See E. L. Hicks, "Inscriptions from Eastern Silicia," *Journal of Hellenic Studies*, 11 (1890): 236–254 and "Inscriptions from Western Silicia," *Journal of Hellenic Studies*, 12 (1891): 225–273. Cited in Fairchild, op. cit., 65.

10. Josephus Flavius, *Antiquities of the Jews*, Book 14, Chapter 7, Section 2.

11. Snyder, op. cit., 9–17.

12. See, for example, Acts 18:1–17 and Acts 19:8.

13. Kraemer, op. cit., 273.

14. Morton Smith, *Jesus the Magician*, 26.

15. James D. Tabor, *The Jesus Dynasty* (New York: Simon & Shuster, 2006), 49–51.

16. The oral Torah, as recorded in the Talmud, states that this prohibition only involves male Moabites (*Yevamoth* 76b).

17. See *The Proto-Gospel of James* (also known as *The Infancy Gospel of James*) in Bart D. Ehrman, *Lost Scriptures*, 70. In this episode, a midwife comes out of the cave in which Jesus was born and says to Salome, "Salome, Salome, I can describe a new wonder to you. A virgin has given birth, contrary to her natural condition." Salome replied to her, "As the Lord my God lives, if I do not insert my finger and examine her condition, I will not believe that the virgin has given birth." She then proceeds to conduct the examination.

18. Ibid., 63–72. In this mid-2nd-century C.E. writing, an angel of the Lord appears to Anna, Mary's mother, and tells her "You will conceive a child and give birth, and your offspring will be spoken of throughout the entire world." At this time, Anna's husband, Joachim, is away from home. This is the origin of the Catholic doctrine of the immaculate conception of the Virgin Mary, i.e., Jesus' mother was also born without male involvement. As with *Joseph and Aseneth*, there are always "angels" present at the moment of conception.

19. Bruce Chilton, *Rabbi Jesus* (New York: Doubleday, 2000), 13.

20. Talmud, *Shab.* 104b. Also see Peter Schäfer, *Jesus in the Talmud*, 20, 98, 138, 141, 158 n.9.

21. *Tosefta Hulim* 2,22 and 2,24. Also *Qohelet Rabbah* 1:8(3).

22. Celsus, *True Discourse*, written in approximately 178 c.e.

23. The name is spelled differently in different sources: Pantera, Panteri, Panthera, Pandera, Panter. In several places the Talmud refers to "Jesus, son of Panteri" or "Jesus, son of Panter."

24. See Tabor, op. cit., 69. Also see Rousseau and Arav, op. cit., 223–225.

25. See Israel Knohl, *Messiahs and Resurrection in "The Gabriel Revelation"* (New York: Continuum, 2009).

26. Josephus Flavius, *Jewish War*, 2.57–59 and 2.43. *Antiquities of the Jews*, 17.278–284.

27. It is possible that the Hebrew/Canaanite word "Abdes," i.e., "slave" on the tombstone refers to Pantera's religious beliefs, not his former status as a slave. Meaning, what testifies to the fact that he was a slave recruited into the Roman army is the adopted name "Tiberius," not the word "Abdes." The latter might refer to his status as a believer in the goddess Isis. This would mean that Pantera was a Canaanite, not a Jew, and might explain the influence on Jesus of the cult of Artemis-Isis. It would also explain Jesus' ambiguous status in Jewish society.

28. See the Shulchan Haruch, *Even Ha Ezer*, Chapter 4, Section 29.

29. As Eldad Keynan has pointed out, a marriage between a Jew and a non-Jew is not technically kosher according to Jewish law. Having said this, Jesus was probably married to Mary the Magdalene in the sense of making her *koinonos*, i.e., his companion. That way, their children could be converted to Judaism and not be *mamzers*. If Mary the Magdalene had converted, then Jesus couldn't marry her and their children would be *mamzers*. We can still, however, speak of a marriage in a sense that Jesus and Mary the Magdalene lived as husband and wife, spiritually married as described in *Joseph and Aseneth*. For the various marriage strategies available to a *mamzer*, see Eldad's Keynan paper "The Holy Sepulcher, Court Tombs, and Talpiot Tomb in Light of Jewish Law" in James Charlesworth, *The Tomb of Jesus and His Family? Exploring Ancient Jewish Tombs Near Jerusalem's Walls* (Eerdmans, 2013), 424–433.

30. "Now on the first *day* of the week Mary the Magdalene came early to the tomb, while it was still dark, and saw the stone *already* taken away from the tomb" (John 20:1).

31. The idea that Mary the Magdalene was a reformed prostitute was put forward by Pope Gregory the Great in the 6th century and only reversed by the Vatican in 1969. If she was indeed a prostitute, her role as one of the major underwriters of the Jesus mission would have meant that both Jesus and the disciples lived off the avails of prostitution. Surely, this is not a conclusion that Pope Gregory would have wanted us to reach.

32. Quoted in Dan Burnstein and Arne J. de Keijzer, op. cit., 67.

33. See Kraemer, op. cit., 260–261.

34. Ibid., 261.

35. Ibid., 263.

36. Ibid.

37. For example, Eusebius reports that the church father Origen castrated himself in order to be able to tutor young women and still remain above suspicion.

38. Eusebius, *Ecclesiastical History*, Book 3, Chapter 11: "After the martyrdom of James and the capture of Jerusalem which immediately followed, the report is that those of the apostles and the disciples of our Lord who were yet surviving came together from all parts with those who were related to our Lord according to the flesh, for the greater part of them were yet living." He goes on to indicate that Simeon, a relative of Jesus, was elected bishop.

39. Eusebius, ibid., Book 4, Chapter 5, Sections 3, 4.

40. It's possible that some Jews—probably very Hellenized ones—conceived of Jesus as a divine, angel-like figure early on. There is a tradition, usually identified with the *Book of Enoch*, which allows for the "ascent" to heaven of certain humans, e.g., Enoch of the Book of Genesis, and their transformation there. By the 3rd century this tradition is identified with the angel Metatron. Furthermore, there is recent New Testament scholarship that argues for early Christology (i.e., that Jesus claimed to be divine early on in his ministry),

appropriating for himself "the Name" (i.e., the Tetragrammaton) or the ineffable name of God. This is not the place to elaborate on all this. Suffice it to say that even if some Jews elevated Jesus during his lifetime, or immediately after the crucifixion, to some kind of divine or semi-divine status, this was not a mainstream Jewish position inside or outside the original Jesus movement. For discussions of early Christology, see April D. DeConick, "How We Talk About Christology Matters" in David B. Capes et al., *Israel's God and Rebecca's Children: Christology and Community in Early Judaism and Christianity* (Baylor University Press, 2007), 1–25. Also, Charles A. Gieschen, *The Divine Name in Ante-Nicene Christology, Vigilliae Christianae*, Vol. 57, No. 2 (Brill, 2003): 115–158. For the Enoch context see Daniel Boyarin, *The Jewish Gospels: The Story of the Jewish Christ* (The New Press, 2012), 91–95. For Metatron see ibid., 51 and Alan Segal, *Two Powers in Heaven: Early Rabbinic Reports About Christianity and Gnosticism* (Brill, 2002), 61–68.

41.   See Eisenman, op. cit., 47–48. Paul is at pains in some of his letters to defend himself from the charge of lying—see, for instance, 2 Corinthians 11:31; Galatians 1:20.

42.   "I pursued them even to foreign cities" (Acts 26:11).

43.   "Up to this point they listened to him, but then they shouted, 'Away with such a fellow from the earth! For he should not be allowed to live'" (Acts 22:22). Note that it is part of the agenda of the author of the Book of Acts to heighten the resistance of Jesus' first followers toward Paul, the hero of this writing.

44.   Eusebius, op. cit., Book 3, Section 27 ("The Heresy of the Ebionites").

45.   See Acts chapter 15 and Galatians chapter 2. The meeting between James and Paul is known by the confusing term *Apostolic Conference*, or The Council of Jerusalem. Essentially, as the Book of Acts makes clear, it was a failed attempt by the Jesus movement to control Paul and his new brand of Christianity.

46.   Some members of the original Church of the Gentiles must have also observed the Sabbath, keeping it as a day of rest, a holy day. After all, this was enjoined upon the Jewish people in the Ten Commandments, which many God-fearers honored.

47.   Meyer suggests that *Joseph and Aseneth* uses terminology similar to the pagan mysteries as well as to the Dead Sea Scrolls and the Gospel of John. Scholars and researchers should follow up on his suggestion. Marvin W. Meyer, ed., *The Ancient Mysteries: A Sourcebook of Sacred Texts*, 227.

48.   We wish to thank Michael LaFond for drawing our attention to this important text. LaFond, in an as-yet-unpublished book, *Kingdom Come, Christ Divided* suggests that the "lady" in question may be Mary the Magdalene and that *kyria* in Greek, i.e., lady, is the same as the Aramaic "Mara," a title that is repeatedly associated with Mary the Magdalene.

49.   Marvin Meyer notes that "a reasonable case can be made for a first century date for a first edition of the *Gospel of Thomas*" (*The Gnostic Gospels of Jesus*, 5).

50.   Ariel Sabar, "The Gospel According to King," *Smithsonian Magazine* (November 2012): 82.

CHAPTER 13

1.   Quoted in Pagels in Dan Burnstein and Arne J. de Keijzer, op. cit., 5.

2.   Quoted in Dan Burnstein and Arne J. de Keijzer, op. cit., 86.

3.   It is interesting that Rivka Nir, who astutely places the *Joseph and Aseneth* story in a Christian context, totally misses the point when it comes to "Pharaoh's son." The reason for this is that while Nir is willing to look at the Christian symbols behind the text, she's not willing to look at the historical figures behind the symbols. In this way, she's quite prepared to say that Aseneth stands for the church, but does not investigate the possibility that there's a real historical female who stands behind the Church of the Gentiles. For Nir, everything remains on a symbolic level. In other words, she's willing to say that *Joseph and Aseneth* is a Christian text, but she does not even consider the possibility that it is a lost gospel preserving the history of Christian origins.

This creates problems for her. For example, she's convinced that the bees represent virginity, which they do, but she does not consider the possibility that we are dealing with a non-Pauline understanding of virginity. Because of this, she cannot reconcile the virginity that Aseneth supposedly represents, with the sexual intercourse that immediately follows her marriage to Joseph/Jesus. The same problem plagues her in her analysis of "Pharaoh's son." Since she is not looking at the text as history, she accounts for the clearly non-symbolic and straightforward treatment of this part of the story by imagining two different authors for *Joseph and Aseneth* (p. 160). According to Nir, one author wrote all the symbolism up to the "Pharaoh's son" section, and another wrote the "Pharaoh's son" story. When she has to account for what the story is telling us, she falls back on cliché, i.e., that the whole purpose of the meticulously detailed "Pharaoh's son" section is to teach the reader that Christians should have "love for the enemy" (op. cit., 168). At the end of the day, Nir has to account for why the text is written mostly in code. If it's not hiding anything, why is it written that way? She answers by quoting the *Gospel of Philip*, which says of symbols that "truth did not come into the world naked" (ibid., 179). In other words, *Joseph and Aseneth* is written in code because it's cooler to write in code, even if you have no secret to encode.

4.   S. G. F. Brandon, *Jesus and the Zealots: A Study of the Political Factor in Primitive Christianity* (New York: Charles Scribner's Sons, 1967).

5.   In Matthew 8:14–17, Jesus is described as curing Peter's mother-in-law. Similarly, Paul mentions that Peter, Jesus' brothers, and other apostles were married (1 Corinthians 9:5) and that their wives accompanied them on their travels. *The Acts of Peter* also demonstrates a commitment to family ties. Here, Peter is portrayed as married and showing concern for his daughter. This is one of the few apocryphal stories that makes mention of the child of an apostle. See Brock, op. cit., 117.

6.   1QH 10:34–11:7, quoted in Wise, op. cit., 62–63.

7.   Jesus began his mission by proclaiming that "the time is fulfilled, and the kingdom of God has come near" (Mark 1:15). Jesus also told his audiences that "Truly I tell you, there are some standing here who will not taste death until they see that the kingdom of God has come with power" (Mark 9:1).

8.   Jesus tells his disciples that "at the renewal of all things, when the Son of Man is seated on the throne of his glory, you who have followed me will also sit on twelve thrones, judging the twelve tribes of Israel" (Matthew 19:28). Like Jesus, the Davidic king in the messianic era, the twelve disciples expected a political role as princes within the Kingdom of God. They, along with Jesus, would form the new Israel, the new world government of God's kingdom.

9.   Geza Vermes, *The Complete Dead Sea Scrolls in English* (New York: Penguin, 1997), 220–228.

10.   "But the Pharisees went out and conspired against him, how to destroy him" (Matthew 12:14).

11.   Jesus references this view in his Sermon on the Mount (Matthew 5:43), the only clear place where he mentions a distinctive Essene teaching.

12.   The Essene graves in Jerusalem are less than a kilometer from the controversial "Jesus Family Tomb."

13.   Eisenman identifies this teacher with James the Just, brother of Jesus. This would mean that at least some of the writings postdated the crucifixion. See his *The Dead Sea Scrolls and the First Christians* (Castle Books, 2004).

14.   Marvin W. Meyer, op. cit., 10.

15.   Many read *Iscariot* as *ish karayiot*, i.e., "man of the city." This has no precedent or parallel. We doubt that Judah was called "man about town." On the other hand, *Judah the Sicarius* makes sense. The Greek inversion of *Sicarii* to *Iscari* is also consistent with other such inversions in translation. Finally, Judah's suicide in Matthew 27:3–10 is not consistent with mainstream Judaism, but totally consistent with Sicarii practices such as the suicide of the nearly one thousand Sicarii at Masada (see Eisenman, *The New Testament Code*, 169). We suspect the *ish karayiot* rendering is an attempt to avoid troubling questions that arise if one of Jesus' twelve disciples was a revolutionary assassin.

16.   A Zealot disappointment in Jesus would also explain the tradition that they preferred Bar Abba to Jesus in the famous incident where Pilate offers to release one of the Jewish leaders arrested by the local Roman authorities (see Matthew 27:15–23).

17. Josephus Flavius, *Antiquities of the Jews*, Book 18, Chapter 6, Section 9.

18. Jesus and Herod Antipas eventually do meet face-to-face. According to the Gospel of Luke, after Jesus' arrest, Pilate, on hearing that Jesus was a Galilean, sent him briefly to Herod Antipas, who happened to be in Jerusalem for Passover. Matthew notes that Herod was eager to meet Jesus, hoping that he'd perform some sign, and he questioned him at length. Jesus, however, refused to perform or be drawn into debate. Herod then mocked him in front of the priests and scribes who had accompanied him, and he returned Jesus to Pilate (Luke 23:6–12).

19. Matthew 4:15, quoting Isaiah 9:1–2 ("Galilee of the Nations").

20. At the time of Jesus, the Jews didn't like the residents of Samaria, who we know as Samaritans. Though these people saw themselves as descendants of the tribes of Israel, the Jews saw them as interlopers who didn't belong. One of the ironies of the Gospel stories is that the story of the "Good Samaritan" is provided as an example of the exception to the rule, i.e., even Samaritans can sometimes be good. Now the Samaritans have become synonymous with goodness.

21. Harold W. Hoehner, "The Withdrawals of Jesus," in *Herod Antipas* (Cambridge, UK: Cambridge University Press, 1972), Appendix IX.

22. From the beginning of history, the most effective way of killing a ruler and getting away with it has been poison. For example, we see this reflected in the Book of Genesis when Joseph finds himself in jail with two individuals who are described as Pharaoh's "baker" and wine "steward" (Genesis 41:23). It's clear from the context that both these positions involved security responsibilities, and that one of them had attempted to assassinate the ruler. After an investigation, the "steward" is restored to the confidence of the Pharaoh, and the "baker" is decapitated.

23. Soon after Jesus' crucifixion, an early leader of the Jesus movement in Antioch was Manaen, a close relation, possibly a stepbrother, of Herod Antipas (Acts 13:3). Along with others in Antioch (Barnabas, Simeon, Lucius of Cyrene), Manaen plays a role in ordaining Paul. In other words, here too we see that Jesus and his movement—and, later on, Paul—were well known within governmental circles of the time and were very well connected with the highest echelons of power.

24. In 37 B.C.E., King Herod used a staurogram—the superimposed Greek letters *tau* and *rho* which later Christians identified as a "symbol of the Christ"—on a coin. Why did King Herod use this symbol nearly seventy years before Jesus' crucifixion? According to David Wray, author of *The Secret Roots of Christianity: Decoding Religious History with Symbols on Ancient Coins* (Numismatics & History, 2012), the staurogram was on King Herod's coin because Herod was claiming to be the anointed one, i.e., the Christ. See Simcha Jacobovici, "King Herod a Messiah?" *SimchaJTV*, accessed April 2014, simchajtv.com/king-herod-a-messiah/.

25. The Gospels tell us that Herod's motivation for killing John was revenge for John's criticism of his marriage to Herodias (Luke 3:19). In contrast, Josephus attributes Herod Antipas' motivation to fear of John's popularity and concern for the stability of his rule (*Antiquities* 18:5–2). Both motivations are plausible. According to Josephus, Herod Antipas imprisoned John the Baptizer in Machaerus, a fortress in Peraea, a few miles east of the Dead Sea. The Gospel of Matthew informs us that the daughter of Herodias, Salome, famously danced before Herod at a festive occasion. Being impressed with her, he promised to give her whatever she desired. Prompted by her mother, she requested John's head (Matthew 14:1–12). In fulfillment of his vow, Herod had John beheaded. Some of John's disciples— notably Andrew and Simon Peter—migrated to Jesus' movement. Whatever his reasons, Herod Antipas appears to have feared not only John but also his cousin Jesus. The Gospels explicitly tell us that Herod Antipas wondered out loud if Jesus was John raised from the dead (Matthew 14:2). In other words, it seems that Herod Antipas thought that to put an end to John's movement, he might also have to kill Jesus.

26. Josephus Flavius, *Antiquities of the Jews*, Book 18, Chapter 5, Section 2.

27. For a novel about Sejanus, see Chris Seepe, *The Conspiracy to Assassinate Jesus Christ* (Syncronopedia, 2012).
28. Mark 12:17; Matthew 22:21; Luke 20:25.
29. Josephus writes that Agrippa appeared before his people dressed in a garment made wholly of silver that reflected the sun's rays. At that point, he was declared a messiah by some of his followers. See Josephus Flavius, *Antiquities of the Jews*, Book 19, Chapter 8:2.
30. Sometimes even common citizens had imperial access. All kinds of delegations went to Rome. Josephus reports that he too went to Rome prior to the Jewish revolt and got access to the emperor through the emperor's wife, by befriending a Jewish actor that she liked. See Josephus Flavius, *Life*, 16.
31. Josephus Flavius, *Antiquities of the Jews*, Book 18, Chapter 7 (2).
32. "Pontius Pilate was the fifth Roman prefect . . . he was a friend of . . . Sejanus, whose position as praetorian prefect of Rome was rendered even more powerful by Tiberius's absence on Capri." John Dominic Crossan, *The Cross That Spoke: The Origins of the Passion Narrative* (New York: Harper & Row, 1988), 33.
33. Geza Vermes, *Who's Who in the Age of Jesus* (New York: Penguin, 2005), 211–215.

CHAPTER 14
1. Luke 23:7–11.
2. Luke 13:31–33.
3. Luke 8:2–3. Luke seems to be very familiar with the Antipas connection.
4. The Gospel of Mark (6:17), followed by Matthew (14:3), calls his brother "Phillip," but does not identify him as Phillip the Tetrarch. The story is told in Josephus Flavius, *Antiquities of the Jews*, 18. See also F.F. Bruce, "Herod Antipas, Tetrarch of Galilee and Perea," *The Annual of Leeds University Oriental Studies*, 5 (1963/65): 6–23.
5. She probably insisted that their subjects call him "king," hence the confusion in Mark and, to some extent, in Matthew where he is called "King Herod" (Mark 6, 14, 22, 25, 26, 27; and Matthew 14:9). He was no king, a mere Tetrarch.
6. Lucius Aelius Lamia was ostensibly the Roman governor during that entire period, but he never left Rome. Sejanus held him back and then sent Pilate to Judaea. Once Pilate was in place, Lamia continued to stay in Rome, making Pilate the *de facto* governor of Syria, as well as Judaea.
7. Werner Eck, *The Age of Augustus* (Oxford: Blackwell Publishing, 2003).
8. Suetonius, *Tiberius*, 39.
9. Ibid., 43.
10. Agrippa was probably in a position to know, having been close to Antipas and his wife Herodias.
11. For these women, Jewish beliefs were not peripheral. See Green, op. cit., 15, ". . . there were women of very high rank with connections at [the Roman] court who were attracted to Jewish belief." Green also states that "Judaism must have been seen as eminently respectable in certain elite circles." (op. cit., 16.) The stage had already been set for Jesus and Mary the Magdalene. Later, Paul sends greetings "from those of the emperor's household" (Philippians 4.21), which suggests that Christianity was rife among the staff in the imperial service. See Green, op. cit., 43.
12. See Josephus, *Antiquities* 19: 343–350. Right after being declared Messiah by a huge crowd, he suddenly began suffering extreme cramps, keeled over and, basically, died. In retrospect, he might have been poisoned. A violent death seems to have been an occupational hazard with would-be Messiahs.
13. Paul L. Maier, *American Society of Church History*, Vol. 37, No. 1 (Cambridge University Press, March 1968), 3–13.
14. Maier, op. cit., 12.
15. Josephus Flavius, *Antiquities of the Jews*, Book 18, Ch. 6.

16. In 23:5 he says to Simon and Levi ". . . if you hesitate . . . behold the point of my own spear is drawn before you."

17. But when Simon and Levi respond by attacking him, he cowers before them: "Pharaoh's son was much afraid. He trembled and fell out of fear upon the ground before the feet of Simon and Levi" (23:15).

18. *The Twelve Caesars*, Tiberius, Section 52. Suetonius indicates that Tiberius had no paternal feelings for his natural son, Drusus, let alone for his adopted son, Germanicus.

19. Tacitus, *Annals II.*

20. Ibid.

21. Ibid.

22. Aretas IV ruled Nabataea, a border state outside the Roman Empire, from approximately 9 B.C.E. to 40 C.E.

23. Matthew 14:2.

24. *Annals II.* With respect to magical spells written on bowls and placed on the floors and in the walls of houses, we have hundreds of archaeological samples mostly from the area of modern Iraq. As part of the incantations, many of them have the word *Jesus* written on them (see Dan Levene, *A Corpus of Magic Bowls*, Routledge, 2002).

25. Kraemer, op. cit., 138.

CHAPTER 15

1. This identification is also made in Pope Benedict XVI, *Jesus of Nazareth, Part II*, San Francisco: Ignatius Press, 2011.

2. A few years later, Agrippa also experienced this type of dramatic and positive reversal of fortune. One day he was sitting in a Roman jail, incarcerated for sedition at the order of Tiberius himself; the next day—after Tiberius' death—he was at the right hand of the new emperor, Caligula, and about to be crowned King of the Jews (see Josephus Flavius, *Antiquities of the Jews*, 18:6).

3. Despite the secrecy, armed with our new gospel, we can compare text to facts, so as to ascertain whether there is, or is not, a fit or synchronicity. The more specific the event, the more likely the match, e.g., the presence of a Roman emperor's son in the Galilee during the time of Jesus' increasing fame, and a ruler referred to in *Joseph and Aseneth* and in Josephus as the "lion."

4. More precisely, it was often led behind the scenes by Caiaphas' father-in-law, the High Priest Hanania, Annas in the Gospels.

5. Josephus Flavius, *Antiquities of the Jews*, 18; 1.1; 17.10.4, *War* 2,4.

6. See Israel Knohl, op. cit.

7. See Morton Smith, *Clement*, op. cit., 248.

8. See also Acts 6:14 where Stephen is charged for having said that Jesus would destroy the temple and change the Law of Moses.

9. This explains why Judas "betrayed" Jesus. Although, given the circumstances, he must have thought that Jesus would be arrested but not crucified; after all, Jesus now had the rulers on his side. When Sejanus fell and Jesus was crucified, in Sicarii fashion, Judas committed suicide.

10. See Schäfer, op. cit., 65.

11. Mark 1:12–13; Matthew 4:1–11; Luke 4:1–14.

12. In Matthew 4:5, Satan specifically takes Jesus to Jerusalem and to the highest point of the temple.

13. Josephus, *War* 10:1.

14. Luke 22:36–38.

15. Matthew 26:52.

16. Brandon, op. cit.

17. In the *Jewish Wars* book 6, chapter 2, Josephus tells us that he was willing to abandon the revolution and play the traitor, if this could save the temple. He describes how he stood

outside Jerusalem's city walls and, speaking in Hebrew, he talked to the defenders: ". . . so he earnestly prayed them to spare their own city, and to prevent that fire which was just ready to seize upon the temple, and to offer their usual sacrifices to God therein."

18. John 11:35.
19. Mark 11:9; Matthew 21:9.
20. 12:13.
21. Until recently, the Good Friday prayer of the Roman Catholic Rite had Catholics praying for the conversion of the "perfidious Jews."
22. Mark 11:16. The day before he shut the temple down, Jesus scouted the territory. See Mark 11:12–25.
23. John 18:13.
24. See John 18:28.
25. *Lives of Illustrious Men*, ch. 2.
26. So much for the notion that Jesus' followers did not kneel in prayer.
27. Josephus, *Wars* 5:13. This also fits with the notion in *Joseph and Aseneth* that the goal of the anti-Jesus/Mary the Magdalene forces was to kill Jesus, but not before murdering his children before his eyes.
28. Josephus Flavius, *Antiquities of the Jews*, 20, ch. 8.
29. Josephus Flavius, *War* II, ch. 20 and *War* IV, ch. 5.
30. Robert Eisenman, *James the Brother of Jesus* (Penguin Group, 1997), 963.
31. Matthew 27:57–59; Mark 15:42–46; Luke 23:50–54; John 19:38–42.
32. Mark 15:34.
33. Eusebius, *Ecclesiastical History*, Book 3, ch. 12.
34. Ibid., Book 3, ch. 19, 20.
35. Ibid., Book 3, ch. 32.

CHAPTER 16

1. In fact, they may have given rise to Islam. If one examines the Koran's view of the "Old Testament," it seems to have been distilled by early Judeo-Christians. The Koran's view of Jesus, for example, as a prophet but not a god does not come from mainstream Judaism or Christianity—it is pure Ebionite theology.
2. Morton Smith, *Clement of Alexandria and a Secret Gospel of Mark*, 256.
3. Ibid.
4. Ibid., 257.
5. Ibid.
6. Ibid. (emphasis added).
7. Ibid. (emphasis added).
8. See Rabia Gregory, "Marrying Jesus: Brides and the Bridegroom in Medieval Women's Religious Literature," 2007, Ph.D. Dissertation, University of North Carolina at Chapel Hill.
9. Surveys of medieval Bride-of-Christ literature normally begin with Bernard of Clairvaux's *Sermons on the Song of Songs* (1136). But they really seem to coincide with the earliest Latin translation of *Joseph and Aseneth*, which was popularized in a condensed form by Vincent of Beauvais. No doubt the Song of Songs helped influence the medieval Bride-of-Christ phenomenon, but it doesn't explain it. (As we've stated, *Joseph and Aseneth* is a kind of Christian Song of Songs.) The term *Bride of God* does not appear anywhere in the Song of Songs. It appears only in *Joseph and Aseneth*.
10. Gregory, op. cit., 4.
11. Ibid., ix and 107.
12. Quoted in ibid., 110–112.
13. Quoted in ibid., 115.
14. Quoted in ibid., 122.
15. Ibid.

16. Quoted in ibid., 132.

17. Ibid., 139.

18. Quoted in ibid., 140.

19. Quoted in ibid., 141. This "mouth on mouth" kissing is later always associated with the mother, not the wife. For example, in the *Homily on the Dormition* attributed to Evodius of Rome: "Mary, his mother, came in a rush, and she advanced to him and kissed him, mouth on mouth" (Shoemaker, *Ancient Dormition*, op. cit., 403). We suspect this kind of kissing is an echo of Jesus' relationship with Mary the Magdalene, not his mother.

20. Gregory, p. 170.

21. Ibid., 171.

22. Ibid.

23. Ibid., 176.

24. Ibid., 177.

25. Ibid., 182.

26. Ibid., 225.

27. Ibid., 215.

28. Ibid., 273.

29. Ibid., 288.

30. Gregory, op. cit., 156. As another example, the patron saint of Spain, St. Teresa of Avila (16th century), wrote of her encounter with an angel as follows: "I saw in his hand a long spear of gold, and at the iron's point there seemed to be a little fire. He appeared to me to be thrusting it at times into my heart, and to pierce my very entrails; when he drew it out, he seemed to draw them out also, and to leave me all on fire with a great love of God. The pain was so great, that it made me moan; and yet so surpassing was the sweetness of this excessive pain, that I could not wish to be rid of it" (quoted in *Autobiography*, ch. 29, part 17). St. Teresa was drawing on the erotically charged language of church father Origen, who describes his soul in female terms and who states that Jesus "pierced" it with "the loveworthy spear of his knowledge" (quoted in Jonathan Hill, op. cit., 143). The famous Renaissance sculptor Gian Lorenzo Bernini depicts St. Teresa and the spear-carrying angel in a marble statue housed in the chapel of the Santa Maria della Vittoria Church in Rome. Well before Freud, commentators on the statue pointed out that St. Teresa seems to be having an orgasm.

  Bernini depicted another Bride of Christ in the midst of a holy orgasm in his sculpture of Ludovica Albertoni (1675). Albertoni was a Roman noblewoman who lived during the Renaissance. She was famous for her works of charity and religious ecstasies. Her statue is housed in the Church of St. Francis of Assisi a Ripa in Rome. Most commentators describe the look of ecstasy on her face as her death throes. But the orgasm could not be more explicit; her right hand is on her breast and the folds of her dress create a vulva in her crotch. See Fr. Antonio Del Vasto OFM, *Church S. Francis of Assisi a Ripa Grande and its Saints Historical Artistic Guide*, Rome (2009), 76–77.

31. Caroline Walker Bynum, *Holy Feast and Holy Fast: The Religious Significance of Food to Medieval Women* (University of California Press, 1988), 174–175.

32. Ibid., 204.

33. Russell Peck, ed., *The Storie of Asneth*, originally published in *Heroic Women from the Old Testament in Middle English Verse* (Kalamazoo, Michigan: Medieval institute Publications, 1991). Available: lib.rochester.edu/camelot/teams/asnint.htm.

34. See http://www.lib.rochester.edu/camelot/teams/asnint.htm, p. 3.

35. Ibid., p. 5.

36. Ibid., p. 7.

37. Henry Noble MacCracken, "The Storie of Asneth. An Unknown Middle English Translation of a Lost Latin Version," *The Journal of English and Germanic Philology*, Vol. 9, No. 2 (April 1910): 224–264; 235, line 200.

38. "The medieval interpretation presumed that all souls were feminine, whether they were associated with male or female bodies." (Gregory, op. cit., 13.)

39. Theologically speaking, an illustrated 12th-century commentary on the Biblical Song of Songs by Honorius Augustodunesis suggests that there were, in fact, four brides of Christ corresponding to four Biblical epochs and, in the end, Jesus would wed the antichrist. Here, again, we see a Gnostic interpretation of Jesus' ultimate union with a wayward force (the antichrist) for the purpose of redemption. This metaphysical marriage is based on previous marriages. Anne E. Matter, *The Voice of My Beloved: The Song of Songs in Western Medieval Christianity* (Philadelphia, PA: University of Pennsylvania Press, 1990), 58–64.

40. *The Gospel of Thomas, Saying* 61. Translation based on B. Blatz, The Coptic Gospel of Thomas, W. Schneemelcher, ed, New Testament Apocrypha, English translation by R. McL. Wilson, James Clarke & Co. Ltd.; Westminster/John Knox Press, Cambridge; Louisville, 1991, 110-133 (emphasis added).

41. George W. MacRae, trans., "The Thunder, Perfect Mind" in James M. Robinson, ed., *The Nag Hammadi Library*, revised edition (HarperCollins, San Francisco, 1990).

CHAPTER 17

1. Harvard Divinity School, "The Gospel of Jesus's Wife: A New Coptic Gospel Papyrus," 2012, hds.harvard.edu/faculty-research/research-projects/the-gospel-of-jesuss-wife.

2. Meyer, *Gnostic Gospels of Jesus*, 40.

3. Ibid., 25.

4. Ibid.

5. Ibid., 63.

6. Karen King would later give a very "academic" explanation for this surprising silence in the face of a momentous discovery: "people interested in Egyptology tend not to be interested in Christianity . . . they're into Pharaonic stuff" (Ariel Sabar, op. cit., 82). We think not.

7. Karen L. King (2014). "Jesus said to them, 'My wife . . .'": A New Coptic Papyrus Fragment. *Harvard Theological Review*, 107, p 154. doi:10.1017/S0017816014000133.

8. Morton Smith, *Jesus the Magician*, 3.

9. This parable too may be referring to sacred sex. To the modern ear, mustard seeds are all about being tiny, and Jesus is talking about a lowly seed growing into a giant tree (Matthew 13:31–32, Mark 4:30–32, Luke 13:18–19). But in the Hellenized world of the Galilee, the parable may have meant something altogether different. Colewort, a plant of the mustard family, was thought by the Romans to have erection-enhancing properties. A poem that survives from Imperial Rome has a man saying to his woman that he would love to rub "ten handfuls" of colewort into "the ditches of [her] groin." Suddenly, Jesus talking about a man sowing mustard seed in the furrows of his field has a different connotation, especially since he likens this act to the Kingdom of God. See David Friedman, op. cit., 27.

10. Quoted in Morton Smith, op. cit., 1–2.

11. Kraemer, op. cit., 291.

12. Mark Goodacre, "The Bride of God or the Lost Gospel of Joseph and Asyath, Richard Bauckham," *NT Blog*, accessed March 2014, ntweblog.blogspot.ca/2013/10/the-bride-of-god-or-lost-gospel-of.html

13. David Friedman, op. cit., 5.

14. Josephus Flavius, *Antiquities of the Jews*, Book 20, Chapter 9, 1.

SUGGESTIONS FOR FURTHER READING

The following is not intended as a complete bibliography of works consulted or cited, but as suggestions for further reading.

BIBLE

The New Oxford Annotated Bible with the Apocrypha, New Revised Standard Version. New York: Oxford University Press, 1994.

JPS Hebrew-English Tanakh. Philadelphia: The Jewish Publication Society, 1999.

BY THE AUTHORS

Jacobovici, Simcha, and Charles Pellegrino. *The Jesus Family Tomb.* New York: HarperSanFrancisco, 2007.

Tabor, James D., and Simcha Jacobovici. *The Jesus Discovery.* New York: Simon & Shuster, 2012.

Wilson, Barrie A. *How Jesus Became Christian.* New York: St. Martin's Press; Toronto: Random House; London: Orion Publishing, 2008.

———. *About Interpretation: From Plato to Dilthey—A Hermeneutic Anthology.* New York: Peter Lang, 1989.

———. *Hermeneutical Studies: Sophocles, Plato, Bultmann.* Lewiston, NY: Edwin Mellen Press, 1990.

———. "Bardaisan: On Nature, Fate and Freedom," in Barrie Wilson, *Hermeneutical Studies*, 131–155.

BY TONY BURKE

Burke, Tony. *Secret Scriptures Revealed. A New Introduction to the Christian Apocrypha.* London: SPCK, 2013.

———, ed. *Ancient Gospel or Modern Forgery? The Secret Gospel of Mark in Debate. Proceedings from the 2011 York University Christian Apocrypha Symposium.* Eugene, OR: Cascade Books, 2012.

———. *De Inantia Iesu euangelium Thomae graece. Corpus Christianorum Series Apocryphorum.* Turnhout: Brepols, 2010.

THE SYRIAC MANUSCRIPT

British Library Manuscript 17,202 was transcribed by J. P. N. Land in *Anecdota Syriaca*, vol. 3. E. J. Brill, 1870.

APHRAHAT

Demonstration 21 (Of Persecution). newadvent.org/fathers/370121.htm.

APOCRYPHA AND PSEUDEPIGRAPHA

Charlesworth, James H. *The Old Testament Pseudepigrapha*, Volumes 1 and 2. New York: Doubleday, 1983–1985.

Sparks, H. F. D. *The Apocryphal Old Testament*. New York: Oxford University Press, 1984.

Wills, Lawrence M. *Ancient Jewish Novels: An Anthology*. Edited and translated by Lawrence M. Wills. New York: Oxford University Press, 2002.

ARTEMIS

d'Este, Sorita. *Artemis: Virgin Goddess of the Sun & Moon*. London: Avalonia, 2005.

Kampen, John. "The Cult of Artemis and the Essenes in Syro-Palestine." *Dead Sea Discoveries* 10, no. 2 (2003): 205–220.

DEAD SEA SCROLL COMMUNITY/ESSENES—TEXTS AND INTRODUCTION

Vermes, Geza. *The Complete Dead Sea Scrolls in English*. New York: Penguin, 1998.

Wise, Michael O., Martin Abegg, and Edward M. Cook. *The Dead Sea Scrolls—Revised Edition: A New Translation*. New York: HarperOne, 2005.

DEAD SEA SCROLL COMMUNITY/ESSENES—SELECTED STUDIES

Eisenman, Robert. *The Dead Sea Scrolls and the First Christians*. Edison, New Jersey: Castle Books, 2004.

Jones, Allen H. *Essenes: The Elect of Israel and the Priests of Artemis*. Lanham: University Press of America, 1985.

Vanderkam, James, and Peter Flint. *The Meaning of the Dead Sea Scrolls: Their Significance for Understanding the Bible, Judaism, Jesus, and Christianity*. New York: HarperOne, 2004.

Wise, Michael O. *The First Messiah: Investigating the Savior Before Jesus*. New York: HarperSanFrancisco, 1999.

EARLY CHRISTIANITY/JESUS

See especially:

Wilson, Barrie. *How Jesus Became Christian*. New York: St. Martin's Press, 2008.

Tabor, James D. *The Jesus Dynasty*. New York: Simon & Schuster, 2006.

Tabor, James D. *Paul and Jesus: How the Apostle Transformed Christianity*. New York: Simon & Schuster, 2012.

Ehrman, Bart D. *Jesus: Apocalyptic Prophet of the New Millennium*. New York: Oxford University Press, 1999.

———. *Lost Christianities: The Battles for Scripture and the Faiths We Never Knew*. New York: Oxford University Press, 2003.

———. *Lost Scriptures: Books that Did Not Make It into the New Testament.* New York: Oxford University Press, 2003.

Smith, Morton. *Jesus the Magician.* San Francisco: Harper & Row, 1978.

Bütz, Jeffrey J. *The Brother of Jesus.* Rochester, VT: Inner Traditions, 2005.

———. *The Secret Legacy of Jesus.* Rochester, VT: Inner Traditions, 2010.

Also see:

Beavis, Mary Ann. *Jesus & Utopia: Looking for the Kingdom of God in the Roman World.* Minneapolis: Fortress Press, 2006.

Chilton, Bruce. *Rabbi Jesus.* New York: Image Books, 2000.

Eisenman, Robert. *The New Testament Code: The Cup of the Lord, the Damascus Covenant, and the Blood of Christ.* London: Watkins Publishing, 2006.

Roth, Wolfgang. *Hebrew Gospel: Cracking the Code of Mark.* Oak Park, Illinois: Meyer Stone Books, 1988.

Rousseau, John J., and Rami Arav. *Jesus and His World: An Archaeological and Cultural Dictionary.* Minneapolis: Augsburg Fortress, 1995.

Schäfer, Peter. *Jesus in the Talmud.* Princeton: Princeton University Press, 2007.

EPHREM THE SYRIAN

Ephrem, *Sermon on Joseph the Most Virtuous.* Anastasis.org.uk/Joseph.pdf.

McVey, Kathleen E. (trans.). *Ephrem the Syrian: Hymns.* New York: Paulist Press, 1989.

Murray, Robert. *Symbols of Church and Kingdom.* Cambridge: Cambridge University Press, 1975.

EUSEBIUS

Cruse, C. F. (translator). *Eusebius' Ecclesiastical History.* Peabody, Massachusetts: Hendrickson Publishers, 2001.

GNOSTIC WRITINGS

DeConick, April D. "The True Mysteries: Sacramentalism in the Gospel of Philip." *Vigiliae Christianae* 55 (2001): 225–261.

———. "The Great Mystery of Marriage: Sex and Conception in Ancient Valentinian Traditions." *Vigiliae Christianae* 57 (2003): 307–342.

Meyer, Marvin. *The Gnostic Gospels of Jesus.* New York: HarperOne, 2005.

Pagels, Elaine. *The Gnostic Gospels.* New York: Vintage Books, 1979.

Translations of Gnostic writings available at gnosis.org/naghamm/nhl.html.

HEROD ANTIPAS

Hoehner, Harold W. *Herod Antipas: A Contemporary of Jesus Christ.* Grand Rapids, Michigan: Zondervan Publishing House, 1980.

JOSEPH AND ASENETH—ENGLISH TRANSLATIONS—ALL BASED ON GREEK MANUSCRIPTS LATER THAN THE SYRIAC.

Brooks, E. W. *Joseph and Asenath: The Confession and Prayer of Asenath Daughter of Pentephres the Priest.* London: Society for Promoting Christian Knowledge, 1918.

Burchard, C. "Joseph and Aseneth," in James H. Charlesworth (ed.), *The Old Testament Pseudepigrapha*, Volume 2. New York: Doubleday, 1985.

Cook, D. "Joseph and Aseneth," in H. F. D. Sparks, *The Apocryphal Old Testament.* Oxford: Clarendon Press, 1984. ntgateway.com/aseneth/translat.htm.

"The Marriage and Conversion of Aseneth." Translated and edited by Lawrence M. Wills, *in* Lawrence M. Wills, *Ancient Jewish Novels: An Anthology*. New York: Oxford University Press, 2002.

JOSEPH AND ASENETH—SELECTED STUDIES
See especially:
Kraemer, Ross Shepard. *When Aseneth Met Joseph*. New York: Oxford University Press, 1998.
Nir, Rivka. *Joseph and Aseneth: A Christian Book*. Sheffield: Sheffield University Press, 2012.
———. "Aseneth as the 'Prototype of the Church of the Gentiles'." *Annual Meeting of the Society of Biblical Literature* (2007).
———. "The Conversion of Aseneth in a Christian Context." *Annual Meeting of the Society of Biblical Literature* (2006).
Philonenko, Marc. *Joseph et Aséneth: Introduction texte critique traduction et notes*. Leiden: E. J. Brill, 1968. [Introduction and French translation from later Greek manuscripts]
Also see:
Kasyan, Maria. "The Apocalyptic Scene in the Apocryphal Story *Joseph and Aseneth* and Artemis of Ephesus." Paper presented at the International Conference on the Ancient Novel, Lisbon, July 21–26, 2008.

JOSEPHUS
Josephus. *The New Complete Works of Josephus*. Revised and expanded edition. Translated by William Whiston, commentary by Paul L. Maier. Grand Rapids, Michigan: Kregel Publications, 1999.

MARY THE MAGDALENE
See especially:
Starbird, Margaret. *The Woman with the Alabaster Jar*. Rochester, Vermont: Bear & Company, 1993.
———. *Mary the Magdalene, Bride in Exile*. Rochester, Vermont: Bear & Company, 2005.
Brock, Ann Graham. *Mary the Magdalene, The First Apostle: The Struggle for Authority*. Cambridge Massachusetts: Distributed by Harvard University Press for Harvard Theological Studies, Harvard Divinity School, 2003.
Burstein, Dan, and Arne J. de Keijzer. *Secrets of Mary the Magdalene: The Untold Story of History's Most Misunderstood Woman*. New York: CDS Books in association with Squibnocket Partners LLC, 2006.
Chilton, Bruce. *Mary the Magdalene: A Biography*. New York: Doubleday, 2005.
Schaberg, Jane. *The Resurrection of Mary the Magdalene: Legends, Apocrypha, and the Christian Testament*. New York: Continuum, 2004.
———. *Mary the Magdalene Understood*. New York: Continuum, 2006.

MARY, MOTHER OF JESUS
Ionescu, Carla. *The Enduring Goddess: Artemis and Mary, Mother of Jesus*. Ph. D. dissertation, York University, Toronto, in preparation.

MISCELLANEOUS EARLY CHRISTIAN WRITINGS
Acts of (Judas) Thomas. earlychristianwritings.com/text/actsthomas.html.
Acts of Pilate. earlychristianwritings.com/actspilate.html.

Infancy Gospel of James, *in* Robert J. Miller (ed.), *The Complete Gospels*. New York: HarperSanFrancisco, 1994 and, under the name "The Proto-Gospel of James," *in* Bart D. Ehrman, *Lost Scriptures: Books that Did Not Make It into the New Testament*. New York: Oxford University Press, 2003.

NEW TESTAMENT — CRITICAL INTRODUCTION — SELECTED STUDIES
Ehrman, Bart D. *The New Testament: A Historical Introduction to the Early Christian Writings*, 3rd edition. New York: Oxford University Press, 2004.
Mason, Steve, and Tom Robinson. *An Early Christian Reader*. Toronto: Canadian Scholars' Press Inc., 1990.

NEW TESTAMENT — TEXTUAL TRANSMISSION
Ehrman, Bart D. *Misquoting Jesus*. New York: HarperSanFrancisco, 2005.

PAUL
Crossan, John Dominic, and Jonathan L. Reed. *In Search of Paul*. New York: Harper-SanFrancisco, 2004.
Holmen, R. W. *A Wretched Man: A Novel of Paul the Apostle*. Minneapolis: Bascom Hill, 2009.
Lüdemann, Gerd. *Paul: The Founder of Christianity*. Amherst, NY: Prometheus Books, 2002.
Maccoby, Hyam. *The Myth-Maker: Paul and the Invention of Christianity*. San Francisco: Harper & Row, 1986.
Murphy-O'Connor, Jerome. *Paul: His Story*. Oxford: Oxford University Press, 2004.
Voskuilen, Thijs and Rose Mary Sheldon. *Operation Messiah: St. Paul, Roman Intelligence and the Birth of Christianity*. Portland, OR: Vallentine Mitchell, 2008.
Plus, books already cited by James D. Tabor and Barrie Wilson.

SECRET MARK
Smith, Morton. *The Secret Gospel: The Discovery and Interpretation of the Secret Gospel According to Mark*. New York: Harper & Row, 1973.

Burke, Tony, ed. *Ancient Gospel or Modern Forgery?: The Secret Gospel of Mark in Debate*. Eugene, OR: Wipf and Stock Publishers, 2013.

SEJANUS
Seepe, Chris. *The Conspiracy to Assassinate Jesus Christ*. Toronto: Synchronopedia Corp., 3 edition, 2012.

SUETONIUS
Suetonius. *The Twelve Caesars*. Translated by Robert Graves, revised by J. B. Rives. New York: Penguin, 2007.

TACITUS
Tacitus. *The Annals & The Histories*. Introduction by Shelby Foote; translated by Alfred John Church and William Jackson Brodribb; edited by Moses Hadas; notes by James Danly. New York: The Modern Library, 2003.

ACKNOWLEDGMENTS

SIMCHA

I would like to thank my co-writer and friend Professor Barrie Wilson. They say co-writing can be a difficult process, but Barrie made it always enjoyable and a learning experience. He's driven by nothing less than a search for the truth. I also want to thank Professor Tony Burke for his masterful translation of the Syriac text and for his patient and detailed notes on our book. I would like to thank my assistant Nicole Austin who literally spent hundreds of hours on the text, flying to different corners of the world trying to catch up with me, researching, editing and generally making the whole endeavor possible. Thank you also to Suzan Yum for her meticulous research.

I am fortunate to have not one but two great agents, Elaine Markson and Joelle Delbourgo. Elaine has been a friend, strategist, supporter and ally for years, and Joelle stepped up to the plate when we needed her most with both professionalism and grace. I'm also fortunate to have two great editors: in Canada, Jim Gifford (HarperCollins) and in the US, Jessica Case (Pegasus). They have been patient, supportive and insightful.

I have been blessed with friends who dare to think, many of them scholars who have selflessly given me their time and shared with me their vast knowledge. Thank you James Tabor, Rami Arav, Richard Freund, James Charlesworth, Noam Kuzar and Eldad Keynan.

I learned the art of thinking outside the box at the supper table growing up. My father Joseph, of blessed memory, my mother Ida, my sister Sara and I were an ongoing forum for debate and intellectual argumentation. I thank them; especially my mother who taught me a love of books and my father who taught me to take nothing for granted and examine every issue from multiple perspectives. I want to thank my children: Ziva, Nava, Iosefa, Adin and Michaela who enrich my life, provide me with invaluable feedback, make me so proud and tolerate a dad who is constantly on the phone debating strange ideas such as the meaning of virginity in the Mary the Magdalene tradition.

Finally, I want to thank my wife Nicole without whom nothing would be possible.

Jerusalem, Israel

Shevat 22, 5774

BARRIE

When we started this project, we agreed we would follow the ancient manuscript wherever it led. Manuscript #17,202 took us on a remarkable journey and there were many surprises along the way. I've enjoyed traveling this fascinating route with my friend and co-author, Simcha Jacobovici. His honesty, integrity and insights have immensely enriched our work. His breadth of knowledge is truly phenomenal, drawing upon the resources of a huge variety of texts buttressed by first-hand knowledge of archeological sites in Israel and around the world. He is a remarkable detective. A special thanks to Simcha's assistant, Nicole Austin, who did travel far and wide, as we wove together our narrative and spliced together various additions and changes. She was literally the gatekeeper of the book manuscript and we owe her immense gratitude. Her cheerful and dedicated commitment to the project was truly amazing. Also sharing the journey has been Tony Burke. His Syriac to English translation, based on the most accurate restoration of the original text using state-of-the-art digital imaging techniques, represents an enormous contribution to the study of *Joseph and Aseneth*.

We are fortunate to have an excellent publishing team. My agent—and, subsequently, Simcha's agent as well—Joelle Delbourgo, stood with us along the way, as our manuscript evolved and our insights proliferated. With good humor, persistence and the occasional nudge, she helped keep us focused on the task at hand, to complete the book in a timely fashion. Through her efforts, we were steered to two very supportive and enthusiastic editors, Jim Gifford at HarperCollins Canada and Jessica Case at Pegasus in the US. They—literary agent and editors—are a publishing "dream team."

My children are now grown up and they have their families. I thank them and their spouses for constantly asking, "How is the book coming along?" I have appreciated their sustained interest along the way. Thanks, too to the many friends, students and scholars who in their own way have tried to keep track of the book's progress.

I'd like to dedicate my portion of this book to my young grandchildren, Jacob, Noah, Eden, Thalia, Jackson and Ryder and to those grandchildren yet to be born. Hopefully some day they will read this book and finally understand what "Saba" was doing during the day when they were at school.

A special thanks goes to my wife, Linda, who has been involved in every phase of the project from the start. Her good humor, patience and critical interest has been evident throughout the process as we opened up and explored various avenues along the way. Months ago, she asked the toughest question, "So what is it that we now know that we didn't know before?"

My final thanks are to you, the reader of this book, for having journeyed with us. You are now best equipped to answer Linda's question.

Toronto, Canada

January 23, 2014

ABOUT THE AUTHORS

SIMCHA JACOBOVICI, co-author of *The Jesus Family Tomb*, is a three-time Emmy-winning Israeli-Canadian documentary filmmaker and a widely published writer and lecturer. He is also an adjunct professor in the department of religion at Huntington University in Sudbury, Ontario. His articles have appeared in publications such as the *New York Times* and the *Los Angeles Times*. Jacobovici is the host of *The Naked Archeologist* on the History Channel. He resides in Israel with his wife and five children. Visit Simcha on his blog at: www.simchajtv.com or on Facebook: https://www.facebook.com/SimchaJTV

BARRIE WILSON, Professor, Religious Studies at York University in Toronto, specializes in early Christianity. His book *How Jesus Became Christian* was long-listed for the Cundill International Prize in History and won the Joseph and Faye Tanenbaum Award. He lives in Toronto.

INDEX

Transmutation, 175
Trinitarian disputes, 36
Trinity, doctrine of the, 24
Tucher, Katharina, 286–287
The Twelve Caesars (Suetonius), 243
Typology, 49, 50, 51, 52, 54, 60, 61, 127, 146, 302
Tyre, 71, 72

U
U2, xv

V
Valentinian Gnosticism. *See also* Gnosticism
  bridal chamber and, 34–35, 171
  focus on celebrating vitality and offspring, 186–187
  Joseph and Aseneth in, 186–187
  marriage as central to, 170
  marriage of Jesus and Mary the Magdalene and, 153, 187–189, 302
  as metaphorical, 167
  rejection of virgin birth, 170
  sexual intercourse and, 165
  theology in, 163, 216
  virginity for, 170
Valentinians, 160–161
Valentinus, 34, 70, 160–161, 162, 214, 303
  birth of, 215
Valerius Gratus, 251, 259, 271
Varius, 261
Vatican, 107, 140
  Institutum Patristicum Augustinianum, 294
Ventris, Michael, 105
Vespasian (Roman emperor), 97, 266, 276
Via Maris, 93, 253
Virgin birth, 128, 170, 196–201. *See also* Immaculate Conception
  menstrual blood and, 179
Virginity, 170
  Aseneth as symbol for, 63
Vitellius, Roman governor of Syria, 232
A Volume of Records of Events Which Have Shaped the World, 3, 19, 24–25, 309–310

W
War Scroll, 225–226
Wedding celebrations, length of, 156
Weeping, Mary the Magdalene and, 90
Western Christian orthodoxy, 63
The Wisdom of Faith, 219
"Woman in the window" motif, 90–91
Word incarnate, 129
Wright, William, 310

X
Xenophon of Ephesus, 117–118

Y
Ya'akov (James, brother of Jesus), 153, 273
Yaldabaoth, 161–162
Yehudah, Rabbi, 155
Yeshua, 151
Yosé (Joseph) (brother of Jesus), 153

Z
Zaccheus, as leader of Jesus Movement, 211
Zacharias, 19. *See also* Pseudo-Zacharias Rhetor; Second Zacharias
  as Bishop of Mytilene, 24
Zacharias Rhetor, 19, 24
  Church History, 24, 25
Zadok, 261
Zadokites, 260–261
Zealots
  as enemies of Jesus, 226–228, 263–264
  ideology of, 263
Zechariah (father of John the Baptizer), 153
Zeus, 107, 119
Ziggurats, 73
Zimri, 116
  heresy of, 168
Zodiac
  Helios and, in ancient Jewish synagogues, 134–140
  sign of, 84